D1064408

THE HISTORY OF WISCONSIN

THE HISTORY OF WISCONSIN

VOLUME V

War, a New Era, and Depression, 1914–1940

PAUL W. GLAD

WILLIAM FLETCHER THOMPSON
General Editor

1990
STATE HISTORICAL SOCIETY OF WISCONSIN
MADISON

Manufactured in the United States of America by
Worzalla Publishing Company, Stevens Point, Wisconsin

Library of Congress Cataloging-in-Publication Data
(Revised for Volume VI of The History of Wisconsin)
THE HISTORY OF WISCONSIN
Includes bibliography and index.
CONTENTS: v. 1. From exploration to statehood, by Alice E. Smith. v. 2. The Civil War era, 1848–1873, by Richard N. Current. v. 3. Urbanization and industrialization, 1873–1893, by Robert C. Nesbit. v. 5. War, a new era, and depression, 1914–1940, by Paul W. Glad. v. 6. Continuity and change, 1940–1965, by William F. Thompson.
1. Wisconsin—History.

ISBN 0-87020-260-X

F581.H68 977.5 72-12941

For
STEPHANIE *and* ELISABETH,
ERIC *and* KARIN,
JESSICA *and* KRISTIN,
JENNIFER *and* MATTHEW,
and for all who, like them, take delight
in watching the paper airplanes
that fly from a study window.

PREFACE

ONCE UPON A TIME, in the distant past when this fifth volume of *The History of Wisconsin* still remained in the planning stage, I was concentrating intensively on how I might organize the voluminous source materials on which it is based. Reading through Aldo Leopold's *A Sand County Almanac*—in much the same way that the ancients once consulted oracles—I found a passage that resonated to my call for help. In "Good Oak," the essay that Wisconsin's poetic ecologist thought appropriate for February, he inserted an "allegory for historians" on the functions of various woodsman's tools.

Leopold elaborated on three instruments necessary in the making of wood: the saw, the wedge, and the axe. "The saw," he wrote, "works only across the years, which it must deal with one by one, in sequence." As the saw cuts, "little chips of fact . . . accumulate in little piles. . . ." Woodsmen call them sawdust, and historians call them archives, observed Leopold, but to both they are samples of what lies within. With the transect completed, "the tree falls, and the stump yields a collective view of a century." Unlike the saw, the wedge has utility "only in radial splits" that provide "a collective view of all the years at once, or no view at all, depending on the skill with which the plane of the split is chosen." The axe cuts "only at an angle diagonal to the years, and this only for the peripheral rings of the recent past." The axe is indispensable in lopping limbs, a purpose for which saw and wedge have little value.

Leopold emphasized that all three tools "are requisite to good oak, and to good history." The longer I thought about the allegory, the more profound it seemed as a guide to the task that lay ahead of me. "By its fall," wrote Leopold, "the tree attests the unity of the hodge-podge called history." If I have fulfilled my responsibilities as it has seemed to me that they should be fulfilled, the publication of this volume stands as an event analogous to the felling of a tree. The volume itself should attest to the unity of the history of Wisconsin between 1914 and 1940. It should provide a collective view of that quarter-century, seen year by year, all at once, and trimmed of suckers.

The plan for these volumes, stipulating only that each should concentrate on a given span of time in the history of the state, has imposed neither methodological nor substantive directives to limit the authors. In preparing Volume V, I have felt so uninhibited by the patterns of other volumes or by the wisdom of other historians that I have, I know, added unduly to the burdens that William F. Thompson has had to bear as the general editor of the series. Yet graceless though I may have been in insisting upon having my way, he has not lunged at me swinging a woodsman's axe, though he must have been sorely tempted. He has, rather, used his editorial axe discreetly and with surgical precision to lop off wild shoots and suckers that contributed nothing to the making of wood. If readers are able to find good oak in this volume, they will have reason to join me in thanking Bill Thompson.

Paul Hass, who has shared editorial responsibilities, has demonstrated a quiet wisdom through every stage in the preparation of *War, a New Era, and Depression.* By reason of his candor, his unfailing good humor, and his modesty, he has forfeited an opportunity to become the éminence grise of this series. On the other hand, his benign influence is quite literally evident from cover to cover of this volume, and I am grateful for that influence.

As one who has needed assistance from a great many people, I have compiled an extensive list of persons to whom I acknowledge my indebtedness. Jack Holzhueter has contributed valuable information from religious groups and other associations, and he has performed indispensable though not necessarily silent service in checking the accuracy of both footnotes and manuscript. Other members of the research staff who merit recognition are Kay Johnson, Stanley Mallach, Mari Jo Buhle, Dale Treleven, Ted Pearson, and Jeanne Delgado. For contributions that extend far beyond any assistance for which I had a right to ask, I am forever obligated to Richard Haney, David Shepard, Jim Voegeli, and George Roeder. Dick pored over small-town newspapers to locate items of interest; he also served as an invaluable source of inside information on Wisconsin politics. David offered his unique perspectives on a variety of subjects. Jim provided yeoman service in enriching my understanding of ecological issues. With a mastery of many areas, George was able to collect materials in Wisconsin agriculture with an eye to their broad significance. He also compiled an impeccably organized set of notes on rural Wisconsin.

Many colleagues and friends have read the manuscript, and their criticisms have brought significant improvements. I am especially grateful to Merle Curti, Morton Rothstein, and Allan Bogue, with whom I served in the department of history at the University of Wisconsin during the 1960's and 1970's. At the University of Oklahoma, I have drawn upon the expertise of Russell D. Buhite, Paul Varg, Richard Lowitt, Robert E. Shalhope, William W. Savage, Jr., and Gary Cohen. Paul Sharp, who shares associations with both Wisconsin and Oklahoma, reviewed the entire manuscript. Two research assistants at the University of Oklahoma, Duncan Aldrich and Robert C. Cottrell, were indefatigable in carrying out a variety of tasks. My colleague Leon Zelby, an expert in computer sciences, approved my application of quantitative techniques. Pastor David J. Klumpp of University Lutheran Chapel, Norman, Oklahoma, has helped improve my understanding of Lutheran theology and church history. As a beneficiary of support generously granted to the University of Oklahoma by the Merrick family, I am pleased to acknowledge my gratitude especially to Elizabeth Merrick Coe and Ward S. Merrick, Jr.

From my first year of teaching at a small college in Nebraska to more recent assignments in the United States and abroad, I have acquired obligations greater than my capacity to repay. For nearly forty years I have cherished professional and personal association with Jay Jones, a native of Wisconsin and a graduate of Carroll College. With his reading of the manuscript he has again come to my assistance as he has through four decades. During a Fulbright year at the University of Graz, Austria, in 1987–1988, I broadened my perspective through association with Greta Walter-Klingenstein, Walter Hölbling, Ingomar Weiler, and Siegfried Beer.

Thomas K. McCraw of Harvard University and David W. Levy of the University of Oklahoma merit special thanks and recognition. Their painstaking thoroughness in criticizing the manuscript, their remarkably telling analyses of crucial questions, and their extraordinarily helpful suggestions were the basis for many improvements in the final product. Their extensive notes and comments—often reassuring and supportive—proved indispensable during the long, agonizing months when Volume V was undergoing revision.

In naming the colleagues and associates to whom I am deeply indebted, I have not recognized by name many archivists and librarians at the universities of Wisconsin and Oklahoma, the State Historical Society of Wisconsin, the Minnesota Historical Society, the Houghton Library of Harvard University, and the Library of Congress. I am, of course, appreciative of all the assistance I have received.

The one person I wish to thank above all others is my wife, Carolyn. Together we have experienced joys and sorrows, gains and losses, triumphs and defeats. She neither shifts with the winds nor stubbornly refuses to change. Graciously she has received applause from those who know her best, but she has refused to glory in the praise accorded her. I have upon occasion tried her patience, but she has never let the sun go down upon her wrath. For nearly half a century she has been my preceptor, my partner, my inspiration. She is the love of my life.

PAUL W. GLAD

Norman, Oklahoma

CONTRIBUTORS

THE STATE HISTORICAL SOCIETY OF WISCONSIN

THE UNIVERSITY OF WISCONSIN

WESTERN PUBLISHING COMPANY, INC.

FIRST WISCONSIN FOUNDATION, INC.

THE JOURNAL COMPANY

THE NORTHWESTERN MUTUAL LIFE INSURANCE COMPANY

PABST BREWERIES FOUNDATION

SCHLITZ FOUNDATION, INC.

APPLETON COATED FOUNDATION, INC.

APPLETON WIRE WORKS CORP.

BANTA COMPANY FOUNDATION, INC.

BERGSTROM FOUNDATION

THE FALK CORPORATION

FOX RIVER PAPER CO.

KIMBERLY-CLARK FOUNDATION, INC.

THE MARINE FOUNDATION, INC.

MARSHALL & ILSLEY BANK FOUNDATION, INC.

THILMANY PULP AND PAPER COMPANY

WISCONSIN ELECTRIC POWER COMPANY

THE JOHNSON'S WAX FUND, INC.

MILLER HIGH LIFE FOUNDATION, INC.

NEKOOSA-EDWARDS FOUNDATION INCORPORATED

WISCONSIN MICHIGAN POWER COMPANY

WISCONSIN NATURAL GAS COMPANY

WISCONSIN PUBLIC SERVICE CORPORATION

CHARLES W. WRIGHT FOUNDATION OF BADGER METER, INC.

CONTENTS

Preface vii

Contributors xi

List of Maps xv

Note on Citations xviii

Part I: The Great War and Its Aftermath 1

1 Wisconsin, Neutrality, and Belligerency 3

2 An Uneasy Peace Comes to Wisconsin 55

3 Dreams, Illusions, and Disappointments of the Postwar Decade 83

Part II: The New Era 127

4 Complexities of Industrial Expansion 129

5 Agriculture, Scientific Research, and the Dissemination of Knowledge 165

6 City and Hinterland: Tensions of the New Era 195

7 Leisure, Education, and Politics 248

8 The Progressive Tradition and Political Behavior in Wisconsin 296

Part III: The Great Depression 346

9 The Challenge of Economic Depression 348

10 Cries of Protest, Murmurs of Discontent, and Formation of the Progressive Party of Wisconsin 398

11 Wisconsin and the New Deal 448

12 Controversies Along the Middle Way 483

13 Man CAN Have Work AND Be Free 524

Epilogue: The Land Remembers 566

Appendix A: The Governors of Wisconsin, 1914–1940 569

Appendix B: Analysis of the La Follette Elections 571

Essay on Sources 589

Index 621

ILLUSTRATIONS

Following pages 78, 270, and 366 are selections of photographs depicting Wisconsin people and events during the period 1914–1940. Unless otherwise noted, all illustrations are from the Iconographic Collections of the State Historical Society of Wisconsin.

MAPS

Designed by
John Krygier

Prepared by
The University of Wisconsin Cartographic Laboratory

County Seats and Other Places, 1930 — 7

German-Born in Wisconsin, 1920 — 13

Population Change, 1910–1920 — 85

Population Change, 1920–1930 — 86

Population Change, 1930–1940 — 87

Scandinavian-Born in Wisconsin, 1930 — 92

Paved Road Network, 1924 — 212

Paved Road Network, 1940 — 213

Urban Population, 1930 — 221

La Follette Elections, 1916–1940 — 330–341

Changes in Farm Value, 1910–1920 — 359

Changes in Farm Value, 1920–1930 — 360

Changes in Farm Value, 1930–1940 — 361

Impact of the Great Depression, 1935 — 371

THE HISTORY OF WISCONSIN

Note on Citations

LRL	Legislative Reference Library (1901–1963).
LRB	Legislative Reference Bureau (after 1963).
WMH	*Wisconsin Magazine of History.*
WSA	Wisconsin State Archives.
UW	University of Wisconsin. (Any use of this term without a specific campus designation denotes the University of Wisconsin–Madison.)

Unless otherwise indicated, all government publications are those of the State of Wisconsin.

Unless otherwise indicated, all manuscripts, pamphlets, and government publications cited are in the collections of the State Historical Society of Wisconsin.

PART I

The Great War and Its Aftermath

DURING the first years of the twentieth century, a popular and pervasive belief throughout western society held that the progress of civilization had made possible the elimination of war. Then came the Great War of 1914–1918. After hostilities began, the brutality of the conflict shattered confidence in the advance of civilization. At the same time, the viciousness of the struggle increased the urgency of finding means to restore peace. Perceiving themselves as conservators of fundamental truths in a world gone awry, Americans at first sought to steer clear of the fighting in Europe. Avoiding conflict, ran the argument for neutrality, would provide a model of international behavior for peoples of the world and preserve the benefits of peace for American citizens.

Yet the United States was an important source of supplies the belligerents needed for waging war. British control of the sea assured Allied access to American markets, and American loans made possible a thriving trade. To compensate for British superiority in conventional fighting ships and to disrupt the flow of war materiel from the United States, Germany employed its new *Unterseeboote*, or submarines. Yet the submarine seemed a particularly reprehensible instrument of warfare, and effective as it was, the new weapon encouraged sympathetic American support of the Allies. The Germans therefore agreed in 1916 to suspend U-boat operations. The suspension turned out to be temporary, however, for early the next year, the Germans decided to launch a full-scale offensive for the purpose of quickly defeating the Allies and ending the war. The peace offensive of the Central Powers did not succeed, but it did bring the United States into the conflict as one of the Allies.

With Wisconsin's sizable population of German and Austrian ancestry—and with Wisconsin's Progressives and Socialists generally opposed to American belligerency—the state experienced unusual tensions during the years of conflict. Tensions of wartime, in turn, affected political alignments in the state. The most famous of Wisconsin's political leaders, Senator Robert M. La Follette, risked his reputation and his influence, first in supporting the abortive effort to prevent American entry into the war, and then in aiding the successful effort to prevent ratification of the settlement drafted at the Peace Conference. The senator felt vindicated during the early 1920's, but the influences that brought vindication for La Follette also brought disillusionment for people who expected a rational world order to emerge from the ruins of war.

However citizens of Wisconsin were to assess the Great War after the return of peace, several groups in the state had sought to use the international crisis to their advantage. Prohibitionists and suffragists, for example, emphasized the nation's wartime emergency needs in working for ratification of the Eighteenth and Nineteenth Amendments to the United States Constitution. Those amendments, and the reforms they represented, did much to shape the development of Wisconsin society during the era of the 1920's. So also did wartime "Americanization" efforts continue to affect Wisconsin attitudes. Chambers of Commerce, the Ku Klux Klan, and other organizations sought in various ways and for various reasons to maintain the patriotic commitment of 1917–1918. Echoes of the Great War thus continued to reverberate across the Wisconsin countryside long after the guns had ceased firing in Europe.

1

Neutrality and Belligerency

LATE in 1918, shortly after the guns had ceased firing across no-man's land in France, University of Wisconsin sociologist Edward Alsworth Ross reflected on the nation's wartime experience. He was impressed by the unity of mind and purpose that had come to dominate American society, and he could not help but contrast it with the divisions that existed when war had first broken out in Europe. "It is plain that a society so politically heterogeneous and mentally confused as ours would have been utterly unable in 1914–1915 to make such a patriotic effort as was made by European belligerents," he wrote. Ross believed that had the United States been attacked in 1914, "we would have collapsed lamentably, owing chiefly to want of like-mindedness." While he exaggerated the solidarity of other countries as well as the likely consequences of an attack, Professor Ross did not misrepresent the diversity of American opinion on the war.[1]

More so than their fellow countrymen, citizens of Wisconsin viewed the European conflict from a variety of perspectives. Indeed, with the state's reputation for innovative leadership jealously nurtured by spokesmen of the Progressive movement, its conservative tradition revitalized in the elections of 1914, its vigorous Socialist contingent optimistic about future victories, and its heavy proportion of German immigrants deeply concerned about the fate of the Fatherland, Wisconsin encouraged a wide array of attitudes towards the war.

The citizenry of the state also held firm convictions about the war. Some were convinced that it represented a return to barbarism; for them, western civilization seemed to have met disaster when leaders of both sides allowed the war to occur. So great was their

[1] Ross to John P. Gavit, December 5, 1918, in the Edward Alsworth Ross Papers.

horror that they worked diligently, often imaginatively, to find means of ending the carnage. Some believed that the conflict in Europe was the culmination of class and economic rivalries; they held that privileged economic interests ruthlessly sent men to their slaughter in order to enlarge their own markets and profits. Some were partial to the Central Powers, either because of ethnic ties with Germany or because they accepted the argument that British imperialism represented the most pernicious form of economic exploitation. Partisans of the Allied cause, on the other hand, leaned towards the view that the progress of civilization had been interrupted the moment German troops had marched across the Belgian border. Those who supported the Allies favored "preparedness" on the theory that it would enable the United States to avoid calamities that had befallen other countries.

* * *

Even before the various responses to the war became evident, seekers after peace were hard at work in Wisconsin. The impulse to do good that animated the prewar Progressive movement also found expression in the formation of peace societies and peace programs. Most noteworthy of the proposals designed to stop the fighting in Europe was one developed by Julia Grace Wales, a young instructor of English at the University of Wisconsin. Returning to the campus for the opening of classes in the fall of 1914, Wales was dismayed by news about the guns of August. She soon found herself devoting much more time to international problems than to her own scholarly interests. Contemplating the evils of war and how to bring them to an end, she wrote the draft of a proposal that in February, 1915, the Wisconsin Peace Society printed and circulated under the title, *Continuous Mediation Without Armistice*.[2]

The Wales plan called for forming a Peace League, in which all neutral nations were to have representation to consider means of resolving the issues that had led to war. Wales proposed that the league discuss peace terms without consulting belligerents and with-

[2] Julia Grace Wales, "The Record of the Wisconsin Peace Plan," and Louise P. Kellogg, "Brief Sketch of the Life and Work of Julia Grace Wales," both in the Julia Grace Wales Papers; Jack Frooman, "The Wisconsin Peace Movement, 1915–1919" (master's thesis, University of Wisconsin, 1949), 29–30. Canadian-born, Wales received her bachelor's degree from McGill University in 1906. After obtaining her M.A. from Radcliffe, she joined the University of Wisconsin faculty in 1909. She completed the work for her Ph.D. degree at the University of Wisconsin in 1926.

out prior agreement to an armistice. Once neutral states had agreed to a proposal that was reasonable, the league would submit it simultaneously to all warring nations with the question, "Will you agree to adopt or consider the accompanying proposition as a basis of peace if and when the governments of the other warring powers will agree to do likewise?" If any power replied in the negative the league would continue in session, formulating new proposals to meet the reluctant nation's objections. Ultimately, thought advocates of the plan, the league could effect a settlement. For her part, Julia Wales believed that she had hit upon a workable formula, "a radical plan . . . which, if it could shorten the present war, would tend also to prevent similar wars in the future." At times she lapsed into sentimental paraphrase of Mary Tudor. "When I die," she remarked more than once, "you will find *Continuous Mediation Without Armistice* written on my heart."[3]

Response to her peace plan was immediate and impressive. Stanford University Chancellor David Starr Jordan, a veteran of the peace movement, thought it "the most forceful and practical thing" he had yet seen. An Emergency Peace Conference held in Chicago on February 27–28, 1915, and attended by such dignitaries as Jane Addams, Morris Hillquit, and Hamilton Holt, formally adopted the plan and appointed a special delegation to carry it to President Woodrow Wilson and the U.S. Congress. In the meantime, encouraged by national success, Wisconsin supporters of the proposal set about lobbying with the state legislature. Both houses ultimately endorsed the plan and requested that President Wilson take appropriate action.[4]

With the plan for continuous mediation winning converts daily, Wales and her friends looked for means to broaden its appeal. An opportunity to advertise the proposal presented itself when women of the Netherlands organized an International Congress of Women that met at The Hague in April, 1915. With encouragement from

[3] Julia Grace Wales, *Continuous Mediation Without Armistice* (1915), 3–6, and Kellogg, "Brief Sketch," both in the Wales Papers. Several versions of *Continuous Mediation*, reprinted by the American Delegation to the International Congress of Women at The Hague, appear in the Wales Papers. Citations are to the pamphlet printed in 1915 under the auspices of the Wisconsin Peace Society.

[4] Jordan to John K. Bonnell, February 16, 17, 1915, and Wales, "Record of the Wisconsin Peace Plan," 4–8, all in the Wales Papers; Frooman, "Wisconsin Peace Movement," 43–45; *Wisconsin State Journal*, February 27, 28, 1915; Chicago *Tribune*, February 28, 1915; Louise P. Kellogg, diary, March 1, 1915, in the Louise P. Kellogg Papers.

Jane Addams and University of Wisconsin President Charles R. Van Hise, Wales attended the congress as a delegate. She was on hand when the congress protested against "the madness and the horror of war" and adopted the principle of *Continuous Mediation Without Armistice*. She also accompanied a committee that presented resolutions of the congress to the governments of other nations. Despite her hopes, however, her activities early in 1915 marked the high point of Wales's involvement with the cause of peace. Late in the year she again traveled to Europe when she sailed on Henry Ford's "Peace Ship." Yet the Ford mission soon fell into disarray, and high-minded participants in the independent peace movement came to appear more and more quixotic.[5]

Back home, citizens of Wisconsin undertook a variety of activities to match peace efforts abroad. On the campus of the University of Wisconsin, the War and Peace Society, made up of fifty male juniors and seniors, carried on discussions and sponsored rallies for peace. Not to be outdone, university women quickly formed an organization of their own, and peace became a major topic of discussion at student gatherings. Music school professor Peter W. Dykema, a member of the National Choral Peace Jubilee Committee, organized a peace pilgrimage to the Pacific Coast. He intended to start Americans singing and "get the nation as a whole into a different [and presumably a more pacific] state of mind." Dykema's junket was only one effort to proclaim the cause of peace beyond the limits of Madison. In September, the Wisconsin Peace Society managed to persuade the Madison Board of Commerce to send out a circular letter to the secretaries of every commercial organization in the state. The document espoused continuous mediation as a plan that would "establish a world brain, so that an adjustment may be scientifically made, that will appeal to both the warring and neutral peoples." Later that fall, David Starr Jordan visited Wisconsin on his way to Washington, where he hoped to convince President Wil-

[5] Madison *Democrat*, March 16, 18, April 2, 1915; *Wisconsin State Journal*, March 15, April 2, 1915; International Congress of Women, *Report, 28 April–1 May*, and Wales to Louise P. Kellogg, April 30, 1915, both in the Woman's Peace Party Papers; Chicago *Tribune*, April 13, 1915; Van Hise to Wales, April 5, 1915, International Congress of Women, *Report*, 12, 16–18, and *Manifesto, Issued by the Envoys of the International Congress of Women at The Hague, to the Governments of Europe, and the President of the United States*, all in the Wales Papers.

The story of the Ford venture is told in Allan Nevins and Frank Ernest Hill, *Ford. Volume 2: Expansion and Challenge, 1915–1933* (New York, 1957), 26–54. For Julia Wales's part, see Frooman, "Wisconsin Peace Movement," 205–216.

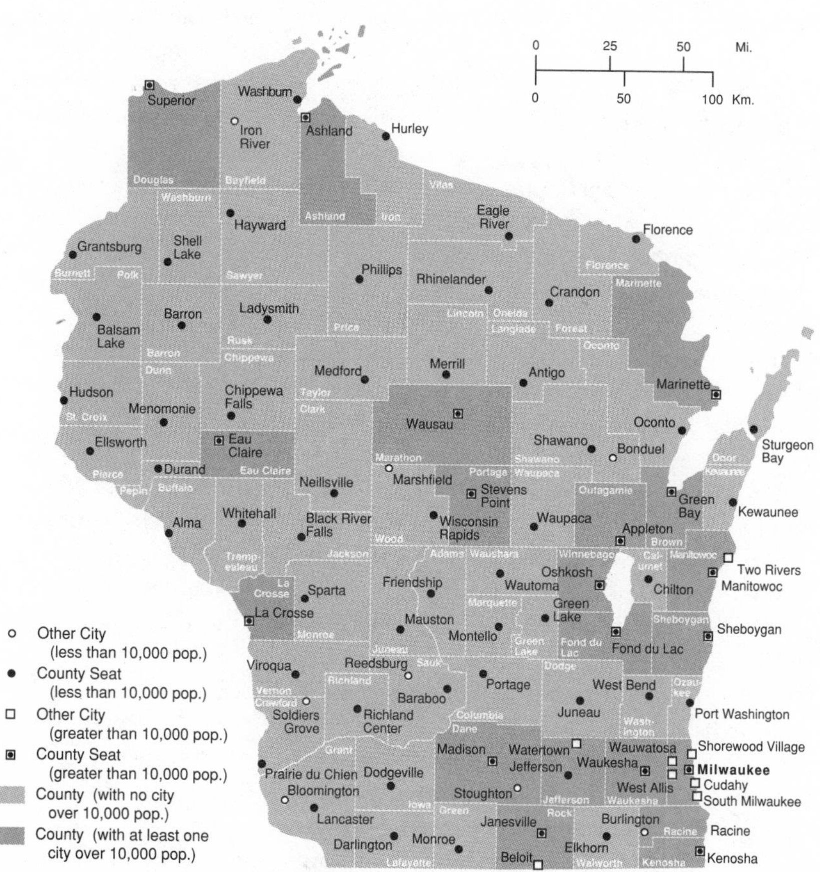

County Seats and Other Places, 1930

son that the Wisconsin plan offered a practical way to end the war. He spoke to a gathering of 4,000 people in the Old Red Gym on the university campus, emphasizing the evils of war and praising the work of Julia Wales.[6]

[6] Frooman, "Wisconsin Peace Movement," 129; H. E. Erdman to Paul O. Husting, May 13, 1915, and Husting to Erdman, May 25, 1915, in the Paul O. Husting Papers; *Wisconsin State Journal*, June 13, 1915; Madison Board of Commerce, circular letter to

Unfortunately, Jordan had no more success with the President than Wales had on the Ford peace mission. The peace movement seemed quickly to lose its momentum, and had it been entirely dependent on the Wisconsin plan it might have come to a halt. But to the seekers after peace, the Wisconsin plan never became an *idée fixe*, nor did the peace movement itself ever become the exclusive property of any particular group. Although interest in the restoration of peace appeared to be lagging in the early months of 1916, the appearances were deceiving.

A major influence in revitalizing the peace movement was the Woman's Peace party, which had begun to organize in Wisconsin during the summer of 1915 under the leadership of Ella H. Neville of Green Bay. Louise Phelps Kellogg, research scholar of the State Historical Society of Wisconsin and a friend of Julia Wales, assisted in setting up the party organization. Others were eager to help, and in Milwaukee a group calling itself the Milwaukee Peace League sought affiliation with the party. In fact, Meta Berger, vice-president of the league, urged that it go further and make common cause with all the peace organizations of the state. A branch of the Woman's Peace party began to form in Madison during the summer of 1916. When women of the capital city held their first meeting in November, they listened to Belle Case La Follette, wife of the U.S. senator, speak on the aims and history of the party. All over Wisconsin women worked for peace, and their perseverance was remarkable. Even after the eventual break in diplomatic relations between Germany and the United States, they remained active in the Do Our Bit Club, organized to send out chain letters for peace. The letters requested that each recipient write the President urging him to resolve the international conflict without resorting to military intervention. Not until after Wilson had read his war message to Congress early in April, 1917, did the Woman's Peace party disintegrate.[7]

---

secretaries of commercial organizations in Wisconsin, September, 1915, in the Woman's Peace Party Papers; Madison *Democrat*, November 10, 1915; Kellogg, "Brief Sketch," in the Wales Papers.

[7] Louis P. Lochner to Wales, November 13, 1915, with enclosed typescript from Lochner, "Strictly Private and Confidential Additional Data Regarding Our Interview," dated November 12, 1915, in the Wales Papers; Eleanor G. Karsten to Kellogg, February 21, 1917, Annette Roberts to Kellogg, March 6, 1917, minutes of the November 18, 1916, meeting of the Madison Branch of the Woman's Peace Party, and "Do Our Bit Club" minutes, c. February 21, 1917, all in the Woman's Peace Party Papers.

Carried on largely by amateurs, the peace movement in Wisconsin manifested qualities of artlessness and naïveté. Yet despite the inadequacies of amateur solutions for complex international problems, the peace movement received a measure of support from most of the state's political practitioners. No one sought identification as a warmonger. That Wisconsin's congressional delegation voted heavily against declaring war on Germany in 1917 indicates that its members were committed to the goal of peace, or at least to maintaining neutrality. The most influential of the state's political leaders, Senator Robert M. La Follette, was also the most prominent in opposing American intervention into what he regarded as essentially a European conflict. Never a true pacifist in the sense that his wife was, La Follette did not condemn all wars. At the same time, he did not think that the nation would be well served by entering this one.[8]

La Follette had become increasingly disenchanted with Wilson's handling of foreign affairs. During the early months of the conflict he had strongly supported the President's plea for neutrality in thought and action, but when the United States seemed to move towards involvement he began to resist presidential leadership. By 1916 he was hammering away at the idea that the old domestic foe, an unscrupulous pack of powerful and predatory special interests, had aligned itself behind the campaign for preparedness. La Follette favored nationalizing all arms industries, placing an embargo on the shipment of arms and ammunition to belligerents, and establishing government ownership of maritime transportation. Take away the possibility of war profits, he reasoned, and you reduce the possibility of war itself. In following that line of thought, La Follette did his best to identify Progressivism with peace and economic privilege with war.[9]

Meanwhile, Wilson's dealings with the factions struggling for power in the Mexican Revolution increased the senator's distrust of the President. That distrust led him to search for a means of preserving American neutrality. When the United States Navy seized Vera Cruz in 1914, La Follette began to worry about the President's creating a war crisis without consulting Congress. Two years later,

[8] Summary of interview with Isabel Bacon La Follette, March 11, 1969, copy in both the author's and project files.

[9] *La Follette's Magazine*, January and March, 1916; Herbert F. Margulies, *The Decline of the Progressive Movement in Wisconsin, 1890–1920* (Madison, 1968), 174–175.

after Wilson threatened direct intervention in Mexican affairs, La Follette reacted by accusing the Senate of meekly dodging its constitutional responsibilities. Congress, he argued, should reassert its duties of advice and consent before Wilson could bring about a state of war.[10]

As if relations with Mexico were not bad enough, German-American tensions increased when a German submarine torpedoed an unarmed French channel steamer, the *Sussex*, in March, 1916. La Follette promptly introduced a war referendum bill in the Senate. It provided that "whenever the President shall sever diplomatic relations with any foreign government and one per cent of the electorate of 25 states shall file petitions with the Director of the Bureau of the Census, then he shall ascertain the number of electors for and against a declaration of war against such foreign government." The La Follette referendum did not require a constitutional amendment, and it could have been made operative without going through a long ratification process. Nothing came of a Senate discussion of the bill, however, for interest in the referendum died with the passing of the *Sussex* crisis. La Follette, to be sure, continued to resist the moves that in his view took the nation closer to war. But he did so largely on a tactical, ad hoc basis.[11]

If a well-formulated analysis of war's causes was vital to an effective peace movement, then socialists should have been better prepared to carry on such a movement than either the peace societies or the politicians. Reduced to its barest essentials, Marxian theory held that a capitalistic economy must be expansive, that eventually the potential for expansion within national boundaries would decrease, and that capitalism would then have no choice but to become imperialistic. War, according to socialist reasoning, resulted from the rivalry of capitalistic-imperialistic powers seeking opportunities for exploitation.

[10] Robert E. Quirk, *An Affair of Honor: Woodrow Wilson and the Occupation of Veracruz* (Lexington, Kentucky, 1962); Arthur S. Link, *Woodrow Wilson and the Progressive Era, 1910–1917* (New York, 1954), 129–137, and *Wilson. Volume 4: Confusions and Crises, 1915–1916* (Princeton, 1964), 208–209; Belle Case La Follette and Fola La Follette, *Robert M. La Follette* (2 vols., New York, 1953), 1:558–560.

[11] Ernest R. May, *The World War and American Isolation* (Cambridge, 1959), 190–194; Karl E. Birnbaum, *Peace Moves and U-Boat Warfare: A Study of Imperial Germany's Policy Towards the United States, April 18, 1916–January 9, 1917* (Stockholm, 1958), 70–92; *Congressional Record*, 64 Cong., 1 sess., 7451–7455. See also Ronald P. Formisano, "The Demand for a War Referendum, 1914–1917" (master's thesis, University of Wisconsin, 1962), 30ff.

Unfortunately for the socialists, the emotional and political realities of the war made application of this theory troublesome, and development of a generally accepted program for peace well-nigh impossible. A part of the socialists' difficulty was that the predominantly middle-class peace societies and their members could not accept the socialist analysis of the causes of war. Furthermore, American socialists had no end of trouble explaining why so many of their European comrades went to war. They could scarcely admit, much less approve, the fact that for some of their number national loyalties took precedence over class loyalties.[12]

Members of the Socialist party in Milwaukee, like socialists everywhere, opposed the war but disagreed among themselves on what should be done about it. Victor Berger, editor of the Milwaukee *Leader*, took his stand in opposition to American involvement when in the spring of 1917 he went as a delegate to a special emergency party conclave in St. Louis. Called to determine policy in the event that the United States abandoned neutrality, the meeting actually convened just one day after Congress had passed a war resolution. Berger served on the committee that drafted a report branding the American declaration of war "a crime of our capitalist class against the people of the United States and against the nations of the world." Adopted by the convention, the report also pledged "continuous active and public opposition to the war, through demonstration, mass petition, and all other means within our power." Although Berger thought some of the language extreme, he signed the St. Louis Proclamation. Other socialists agreed with him. When the report went out to party members in a national referendum, they approved it by a three-to-one margin.[13]

Not everyone in the Milwaukee Socialist organization followed Berger's lead. Algie M. Simons, who had worked on the staff of the *Leader*, had long thought the party too pro-German. Refusing to vote for the proclamation, he left the party, became director of the Bureau of Literature in the Wisconsin Loyalty Legion, and set about whooping it up for the war effort. The Socialist party mayor

[12] M. E. M. [Mary E. Marcy], "Socialist Unpreparedness in Germany," in the *International Socialist Review*, 15 (October, 1914), 245; David A. Shannon, *The Socialist Party of America: A History* (New York, 1955), 82–83, 87–88.

[13] Milwaukee *Leader*, April 11, 1917; Nathan Fine, *Labor and Farmer Parties in the United States, 1828–1928* (New York, 1928; reprinted, New York, 1961), 310–314; Shannon, *Socialist Party of America*, 98.

of Milwaukee, Daniel Hoan, occupied a more moderate position. In July, 1916, he marched at the head of what he insisted on calling "a national civic demonstration," but what to all intents and purposes amounted to a preparedness parade. He also refused to endorse the St. Louis Proclamation. On the other hand, he stood by the party's city platform, which blamed the capitalist class for America's entry into war and proposed that profiteers pay the costs of American military operations.[14]

Lack of unity presented fewer problems to Germans, who viewed with horror the possibility of war with the Fatherland. The combined German-Austrian population in Wisconsin was sizable: about 700,000 out of 2,334,000 people in 1918. It was well organized under the leadership of the German-American Alliance, with approximately 37,000 members in the state. During the first dozen years of its existence before the war, the alliance placed great emphasis on its cultural program, stressing the teaching of German in public schools, encouraging physical training after the pattern of the *Turnvereine* (gymnastics clubs), and studying the distinctive German contributions to American history. Like most other ethnic associations, the alliance also assisted immigrants in their quest for citizenship.[15]

On the negative side, the alliance soon associated itself with the fight against prohibition. Indeed, its members sometimes saw prohibitionists as their principal political adversaries. "In order to gain for the Germans of America that place in the sun which has hitherto always been denied them," contended the monthly bulletin of the association, "it is absolutely necessary that they enjoy personal liberty, and that this shall not be whittled away by the attacks of the prohibitionists and the persecutors of the foreign-born." After 1914, of course, opposition to prohibition lost some of its importance—but not all. In the midst of plots and rumors, the whole German community fell under suspicion, and many Americans came

[14] Algie M. Simons, "The Future of the Socialist Party," in the *New Republic*, December 1, 1916, pp. 118–120; Richard T. Ely to Edward C. Marsh, June 13, 1918, in the Richard T. Ely Papers; Robert C. Reinders, "Daniel W. Hoan and the Milwaukee Socialist Party During the First World War," in the *Wisconsin Magazine of History* (hereinafter cited as the *WMH*), 36 (Autumn, 1952), 49, 52; Bayrd Still, *Milwaukee: The History of a City* (Madison, 1948; reprinted, 1965), 524; Margulies, *Decline of the Progressive Movement*, 200–201.

[15] Madison *Capital Times*, May 6, 1918; Clifton J. Child, *The German-Americans in Politics, 1914–1917* (Madison, 1939), 3–4.

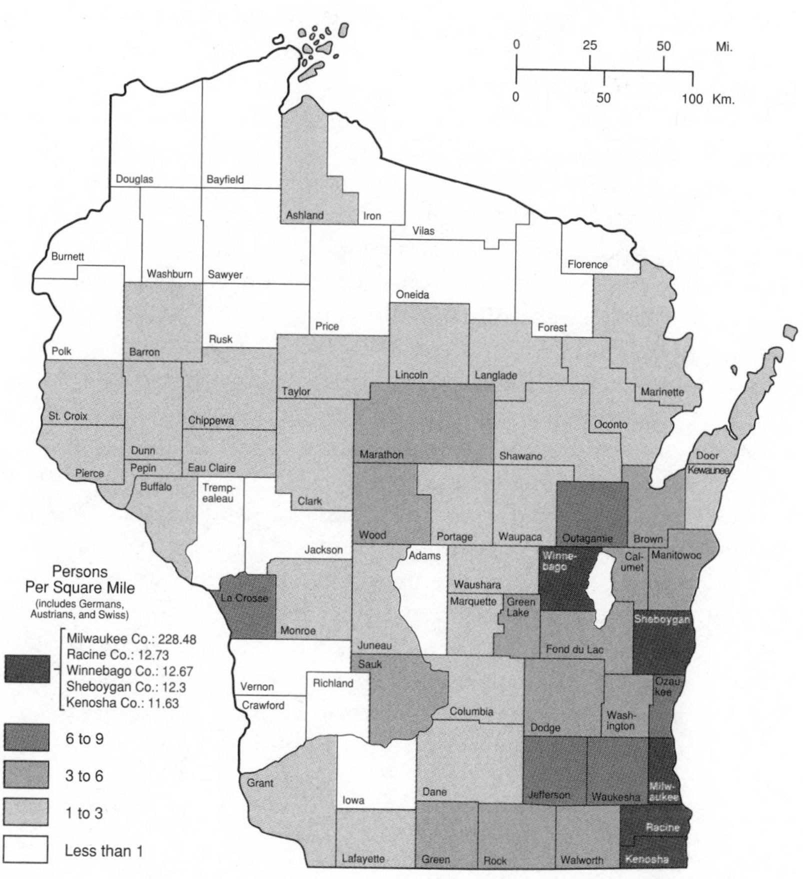

German-Born in Wisconsin, 1920

to believe that German clubs and societies operated under orders from Berlin. That the alliance continued to emphasize its opposition to prohibition after 1914 is in itself evidence that the organization was by no means an instrument of pan-Germanism. Prohibition was primarily an American issue, one that befuddled the German government. The alliance position suggests that its orientation was towards American society and domestic politics. As the war progressed, Wisconsin's Germans became increasingly concerned about international problems, but never did those problems destroy their consciousness of a need to make their own way under conditions of life in the United States.[16]

When war broke out in 1914, then, a sense of alienation combined with genuine pride in their cultural heritage led Wisconsin's German population to support President Wilson's appeal for "a true spirit of neutrality." As members of an ethnic group seeking to maintain both its identity and its position in American society, they readily associated themselves with the consensus opposing war. As late as the summer of 1915 Francis Hackett, an editor of the *New Republic*, could write of the Milwaukee Germans: "As between Germany and the Allies, they are for Germany, but this does not mean that the bulk of them desire at practically any cost, even to America, the triumph of German arms." Yet by that time most Germans had moved with La Follette to the conviction that Wilson himself was not steering a neutral course. What most troubled members of the German community was the exportation of munitions to belligerents. They were keenly conscious of the fact that British control of the seas assured delivery of those munitions into Allied hands exclusively. They therefore insisted that if the United States was to be neutral in fact as well as in rhetoric the nation would have to impose an embargo on arms. La Follette supported the idea. So did Wisconsin's conservative Republican governor, Emanuel Philipp. But efforts to stop the shipment of munitions proved abortive when the Wilson administration stood fast by the legality of the trade. "If it came to the iast analysis," wrote Colonel Edward M. House to Wilson, "and we placed an embargo on munitions of war and foodstuffs . . . our whole industrial and agricultural machinery would cry out against it."[17]

[16] Deutsch-Amerikanischen National-Bundes der Vereinigten Staaten von Amerika (National German American Alliance), *Mitteilungen* (*Bulletin*), August, 1915, p. 4, as quoted in Child, *German-Americans in Politics*, 11; John Higham, *Strangers in the Land: Patterns of American Nativism, 1860–1925* (New Brunswick, New Jersey, 1955), 196–197; U.S. Senate, Subcommittee of the Committee on the Judiciary, *National-German American Alliance: Hearings Before the Subcommittee . . . on S. 3529 . . . February 23–April 13, 1918*, 65 Cong., 2 sess. (1918), 140–141.

[17] Francis Hackett, "How Milwaukee Takes the War," in the *New Republic*, July 17, 1915, p. 272; Milwaukee *Sentinel*, April 10, 1915; *Congressional Record*, 63 Cong., 3 sess., 3632–3633; Charles Seymour, ed., *The Intimate Papers of Colonel House: From Neutrality to War, 1915–1917* (4 vols., Boston, 1926–1928), 2:58; *Correspondence Between the Secretary of State and the Chairman of the Committee on Foreign Relations*, published as no. 716 in *Senate Documents*, 63 Cong., 3 sess. (serial 6783).

Meanwhile, the Germans of Wisconsin had been doing more than urging passage of an embargo. They established a committee to assure proper dissemination of news and information about the German cause. They protested what they regarded as anti-German passages in a textbook used in French courses at the University of Wisconsin and elicited an apology through President Van Hise. They readily contributed to a national fund-raising campaign for relief work in Germany, a campaign launched by the German-American Alliance in the fall of 1914. More than $67,000 had come from Wisconsin, $61,000 from Milwaukee alone, by the end of January, 1915. The alliance sold pictures of Kaiser Wilhelm II and Emperor Francis Joseph, and in exchange for jewelry and other valuables it distributed more than 7,000 iron rings bearing inscriptions such as the following:

Dem alten Vaterland
Die Treue zu beweisen
Gab ich in schwerer Zeit
Ihn Gold für dieses Eisen.

Did these activities violate the spirit of neutrality for which the President had pleaded at the outset of the war? "I should like to know," commented Dr. Leo Stern, an assistant superintendent of the Milwaukee public schools and president of the Wisconsin alliance, "why I should not love the country where my parents are buried, and where my sisters are buried, where I received my fundamental education."[18]

For many non-German residents of the state the attitude of Stern and the activities of the alliance raised doubts about the fidelity of Germans. Wisconsin's junior senator, Paul O. Husting, spoke for some of his constituents when he began charging the Wisconsin Germans with disloyalty. Referring to their criticism of American trade policies, he accused them of having made "a very coarse,

[18] Merle Curti and Vernon Carstensen, *The University of Wisconsin: A History, 1848–1925* (2 vols., Madison, 1949), 2:323–324; Child, *German-Americans in Politics*, 37–38; *The Fatherland [Fair Play for Germany and Austria Hungary]*, 2 (April 7, 1915), advertisement on p. 30 (cataloged as *American Monthly*); Hackett, "How Milwaukee Takes the War," *New Republic*, 3:272. The verse can be translated as follows:

To demonstrate fidelity
To the ancient Fatherland,
In a time of difficulty,
I gave gold for this iron.

vituperative, un-American attack on President Wilson and his administration."[19]

The development that most stirred anti-German feeling was the U-boat sinking of the *Lusitania* on May 7, 1915, with a loss of 1,198 lives. Four days before the ship went down, the Milwaukee *Germania-Herold* had argued the right of German submarines to sink it. Contending that the *Lusitania* carried a contraband cargo of more than 5,000 cases of ammunition, and that the British Admiralty had failed to provide adequate protection, the *Herold* article established the main line of justification for the attack. A national wave of criticism nevertheless overwhelmed all Germanic argument and threw Germans on the defensive as never before. Throughout the long *Lusitania* negotiations and beyond, the best they could hope for was avoidance of direct military involvement of the United States. Unlike many opponents of war who supported Wilson's efforts to maintain American neutrality, however, Germans had grown increasingly critical of the President and his policies. By their criticism they lent credibility to charges of disloyalty and thereby helped bring about the anti-German hysteria that swept the country after the United States had declared war.[20]

* * *

The *Lusitania* incident had another important consequence. It provided an argument and a stimulus for those urging an American military buildup. The awkwardly labeled "preparedness" movement had its organizational beginnings in December of 1914 with the formation of the National Security League in New York, and it soon won enthusiastic adherents in Wisconsin. Milwaukee boasted the largest branch of the National Security League in the Middle West outside Chicago, and preparedness parades became a common occurrence in many Wisconsin cities. The Milwaukee parade in mid-July, 1916, with its 28,253 participants and forty-five bands, drew an estimated 150,000–175,000 spectators.

Preparedness was a cause that appealed to the pride of Wisconsin citizens, and they were pleased with their showing. Nevertheless few of them agreed with former President Theodore Roosevelt, best known of the advocates of preparedness, that war with Germany

[19] Husting to Andrew Noll, May 14, 1915, in the Husting Papers.

[20] Milwaukee *Germania-Herold*, May 3, 1915, cited in Child, *German-Americans in Politics*, 67–84.

was in the national interest. Governor Philipp, who had backed Julia Grace Wales's peace plan and the embargo on arms shipments, was among the first to be persuaded of the need for a stronger military establishment. But he drew a distinction between preparation for war and preparation as a guarantee of neutrality. Speaking at Monroe in October, 1915, he argued that a trained citizenry was better able to preserve its neutrality than was a disorganized populace. He warned that the people of Wisconsin wanted an "honest neutrality" with no evidence of partisanship.[21]

President Wilson also became a convert to preparedness. In the fall of 1914 he had scoffed at the movement, and in his annual message of that year he had said that the position of his administration would not change simply because some Americans were "nervous and excited." By the summer of 1915, after the *Lusitania* affair, he had shifted his ground, and in November he called for expenditure of $500 million in ship construction as well as significant increases in the Regular Army. In May of the following year, after a bitter legislative struggle, Congress passed a measure that more than doubled the size of the Regular Army and authorized a five-year increase in National Guard strength to 17,000 officers and 440,000 men. The Naval Appropriations Act, marking a triumph for "big navy" enthusiasts, followed in August.[22]

The Wisconsin National Guard had long enjoyed respect throughout the state, perhaps in part because, after labor disturbances of the 1880's, it had not again intervened in labor strikes. The Guard had other qualities to recommend it. It retained officers until they reached the age of sixty-four, and inasmuch as officers did not face replacement with every new state administration, the Guard did not become a haven for political appointees. Robert La Follette, who as governor had helped take the Guard out of politics and establish its efficiency standards, thought it the equal of any in the country. Nevertheless the Wisconsin National Guard had weaknesses too.

[21] Link, *Wilson and the Progressive Era*, 177–178; John P. Finnegan, "Preparedness in Wisconsin: The National Guard and the Mexican Border Incident," in *WMH*, 47 (Spring, 1964), 200; Milwaukee *Journal*, July 15 and 16, 1916; Milwaukee *Daily News*, June 13, 1916; William H. Harbaugh, *Power and Responsibility: The Life and Times of Theodore Roosevelt* (New York, 1961), 447; John Morton Blum, *The Republican Roosevelt* (Cambridge, 1954), 152; *Wisconsin State Journal*, October 13, 1915; Robert S. Maxwell, *Emanuel L. Philipp: Wisconsin Stalwart* (Madison, 1959), 114–115.

[22] Link, *Wilson and the Progressive Era*, 177–180, 188–190; Maxwell, *Emanuel L. Philipp*, 115; Edward M. Coffman, *The War to End All Wars: The American Military Experience in World War I* (New York, 1968), 17–18.

Guardsmen received no pay for drill and so felt little compulsion to attend. Prior to 1916 the President had no power to call the Guard into service; he could only request enlistment en masse. Adjutant General Charles Boardman, who served Wisconsin under five governors between 1897 and 1913, believed that these weaknesses could be eliminated with establishment of a federal militia. If Congress appropriated funds for paying guardsmen, then it would have every right to set standards for each unit and place personnel under obligation to the federal government as well as to the state.[23]

The National Defense Act of 1916, by making the National Guard a component of the military forces of the United States, met most of Boardman's desires. That the act by no means eliminated all defects in the system, however, became abundantly clear within a month after its passage. During the winter of 1915–1916, while the preparedness movement had been building momentum, relations with Mexico deteriorated. They grew still worse after Francisco Villa's March 9 raid on Columbus, New Mexico. By late spring, war seemed imminent, and on June 18 the President called into service almost all of the National Guard. Yet neither country wanted war, and with the appointment of a Joint High Commission to investigate and make recommendations for the resolution of difficulties, tensions relaxed.[24]

If the Mexican crisis could be regarded as a dress rehearsal for military action in Europe, as it was by many Americans, then the commanders of National Guard units must have faced the future with apprehension. The Wisconsin Guard, supposedly capable of assembling at Camp Douglas in Juneau County in a matter of twelve to eighteen hours, actually took four days to do so. The delay was not serious, but other problems were abundant, and the red tape began to pile up. Because Congress had just passed the National Defense Act, nobody knew what oath to administer, and some guardsmen never did take the proper one. The men had just undergone their regular physical examinations, but they had to go through them again when they reached camp. Then the army in-

[23] Finnegan, "Preparedness in Wisconsin," in *WMH*, 47:200–201. For a fuller treatment of preparedness and the Wisconsin National Guard, see John P. Finnegan, "The Preparedness Movement in Wisconsin, 1914–1917" (master's thesis, University of Wisconsin, 1961).

[24] Link, *Wilson and the Progressive Era*, 136–144.

sisted on yet another examination with its own reserve doctors wielding the stethoscopes. The inevitable difficulties with training and supplying new recruits produced their full quota of stories to write home about. Finally, with some semblance of order, the guardsmen boarded the slow train for Texas. Dressed in their olive-drab wool uniforms, they arrived at the border in 100-degree heat. They saw no military action but, as a Milwaukee *Journal* reporter put it, they "stayed to pitch tents in six-inch gumbo, fight scorpions, and break untamed broncos for mounts." They also drilled endlessly, cursed some, played poker when they could, and eventually returned home. They had not covered themselves with glory, but they came back with the understanding that it took more than preparedness parades to develop an effective fighting force.[25]

* * *

The year 1916 was also one of general elections for both state and national offices, and political affairs in Wisconsin reached a state of considerable uncertainty. Some of the perplexity people experienced was attributable to the war, of course, but a part of their uncertainty derived from political developments that had taken place in Wisconsin during the previous twenty years. From the Civil War to the economic depression of the 1890's, a two-party system had prevailed in the state. Although the Republican party had gained a majority of votes in most elections, the Democrats had won the state for Grover Cleveland in 1892, and they had three times sent a Democrat to the governor's mansion. The Democrats had, in other words, provided voters with an alternative to the dominant party. Beginning in 1894, however, the Democratic party had gone into decline, and the Republicans had gained almost complete control over the state legislature and the state congressional delegation as well as the office of governor. Nevertheless, Republican domination had not eliminated political conflict from Wisconsin. What had happened, rather, was that Stalwart and Progressive factions struggled for control of the Republican party. The most important leader of the Progressives, Robert M. La Follette, sought always to identify his opponents with special interests and

[25] Newton D. Baker to Emanuel L. Philipp, telegram, June 18, 1916, in the Emanuel L. Philipp Papers; Finnegan, "The Preparedness Movement in Wisconsin," 88–89; Adjutant General's Office, *Biennial Report*, 1914–1916, p. 12; Milwaukee *Journal*, June 27, July 1, 3, 1916; Coffman, *War to End All Wars*, 14.

his own cause with righteous reform. He had been spectacularly successful, winning three gubernatorial elections in 1900, 1902, and 1904, and then gaining a seat in the United States Senate in 1905. Factional struggles had not ended there. La Follette had never had complete confidence in James Davidson, his successor as governor, and in 1910 the Progressive support went to Francis McGovern, who had won his political spurs in Milwaukee. The success of the Progressives was remarkable during McGovern's first term as governor, and the legislation of 1911 marked the high point of Progressive achievement in Wisconsin. Yet personal rivalries again destroyed Progressive unity, and the Stalwarts registered an important victory when Emanuel Philipp won the gubernatorial race of 1914. With intelligence and good sense, Philipp reached accommodation with the Progressives, but pressures of the Great War were beginning to influence politics in Wisconsin as Philipp prepared to seek re-election.[26]

Neutrality and preparedness issues occupied an important place in the minds of voters throughout the nation in 1916. Yet Philipp's campaign for a second term as governor coincided with La Follette's quest for a third term in the United States Senate, and political discussion in Wisconsin therefore encompassed the old Progressive-Stalwart issues as well. The first showdown between the two factions of the party, the contest for delegates to the Republican National Convention in Chicago, proved inconclusive. Wisconsin sent a split delegation, with fifteen of the state's twenty-six votes pledged to La Follette. A month after the Republicans nominated Charles Evans Hughes for President, the Stalwarts met in Madison and endorsed both Philipp and Hughes. La Follette returned to Wisconsin to campaign for himself, and he soon demonstrated that congressional struggles had quenched none of his rhetorical fire. Apparently unimpressed by the fact that Philipp's honesty and balance had led him down the paths of moderation since 1914, La Follette attacked the governor as though he were a venal corruptionist, a puppet of the interests. Philipp, recovering from an emergency appendectomy, limited himself to a few speeches in which he de-

[26] David L. Brye, *Wisconsin Voting Patterns in the Twentieth Century, 1900 to 1950* (New York, 1979), 163–185, 225–232; Leon D. Epstein, *Politics in Wisconsin* (Madison, 1958), 35–40; Margulies, *Decline of the Progressive Movement*, 83–123; Robert C. Nesbit, *Wisconsin: A History* (Madison, 1973), 408–440.

fended his administration and denounced the "La Follette lobby" that had stood in the way of even greater achievement.[27]

Results of the fall primary indicated that Stalwarts and Progressives remained in equilibrium. Both La Follette and Philipp won overwhelming victories, and each refrained from attacking the other in the weeks before the November election. Clearly, none of the old factional issues seemed particularly important to voters in 1916. And in matters of foreign policy, on which Progressives and Stalwarts might have taken conflicting positions, divergent opinions could be found within each faction. The Republicans, then, buried their differences and coasted to victory as La Follette and Philipp trounced their Democratic opponents. The vote for Charles Evans Hughes was less impressive, though he ran nearly 30,000 votes ahead of Wilson in the state. The voters of Wisconsin obviously wanted President Wilson to continue on a neutral course. Early in 1917, the Oshkosh *Northwestern* accurately expressed their feelings when it wistfully hoped that the nation might "pass through this crisis without becoming involved in the war maelstrom."[28]

The choice between neutrality and war, however, did not rest entirely with Wilson. On January 31, 1917, the German government announced the removal of restrictions on submarine warfare that had been in effect since the *Sussex* crisis of early 1916. The President responded by breaking off diplomatic relations, but he resisted taking the further step of arming merchant ships. Then the British secret service turned over a dispatch it had intercepted and decoded. Containing instructions from the German foreign minister to his minister in Mexico, it proposed a German-Mexican alliance in case of war with the United States. The next day Wilson went before Congress to ask for authority to arm merchant ships. He did not receive it. Eleven senators, led by La Follette, filibustered the bill to death. Calling them "a little group of willful men, representing no opinion but their own," and confident of public support, the President went ahead and armed the vessels anyway. The move did not prevent U-boats from sinking nearly 600,000 tons of Allied and neutral shipping during the month of March, and Wilson

[27] Maxwell, *Emanuel L. Philipp*, 121; Margulies, *Decline of the Progressive Movement*, 183; La Follette and La Follette, *La Follette*, 1:581–585; *La Follette's Magazine*, August, 1916, p. 10.

[28] Margulies, *Decline of the Progressive Movement*, 189–190; *Wisconsin Blue Book, 1917*, pp. 218, 282–287; Oshkosh *Northwestern*, January 23, 1917.

called Congress into special session on April 2, 1917, to ask for a declaration of war.[29]

Nine of Wisconsin's eleven congressmen were among the fifty who voted against the declaration, and La Follette was one of six senators who opposed it. Shocked that war had finally come, a majority of Wisconsin citizens would doubtless have sympathized with Congressman John M. Nelson's poignant inability to articulate his feelings. "I did the very best I could to keep us out of the European war," he wrote privately. "I have two boys who will undoubtedly be called. You can imagine how Mrs. Nelson and I feel about it. We would gladly give them in defence of the country or any great principle, but—." Within a matter of hours after the declaration, though, the state had begun to mobilize, and champions of a united war effort had set to work dispelling doubts.[30]

The Wisconsin experience in the period from 1914 to 1918 appeared to validate the observation that stirring up sentiment for war is easier than promoting the cause of peace. In itself the observation is a commonplace, but it suggests comparisons that are worth examining. War provided a clear-cut objective that could be stated in simple terms: defeat the Hun. No ambiguity surrounded the demands of Mars. War did not involve ordinary citizens in the hard choices of military strategy or diplomatic maneuver; it simply demanded sacrifice, work, and obedience. On the other hand, the peace movement, which envisioned a world free of wartime imperatives, contained more subtle imperatives of its own. Its success required that leaders of the movement demonstrate the practicality of their proposals. But doing that meant analyzing international relations and the causes of war; and, disconcerted by the complexities of these problems, the peace movement inevitably wandered off into a realm where no argument was verifiable or entirely credible. Just as inevitably, then, the peace movement followed a route that led from hope through uncertainty to frustration.

Those who wanted the United States to stay out of war therefore tended to emphasize American neutrality rather than world peace. But while neutrality may have been realistically possible, it could not project the shining goal that had inspired the peace movement. A policy intended to make possible American avoidance of war was,

[29] Link, *Wilson and the Progressive Era*, 266–278; Robert M. La Follette, "The Armed Ship Bill Meant War," in *La Follette's Magazine*, March, 1917, pp. 1–4.

[30] Nelson to Ada James, April 7, 1917, in the Ada James Papers.

by its very nature, a negative one. Avoidance of war called for responding to developments abroad rather than shaping the course of events. In concrete situations, the responses required of a neutral power were not always clear. Specific proposals, such as the sale of munitions, gave rise to interminable discussions of what neutrality really involved. And neutrality, like the peace movement, was doomed.

Perhaps the United States could have stayed out of war had the Wilson administration responded differently. But more important, at least so far as the climate of opinion in wartime Wisconsin was concerned, was that nearly three years of neutrality had eroded a popular sense of mastery and control. People felt buffeted by events—until America's entry into the war. That move restored the *sense* of mastery, if not its substance. Citizens could again believe that they held destiny in their hands, and much of what they heard and read during the war period reinforced that belief. Small wonder that people exasperated by a feeling of impotence during the years of neutrality should lash out at those who threatened to destroy their newfound sense of control. Small wonder that they self-righteously launched a crusade against heresy. Edward Alsworth Ross exaggerated the unity of mind and purpose that the Great War brought to the people of Wisconsin. Yet for a time they were engulfed in a surge of patriotism, the most selfless, admirable, and dangerous emotion that war could stimulate.

* * *

On April 6, 1917, Congress voted to declare war on the Central Powers, and the young men of Wisconsin prepared to answer the call to the colors. The Wisconsin National Guard once more took up arms, and by August 5 Guard units had assembled at Camp Douglas for preliminary organization and training. It required spirited initiative on the part of Governor Philipp to meet their basic needs. Despite the preparedness program and military reforms of the previous year, the War Department found itself embarrassed for lack of both funds and equipment to outfit the many guardsman called into service. Fearing interminable delay if soldiers had to wait for the Army to solve its supply problems, Philipp sent Adjutant General Orlando Holway to New York to buy on the open market some $700,000 worth of clothing, blankets, tents, and mess kits. That done, the Guard trained at Camp Douglas until September, when most of the troops were transferred to Camp MacArthur near Waco, Texas. There, as part of the War Department's reorganization program, guardsmen from Wisconsin joined those from Michigan to form the 32nd, or "Red Arrow" Division.[31]

Manpower needs of the Army were greater than the National Guard could fill, of course, and for six weeks state and national leaders debated how best to meet them. Essentially, they argued over whether there should be a volunteer army or a system of conscription. Wilson, the War Department, and the general staff favored a nationwide draft, and Wilson's supporters in Congress introduced measures for authorizing it. La Follette surprised no one by leading the opposition to conscription, which he denounced as unconstitutional. Governor Philipp also opposed compulsory service, but for different reasons. He thought it unnecessary, and he sent Wilson a telegram telling him so: "The volunteer system will leave a good feeling at home, while conscription at this time would, in my judgment, have a tendency to make the war unpopular." Congressional proponents of a draft law eventually overcame such contentions, and the first registration took place on June 5. Governor Philipp proclaimed the date "duty day" in Wisconsin, but he did not totally reject the possibility of resistance and disorder. He wired Provost Marshal General Enoch Crowder, "All is quiet today and I feel confident that no situation will arise that we shall not be able to handle fully." As it turned out, men registered calmly in all sections of the state, and draft officials reported no disturbances.[32]

With mobilization well under way by the end of the summer, troops of the newly formed 32nd Division were eager to learn what

[31] Maxwell, *Emanuel L. Philipp*, 132–133; Fred. L. Holmes, *Wisconsin's War Record* (Madison, 1919), 20–21; *Wisconsin Blue Book, 1919*, p. 308.

[32] Philipp to Wilson, unidentified newsclipping, April 10, 1917; Philipp to New York *American*, April 18, 1917; J. H. Davidson to Philipp, April 11, 1917; Philipp to Crowder, telegram, June 2, 1917, all in the Philipp Papers; Milwaukee *Sentinel*, May 24, 1917; Edward A. Fitzpatrick, *McCarthy of Wisconsin* (New York, 1944), 208–209. In disagreeing with Philipp, E. A. Ross advanced a eugenic argument for conscription: "What clinched me was perceiving how young men in groups—such as we find them in our higher institutions of learning—are subject to mass impulses and volunteer readily; whereas isolated young men on the farms hang back. Now the grouped young men are a highly selected body. Only about one young man in sixty in this country obtains a college education—and it is dead against the interests of social leadership and of eugenics that these young men should expose themselves to the hazards of war more than other young men. The volunteer system is hap-hazard, irrational and diseugenic." Ross to J. W. Beatson, April 23, 1917, in the Ross Papers.

lay in store for them. After several months of training and marking time, they finally sailed for France in January and February, 1918, the sixth of forty-two divisions to be sent overseas. They arrived at Brest early in March. The division was first used for replacement and noncombat duty, but in July it received orders to relieve the American 3rd Division near Château-Thierry. It reached the front just in time to participate in turning back a powerful offensive that the German high command had hoped would end the war. The commander of the French 38th Corps, under whose orders the men of the Red Arrow were serving at the time, was properly impressed with their fighting qualities. "Les Terribles," he called them, and the sobriquet became a part of Red Arrow legend. The division also took part in the Oisne-Aisne offensive, and during the fall it spent twenty days in the Argonne. "Les Terribles" were in action east of the Meuse when the Armistice was signed in November, and before returning home in 1919 they served with the army of occupation in the Coblenz area. In all, more than 800 officers and men of the 32nd Division were decorated by the American, French, and Belgian governments, but the division sustained heavy losses: 2,660 men killed and total casualties of nearly 14,000.[33]

The sacrifices of the American Expeditionary Force required justification. Wishing to live comfortably with themselves, President Wilson and many other Americans felt compelled to believe wholeheartedly in the cause for which so many men died. Demands of conscience—as well as a sense of mastery over the fate of the world—help to account for the intensity of patriotic fervor that accompanied "the war to end all wars." To men such as Ray Stannard Baker, a prominent muckraking journalist who worked closely with the President and with the Committee on Public Information, dedication to Wilsonian idealism was an essential element in the Amer-

[33] The activities of the 32nd Division are detailed in the following: War History Commission, *The 32nd Division in the World War, 1917–1919. Issued by the Joint War History Commissions of Michigan and Wisconsin* (Milwaukee, 1920); U.S. American Battle Monuments Commission, *32d Division, Summary of Operations in the World War* (1943); and Rutherford B. Pixley, *Wisconsin in the World War . . .* (Madison, 1919). For a superb memoir by a Wisconsin veteran, see Ira Berlin, ed., "A Wisconsinite in World War I: Reminiscences of Edmund P. Arpin, Jr.," in *WMH*, 51 (Autumn, 1967), 3–25, (Winter, 1967–1968), 124–138, and (Spring, 1968), 218–237. An excellent general account is in Coffman, *War to End All Wars*, especially pp. 54–85. William F. Raney in *Wisconsin: A Story of Progress* (New York, 1940), p. 310, notes: "Among twenty-nine combat divisions it [the 32nd Division] stood seventh in total casualties and fourth in the number of battle deaths."

ican war effort. That was why Baker felt troubled after a visit to Wisconsin in June, 1917. He had grown up in St. Croix Falls, and while he thought the Middle West generally lacking in enthusiasm, he found Wisconsin "really the most backward state I've struck in its sentiment toward the war." Perhaps observers such as Baker saw only what they expected to see. Perhaps the publicity given La Follette and other opponents of war, along with the obvious presence of a large and active German population, led them to assume that Wisconsin would be laggard in its war contributions. Yet Baker was too good a reporter not to detect "strong patriotic fevers also at work" even as he wrote about the state's backwardness.[34]

What Baker actually witnessed in Wisconsin during that early summer of 1917 was a traumatic conflict of loyalties and principles. In the neutrality period, citizens made much of their convictions and their principles; as the nation readied itself for war, supporters of mobilization began placing greater emphasis on their patriotism and their loyalty. The shift involved more than playing with words. Under the pressures of international crisis, long-standing associations broke down; and under the same pressures, fresh alliances began to form.

The Wisconsin Defense League, which originated in Milwaukee with a self-appointed citizens' committee of businessmen, lawyers, and bankers, took the lead in promoting a statewide consensus supporting the American effort on the western front and opposing the likes of Robert M. La Follette and Victor Berger at home. Far from sharing in the backwardness that Baker observed, the league had formally organized on March 24, two weeks before the United States joined the Allies in the war. With Wheeler P. Bloodgood as its state chairman—he had followed the call of the Bull Moose in 1912, and, remaining faithful to the bellicose Theodore Roosevelt, he could claim some experience in rallying 'round the flag—the Wisconsin Defense League was primed and ready to set off on its loyalty campaign at the very outset of war.[35]

The campaign encompassed a variety of activities directed towards both winning the hearts and minds of Wisconsin and cen-

[34] Baker to William Allen White, June 8, 1917, in the William Allen White Papers, Library of Congress.

[35] Lorin Lee Cary, "The Wisconsin Loyalty Legion, 1917–1918," in *WMH*, 53 (Autumn, 1969), 35; Dana Lee Gisselman, "Anti-radicalism in Wisconsin, 1917–1919" (master's thesis, University of Wisconsin, 1969), 12–13.

suring the opponents of war. The league sent out a flood of pamphlets detailing the steps by which Kaiser Wilhelm II had initiated hostilities in violation of treaty commitments and of morality. It assisted in organizing county councils of defense and in registering men for the draft. It established a cadre of patriotic speakers, the "Four Minute Men," who were prepared to burst forth with brief orations at a moment's notice. It helped to identify and register enemy aliens residing in the state; it also sought to identify members of the radical labor organization, the Industrial Workers of the World (IWW). Joseph Moriarity, a Milwaukee public relations man who served as secretary of the state organization, produced a movie, *The Slacker*, which proved popular at league-sponsored gatherings. Yet no one in the Defense League said very much about the object of the loyalty it hoped to stimulate. Most of the leaguers doubtless assumed that the term meant fidelity to the United States, but in order to cast its nets as broadly as possible the organization avoided particulars. The campaign was a perfect example of the way in which war could reinforce a sense of mastery while depriving people of opportunities to make meaningful choices.[36]

The league succeeded in bringing together a disparate group for whom loyalty alone—undirected and therefore sometimes misapplied—was sufficient. Motorcycle manufacturer Walter Davidson and meat-packer John Cudahy served on the executive committee. Their Stalwart Republican connections and their economic conservatism prevented neither Socialist Algie M. Simons nor Progressive Merlin Hull from joining their ranks. Democratic Senator Paul O. Husting found many ways to assist the league, from encouraging the formation of a branch in Fond du Lac to passing on information he picked up in Washington. Irvine L. Lenroot, once a La Follette protégé but one of the two Wisconsin congressmen to vote for war, gave his support to the loyalty cause. So did future congressman Hubert H. Peavey, president of a land company, who worked to organize the patriots of Bayfield County. John

[36] W. H. Dougherty to Wisconsin Defense League, May 15, 1917 (filed under Rock County); Burt Williams to Wheeler P. Bloodgood, August 14, 1917 (filed under Organization, Loyalty Legion); Bloodgood to various firms such as the Armour Company, Stegman Motor Company, American Candy Company, Dahlman and Inbush Company, Edward Dewey Company, and the Milwaukee Vinegar Company, August 29 and 30, 1917, all in the Wisconsin Defense League General Correspondence, 1917–1918, Series 1705, Records of the War History Commission, WSA. See also Cary, "Wisconsin Loyalty Legion," in *WMH*, 53:35.

W. Reynolds, who was later to become state attorney general and whose son was to become governor, served as secretary of the Brown County Defense League. Second District Congressman Michael E. Burke helped to organize the Dodge County branch.[37]

With justification, then, chairman Bloodgood could boast in August of 1917 that "men of every political faith—Republicans, Democrats, Socialists—have joined hands in this organization." And in the same month a Green Bay attorney, Patrick H. Martin, could indulge in sentiments worthy of the most bellicose citizen of the land. "No mercy should be shown to the traitors who are working in behalf of Germany," he told the Milwaukee branch of the Wisconsin Defense League. "The man who by his seditious talk or actions strikes at the American boys in uniform or who says or does anything that will keep them there a day longer than is necessary, should be shot down or hanged to the first lamp post."[38]

Such speeches were raucous and strident, to be sure, and there were many more of them to come. But they never overpowered the forces of moderation. Within a week after the declaration of war, when the ardent spirits of the Defense League began to quiver with rage against Teutonic diabolism, the legislature passed an act establishing the State Council of Defense. Set up to work in coordination with the National Council of Defense, which was already in operation, the State Council received broad powers to supervise and regulate war activities. Although in no sense designed to compete with the Defense League, the State Council brought both worry and confusion to league ranks. For one thing, the similarity in name meant that ordinary citizens had difficulty in distinguishing between the two bodies. For another, the governor's appointments to the eleven-man council brought dismay to the leaguers. The council represented a cross section of Wisconsin interests, but none of the eleven personified a star-spangled, jingoistic chauvinism.[39]

[37] B. A. Husting to Wisconsin Defense League, April 21, 1917 (filed under Fond du Lac County); M. E. Burke to Bloodgood, April 24, 1917 (filed under Dodge County); Peavey to Joseph E. Moriarity, May 1, 1917 (filed under Bayfield County); Reynolds to Bloodgood, May 3, 1917 (filed under Brown County); minutes of the Wisconsin Defense League meeting, Milwaukee, August 15, 1917, all in the Wisconsin Defense League Correspondence, Series 1705, WSA.

[38] Statement of Purpose in minutes, August 22, 1917, in *ibid.*; Milwaukee *Evening Wisconsin*, August 21, 1917.

[39] Maxwell, *Emanuel L. Philipp*, 141; Emanuel L. Philipp to W. S. Gifford, telegram, April 18, 1917, and Andrew H. Melville to Philipp, April 20, 1917, both in the Philipp Papers; *Wisconsin Blue Book, 1919*, pp. 371–378.

The initial task of the Council of Defense was the organization of county committees to assist in carrying out its program, and in most localities the Defense League co-operated with the State Council in establishing county councils. Governor Philipp was well aware of the possibility that such co-operation could lead to domination, however, and he rejected all suggestions that the Council of Defense have any structural relationship to the Defense League. At several points the council's activities ran parallel to those of the league, but the council faced problems of considerable real importance. Furthermore, since members of the council had official status, they could be held accountable for their actions. In this sense they were more responsible than were members of the league, a volunteer organization.[40]

The minutes of the council meetings reveal the breadth of its interests and activities. One subject concerned the allocation of labor to critical projects. After discussing the problem with several authorities, including John R. Commons, the university's distinguished labor economist, the council decided to work through the Wisconsin Industrial Commission, the United States Employment Service, and other such agencies. As the principal wartime co-ordinating body of an important agricultural state, the council also became deeply interested in solving the national food crisis that developed in 1917. Before Congress created the Food Administration, council chairman Magnus Swenson of Madison was promoting the idea of food conservation. With the assistance of the county councils he attacked food hoarding, urged citizens to cultivate their own vegetable gardens, and instituted wheatless and meatless days in the state. When Herbert Hoover took over as food administrator for the nation, he not only adopted some of Swenson's innovations but also appointed him food administrator for Wisconsin. With vigorous enthusiasm Swenson managed to persuade both Philipp and the legislature that the council should exercise the right of eminent domain and buy stores of foodstuffs to be distributed at its discretion. The wartime fuel shortage in Wisconsin, with its long

[40] Ralph F. Brown to Wheeler P. Bloodgood, April 21, 1917 (filed under Ashland County); O. J. Hohle to Bloodgood, April 29, 1917, and Wisconsin Defense League [Algie M. Simons] to Hohle, May 5, 1917 (both filed under Pierce County); Wisconsin Defense League [Joseph E. Moriarity] to A. C. Moors, May 8, 1917 (filed under Adams County), all in the Wisconsin Defense League Correspondence, Series 1705, WSA; Janesville *Gazette*, April 28, 1917.

winters and dearth of fuel resources, was another matter that attracted the council's attention. It was the governor rather than the council, however, who managed to facilitate delivery of the necessary supply of coal during the harsh winter of 1917–1918.[41]

* * *

The Defense Council concentrated most of its attention on practical problems such as the allocation of resources and the production of war materiel, but because it was the official state agency most directly concerned with the war effort, its involvement in loyalty problems was unavoidable. Watchdogs of patriotism, many of them writing anonymously, sent scores of letters to the council with accusatory hints and suggestions about neighbors they considered "unreliable." To its great credit, the council prepared a standard reply discounting rumor and unsupported allegations. In December, 1917, it sent out a special bulletin detailing its position:[42]

> Report cases of disloyalty to the State Council of Defense. But be sure that you report FACT and NOT HEARSAY. Charges of disloyalty, treason, and sedition are very serious matters and should be carefully considered.
>
> When you report a case of disloyalty, be sure to give VERBATIM QUOTATIONS from the man's speech, or give a statement of his actions from eye witnesses. Whenever it is possible to do so, SECURE AFFIDAVITS. . . .
>
> Our daily mail contains letters, some of them unfortunately anonymous, which report cases of disloyalty, sedition, or treason. Investigation discloses that the majority of these reports are based on mere hearsay

[41] Minutes of the meetings of April 27, May 2, 8, 23, 31, June 12, 20, 23, July 31, 1917, and January 2, September 17, October 15, 29, November 19, 1918, all in Minutes, 1917–1919, Series 1641, Records of the State Council of Defense, World War I, WSA; Woodrow Wilson to Emanuel L. Philipp, August 16, 1917, Philipp to Harry A. Garfield, telegram, December 21, 1917, John A. Grimm to Philipp, January 2, 1918, W. N. Fitzgerald to Philipp, telegram, January 10, 1918, Philipp to W. H. Groverman, telegram, January 14, 1918, Philipp to James T. Clark, telegram, January 15, 1918, Philipp to W. H. Groverman, January 16, 1918, and Philipp to Swenson, April 17, 1918, all in the Philipp Papers; Maxwell, *Emanuel L. Philipp*, 142–143; *Wisconsin Blue Book, 1919*, p. 390; *Laws of Wisconsin*, 1917, pp. 920–922 (Chapter 561). For a general discussion of early activities of the State Council of Defense, see the council's report, July 26, 1917, also in the Philipp Papers. A discussion of activities at the county level may be found in the Report of the Dane County Council of Defense, May 1 to November 1, 1917, in the John S. Donald Papers.

[42] Special Bulletin No. 121, December 14, 1917, in Bulletins and Circulars, 1917–1919, Series 1644, Records of the State Council of Defense, World War I, WSA; State Council of Defense [Henry A. Burd] to Charles Barry, December 12, 1917, and to James A. Andrews, March 27, 1918, both in General Correspondence, 1917–1918, box 16, file S23, Series 1642, Records of the State Council of Defense, World War I, WSA.

> and have no foundation in fact. You will readily understand that the legally constituted authorities of the Government cannot proceed in matters of this sort without a basis of fact on which to stand.

Unfortunately, the council did not always remember its own warnings. On frequent occasions it sent threatening letters to people suspected of having antiwar attitudes. "It has been reported to this office that you are guilty of sedition in talking against the Government and its best interests in the war," the council admonished one such unfortunate, adding that it expected him "to call at this office within the next day or two to explain your attitude in this matter." At times the council could be self-righteously didactic in lecturing those whose behavior had aroused criticism. "We are living in serious times, Mr. Burmeister, times in which men's souls are being stirred," it informed an alleged author of pro-German remarks. "It is a serious matter for any individual even to be suspected of disloyalty to the Government which protects him and furnishes him a home and a livelihood, although that suspicion may grow out of words which were spoken more or less thoughtlessly in an unguarded moment."[43]

While the ardor of council members sometimes overcame their good judgment, they seldom became frenzied in their patriotism. Governor Philipp saw to that. He deplored the wave of vigilante activities in Wisconsin that accompanied the war crisis. He constantly urged local authorities to uphold the law, and he insisted that they provide protection for all persons. When the American Protective League organized as a voluntary adjunct of the United States Department of Justice to assist in tracking down delinquents and deserters—"slackers," in the slang of the day—Philipp sent out a word of advice to draft boards. "There is a danger in an agency like the American Protective League to become a busy-body or to do detective work of a very amateur quality," he warned. The governor resisted intimidation in the name of patriotism. After a farmer from Jump River wrote him that his life had been threatened by a deputy sheriff, Philipp publicly reiterated his opposition to lynching bees. He assured the farmer that "no sheriff or other officer in the state of Wisconsin has any right to threaten to hang anyone."[44]

[43] State Council of Defense [Henry A. Burd] to John Cobb, March 2, 1918, and to Wm. Burmeister, December 28, 1917, both in State Council of Defense Correspondence, box 16, file S23, Series 1642, WSA.

[44] Emanuel L. Philipp, Memorandum No. 1235 and Supplement, April 10, 1918, in

Yet zealous patriots often practiced as well as threatened violence in wartime Wisconsin. "There can be no doubt that the present war is made the excuse for many abuses which would not be countenanced during times of peace," a concerned citizen wrote the governor. Philipp agreed, but it was not always easy for state officials to hold anti-German hysteria in check. The patriots of Ashland County, for example, carried out a series of tar-and-feather parties against persons suspected of opposing the war effort. Philipp appointed an attorney and a corps of detectives to investigate the episodes and wrote the mayor of Ashland a letter of admonition. Little came of the investigation, but Philipp announced that if necessary he would use every resource at his command to restore order. "Mob law is a dangerous institution," he cautioned. "It has no place in a civilized state, and when it gets underway, no man is safe." Whether or not its citizens agreed, Ashland became a quieter city and the hysteria passed.[45]

A public sentiment that could countenance tar-and-feather parties was one that sometimes had difficulty drawing nice distinctions and exercising discriminating judgment. The governor could temper moods and discussions of the State Council of Defense sitting in Madison, but county councils were less amenable to reason, if only because there were fewer opportunities for responsible state officials to discuss problems with them. In some localities, anything Germanic was automatically suspect. In northern Wisconsin a county council notified the Washburn German Lutheran Church that it believed "the holding of services at which the German language is spoken exclusively tends to engender hate and enmity in the hearts and minds of true loyal Americans." Its demand that services be conducted in English or not at all led the pastor to appeal to Governor Philipp. Characteristically, the governor replied that "he who worships his Deity may do so in the language of his own choice," and he notified the State Council of Defense that the county council had acted "entirely outside the province of that organization."[46]

Selective Service in Wisconsin, 1917–1919, box 2, Series 1696, Records of the War History Commission, WSA; *Capital Times*, April 17, 1918.

[45] Irvin Strauss to Emanuel L. Philipp, September 20, 1918, and Philipp to Strauss, September 28, 1918, both in the Philipp Papers; *Capital Times*, July 9, 10, 18, 25, August 3, 24, 1918; Ashland *Press*, July 16, 17, 27, August 1, 20, 1918.

[46] R. Krenke to Emanuel L. Philipp, October 21, 1918, Philipp to Krenke, October 24, 1918, and Philipp to W. S. Heddles, October 24, 1918, all in the Philipp Papers.

To many hyperpatriots, their indignation inflamed by war propaganda, the attitude of Governor Philipp and the State Council of Defense seemed weakness itself. As a result, the council received several letters threatening forceful and direct action. A Cumberland resident gave notice that unless responsible officials prosecuted disloyal and traitorous rascals more vigorously than they had, "we'll look after them in a different way up here." Another correspondent was more explicit: "I helped drive the La Follette pacifist bunch out of Hudson last fall and if the state authorities do not take care of these cases, we will use part of Wis. hemp crop to make neckties." Despite his efforts to encourage temperance and moderation, Governor Philipp could not persuade all citizens of the state that cool reason was either appropriate or sufficient unto the day.[47]

For those whose prejudices demanded something more exhilarating, the Wisconsin Loyalty Legion supplied programs of passionate patriotism. The legion began to form in the summer of 1917 as the Council of Defense assumed official responsibility for co-ordinating wartime activities in the state. Although the voluntary Defense League had sought to share that responsibility, it had been rebuffed, largely because of the governor's mistrust of fanaticism. But leaders of the Defense League, along with kindred spirits throughout the state, refused to be subdued; they wanted to believe that they were doing something more for the war effort than growing vegetables and buying Liberty Bonds. They also wanted to counteract the effects of what they characterized as La Follette's un-American antiwar speeches, Berger's socialist scribblings, and the pacifists' naïve and unrealistic indifference to national needs. They were profoundly stirred by suggestions—such as those of Ray Stannard Baker—that patriotism burned with a weak and flickering flame in their state. "That Wisconsin stands impugned in the eyes of the country," wrote the journalist and author Samuel Hopkins Adams early in 1918, "none understands better than her own loyal sons." According to Walter Goodland, a Racine newspaperman who was to become governor during World War II, it was concern for Wisconsin's reputation that justified the legion. The organization, he asserted, was "prepared to refute the slander that Wisconsin is a

[47] W. N. Fuller to State Council of Defense, March 25, 1918, and W. C. Bradley to Andrew T. Melville, May 24, 1918, both in State Council of Defense Correspondence, box 16, file S23, Series 1642, WSA.

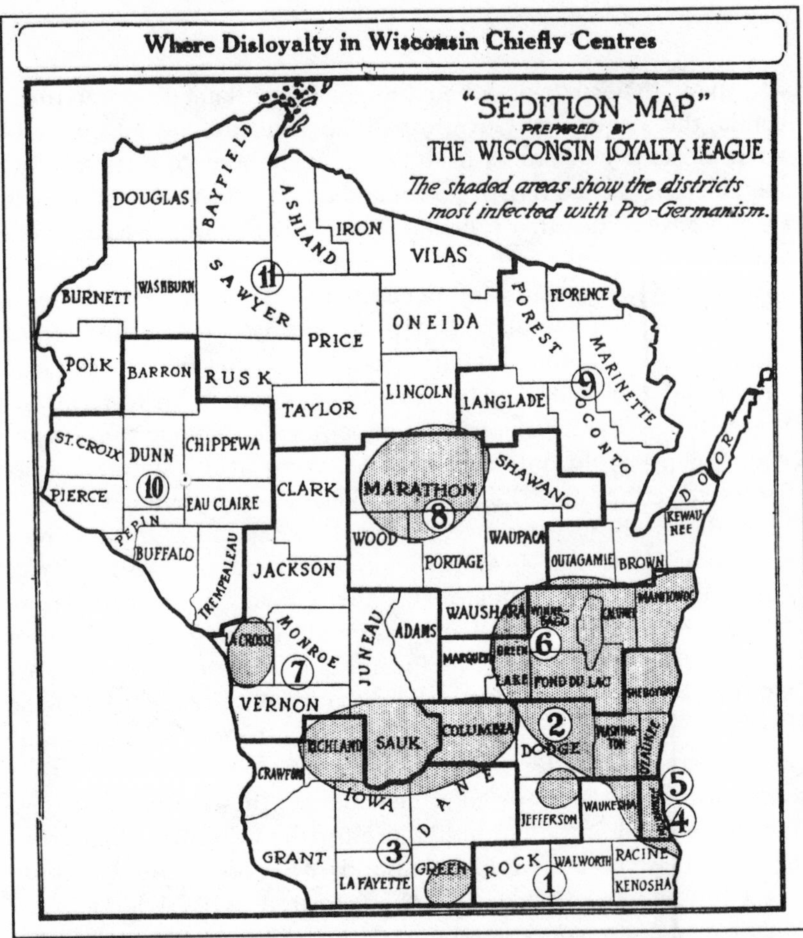

This so-called "sedition map" from the New York *Sun* of March 21, 1918, indicates how Wisconsin was viewed by much of the nation during the period of wartime hysteria. The shaded areas represent "pro-German" voting in the spring primary election for a seat in the U.S. Senate. Old Bob La Follette's candidate, James Thompson, and Victor Berger, Socialist congressman from Milwaukee, fared especially well in the "disloyal" areas. (The circled numbers refer to congressional districts.) Source: *Loyalty Issue Clippings, 1917–1919, in Wisconsin in World War I, Series 1699, Records of the War History Commission, WSA.*

'traitor state' and to demonstrate beyond controversy that the great mass of its citizens are patriotic to the core."[48]

The directors of Loyalty Legion affairs—generally the same per-

[48] Samuel Hopkins Adams, "Invaded America: Wisconsin Joins the War," in *Everybody's Magazine*, January, 1918, p. 28; Walter Goodland to Alfred Bench, September 12, 1917, in Wisconsin Loyalty Legion Correspondence and Miscellaneous Papers, 1917–1919, box 1 (filed under Patriotic Press Association), Series 1706, Records of the War History Commission, WSA. See also Cary, "Wisconsin Loyalty Legion," in *WMH*, 33–50.

sons who had led the Defense League—were doubtless sincere in thinking that an effective war effort required greater efficiency in stamping out disloyalty and dissent. The Congress of the United States lent credence to that belief when it passed the Espionage Act in June, 1917. Congressman Edwin Y. Webb of North Carolina, who steered the bill through the House, argued that its purpose was to safeguard military secrets, but both in wording and application the act went much further than that. It provided a maximum penalty of twenty years in prison and a $10,000 fine for anyone who willfully made false statements interfering with the war effort, attempted to promote insubordination within the armed forces, or obstructed efforts to recruit soldiers and sailors.

Armed with the Espionage Act the government could, in the words of Harvard law professor and legal historian Zechariah Chafee, render "civilians severely punishable during a war for questioning its justifiability or the methods of conducting it." The Espionage Act had important consequences even before anyone came to trial under its provisions. Patriots of the Defense League and the Loyalty Legion could argue that Congress had recognized disloyalty as a genuine threat and in so doing had given its blessing to organizations pledged to combat the pro-German menace. Both organizations made the most of the opportunity. A circular letter sent to Wisconsin chapters during August, 1917, described the heroic efforts of the Defense League, the emergence of the State Council of Defense, and the multiplying iniquities of Socialist, pacifist, and pro-German forces. "The time has now come . . . ," it announced, "when a decided stand must be taken to offset the work of the anti-American party, who under the guise of 'peace' meetings are spreading dissention [*sic*] and disloyalty in all parts of the state."[49]

Finally, in September, 1917, the Loyalty Legion formally took

[49] Horace C. Peterson and Gilbert C. Fite, *Opponents of War, 1917–1918* (Madison, 1957), 15–17; *Congressional Record*, 65 Cong., 1 sess., 1599; Zechariah Chafee, Jr., "Sedition," in the *Encyclopedia of the Social Sciences*; Statement of Purpose in minutes of the Wisconsin Defense League meeting, August 22, 1917, in the Wisconsin Defense League Correspondence, Series 1705, WSA. See also Harold M. Hyman, *To Try Men's Souls: Loyalty Tests in American History* (Berkeley, 1959), 268. Hyman points out that the Espionage Act did not specifically cover individual oral or written antiwar sentiments. The Wilson administration, under severe pressure to silence pacifists and soapbox orators, approved an amendment to strengthen the Espionage Act, and Congress passed it in May, 1918. Known as the Sedition Act, it provided great latitude in the suppression of dissent.

the place of the Defense League as Wisconsin's most important voluntary patriotic association. The legion participated in almost every phase of the state's war effort. The activities that absorbed most of its energies included schemes to identify the disloyal and punish them for their sins, projects to educate people on American war aims and stimulate enthusiasm for the Allied cause, and programs to promote Liberty Bond sales, Red Cross services, and other patriotic work.[50]

The first task to which the legion set itself was that of separating loyal sheep from disloyal goats. The device employed to carry it out was a loyalty petition to Congress. All members and prospective members were invited to affix their signatures; so were the unaffiliated. Those who signed the petition identified themselves as citizens who were "grieved and humiliated by the fact that deliberate and concerted efforts are being made to represent this patriotic commonwealth [of Wisconsin] to the people of the United States as disloyal to the American government in its hour of peril and need." Expressing their faith in American institutions and their conviction that the war was necessary to preserve vital principles of American democracy, they concluded by pledging support to the American government. Anyone who could not agree to such sentiments was obviously not to be trusted, and those refusing to sign up were reported to legion headquarters. Much later, at the very end of the war, the legion began to exchange information with that U.S. Justice Department adjunct, the American Protective League, and some of the names found their way into APL files.[51]

By the end of 1917, the Loyalty Legion claimed to have 150,000 signatures on its petition, and since non-signers made up a convenient list of suspects who could be investigated, legion leaders believed the technique a useful one. They continued to apply it in modified forms, most commonly by using loyalty pledges in place of the petition. Such pledges said more than either their authors or their signers intended. Indeed, nothing so clearly reveals the obsessions and anxieties that gave the loyalty movement in Wis-

[50] *Wisconsin Blue Book, 1919*, pp. 415–416; Racine *Times-Call*, May 17, 1919.

[51] Merlin Hull to the Wisconsin Loyalty Legion, September 5, 1917; Roy I. Hannan to the Wisconsin Loyalty Legion, September 21, 1917; Walter Goodland to J. J. Handley, October 6, 1917; B. K. Miller to George Kull, November 2, 8, 1918; and Kull to Miller, November 6, 1918 (the last three with American Protective League correspondence under "September, 1918," in box 3), all in Wisconsin Loyalty Legion Correspondence and Miscellaneous Papers, Series 1706, WSA.

consin its curiously parochial character. The pledge used by the legion's Madison chapter provides a case in point. It began by binding its signers to support the legion "in its state-wide work to stamp out disloyalty, and to stimulate those whose loyalty is weak and thin into a militant love for our country and the principles for which it stands." It vowed full support to the President, to the American flag, and to the Allies. It also expressed a belief in the justice and the expediency of both the Espionage Act and the Selective Service Act. The pledge then reached its climax with an attack on the man legion members considered most responsible for Wisconsin's shame:[52]

> We condemn the war attitude of Robert M. La Follette as being against the best interest of our country.
>
> We pledge ourselves to work against La Folletteism in all its anti-war forms, realizing that any encouragement to the supporters of La Follette is in fact support of La Follette himself.

In the minds of Loyalty Legion members, promoting war activities necessarily involved a massive education offensive. In part through the influence of the state's junior senator, Paul O. Husting, the legion became Wisconsin's chief distributing agency for pamphlets emanating from the Committee on Public Information in Washington. Along with materials provided by the Universal Military Training League, the National Security League, the YMCA, and the Red Cross, the pamphlets went out in prodigious quantity. Husting also had a hand in promoting the Patriotic Press Association, a newspaper alliance established under Loyalty Legion auspices to counteract "newspapers which are for our enmies [*sic*] first and last and against their country all the time." The legion considered the spoken word just as important as the written. Its speakers' bureau dispatched lecturers to patriotic rallies, and it assumed the expenses

[52] Pledge of the Madison Chapter, Wisconsin Loyalty Legion (1918), in the Richard T. Ely Papers. For similar pledges, see George Kull to George Chamberlain, April 18, 1918, and a Milwaukee *Journal* clipping dated November 3, 1917, both in Wisconsin Loyalty Legion Correspondence and Miscellaneous Papers, box 2, Series 1706, WSA. The pledge of the state organization appears in the *Wisconsin Blue Book, 1919,* p. 416. Professor A. R. Hohlfeld of the German department at the University of Wisconsin had the courage to oppose the Madison chapter's pledge. He objected to "those critical or negative features which, in vague and sweeping terms, condemn our congressmen, Senator La Follette, and even so-called supporters of La Follette. These statements seem to me to have to do far more with the field of party politics than with that of a constructive patriotism in which it ought to be our endeavor at this time to unite all loyal citizens of the state." Hohlfeld to Richard T. Ely, February 8, 1918, in the Ely Papers.

as well as the work of co-ordinating efforts of the state's Four Minute Men. The legion asked 25,000 speakers to make presentations as part of the Four Minute program, and almost all of them were only too happy to serve. Octogenarian Edward Cronon, a Civil War veteran from La Crosse, considered it "a high honor for one of my age—it shows that I am not a back number or a has been." Superior, Stevens Point, and Sheboygan seem to have had especially strong Four Minute speakers, though of course some were more effective than others. "The work seems to be taking well here," wrote one Four Minute Man from Superior. "I find that patrons of the theater frequently go up to the ticket window to inquire what four minute man is going to speak there . . . before purchasing their tickets."[53]

While the legion was interested in educating the general public, it was also concerned with patriotic instruction in the schools. It urged that high school history courses include study of the war, and it offered to send out literature from the Committee on Public Information for supplementary reading. The widespread movement to ban use of the German language in public school instruction was not exclusively a legion project, but the organization certainly did not oppose the idea. More positively, the legion supported various extracurricular projects such as the Boys Working Reserve, a pool of high school students set up to provide replacements for agricultural workers called into military service. J. E. Roberts, su-

[53] Husting to Walter Goodland, September 18, 1917; Goodland to Guy D. Stanton, September 20, 1917; Husting to Goodland or Wheeler P. Bloodgood, telegram, September 3, 1917; Goodland circular letter to Fellow Editor, c. August 29, 1917; minutes of the Wisconsin Patriotic Press Association, September 3, [1917], all in the Wisconsin Loyalty Legion Correspondence and Miscellaneous Papers, box 1, Series 1706, WSA. George F. Kull, executive secretary of the Wisconsin Loyalty Legion, later estimated that the legion had distributed more than 4 million pieces of literature for the Committee on Public Information. Racine *Times-Call*, May 17, 1919.

See also: [Roger Flanders] to R. B. Way, February 9, 1918; Flanders to George Borum, March 1, 1918; J. J. McGillivray to Flanders, March 11, 1918; and [Flanders] to Chapple, June 5, 1918 (all in box 1); John P. McGalloway to Flanders, March 9, 1918 (in box 2); W. M. Steele to Flanders, September 17, 1917 (in box 4), all in Four Minute Men General Correspondence, 1917–1919, Series 1709, Records of the War History Commission, WSA; and Cronon to John J. Esch, September 7, 1917, in the John J. Esch Papers. Roger Flanders served as state chairman of the Four Minute Man organization.

Not all Four Minute groups were as successful as the three named. Both Fond du Lac and Black River Falls found that speakers were talking to the same groups repeatedly and producing more yawns than huzzahs. Ashland's John C. Chapple, who was supposed to be in charge of that city's Four Minute contingent, so neglected his responsibilities that he was dismissed from the organization.

perintendent of schools in Fond du Lac, wrote the legion to describe programs of the Junior Patriotic leagues in his schools. During the summer, he noted, girls worked with the Red Cross or canned fruits and vegetables while boys planted gardens and took jobs as farmhands. Waukesha High School introduced military training, using officers and cadets from St. John's Military Academy as instructors.[54]

Such projects led legion leaders to favor setting up a Junior Loyalty Legion to disseminate war information and patriotic ideas to high school students. When legion executive secretary George F. Kull asked the advice of school principals and superintendents, however, he encountered a mixed reaction. J. G. Moore, superintendent of schools in Superior, was enthusiastic, but he questioned the advisability of dues. The Janesville superintendent seemed to prefer a Junior Red Cross. F. J. Shannon of Ashland thought "there is a danger of having too many of these kind of organizations with the result that not any one of them will be doing effective work or if they do effective work the work of the school must inevitably suffer." To a man of Kull's temperament, such reluctance exemplified the distressing persistence of pro-German sentiment. Seeking to prove the need for an even more vigorous campaign against disloyalty, in April, 1918, he made out a bill of particulars that included: "Refusal on the part of many school teachers and members of school boards to permit the teachers to use in their schools the patriotic material sent out from our office and printed under the auspices of the Department of Public Information."[55]

Although the response of some secondary schools to Loyalty Le-

[54] George F. Kull, form letter to "High School Principal," October 14, 1918; Kull to "History Teacher," November 14, 1918 (both in box 4); Kull to Myrta D. Cuenot, October 15, 1918 (in box 3); minutes of a statewide Loyalty Legion meeting, Milwaukee, March 23, 1918, and J. E. Roberts to Kull, January 14, 1918 (both in box 2), all in the Wisconsin Loyalty Legion Correspondence and Miscellaneous Papers, Series 1706, WSA; and minutes of the meeting of September 17, 1918, in State Council of Defense Minutes, Series 1641, WSA. See also the *Wisconsin Blue Book, 1919*, p. 397, and Department of Public Instruction, *Educational News Bulletin*, December 1, 1917.

[55] Moore to Kull, January 11, 1918; H. H. Faust to Kull, January 17, 1918; Shannon to Kull, January 14, 1918; and Kull to George Chamberlain, April 18, 1918 (all in box 2); and Secretary, Milwaukee County Division of the Wisconsin Loyalty Legion to Fred Hemke, Henry Roudow, and David Heidrich, April 4, 1918 (filed under "Milwaukee County Ward and Precinct Chairmen" in box 5), all in the Wisconsin Loyalty Legion Correspondence and Miscellaneous Papers, Series 1706, WSA. The last letter demonstrates that the legion watchdogs were always ready to demand more patriotic instruction in the schools.

gion endeavors may have been disappointing, the University of Wisconsin's faculty seemed eager to outdo the state's populace in demonstrating its patriotism. "Of course, we must admit that there is unfortunately a great deal of disloyalty in the state, but on the other hand that quickens the loyalty of the large majority of the loyal element," Professor Richard T. Ely wrote his friend and fellow economist, Alvin H. Hansen. The faculty was "almost unanimously loyal," and Ely could find little fault with his colleagues. "Moreover," he added, with a touch of the martyr complex that tended to shape his view of the world, "there is a fine courage on the part of the faculty, a willingness to nail the flag to the mast and go down with the ship if necessary." Edward Alsworth Ross agreed. Writing in 1919, he thought the university had been "intensely pro-Ally" from the beginning and "intensely patriotic" after American entry into the war.[56]

Ely, who served as president of the Loyalty Legion's Madison chapter, taught a "war aims" course, using his book, *World War and Leadership in a Democracy*, as a text. He also required that students read supplementary materials obtained from the Committee on Public Information. Not satisfied that one such course would be sufficient, Ely was instrumental in securing the appointment of Don D. Lescohier as a specialist in Americanization. "He is not to have the title Associate Professor of Americanization, but I think probably Associate Professor of Political Economy," Ely confidentially informed Charles A. Williamson of the Carnegie Corporation. "Probably our work will be done largely under some other name, and that for very obvious reasons."[57]

Other faculty members also put their talents to work. During the academic year 1917–1918, several of them—including John R. Commons, Frederick Ogg, George C. Sellery, Edward B. Van Vleck, Carl Russell Fish, and Charles S. Slichter—wrote and distributed a series of papers under the general title *University of Wisconsin War Pamphlets*. Later collected and published as the *War Book of the University of Wisconsin*, the papers by and large duplicated arguments appearing in the "Red, White, and Blue" pamphlets issued

[56] Ely to Hansen, April 23, 1918, in the Ely Papers; Ross to Edward Anderson, March 3, 1919, in the Ross Papers.

[57] Ely to Charles Ellwood, September 26, 1918; Ely to Hansen, October 25, 1918; Ely to Williamson, August 7, 1918; and Ely to John P. Gavit, December 14, 1918, all in the Ely Papers.

by the Committee on Public Information: the war had resulted from two decades of Teutonic planning and scheming to secure for Germany certain imperial objectives; Great Britain and France had struggled desperately "to avert a catastrophe which (as they could not know at the time) had been fully determined by their opponents in advance"; the German invasion of Belgium was a crime against civilization exceeded only by the policy of *Schrecklichkeit*, or frightfulness, that employed atrocities to break the spirit of Germany's enemies. The German intellectual tradition had contributed to "the more repulsive forms of militaristic ideals" and had encouraged "a feeling of the necessity, the beauty, and the glory of war." If Germany won, Americans would "always have to reckon with the danger of the ultimate extinction of our democratic form of government, and even of the submergence of our separate national existence into a new World Empire, as despotic and all-embracing as was that of Rome." Obviously, then, "our sympathies and our concern for our own future alike call us to make common cause with the world's democracies."[58]

The University of Wisconsin, to be sure, shared in some of the disloyalty charges leveled at Wisconsin in general. Out-of-state speakers who journeyed to Madison to whip up enthusiasm for the war perhaps expected to be greeted with indifference. In any event, Princeton's Robert McNutt McElroy, a representative of the National Security League, drew attention to the University of Wisconsin when he published a captious account of a campus loyalty meeting he addressed in April, 1918. That students had paraded through drizzling rain to get to the Stock Pavilion, that his audience was cold and uncomfortable, and that his address was overly long did not seem to McElroy sufficient reasons for restlessness. He called the students "a bunch of damned traitors!" and thereby initiated a noisy public debate over Badger patriotism.

The controversy proved little, but defenders of the university could point to significant contributions it was making to the war effort. Its chemists, physicists, and engineers conducted important research on gases and explosives, submarines and aircraft. The college of agriculture worked with farmers to increase crop production. Geologists used their learning to increase stocks of vital metals

[58] University of Wisconsin, *War Book of the University of Wisconsin: Papers on the Causes and Issues of the War by Members of the Faculty* (Madison, 1918), 11–14.

such as manganese, iron, and nickel. The university sent more of its faculty to serve as officers in the armed forces than did any other institution of higher education in the country. When classes opened in the fall of 1918, the Student Army Training Corps was a flourishing campus organization, and the university's extension service was busily training Red Cross workers.[59]

* * *

Such contributions were impressive, but to members of the Loyalty Legion the university's finest hour came early in 1918 with the repudiation of Wisconsin's senior senator by an overwhelming majority of the faculty. In managing that coup, the hyperpatriots employed a round-robin resolution protesting "those utterances and actions of Senator Robert M. La Follette which have given aid and comfort to Germany and her allies in the present war" and deploring "his failure loyally to support the government in the prosecution of the war." Nearly all of the faculty, including La Follette's old friend and classmate, President Charles R. Van Hise, signed the resolution. Disappointed though he surely was, La Follette had been forewarned that something was in the wind. Charles H. Crownhart, who had served as his campaign manager in 1916, had written to give notice that there was "a very evident conspiracy on here . . . to keep the people aroused against you and to influence the action of the United States Senate." Yet neither La Follette nor Crownhart was ever fully aware of the lengths to which some faculty members went in their opposition.[60]

The leader of the sub-rosa movement to destroy La Follette was none other than the shining light of the Madison Loyalty Legion, Richard T. Ely. "What we need now above everything else and need very quickly is to get together facts about La Follette's activities in this country and other countries," he wrote Princeton historian and former colleague Dana C. Munro in January, 1918, after the round robin had begun circulating among the faculty. "We want to show that his influence has been pernicious, and that he has been encouraging our foes and discouraging the government in its war activities." What Ely wanted in particular was a search of German

[59] Curti and Carstensen, *The University of Wisconsin*, 2:111–121; Peterson and Fite, *Opponents of War*, 107–108.

[60] An account of the resolution and the machinations of those who promoted it may be found in La Follette and La Follette, *La Follette*, 2:842–852.

newspapers, hoping that they might contain articles proving La Follette's complicity in efforts to aid the enemy. Munro dutifully forwarded Ely's letter to the educational division of the Committee on Public Information, which in turn handed it over to a private group that specialized in rummaging through German newspapers. Ely was delighted; he began to think of titles for the pamphlet he might write from the materials he expected to receive. The search nevertheless proved disappointing. As one of the investigators reported, "the German press is giving very little attention indeed to internal affairs in America." The most damning item the investigators could turn up referred to a La Follette statement indicating that the *Lusitania* had, in fact, carried munitions. So it was, then, that Ely and his associates found themselves committed to the round robin's unproved assertion that La Follette had given aid and comfort to the Central Powers.[61]

La Follette's opposition to the war, thought many of Wisconsin's hyperpatriots, provided a partial explanation for the state's poor showing in the first two Liberty Loan campaigns. In point of fact, the Liberty Loan drives encountered difficulties throughout the country. Secretary of the Treasury William Gibbs McAdoo regarded the loans as a means of diverting individual savings into the war effort. To achieve that objective at minimum cost, he sought to keep interest rates low. Low interest rates, however, resulted in a marketing strategy that placed more emphasis on patriotism than on profitable investment. To attract support from investors for whom patriotism alone was an insufficient reason for buying bonds, McAdoo offered special inducements: installment plans, tax exemption features, and convertibility guarantees. Such inducements proved advantageous to persons of more than average means, while for low-income groups, McAdoo advised the purchase of war savings stamps or war savings certificates. Inevitably, linking bond sub-

[61] Ely to Munro, January 20, 1918; Guy Stanton Ford to Ely, January 30, February 13, 1918; Ely to Ford, February 6, 1918; Vincent Clark to John S. P. Tatlock, February 14, 1918; Tatlock to Ely, February 16, 1918; and James G. Randall to Tatlock, February 16, 1918, all in the Ely Papers. Hostility to La Follette was not, of course, limited to Wisconsin. Shortly after the declaration of war, for example, Alton B. Parker, Democratic presidential candidate in 1904, wired William Jennings Bryan: "If you and your friend Senator La Follette and all of your joint followers and sympathizers had gone to heaven three years ago, Germany would not have attempted to drive the United States from the seas or to conspire with other nations to make war upon her, for we should by now have been well prepared to defend ourselves. . . ." Parker to Bryan, March 4, 1917, in the William Jennings Bryan Papers, Library of Congress.

scriptions with loyalty made prosperous investors appear more patriotic than people who could afford only the stamps.[62]

From the beginning, the State Council of Defense assumed responsibility for directing the drives, although several organizations lent their assistance. In Madison, for example, the Boy Scouts conducted a house-to-house solicitation. For all of the council's careful planning and for all the community involvement, however, Wisconsin fell $10 million short of its $44 million quota in the first drive conducted during the summer of 1917. Those who felt shamed by the results talked about pro-German influence, but painstaking postmortems revealed that bond buying had little to do with ethnic configurations. Milwaukee, Kenosha, and Racine counties, which were heavily German, oversubscribed their quotas, while most of the northern rural counties failed to meet theirs. The pattern of the second drive, held in the fall of 1917, was much the same. Kenosha led the nation in percentage of subscriptions as compared with quota, population, and banking resources. But again the rural areas, in a less favorable economic position to invest in Liberty Bonds, brought the state subscription rate down. And again Wisconsin fell short of its quota.[63]

When it came time to launch the third loan drive in the spring of 1918, state officials and public alike were determined to do better. Wisconsin had experienced an important change in mood, or so it seemed. War rallies, four-minute speeches, and dissemination of war information all appeared to have had an effect. The confusion of role and responsibility between the Defense League and the Council of Defense had been resolved with the formation of the Loyalty Legion. As people became involved in Red Cross programs, food production programs, and war labor programs, they may have begun to develop greater awareness of what meeting the crisis entailed. News of American sacrifices in France probably en-

[62] Charles Gilbert, *American Financing of World War I* (Westport, Connecticut, 1970), 117–124; William G. McAdoo, *Crowded Years: The Reminiscences of William G. McAdoo* (Boston, 1931), 380–382; Alexander D. Noyes, *The War Period of American Finance, 1908–1925, Being the Continuation of 'Forty Years of American Finance'* (New York, 1926), 171–175.

[63] Wisconsin State Council of Defense [Magnus Swenson] to R. B. Dudgeon, June 4, 1917 (in box 21); Alfred L. P. Dennis to chairmen and secretaries of the county councils of defense, May 19, 1917 (in box 2); and Wisconsin State Council of Defense [Andrew H. Melville] to George F. Porter, September 6, 1917 (in box 22), all in the State Council of Defense Correspondence, Series 1642, WSA; *Wisconsin Blue Book, 1919*, pp. 420–421.

couraged a willingness to make greater sacrifices at home. Wisconsin citizens—or at least some of them—had been thoroughly conditioned to respond generously to any appeal for bond subscriptions. But more significantly, McAdoo and other responsible officials introduced measures to attract a larger number of middle-income investors. The most important of the new terms were an increase in the interest rate to 4½ per cent and a provision for the use of bonds in the payment of estate and inheritance taxes.

As the Council of Defense and affiliated groups promoted an efficient, high-pressure campaign in Wisconsin, the third Liberty Loan became an arduous, demanding chore for many ordinary people who really wanted to do their part. At the same, vigilantes and busybodies enjoyed a field day. With the willing assistance of the Loyalty Legion, local workers sent out questionnaires which were used to determine the bond-buying capability and past performance of every adult citizen. Then, armed with this information, committees went out to call on prospects. Anyone who proved reluctant to buy bonds received an invitation to appear before the county's Council of Defense to explain. In more than one instance, high-pressure tactics became inhuman coercion. A Rock County mob furnished an example of what was an altogether too common occurrence when it seized a retired banker, jostled him about, and smeared his back with yellow paint. Many people, Governor Philipp among them, objected to such methods, but few would argue that they did not produce results. Wisconsin oversubscribed its third Liberty Loan quota of $54 million by a sensational $34 million margin. And when the books were closed on the fourth of the wartime loans later in 1918, the state had subscribed more than $300 million in bonds over the course of the four drives, an amount slightly in excess of its quotas.[64]

At the same time that patriots were building up momentum for the third Liberty Loan, politicians of Wisconsin were preparing for a special election occasioned by the death of Senator Paul O. Husting. Killed in a hunting accident in October, 1917, Husting had

[64] The *Wisconsin Blue Book, 1919*, pp. 420–421, contains obvious errors in tabulation of data on Wisconsin's performance in the four Liberty Loan drives, as well as the Victory Loan after the war in 1919. Compare the tables in the *Wisconsin Blue Book, 1919*, with U.S. Secretary of the Treasury, *Annual Report*, 1919, pp. 253–254. A summary of the national response to the five loan drives may be found in Gilbert, *American Financing of World War I*, 139–142.

been a great favorite of the Loyalty Legion and of Democrats in the state. His passing invited comparison of his record with that of the senior senator, and a good many voters apparently agreed with the University of Wisconsin alumnus who proclaimed that he would rather be Senator Husting "dead in his glory" than Senator La Follette "alive in his shame." Fearing that passions of the electorate could get out of hand, Governor Philipp asked the state legislature to grant him power to appoint Husting's successor. Legislators supported by the Loyalty Legion would not hear of it; they believed an election would serve as a popular referendum to demonstrate Wisconsin's loyalty. Progressives also opposed the grant of appointive power, chiefly because they distrusted the governor. Philipp therefore called for primaries on March 19, to be followed by an election on April 2, 1918. Meanwhile, by passing a resolution condemning "Senator Robert M. La Follette and all others who have failed to see the righteousness of our nation's cause," the legislature tried to ensure that loyalty would be a major issue in the campaign.[65]

Voters of every persuasion on that issue had opinions about who could best take Husting's place, and several candidates entered the lists. Irvine L. Lenroot was the choice of most Stalwart Republicans and of Philipp himself. Having voted for the war as a congressman from the Eleventh District, he also received support from the Loyalty Legion. But former governor Francis E. McGovern, who like Lenroot had once been close to La Follette, was too much a maverick to permit an uncontested nomination. Only after a Milwaukee conference endorsed Lenroot, and after intense pressure from Republicans who saw Lenroot as a harmony candidate, did McGovern withdraw from the race. That left James Thompson, who had La Follette's support, as the only other contender for the Republican nomination. Even though he called for "a united country to prosecute the war vigorously and effectively until peace shall be declared," Thompson was tarred with the same brush that hyperpatriots had used on La Follette. In the eyes of Loyalty Legionnaires

[65] Milwaukee *Journal*, October 22, 1917; La Follette and La Follette, *La Follette*, 2:846; *Wisconsin State Journal*, February 23, March 1–6, 1918; *Wisconsin Assembly Bills*, Special Session, 1918, amendment 2S to joint resolution 3A; *Wisconsin Senate Journal*, Special Session, 1918, pp. 78–79; *Supplement to the Wisconsin Senate Journal*, Special Session, 1918, pp. 80–81; *Wisconsin Assembly Journal*, Special Session, 1918, pp. 95–130; *Supplement to the Wisconsin Assembly Journal*, Special Session, 1918, pp. 141–165.

and their kind, that made him as dangerous as Victor Berger, the candidate of the Socialists.[66]

Rivalry also appeared in the Democratic camp before the primary. Joseph E. Davies, a friend of Husting and a supporter of President Wilson, resigned from the Federal Trade Commission to become a candidate. His chief opponent was Charles McCarthy, who could cite impressive credits in his record of service to the state: founder and chief of the Legislative Reference Library; author of *The Wisconsin Idea* (1912); earnest advocate of farm cooperatives, of government agricultural programs, of extension, adult, and vocational education; and one of the founders of the state's Council of Defense. Yet McCarthy had never been prominent in Democratic circles. Indeed, Otto La Budde, chairman of the Democratic state central committee, denied that McCarthy had ever been affiliated with the party at all. Why he became a candidate was never entirely clear, but he probably thought that he stood a better chance with farmers and laborers than did the aristocratic Davies. He used the slogan, "Back the President to the Finish," but the President did not back him in return. If McCarthy's candidacy had any influence it was scarcely noticeable, although he may have prevented some Democrats from crossing over to vote for Thompson on the Republican side.[67]

The day before voters went to the polls in the primary that had been billed as a great loyalty referendum, Richard Lloyd Jones offered his counsel and advice in a *Wisconsin State Journal* editorial. "Neither Thompson nor Berger are [*sic*] fit men to now send to the Senate of the United States," he warned as editor. "One admits that he doesn't know what the war is about. That condemns him.

[66] *Wisconsin State Journal*, February 28, March 1, 5, 12, 15, 1918; James A. Stone to O. D. Whitehill, March 9, 1918, in the James A. Stone Papers; Margulies, *Decline of the Progressive Movement*, 216–217, 221; *La Follette's Magazine*, February and March, 1918, *passim*; Thompson's platform, March 19, 1918, in the James Thompson Papers. Thompson received support from William T. Evjue's Madison *Capital Times*. Evjue had left the *Wisconsin State Journal* the previous fall, and with the help of La Follette progressives had established his new paper in December, 1917. See William T. Evjue, *A Fighting Editor* (Madison, 1968), 274ff.

[67] Milwaukee *Journal*, February 21, March 8, 1918; Charles A. Nelson, "Progressivism and Loyalty in Wisconsin Politics, 1912–1918" (master's thesis, University of Wisconsin, 1961), 113; McCarthy to John Walsh, telegram, February 23, 1918; McCarthy to T. J. Mahon, telegram, February 24, 1918; McCarthy to Louis Wehle, February 24, 1918; McCarthy to Vance McCormick, telegram, February 25, 1918; McCarthy to Charles Lyman, February 25, 1918; McCarthy to Louis D. Brandeis, March 18, 1918; and McCarthy to J. S. Cullinan, March 22, 1918, all in the Charles R. McCarthy Papers.

The other is openly pro-German. Wisconsin must have a man in the United States Senate who is every inch PRO-AMERICAN, who KNOWS what we are fighting for and why we have to fight." The *State Journal* endorsed Lenroot as the only candidate worthy of a patriot's vote.[68]

Jones and others who saw the primary as the consummate test of Wisconsin's loyalty could take but moderate satisfaction in the results. Although Lenroot defeated Thompson, his margin was only 2,414 votes out of 143,958 cast. The much-maligned Thompson had polled 49.2 per cent of the Republican vote. Lenroot won in fifty counties; his greatest strength lay in those that were predominantly agricultural and Scandinavian. By contrast, Thompson's twenty-one counties included those with the heaviest urban and German concentrations, counties such as Milwaukee, Sheboygan, Manitowoc, Jefferson, and Ozaukee. In the Democratic primary Davies employed the party machinery to good effect in overwhelming McCarthy, 57,282 to 13,784. Berger ran without opposition on the Social Democratic ticket, and he did surprisingly well in capturing 38,564 votes. From the point of view of those who equated loyalty with enthusiastic support of the war, the best that could be said for the primary was that it eliminated Thompson from consideration in the April election.[69]

As hyperpatriots viewed the political scene after the primary, Berger stood out as a major threat. Members of the Loyalty Legion tortured themselves with the thought that Thompson's supporters might now switch to Berger and provide him with the margin of victory, while Davies and Lenroot would split the "loyal" vote and go down to defeat. To some of the legionnaires, that possibility seemed so frightening and so likely that they urged either Lenroot or Davies to withdraw from the race. The Milwaukee *Journal* attempted to force Lenroot's departure by attacking his record on preparedness. The day after the primary it published a letter from Wilson in which the President praised Davies for having been true when "the McLemore resolution, the embargo issue and the armed

[68] *Wisconsin State Journal*, March 18, 1918. The Loyalty Legion agreed with Jones but had to be more circumspect to maintain its nonpartisan stance. See Willet M. Spooner to George F. Kull, March 13, 1918, and Kull to Spooner, March 15, 1918 (both in box 2), and Kull to Chapter Secretaries, March 7, 1918 (in box 4), all in Wisconsin Loyalty Legion Correspondence and Miscellaneous Papers, Series 1706, WSA.

[69] *Wisconsin Blue Book, 1919*, p. 45; Herbert F. Margulies, *Senator Lenroot of Wisconsin: A Political Biography, 1900–1929* (Columbia, Missouri, 1977), 237–247.

neutrality measure presented the first opportunities to apply the acid test in our country to disclose true loyalty and genuine Americanism." Lenroot had failed that test, and even some members of his own party thought he should pull out. Governor Philipp would tolerate no such nonsense. He had never been taken in by claims of "superior loyalty," and he found the boasting of Democratic breast-beaters particularly irksome. Other Republicans shared the governor's annoyance. Lenroot remained in contention for the Senate seat.[70]

Clumsiness in using the loyalty lever as a tool to build a pro-Davies coalition was matched by the crudity of maneuvers to destroy Berger. Postmaster General Albert S. Burleson had been the first to act when, in September of 1917, he had charged the *Leader* with violation of the Espionage Act and had revoked its second-class mailing privilege. Then Berger himself was indicted under the same act on February 2, 1918, although announcement of his indictment did not come until March 9 during the heat of the primary campaign. Berger believed, perhaps correctly, that the delay was "a political move, pure and simple." And like the criticism of Lenroot's loyalty, it boomeranged. Sympathy for the harassed editor began to build. In the election on April 2 Berger increased his vote to 110,487, or 26 per cent of the total.[71]

In the contest between Lenroot and Davies, Lenroot emerged the winner, but the Republican victory by no means laid to rest the loyalty question in Wisconsin. Congressman John J. Esch spoke for many citizens when he expressed his regret that Berger had done so well. "Normally there are some 30,000 Socialists in our State, as disclosed in the votes of previous elections," he wrote. "Opposition to war is a fundamental socialistic doctrine and the party, therefore, would be opposed to war with any other nation as well as Germany, but the other 70,000 citizens who voted for

[70] Milwaukee *Journal*, March 20, 1918; Margulies, *Decline of the Progressive Movement*, 227; Madison *Democrat*, March 23, 1918; Maxwell, *Emanuel L. Philipp*, 163. Failing to secure withdrawal of either candidate, the Loyalty Legion expressed satisfaction with both Lenroot and Davies. It urged only that its chapters get out the "loyal 'stay-at-homes.'" See George F. Kull to Chapter Secretaries, March 28, 1918, in Wisconsin Loyalty Legion Correspondence and Miscellaneous Papers, box 4, Series 1706, WSA.

[71] U.S. House, Special Committee on Victor L. Berger Investigation, *Hearings Before the Special Committee . . . Concerning the Right of Victor L. Berger to be Sworn in . . .*, 66 Cong., 1 sess. (1919), 2 vols., 1:505–513, and 2:564–573; John M. Work, "The First World War," in *WMH*, 41 (Autumn, 1957), 32–44; Peterson and Fite, *Opponents of War*, 164–165.

Berger were persuaded so to do because they were either inborn pacifists or were opposed to the war with Germany." As Esch saw it, the Berger vote "behooves every patriotic citizen to exert himself to the utmost in order that these 70,000 may see the error of their ways and be brought to a realizing sense that the fate of America is now involved and their country needs their undivided and loyal support." Loyalty continued to be a dominant issue during the gubernatorial and congressional campaigns of 1918, and it had a powerful influence on the elections in November. But diverse concerns also had their effect and helped to prevent a loyalty monomania from wiping out all the ideological, ethnic, and other interests that were important influences in the changing alignments of Wisconsin politics.[72]

The first to throw his hat into the gubernatorial ring in 1918 was Republican state senator Roy P. Wilcox of Eau Claire, chief sponsor of the resolution condemning La Follette. Proclaiming that "politics this year is patriotism," he sought and received support from pro-war extremists, disaffected Progressives, and Stalwarts disenchanted by Philipp's moderation. In an effort to project an image of himself as the "All-American candidate," he campaigned on a platform that included reforms such as woman suffrage, agricultural co-operatives, a marketing commission, and taxation based on ability to pay. While he endorsed measures designed to please Progressives, however, Wilcox also launched a ferocious attack on Philipp's loyalty: "The present Governor who advocated an Embargo, opposed conscription . . . openly took the position that we are not interested in the causes of the war, and should not sacrifice American life on European soil. . . . certainly has no claim that he is a 'War Governor.' "[73]

Philipp had not intended to run for a third term, but he could ignore neither the pleas of friends nor his own conviction that the times required a steady hand at the helm. He announced his candidacy and suggested that his experience in office would be invaluable to Wisconsin during the continuing war crisis. In the primary campaign he responded to the charge that he had not been

[72] Esch to Frank Drew, April 8, 1919, in the John J. Esch Papers. Lenroot beat Davies 163,983 to 148,923, but he won less than 39 per cent of the total vote. See the *Wisconsin Blue Book, 1919*, p. 46.

[73] Wilcox to James A. Stone, August 29, 1918, in the Stone Papers; Milwaukee *Sentinel*, August 14, 21, 1918; Nelson, "Progressivism and Loyalty in Wisconsin," 123–124.

sufficiently patriotic in 1915–1916 by pointing out that Wilson himself had favored neutrality. He cited past editorials from newspapers that were most vicious in condemning his record—the *Wisconsin State Journal*, the Milwaukee *Journal*, and the Eau Claire *Telegram*—to show that they too had wanted to stay out of war in 1916. More than anything else, however, Philipp spoke for reason and good sense. He announced that he had "no intention of going about the state denouncing the people along racial [i.e. nationality] lines," and he advised voters to "shun all men" who presumed to judge the patriotism and loyalty of others. "If my opponent, Mr. Wilcox, wishes to stand before the people as the Tar and Feather Candidate, he may do so," he remarked. "I shall stand for law and order."[74]

Meanwhile, the La Follette wing of the Republican party was having great difficulty in finding a candidate. James Thompson, a favorite of Progressives, refused to run, and no one else attracted any significant support. Finally, James N. Tittemore stepped into the breach. He had had little political experience, but as president of the Wisconsin Society of Equity he could claim a following among farmers and laborers. Organizing a convention made up of 500 delegates from Equity, labor, the Grange, and the newly formed Nonpartisan League, Tittemore engineered a gubernatorial nomination for himself. The convention also supported two Progressives for state offices: Merlin Hull for re-election as secretary of state, and John J. Blaine for attorney general. To some old-line Progressives the Tittemore candidacy seemed almost farcical, but it was significant in at least two respects. For one thing, it foreshadowed the Farmer-Labor Progressive coalition that was to become increasingly important until it reached its apogee during the Depression thirties. More immediately, it provided La Follette supporters with a means of joining in the effort to defeat the hyperpatriotic Wilcox,

[74] Philipp, speeches at Marshall, June 27, 1918, and Waukesha, August 6, 1918, both in the Philipp Papers; Milwaukee *Sentinel*, August 7, 25, September 1, 1918; *Wisconsin State Journal*, June 29, 1918. Members of the Loyalty Legion disagreed on whether or not to oppose Philipp openly. Wheeler P. Bloodgood urged that "we take an active part in defeating him for re-election." But others thought such a position would involve more partisan politics than the legion could afford. See Bloodgood to George F. Kull, October 9, 1918; Otto A. LaBudde to Kull, October 10, 1918; John M. Whitehead to Kull, October 10, 1918; Carroll E. Gray to Kull, October 11, 1918; Richard Lloyd Jones to Kull, October 12, 1918; J. E. McConnell to Kull, October 15, 1918; and W. N. Fuller to Kull, October 19, 1918, all filed under "Loyalty Legion Minutes, 1917–1918" in the Wisconsin Loyalty Legion Correspondence and Miscellaneous Papers, box 1, Series 1706, WSA.

and it thus opened the way for co-operation between La Follette and Philipp.[75]

Although Progressives had doubts about Tittemore's entry into the primary campaign for the Republican nomination, many of them believed that their only reasonable alternative was to endorse him. "It makes me mad all over to find Progressives everywhere, down here, supporting Wilcox," wrote Charles Rosa from Beloit. And if Wilcox should win the GOP nomination, it would be "the last straw." Rosa considered the Loyalty Legion's hero "five times as vicious as Governor Philipp, from the standpoint of Progressive Republicanism." William T. Evjue of the *Capital Times* also believed Philipp less wicked than Wilcox. Along with other Progressives, he joined Rosa in the Tittemore cause, hoping that the move would help win enough votes away from Wilcox to assure Philipp's nomination.[76]

The strategy proved successful, but the primary was a cliff-hanger. Voters had to wait a week for all the returns to come in before they learned that Philipp had defeated Wilcox by a scant 440 votes out of nearly 200,000 votes cast for the several Republican candidates. He carried only twenty-three counties as opposed to thirty-two for Wilcox and sixteen for Tittemore; had it not been for his victories in Milwaukee and several other German counties he would have lost. Comparison of the vote in the fall gubernatorial primary with returns of the March senatorial primary suggests that many German voters who had supported Thompson and Berger in the spring cast their ballots for Philipp in September. Hull won renomination for a second term as secretary of state, and Blaine easily defeated the Republican incumbent to win the nomination for attorney general.

The election provided evidence of a new political alignment in the making as Progressives gained strength in German areas that had opposed them before the war; and when it reached fruition it helped make possible La Follette's return to respectability. In the fall of 1918, however, only the most sanguine of the senator's fol-

[75] James A. Stone to Herman E. Sachtjen, April 26, 1918, in the Stone Papers; *Capital Times*, May 1, 2, 1918; Theodore Saloutos, "The Wisconsin Society of Equity," in *Agricultural History*, 14 (April, 1940), 78–95.

[76] Evjue to Rosa, July 23, 1918, in the Charles D. Rosa Papers; Rosa to James Thompson, August 2, 1918, in the Thompson Papers; Rosa to James A. Stone, August 12, 1918, in the Stone Papers; *Capital Times*, July 22, 25, August 16, 22, 1918.

lowers dared entertain such a hope. Unsuccessful though the hyperpatriots may have been in their efforts to terminate Philipp's career, they still wielded considerable power. That became evident when they organized during the primary campaign to defeat the congressmen who had voted against American entry into the war. As a result of their opposition, Henry Allen Cooper, John M. Nelson, and William J. Cary were all unseated. Only James A. Frear managed to survive.[77]

The general election in November lacked both the interest and the importance of the Republican primary. The influenza epidemic that swept the country that fall forced a curtailment of public gatherings, and campaign orators rested their vocal cords. The Wilson administration did its best to get Democrats into office, but they failed miserably. Philipp won an easy victory over Henry Moehlenpah. The entire Republican state ticket coasted into office, with La Follette Progressives registering impressive victories. Edward Dithmar and Merlin Hull won re-election as lieutenant-governor and secretary of state respectively, while John Blaine won the race for attorney general.

The GOP also captured ten of the state's eleven seats in Congress. Victor Berger, folk idol of the Fifth District, won election to the remaining seat, but when he sought to claim it the House rejected him. Congressmen considered him too disloyal to take the oath of office, and even though his constituents re-elected him, the House had its way. Not until 1922, after his third victory at the polls and after wartime passions had cooled, was the Milwaukee Socialist finally seated.[78]

Berger's difficulties demonstrated that down to the end of the war and beyond, questions of loyalty continued to trouble many people. Even as voters went to the polls on that November day in 1918, however, the war crisis seemed to be spinning itself out.

[77] *Wisconsin Blue Book, 1919*, p. 93; *Capital Times*, June 8, September 4, 5, November 15, 1918; Milwaukee *Sentinel*, September 18, 1918; Margulies, *Decline of the Progressive Movement*, 238–239; Brye, *Wisconsin Voting Patterns*, 277–278. See also Frear to Dear Friend, August 10, 1918, in the James A. Frear Papers.

[78] Maxwell, *Emanuel L. Philipp*, 179; *Wisconsin Blue Book, 1919*, pp. 149, 155; *House Reports*, 66 Cong., 1 sess., no. 413 (serial 7595), *Case of Victor L. Berger, of Wisconsin.* Algie Simons thought Berger's strength "almost exactly proportioned to the German born population, and not in any way proportionate to the labor element or the radical forces." William English Walling to Simons, January 8, 1919, and Simons to Walling, January 12, 1919, both in the Algie M. Simons Papers. See also Hyman, *To Try Men's Souls*, 319; and Peterson and Fite, *Opponents of War*, 165–166.

"Germany stands alone, her allies having quit," Philipp wrote his sailor son. "I look for an armistice in a short time."[79]

Richard Ely did not share the governor's sense of relief; his mind was preoccupied with the need to punish Germany. "I can not make it seem right to me that after Germany has devastated Belgium and a large part of France, that the war should close without an invasion of her own territory," he scribbled with a mixture of pride and sanctimony. "She ought to be made to taste the kind of food she had been handing out to others. She needs it for her soul's good." Professor Ely knew a profitable fad when he saw it, however, and he was soon off on another enterprise. "Bolshevism," he observed a few days after the armistice, "is as much opposed to any real freedom as were the Kaisers who have lost their thrones." While members of the United State House of Representatives were beginning to think about what they should do with Victor Berger, Ely was beginning to think about a book to which he gave the tentative title "Democracy the Hope, Bolshevism the Menace of Civilization." Writing his publishers to describe what he had in mind, the professor primly noted that "in our work in this state we have three watch words, namely, patriotic, sanely progressive and anti-Bolshevik."[80]

[79] Philipp to Cyrus Philipp, November 5, 1918, in the Philipp Papers.

[80] Ely to Samuel H. Marshall, November 4, 1918; Ely to William H. Short, November 16, 1918; and Ely to Edward C. Marsh, January 28, 1918, all in the Ely Papers.

2

An Uneasy Peace Comes to Wisconsin

AFTER four years of war, Allied armies were winning on every front by the summer of 1918. Kaiser Wilhelm's commanders informed him that Germany had little hope of victory, and negotiations for a settlement began in October. Finally, on November 11, President Woodrow Wilson announced that the anticipated armistice had at last ended military operations. "Everything for which America fought has been accomplished," he assured the nation. "It will now be our fortunate duty to assist by example, by sober, friendly counsel and by material aid in establishment of just democracy throughout the world." Across the land, Americans greeted the news with a profound sense of relief that the trial by battle had ended and that the Allies had defeated the Central Powers. Along with their compatriots, citizens of Wisconsin rejoiced as they looked forward to the return of peace. According to a reporter's account of the triumphant merrymaking in Wisconsin's beer capital, celebrants lined up two deep at the bar of Henry Wehr's establishment on West Water Street. And as if to summarize the social changes war had accelerated, the reporter noted that "several women were placing their feet on the 'rail' beside the men and taking 'theirs' in the true spirit of democracy."[1]

The extent to which women had won liberation from prewar strictures is debatable, but the people of Wisconsin unquestionably anticipated returning to the daily routine they had followed before 1914. With the dreadful experience of war behind them, they relished thoughts of a contented existence in the tranquil setting of their home state. "We have lived with an awful fear in our hearts for our beloved boys so long that as we begin to come back toward

[1] Burl Noggle, *Into the Twenties: The United States from Armistice to Normalcy* (Urbana, 1974), 3; New York *Times*, November 12, 1918; Milwaukee *Journal*, November 11, 1918.

normal life and conditions . . . ," Senator Robert La Follette wrote his family, "I want to pray or cry or sing my thankfulness for all our blessings." The *Pierce County Herald* of Ellsworth expressed the same idea in a homely query: "Lordy, but doesn't that white bread look good on the table?"[2]

Despite many expressions of joy and gratitude, however, an undercurrent of apprehension prevented people from being swept away in their eagerness for a resumption of peacetime activities. Some of their anxiety was attributable to a sense of what the war had cost in lives and resources, coupled with a general awareness of difficulties they might confront in establishing a "just democracy throughout the world." La Follette joined in the celebration of victory, but he did not yield to enthusiasms of the moment. Writing to his family two days after the Armistice, he fretted over Wilson's planning to closet himself in confidential sessions with Allied leaders in Europe as they made arrangements for drafting a treaty; he expressed his concern over the President's holding in abeyance the principle of freedom on the high seas; and he explained his anxiety over territorial changes resulting from secret treaties made among the Allies during the war. A man stirred neither by Wilsonian rhetoric nor by arguments that the United States might benefit from the war, the old Progressive campaigner concluded that "about all we [are] going to have left is—*peace*[,] a big war debt and *Wilsons* [*sic*] *speeches. . . .*"[3]

* * *

Back in Wisconsin, many of La Follette's admirers shared his concerns. His detractors, most of whom backed Wilson's wartime policies, sought to counteract the senator's influence by organizing support for the President in his effort to secure a treaty that would assure a lasting peace. A great debate over America's place in world affairs began shaping up in Wisconsin as well as in the nation. In the meantime, however, residents of the state confronted a more immediate problem.

[2] Robert M. La Follette to Belle Case La Follette, Robert M. La Follette, Jr., and Mary La Follette, November 15, 1918, in box A-24, the La Follette Family Papers, Library of Congress; Belle Case La Follette and Fola La Follette, *Robert M. La Follette* (2 vols., New York, 1953), 2:908; *Pierce County Herald* (Ellsworth), November 21, 1918.

[3] Robert M. La Follette to Belle Case La Follette, Robert M. La Follette, Jr., and Mary La Follette, November 11, 13, 1918, in box A-24, the La Follette Family Papers; La Follette and La Follette, *La Follette*, 2:907–908.

A deadly influenza virus had entered Wisconsin, probably carried by sailors from the Great Lakes Naval Training Station north of Chicago, and it was clear that silencing the guns of war in Europe did little to quiet the fear of mortality at home. A pandemic of the disease—causing, according to one estimate, 20 million deaths worldwide—was at the height of its virulence. No one knew much about the Spanish influenza virus, and medical practitioners were uncertain about what treatment to advise. In Wisconsin, a common belief held that munching Horlick's malted milk tablets (manufactured in Racine) increased resistance to the disease, and physicians recommended bed rest and castor oil for flu victims. But nothing appeared effective in counteracting influenza once it had struck. In the worst cases it produced severe inflammation of the respiratory passages, pneumonia, and death in a matter of days. The one characteristic of the flu that seemed certain was that it spread through human contact. City health commissioners therefore closed schools and theaters and canceled public gatherings across the state during much of October, 1918. Teachers joined Red Cross volunteers in providing ambulance and other assistance to stricken families. Such measures proved effective. Milwaukee's death rate between September 14 and December 21, 1918, was 0.6 per 1,000 population, lower than that of any other major American city. By January of 1919 the worst was over.[4]

The contagious character of the flu gave rise to various theories about the pandemic's causes; it also elicited support for immigration restriction and the prohibition of alcoholic beverages as public health measures. Some authorities reasoned that the merging of displaced populations during the war had helped to spread the disease. Others blamed the Germans. A New York *Times* article, for example, suggested the hypothesis that U-boats had delivered vials of the virus to German agents in key places. Those who believed the Germans capable of every sort of crime (they had, after all, employed poisonous gas on the battlefields) suspected the Kaiser

[4] Edwin O. Jordan, *Epidemic Influenza: A Survey* (Chicago, 1927); Milwaukee *Journal*, October 19, 21, 22, 1918; William R. Noyes, "Influenza Epidemic, 1918–1919: A Misplaced Chapter in United States Social and Institutional History" (doctoral dissertation, University of California, Los Angeles, 1968); Mary Bradford, *Memoirs of Mary Bradford: Autobiographical and Historical Reminiscences of Education in Wisconsin, Through Progressive Service from Rural School Teaching to City Superintendent* (Evansville, Wisconsin, [1932]), 435–438; Judith W. Leavitt, *The Healthiest City: Milwaukee and the Politics of Health Reform* (Princeton, 1982), 229–237.

of using biological warfare. The Armistice did little to allay fear that the arrival of disease-bearing immigrants might well jeopardize the health of the American people.[5]

Anxieties over the Spanish flu also provided prohibitionists with new arguments for closing the saloons, and a committee of the Anti-Saloon League visited Governor Emanuel Philipp to make its case. The cessation of other activities, ran the argument, caused people to congregate in saloons to a greater degree than ever before. Holding that the contagion was even more likely to infest barrooms than it was other public meeting places, the Anti-Saloon League unsuccessfully urged Philipp to lock the doors of all public houses dispensing alcoholic beverages. Saloons remained open for a time, but influenza morbidity nevertheless gradually declined.[6]

Even as the threat to public health in Wisconsin subsided, President Wilson traveled to Europe to conclude a treaty that would mark, in his words, "the greatest success or the supremest tragedy in all history." The program that Wilson took with him included a League of Nations to provide a forum for diplomatic discussion and means to keep the peace. The idea for an organization such as the league was not Wilson's alone. Advocates of peace had discussed a parliament of mankind long before Sarajevo, and the failure of efforts to mediate peace among belligerents increased the urgency of arguments for an international order. While politicians and statesmen differed over its specific features, even political enemies of the Wilson administration could agree on the need to create an agency for international co-operation. Both William Howard Taft and Theodore Roosevelt, for example, came out in favor of an association of nations with enough power to prevent or control an outbreak of hostilities.[7]

Before American entry into the war, the impulse to organize had produced the League to Enforce Peace, founded in Philadelphia during the summer of 1915. Appealing to all who recognized the need for order in a war-torn world, league organizers established affiliates throughout the nation. In Wisconsin they won support

[5] New York *Times*, September 19, 1918; Noyes, "Influenza Epidemic," 100.

[6] Milwaukee *Journal*, October 19, 1918.

[7] Arthur Walworth, *America's Moment, 1918: American Diplomacy at the End of World War I* (New York, 1977), 136; Frederick H. Lynch, "Taft's Labors for International Peace," in *Current History*, 32 (May, 1930), 297; Theodore Roosevelt, *America and the World War* (New York, 1915), 80; Theodore Roosevelt, "Utopia or Hell," in *The Independent*, January 4, 1915, p. 13.

primarily from those who rejected pacifist contentions and opposed German influence in the state. Prominent members of the Loyalty Legion became prominent members of the League to Enforce Peace as well, and Richard T. Ely of the University of Wisconsin became a dominating influence in the co-operative activities of the two groups.[8]

In May, 1918, Ely traveled to Philadelphia, where he attended the league's second national convention. The meeting generated widespread enthusiasm for scheduling state and county conventions to promote international organization under the slogan "win the war for permanent peace." With characteristic vigor, Ely plunged into the work of organizing a state rally to be held in Madison. From President Charles R. Van Hise he secured a promise of support from the University of Wisconsin, and from Taft a commitment to deliver the major address. Broadcasting invitations throughout the country, especially in the Middle West, he saw in the rally an opportunity to restore Wisconsin's good name as a patriotic and loyal state. Indeed, the Wisconsin legislature endorsed it in a joint resolution, and the convention came off without a hitch on November 8–10, 1918. Although news of the Armistice was to dominate headlines after it adjourned, the Madison conclave offered an opportunity to promote the idea of international organization. Van Hise delivered a reasoned argument for a league of free nations, and Taft urged patriotic citizens to support such a league as the best means of achieving progress without resorting to radical programs.[9]

Although not every supporter of the League to Enforce Peace wished to become identified as a follower of Woodrow Wilson, the organization did become associated with ideas the President introduced at the peace conference in Paris. Partly as a result of league efforts, sentiment in Wisconsin was running in favor of some sort of international organization at the time peacemakers were con-

[8] Ruhl J. Bartlett, *The League to Enforce Peace* (Chapel Hill, 1944), 34–41; Selig Adler, *The Isolationist Impulse: Its Twentieth-Century Reaction* (New York, 1957), 40–41; Denna Frank Fleming, *The United States and the League of Nations, 1918–1920* (New York, 1932), 8–9.

[9] Ely to Charles A. Ellwood, May 22, 1918, Ely to Franklin H. Giddings, August 8, 1918, and Ely to William H. Short, September 26, 1918, all in the Richard T. Ely Papers; Benjamin G. Rader, *The Academic Mind and Reform: The Influence of Richard T. Ely in American Life* (Lexington, Kentucky, 1966), 188; Merle Curti and Vernon R. Carstensen, *The University of Wisconsin: A History, 1848–1925* (2 vols., Madison, 1949), 2:120; Bartlett, *League to Enforce Peace*, 96.

ferring. Most of the state's newspapers favored a League of Nations, and most of them were confident of support for a new international order. "You must know that we are very strong for the League of Peace out here," wrote Professor Edward Alsworth Ross to George P. Morris, assistant editor of the *Advocate of Peace*. Commenting on attitudes in Wisconsin, he predicted, "We will be far in advance of any other state in organization of the League to Enforce Peace."[10]

In the meantime, before the conclusion of negotiations in Paris, attention shifted towards the United States Senate, where a struggle over ratification of the treaty was beginning to take shape. With the death of Senator Paul Husting and his replacement by Irvine Lenroot in April, 1918, the Republican party had gained a seat at Democratic expense. Later, in the November off-year elections, Republicans had scored victories in enough other states to assure control over both houses when the Sixty-sixth Congress convened the following March.[11]

Victories at the polls, however, did not assure Republican unanimity in responding to the work of the peace conference. The attitudes and experiences of senators differed widely, and so did their perspectives on the treaty. Wisconsin's senators, La Follette and Lenroot, were eventually to cast their votes against ratification of the treaty as Wilson submitted it, unqualified by reservations that would limit its application. Nevertheless, Lenroot's path to rejection was by no means the same as La Follette's. A longtime supporter of international organization, La Follette was to be identified with the so-called "irreconcilables," a group of sixteen senators who had little use for the international order that Wilson and other heads of state worked out in Paris. During the treaty debate, Lenroot was to become a leader of the "mild reservationists" who sought compromise so as to secure ratification of the League of Nations.[12]

After the 1918 elections, La Follette played a restrained role in early discussions of the treaty negotiations. Charged with disloyalty during the war, he was still under investigation by the Senate Com-

[10] Ross to Morris, January 15, 1919, in the Edward Alsworth Ross Papers.

[11] Seward W. Livermore, *Politics Is Adjourned: Woodrow Wilson and the War Congress, 1916–1918* (Middletown, Connecticut, 1966), 224–226; Thomas A. Bailey, *Wilson and the Peacemakers* (2 vols., New York, 1947), 2:61–62.

[12] David P. Thelen, *Robert M. La Follette and the Insurgent Spirit* (Boston, 1976; reprinted, Madison, 1986), 150; Ralph Stone, *The Irreconcilables: The Fight Against the League of Nations* (Lexington, Kentucky, 1970), 33; Herbert F. Margulies, *Senator Lenroot of Wisconsin: A Political Biography, 1900–1929* (Columbia, Missouri, 1977), 267.

mittee on Privileges and Elections when the war ended. Though the Senate voted in January, 1919, to dismiss the charges, La Follette may have been reluctant to antagonize his colleagues unnecessarily. Whatever the reason, his thoughts on the peace conference were for a time restricted largely to letters he wrote his family. Distrustful of the Paris peacemakers from the very beginning, he believed that "none of them want to pay the price of war" but that all of them wanted to achieve their own particular objectives. He anticipated an unseemly scramble for spoils. "What a joke it would be," he commented wryly, "if they should find that they had grabbed such a hand-full of sugar lumps that they couldn't get their big fist out of the bowl without dropping it all."[13]

La Follette's colleagues in the Senate tended to split into four groups that became increasingly discernible as the peace conference drew to a close. Wilson's supporters, mainly Democrats, favored ratification of the treaty without reservation. At the other end of the senatorial spectrum were the "irreconcilables" who expected to hold out against the treaty until the bitter end, whatever changes might be introduced. Between those two groups were the "strong reservationists," who wished to restrict operations of the league severely, and the "mild reservationists," who approved the league but favored attaching some blandly worded reservations.

While the peacemakers worked to complete the treaties, the apprehensions that had been nagging at La Follette increased. Wilson, he thought, was "turning flip flops with marvelous agility" in sacrificing self-determination, open diplomacy, and an impartial settlement of colonial claims. By the time a final draft of the treaty had been drawn up, La Follette believed that nothing remained from Wilson's Fourteen Points program "that couldn't be covered with a postage stamp." In the meantime, while La Follette's concerns led him to consort with the irreconcilables, Lenroot was working to secure ratification. He thought the best way to accomplish that end was to qualify American participation through the adoption of reservations on domestic questions, the Monroe Doctrine, and collective security. The last, Lenroot believed, was the most important. The peacemakers had placed a formula for collective security in Article X of the league covenant, which pledged member

[13] La Follette and La Follette, *La Follette*, 2: 926–931; Arno J. Mayer, *Politics and Diplomacy of Peacemaking: Containment and Counterrevolution at Versailles, 1918–1919* (New York, 1967), 560–561; Stone, *The Irreconcilables*, 186.

nations to "respect and preserve as against external aggression the territorial integrity and existing political independence of all members of the league." Committed as he was to a plan for peace, Lenroot never wavered in his insistence upon a reservation to prevent the possibility of the United States being involved under Article X in a war against the national interest and perhaps even against American principles of justice.[14]

On July 10, 1919, the President took a copy of the treaty to the Senate. "The stage is set, the destiny disclosed," he told the senators. "It has come about by no plan of our conceiving, but by the hand of God who led us into this way." In the months that followed, Wilson was to have reason to think that the Almighty had abandoned him. The treaty went immediately to the Senate Foreign Relations Committee, where the chairman, Senate majority leader Henry Cabot Lodge, worked assiduously to maintain Republican party unity. To prevent enthusiasms of the moment from overwhelming committee deliberations, Lodge insisted on reading aloud the 268-page document with painstaking attention to every detail. This laborious process required a fortnight, and then Lodge held public hearings for another six weeks. Not until September 10 did the committee report the treaty, heavily encumbered with amendments and reservations. The amendments were easily defeated, for passing them would have changed the treaty and required reconvening the peace conference to approve the changes. The reservations fared better. By November 18, fourteen of them had been adopted, and the Senate prepared to vote on ratification.[15]

* * *

The peace settlement became a major topic of discussion throughout the country. Generating enthusiasm for an international organization at the time of the Armistice, the League to Enforce Peace had done its work well. In Wisconsin, as elsewhere, most people assumed that Wilson's Fourteen Points would form a basis for the

[14] La Follette and La Follette, *La Follette*, 2:954–955; Paul Birdsall, *Versailles Twenty Years After* (New York, 1941; reprinted, Hamden, Connecticut, 1962), 132–147; Margulies, *Senator Lenroot*, 266–267; Bailey, *Wilson and the Peacemakers*, 2:385.

[15] Ray Stannard Baker and William E. Dodd, eds., *The Public Papers of Woodrow Wilson* (6 vols., New York, 1925–1927), 5:551; Chicago *Tribune*, July 11, 1919; Arthur C. Walworth, *Woodrow Wilson. Volume 2: World Prophet* (New York, 1958), 333–354; Margulies, *Senator Lenroot*, 272–294; Stone, *The Irreconcilables*, 123–125, 143–146; Beloit *Daily News*, September 25, 1919.

treaty; few doubted that the League of Nations would, for good or ill, become a reality. Confident of the future, proponents of such a league expressed their confidence in high moral abstractions. At the same time, they displayed a reluctance to debate particulars of the new international order. "In so vital a matter as the League of Nations," argued the *Wisconsin State Journal*, "it is not wise to take the decision away from the men who are best informed on the subject and whose business it is to study it." The United States Senate, the *State Journal* insisted, was "the body best fitted to ratify the League of Nations covenant in its final form."[16]

The growth of a critical attitude within the Senate—one more vigorous than most Americans had anticipated—was a disappointment to the advocates of international organization. Assuming that the patriotic endeavors of 1917–1918 had produced support for international order, proponents of a formal international structure were surprised at the depth of opposition to the league proposal. In Wisconsin, with its Old World antecedents, discussion of the league sometimes echoed with phrases from half-remembered debates of earlier times. Wisconsin Synod Lutherans, for example, found no difficulty in stating their case against the league in theological terms. An editorial in the *Northwestern Lutheran* acknowledged that "the League of Nations in its noblest aspects was a godly idea which man is everlastingly unable to carry out." The good German Lutherans of this persuasion had known all along that man's sinfulness would always prevent realization of a heaven on earth; only on the day of Grace would perfection become attainable under God. Until then, man's puny efforts could at best establish a League of Nations "in some diluted, wordy form"; the league itself would amount to nothing because it represented a work of man, not a work of the Heavenly Father.[17]

For the most part, however, the opposition to the League of Nations in Wisconsin derived from a secular heritage that was more characteristically mid-American in nature. Readers of the *Kickapoo Scout*, the Soldiers Grove weekly newspaper, learned that support for the league resulted from "widespread and insidious propaganda, aparently [*sic*] well financed in behalf of internationalism as

[16] *Wisconsin State Journal*, May 6, 1919.

[17] H. K. M., "The League of Nations," in the *Northwestern Lutheran*, 6 (February 9, 1919), 18; Austin J. App, "The Germans," in Joseph P. O'Grady, ed., *The Immigrants' Influence on Wilson's Peace Policies* (Lexington, Kentucky, 1967), 50–55.

against nationalism." Having fought the American Revolution "to free ourselves from the European yoke," the people of the United States could commit no greater folly than to place themselves under the "command of a league . . . representing interests in almost every instance diverse from ours." The Madison *Capital Times* agreed, expressing its skepticism of the sophisticated and cynical diplomats who drafted the treaty: "President Wilson alone went [to Paris] with ideals. The rest of them went to look out for No. 1." Except for Wilson, none of the diplomats spoke for the peoples of the world, "and Wilson was beaten at the peace table." Shortly before the President turned the treaty over to the Senate, *Capital Times* editor William T. Evjue reprinted a comment on "The Madness of Versailles" from the pen of Oswald Garrison Villard, editor of *The Nation*. According to Villard, Wilson had "repaid the confidence which the people gave him" by helping to enthrone "an arrogant and self-sufficient autocracy of . . . Great Powers." For that betrayal, "the one-time idol of democracy stands today discredited and condemned."[18]

The Beloit *Daily News* avoided recriminations, but after publication of the treaty it came out with an editorial that expressed some of the concerns troubling people throughout the state. It argued that in basing the league covenant on abstract principles of right and justice, Wilson had ignored nationalistic feuds and rivalries of long standing. The opinion of the *Daily News* was that, given Article X, the American people should be very clear about how they would respond to international problems if the treaty were ratified. Through their chosen representatives in the Senate, they should unambiguously state "how far the nation will commit itself to the proposed league and what reservations it deems necessary while entering into its new obligations." But Wilson could not bring himself to compromise with even the mildest of the reservationists, and he urged "all true friends of the treaty" to vote against ratification with reservations. Summing up the attitude that appeared to predominate in Wisconsin at the end of September, the Milwaukee *Sentinel* observed that "the plain citizen is beginning to feel that a tremendous pother is being kicked up over the treaty which

[18] *Kickapoo Scout* (Soldiers Grove), February 13, 1919; Madison *Capital Times*, May 12, 24, 1919.

could be avoided by some comparatively slight concessions on the part of the President."[19]

Senator La Follette wrote Oswald Garrison Villard in October to warn that "the mild reservationists are more or less in a strategic position." Having by that time determined to vote against ratification, La Follette feared that "milk and water reservations may prevail." The way attitudes were forming in Wisconsin may have reinforced his fears. Lenroot had returned home for a few days to speak at the state fair, where he talked confidently about the likelihood of agreement on Article X and prompt ratification of the treaty within two weeks. The Wisconsin branch of the League to Enforce Peace had increased its activity in support of the treaty, even going so far as to hire a professional campaign manager, William W. Powell. Under league auspices, several notable Americans—including diplomat Henry Morgenthau, former president Taft, Harvard president A. Lawrence Lowell, and Kansas editor William Allen White—were stumping the state for the treaty. Protesting against amendment of it, but not against reservations or interpretations, the League to Enforce Peace pleaded for "immediate ratification without delay."[20]

Most of the speakers who came into Wisconsin for pro-treaty rallies adopted the position taken by the national organization, advocating ratification with reservations. William Allen White, for example, conceded that Wilson had compromised his Fourteen Points and that some of the compromises were bad ones. Nevertheless, he argued, it was better to accept a covenant that was partly bad than it would be "not to take it at all." By ratifying the treaty with reservations, the Senate would place the United States in a position to benefit from association with the League of Nations without sacrificing American interests. While some of White's listeners thought him too willing to acknowledge the flaws in the treaty, Powell considered the lecture series a "splendid success." He

[19] Beloit *Daily News*, July 17, 1919; Walworth, *Woodrow Wilson. Volume 2*, 361–373; Bailey, *Wilson and the Peacemakers*, 2:105–114, 177–179; Margulies, *Senator Lenroot*, 275, 283; Milwaukee *Sentinel*, September 13, 1919.

[20] La Follette to Villard, October 11, 1919, in the Oswald Garrison Villard Papers, Houghton Library, Harvard University; William Harrison Short to Richard T. Ely, August 27, 1919, in the Ely Papers; Margulies, *Senator Lenroot*, 280; Milwaukee *Sentinel*, September 12, 1919; Rader, *The Academic Mind and Reform*, 188–189. By comparison with some of his incoming correspondence, La Follette's letter to Villard was restrained. See, for example, Amos Pinchot to La Follette, September 22, 1919, in the Amos Pinchot Papers, Library of Congress.

thought that White had spoken candidly and persuasively, and had so skillfully explained the difficulties encountered by the President that he was able "to remove in a large measure the heretofore expressed prejudices against the league as a Wilson product."[21]

Whatever the shadings and nuances of public opinion in Wisconsin, on November 19 the U.S. Senate voted on the treaty with reservations. The count showed that all but four Democrats had joined the Republicans who opposed the settlement, and the Senate had rejected the treaty with reservations, 39 ayes to 55 nays. Requiring a two-thirds vote for ratification, the treaty failed to get a simple majority. A second vote on the same motion suffered a similar fate. In yet a third vote, on a resolution to approve the treaty without reservations, the result was again negative, this time by a 38-to-53 margin. The treaty had gone down to defeat. That night the irreconcilables joined the strong reservationists in a victory celebration at the home of Alice Roosevelt Longworth.[22]

Neither Wisconsin senator did much celebrating. La Follette predicted that the treaty fight would be renewed during the next session of Congress, and he prepared to do battle. "I am hoping that the milk and water fellows on the Republican side will return with a little iron in their blood," he wrote his friend, Robert F. Paine. "If they do, we may be able to establish a precedent which will make presidents hesitate in the future before they violate the Constitution with such contempt for its meaning."[23]

For his part, Lenroot continued to work for a compromise that would satisfy both the irreconcilables and the President. Holding fast to his position that reservations were essential, he sought vainly for the formula that might bring about ratification before the 1920 political campaign began in earnest. He was fighting a lost cause. From his point of view the problem was not too little iron in the blood of his senatorial colleagues, but too much of it. And Wilson could be as stubborn as they. "I hear of reservationists and mild reservationists," declared the President, "but I cannot understand the difference between a nullifier and a mild nullifier."[24]

[21] *Wisconsin State Journal*, August 31, September 6, 1919; A. L. Hougen to Richard T. Ely, September 5, 1919, and William W. Powell to W. R. Boyd, September 11, 1919, both in the Ely Papers.

[22] *Congressional Record*, 66 Cong., 1 sess., 8786, 8802–8803; Bailey, *Wilson and the Peacemakers*, 2:190–194; Alice Roosevelt Longworth, *Crowded Hours: Reminiscences of Alice Roosevelt Longworth* (New York, 1933), 292; Stone, *The Irreconcilables*, 145–146.

[23] La Follette and La Follette, *La Follette*, 2:983.

[24] Stone, *The Irreconcilables*, 166; Walworth, *Woodrow Wilson. Volume 2*, 392.

The treaty came up for ratification with reservations one last time on March 19, 1920. The final tally showed 49 senators voting for it with 35 against, and ratification thus fell seven votes short. Both Wilson and the bitter-enders expected the 1920 elections to become, in Wilson's words, "a great and solemn referendum, a referendum as to the part the United States is to play in completing the settlements of the war." Again disappointment awaited proponents of the league, and in Wisconsin people turned to other matters: snowstorms, the University of Wisconsin's athletic contests, the price of sugar, or the opening of trout season. Six weeks before the treaty came up for a vote in March, the *Pierce County Herald* posed what may have seemed a more important question: "How About a Pierce County B.B. League?" The voters of Wisconsin were in no mood for a solemn referendum, and neither were the voters of other states.[25]

* * *

As Americans resumed peacetime activities, their anxieties over German autocracy and German-American disloyalty quickly diminished. Nevertheless, the wartime experiences of the United States left a residue of uneasiness over the subversive influence of radical ideas and radical organizations. Having successfully fought to defeat the Hun, the nation now appeared to be confronted with a new challenge growing out of the triumph of communism in Russia. Fears and misgivings about a Bolshevik threat to American society reached a peak in 1919. The intensity of popular alarm in many parts of the country was a measure of the deep longing for order at home. At the same time, the furor over dangers from the left betrayed doubts about the possibility of achieving either peace or stability.

The Red Scare that swept the country in 1919–1920 resulted in part from a long tradition of opposition to social democratic (socialist) parties and from efforts directed at circumventing progressive reform. Associated with stresses that came with waging the Great War and drafting the peace treaties, it represented a cathartic release of national trepidations that had been rising for years. The hysteria itself dissipated in 1920, but it was to become profoundly

[25] Margulies, *Senator Lenroot*, 302–307; Baker and Dodd, eds., *Public Papers of Woodrow Wilson*, 6:455; *Pierce County Herald* (Ellsworth), February 12, 1920. The *Herald* was campaigning for a baseball league.

influential in shaping patterns of thought that dominated the decade following the Armistice.[26]

Although the postwar fear of radicalism that permeated Wisconsin as well as other states was real, circumstances and a concern for the rights of citizens mitigated its effects within the state. The wartime campaign against German-Americans and alleged traitors had, in a sense, inoculated Wisconsinites against the nervousness that produced red-baiting. After the return of peace, most Wisconsin citizens arrived at the realization that having German ancestors did not necessarily make a person a traitor; and they welcomed an opportunity to attend to healing the psychic wounds inflicted during the war years.

Milwaukee's experience with Victor Berger's Social Democratic party provides an indication of why the state managed to escape extreme anti-radical hysteria. Occupying a position to the right of most Socialists nationally, Berger had long been actively involved in municipal government, and the party had become an effective element in the city's political system. While the Social Democratic party of Milwaukee had made Marx respectable, it stood high on the list of organizations thought to be "un-American" by various groups worried about threats to the Republic. That Wisconsin's Fifth Congressional District twice re-elected Berger after the House of Representatives had refused to seat him suggests that, in Milwaukee, resentment of congressional interference with the right of a locality to choose its own representatives aroused greater concern than did a fear of radicalism.[27]

While the Red Scare never became a serious menace in Wisconsin, its citizens were not inattentive to the events that provided a context for the anti-radical hysteria. When Czar Nicholas II abdi-

[26] John Higham, *Strangers in the Land: Patterns of American Nativism, 1860–1925* (New Brunswick, New Jersey, 1955), 175–177, 222–228; Robert K. Murray, *Red Scare: A Study of National Hysteria, 1919–1920* (Minneapolis, 1955), 3–4; Noggle, *Into the Twenties*, 100–101; Stanley Coben, "A Study in Nativism: The American Red Scare of 1919–20," in the *Political Science Quarterly*, 79 (March, 1964), 59–63.

[27] David A. Shannon, *The Socialist Party of America: A History* (New York, 1955), 21–23; Roderick Nash, "Victor L. Berger: Making Marx Respectable," in *WMH*, 47 (Summer, 1964), 301–306; Edward J. Muzik, "Victor L. Berger: Congress and the Red Scare," in *WMH*, 47 (Summer, 1964), 316–318; Robert Mikkelsen, "The Social Democratic Party of Milwaukee, Wisconsin: A Study of Ethnic Composition and Political Development" (candidatus philologiae [master's] thesis, University of Oslo, 1976), 109. The Wisconsin State Federation of Labor supported Berger in his effort to be seated, but so did Governor Philipp. See the Milwaukee *Sentinel*, July 19, 1919, and the Madison *Democrat*, January 4, 1920.

cated his throne in March, 1917, Americans greeted his downfall as a victory over despotism. Yet as Lenin and his Bolshevik followers gained ascendancy in Russia, Woodrow Wilson came to see the revolution as a threat of global proportions, and he dispatched 5,000 troops to join British forces at Murmansk, ostensibly to guard military supplies. In January, 1919, ten days before the peacemakers met in Paris, Robert M. La Follette spoke in the Senate "on our soldiers in Russia—what they are there for and why they are fighting the Russian people with whom we are *not at war*." Prompted by a New York *Times* report of an engagement near Archangel in which Wisconsin troops had been involved, the senator maintained that the kind of polity ultimately prevailing in Russia depended on decisions made by Russians, not Americans.[28]

While La Follette was raising questions about the Allied intervention in Russia, Charles McCarthy of the Wisconsin Legislative Reference Library wrote a memo to Matthew S. Dudgeon, secretary of the Wisconsin Free Library Commission. "There is no use trying to supress [*sic*] the Bolsheviki ideas," insisted McCarthy, "they can't be supressed [*sic*]." The struggle of the Bolsheviks was part of "an age old fight"; they were "stupidly but with a wisdom which does not appear at first sight" attempting "to get a greater share for those who toil." The means to that end was "set forth in the theory that all the workers should own that which they work to build up." In McCarthy's opinion, it was by no means a strange doctrine, even though "the so-called middle class strenuously object." Indeed, the basic problem as he saw it was that "our people have such a poor knowledge of economics and our capitalists are so ignorant that instead of studying the question they are trying to fight it."[29]

For several reasons, the fight became critical during 1919. The coming of peace meant cancellation of war contracts, and that in turn brought hardship to laborers who lost their jobs at a time when living costs were rising. Gains made during the war had led workers to believe that victory over the Central Powers would also bring victories for labor unions in their long effort to gain recognition, higher wages, and better working conditions. But with discharged soldiers returning to the labor market and with employers determined to oppose union activities, amicable industrial

[28] La Follette and La Follette, *La Follette*, 2:921–922; New York *Times*, January 2, 1919; *Congressional Record*, 65 Cong., 3 sess., 1102–1103.

[29] McCarthy to Dudgeon, January 8, 1919, in the Matthew S. Dudgeon Papers.

relations appeared to be in jeopardy. As unemployment increased to an estimated 3 million workers by February, 1919, the United States Employment Service, a wartime agency, found itself deprived of the appropriations necessary to meet the needs of the jobless. Workers took matters into their own hands, and 1919 became a year of labor unrest and strikes.[30]

Attempting to discredit the strikers, employers throughout the country sought to tar organized labor with the brush of radicalism. For several months they were spectacularly successful, in part because a series of mysterious bombings lent plausibility to charges that radical terrorists within the labor movement posed a serious threat to the nation. Fortunately, most of the bombs sent through the mail were intercepted, but on June 2, 1919, a new series of explosions occurred within the same hour in eight different cities. Although they destroyed property and killed two people in what was obviously a co-ordinated attack, no one was ever able to detect a pattern in the selection of targets. The mystery surrounding the bombings contributed to the intensity of social shock waves that followed. A tendency to associate violence in the United States with Bolshevik success in Russia was hard to resist, and the pressure for effective anti-radical measures rapidly increased.[31]

United States Attorney General A. Mitchell Palmer, whose Washington house had been dynamited, decided by early fall that it was time for dramatic action. In November, 1919, his agents began a series of raids to round up people associated with un-American ideas and activities. Of the persons seized, 249 were aliens and were subject to deportation. After a hurried screening, they were sent to Russia via Finland on the U.S.S. *Buford*, an army transport iden-

[30] E. Jay Howenstein, Jr., "Lessons of World War I," in the American Academy of Political and Social Science, *Annals*, 238 (March, 1945), 180–187; Noggle, *Into the Twenties*, 68–73, 75–76; U.S. National Resources Planning Board, *After the War, 1918–1920: Military and Economic Demobilization of the United States, Its Effect upon Employment and Income*, comps. Paul A. Samuelson and Everett E. Hagan (1943), 5–14; James R. Mock and Evangeline Thurber, *Report on Demobilization* (Norman, 1944), 170–181; U.S. Council of National Defense, Reconstruction and Research Division, *Readjustment and Reconstruction Information. Volume II: Readjustment and Reconstruction Activities in the States* (1919), 350–364, for Wisconsin discussion.

[31] David Brody, *Labor in Crisis: The Steel Strike of 1919* (Philadelphia, 1965), 128–130, 151; *Weekly Bulletin*, December 22, 1919, in the Wisconsin Manufacturers' Association Records, 1910–1975; Bayrd Still, *Milwaukee: The History of a City* (Madison, 1948; reprinted, 1965), 487; Murray, *Red Scare*, 69–73, 78–80; Horace C. Peterson and Gilbert C. Fite, *Opponents of War, 1917–1918* (Madison, 1957), 286–287; Patrick Renshaw, *The Wobblies: The Story of Syndicalism in the United States* (New York, 1967), 238–241.

tified in the press as the "Soviet Ark." On January 2, 1920, a more extensive raid involving thirty cities resulted in the arrest of some 4,000 persons, more than 500 of whom were eventually deported. Watching agents apprehend people he had known for years, the sheriff of Milwaukee County reportedly remarked that the federal authorities were "a bunch of nuts." The Red Scare was already beginning to fade when Palmer announced that the communists were planning a reign of terror on May Day. He had relied on informants of dubious credibility, however, and nothing unusual occurred. Newspapers across the country, including the Chicago *Tribune*, suggested that Palmer was subject to hallucinations. By fall the Red Scare had all but disappeared.[32]

The national hysteria of course had affected Wisconsin, and throughout 1919 and the early part of 1920 the federal attorney general could rely on supporters in the state. Their attitude was well expressed in a Kewaunee *Enterprise* editorial published just as the Red Scare began to build up. "Autocracy is government by the worst elements at the top," lectured the editor; "Bolshevism is government by the worst elements at the bottom." Both systems were "bitter enemies of Democracy," and the defeat of Germany would prove useless if Europe were delivered into the hands of the Bolsheviks. As for the United States, long "the sanctuary of the oppressed," it had lately become "the sanctuary of too many would be oppressors." Most of the nation's problems were imported. "From our silly system of smart society . . . down to our bogus Socialism, made in Germany and Russia . . . our worries are due to our carelessness as to who and what comes to America." One might argue that American industry required an influx of labor to keep factories producing and to expand commerce, but "what shall it profit us to have all the commerce of the world if in the end we blow up in one grand Bolshevik bust?" Policy makers would be well advised "to go just a little slower" and "to educate what unassimilated labor we have into American citizenship." Rotten men, like rotten food, should be sent to the dump. "So in planning our new

[32] Murray, *Red Scare*, 193–198, 207, 213, 251; "The Deportations," in *Survey*, 41 (February 22, 1919), 722–724; Louis F. Post, *The Deportations Delirium of Nineteen-Twenty: A Personal Narrative of an Historic Official Experience* (Chicago, 1923), 56, 77–78; Edwin P. Hoyt, *The Palmer Raids, 1919–1920: An Attempt to Suppress Dissent* (New York, 1968), 93; Stanley Coben, *A. Mitchell Palmer: Politician* (New York, 1963), 211, 217–219, 221–223, 227–234; Higham, *Strangers in the Land*, 232–233; Noggle, *Into the Twenties*, 111.

list of imports let us include only desirables," concluded the editor. "In planning our new list of exports let us head it with undesirables." The United States could then become a nation "for Americans and men who want to be Americans."[33]

Other Wisconsin newspapers noted with approval the anti-radical activities of 1919–1920, and so also did some organizations. Press comment rang the changes on the theme of radical threats to the country: "most of the Bolsheviki leaders have lived in the United States and, while here, studied political economy under the I.W.W. [Industrial Workers of the World]"; "it is time a halt be called upon such nonsense" as "the epidemic of insane notions that has developed within or [*sic*] borders"; the assistance of "dilettante reformers in providing funds for spreading the Russian revolutionary propaganda constitute a distinct menace and the tolerant amusement with which they have been regarded should give place to righteous wrath and a stern squelching of their activities"; "to the alien we need not extend too liberally our constitutional guarantees"; the bomb plot "shows the need of more drastic action against I.W.W., anarchists, etc."; the deportation of aliens was justified, for "the melting pot had to be skimmed of its scum to protect its contents from constant pollution."[34]

Patriotic organizations and chambers of commerce added their voices to the anti-radical chorus. The Wisconsin Loyalty Legion officially disbanded in March, 1919, but other groups were prepared to carry on Americanization efforts. The American Constitutional League, for example, sought to uphold "the basic principles of Americanism": the family, the church, private property, and constitutional government. The newly formed American Legion established posts in the state, and Wisconsin Legionnaires took a strong stand against "those who are planning the destruction of our form of government." The Wisconsin Manufacturers' Association and associations of commerce also sought to preserve American institutions against the influence of foreign ideologies.[35]

[33] Kewaunee *Enterprise*, January 3, 1919.

[34] Wausau *Record-Herald*, quoted in the Beloit *Daily News*, May 20, 1919; Iron River *Pioneer*, December 11, 1919; Milwaukee *Sentinel*, November 13, 1919; *Wisconsin State Journal*, January 13, 1920; Burlington *Standard-Democrat*, May 16, 1919; *Kickapoo Scout* (Soldiers Grove), January 1, 1920.

[35] Minutes of the March 24, 1919, meeting, in Minutes, 1917–1919, Series 1641, Records of the State Council of Defense, World War I, WSA; "An Invitation," American Constitutional League flyer [undated, ca. 1921–1922], in "Socialism" clipping file, Leg-

Yet the anti-radical efforts of Wisconsin's business and patriotic organizations took a much milder form than might have been anticipated. In June, 1919, the legislature passed a "Red Flag" bill similar to laws enacted in several other states. Intended to prevent riots such as those that occurred in Boston, New York, and Cleveland on May Day that year, the law prohibited displaying "the red flag or any other flag, banner or emblem, symbolizing a purpose to overthrow, by force or violence . . . the government of the United States or of the state of Wisconsin." Yet the legislature tempered its action by specifying that violation of the law constituted only a misdemeanor punishable by a ten-dollar fine. At the height of the Red Scare, to be sure, Palmer's agents raided centers of alleged un-American activity in Milwaukee and nearby cities, but such raids were carried out under the aegis of the United States Department of Justice, not by the state government. The major attempt to control radicalism in Wisconsin concentrated not on raids to seize radical agitators and radical literature, but on programs for the Americanization of immigrants and ethnic groups that had a preference for the language and customs of their mother countries.[36]

* * *

Americanizers typically emphasized the importance of education for citizenship in factories, churches, and clubs as well as in the schools. "The best antidote for the menace of Bolshevism is Americanism," argued E. L. Harvey, publicity director of the National Security League. "Americanism is purely a matter of education." A *Waupaca County Post* editorial reiterated that theme in making a case for the social importance of learning and morality: "Vicious tendencies depend on crude understanding for growth; Red anarchy disappears when morality, good sense and education are combined in treating social, commercial and political questions."[37]

---

islative Reference Bureau; Milwaukee *Leader*, July 29, 1922; Iron River *Pioneer*, December 4, 1919; *Weekly Bulletin*, March 15, 1920, in the Wisconsin Manufacturers' Association Records; Appleton Chamber of Commerce, *Proceedings*, July 23, 1920, p. 241, in Appleton Association of Commerce Records, Oshkosh Area Research Center; *Civics and Commerce*, August, 1919, p. 28.

[36] Laws of Wisconsin, 1919, pp. 547–548 (Chapter 369); Murray, *Red Scare*, 234–235; Milwaukee *Sentinel*, November 8, 1919; *Wisconsin State Journal*, January 3, 1920. William T. Evjue's newspaper vigorously opposed the bill. See the *Capital Times*, February–June, 1919, *passim*.

[37] Harvey to Richard T. Ely, April 11, 1919, in the Ely Papers; *Waupaca County Post* (Waupaca), July 31, 1919.

In Milwaukee, the Association of Commerce took the lead in establishing an Americanization Council to co-ordinate activities for "the Americanization and assimilation of the large foreign born and foreign language speaking portion of Milwaukee's population." A few of the city's manufacturers became directly involved in the education of their workers. The Chain Belt Manufacturing Company, for example, offered classes on Tuesday and Thursday evenings, providing a free supper in the company cafeteria. The students, all of them Polish and all of them male, learned practical lessons on how to make out a budget and how to save money; guest speakers lectured on civics, health care, and other subjects of immediate interest. The Pfister and Vogel Leather Company offered English instruction and, in its advanced course, citizenship training.[38]

While the Milwaukee Association of Commerce and the proponents of Americanization strongly approved of courses for workers, the enterprise enjoyed indifferent success, in part because workers suspected that it served the purposes of employers rather than their own. The established institutions of learning provided a better environment for Americanization activities. Public school courses in civics and citizenship, many of them instituted during the war years, won support in many Wisconsin communities and from the state department of public instruction. The University of Wisconsin's program in Americanization continued through the Red Scare, and it served to correct a common misapprehension that social scientists on the faculty viewed the world from a radical perspective.[39]

Citizenship training represented the most positive side of the Americanization movement. Its negative side began to predominate when it made common cause with the opponents of Bolshevism during the hysteria of 1919–1920. Americanizers then became more shrill in supporting immigration restriction, the deportation of aliens, the elimination of foreign-language courses in schools, and the exclusive use of English in all courses. Grumbling that attempts to enforce teaching in the English language had met with

[38] *Civics and Commerce*, December, 1919, pp. 46–47; Isabelle L. Hill, "Americanization Work in Milwaukee" (bachelor's thesis, University of Wisconsin, 1920), 22–24; Department of Public Instruction, *Biennial Report*, 1916–1918, pp. 141–142; Gerd Korman, *Industrialization, Immigrants, and Americanizers: The View from Milwaukee, 1866–1921* (Madison, 1967), 182–194.

[39] Richard T. Ely to Charles A. Williamson, August 7, 1918, in the Ely Papers; Curti and Carstensen, *University of Wisconsin*, 2:340–341.

evasion and indifference, the *Wisconsin State Journal* demanded that the legislature face "this vital American issue." The newspaper hoped to see Wisconsin become "such a 100 per cent American state that if ever again we had to go thru the history of the last two years . . . we would not have to keep Wisconsin's record right by forcing some of our 'citizens' to support our flag." While many educators may have been intimidated by such pronouncements, the institutions that some German Lutherans thought most threatened were their own parochial schools.[40]

Catholic schools were relatively secure from the postwar Americanization offensive, in part because the church's opposition to radicalism was so well established. To Catholic leaders, Bolshevism was the real enemy because it was the enemy of all organized religion. "Our Church is preeminently the Church of the poor—and the problems of the poor, of the so-called lower classes, should closely touch our hearts," ran an editorial in *The Salesianum*, a church publication. But Bolshevism was a "false remedy for social ills," and the editor suggested that radical successes demanded greater effort on the part of Catholics to prevent Bolshevism "from reaching out and grasping in its hold those who, discontented with existing conditions, are ready to turn upon what is held out to them as their great arch-enemy—Capitalism." In April, 1919, Archbishop Sebastian Messmer sent out a circular letter to the pastors of Milwaukee County, suggesting among other things that they prepare a sermon on socialism. "Priests," he observed, "are in duty bound to instruct the people . . . on this anti-Christian and anti-social movement which is making such terrible inroads not only among Protestants but unfortunately also among Catholics."[41]

In deploring the socialist influence among Catholics, the archbishop may have been thinking about his prewar struggles with critical and sometimes anticlerical factions of the Polish community in Wisconsin. At the turn of the century, while bishop of Green Bay, Messmer had ordered all parishes in the diocese to increase the instruction of English in the schools and to use English more extensively in worship services. Polish immigrants, many of them recently arrived in the United States and struggling to preserve

[40] Higham, *Strangers in the Land*, 259–261; *Wisconsin State Journal*, June 10, 1919.

[41] "Civic Education of Catholics," in the *Salesianum*, 14 (January, 1919), 37; Archbishop Sebastian Messmer to Pastors of Milwaukee County, April 7, 1919, in old file 87, Milwaukee Archdiocesan Archives, St. Francis Seminary, Milwaukee.

their Polish identity in the New Land, resisted the church's program of assimilation. The Reverend Wenceslaus Kruszka, from his remote parish in Ripon, began a campaign for the nomination of Poles to ecclesiastical posts. Later named pastor of St. Adalbert's parish in Milwaukee, he continued his efforts over a broader field. Although a fifth of the Catholic population in the United States had Polish antecedents, Kruszka pointed out, it was Irish and, to a lesser extent, German influences that predominated within the hierarchy. Associated with Father Kruszka in promoting Polish self-consciousness and ethnic diversity was his half-brother, Michael Kruszka. As editor and publisher of the influential Milwaukee Polish-language newspaper, *Kuryer Polski,* Michael Kruszka championed Polish causes for thirty years until his death in 1918.

While the *Kuryer Polski* often took a position that placed it in opposition to Archbishop Messmer in matters of ecclesiastical policy, the newspaper also questioned reliance on the Democratic party as the best way to advance the secular well-being of Polonia.* During the years before the Great War, Michael Kruszka urged *Kuryer Polski* readers to act independently in politics. By gaining influence as a voting bloc within the Socialist party or within the Progressive faction of the Republican party, ran his argument, the Poles of Wisconsin could gain far more than by relying solely upon the Democrats to serve their interests. As the influence of the *Kuryer Polski* increased, Kruszka won several important victories for cultural pluralism. One of the most noteworthy came in 1907, when Milwaukee's school commissioners approved Polish language classes in the public schools of Polish neighborhoods.

World War I, in many ways a divisive influence among the Germans of Wisconsin, had the effect of uniting the Poles and silencing their quarrels. Woodrow Wilson's inclusion of an independent Poland as the thirteenth of his Fourteen Points stirred Polish-Americans to patriotic enthusiasm for the common objectives of both nations. United in the good cause that Wilson articulated, the battling factions of Polish Wisconsin moved again towards unity in the Democratic party and in the Catholic church. Thus the wartime response of Polonia was all that the Americanizers could ask, even

* "Polonia" refers to the distinguishing characteristics and qualities of Polish peoples and also to a population of Polish origin in a non-Polish country or governmental subdivision within a non-Polish country. It is the Polish equivalent of Deutschtum or Germanism in the United States.

though the events of 1917–1919 stirred pride in Poland as much as in the United States. Throughout the Great War and after, Polish nationalism seemed far more consistent with American ideals than did German nationalism.[42]

To German Lutherans, pressure from the Americanizers sometimes appeared as a threat to religious convictions as well as to ethnic identity. Too hasty an abandonment of German instruction in Lutheran schools, many of the faithful believed, might well mean depriving them of the German language in worship, and—even more awful to contemplate—depriving communicants of a thorough understanding of those Reformation writings upon which the Lutheran confessions rested. The homogenizing influence of the English language, in the view of both the Missouri and Wisconsin synods, helped to explain the imprecision of religious belief in America. And if there was one thing these German Lutherans wished to avoid above all else it was a deterioration of doctrine. Back in 1889–1890 they had successfully resisted the Bennett Law, a measure that would have required the teaching of reading, writing, arithmetic, and United States history in the English language in all Wisconsin schools, both public and private. In 1919, despite the popular tendency to associate disloyalty and Bolshevism with wartime policies of the Kaiser, an influential proportion of German Lutherans still preferred using the German language in their parishes and in church-related institutions. All synods with ethnic ties acknowledged that their capacity to survive in the United States depended on their ability to adapt to American society. Yet German Lutherans who had studied Luther's Small Catechism and the Augsburg Confession in German were particularly desirous of retaining the language of their ancestors in the religious instruction of their children.[43]

The wartime experience of the German Lutherans in Wisconsin had reinforced another traditional Lutheran predilection: accept-

[42] Donald Pienkos, "Politics, Religion, and Change in Polish Milwaukee, 1900–1930," in *WMH*, 61 (Spring, 1978), 196–208; Victor R. Greene, *For God and Country: The Rise of Polish and Lithuanian Ethnic Consciousness in America, 1860–1910* (Madison, 1975), 130–142; Philip Gleason, *The Conservative Reformers: German-American Catholics and the Social Order* (Notre Dame, 1968), 49–50.

[43] Dean Wayne Kohlhoff, "Missouri Synod Lutherans and the Image of Germany, 1914–1945" (doctoral dissertation, University of Chicago, 1973), 14; Paul Kleppner, *The Cross of Culture: A Social Analysis of Midwestern Politics, 1850–1900* (2nd ed., New York, 1970), 158–167; Robert C. Nesbit, *Wisconsin: A History* (Madison, 1973), 377–378.

ance of the authority of the state in matters other than faith and doctrine. Thus, when advocates of "100 per cent Americanism" were pressuring the states to pass legislation eliminating from the schools all languages other than English, Wisconsin managed to avoid hostile confrontation over the issue. Neither side believed that it had much to gain from a major battle. The Americanizers did not wish to repeat the political mistake of 1889–1890, when a hostile German vote brought heavy losses to the Republican party in Wisconsin. The Missouri Synod and Wisconsin Synod Lutherans, on the other hand, were beginning to think that Lutheran traditions could suffer more damage from a struggle with the state than from using English in the classrooms of parochial schools.

The basis for an understanding between the Lutherans and the Americanizers was evident at a meeting held in Milwaukee early in 1919. May Wood Simons, who had chaired the Milwaukee County Council of Defense during the war, observed that so far as she knew the Lutheran schools were using English in teaching secular courses and that she had been impressed by their hearty co-operation in her work. W. E. Holmes, regional director of the United States Department of Interior's Americanization division, then presented his interpretation of the position taken by Interior Secretary Franklin K. Lane. Lane opposed a law against teaching foreign languages, reported Holmes, and he believed that "the various denominations should be permitted to preach and teach religion in any language. . . ." The secretary hoped, a report on the meeting continued, that the denominations "would recognize the danger to the church, primarily, in continuing the teaching of religion in a foreign language and would also recognize that one language is a great aid to a united country." At least some of the Lutherans present at the meeting endorsed the hypothesis "that the sooner the Lutheran Church makes the transition from the foreign language to the English in its schools, parochial and Sunday, the better it will be for the Church in aiding [it] to keep the young people and to unite the Church."[44]

Although the Lutherans and the Americanizers drafted no formal compromise, the effectiveness of their mutual understanding became apparent when a bill to prohibit the teaching of foreign lan-

[44] E.v.B., "No Legislative Compulsion," in the *Northwestern Lutheran*, 6 (February 9, 1919), 21.

WHi(X3)45192

ABOVE: Pulling stumps in the Cutover the old-fashioned way, c. 1920. BELOW: The Richard Pollack farm near Ripon, c. 1930.

WHi(X3)45195

WHi(D749)11265

ABOVE: Loading a horse-drawn hay wagon, Green County, 1938. BELOW: Morning coffee, River Falls vicinity, c. 1910.

Jacobson 18/4

WHi(X3)33150

ABOVE: Emil Seidel (left), first Socialist mayor of Milwaukee, in front of his home at 1154 20th Street, c. 1910. BELOW: The main street in Yuba, 1921.

WHi(G5)2145

EYE VIEW
PLAINS, WIS.
1300

WHi(G5)574

ABOVE: View of Cross Plains, c. 1916. BELOW: Lower campus of the University of Wisconsin, Madison, looking westward towards Bascom Hall, 1927.

WHi(D487)93

4

/Hi(X3)18818

ABOVE: Wisconsin National Guardsmen in training at Camp Douglas, 1914. BELOW: Contingent of draftees departing Black River Falls, c. 1917.

WHi(V2)1915

WHi(X3)45062

ABOVE: Camouflaged trucks produced for the Army at Hartford, c. 1918. BELOW: Fourth Liberty Loan parade, Waupun, 1918.

WHi(X3)21

ukee Public Museum Photo

Homecoming parade on Wisconsin Avenue, Milwaukee, 1919.

WHi(X3)19820

ABOVE: The Moonlight Outing Club, Muskego Lake, 1913. (The photo was part of a legislative investigation of the liquor traffic.) BELOW: Art Janik's Balcony Inn at Lincoln and 33rd, Milwaukee, during prohibition.

WHi(X3)379

guages came before the state legislature in February, 1919. Axel Johnson, the author of the measure, obtained very little support, and as a result the bill was tabled. Lutherans of the German synods could rejoice that the Wisconsin legislature had not violated "the basic law of our land," which included "the right of citizens to train their children in the tenets of their own religion." Simultaneously, now that the war had ended, they could credibly profess their patriotism. "If the members of a Church which had long been established in this country at a time when there were only thirteen States in the Union, are not Americans, then who is an American?" queried a writer in the *Lutheran Witness*. Proceeding from his rhetorical question as if setting to rest the whole loyalty question, he concluded that the war record of German Lutherans was "eloquent testimony to their thoroughgoing Americanism."[45]

* * *

The understanding on parochial school questions and the reintegration of Germans as unembarrassed participants in Wisconsin affairs came about with relative ease. The Great War produced many new problems in the state—and exacerbated many old problems—that proved more difficult to resolve. Americans had gone to war to make the world safe for democracy, but during the twenty-year period after 1919 it became increasingly evident that the world remained dangerous and that the wartime slogan remained unfulfilled. Citizens of Wisconsin and of the nation recognized in their realistic moments that something deep and fundamental prevented the achievement of a heaven on earth. Fallible human beings, whatever they might accomplish through seriousness of purpose and strenuous endeavor, were compelled always to grapple with their own shortcomings and with those of society.

That was the theme of a novel that bore the captivating title *Night Outlasts the Whippoorwill*. The author, Sterling North, was a native of Rock County, Wisconsin. After studying at the University of Chicago, he worked most of his life as a literary editor, first with the Chicago *Daily News* from 1933 to 1943, and later with the New York *Post* and the New York *World-Telegram and Sun*. He also wrote fiction of his own, basing it upon the lives of people he had known during his youth. *Night Outlasts the Whippoorwill*, published in 1936,

[45] *Capital Times*, February 13, 27, 1919; "Un-American Legislation," in the *Northwestern Lutheran*, 6 (March 23, 1919), 45, reprinted from the *Lutheran Witness*.

"The Joke," a cartoon by H. T. Webster (1885–1952) which nicely captures the spirit of disillusionment which prevailed during the New Era. (This drawing was published on November 14, 1921.) More than 5,000 of Webster's original cartoons reside in the collections of the State Historical Society of Wisconsin.

is the story of how a small Rock County community responded to the pressures and demands of World War I. Its principal characters are a cub reporter for the local newspaper and the young wife of a farmer, who, in a moment of impulsive bravado, enlists in the army. A reviewer for the New York *Times* found the novel "a superior but very familiar bit of sentimental American story-telling," and *Time* magazine noted only that it offered "a diffuse description of how a small Wisconsin town carried on during the War."[46]

The reviewers provided an accurate assessment of the novel's merits, but it is not merely a sentimental study of a small town. Neither is it a typical product of the literary revolt against values of the middle-western village, even though the cub reporter could have appeared in Sherwood Anderson's Winesburg, Ohio, as plausibly as in the Rock County community he calls home. The soldier's wife who emerges from North's pages is a young woman of extraordinary self-sufficiency, business acumen, and social sensitivity. It is her strength of character, her tough-minded resilience, that lifts the novel above sentimentality. One night, before her husband sails for France and his first encounter with the enemy, she dreams of hearing the call of a whippoorwill far down a dark ravine. To be sure, the bird's monotonous shrieking in the darkness sounds an ominous note appropriate for a gothic novel, but Sterling North used the bird's weird, haunting cry as something more than a premonition of disaster for the Wisconsin soldier and his wife. He implied that just as the night was to outlast the whippoorwill's nocturnal enthusiasm, so also were mysterious, sinister forces to outlast repeated, clamorous efforts to use the war crisis as a rationale for desirable social and economic objectives.

The young Rock County farmer, who leaves his wife to fend for herself while he performs heroic deeds of war, returns home with an empty sleeve sewn into his right coat pocket. That empty sleeve, "which kept its knife-edge press too easily and too long," becomes a symbol of the war's consequences. Eventually, by the time they reach middle age, the soldier and his wife appear to take no notice of it. But in 1936, while waiting in line to cash veterans' bonus bonds, the wife looks at the men around her and thinks of the Civil War veterans she remembers from her childhood: "old men in faded

[46] Sterling North, *Night Outlasts the Whippoorwill* (New York, 1936); *Time*, November 2, 1936. Fred T. Marsh reviewed the book in the New York *Times*, November 1, 1936.

uniforms bragging of Shiloh and Gettysburg, tottering along behind the flag on Memorial Day."

Was there, then, no ultimate, definitive victory over evil? Were the celebrations of those who fought the battle turning out to be a grotesque charade? Was the dark of the night always to outlast the whippoorwill? The hopes of Americans did not suddenly vanish in the months after the Armistice, but neither did the flaws of society and the shortcomings of individual persons cease to create difficulties for the people of Wisconsin. The years between the two world wars were unsettling. During the 1920's the rate of change in American life accelerated rapidly, and during the 1930's the Great Depression raised doubts about the direction of change. Overall, the peace that prevailed during the interwar period was an uneasy peace.

3

Dreams, Illusions, and Disappointments of the Postwar Decade

WHEN the Great War ended, most Wisconsin citizens anticipated returning to peaceful pursuits at home. Others, more restless, hankered after the excitement, the sophistication, or the economic opportunities they associated with urban centers such as Chicago or New York. Still others, fewer in number and more interested in the arts and literature, believed that only through residence abroad could they achieve the perspective they needed to see their nation and themselves in appropriate dimension. In a celebrated hegira, Wisconsin writers and artists joined other creative Americans who flocked to Paris, London, Florence, and sometimes Berlin for intellectual and esthetic stimulation.

One of Wisconsin's best-known expatriates was Glenway Wescott. Born in 1901 in Kewaskum near the Kettle Moraine in Washington County, he studied at the University of Chicago and began his career as a writer in 1920 with the publication of a small collection of lyric poems, *The Bitterns*. Turning from poetry to fiction, the young author chose eastern Wisconsin as the setting for his novel, *The Apple of the Eye*. Reviewers praised the book, hailing it as a work that provided new insights into images and myths about the Middle West. But Wescott aspired to become more than a regional writer. In 1925 he moved to France, where he lived for eight years. There he wrote *The Grandmothers*, an imaginative novel in which he examined his roots and the ground of his being.[1]

[1] William H. Rueckert, *Glenway Wescott* (New York, 1965), 17–18, 23–25, 39–45, 59–61. Ira Johnson, *Glenway Wescott: The Paradox of Voice* (Port Washington, New York, 1971) provides a detailed analysis of Wescott's fiction, and Sy M. Kahn, "Glenway Wescott: A Critical and Biographical Study" (doctoral dissertation, University of Wisconsin, 1957) contains important information on Wescott's life.

Though making his home in France, Wescott returned to visit his family several times during the years of his expatriation. In 1928, after one such holiday, he published *Good-Bye Wisconsin,* a collection of short stories with an introductory essay in which he tried to explain the necessity of his returning to Europe. Confessing that he wished to write "a book about ideal people under ideal circumstances," he attempted to show why Middle America could not sustain an ambitious young writer like himself. "The Middle West is nowhere," he wrote, "an abstract nowhere." He thought it a part of the world that had "no fixed boundaries, no particular history; inhabited by no one race, always exhausted by its rich output of food, men and manufactured articles; loyal to none of its many creeds, prohibitions, fads, hypocrisies; now letting itself be governed, now ungovernable."[2]

Wescott was telling his Wisconsin readers little they did not already know about their state. Much as they may have appreciated its serene beauty, they would have been the first to admit that their circumstances were not ideal and that they were certainly not an ideal people. Nevertheless, they too had their dreams. And a prevailing theme in all of them was the theme of improvement and progress. In compliance with the state motto "Forward," citizens of Wisconsin sought to move ahead. Yet they were human and fallible, and the course that some of them charted for themselves did not always lead forward. Dreams could become illusions, and in a time of rapid social and economic change it was not easy to discern which of many roads led in the right direction.

Debates over the League of Nations set the tone of public discourse during the postwar decade. Woodrow Wilson believed the league necessary for achieving his goal of peace in a world made safe for democracy; his opponents believed the league likely to draw the United States into international affairs in a way that threatened democracy at home. A twofold concern for ideals and practicalities also became apparent in discussions of prohibition, woman suffrage, the norms of Wisconsin society, and economic development of the state during the 1920's. Prohibitionists, believing that the war experience demonstrated the need for Americans to set their own house in order, concentrated on eliminating the evil that to them

[2] Glenway Wescott, *Good-Bye Wisconsin* (New York, 1928), 38–39, 42; Rueckert, *Glenway Wescott*, 69–71.

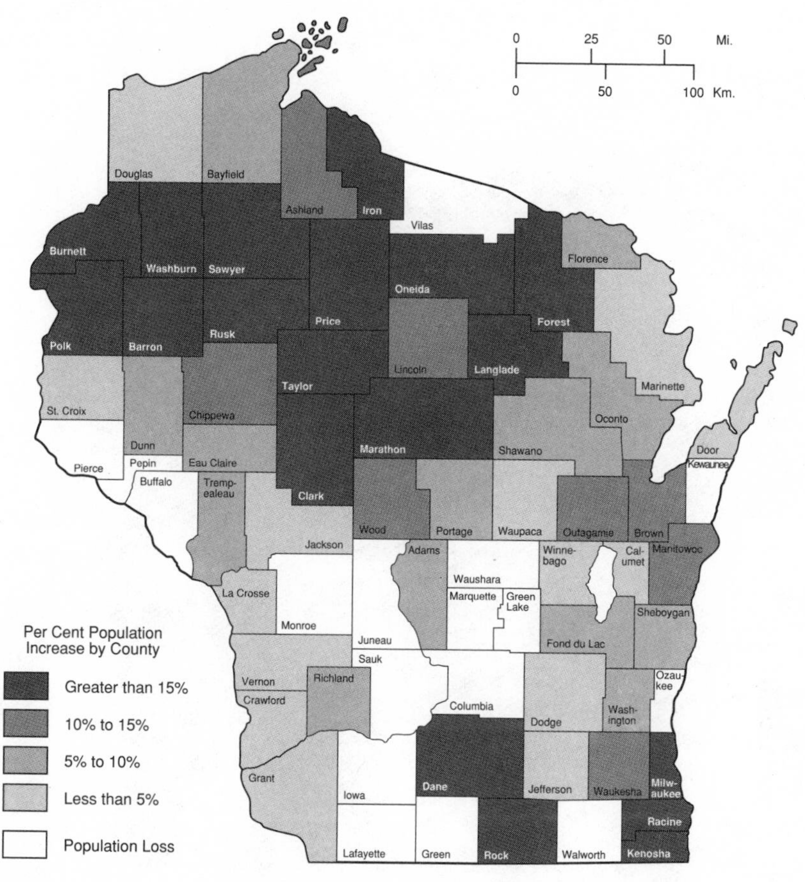

Population Change, 1910–1920

represented a principal cause of both social injustice and personal failure. Feminists and suffragists, believing that the wartime contributions of women demonstrated the functional absurdity of sex discrimination, united to gain recognition of equality for all citizens at the polls. The Ku Klux Klan, believing that the war had rocked Wisconsin society to its foundations, sought to preserve its particular notion of fundamental Christian values from the insidious in-

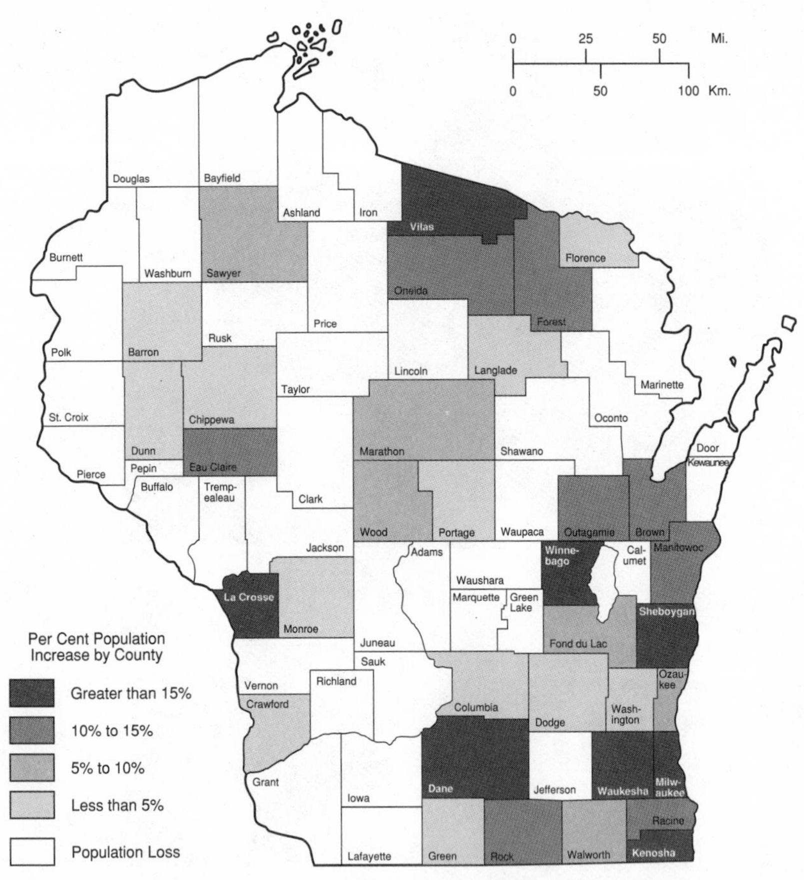

Population Change, 1920–1930

fluence of alien creeds. Negro sharecroppers in the South, believing that opportunities for social and economic advancement awaited them in the North, undertook a great migration to northern cities. Wisconsin business people, believing that the return of peace meant liberation from restrictive wartime regulations and demands, welcomed a new era of freedom for the development of new economic opportunities.*

* Editor's note: The decision was made, beginning with the first volume in this series,

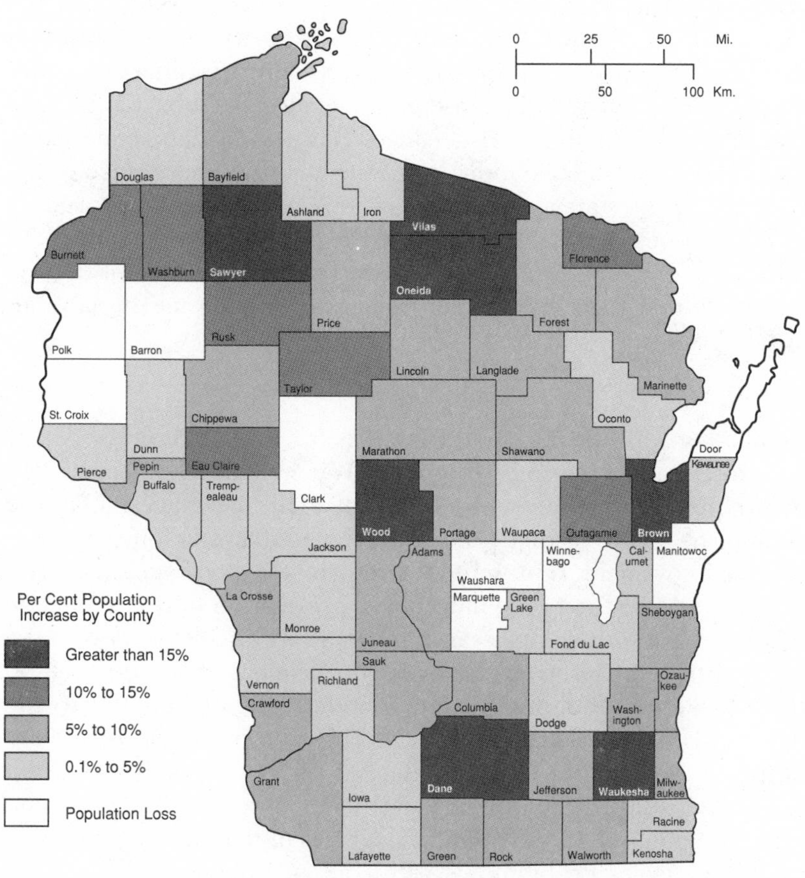

Population Change, 1930–1940

Above all, apologists for these various beliefs dreamed of success, and for a time their dreams seemed extensions of reality. The Eighteenth Amendment and the Volstead Act of 1919 closed the saloons and provided sanctions for sobriety. The Nineteenth Amendment,

to refer to all groups of people by the names by which they were commonly known *at the time*, rather than to use those later names which were more acceptable to the sensitivities in the 1970's and 1980's—for example, Germans rather than German-Americans, Indians rather than Native Americans, and Negroes rather than blacks.

adopted in 1920, ensured votes for women, and the women of Wisconsin began taking a more active part in affairs outside the home. The Wisconsin Klan added greatly to its membership and threw its influence behind restrictive legislation. Southern Negroes moved to Milwaukee in increased numbers to take jobs that became available when immigration declined. Business leaders, conducting their affairs with imagination, acknowledged the importance of agriculture in the state's economy and took credit for the prosperity of the twenties. Nevertheless, before the postwar decade ended, the dreamers confronted new realities that forced them to consider the possibility that their visions had in fact never been more than fantastic illusions.

* * *

Competing with the League of Nations for the attention of American voters at the close of the Great War was an all-out campaign to prohibit production and sale of alcoholic beverages. Like the attempt to secure lasting peace in international relations, the prohibition movement represented a reform effort of venerable tradition. And like the peace movement, prohibition bore a symbiotic relationship to other American reform movements with roots in the nineteenth century. After the Civil War, leaders of the Prohibition party looked to abolitionism for a model they could adapt to the new needs of the American society. Thus the party platform demonstrated concern for a broad range of issues, and during the economically troubled 1890's the party made advances towards fusion with the Populists. In the political struggles of that decade, however, the broad-gauge Prohibitionists lost out to a faction of the party that emphasized the single issue symbolized in the saloon. The campaign against the saloon gathered momentum, and by the time prosperity returned at the close of the century, control over the prohibition movement had passed to the Anti-Saloon League.[3]

When the prohibitionists focused attention on doing away with the sleaziest of the establishments dispensing alcoholic beverages, they were in effect avoiding serious challenge to the social and

[3] Jack S. Blocker, Jr., *Retreat from Reform: The Prohibition Movement in the United States, 1890–1913* (Westport, Connecticut, 1976), 77–78, 103–106; Andrew Sinclair, *Prohibition: The Era of Excess* (Boston, 1962), 84–85. This discussion of prohibition in Wisconsin uses much of the material contained in my article, "When John Barleycorn Went into Hiding in Wisconsin," in *WMH*, 68 (Winter, 1984–1985), 119–136.

economic standards of middle-class Americans. Respectable people, who did not ordinarily patronize such places, encountered no conflict of principle in supporting the elimination of agencies associated with the degradation of the working classes. Appealing to concerned middle-class Americans, the Anti-Saloon League achieved astonishing success in mobilizing dry voters across the country during the first decade of the twentieth century.[4]

Whatever its success elsewhere, however, the league met stubborn resistance in Wisconsin. The brewing industry, centered in Milwaukee, had grown since its origins in the 1840's to become one of the state's most important industries. By 1910, Wisconsin ranked third among the states in the production of malt liquors and second in the production of malt. An economic interest of such size could not be expected passively to accept a program for bringing about its destruction, and the Wisconsin Brewers' Association exerted considerable influence against the Anti-Saloon League. Allied with the brewers were various ethnic groups, particularly the Germans. During the years before 1914 the *Deutsch-Amerikanische National-Bund*, or German-American Alliance, took aggressive pride in all things German, including the *Gemütlichkeit* of the beer hall. As George Sylvester Viereck, editor of *The Fatherland*, later observed, leaders of the alliance "appealed exclusively to Deutschtum, but the Golden Grail of their idealism was filled to the brim with lager beer."[5]

The dominant religious affiliations among Germans, the Catholic and Lutheran churches, also influenced attitudes towards prohibition in Wisconsin. Throughout the nation, the Anti-Saloon League secured its most enthusiastic support from Protestant denominations that emphasized the importance of religious sanctions in maintaining a decent society. To some of the pious—those believing in the fundamental urgency of "getting right with God"—pledges of abstinence may have come to hold a special place as passports to eternal bliss. Others, the advocates of a social gospel, felt obliged to meliorate conditions of this world by eliminating

[4] Blocker, *Retreat from Reform*, 207–208; Jeffrey Lucker, "The Politics of Prohibition in Wisconsin, 1917–1933" (master's thesis, University of Wisconsin, 1968), 1–2; Robert H. Wiebe, *The Search for Order, 1877–1920* (New York, 1967), 89–90.

[5] *Thirteenth Census of the United States, 1910: Abstract with Supplement for Wisconsin*, 667; George S. Viereck, *Spreading Germs of Hate* (New York, 1930), 236; U.S. Senate, Subcommittee of the Committee on the Judiciary, *National-German American Alliance: Hearings Before the Subcommittee . . . on S. 3529 . . . February 23–April 13, 1918*, 65 Cong., 2 sess. (1918), 224; Lucker, "Politics of Prohibition," 3; Sinclair, *Prohibition*, 119–120.

evils that produced intemperate behavior of all sorts. By contrast, neither Catholics nor Lutherans placed much emphasis on revivalistic enthusiasms; nor did they hold out much hope for the creation of a new heaven on earth. The theological perspectives of Catholic and Lutheran churches in Wisconsin thus made possible the growth of an opposition to prohibition among the German membership.[6]

There were, of course, variations of attitude towards prohibition within the two denominations. In the Catholic church the fight over alcohol usage was part of the broader battle over Americanization, with the Americanizers urging total abstinence as a way of overcoming stereotypes that associated drunkenness with certain immigrant groups. During the nineteenth century the Irish, in particular, had gained notoriety as hard drinkers. When the prohibition movement grew in strength under Anti-Saloon League leadership after 1900, Irish acculturationists began to favor it as a means of overcoming the Irish reputation for insobriety. Identifying themselves with liberal Catholics who worked for adaptation to American society, they won some important victories for Irish "respectability."[7]

The Irish Catholic reformers proved so persuasive, in fact, that even some Germans began to consider the merits of their arguments. By 1913 the Central-Verein, the principal organization of German Catholics in the United States, had conceded that alcoholism was "a very grave danger to the welfare of our people" and had recommended that it be opposed within the Catholic church. Most German Catholics, however, found a great difference between the whiskey-swilling Irish reprobate and the honest burgher enjoying his "continental Sunday" in the *Biergarten*. Though living in a new land, they were reluctant to forsake customs that in Germany

[6] James H. Timberlake, *Prohibition and the Progressive Movement, 1900–1920* (Cambridge, 1963), 18–21, 23–29; Sinclair, *Prohibition*, 64–68; Peter H. Odegard, *Pressure Politics: The Story of the Anti-Saloon League* (New York, 1928), 30–35; Blocker, *Retreat from Reform*, 165–166; Martin E. Marty, *Righteous Empire: The Protestant Experience in America* (New York, 1970), 212–213.

[7] Timberlake, *Prohibition and the Progressive Movement*, 31–32; Philip Gleason, *The Conservative Reformers: German-American Catholics and the Social Order* (Notre Dame, 1968), 37; Joan Bland, *Hibernian Crusade: The Story of the Catholic Total Abstinence Union of America* (Washington, 1951), 267; Dennis J. Clark, "The Irish Catholics: A Postponed Perspective," in Randall M. Miller and Thomas D. Marzik, eds., *Immigrants and Religion in Urban America* (Philadelphia, 1977), 61; Robert F. Bales, "Attitudes Toward Drinking in Irish Culture," in David J. Pittman and Charles R. Snyder, eds., *Society, Culture, and Drinking Patterns* (New York, 1962), 157–187.

had seemed consistent with decent living as well as church teaching. More than their Irish coreligionists, therefore, Germans tended to follow traditional practices. And the most liberal of German Catholics tended to be far less amenable to prohibition than were the liberal Irish.[8]

For different reasons, the Lutherans also divided along the lines of national origin in their attitudes towards prohibition. Influenced by a nineteenth-century pietistic reform movement in Scandinavia, the Scandinavians in Wisconsin as elsewhere had moved much closer to the revivalistic denominations of the United States than had the Germans. Swedish Lutherans of the Augustana Synod were the most committed, first to temperance reform, then to prohibition. Augustana Lutherans had long been troubled by spiritual complacency and clerical conservatism in the established church in Sweden; with migration to the United States they found abundant opportunity for their religious fervor, and they made the most of it. Joining the Swedes in the campaign against insobriety were some of the Norwegians and the General Synod, an association of older, primarily English-speaking Lutherans.[9]

Unlike the Scandinavians, the German Lutherans were not given to emotional enthusiasm. They were, instead, preoccupied with working out clear statements of doctrine. Beginning with insistence upon both the Old and New Testaments as the written Word of God and as the only rule of faith and life, most German Lutherans held to traditional Lutheran confessional writings of the sixteenth century as the pure, unadulterated explanation of the Word of God. They resisted vigorously such deviations as pietism, rationalism, and modernism, and they could accept neither prohibition nor the social gospel as having anything to do with the efficacy of God's love, the

[8] Gleason, *Conservative Reformers*, 37–39, 157; Robert D. Cross, *The Emergence of Liberal Catholicism in America* (Cambridge, 1958), 71, 89–90, 108, 124–129; Timberlake, *Prohibition and the Progressive Movement*, 31–32, 118–119; Joseph R. Gusfield, *Symbolic Crusade: Status Politics and the American Temperance Movement* (Urbana, 1963), 56–57.

[9] George M. Stephenson, *The Religious Aspects of Swedish Immigration: A Study of Immigrant Churches* (Minneapolis, 1932), 7–8, 17–22, 374; Timberlake, *Prohibition and the Progressive Movement*, 5–6; Eugene L. Fevold, "Coming of Age, 1875–1930," in E. Clifford Nelson, ed., *The Lutherans in North America* (Philadelphia, 1975), 326–327, and Fred W. Meuser, "Facing the Twentieth Century, 1900–1930," in *ibid.*, 417–418; Sten Carlsson, "Chronology and Composition of Swedish Emigration to America," in Harald Runblom and Hans Norman, eds., *From Sweden to America: A History of the Migration* (Minneapolis, 1976), 116–119; Lawrence N. Crumb, "Religion," in Nicholas C. Burckel, ed., *Racine: Growth and Change in a Wisconsin County* (Racine, 1977), 498.

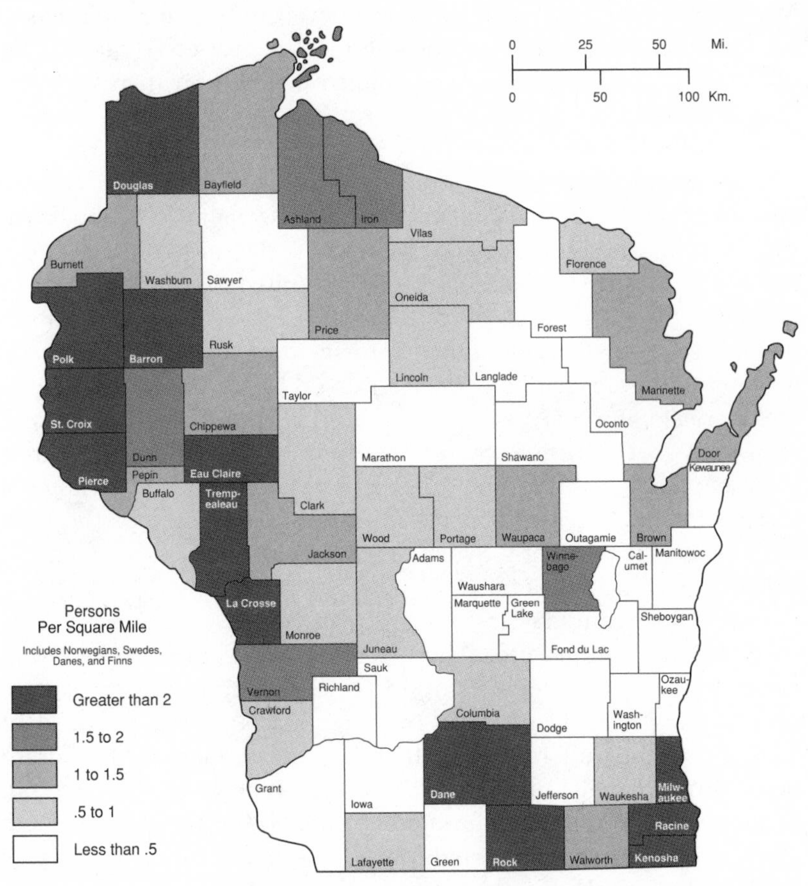

Scandinavian-Born in Wisconsin, 1930

only means by which a sinful mankind might be saved. Thus the German Lutherans of the Ohio, Buffalo, Missouri, Iowa, and Wisconsin synods remained discrete, isolated from other Lutherans as well as from Anti-Saloon League efforts to purify America by destroying the liquor traffic. Opposing the Catholic church with increasing virulence as the four hundredth anniversary celebration of the Reformation approached, the German Lutherans nevertheless found themselves united with German Catholics in their antagonism towards Anti-Saloon League objectives.[10]

Whether German hostility to prohibition was primarily ethnic or whether it was religious, the coming of World War I sharply diminished German influence in American society. With anti-German sentiment running high and with wartime needs for men and materiel a prime consideration, many Americans became amenable to patriotic coercion. In a famous essay published in the *New Republic*, philosopher John Dewey argued that the war represented a "plastic juncture" in history. Coercion could become a threat, to be sure, but Dewey thought that the war had brought the creation of agencies to promote "the public and social interest over the private and possessive interest." In short, the war experience could teach "intelligent men" how to construct a better world. Among other things, wartime needs "added to the old lessons of public sanitary regulation the new lesson of social regulation for purposes of moral prophylaxis," and Dewey cited new efforts to control the traffic in alcoholic beverages as a part of the same war-inspired impulse.[11]

War had come, in fact, just as the Anti-Saloon League was mounting a major offensive of its own. Responding to "dry" pressure in 1913, Congress had passed the Webb-Kenyon Act, a measure that prevented interstate commerce in alcoholic beverages where state laws prohibited such beverages. Fearful that the cause might languish if prohibitionists settled for such limited legislation, league leaders determined to press on towards a constitutional amendment to prohibit the sale and consumption of alcohol. With American entry into the war, they campaigned for closing the saloons as part of an efficient war effort. Professor Irving Fisher, a Yale economist, wrote E. A. Ross at the University of Wisconsin to suggest that prohibition "would save enough grain alone to make a loaf of bread for each of eleven million fighting men." Prohibition would also allow army and navy physicians "to reduce greatly those contagious diseases that are the most prevalent among both soldiers and sailors."[12]

[10] Myron A. Marty, *Lutherans and Roman Catholicism: The Changing Conflict, 1917–1963* (Notre Dame, 1968), 4–5; August R. Suelflow and E. Clifford Nelson, "Following the Frontier, 1840–1875," in Nelson, ed., *Lutherans in North America*, 173–185; Dean Wayne Kohlhoff, "Missouri Synod Lutherans and the Image of Germany, 1914–1945" (doctoral dissertation, University of Chicago, 1973), 32–33, 152–154, 179.

[11] John Dewey, *Characters and Events: Popular Essays in Social and Political Philosophy*, ed. Joseph Ratner (2 vols., New York, 1929), 2:551–560.

[12] Timberlake, *Prohibition and the Progressive Movement*, 159–163; Blocker, *Retreat from*

Having committed the nation to war, Congress quickly passed a series of acts to facilitate victory. It had already enacted prohibition laws for Alaska and the District of Columbia, as well as a law to eliminate liquor advertisements. Then, with the passage of the Selective Service Act in May, 1918, it set up "dry zones" around every military installation and forbade selling or giving liquor to any member of the armed forces. In an amendment to the Lever Food and Fuel Control Act, it forbade the use of foodstuffs in the manufacture of distilled spirits for beverage purposes. By presidential proclamation, Woodrow Wilson limited the alcoholic content of beer to 2.75 per cent. Along with such measures, Congress passed a resolution calling for a constitutional amendment to prohibit the manufacture, sale, transportation, and exportation of intoxicating liquors. Transmitted to the states in December, 1917, the proposed amendment brought on the climactic debate over prohibition in an atmosphere of wartime tension and acute hostility towards Germany and all things German.[13]

True to form, and despite the risk of finding themselves misunderstood, most Germans in Wisconsin opposed the prohibition amendment. Lay and clerical leaders alike urged their followers to be temperate in all things, but they worried about the threat to freedom they detected in the constitutional tinkering of the Anti-Saloon League. During the summer of 1918, Archbishop Messmer of Milwaukee became concerned about the possible elimination of wine from the Eucharist, and he sent out a circular letter arguing

---

Reform, 214–217, 227–229; Peter R. Weisensel, "The Wisconsin Temperance Crusade to 1919" (master's thesis, University of Wisconsin, 1965), 142; Lucker, "Politics of Prohibition," 3–8; William T. Evjue, *A Fighting Editor* (Madison, 1968), 263–264, 271–273; Anti-Saloon League of America, *Year Book*, 1918, p. 322; Fisher to Ross, April 23, 1917, in the Edward A. Ross Papers; Julius Weinberg, *Edward Alsworth Ross and the Sociology of Progressivism* (Madison, 1972), 169–170. "Every possible advantage should be taken to make America's assistance in the war immediate and effective," commented the *Waupaca County Post* (Waupaca) on April 18, 1918, "and one of the most apparent changes needed to secure efficiency and results is the need of abolishing every saloon and brewery in the nation."

[13] Norman H. Clark, *Deliver Us from Evil: An Interpretation of American Prohibition* (New York, 1976), 118–130; Ernest H. Cherrington, *The Evolution of Prohibition in the United States of America: A Chronological History of the Liquor Problem and the Temperance Reform in the United States from the Earliest Settlements to the Consummation of National Prohibition* (Westerville, Ohio, 1920; reprinted, Montclair, New Jersey, 1969), 318, 332, 353, 354–355; Mark E. Lender and James Kirby Martin, *Drinking in America: A History* (New York, 1982), 124–131; John Kobler, *Ardent Spirits: The Rise and Fall of Prohibition* (New York, 1973), 206–212; *Congressional Record*, 65 Cong., 1 sess., 5548–5560, 5585–5590; *ibid.*, 65 Cong., 2 sess., 338, 422–470, 477–478, 490.

that "there is a strong sectarian power back of the present prohibition movement." Suspecting that sinister enemies of the Catholic church were using the reform as a stalking horse to attack her "in the most sacred mystery entrusted to her," he forbade "pastors of parishes in this Archdiocese from allowing any prohibition speeches to be given on any premises, be it the church, the school or a hall."[14]

Lutheran congregations of the Missouri and Wisconsin synods took a similar position. "We can see no good whatever in a church's espousing any outside cause," commented a writer in the *Northwestern Lutheran,* "least of all so messy a cause as prohibition, involved as it is with plots and counterplots, with spying and detective work, with smug hypocrisy and cant." Later, after the Eighteenth Amendment had been ratified, the same commentator suggested that three interests were behind the facade of the Anti-Saloon League's moral reform. The first was the Rockefeller interest, which "absorbs the corn output and by removing the brewer and distiller hopes to buy all the corn at lowest prices." Second were the meatpackers, who expected cheaper meat and greater profits to result from lower grain prices, and the canners, who looked forward to new markets in "grape-juice and other products to take the place of the vanished cheer." The third interest behind prohibition included "the manufacturers of certain beverages, such as Coca-Cola, which is said to contain habit-forming drugs." From the Lutheran perspective, the proper work of the church was preaching the Gospel; identifying the Kingdom of God with a saloonless society reduced the church's responsibility to "the perforation of bungholes," an activity that served not God but mammon.[15]

Wisconsin's brewers and distillers also opposed the amendment, of course, and their arguments are worth notice. An advertisement of the Wisconsin Brewers' Association, for example, suggested that

[14] Archbishop Sebastian G. Messmer to all priests of the archdiocese, June 17, 1918, in the Milwaukee Archdiocesan Archives, St. Francis Seminary, Milwaukee.

[15] H. K. M., "A Few Results of Prohibition," in the *Northwestern Lutheran,* 6 (November 7, 1916), 162, and H. K. M., "The Prohibition Amendment Is Winning," in *ibid.,* 6 (January 26, 1919), 9–10. At least one prominent dry, William T. Evjue of Madison, agreed with H. K. M. Elected to the state assembly in 1916, Evjue had sponsored a bill calling for a statewide referendum on prohibition. By 1918, however, he had become disillusioned with the Anti-Saloon League because he thought it represented reactionary interests. See Evjue, *Fighting Editor,* 269; and Madison *Capital Times,* April 11, 27, 1919. See also Lucker, "Politics of Prohibition," 15; and Kohlhoff, "Missouri Synod Lutherans," 152–153, quoting from the *Lutheran Witness,* 40 (January 18, 1921), 25.

the war crisis had led to an increase in the power of the national government in Washington, but that sound policy demanded the return of powers surrendered by the states. Another advertisement pointed out that "the United States government is today collecting from the liquor industry alone in internal revenue more than enough money to pay each year [the] interest charge on all three Liberty Loans."[16]

In wartime Wisconsin, however, the most telling arguments were those of the Anti-Saloon League and its allies. "We have German enemies across the water," charged one prohibitionist in denouncing the brewers. "We have German enemies in this country too. And the worst of all our German enemies, the most treacherous, the most menacing are Pabst, Schlitz, Blatz, and Miller." Prohibitionists condemned "Schlitzville-on-the-Lake" for producing "Kaiser brew," and argued that German brewers contributed only to industrial disorder at a time when efficiency of production was essential for national survival.[17]

In the end, it was not just argument but incessant campaigning and political pressure that produced ratification of the Eighteenth Amendment in Wisconsin. R. P. Hutton, Anti-Saloon League superintendent for the state, detailed the magnitude of his organization's effort. "We put on a country schoolhouse campaign. . . . We put factory experts to speak in factories and got the companies to pay the men for listening. We built up a Council of One Thousand to back us—business and labor leaders. . . . We sold the factories billboards and posters which were changed bi-weekly. . . . We staged the biggest demonstration in Madison the state has ever seen. We ratified! and in the archives in Washington, Wisconsin was one of the thirty-six! We put it over."[18]

Hutton claimed too much. Wisconsin was not one of the thirty-six states necessary for ratification. It was the thirty-ninth state to ratify, but the point is inconsequential. The Eighteenth Amendment was ratified, and the Constitution provided that after January 16,

[16] Kewaunee *Enterprise*, July 12, 26, August 2, 9, 1917.

[17] Thomas C. Cochran, *The Pabst Brewing Company: The History of an American Business* (New York, 1948), 320; *The American Issue (Wisconsin Edition)*, April, 1918; Odegard, *Pressure Politics*, 70.

[18] Anti-Saloon League of America, *Proceedings*, 1919, p. 322; Odegard, *Pressure Politics*, 179–180.

1920, the manufacture, sale, and transportation of intoxicating liquors were to be prohibited.[19]

The Constitution also provided that Congress and the several states should have concurrent power to enforce the article, although it specified no mechanism by which the concurrent power might be exercised. While the Wisconsin legislature deliberated a bill introduced by Senator Charles Mulberger of Watertown, Congress considered a bill introduced by Minnesota Representative Andrew J. Volstead. Passed over the President's veto in October, 1919, the Volstead Prohibition Enforcement Code defined as intoxicating any liquor containing 0.5 per cent alcohol, and to prevent the use of such liquor, trafficking in it was prohibited. Yet the law did not make the purchase of intoxicating liquor an act subject to prosecution. Other loopholes appeared in the form of several important concessions to drinkers. In the privacy of their own homes they could serve any intoxicating liquors acquired before passage of the Volstead Act. The thirsty could also produce cider, fruit juices, and other drinks for use in their own homes. These beverages were to be considered intoxicating only if a jury in each case determined that they were intoxicating in fact, whatever their alcoholic content. Finally, the Volstead Act permitted the sale of alcohol for medicinal, sacramental, and industrial purposes.[20]

In the meantime, the Wisconsin legislature had passed the Mulberger Act in July, 1919. A disappointment to the drys, it legalized beer containing 2.5 per cent alcohol. Yet it also provided that the alcoholic content established by Congress was to be accepted under state law. When the United States Supreme Court upheld the authority of Congress to define "intoxicating liquor," the Volstead definition prevailed, and the Anti-Saloon League supported the Mulberger Act. In a statewide referendum held at the time of the November elections in 1920, citizens of Wisconsin voted overwhelmingly to approve the statute. They also elected John J. Blaine as governor. Blaine was not ardently wet, but neither was he an advocate of sumptuary legislation. As governor, his principal con-

[19] Anti-Saloon League of America, *Year Book*, 1920, pp. 88, 212; Charles Merz, *The Dry Decade* (Garden City, New York, 1931), 315–316.

[20] *Congressional Record*, 66 Cong., 1 sess., 2139, 2281, 2301, 2426–2443, 2445–2486, 2552–2573, 2775–2808, 2856–2905, 2949–2977, 2982, 3005, 3920, 4836–4852, 4892–4896, 4903–4908, 6681–6698, 6955, 7611, 7633–7634; Anti-Saloon League of America, *Year Book*, 1920, pp. 89–95; Sinclair, *Prohibition*, 168–169.

cern was with enforcement of the law, and he wanted unambiguous legislation he could enforce. Introduced by Senator Herman J. Severson of Iola, a new law passed the legislature and became effective on July 1, 1921. Because it allowed people to make their own wine and brew their own beer, Blaine noted that "there can be no invasion of the home or any spying on family life under the bill, and it provides simplified machinery for enforcement."[21]

* * *

With legislation for carrying out the intent of the Eighteenth Amendment in place, enforcement turned out to be more difficult than either Blaine or the Anti-Saloon League anticipated. Later a University of Wisconsin student from Viroqua described the problem confronting enforcement officers when he wrote a term paper on his home town. A lively section of that paper bore the heading "The Prohibition Question," and the young author introduced his discussion with remarks suggesting that he might have been an admirer of H. L. Mencken. "There is no Prohibition question in Viroqua," he wrote. "There can't be. There is no Prohibition." He then proceeded to provide in great detail the evidence to support his thesis, listing fifty-one persons and establishments engaged in selling liquor to the citizenry. Some of the town's tipplers were notable enough to merit brief characterizations. "Put a couple of cloves in [Clarence's] nose and it would be mistaken for a ham." Harold had eyes "like a couple of fried eggs." Yet it was Skinny who best served as Viroqua's "standing argument for prohibition." His one great ambition: "to get as drunk as he can as quick as he can and stay that way as long as he can." For years Skinny had been "an absolute martyr to this ambition." While such persons had no difficulty in obtaining strong drink, the student reported, there were no speakeasies in the community. "If you should happen by a dispensary and hear the wassail, lusty songs and feminine laughter that is always in evidence, speakeasy is the last term you would think of."[22]

[21] *Wisconsin Senate Journal*, 1919, pp. 1243–1262; *Laws of Wisconsin*, 1919, pp. 843–851 (Chapter 556), and p. 1236 (Chapter 685); Robert S. Maxwell, *Emanuel L. Philipp: Wisconsin Stalwart* (Madison, 1959), 182–183; *Capital Times*, May 27, 1921; Milwaukee *Journal*, June 7, 1921; Blaine to D. F. Burnham, June 30, 1921, Blaine to Annie Wyman Warren, February 10, 1925, and P— to Robert M. La Follette, Sr., January, 1924, all in the John J. Blaine Papers.

[22] Cyrus M. Butt III, "Viroqua," undergraduate term paper in Student Records for

Although the student's paper greatly exaggerated the prevalence of drunkenness in Viroqua at the end of the decade, citizens of Wisconsin were skeptical of prohibition from the very beginning. When Wisconsin newspapers reported the passage of the Volstead Act in 1919, many of them clearly did not expect the state to become a Sahara. The Rhinelander *New North* innocuously reminded readers that there was "still plenty of water in the old Wisconsin River," while the *Pierce County Herald* of Ellsworth pointed out that "sweet cider time will have an added significance this season." A year later, with Congress setting up the machinery for prohibition enforcement, the *Herald* posed an editorial query: "How's your dandelion wine coming?" Simultaneously, the Burlington *Standard-Democrat* commented on the vain conceits of the Anti-Saloon League. "A beerless Milwaukee," noted the editor, "is like a beanless Boston—it can't be done. Milwaukeeans will have their favorite beverage even if they have to brew it themselves." In 1921, the United States representative from Wisconsin's Second Congressional District, Edward Voigt of Sheboygan, articulated the same theme with an emphatic variation. "I believe that there is more bad whiskey consumed in the country today than there was good whiskey before we had prohibition," he wrote a constituent, "and of course we have made a vast number of liars and law violators through the Volstead Act."[23]

Both wets and drys were soon commenting on the ancillary effects of prohibition as well as on the way it influenced drinking habits. When a former federal prohibition commissioner spoke in Medford to encourage respect for the Volstead Act, he emphasized the pernicious results of violating the law. "Moonshine," he contended in 1921, "is murdering many of our fellow citizens because the successful defiance of law . . . is encouraging general lawlessness, such as bank robberies, automobile murders, assaults, and other crimes." In 1922, the school board of Mercer in Iron County complained to the governor that children going to and from school were "never free from the menace of moonshine crazed men." Without assis-

---

Class 4 (1930–1932), Experimental College, College of Letters and Science, University of Wisconsin Archives.

[23] Rhinelander *New North*, July 3, 1919; *Pierce County Herald* (Ellsworth), July 3, 1919, July 1, 1920; Burlington *Standard-Democrat*, July 2, 1920; Voigt to Halbert Hoard, March 11, 1921, in the Halbert L. Hoard Papers. The letter is quoted in David E. Kyvig, *Repealing National Prohibition* (Chicago, 1979), 25.

tance in controlling the situation, warned the school board, "we will be justified in adopting some of the methods used by the Ku Klux Klan."[24]

James A. Stone, a Reedsburg attorney and former prohibition director for Wisconsin, expressed the fear that "the number of people who are indulging in moonshine in small places" was increasing during 1923. Perhaps it was such small places that provided a market for products of the Perfect Tinfoil Company of New York. In 1927, Stone reported that the firm was advertising "bottles, cartons, corks and other essentials to go with doctored gin . . . and whiskey." It also offered for sale "capping machines, caps, and bottles stamped . . . 'Hennesy [*sic*] Three Star,' 'Martell Three Star,' and 'Bacardi.' " For its part in the undercover trade, Wisconsin was able to offer a commodity of its own in return. Eastern Wisconsin gained fame during the twenties as the home of packaged wort, a liquid made from malt. The process of manufacturing beer from wort is relatively simple, requiring mainly the addition of yeast.[25]

While the Eighteenth Amendment created some problems for Wisconsin's brewers, the large breweries had less difficulty than did smaller ones. Sizable pre-prohibition profits enabled the major brewers to trim capital structures and shift product lines while retaining name advantage. Small plants were more likely to lease their properties and become inactive. Many of the breweries turned to the manufacture of near beer, and some changed to soft drinks, cheese, ice cream, and other food products. The large breweries, in short, adapted well to prohibition, and they were in good condition to resume beer production after repeal. Even with its beer output sharply reduced, Wisconsin found ways to satisfy the thirsty. By 1928, according to an article in the Burlington *Standard-Democrat*, Wisconsin was accounted "one of the wettest states west of the Alleghenies" despite the "thrift, industry and intelligence" of its citizens. Alcohol flowed among all classes in all parts of the state. "In some of the staid, old communities . . . ," noted the *Standard-Democrat*, "one often finds old fashioned places with the old mahogany and the brass rail where beer is drawn at 25 cents a stein."[26]

[24] *Taylor County Star News* (Medford), November 10, 1921; Ida M. Harper, Fred E. Lee, and W. H. Hoffman to the governor, attorney general, and state superintendent of schools, October 25, 1922, in the James A. Stone Papers.

[25] Stone to Roy A. Haynes, April 16, 1927, in the Stone Papers.

[26] Robert Beyer, "Financial Policy of the Wisconsin Brewing Industry, 1916–1933"

Many Americans, including some who were not prohibitionists, found such reports of lawlessness disturbing. In one of his first acts as President, Herbert Hoover in 1929 appointed a commission to consider the problem of criminal justice and to make recommendations for improving the administration of federal laws. Headed by George Wickersham, a former United States attorney general, the commission completed its investigation in 1930, and in January of the following year President Hoover transmitted its report to Congress. Although it did not suggest abandonment of the "noble experiment," it did provide a vast amount of information to reinforce the impression that violations of the Volstead Act were endemic.

The *Official Records* of the commission contained a section on Wisconsin which, if anything, indicated that prohibition violations were even more common than anyone thought. According to a summary table in the *Official Records*, only twenty of Wisconsin's seventy-one counties deserved to be called dry. (Even so, one wonders about the accuracy of the label. Viroqua is the county seat of Vernon County, which investigators reported as dry.) The investigator who conducted the survey of Wisconsin visited several towns and cities, and in almost all of them alcoholic beverages could be obtained with ease. Volstead Act violators were treated in a straightforward, candid manner involving few admonitions or recriminations. The investigator attended police court in Superior and observed the daily collection of fines from proprietors of establishments selling booze. Before the judge had finished asking the defendant how he pleaded, "the violator in each case would reach into his pocket, extract therefrom a roll of bills, plead guilty, and place $200 on the desk."[27]

In Madison, the investigator visited the section known as "The Bush." There he identified "an attractive young Italian girl" as "the queen of the bootleggers." She "catered exclusively to a fraternity

(master's thesis, University of Wisconsin, 1935); Burlington *Standard-Democrat*, October 26, 1928. With the adoption of the Eighteenth Amendment, agricultural leaders in Wisconsin urged breweries to convert their operations to food processing. See "Make Good Use of Breweries," in the *Wisconsin Farmer*, March 20, 1919, p. 1, and *Waupaca County Post* (Waupaca), July 1, 1920.

[27] U.S., National Commission on Law Observance and Enforcement, *Enforcement of the Prohibition Laws: Official Records of the National Commission on Law Observance and Enforcement*, in *Senate Documents*, 71 Cong., 3 sess., no. 307 (5 vols., serial 9341), 4:1100–1102.

house clientele." At the University of Wisconsin, the investigator conferred with an assistant dean of women, who told him that she knew of "no drinking or revelry on the part of the young ladies under her supervision." Yet the dean impressed him "as one who would not be likely to be cognizant of such conditions." Ignorance of the lawbreaking, he hinted, was indicative of exceptional naïveté. "Soft drink establishments, dispensing beverages of a harder variety than the name implies," flourished not only in Madison but also in Sheboygan, Manitowoc, Green Bay, Appleton, Racine, and Kenosha. They flourished in Fond du Lac, too, but in that city the authorities frowned on "other forms of vice." Milwaukee had the most efficient police force in the state, according to the report, but in March, 1930, federal prohibition agents seized twenty-four large stills, one of which was capable of producing twenty-five gallons of 190-proof liquor an hour.[28]

Despite the amassing of such evidence, the Wickersham Commission could not agree upon modification of prohibition laws. Two commission members, Newton D. Baker and Monte M. Leman, favored repealing the amendment and returning to the states the responsibility for liquor control. A third, Henry W. Anderson, argued for adopting Sweden's system of government-regulated liquor monopoly, and he won the support of several other commissioners, including Wickersham. Shortly before Hoover released the report, however, he announced that "the commission, by a large majority, does not favor the repeal of the eighteenth amendment as a method of cure for the inherent abuses of the liquor traffic." And he added, "I am in accord with this view." What Hoover did, thought the columnist Walter Lippmann, "was to evade a direct and explicit official confession that federal prohibition is a hopeless failure." Other critics were both puzzled and disappointed. "Is [Hoover's] action either constructive or courageous?" queried *The Nation*. "Is his treatment of the report in his message of transmittal even honest?"[29]

In the end, of course, the Eighteenth Amendment was repealed; but that was after the coming of the Great Depression and after

[28] *Ibid.*, 4:1103–1106.

[29] Herbert Hoover, *The State Papers and Other Public Writings of Herbert Hoover*, ed. William S. Myers (2 vols., New York, 1934), 2:29–31; Kyvig, *Repealing National Prohibition*, 113–114; Walter Lippmann, "The Great Wickersham Mystery," in *Vanity Fair*, April, 1931; "Confusion Worse Confounded," in *The Nation*, February 4, 1931.

Franklin D. Roosevelt had defeated Hoover in 1932. By then, several states had expressed formal disapproval of prohibition, and Wisconsin was one of them. In 1926, Wisconsin had voted overwhelmingly in favor of amending the Volstead Act to permit the manufacture and sale of beer with 2.75 per cent alcohol. Only Congress could amend the act, however, and little came of the referendum. In April, 1929, citizens of Wisconsin voted to repeal the state's prohibition enforcement law, the Severson Act.[30]

A major influence in the passage of these referenda was the Association Against the Prohibition Amendment. Under the leadership of men such as Dr. J. J. Seelman, president of the Milwaukee Medical Society, and Fred Pabst, a heavy contributor to wet campaigns, the state AAPA devoted great energy to repeal of the Severson Act. Governor Blaine, harassed by the problems of prohibition enforcement in Wisconsin, became a useful ally. As early as 1924, he was writing Pabst:[31]

> Wisconsin has very good enforcement of the liquor laws, but if [the drys] are going to have absolute prohibition they will have to find some scheme of uprooting the grapevine, destroying the dandelion, the clover, and the hundreds of fruits out of which is made wine; then, to make the prohibition complete, the prohibition of the growing of corn, rye, barley, and other grains out of which malt and spirituous liquors may be made; and then, to make the prohibition absolutely complete, it would be necessary to have a law that would destroy practically the entire vegetable kingdom. And even when they got through with all this perfection, inventive ingenuity of the human race would probably be able to extract the necessary ingredients from the air, from the soil, or from the water.

In 1926, Governor Blaine campaigned for the U.S. Senate seat occupied by Irvine Lenroot. Pledging loyalty to "the will of the people as expressed in the referendum on the Wet and Dry question," and identifying Lenroot as a tool of special interests, Blaine presented himself as the more Progressive as well as the wetter of the two candidates, and he was successful. He served only one term, but before leaving office he proposed a constitutional amendment for the repeal of prohibition. Modifying the Blaine resolution to satisfy the AAPA and other antiprohibitionists, the Senate passed the measure without delay, and it went to the states for ratification.

[30] U.S., National Commission on Law Observance and Enforcement, *Enforcement of the Prohibition Laws*, 4:1098–1099.

[31] Blaine to Pabst, October 3, 1924, and Blaine to James Couzens, February 6, 1925, both in the Blaine Papers.

On December 5, 1933, Utah became the thirty-sixth state to ratify, and the Twenty-first Amendment became a part of the Constitution of the United States.[32]

With repeal of prohibition, ridiculing the drys and their abortive effort to establish an alcohol-free society became an easy matter. In point of fact, however, prohibition was far more effective in reducing the consumption of alcohol than its opponents were willing to concede. Four decades later, when drug addiction once more stirred national apprehensions, scholars and reformers re-examined the Great Experiment of the 1920's. Many of them reached the conclusion that ridiculing the prohibitionists may have had unfortunate consequences. As anxious citizens again began focusing their attention on alcohol and other dependencies, the prohibitionists' dream of an alcohol-free society no longer seemed ridiculous. Nonetheless, in 1933, the Eighteenth Amendment appeared to be unenforceable, and the hope of eliminating evils resulting from alcohol seemed little more than an outdated conceit of old-fashioned reformers.[33]

* * *

Although American women had exerted an important influence in the long struggle to banish alcoholic beverages in the United States, many of them saw the prohibition movement as only part of a much larger campaign to improve the quality of life in America. In that campaign, measures to assure recognition of women's right to vote and to become involved in the political process were at least as important as prohibition. Two attitudes towards women's voting became apparent among suffragists. One stemmed from the idea that the political equality of citizens is a fundamental principle of a just society, and the aggressive manner in which some suffragists expressed their desire for equality reflected their resentment of the discrimination they confronted at the polls. The other attitude rested on a popular belief that women are more gentle and com-

[32] Grant County Progressive Republican Committee to Fellow Voter of Grant County, campaign letter enclosed in Otto F. Christiansen to Blaine, October 28, 1926, in *ibid.*; Kyvig, *Repealing National Prohibition*, 169–182.

[33] J. C. Burnham, "New Perspectives on the Prohibition 'Experiment' of the 1920's," in the *Journal of Social History*, 2 (Fall, 1968), 51–68; Joseph R. Gusfield, "Prohibition: The Impact of Political Utopianism," in John Braeman, Robert H. Bremner, and David Brody, eds., *Change and Continuity in Twentieth-Century America: The 1920's* (Columbus, Ohio, 1968), 271–308; Lender and Martin, *Drinking in America*, 136–147; Clark, *Deliver Us from Evil*, 209–226.

passionate, yet more principled and moral, than are men. Feminine attributes, argued suffragists who held such beliefs, could exercise a humanizing influence in governance of the American people.[34]

An organization notable for spreading the idea that women's participation might elevate the tone of American politics was the Women's Christian Temperance Union. Formed in Ohio in 1874 during a "women's uprising" against Demon Rum and the saloons that had become outposts of his infernal empire, the WCTU took a broader view of reform than the name of the organization might imply. And its achievements were noteworthy. By 1911 it had enlisted 245,000 members to become the largest women's lobby in the country. The WCTU owed much of its success to Frances Willard, who grew up on a farm near Janesville. Serving as president of the organization until her death in 1898, Willard campaigned tirelessly against drunkenness. Yet she perceived the WCTU as performing important political functions as well, and after the presidential campaign of 1880, she helped organize the Home Protection party to promote what she called the "politics of the mother heart." Within a few years she was commending "the movement that is revolutionizing the outlook . . . through which temperance and the elevation of women are making such progress as seems well-nigh magical."[35]

Willard recognized that she could scarcely rely on magic alone, and that to become effective in the cause of temperance women must exert their influence in the voting booth. She therefore led the WCTU into the effort to secure voting rights for women. Historians of the suffrage movement have associated Willard's point of view with "social feminism," and they have noted that it avoided challenge to the old idea that men and women operated in different spheres. Indeed, the WCTU and Willard's politics of the mother heart provided support for the notion that women's concerns were properly centered in the home. It was precisely that emphasis that made social feminism acceptable to conventional people who feared

[34] William L. O'Neill, *Everyone Was Brave: The Rise and Fall of Feminism in America* (Chicago, 1969), 142–144; Carl N. Degler, *At Odds: Women and the Family in America from the Revolution to the Present* (New York, 1980), 326–331; Aileen S. Kraditor, *The Ideas of the Woman Suffrage Movement, 1890–1920* (New York, 1965), 53–74.

[35] Mary Earhart, *Frances Willard, from Prayers to Politics* (Chicago, 1944), 24–39, 195–196, 215–220, 230–244; Ruth B. A. Borden, *Woman and Temperance: The Quest for Power and Liberty, 1873–1900* (Philadelphia, 1981), 117–139.

the social and economic consequences of recognizing gender equality in all areas of life.[36]

The increased use of social feminist arguments for suffrage is understandable, for opponents of woman suffrage were contending that participation in the political process would distract women from their "appropriate" sphere of activity. The strenuous effort to persuade the "antis" that votes for women would disrupt neither the home nor the family proved remarkably effective. Assured that social feminists were merely seeking to bring a woman's perspective into the political process, and that the destruction of American institutions was the last thing on their minds, the opponents of woman suffrage became less obstinate in their resistance.

Other feminists—those who remained adamant in their insistence upon absolute equality of the sexes in all the institutions of society as well as in the voting booth—recognized the practical merit in arguments of the social feminists. Yet the egalitarians refused to compromise their principles. In the final campaign for woman suffrage, independent cohorts of feminists thus adopted different approaches to the same immediate goal. Though they could not subordinate their philosophical disagreements, both were able to claim a share in the victory of 1920.[37]

While the ebb and flow of the national debate had an effect on the suffrage movement in Wisconsin, the state struggle to secure political rights for women took on a distinctive character. In Wisconsin, the same interests that opposed the prohibition of alcoholic beverages also opposed woman suffrage. Worried about the possibility that women might cast enough votes for prohibitionist candidates to dry up the state, brewers and distillers thought they had good economic reasons for opposing woman suffrage. On different grounds, both Catholics and Lutherans also tended to withhold support from the suffragists. The most stubborn opponents of votes for women in both denominations were those who held to the idea that God had placed women in subordinate positions so that they

[36] William L. O'Neill, "Feminism as a Radical Ideology," in Alfred F. Young, ed., *Dissent: Explorations in the History of American Radicalism* (De Kalb, 1968), 276; J. Stanley Lemons, *The Woman Citizen: Social Feminism in the 1920's* (Urbana, 1973), viii–x; Degler, *At Odds*, 341–343, 345–354, 357–360.

[37] William H. Chafe, *The American Woman: Her Changing Social, Economic, and Political Roles, 1920–1970* (New York, 1972), 12–14, 20–21; Susan D. Becker, *The Origins of the Equal Rights Amendment: American Feminism Between the Wars* (Westport, Connecticut, 1981), 5.

might fulfill their proper functions as mothers and as keepers of the hearth. Confronting the combined opposition of unusually powerful religious and economic interest groups, the state's proponents of woman suffrage recognized the enormous problem they confronted. To them, the arguments of the social feminists often seemed ill-suited to the peculiar circumstances in the state and therefore inadequate to the task at hand.[38]

Because the religious bodies and publications of the sizable German population in Wisconsin opposed prohibition, social feminists had difficulty in using their prohibitionist activities as evidence of the superior moral sensitivity of women. In effect, the ethnic alignment on social questions in the state greatly reduced the force of social feminist arguments for woman suffrage. At the same time, other influences strengthened the position of feminists who favored woman suffrage because they believed in political equality. Women affiliated with the Progressive faction of the Republican party tended to identify with the egalitarian feminists, as did women of the Socialist stronghold in Milwaukee. Both the Progressive Republicans and the Socialists, with their resentment of privilege and their sympathy for the underdog, were drawn to the suffragist arguments for human equality.[39]

Resistance the suffragists encountered in Wisconsin nevertheless had a debilitating influence, and during the first decade of the twentieth century, the Wisconsin Woman Suffrage Association appeared to languish. Under the leadership of the Reverend Olympia Brown of Racine, who believed the suffragists had little to gain from stirring up opposition, the state WSA seemed headed for extinction. In 1910, however, militant women in the organization demanded that President Brown either assert herself or relinquish control to someone more dynamic. Refusing to surrender the presidency, Brown instead requested a sympathetic state senator, David G. James of Richland Center, to introduce a suffrage bill. James complied with the request, and the legislature approved a measure

[38] Meuser, "Facing the Twentieth Century," in Nelson, ed., *Lutherans in North America*, 417, 427; Alan Graebner, *Uncertain Saints: The Laity in the Lutheran Church—Missouri Synod, 1900–1970* (Westport, Connecticut, 1975), 85–87; Gleason, *Conservative Reformers*, 183–184.

[39] Elizabeth Cady Stanton et al., eds., *History of Woman Suffrage* (6 vols., various places, 1881–1922), 6:700–706; Belle Case La Follette and Fola La Follette, *Robert M. La Follette* (2 vols., New York, 1953), 2:476–479; Mari Jo Buhle, *Women and American Socialism, 1870–1920* (Urbana, 1981), 231–232.

for submission to voters as a referendum in the general election of 1912.[40]

The referendum stirred suffragists to action as had few events in the history of Wisconsin. Militant women, with little confidence in the state WSA, established the Political Equality League (PEL) in an independent effort to gain the vote. Ada James, daughter of the state senator, won election as president of the PEL, and she set to work with extraordinary political understanding. She sought first to heal the wounds of the militants' opposition to Olympia Brown and the state WSA leadership with assurances that the two organizations could work together. She then consulted prominent men and women of Wisconsin to secure their advice and support. Belle Case La Follette's assistance was invaluable. Drawing on all she had learned from her husband's many political battles in the state, she aided James in a campaign of education that neglected no corner of Wisconsin, however isolated.[41]

Despite the vigor and co-ordination of the campaign for the woman suffrage referendum in 1912, however, the effort proved unsuccessful. Some feminists later argued that given the strength of forces opposing it, the referendum had been ill-advised in the first place. In their historical survey of the suffrage movement, published in 1923, Carrie Chapman Catt and Nettie Rogers Shuler observed that Wisconsin ranked second among the states in the production of malt liquors and that an antagonistic economic interest of such proportions made success unlikely. Yet the referendum campaign registered at least three notable gains. It allowed women who believed in equality to make their case, and in the context of the state's distinctive political economy, that case won significant support from citizens who remained unimpressed by the arguments of social feminists. Egalitarian feminists also gained organizational experience through the Political Equality League, and that experience was to serve them well in the years ahead. The referendum campaign also instructed citizens on various facts of woman suffrage better than had any previous educational effort.

[40] Marilyn Grant, "The 1912 Suffrage Referendum: An Exercise in Political Action," in *WMH*, 64 (Winter, 1980–1981), 108–109; Crumb, "Religion," in Burckel, ed., *Racine*, 514–515; Charles E. Neu, "Olympia Brown and the Woman's Suffrage Movement," in *WMH*, 43 (Summer, 1960), 277–287.

[41] Grant, "The 1912 Suffrage Referendum," in *WMH*, 64:109–116; Stanton et al., eds., *History of Woman Suffrage*, 6:702–703.

Voters rejected the referendum, 227,024 to 135,545, but debate on the issue no longer seemed an exercise in the absurd.[42]

In the end, it was American entry into the Great War that made woman suffrage possible. The pressure for national unity and wartime demands on all citizens led to the involvement of women in every phase of the war effort. Old stereotypes began to seem outmoded, and arguments for women's rights gained new cogency. As women of the National American Woman Suffrage Association worked to make the world safe for democracy, they seized every opportunity to persuade the President and anyone else who would listen that woman suffrage would demonstrate the superiority of the American way of life over German *Kultur*.[43]

Woodrow Wilson finally conceded the point, after having opposed votes for women most of his life. Announcing his support for the suffrage amendment in January, 1918, he used his influence in the Congress to help secure the approval of two-thirds of both houses by June 4, 1919. With their state legislatures acting almost simultaneously on the morning of June 10, Wisconsin and Illinois became the first states to ratify, and less than fourteen months later, Tennessee became the last state needed for inclusion of the Nineteenth Amendment as part of the Constitution of the United States. Women of Wisconsin, like women across the country, prepared to cast ballots in the fall election, 1920.[44]

* * *

Having at last won the victory that they had struggled so long to achieve, suffragist leaders of the crusade for the Nineteenth Amendment sought ways to direct women's enthusiasm into support for continued reform. For that purpose Carrie Chapman Catt, president of the National American Woman Suffrage Association, proposed a new organization, the National League of Women Voters. Although only about a hundred thousand of the 2 million women affiliated with NAWSA joined the NLWV during the 1920's, the

[42] Carrie Chapman Catt and Nettie Rogers Shuler, *Woman Suffrage and Politics: The Inner Story of the Suffrage Movement* (New York, 1923), 186–188.

[43] Lemons, *Woman Citizen*, 4–7, 10–12; Chafe, *American Woman*, 19–20; O'Neill, *Everyone Was Brave*, 199–200, 204–206.

[44] Stanton et al., eds., *History of Woman Suffrage*, 5:639–649; Ernest R. Groves, *The American Woman: The Feminine Side of a Masculine Civilization* (2nd ed., New York, 1944), 354; Inez Haynes Irwin, *The Story of the Woman's Party* (New York, 1921; reprinted, 1971), 419–421.

new organization established branches in the states. Choosing neither to form a political party nor to affiliate with one, the League of Women Voters assumed a nonpartisan stance in working to familiarize both male and female voters with political issues important to women.[45]

All feminists welcomed ratification of the Nineteenth Amendment, but after 1920 some of them were drawn towards the ideas of the National Woman's Party, which had formed in 1916. With less that ten thousand members at the height of its influence, the NWP remained throughout the 1920's a much smaller organization than the League of Women Voters. Yet it received financial assistance from prominent persons of great wealth, including several members of the du Pont family and Alva Belmont, widow of financier O. H. P. Belmont, and with such help, the NWP was able to exert an influence far greater than the size of its membership might suggest.[46]

Before ratification of the Nineteenth Amendment, the National Woman's Party had attracted a small but influential following in Wisconsin. Meta Berger organized an affiliate in 1917, when she invited a sympathetic group of feminists to discuss the matter in her home. She and others committed to full equality for women continued to campaign for that principle after 1920. Joining them in the effort were many of the women who held membership in the Wisconsin Women's Progressive Association, which maintained ties with the Progressive faction of the Republican party.[47]

Other women's groups formed around a wide variety of interests and causes during the years after the Great War. The Wisconsin Federation of Women's Clubs included representatives from the Association of University Women, the Women's Trade Union League, the Consumers' League, the Council of Jewish Women, and the State Conference of Social Workers, as well as the WCTU, the League of Women Voters, and the National Woman's Party. The number of discrete women's organizations, all of them sharing some

[45] Chafe, *American Woman*, 33–36; Catt and Shuler, *Woman Suffrage and Politics*, 386; Stanton et al., eds., *History of Woman Suffrage*, 5:541, 553–554, 683–701.

[46] Becker, *Origins of the Equal Rights Amendment*, 4–5, 27–32, 38–39; Irwin, *Story of the Woman's Party*, 149–159; Lemons, *Woman Citizen*, 182–184.

[47] Berger to Ada James, July 9, 15, September 18, November 4, 1917; Berger to Executive Board, Wisconsin Woman Suffrage Association, November 8, 1917; Harriet Bain to Ada James, July 17, 1917; Gena Thompson to Ada James, October 9, 1920; Zona Gale to Ada James, January, 1921, all in the Ada James Papers.

common ground but each pursuing its own particular objectives, created an impression that women who had united to gain the suffrage were again breaking up into splinter groups.

The apparent fragmentation, combined with meager evidence that women's votes had changed the results of elections during the 1920's, led to the frequently expressed assertion that the Nineteenth Amendment produced no significant alteration in American life. Observers of society in the United States during the postwar era were, of course, conscious of change. Yet they often attributed social change to the flouting of authority that followed the war rather than to activities of women who had campaigned for the suffrage. The much discussed rebelliousness of youth, and violations of the Volstead Act, appeared far more indicative of major social trends than the political issues that interested women voters. It was the flapper, not the feminist, who came to represent the thoroughly modern woman of the New Era.[48]

Were the dreams of the suffragists thus to be cast aside along with the visions of an international order and a society free of alcohol's corrupting influence? Was the reform impulse doomed in a materialistic scramble for wealth and a selfish effort to gratify physical desires? Popular commentaries of the time (and later historical interpretations of the New Era) have left a nearly indelible impression that after ratification of the Nineteenth Amendment, women returned to their accustomed position as second-class citizens generally admired for their femininity but rarely for their intelligence. There they remained in the popular masculine imagination for half a century or more as nearly every form of discourse from advertisements to scholarly publications reinforced popular myths about the place of women in American society.

The power of the myths shaped perceptions of reality among both men and women—for that is the nature of myths—and in the perceptions there was little recognition of the real achievements of women during the years between the two world wars. Indeed, it was not until long after the second of the two great conflicts that

[48] Chafe, *American Woman*, 92–95; Paula S. Fass, *The Damned and the Beautiful: American Youth in the 1920's* (New York, 1977), 17–21; Becker, *Origins of the Equal Rights Amendment*, 6–7, 57–58. Estelle B. Freedman presents an extraordinarily perceptive review of scholarship on the women's movement of the 1920's in "The New Woman: Changing Views of Women in the 1920s," in the *Journal of American History*, 61 (September, 1974), 372–393.

a re-evaluation of the history of women began to reveal the extent to which the American collective memory had become distorted. In point of fact, women of Wisconsin did not scurry mouselike back into political inaction after the suffrage amendment. The influence of egalitarian feminists remained strong enough to secure passage of a state equal rights law in 1921, and women of varying political and feminist persuasions worked for a number of causes that represented advancement extending beyond the suffrage they had secured.

Women of Wisconsin knew that moving beyond suffrage required continued involvement in political processes. In 1920, John J. Blaine campaigned for governor on a platform that included a plank calling for equality, and during the spring following his election the legislature considered a bill to clarify women's rights and to assure equality for all. Mabel Putnam, who headed the Wisconsin branch of the National Woman's Party, sought support for the measure from women's organizations of the state, including the Daughters of the American Revolution, the Polish Housewives League, the Women's Progressive Association, the Consumers' League, the YWCA, the Association of Catholic Women's Clubs, and the League of Women Voters. It was obvious that if legislators were to approve the measure, they would require assurances of support from social feminists as well as women of egalitarian preferences. In leading opposition to the bill, Assemblyman Alexander E. Matheson of Janesville once again raised the specter of social disintegration. "Our civilization is tottering and crumbling and I think we should go slow in passing this kind of legislation," he cautioned. "This bill will result in coursening [*sic*] the fibre of women—it takes her out of her proper sphere."[49]

Confronted anew with that hoary argument, supporters of the legislation settled for compromise. In its original phrasing, the measure amounted to blanket equality legislation; but to satisfy social feminists, legislators inserted a clause exempting protective regulations for women from its provisions. With the backing of social feminist groups as well as the National Woman's Party of the state, the compromise bill passed both houses of the legislature, and Blaine signed it into law in July, 1921. The Wisconsin Equal

[49] Lemons, *Woman Citizen*, 187–188; Milwaukee *Journal*, May 15, 1921; *Capital Times*, June 10, 1921; Milwaukee *Leader*, June 14, 1921.

Rights Law stimulated discussion among women considering similar measures in other parts of the country, and the discussion revealed strong opposition from egalitarian feminists. Favoring equal rights, but believing that the Wisconsin exemptions compromised their position, leaders of the National Woman's Party announced their intention to work for a constitutional amendment that would avoid compromise and complement the Nineteenth Amendment.[50]

Although sympathetic supporters introduced the amendment into both houses of Congress in 1923, neither house took action on the measure. Progressive legislators who might have been expected to vote for it on its merits were troubled by the intentions of those who urged its adoption. The National Association of Manufacturers, sensitive to the usefulness of equal rights principles in formulating a rationale for the open shop, endorsed the amendment. With the NAM behind it, reformers and leaders of organized labor became zealous in their opposition.[51]

While representatives of the National Woman's Party sought the endorsement of prominent persons in Wisconsin, Irma Hochstein of the League of Women Voters cautioned Governor Blaine against supporting the equal rights advocates. Comparing the proposed amendment with the Fourteenth Amendment, she noted that both were drafted to strike down legal barriers to equality. Under the Fourteenth Amendment, state laws that discriminated against an emancipated race became unconstitutional; under the equal rights amendment, laws discriminating against an emancipated sex would become unconstitutional. Yet Hochstein found the wording of both to be "vague and indefinite," and she feared that the equal rights amendment might easily become, like the Fourteenth Amendment, an instrument for achieving purposes having little to do with the purposes for which it had been drafted. Less than 5 per cent of the cases brought under the Fourteenth Amendment prior to 1912 concerned Negro people, she noted, and instead of serving as a safeguard of citizens, the amendment had become a weapon used to defeat state regulation of corporations. Because of ambiguity in

[50] Zona Gale, "What Women Won in Wisconsin," in *The Nation*, August 23, 1922, pp. 184–185; Chafe, *American Woman*, 117–118; Lemons, *Woman Citizen*, 189; Becker, *Origins of the Equal Rights Amendment*, 122–123.

[51] Lemons, *Woman Citizen*, 142–144, 191; Nancy Schrom Dye, *As Equals and as Sisters: Feminism, the Labor Movement, and the Women's Trade Union League of New York* (Columbia, Missouri, 1980), 156–158.

its wording, the proposed equal rights amendment might similarly become a treacherous addition to the armory of corporate interests. Hochstein believed that recognizing equal rights for women through legislation in the states and in Congress would be far less pernicious than "a general vague amendment to the federal constitution may be."[52]

Both the National League of Women Voters and the National Women's Trade Union League joined in the opposition to an equal rights amendment during the 1920's, and in criticizing blanket legislation they also attacked the Wisconsin equal rights law despite its protective clause. Condemned by both sides in debates over theories of protection versus equal rights, the Wisconsin law nevertheless proved to have utility in mitigating grievances. During the postwar recession in 1921, for example, municipal officials of Milwaukee used the law to prevent the state civil service commission from automatically rejecting the job applications of married women and from dismissing married women already employed. In those and other instances, concluded a committee of the Wisconsin Federation of Women's Clubs, the state equal rights law had brought "a greater degree of justice and greater equality of women with men than they had before the passage of the law."[53]

Much of the opposition to equal rights principles after World War I actually came from people who had co-operated to work for ratification of the Nineteenth Amendment. Debates over equal rights in Wisconsin, however, do not suggest that women of the state gave up their hopes for equality. They suggest, rather, that men and women who feared corporate domination believed that business interests were capable of using an equal rights amendment to reduce working men and women to the status of an industrial proletariat. Equality in servility represented a grim alternative. Thus the Wisconsin Progressives, and others who feared that an equal rights amendment could prove more beneficial to business interests than to women, tended to join the social feminists in good causes that might at least consolidate and preserve the gains they had already made.

[52] Hochstein to Blaine, April 18, 1924, in the Blaine Papers. Arguing that the Fourteenth Amendment and the proposed ERA were not comparable, women of the NWP failed to meet Hochstein's objections. See Becker, *Origins of the Equal Rights Amendment*, 123.

[53] Lemons, *Woman Citizen*, 188–189; Chafe, *American Woman*, 118, 125–132.

Throughout the decade of the twenties, the League of Women Voters exercised an important influence in identifying the good causes and in aiding both men and women to become better-informed participants in political processes. Because the LWV defined its principal purpose as educational, it generally spoke with understanding and moderation on issues that concerned both the social feminists and their more militant sisters. Drawing its membership largely from middle- and upper-class women, the LWV usually sought consensus in proceeding gradually towards enlarging the role of women in politics. Patience and moderation seldom inspire headlines, however, and activities of the organization often went unnoticed. For that reason, among others, historians as well as contemporary observers have understated the achievements of women as a political force in the postwar decade.[54]

The LWV's first and most important national victory came in 1921 with the passage by Congress of the Sheppard-Towner Act, a measure that received support from other women's groups as well. The act provided an appropriation of $1,480,000 for fiscal 1921–1922 and $1,240,000 for the five years thereafter to be allocated to the states in matching grants for instruction in the health care of mothers and infants. Although the American Medical Association opposed the act as one that could lead to socialized medicine, the NLWV and its allies prevailed in winning support from legislators concerned about alienating women voters.[55]

In Wisconsin, the LWV became involved in state as well as national affairs. While the suffrage amendment recognized women's right to vote, it did not extend that recognition to other civic responsibilities. During the early years of the post-suffrage decade, the state LWV exerted pressure to gain legislative approval of jury duty for women. At the very end of the 1921 session, the Wisconsin legislature acceded to that pressure. The immediate reaction to the way they performed on juries was overwhelmingly positive. "Our practice and experience . . . have demonstrated that the objections that were formerly urged in relation to having women participate in jury service were rather theoretical and imaginary," reported

[54] Lemons, *Woman Citizen*, 118–119; Degler, *At Odds*, 437; O'Neill, *Everyone Was Brave*, 268–275; Chafe, *American Woman*, 114–115.

[55] Maud Wood Park to Friend of the League, January 25, 1922, in the Wisconsin League of Women Voters Papers; Lemons, *Woman Citizen*, 155–167; Chafe, *American Woman*, 27–28.

Judge Oscar M. Fritz of the second circuit court in Milwaukee early in 1922. "Thus far," he added, "women generally seem to be more appreciative of the seriousness and importance of close attention, and the exercise of an impartial and intelligent judgment in the administration of justice, than was at times true of juries composed entirely of men."[56]

Related to the Wisconsin LWV's pressure for recognizing women's eligibility as jurors was the organization's interest in preparing women for jobs as policewomen and deputy sheriffs. Since before the Civil War, women had worked as matrons having custody of females charged with crimes, but by 1920 the duties of policewomen had also come to include the protection of women and children. Recognizing that such work required special skills, the Wisconsin League of Women Voters began a campaign to establish a school to provide the training policewomen needed. The league's rationale was not that women needed jobs, but that society needed policewomen who knew how to meet their responsibilities. "We do not want to get women on the police force just because they are women," noted Jessie Jack Hooper, the state league's first president, in a circular letter to the organization's membership. "We want fine, trained women who will look after the best interests of our children and protect them from the evils that surround them at the present time."[57]

Eventually, after representatives of the LWV had consulted with officials of the University Extension, women's organizations co-operated to establish a four-month course for policewomen. Persons selected for law enforcement responsibilities, noted Hooper, "should be women with tact and good judgment, and should have training in social service. . . ." She also believed that women contemplating careers in social service would benefit from taking the policewomen's course. In time, the training provided in Wisconsin

[56] Mrs. Ben Hooper to Lavinia Engle, February 14, 1922, and Oscar M. Fritz to Mrs. Ruth Hamilton, February 7, 1922, both in the Wisconsin League of Women Voters Papers. In response to a query about the performance of women jurors, Ruth Hamilton received several letters containing comments similar to those of Fritz. John M. Whitehead, president of the Wisconsin State Bar Association, opposed jury duty for women. See Whitehead to Mrs. O. D. Bates, March 29, 1922, in *ibid.*

[57] Hooper, circular letters to local presidents, Wisconsin League of Women Voters, February 7, March 8, 1922, in *ibid.*; Sophonisba P. Breckinridge, *Women in the Twentieth Century: A Study of Their Political, Social and Economic Activities* (New York, 1933), 205–207.

aided in raising professional standards for policewomen in the nation.[58]

In a campaign that represented yet another effort to change conditions of life during the postwar decade, the Wisconsin League of Women Voters sought to prohibit public schools from granting credits to boys who joined the National Guard. Some members of the league even went so far as to urge that the legislature abolish the Guard altogether. Governor Blaine, who usually supported LWV objectives, backed away from this one. In February, 1923, he sent the legislature a detailed statement justifying the Guard's continued existence. The National Guard was, he argued, "an antidote to militarism" because it minimized the need for professional soldiers. He further contended that persons who wished to abolish the Guard were in effect lending support "to those who want a large standing army, universal compulsory military service, and the administration of government by the sword."[59]

Women of the Wisconsin League of Women Voters were troubled by the governor's position on the National Guard. Zona Gale, who had earned a reputation as one of the state's most prominent authors, wrote Blaine from Portage to explain why she favored disbanding the Guard. Believing that citizens of Wisconsin should never permit war to become respectable, she argued that maintaining the Guard at state expense "tends to stamp physical force with state approval." How much better it would be if citizens of Wisconsin could say through their legislators, "We are done with every form of militarism in our state!" In saying that, mused the Portage reformer, they would be speaking with a voice "heard and echoed round the world." Jessie Jack Hooper, whose views on most political questions were conservative, opposed the National Guard with a conviction matching that of Zona Gale. Indeed, from the campaign against the National Guard in the early 1920's until her death in 1935, Hooper became increasingly involved in efforts to prevent war. Her last act of devotion to peace was her journey to the League of Nations Disarmament Conference in 1934. There, as a member of the General Federation of Women's Clubs, she

[58] Hooper, circular letter to local presidents, Wisconsin League of Women Voters, February 7, 1922, in the Wisconsin League of Women Voters Papers.

[59] Mrs. Ben Hooper to Ruth Hamilton, July 16, 21, 1921; Hooper, circular letter, December 8, 1921; Hooper to Maud Wood Park, January 17, June 23, 1922, all in *ibid.*; Blaine to the Honorable Legislature, February 27, 1923, in the Blaine Papers.

submitted disarmament petitions bearing the signatures of 635,300 American women.[60]

From Julia Grace Wales's campaign to halt the first Great War to Jessie Jack Hooper's efforts to prevent a second great conflict, women of Wisconsin had striven to exert their influence for peace. Yet despite heroic efforts, they failed, as indeed did all who sought to ensure international tranquility. In domestic politics, too, there was disappointment. Although women had secured the ballot, voting patterns appeared to change little as a consequence of the Nineteenth Amendment. Low female turnout at the polls was also beginning to cause concern within the League of Women Voters by the end of the twenties, a decade characterized as well by only a fractional number of women winning election to public office. But four women served in the Wisconsin legislature during the New Era. All of them sat in the assembly; only two remained there beyond a single term.[61]

In the meantime, patterns in the employment of women remained disappointingly static. A larger percentage of married women sought employment after the war, but the total number of working women did not increase sharply during the postwar decade. Although the nature of manufacturing was undergoing change, women made up 16.4 per cent of the persons engaged in the manufacturing industries of Wisconsin in 1919, and in 1929 the percentage was 16.5. More dispiriting was the fact that, in wage scales and salaries, working women encountered as much discrimination as ever. Furthermore, they continued to confront limited job opportunities in occupations considered appropriate only for men. As a result, women tended to avoid the scientific and technical profes-

[60] Gale to Blaine, February 28, 1923, in the Blaine Papers; James Howell Smith, "Mrs. Ben Hooper of Oshkosh: Peace Worker and Politician," in *WMH*, 46 (Winter, 1962–1963), 129–135; Milwaukee *Journal*, December 22, 1929 (article by Hooper), April 14, 24, 1932; Oshkosh *Northwestern*, May 8, 1935.

[61] Cornelia Groth to Mary D. Bradford, February 15, 1930, in the Wisconsin League of Women Voters Papers. The four women who served in the assembly were Helen F. Thompson of Park Falls, Mildred Barber of Marathon, Hellen M. Brooks of Coloma, and Mary Kryszak of Milwaukee. Thompson, Barber, and Brooks won their seats in the election of 1924, but only Thompson was re-elected in 1926. Kryszak, the most successful, won election in 1928 and six times thereafter between 1932 and 1944. See the *Wisconsin Blue Book, 1925*, pp. 664, 668; *ibid., 1927*, p. 718; *ibid., 1929*, p. 561; *ibid., 1946*, p. 54. The extent of political involvement of Wisconsin women differed little from that of American women generally. See Marguerite M. Wells, "Some Effects of Woman Suffrage," in the American Academy of Political and Social Sciences, *Annals*, 143 (May, 1929), 207–216.

sions unless they planned to use their training in the performance of humanitarian activities, in teaching, or in one of the service industries. Outside the professions, working women gravitated towards white-collar and clerical positions, where pay was low and rates of turnover were high.[62]

The pattern of employment among persons who held positions in the state government of Wisconsin seems to have reflected the pattern of American society during the twenties. Official records of the personnel on state boards and commissions indicate that more women worked for the state boards in 1929 than in 1919, but by far the largest number of them held appointments in fields related to health or education. In 1929, the most important concentration of women was in the Board of Health with thirty-two. Twenty-eight of that number were in the bureaus of child welfare, public health nursing, nursing education, and laboratory services.[63]

In November, 1929, when Ada Fuller Crowley prepared to complete her term as regional director of the third district of the Wisconsin League of Women Voters, she wrote her successor about the needs to be fulfilled. Her doleful memo was indicative of a certain disappointment that pervaded women's organizations at the close of the post-suffrage decade. "In the first flare of enthusiasm, it was easy to organize the successful suffragists for the purpose of understanding the problems and responsibilities of their newly acquired voting rights and duties," Ada Crowley recalled, "but neither National nor State had sufficient material to give these new groups." Thus it was no surprise to find smaller local leagues dying from lack of inspiration and guidance, especially in towns distant from informational sources. With "no little chagrin," the retiring director conceded that LWV accomplishments had been negligible and that she could offer few assurances of improvement. Doing her best to take an optimistic view of the future, she could only urge more efficient organization and more citizenship training schools. Better programs of education could accomplish much, but equally im-

[62] *Fifteenth Census of the United States, 1930: Manufactures, 1929, Volume III*, 563. The American Academy of Political and Social Sciences devoted an entire issue of its *Annals*, titled *Women in the Modern World*, 143 (May, 1929), to the position of women in the American economy at the end of the post-suffrage decade. The most comprehensive contemporary study of the subject is Sophonisba P. Breckinridge's *Women in the Twentieth Century*. Chafe provides an impressive historical analysis in Part One of his *American Woman*. See especially pp. 54–61.

[63] *Wisconsin Blue Book, 1929*, pp. 122–128.

portant was the receptivity of participants. Their growth in understanding depended upon the influence of social customs and perspectives as well as upon formal programs of education.[64]

* * *

During the troubled years after the war, when many people worried about radicalism and disloyalty, defenders of Americanism sometimes organized to advance their convictions in a way that brought scant enlightenment. One of the most successful of the legions of the night actually began its operations in 1915, when a few zealots met at the summit of Stone Mountain, Georgia. By the light of a fiery cross, the little group agreed that the time had come to re-create the Invisible Empire of the Knights of the Ku Klux Klan. For five years the new organization grew slowly as Americans concentrated on problems of war and peace in Europe. Then, before the postwar campaign against American radicals had spent itself, Klan leaders solicited help from the Southern Publicity Association, a group that reconstituted itself as the Propagation Department of the Invisible Empire. Cleverly working out arrangements for sharing income from klecktokens (initiation fees), the Propagation Department sent out kleagles (recruiters) across the land to sign up new members in every state of the union.[65]

No one knows for certain how many Americans joined the Klan during the postwar period, but the best estimate is that the order was able to recruit more than 2 million members by the time it reached the peak of its influence in 1925. Of that number, perhaps 15,000 were residents of Wisconsin. The heaviest concentration was in Milwaukee, where estimates indicate that there may have been as many as 6,000 members.[66]

The Klan first appeared in Wisconsin during the fall of 1920, when a select group of business and professional men met on board

[64] Crowley to Mrs. Clark E. Daniels, November, 1929, in the Wisconsin League of Woman Voters Papers.

[65] Robert A. Goldberg, "The Ku Klux Klan in Madison, 1922–1927," in *WMH*, 58 (Autumn, 1974), 31; Kenneth T. Jackson, *The Ku Klux Klan in the City, 1915–1930* (New York, 1967), 9–23; Robert K. Murray, *Red Scare: A Study of National Hysteria, 1919–1920* (Minneapolis, 1955), 90–92.

[66] Jackson, *The Klan in the City*, 236–239, is the source for membership figures cited above. Norman F. Weaver, "The Knights of the Ku Klux Klan in Wisconsin, Indiana, Ohio and Michigan" (doctoral dissertation, University of Wisconsin, 1954), pp. 82–83, places the number of Klansmen in the state at "not more than 75,000 men," which seems far too high.

the U.S. Coast Guard cutter *Hawk*, anchored in the Milwaukee River. The provisional Klan formed at that time functioned principally as a social club, and it was several months before anyone other than the members themselves knew of its existence. Then, in 1921, internal squabbling led to the appointment of a new "king kleagle" for the state. William Wieseman, a Milwaukee insurance broker, accepted the position, and under his leadership the Klan began to grow throughout Wisconsin. Before long, however, Wieseman's greed got the better of him. Provisional Klans ordinarily surrendered a portion of their klecktoken income to the king kleagle, but after a Klan received a charter from the national organization, it retained the entire initiation fee. Of course it was in Wieseman's interest to delay the granting of charters, and that is what he did. Unfortunately for him, he procrastinated so long that in 1924 he stirred up a rebellion in the ranks of the sheet-clad, and national leaders transferred him to an obscure position at Klan headquarters in Washington.[67]

With Wieseman's departure, Charles B. Lewis, the grand dragon (commander) of Michigan, moved into Wisconsin to take over as king kleagle. His was a steadying influence, and the Wisconsin Klan appeared to be well on its way to becoming one of the state's respected fraternal orders. All local Klans with any vitality received charters from the national organization, and in 1925 Lewis was able to secure a state charter for the Wisconsin affiliate. Yet the Klan's precipitous decline had already begun. With little to offer its members other than its adolescent mumbo-jumbo, the Invisible Empire proved able to retain neither the loyalty nor the support of Klansmen. By 1926 it had become an object of ridicule, and by 1928 it had all but disappeared from the state.[68]

After the ignominious demise of the Klan in Wisconsin, people asked why the Invisible Empire aroused so much enthusiasm in the first place. Those who observed Klan activities from outside the organization had always been skeptical of its purposes and distrustful of its self-proclaimed preeminence as the embodiment of true Americanism. Critics had difficulty in understanding why an organization hostile to Catholics, Jews, Negroes, recent immigrants, re-

[67] Weaver, "The Knights of the Ku Klux Klan," 50–52, 56–67; Jackson, *The Klan in the City*, 162; Goldberg, "The Ku Klux Klan in Madison," in *WMH*, 58:32–33.

[68] Weaver, "The Knights of the Ku Klux Klan," 67–69; Jackson, *The Klan in the City*, 251–252.

"Life in the Invisible Empire Is Just One Doggone Thing After Another." Cartoon by H. T. Webster, published September 19, 1921. From an original drawing in the collections of the State Historical Society of Wisconsin.

ligious modernists, freethinkers, and radicals should present itself as a staunch defender of the American democratic faith during the 1920's. Governor Blaine described the Klan as "an organization of hate and haters," and he was able to discover "no good reason for its existence." J. Henry Bennett, a Viroqua lawyer, was able to comprehend the Klan's capacity for beguiling some people, but he doubted that terrorizing the citizenry provided much of a service to communities of the state. Klan leaders in Viroqua, he wrote the governor in 1923, included "a few fanatic Prohibitionists, dishonorably discharged soldiers who not long since were released from Leavenworth, and the riff-raff of the town, with some misguided individuals who should know better."[69]

In organizing its klaverns throughout the state, the Klan never presented a very clear statement of what it did, in fact, represent. Placing recruitment notices in the classified sections of Wisconsin newspapers in 1921, it innocuously announced that it was seeking "fraternal organizers, men of ability between the ages of 25 and 40," that applicants should be "100% Americans," and that Masons were preferred. Charles E. Whelan, past grand master of Wisconsin's Masons, objected to the Klan's advertisement, announcing that it represented an "insidious effort to prostitute the institution of Masonry to a movement entirely out of line with its principles." But the Klan paid scant attention and continued to welcome Masons into the organization.[70]

The reasons for the Klan's preference for Masons are not difficult to fathom. With the negative program it espoused, the Klan was compelled to show that its enemies actually posed a real threat to the people of Wisconsin. Of the organizations and groups on the Klan's list of enemies, the only one sizable enough to exert much influence in the state was the Catholic church, and the Wisconsin Klan therefore went to great lengths in emphasizing its identification with a generalized American Protestantism. Because the Church of Rome had long condemned Freemasonry, the kleagles of the Klan saw the Masonic order as a logical source of new mem-

[69] Blaine to James Laidlaw, April 12, 1924; Blaine to John Fox, May 3, 1926; and Bennett to Blaine, December 19, 1923, all in the Blaine Papers. In 1921, the Milwaukee Common Council had passed a resolution to curb the Klan's influence because it believed the organization to be "an ever-present menace to the good order of the community." See J. J. Weither, Jr., to Blaine, September 22, 1921, in *ibid.*

[70] Goldberg, "The Ku Klux Klan in Madison," in *WMH*, 58:32–33; Weaver, "The Knights of the Ku Klux Klan," 89, 99–100; *Wisconsin State Journal*, October 18, 1922.

bers. In addition to reinforcing their own opposition to the Catholic menace, thought the knights of the Invisible Empire, Masons could assist in developing a structure for the new organization. The Klan's antipathy to Roman Catholicism occasionally served it well, sometimes in unexpected ways. The Socialist party disliked the Church of Rome as much as did the Klan. In Milwaukee, despite the influence of Victor Berger and other party leaders who regarded the Klan with contempt, a surprisingly large number of Socialists found their way into the Invisible Empire.[71]

The Klan's hostility to the Catholic church helped to explain its opposition to the "new" immigrants from southern and eastern Europe, many of whom were devout Catholics. Klansmen were among the most ardent supporters of immigration restriction during the twenties. They saw themselves as contributing towards the continued dominance of native-born Protestant Americans who, they believed, had established the foundations of American greatness. Unwittingly, in backing restrictive immigration legislation, Klansmen were supporting a policy that even before the war had brought a larger number of Negroes into the state. As fewer immigrants entered the labor pool, Wisconsin manufacturers turned increasingly to the Negro population of the agricultural South as a source of cheap labor.[72]

Whatever the Wisconsin Klan hoped to gain by opposing new immigrants and Catholics, knights of the Invisible Empire recognized the importance of providing some sort of service to the communities where they hoped to establish klaverns. The Klan's most compelling enticement in its campaign for new members was its promise to maintain orderliness and, in its own vigilante style, to serve as an effective means of crime prevention. Linking crime with immigrants, the Klan gained some influence in Madison when it concentrated on a campaign to clean up "The Bush," that area of the city Madisonians also called "Little Italy." The Reverend Norman B. Henderson, pastor of the First Baptist Church and president

[71] Weaver, "The Knights of the Ku Klux Klan," 74–78; Milwaukee *Leader*, October 7, 1922.

[72] Murray, *Red Scare*, 90–92, 265–266; Robert A. Goldberg, *Hooded Empire: The Ku Klux Klan in Colorado* (Urbana, 1981), 9–10; Joe William Trotter, Jr., *Black Milwaukee: The Making of an Industrial Proletariat, 1915–45* (Urbana, 1985), 39–45; Bayrd Still, *Milwaukee: The History of a City* (Madison, 1948; reprinted, 1965), 471–472; J.R.W., "Does America, or Milwaukee, Need Another Ku Klux Klan?" in the Milwaukee *Journal*, May 15, 1921.

of the Madison Ministerial Union, commended the Klan for its efforts. In a 1923 sermon, he posed the rhetorical question: "Do We Need the Ku Klux Klan?" Pointing out that the Klan opposed illicit commerce in narcotics and alcohol, the white slave trade, and organized gambling, Henderson concluded that persons such as the knights of the Invisible Empire were indispensable members of any decent community.[73]

Identifying itself with efforts to preserve an orderly community was as close as the Klan came to developing a positive program of service. Holding out the promise of restoring the values of a traditional white, Protestant society, it proved itself unable to prevent social changes that occurred after World War I. In adopting the approach it used, in fact, the Klan helped to undermine the very principles it pledged itself to defend. Unlike the Klans in some other parts of the country, the Wisconsin Klan did not resort to violence. Yet in attempting to achieve its goals through secret and extralegal operations, it did more to weaken the foundations of a democratic society than it did to strengthen them. In the end, it relied mainly on its fraternal activities to retain the loyalty of its members. But those activities—picnics, barbecues, Klan weddings, and the like—were neither intriguing nor useful. Finally, hidden under their hoods and sheets, the klansmen of Wisconsin suffocated from their own boredom as well as from the boredom of people who no longer found them either interesting or challenging.[74]

Boredom was seldom a problem that plagued the Negroes who came to Wisconsin as part of the great migration from the South during and after World War I. Realizing their dream of a decent, comfortable existence for themselves and their families did, however, turn out to be more difficult than many of them may have anticipated. Migrants came in hope, encouraged by reports of jobs open to them in a society free of prejudices that limited their opportunities elsewhere. Commenting on the influx of Negroes from the South in 1917, the Milwaukee *Journal* predicted that with the support of white citizens, the migrants would achieve success in their new environment.[75]

[73] Goldberg, "The Ku Klux Klan in Madison," in *WMH*, 58:34–37; *Wisconsin State Journal*, November 19, 1923.

[74] Weaver, "The Knights of the Ku Klux Klan," 70–72, 106–109, 128–129.

[75] Trotter, *Black Milwaukee*, 8–9, 44–46; Allan H. Spear, *Black Chicago: The Making of a Negro Ghetto, 1890–1920* (Chicago, 1967), 129–130; Milwaukee *Journal*, August 19, 1917.

The *Journal's* encouraging forecast turned out to be only partially accurate. For one thing, the migration to Milwaukee was much smaller than the migration to other northern cities such as Detroit or Chicago, and while Negroes may have fared better in Wisconsin than they had in the South, they remained a small and powerless minority that depended heavily on community good will. For the Milwaukee Federated Trades Council and for the labor unions it represented, good will had economic limits. Viewing the migration as a part of industry's effort to cut labor costs and reduce the bargaining power of unions, organized labor opposed issuing union cards to Negro workers. As a result, most Negro laborers found themselves having to become strikebreakers or to accept only the low-paying, unskilled positions—positions that were most hazardous to mind and body.[76]

In many ways, the Negro experience in Milwaukee became emblematic of the experiences of other groups in Wisconsin during the 1920's. Like the prohibitionists and like the suffragists, Milwaukee Negroes entered the postwar era with high hopes of a better existence; and like others who dreamed of hopes fulfilled, they met disappointment. Confronting the weight of social inertia, the stubbornness of old prejudices and habits, and the harsh realities of American life, they could scarcely avoid the conclusion that their dreams had been little more than illusions. Worse yet, with the arrival of the Great Depression in the 1930's, optimism gave way to despair for countless Americans of every race and creed, and nightmares of anxiety replaced dreams of hope.

[76] Trotter, *Black Milwaukee*, 47–54, 56–57, 63.

PART II

The New Era

THE postwar decade was a time of prosperity in Wisconsin, as it was in the nation. Economic growth reversed a brief postwar recession, and the good years that followed were exciting years of experimentation and development in communities throughout the state. Scientific and technological innovations stimulated industrial expansion, brought increased agricultural productivity, and radically altered conditions of life. The responses of citizens sharpened public awareness of profound changes under way. Not always certain of what the changes meant, and not always confident of what the future might hold, people could at least agree that they had entered a New Era.

Important artifacts and documents of the New Era create an impression of benign discourse within a good society. The rhetoric of the decade, unlike that of the war years, concentrated on neighborliness and the rewards of social accommodation. Business organizations and service clubs emphasized the benefits of co-operation and harmony. Educators talked of teaching the whole child and enriching the lives of all children in the public schools. Residents of small towns and rural areas reiterated a continuing refrain emphasizing the friendliness of villages and the virtues of an unpretentious yeomanry.

Unfortunately, the New Era was not always so benign and felicitous as inflated rhetoric would have it. While business leaders appealed for co-operation in dealing with a changing economy, different economic interests produced genuine divisions and tensions in Wisconsin. By the end of the decade, the prevailing view among settlers of the timber Cutover and laborers of industrial centers was that co-operation amounted to little more than a tender solicitude for commercial activities. That solicitude helped to make the postwar decade a period of prosperity for business enterprise, to be sure, but not all citizens of the state benefited equally from the good times for which business leaders took credit. To residents of

Wisconsin's hinterland, as to industrial workers, the decade often brought frustration with current problems and anxiety about the course of events. Clearly, for many citizens of the state, calls for co-operation were mere cant.

In periods of rapid social and economic transition, communities seldom lack persons who aspire to guide the changes taking place. In company with business leaders seeking to direct the thinking of Wisconsin were political leaders who felt compelled to adapt their programs to changing conditions. The Progressive faction of the Republican party, led first by Robert M. La Follette, and then after 1925 by his sons, again took up the crusade against privilege interrupted by the war. While the Progressives maintained their following, especially in the rural areas of the state where Scandinavian influences were strong, they experienced some difficulty in taking advantage of ideas associated with the New Era. One of the political ironies of the twenties is that Progressive orators continued to ring the changes on issues and beliefs of the years before the war. At the same time, business leaders of New Era Wisconsin, who thought themselves up-to-date, felt a natural affinity with the Stalwarts who made up the Republican faction that Progressives called "reactionary." During the twenties and thirties, the La Follette family was to attract a national following among people of progressive or liberal persuasion. Perhaps sensing something broadly portentous in the La Follette influence, citizens outside Wisconsin were to demonstrate unusual interest in the state's political struggles during the New Era.

4

Complexities of Industrial Expansion

"IT is wonderful how men with great opportunities for gaining wealth are neglecting everything else for patriotic service," rhapsodized Richard T. Ely in March, 1918. His enthusiasm for the war effort had blinded him to the facts. The truth is that business people throughout the state tended to think of the Great War as providing great economic stimuli, and many of them believed that their opportunities for profit would continue to expand when peace returned. "After the war, when Wisconsin . . . once more enters into competition with other states for the markets of the nation and of the world," noted a Council of Defense press release in the summer of 1917, "the state which is the best prepared will lead all others." The release went on to suggest that Wisconsin manufacturers stood to gain immeasurably from their experience in meeting wartime production needs. Factories that had contributed to the war effort would continue to prosper "because manufacturers will have learned how to economize on time and material." War meant sacrifice, to be sure, but with the arrival of peace "the lessons of sacrifice will show their worth."[1]

Whatever the influence of military exigencies, Wisconsin business leaders entered the decade of the twenties with optimism. For a time their hopes seemed justified as the postwar economic cycle began with a frenzied speculative boom. The boom collapsed precipitously in the early summer of 1920, however, and a short, severe depression followed. Soon, the economy righted itself. By 1923 both state and nation had begun to enjoy a period of stability that was to last until 1929. The prosperity of the twenties was marked

[1] Ely to Frank T. Carlton, March 29, 1918, in the Richard T. Ely Papers. The Council of Defense press release, distributed with a June 22, 1917, dateline, appeared in several Wisconsin newspapers. See, for example, the *Kickapoo Scout* (Soldiers Grove), June 28, 1917.

by significant technological changes that had the effect of altering the way people lived and the concerns that dominated the state.

* * *

Reviewing business activity at the close of 1919, Milwaukee banker Oliver C. Fuller observed that "the combination of a world shortage of goods, the possession of more money than they had ever had before by a large number of people, and the national revulsion from the strain of war-time conditions, produced a demand for goods which no artificial movement on the part of the government or of the large purchasing corporations could counteract." While individual persons spent collectively much less than Fuller indicated, actions by the United States government had a far greater influence than he seemed to think. For one thing, because spending exceeded tax receipts, the federal deficit in 1919 was over $4.5 billion. By comparison with deficits after World War II, it was a paltry amount, but the respending of this money produced significant indirect results. For another thing, the Allies continued to receive loans that were used largely for purchases in the United States. Government spending brought expansion of credit and inflationary prices. Credit expanded because government bonds could be used as collateral for bank loans to business and agriculture and because such loans could be rediscounted by federal reserve banks. The increased amount of bank loans to private borrowers, combined with the ending of wartime price controls in 1918, encouraged price increases and speculative activity in nearly every sector of the economy.[2]

Using 1926 prices for purposes of comparison, the U.S. Bureau of Labor Statistics later calculated that the wholesale price index for all commodities rose from 131.3 at the time of the Armistice in November, 1918, to 154.4 in 1920. The cost-of-living index increased more than 30 per cent during the same period, and escalating costs gave rise to bitter jokes and murmuring of a buyers'

[2] Oliver C. Fuller, "Milwaukee Has a Way All Her Own," in Milwaukee, First Wisconsin National Bank, *Business Milwaukee* [annual], 1919, p. 4; George H. Soule, *Prosperity Decade: From War to Depression, 1917–1929* (New York, 1947), 88–90; U.S. National Resources Planning Board, *After the War, 1918–1920: Military and Economic Demobilization of the United States, Its Effect upon Employment and Income*, comps. Paul A. Samuelson and Everett E. Hagan (1943), 23–27; John D. Hicks, *Republican Ascendancy, 1921–1933* (New York, 1960), 6; H. L. Lutz, "The Administration of the Federal Interest-Bearing Debt Since the Armistice," in the *Journal of Political Economy*, 34 (August, 1926), 423.

strike. Yet expectations of further price rises induced business executives to build their inventories in anticipation of greater profits. In June, 1919, the Federal Reserve Board warned member banks against speculation in the stock market and against loans for accumulation of inventories. Nevertheless, loans and investments continued to increase. The estimated growth in business inventories during 1919 was $6 billion, an increase far greater than during any single year of the following decade.[3]

Warnings were clearly ineffective in halting inflation, yet the Federal Reserve Board was reluctant to take further steps to discourage speculation. Committed to aiding the Department of the Treasury in floating the Victory Loan in 1919, it avoided measures that might make money dear and investors hesitant. Nevertheless, the reserve board finally acted. In November, 1919, it began raising the rediscount rate. By the end of the year the Federal Reserve Bank of New York had set its rates at 4¾ per cent. In January, 1920, the general rate advanced to 5½, and in June to 7 per cent. By midyear, the economic picture had altered. Within a few months the federal government had moved from large-scale borrowing to credit restriction, and from budgetary deficit to a treasury surplus. Merchants and manufacturers who could not then finance inventories through bank credit found themselves obliged to dispose of goods at reduced prices. By June, 1921, distress selling and other pressures had brought wholesale prices to 56 per cent of what they had been in May, 1920. Rapid deflation also brought further credit restrictions, and business managers felt compelled to cancel orders and lay off workers.[4]

[3] U.S. Bureau of the Census, *Historical Statistics of the United States: Colonial Times to 1957* (1960), which also appears as *House Documents*, 86 Cong., 1 sess., no. 33 (serial 12216), 116, 126; Paul H. Douglas, *Real Wages in the United States, 1890–1926* (Boston, 1930; reprinted, New York, 1966), 60; Milwaukee *Leader*, June 29, 1920; Soule, *Prosperity Decade*, 90; Wesley C. Mitchell, "A Review," in Conference on Unemployment, Committee on Recent Economic Changes, *Recent Economic Changes in the United States* (2 vols., New York, 1929), 2:852; Joseph S. Davis, *The World Between the Wars, 1919–39: An Economist's View* (Baltimore, 1975), 85–86. A useful table, "Gross National Product and Its Main Components, Changes During 5 Business Cycles, 1919–1938," may be found in Moses Abramovitz, *Inventories and Business Cycles, with Special References to Manufacturers' Inventories* (National Bureau of Economic Research, *Studies in Business Cycles*, no. 4, New York, 1950), 476–477. *La Follette's Magazine*, August, 1919, condemned speculation in food as well as in other products.

[4] Lutz, "Administration of the Federal Interest-Bearing Debt," *Journal of Political Economy*, 34:425; Soule, *Prosperity Decade*, 89–90, 95, 98, 101–102; U.S. National Resources Planning Board, *After the War*, 23. For a critical assessment of Federal Reserve policy,

The depression that followed the postwar boom did not last long, but while it lasted it brought considerable hardship. Excluding salaried employees, the number of wage earners in Wisconsin declined from 263,949 in 1919 to 191,770 in 1921, a 27.3 per cent decrease. The value of products and value added by manufacture declined even more, by 34.2 and 32.3 per cent respectively. Much of the decrease in both employment and production was a result of reconversion to peacetime activities, but the sudden collapse of the economy made things difficult for the worker out of a job or for the farmer who had borrowed money to buy land at inflated prices.[5]

Conditions had begun to appear threatening by the time Warren G. Harding entered the White House in March, 1921, and at the urging of the new secretary of commerce, Herbert Hoover, the President agreed to hold a conference to discuss the problem of unemployment. Beginning their deliberations on September 26, 1921, the conferees recommended no bold program of action on the part of the federal government. Instead, they urged states and communities to undertake co-operative action to find work for the jobless. In the meantime, Wisconsin Governor John J. Blaine received various suggestions for dealing with unemployment. Frank J. Weber of the Federated Trades Council of Milwaukee, for example, wanted the governor to ask Congress for an extensive program of national improvements, and Glenn P. Turner of Madison suggested that the construction of dormitories at the University of Wisconsin would create new jobs.[6]

Finally, in November, Blaine issued a press release outlining a plan to find work for the unemployed. He called for the creation of an *ad hoc* committee in every municipality with a population larger than 3,000. Such committees could then work with the Wisconsin Industrial Commission to improve the effectiveness of eleven free employment agencies already operated by the state. Employment offices could not create jobs, however, and promises of em-

see Milton Friedman and Anna Jacobson Schwartz, *A Monetary History of the United States, 1867–1960* (Princeton, 1963), 231–239.

[5] *Fifteenth Census of the United States, 1930: Manufactures, 1929, Volume III*, 561.

[6] Robert K. Murray, *The Harding Era: Warren G. Harding and His Administration* (Minneapolis, 1969), 231–233; Robert K. Murray, "Herbert Hoover and the Harding Cabinet," in Ellis W. Hawley, ed., *Herbert Hoover as Secretary of Commerce: Studies in New Era Thought and Practice* (Iowa City, 1981), 24–26; Joan Hoff Wilson, *Herbert Hoover, Forgotten Progressive* (Boston, 1975), 90–92; Weber to Blaine, September 28, 1921, and Turner to Blaine, October 13, 1921, both in the John J. Blaine Papers.

ployment were not always fulfilled. In September, 423 persons had registered at the Milwaukee office in response to an announcement of municipal job openings, only to find that not a single work order had been received from city departments.[7]

Fortunately, economic recovery was not long in arriving, and prosperity did indeed appear to be a concomitant of peace. *Business and Financial Comment,* a monthly publication of the First Wisconsin National Bank of Milwaukee, provided a running dissertation on the course of recovery. In June, 1922, it reported that the Milwaukee Employment Bureau had placed nearly 6,000 persons the previous month, and that requests for common laborers far exceeded the number of job seekers. Events of the early summer "confirmed the impression that business is well started on the upward trend." The only danger on the horizon in July was the possibility of another runaway market, and the First Wisconsin was grateful that conservative companies such as the United States Steel Corporation were keeping their prices down and under control. By the end of the year, unfilled orders averaged perhaps 100 per cent higher than at the end of 1921. Nearly all lines of industry shared in the year's improvement, but the leading beneficiaries of better times were those in the automotive group, iron, steel, heavy machinery, boots and shoes, knit goods, paper and pulp, chemicals, drugs, and wood products. In January, 1923, one Milwaukee steel foundry reported that sales were 325 per cent over January, 1922; its unfilled orders were 600 per cent greater.[8]

Only agriculture seemed to lag behind in recovery, despite the bumper crops of 1922. Mail-order sales increased and sales of automobiles and farm implements indicated that farmers bought "substantially more" during the spring of 1923 than they had bought a year earlier. Nevertheless, economic analysts believed that farmers experienced greater hardship during the postwar depression than did other segments of Wisconsin society. "Did you ever know of a time," asked University of Wisconsin Professor E. H. Farrington in a letter to his family, "when the farmer got so hard hit by falling

[7] "Suggestions by Governor Blaine concerning unemployment," November 10, 1921, in the Blaine Papers; Milwaukee *Leader,* September 22, 1921.

[8] *Business and Financial Comment,* June 15, July 15, 1922; January 15, May 15, 1923. This is a monthly publication of the First Wisconsin National Bank, June, 1920, through February 15, 1930, succeeded by Wisconsin Bankshares Corporation's *Bankshares Review,* March 15, 1930, through December 26, 1933, both in the Milwaukee Public Library.

prices of everything he has to sell?" Henry A. Moehlenpah, the Clinton banker who had been the Democratic gubernatorial candidate in 1918, was called to Washington to appear before the Senate banking and currency committee in 1921. "The people of the cities do not appreciate the gravity of the farm crisis," he declared, adding that low prices for farm products and high costs for labor and goods had left farmers "in a worse position than any other class." Dean Harry L. Russell and Professor F. B. Morrison, of the University of Wisconsin College of Agriculture, also reinforced the agriculturists' complaint that deflation had brought greater reduction of prices in farm commodities than in the finished products farmers had to buy. Dante M. Pierce, editor of the *Wisconsin Farmer*, put the case with vivid clarity when he noted that the same farm wagon that cost 114 bushels of corn at Rhinelander in 1914 required 503 bushels in 1921; a gang plow costing ninety bushels of corn at Janesville in 1914 required 302 bushels in 1921.[9]

While farmers did not share adequately in the prosperity that came with business recovery in 1922–1923, the farmers of Wisconsin were generally better off than those of other states. In December, 1923, the American Farm Bureau Federation reported that farm income in Wisconsin was $41.2 million more than the previous year. In 1922–1923, the average gross income per farm in the United States was $1,314, while the gross income per farm in Wisconsin was $1,608. The Farm Bureau pointed out that 81 per cent of Wisconsin farm income was derived from livestock and its products. Because both were relatively more stable than grains, "it is easily apparent that Wisconsin agriculture is on a much more solid base than that of grain crop regions." In every year from 1922 to 1931, gross farm income in Wisconsin surpassed the farm income

[9] Farrington to "Circle," May 10, 1921, in the E. H. Farrington Papers; Milwaukee *Journal*, May 8, 1921; UW Agricultural Experiment Station, *Annual Report*, 1920–1921, published as *Bulletin*, no. 339 (1922); Dante Pierce, "Six Loads of Corn Will Buy Wagon," in *La Follette's Magazine*, January, 1922. See also Harry D. Baker to George A. Nelson, May 12, 1922, in the George Nelson Papers; Charles Rosa to E. H. Kronshage, March 8, 1923, in the Charles Rosa Papers; John J. Blaine to John D. Jones, January 27, 1926, in the Blaine Papers; *Wisconsin Farmer*, 50 (January 13, 1921), 55; Burlington *Standard-Democrat*, May 27, 1921; *Wisconsin Farm Bureau News*, Winnebago County section, October, 1922; *Wisconsin Agriculturist*, May 5, 1923; J. H. Kolb, *Service Relations of Town and Country*, UW Agricultural Experiment Station, *Research Bulletin*, no. 58 (1923); Madison *Capital Times*, January 25, 30, February 5, 1924; *Equity News*, September 1, 1924; and U.S. Department of Agriculture, *Yearbook of Agriculture, 1940: Farmers in a Changing World*, 299–300.

of 1920; in every year save 1924, 1928, and 1930, gross farm income was greater than the year before.[10]

After surveying Wisconsin's economic progress early in 1926, Milwaukee tax consultant Burt Williams drafted an enthusiastic report. "Wisconsin can today challenge any state in the union in the extent, variety and investment, and in the increase of its manufacturing establishments during the past four or five years," he boasted. With an annual value of manufactured products in excess of $1.7 billion, the Wisconsin economy doubled the value of all oil production in the United States and exceeded in value the total world production of precious metals. Forwarding his report to Governor Blaine, Williams noted that his figures "certainly show that Wisconsin is making great strides along manufacturing lines, notwithstanding the attempt of pessimists to show otherwise."[11]

A few farm spokesmen had been voicing similar optimism since 1922, and they had been making efforts to silence calamity howlers in the rural areas. "Better prices are bound to come if we can only remain patient," was the soothing forecast of the *Wisconsin Agriculturist* in the spring of 1923. "More hopeful times are in sight for farmers as well as for the rest of mankind." Later in the year the author promised that "the one thing above all others that is going to carry the farming interests of this country forward to better and more prosperous times is the splendid optimism of the American farmer." At every crossroads, she alleged, farmers of Wisconsin were talking cheerfully, "assuring themselves and others that better times are just around the corner." And everywhere "the leaven of this optimism is working a marvelous change in the future outlook."[12]

The wish for better times was father to the thought that better times were indeed at hand. Although one might find farm mortgage foreclosures and business failures in every area of the state, the tone of public discourse sounded a purposefully optimistic note to

[10] *La Follette's Magazine*, October, 1924; *Wisconsin Farm Bureau News*, December, 1923; Thomas C. McCormick and Paul C. Glick, "Fertility Rates in Wisconsin, 1920–35," in the *American Journal of Sociology*, 44 (November, 1938), 405; Paul C. Glick, "The Effects of the Depression on Wisconsin's Birth Rates" (doctoral dissertation, University of Wisconsin, 1938).

[11] Burt Williams to John J. Blaine, March 27, 1926, in the Blaine Papers; *Wisconsin State Journal*, June 7, 1926.

[12] *Wisconsin Agriculturist*, May 19, November 17, 1923; *Taylor County Star News* (Medford), November 27, 1924.

foster better economic conditions in business and agriculture. "It is our opinion that too many bankers, business men and farmers are engaged in destructive rather than constructive comments on local business conditions," observed the editor of the Bloomington *Record*. "A few bankrupt farmers do not mean that the farmers are all in a bad way," he cautioned, and he reminded his readers that "for every farmer or business man who is not successful anyone can pick out among his own acquaintances twice or three times the number of farmers or business men who are successful and can also give valid reasons, that could have been corrected, if started in time, for the failures." For citizens of Wisconsin, but one course of action seemed appropriate: "Let us all resolve to quit our idle pessimistic gossip and 'do our durndest' to help ourselves and the other fellow along to better times and conditions, and real prosperity will be with us before we know it—if it is not here already."[13]

* * *

A basic influence in the economic changes that took place during the years around World War I was development of the internal combustion engine. By that time, horseless carriages were no longer a novelty. In 1873, Dr. John W. Carhart had mounted a steam engine on wagon wheels and run his vehicle through the streets of Racine. Then in 1878, competing for a prize offered by the state legislature, two steam "road wagons" had raced from Green Bay to Madison. While steam or electricity at first appeared to be the most likely means of improving on horse power, a variety of experiments on both sides of the Atlantic provided reason to believe by 1890 that transportation in the future depended on the internal combustion engine. Before the turn of the century, American inventors sought to improve upon European models, and the sprint for automobility began in earnest. The Office of Road Inquiry was set up in the United States Department of Agriculture in 1893, and by the fall of 1895 the U.S. Patent Office had received more than 500 applications relating to motor vehicles.[14]

[13] Bloomington *Record*, June 10, 1925.

[14] State Highway Commission and United States Public Roads Administration, *A History of Wisconsin Highway Development, 1835–1945* (Madison, 1947), 19; Richard N. Current, *The History of Wisconsin. Volume II: The Civil War Era, 1848–1873* (Madison, 1976), 451; James J. Flink, *The Car Culture* (Cambridge, 1975), 9–11; James J. Flink, *America Adopts the Automobile, 1895–1910* (Cambridge, 1970); James J. Flink, "Three Stages of Automobile Consciousness," in *American Quarterly*, 24 (October, 1972), 452–453; John S. Donald, "Wisconsin's Pioneer Part in the Development of the Motor Vehicle and Farm

Almost from its beginning in the United States, the automobile industry gravitated towards the Middle West. Hardwood forests had long made the region attractive to carriage and wagon manufacturers, and converting to automobiles was a natural transition. When automobile companies later became large-scale business organizations, entrepreneurs concentrated on Detroit as the major center of production. A nucleus of industrial activity of all sorts, Detroit boasted advantages in proximity to both resources and markets that no city in Wisconsin and not even Chicago could claim. Southeastern Wisconsin lay on the periphery of industrial development during the nineteenth century, and auto makers there had difficulty matching the accomplishments of their counterparts in southeastern Michigan.[15]

One of the first Wisconsin manufacturers to try his hand at producing automobiles was Edward Joel Pennington, but he is best remembered for his promotional rather than his technical abilities. In 1895, he joined Thomas Kane and Company to produce the appropriately named "Kane-Pennington Hot Air Engine" at Racine. When the company failed to fulfill its promises, Pennington departed for England where he wound up in bankruptcy court. A far more astute auto maker was Thomas B. Jeffery, who began producing automobiles at Kenosha in 1901. Trained in England as a maker of scientific instruments, Jeffery had emigrated to the United States where he went into business to produce a bicycle he marketed under the name "Rambler." After he opened his Kenosha plant, he used the bicycle name for his automobiles. A man of considerable acumen, Jeffery anticipated Henry Ford in his attempt to produce a rugged, serviceable car for the average family. Though the idea was premature, one of the new automobile journals, *Motor World*, greeted the Rambler's arrival with enthusiasm. "When the fizz and fireworks cease to sizz and splutter . . . ," it predicted, "the firm of T. B. Jeffery . . . will be found well up on the list of the fittest who survived." And survive the company did, though it went through a series of changes in ownership.[16]

Tractor," typescript, and John W. Carhart to Donald, March 5, 1914, both in SHSW chronological manuscripts file for 1914, February 23; John B. Rae, *American Automobile Manufacturers: The First Forty Years* (Philadelphia, 1959), 6–8.

[15] Rae, *American Automobile Manufacturers*, 29, 58–60; John B. Rae, *The American Automobile: A Brief History* (Chicago, 1965), 28–29; Francis F. Bowman, Jr., *Industrial Wisconsin*, Department of Commerce (1939), 111.

[16] Rae, *American Automobile Manufacturers*, 29, 58–60; *Motor World*, 2 (May 2, 1901), 95, cited in *ibid.*, 14; Rae, *The American Automobile*, 11–12.

Other companies joined the scramble to produce automobiles in Wisconsin during the heyday of motor vehicle promotion before World War I. In 1902 the Wisconsin Wheel Works, manufacturer of bicycles in Racine, changed its name to the Mitchell Motor Car Company and turned to the production of automobiles. Eight years later the firm combined with the Mitchell & Lewis Wagon Company to become the largest employer in the city by 1911. In 1917, however, the Mitchell family sold out, and production of automobiles ceased in 1922. Another organization, the Pierce Engine Company, began in 1907 to produce Pierce-Racine automobiles, marketed by the J. I. Case Threshing Machine Company. Case took over the management in 1912 and turned out automobiles for a dozen years before concentrating on tractors and agricultural implements. In the meantime Louis Kissel, an implement and hardware dealer in Hartford, moved into automaking in 1906. His firm's product, the Kisselkar, became famous for its name and its design, infamous for its gluttony at the gasoline pump and its tendency to break down. Whatever the faults of the Kisselkar, the company remained in operation until 1930.[17]

The Hartford firm that manufactured the Kisselkar lasted longer than most small producers of automobiles. During the Great War and after, the tendency was for large companies to absorb smaller ones, and for the large companies to break up and then merge in new ways. By the close of the twenties the manipulations of auto manufacturers left two great companies, Ford and General Motors, producing more automobiles than all other car makers combined. Competitive conditions of the postwar decade, in other words, brought closure of entry into automobile manufacturing and accelerated a movement towards oligopoly.[18]

The oligopolistic trend was to have an important effect on the auto makers of Wisconsin. The Ford Motor Company's vaunted use of mass-production techniques represented but one way to achieve the organization necessary for rising above the competition of small-factory, individualized production. William C. Durant took another

[17] Richard H. Keehn, "Industry and Business," in Nicholas C. Burckel, ed., *Racine: Growth and Change in a Wisconsin County* (Racine, 1977), 293–294; Rae, *American Automobile Manufacturers*, 192; Milwaukee *Journal*, February 27, 1955; David L. Cohn, *Combustion on Wheels* (Cambridge, 1944), 133.

[18] Flink, "Three Stages of Automobile Consciousness," *American Quarterly*, 24:461–462.

approach when he put together the General Motors Company in 1908. The holding company structure allowed him to gain control of thirteen motor vehicle firms, along with several ancillary concerns. Unfortunately for General Motors, Durant's extravagant bullishness, yoked with his limited technical understanding, led to a series of blunders that nearly brought ruin to the new company. It was saved only with the help of a bankers' syndicate headed by James J. Storrow of Lee, Higginson and Company. Bringing Charles W. Nash and Walter P. Chrysler into the top echelons of General Motors, the Storrow regime restored the company to solvency and worked out a much-needed reorganization.[19]

Durant, in the meantime, remained a trustee and a member of the GM board of directors. He also formed the Chevrolet Motor Car Company, later to have an important influence on the economy of Janesville after establishment of an assembly plant there. The company was named after Louis Chevrolet, who had been a racing driver for Buick and who designed the first models for the firm. But it was Durant, not Chevrolet, who achieved a success with the new venture that was remarkable. In two years he sold nearly 16,000 automobiles and attracted favorable attention from Pierre S. du Pont and his brother Irenee. Each began adding General Motors common stock to his portfolio, and when the voting trust that controlled the company expired on October 1, 1915, Durant was ready for a comeback with du Pont assistance. Durant called a meeting of the board of directors the next May to announce that he controlled General Motors.[20]

Distressed by this turn of events, Nash resigned in June. Storrow withdrew from the board of directors at the same time, and the two went out to search for another automobile company in need of their talents. After considering Packard and Mack Motors, they finally settled on the Thomas B. Jeffery Company of Kenosha. In 1916 they paid $5 million and set about reorganizing the firm as the Nash Motors Company. Later in 1924, Nash bought the Mitchell auto company, which had been experiencing difficulties and had gone into receivership. In Racine, Nash first produced the six-

[19] Bernard A. Weisberger, *The Dream Maker: William C. Durant, Founder of General Motors* (Boston, 1979), 133–152; Flink, *Car Culture*, 62–64; Paul W. Glad, *Progressive Century* (Lexington, Massachusetts, 1975), 212.

[20] Weisberger, *Dream Maker*, 160–177, 235–237. The story of Durant's comeback is well-known, but it has been engagingly told by Weisberger, pp. 153–201.

cylinder Ajax, which later became the Nash Light Six. The company shared in the prosperity of the automobile industry during the mid-twenties, and in 1927 it began a $1.2 million expansion program.[21]

The boom in Wisconsin motor vehicle manufacturing was a cause for rejoicing, to be sure, but cautious observers worried about dangers ahead. As early as 1914, Clinton banker Henry A. Moehlenpah warned the Wisconsin Bankers' Association that growth of the automobile industry had proceeded at "a pace too swift to give people time to ask 'whither it takes them.' " The following year the bankers debated the advisability of automobile loans. Some thought that since most purchasers did not have the income to pay for an automobile, manufacturers should carry the paper of their dealers and their dealers' customers. Others thought that an automobile owner possessed an asset that merited consideration for a bank loan. Henry Ford emphatically disagreed with both. Writing to George Bartlett, secretary of the WBA, he observed that it had always seemed to him that "this putting off the day of payment for anything but permanent improvements was a fundamental mistake."[22]

Though Ford was an undoubted genius at production, his opinions on consumer financing carried little weight. Motor vehicle production and sales broke all records in 1923, and installment buying became an important instrument of New Era prosperity. Through easy credit as much as through mass-production techniques, car manufacturers were able to reach down to lower-income groups, and the increased number of consumers justified increased production. Yet even an enlarged market could become saturated, and motor vehicle manufacturers encouraged a tendency to think of the automobile as a social necessity. Advertisements began to emphasize not only the importance of owning a car but also the importance of owning a new car, and consumers readily accepted the message. Indeed, their cravings were insatiable. As one Wisconsin observer noted in 1926, "the appetite of the public is not an appetite simply for an automobile but for the latest model in automobile quality and performance." Whether or not model changes actually brought mechanical improvements, they were an important means of increasing motor vehicle production. And by allowing

[21] Rae, *American Automobile Manufacturers*, 112, 176; Flink, *Car Culture*, 120.

[22] Wisconsin Bankers' Association, *Proceedings*, 1914, pp. 46–47; *ibid.*, 1915, pp. 124–129.

consumers to keep up with a succession of models, the practice of installment buying accelerated a trend towards rapid turnover in automobile ownership.[23]

Wisconsin automakers benefited from financial and marketing practices of the New Era. By 1927 the value of motor vehicle bodies and parts produced in the state was exceeded only by Michigan, Ohio, and New York. Yet Wisconsin bankers could not avoid a certain uneasiness. *Business and Financial Comment* admitted in 1925 that "an industry which can constantly improve its product, sell it at lower prices and still realize good profits has achieved remarkable economies in production." But the article cautioned that this was only "the favorable side of the automobile situation." On the other side was the severe competition that led automakers to overload markets and force the pace of commerce. While the system worked well enough when credit terms were liberal, bankers knew that ample supplies of credit would not always be available, and they feared that credit restrictions might well force unpleasant readjustments.[24]

The Wisconsin Bankers' Association was attentive to economic problems of the automobile industry, but more often than not it avoided proposing economic solutions for them. The bankers suggested, instead, that after the war Americans had become hedonists who grasped for every extravagance that came to their attention. "The creation of conditions following a world war have [*sic*] given us a false philosophy and a distorted vision of things," intoned W. H. Doyle in his presidential address to the association in 1925. "This is the age of the wireless telegraph, the radio, the automobile, the flying machine, and it is also the age of reckless extravagance in nation, state, community, and home. . . . The well-to-do and many others not so well-to-do, mortgage their homes to buy automobiles and luxuries, while the rank and file of those less blessed with worldly goods struggle along in a vain effort to keep pace with their neighbors." Like many other pundits of the twenties, Doyle was arguing that Americans had lost their spiritual moorings. Economic

[23] *Business and Financial Comment*, October 15, 1923, January 15, 1925, and July 15, 1926, in the Milwaukee Public Library.

[24] *Ibid.*, December 15, 1925, November 15, 1926; Wisconsin Manufacturers' Association, *Statistical History of Industrial Development and Growth in Wisconsin from 1850 to 1929 Inclusive* (mimeographed, Madison, [1930]), in the LRB, microfilm copy in the SHSW.

measures were unnecessary, he believed, for "every unfavorable condition that today exists may be overcome by the energy, courage and thrift of our people." Two years later, Eau Claire banker Knute Anderson was less moralistic, but he too provided few concrete suggestions for solving the problems of industry. He urged only that Wisconsin bankers resist the temptation to sacrifice "sound banking principles."[25]

By 1927, the automobile industry was in trouble not only in Wisconsin but in the nation as well. As a new industry, motor vehicle manufacturing had experienced phenomenal growth during the postwar period, but even with installment buying there were limits to the number of automobiles that could be sold. Eventually the saturation that worried bankers and credit agencies actually occurred. The output of new cars decreased by 22 per cent in 1927, and 59 per cent of the automobiles sold that year were replacement sales. Auto makers of Wisconsin had fallen far behind Michigan manufacturers by 1927, but that may have been a blessing in that it prevented too heavy a reliance upon one form of consumer durable. Because the consumption of durable goods is easily postponed during times of stress, industries producing such goods were especially hard hit by the economic depression that began in 1929. With industrial diversification, Wisconsin was better prepared to meet the challenge of hard times than it might have been had the state's automobile producers won out in competition with the car manufacturers of Michigan.[26]

* * *

Ever since the heyday of Populism, rural people had insisted that husbandry was as much a business as any other calling. It was therefore logical that farmers should apply business principles and practices in their daily work. As evidence that they were indeed becoming efficient business operators, the *Wisconsin Farmer* noted in the spring of 1920 that "progressive farmers everywhere have offices on their farms with all the latest equipment." They were buying office chairs and desks, filing cabinets and card indexes, typewriters and letterhead stationery. Wisconsin copyright law protected farm names, and agricultural producers were beginning to appreciate

[25] Annual presidential addresses of W. H. Doyle and Knute Anderson in the Wisconsin Bankers' Association, *Proceedings*, 1925, pp. 51–52, 57, and 1927, p. 52.

[26] Soule, *Prosperity Decade*, 286.

the value of advertising. "Wisconsin's agricultural products can go around the world" was the intoxicating supposition of Ernest L. Luther, superintendent of the university's farmers' institutes. With effective advertising, Wisconsin pedigree grains and livestock could conquer markets at home and abroad.[27]

The *Wisconsin Farmer* greatly exaggerated the degree to which rural homesteads were beginning to resemble urban business offices, but there is little doubt that farmers were becoming more businesslike. Wartime labor shortages, combined with the development of agricultural machinery and a transportation revolution, wrought fundamental changes in the Wisconsin countryside. In 1918, the Wausau *Record-Herald* marked the changed conditions and predicted that "farming will necessarily become more and more a scientific business." Shiftless operators would not be able to survive, for "the farmer must invest too much money in order to farm at all, to permit the land to be poorly cultivated and produce correspondingly poor crops." And having invested in new and unfamiliar machinery, he found that if he himself did not learn new technical skills he had to rely on the specialized training of others. In either case his links to a growing industrial complex grew stronger through his need for such items as parts and fuel. He also became linked to a dynamic commercial complex through a new, rapidly advancing distributive system.[28]

Motor vehicle manufacturers in Wisconsin could not produce automobiles on a scale with Michigan auto makers, but the same generalization does not apply to the production of tractors and agricultural implements. Located closer to the grain belt of the West, and with rail lines extending from the Chicago-Milwaukee industrial area into the North American breadbasket, Wisconsin and Illinois manufacturers enjoyed an advantage in the tractor and agricultural implement market that was comparable to the advantage Detroit found in the market for automobiles. By 1930 the states that led all others in the percentage of farms having tractors were North and South Dakota, Montana, and Kansas. Of the ten states with tractors on at least a fourth of the farms, only New Jersey and California lay outside the Upper Middle West and Northern Plains

[27] *Wisconsin Farmer*, 49 (April 15, 1920), 800, and 45 (July 13, 1916), 900; Burlington *Standard-Democrat*, May 28, 1920; "The Farmer of Today," in the *Wisconsin Agriculturist*, November 13, 1926.

[28] Wausau *Record-Herald*, June 3, 1918; *Wisconsin Farmer*, 48 (February 6, 1919), 197.

regions. By 1940 the states in which at least a third of the farms had tractors were the Dakotas, Iowa, Kansas, Nebraska, Illinois, Minnesota, Montana, New Jersey, Wisconsin, Wyoming, Colorado, Indiana, Ohio, New York, California, and Michigan. The predominance here of states in the American interior between the Milwaukee-Chicago area and the Rocky Mountains suggests that tractors were more cost effective in cash grain production than in other types of agriculture. They were also more cost effective on large farms than on smaller farms. In any case, World War I brought greater demand for wheat than for any other crop, and high grain prices along with a shortage of farm labor encouraged mechanization in the wheat belt. Manufacturers of gasoline-powered tractors were enticed by possibilities on the Plains as well as in the corn- and feed-producing Middle West.[29]

During the thirty years before the war, to be sure, steam engines had provided a major source of draft power on mechanized farms. But they were too heavy to handle easily on rough or rain-soaked terrain. They were also dangerous, sometimes exploding when boilers were carelessly constructed or inadequately attended, and sometimes causing fires when hot coals fell from the ash box or when sparks from the stack blew across dry fields. So great was the demand for mechanical traction, however, that the market for steam engines did not entirely disappear until the mid-1920's. During the half-century after 1876, the J. I. Case Threshing Machine Company of Racine produced nearly 36,000 agricultural steam engines and led all competitors.[30]

Nonetheless, the future belonged to the internal combustion engine. As with other farm-related inventions and innovations—the butterfat test and the discovery of vitamins, for example—the University of Wisconsin generated important work. In 1896 two engineering students, Charles W. Hart and Charles H. Parr, collaborated on a thesis dealing with gasoline engines which became the

[29] *University of North Carolina News Letter*, November 12, 1941, in "Farm Machinery" clipping file, LRB; Harold Barger and Hans H. Landsberg, *American Agriculture, 1899–1939: A Study of Output, Employment and Productivity* (National Bureau of Economic Research, *Publications*, no. 42, New York, 1942), 201–202; Theodore Saloutos and John D. Hicks, *Agricultural Discontent in the Middle West, 1900–1939* (Madison, 1951), 90–92; U.S. Department of Agriculture, *Yearbook of Agriculture, 1940*, pp. 280–284.

[30] Reynold M. Wik, *Steam Power on the American Farm* (Philadelphia, 1953), 100–101, 131–140, 180–181; Stewart H. Holbrook, *Machines of Plenty: Chronicle of an Innovator in Construction and Agricultural Equipment*, updated by Richard G. Charlton (2nd ed., New York, 1976), 48–50, 55–62, 89–90.

foundation of a new industry. After operating a stationary engine plant in Madison for a brief period, the two friends secured financial backing and moved to Charles City, Iowa. There they formed a company and began building gasoline-powered tractors. The idea caught on, other firms entered the competition, and by 1907 there were about 600 tractors working American fields. A third of those were Hart-Parrs, which gained a deserved reputation for durability. Five of the fifteen tractors built by the company in 1903 were still being used in 1930, though by that time Hart-Parr had become part of the Oliver Farm Equipment Company.[31]

The merits of Hart-Parr tractors did not obscure the difficulties that affected the industry in its early years. The first internal combustion tractors, many of them built on the same pattern as steam traction behemoths, proved as ill-suited for small farm operations as were the J. I. Case steam prototypes. Some of them weighing as much as 50,000 pounds, these dinosaurs of the new industry damaged fields when they did not break down or become mired in mud. Too large and cumbersome to be used in the cultivation of row crops, they were marked for extinction after the war. Plowing contests at state and county fairs, and the international tractor exhibitions held at Winnipeg, Manitoba, from 1909 to 1912 had already demonstrated the superiority of lighter tractors. The first entry into the light tractor market, introduced by the Bull Traction Machine Company of Minneapolis in 1913, was powered by a small twelve-horsepower engine and advertised as "The Bull with a Pull." It appealed to manufacturers who were attentive to lessons of the Winnipeg and other competitions, and the little Bull set a new trend in tractor design.[32]

Henry Ford, who attended the Manitoba plowing trials in 1910, moved into the small tractor business five years later with the Fordson. Turned out through the system of mass production employed in the manufacture of automobiles, the Fordson enjoyed great popularity during the war and into the postwar period. The design of

[31] Merle Curti and Vernon Carstensen, *The University of Wisconsin: A History, 1848–1925* (2 vols., Madison, 1949), 2:461–462; Holbrook, *Machines of Plenty*, 166–168; Wik, *Steam Power on the American Farm*, 203–204; U.S. Department of Agriculture, *Yearbook of Agriculture, 1960: Power to Produce*, 31.

[32] Barger and Landsberg, *American Agriculture, 1899–1939*, pp. 206–207; Wik, *Steam Power on the American Farm*, 205–206; Reynold M. Wik, "Mechanization of the American Farm," in Melvin Kranzberg and Carroll W. Pursell, Jr., eds., *Technology in Western Civilization. Volume II: Technology in the Twentieth Century* (New York, 1967), 360.

the first Fordson featured a four-cylinder motor bolted to the transmission housing, and it could burn either kerosene or gasoline. Weighing but 2,500 pounds, the tractor was less than five feet high and could turn a twenty-one-foot circle. Ford sold more than 34,000 tractors in 1918, more than 100,000 in both 1923 and 1925. Fordson officials were not far off the mark in the mid-1920's when they claimed to have produced more than half the tractors in the country. Widely used in Wisconsin, the diminutive Fordson solved many old problems, but it also presented farmers with new ones. Most distressing was its tendency to flip over backwards if unexpected resistance on the drawbar (or beam to which the farmer might hitch implements) created too much torque in the transmission. There were problems for the manufacturer as well. Sales did not meet Ford's expectations during the postwar recession, and then, with the promise of better times for American farmers, competitors began to gain entry into the market. The lightweight Fordson fell short of meeting the need for an all-purpose tractor, and in 1927 Ford officials decided to halt production in the United States.[33]

Like Ford, William C. Durant was intrigued by thoughts of capturing the market for light tractors, and in 1917 General Motors bought the Samson Sieve-Grip Tractor Company of Stockton, California. Then, almost immediately, the corporation added the J. A. Craig Company of Janesville. Persuaded that a midwestern location was best suited for production of agricultural implements, Durant next transferred his tractor plant to Wisconsin. Quickly moving into production, Janesville turned out 3,000 Samson Model M tractors in 1919. It was an auspicious beginning, but Durant soon came across what he thought was a better idea. He bought the patent rights to a tractor that could be managed with a pair of reins connected to control levers. The ingenious machine allowed a farmer without assistance to attend to raking, mowing, or binding without climbing in and out of a driver's seat. Durant named his curious contraption the Iron Horse and proceeded to demonstrate its versatility at the Wisconsin State Fair in 1919. Unfortunately for General Motors, the idea came a cropper. Trouble with the trans-

[33] Reynold M. Wik, *Henry Ford and Grass-Roots America* (Ann Arbor, 1972), 87–89, 94–97; Holbrook, *Machines of Plenty*, 170; Allan Nevins and Frank Ernest Hill, *Ford. Volume 2: Expansion and Challenge, 1915–1933* (New York, 1957), 685; U.S. Department of Agriculture, *Yearbook of Agriculture, 1960*, pp. 32–33.

mission belts set the Iron Horse to meandering fecklessly and uncontrollably, and the small number of Horses produced by Samson had to be recalled. General Motors abandoned tractor production, and Chevrolet acquired the Janesville factory for an automobile assembly plant.[34]

The advantages of internal combustion engine tractors had been well established by the end of the war, as had the fundamental principles of engineering and design. Yet the large tractors that predominated between 1910 and 1920 had limited use; they could only plow, drive threshers, and pull large headers. Light tractors such as the Fordson or the Iron Horse were equally limited; they simply could not perform all the functions required of them. Thus the postwar period became one of search and experimentation to find a tractor that would meet a variety of needs. An important consequence of that experimentation was development of a practical power take-off by the International Harvester Company in 1918. Power take-off meant the direct transmission of power from the engine to other equipment such as mowers or sprayers. Because it greatly increased the tractor's versatility and usefulness, most manufacturers began immediately to equip field machines with take-off mechanisms. Finally, in 1924, International Harvester produced the Farmall, the first really successful all-purpose tractor, capable of plowing, cultivating, and with appropriate attachments performing other tasks.[35]

The J. I. Case Company also took an active part in the improvement of tractors. The Racine firm was already the leading producer of steam traction engines in 1892, when it began testing gasoline tractors. Finally, in 1911, it produced the Case 30-60 and the 20-40 a year later. While the 1912 model captured the gold medal at the Winnipeg trials, Case officials did not rest on their laurels. In 1915 the company built its first four-cylinder vertical engine tractor. Its three wheels functioned in different ways: the single one in front was for steering, the right rear was a driver, and the left rear an idler. In the meantime, the company itself seemed to lose its uni-

[34] John W. Alexander, "Geography of Manufacturing in the Rock River Valley" (doctoral dissertation, University of Wisconsin, 1949), 168–169; Weisberger, *Dream Maker*, 235–237.

[35] U.S. Department of Agriculture, *Yearbook of Agriculture, 1960*, pp. 32–35; Barger and Landsberg, *American Agriculture, 1899–1939*, p. 207; Eugene G. McKibben and R. Austin Griffin, *Changes in Farm Power and Equipment: Tractors, Trucks, and Automobiles* (Philadelphia, 1938), 6.

formity of purpose when it experimented with the manufacture of automobiles. The Case motor department produced good automobiles, including some excellent racers, but they were to all intents and purposes custom-built and were never profitable.[36]

Just as the company appeared to be floundering, it acquired new leadership. In 1924, the year International Harvester began marketing the Farmall, Leon R. Clausen left John Deere to take over as president at Case. "When I came to Racine," he later recalled, "Case's tractor line was obsolete in both appearance and performance. I believed then, as I believe now, that almost anybody can make a pretty good automobile but that a tractor is something else. A good tractor is far more difficult to design and produce. We simply had to have a good tractor to hold our own or better in the race." Clausen, a native of Fox Lake and a graduate of the University of Wisconsin, brought back to the J. I. Case Company a badly needed sense of direction. He was to remain at the helm until after World War II.[37]

Another industrial executive who exercised great influence in developing tractors to serve the needs of American farmers was Otto H. Falk. Educated at Northwestern College in Watertown and at the Allen Military Academy in Chicago, Falk had seen military service during the Spanish-American War and after that in the Wisconsin National Guard. As vice-president of the Falk Corporation, a family-owned steel foundry, he had become a leader of the Milwaukee business community during the first decade of the twentieth century. When Allis-Chalmers Manufacturing Company went into receivership after a series of mergers and internal conflicts, it was Falk who became president and in 1913 began a careful rebuilding of the corporation. Profiting greatly during the years of wartime prosperity, Allis-Chalmers looked forward to continued success when peace returned.[38]

Falk recognized the importance of improving product lines, and

[36] U.S. Department of Agriculture, *Yearbook of Agriculture, 1960*, p. 33.

[37] Holbrook, *Machines of Plenty*, 189–190; Wayne G. Broehl, Jr., *John Deere's Company: A History of Deere & Company and Its Times* (Garden City, New York, 1984), 451–452.

[38] Walter F. Peterson, *An Industrial Heritage: Allis-Chalmers Corporation* (Milwaukee, 1978), 149–154. Because of Falk's German ancestry, war materiel production at Allis-Chalmers was particularly offensive to the German-American Alliance in 1915. Falk made clear, however, that he intended to act in the best interests of the company "as a representative American manufacturing concern which takes no part and has no prejudices for or against either side in the present European war." *Ibid.*, 167–168; Milwaukee *Journal*, March 20, 1915.

during the postwar decade he led his company into a program of research and development in a variety of fields such as flour milling, sawmilling, mining, electric power, concrete and other types of construction. Yet outside the heavy industries the Allis-Chalmers name meant little, and Falk began searching for new opportunities elsewhere. He finally decided to concentrate on the production of farm equipment, and to emphasize tractors in particular. Allis-Chalmers engineers were already experimenting with tractor designs in 1919, when Falk persuaded the executive committee and the board of directors of the company to establish a separate tractor department with its own shop.[39]

Despite Falk's enthusiasm and an advertising campaign that included the first use of the radio to publicize Allis-Chalmers products, initial sales were disappointing. Then, in 1926, the company hired Harry C. Merritt as manager of the tractor department. It was a happy choice. With great care he and his engineers disassembled an entire 20-35 A-C tractor, spread the parts on the floor, and set about perfecting the machine piece by piece. The result was the clean, lively 1927 model that was half a ton lighter and that featured a motor sealed against dirt and grit, with oil and gas filters as standard equipment. Best of all from the farmer's perspective, the improved tractor was reduced in price from $1,950 to $1,295.

Allis-Chalmers had cut profits to about 4 per cent as compared with 6.7 per cent for International Harvester and 18 per cent for Deere and Company, but on the other hand, sales increased dramatically. In 1927 the company sold nearly three times as many tractors as in 1925, and the next year it sold 4,867 of them to more than double the record of 1927. Falk's confidence in the future of the tractor and Merritt's skill in perfecting the 20-35 had placed Allis-Chalmers in a position to weather the economic storms that were to come. In 1932, at the depth of the Great Depression, the company began turning out tractors equipped with rubber tires and sent racing drivers Ab Jenkins, Lou Meyer, and Barney Oldfield to demonstrate them at county fairs. In 1933, the year the Century of Progress exhibition opened in Chicago, an Allis-Chalmers tractor took but five hours to make the eighty-eight-mile run from Milwaukee. In 1934, Merritt introduced the first tractors specifically

[39] Peterson, *Industrial Heritage*, 237, 244–245.

designed for pneumatic tires. They proved enormously popular among farmers, and long before the close of the decade Allis-Chalmers had become the nation's third-largest tractor manufacturer, trailing only International Harvester and John Deere. Although Wisconsin had long before lost the automobile industry to Michigan, the Milwaukee *Sentinel* observed in 1929 that Allis-Chalmers had taken good advantage of Ford's withdrawal from tractor production in the United States. Having stepped in at the "psychological moment," the newspaper enthused, Milwaukee had "assured itself of being the tractor center of the nation."[40]

Assessing the importance of the Allis-Chalmers tractor division requires more than an examination of sales figures. In fact, while tractors accounted for increasing percentages of company profits, Allis-Chalmers continued to rank below International Harvester, John Deere, and J. I. Case in its share of the total farm machinery market. Yet in becoming a full-line producer of agricultural implements, Allis-Chalmers managed to avoid a fragmentation of effort. While taking advantage of opportunities in diversification, the company never sacrificed overall corporate objectives.[41]

With improvements in internal combustion tractors generally, and with the development of small tractors in particular, came important changes in the designing of other agricultural implements. For Wisconsin implement manufacturers, the most important new machine after the tractor was a harvester that farmers could use for a variety of crops. In 1930, Allis-Chalmers bought rights to a small combine manufactured in California. A year later, the company purchased the financially troubled Advance-Rumely Corporation of La Porte, Indiana, long a producer of harvesting and threshing machinery. After painstaking experimentation, Allis-Chalmers finally produced the All-Crop harvester. A small combine well-suited to cornbelt agriculture, the innovative implement was capable of harvesting "everything from bird seed to beans," as one enthu-

[40] *Ibid.*, 247–250; "Allis-Chalmers: America's Krupp," in *Fortune*, May, 1939, pp. 53–58, 148–150; "Life and Death of Harry Merritt: An Industrial Leader," in *Implement & Tractor*, December 4, 1943, pp. 30, 59, and "A Tribute to H. C. Merritt," in *Farm Implement News*, August 29, 1935, pp. 40–42, both in the Center for Research Libraries, Chicago; Robert C. Williams, *Fordson, Farmall, and Poppin' Johnny: A History of the Farm Tractor and Its Impact on America* (Urbana, 1987), 92–93; Michael Williams, *Great Tractors* (Poole, Dorset, United Kingdom, 1982), 74–75; Milwaukee *Sentinel*, March 14, 1929.

[41] *House Documents*, 75 Cong., 3 sess., no. 702 (serial 10261), Federal Trade Commission, *Report on the Agricultural Implement and Machinery Industry. Part I: Concentration and Competitive Methods* (1938), 124–126, 150–153.

siast put it, and Allis-Chalmers implement sales rose dramatically. In 1935 the company gained 14 per cent of the market in combines, and in 1936 its share skyrocketed to more than 45 per cent. Allis-Chalmers' leadership, diversity of operations, and emphasis on research were to assure the company's survival during the hard times of the Great Depression.[42]

* * *

In the meantime, during the New Era when few people anticipated the economic calamities of the 1930's, concerned citizens had reason to be anxious about trends in Wisconsin agriculture. The University of Wisconsin College of Agriculture had long emphasized the importance of efficient farming, and the mechanization of operations greatly increased productive capabilities on farms of the state. Yet the emphasis on production met resistance, especially during the recession of 1920–1921. Many rural people believed that in urging farmers towards greater production, the College of Agriculture and the Extension Service were in reality performing an economic disservice. To increase yields and output, ran the argument, was to ensure lower prices for agricultural products. At the same time, the costs of production increased in direct proportion to the growing sophistication of the agricultural system.

In the view of many farmers, the real beneficiaries of the new mechanized and scientific agriculture were the manufacturers of agricultural implements and business interests generally. It was those interests that set high prices for what farmers had to buy while allowing increased production to drive down the prices of agricultural commodities. "We have built up in this country an artificial business structure which throttles the natural law of supply and demand," was Robert La Follette's way of putting the case for the farmer in 1923. The price of steel, of cloth, of virtually all manufactured goods was fixed by a few private interests, but "conservatives, so called, have nothing to say about that." The senator thought that only when confronted with a proposal to fix agricultural prices in order to "save from destruction the great agricultural industry, upon which the country is absolutely dependent" did the profiteering interests "throw up their hands in terror."[43]

[42] *Ibid.*, 124–126, 150–153, 180–182; Peterson, *Industrial Heritage*, 257, 266–270; Williams, *Fordson, Farmall, and Poppin' Johnny*, 94–96.

[43] Baltimore *Sun*, July 28, 1923, cited in Saloutos and Hicks, *Agricultural Discontent*, 367.

Resistance to "profiteering" by industrialists at the expense of agriculture gave rise to various plans for improving the economic position of farmers. One reason for the great popularity of the co-operative movement in the years before World War I was that it provided a means by which farmers could gain at least some control over markets. Improving agricultural prices through legislation also seemed an attractive possibility to some Wisconsin farmers, particularly grain growers, during the 1920's. In 1924, Senator Charles McNary of Oregon and Representative Gilbert N. Haugen of Iowa first introduced a bill embodying a plan developed by George N. Peek and Hugh Johnson, executives of the Moline Plow Company. To restore farm prosperity, Peek and Johnson proposed eliminating agricultural surpluses from the domestic market and dumping them abroad at world prices. Losses encountered from foreign sales were to be shared by producers through an "equalization fee." The plan was to be administered by a government corporation in a manner that would assure parity for agriculture as compared with other industries.[44]

Although the proposal won the support of Secretary of Agriculture Henry C. Wallace and was popular among farmers of the Upper Middle West, the McNary-Haugen Bill met defeat in the House. Proponents of parity for farmers did not give up. Similar bills were defeated in 1925 and 1926, but with changes in the language of yet another bill, Congress finally passed it in 1927. President Calvin Coolidge vetoed the legislation because he thought it would be difficult to administer, and in any case he believed its equalization fee to be unconstitutional. He also argued that allowing the measure to stand would be to benefit grain farmers at the expense of dairy farmers and producers of products other than grains. With another revision intended to meet Coolidge's objections, the bill passed again in March, 1928. Coolidge was not impressed. Again he vetoed the bill, bringing to an end the pre-New Deal effort to achieve equality for agriculture by means of congressional legislation.[45]

[44] Excerpts from George N. Peek and Hugh S. Johnson, *Equality for Agriculture* (Moline, 1922), 5–7, 11, 14–19, 22–25, 27–31, 37, 40, reprinted in Wayne D. Rasmussen, ed., *Readings in the History of American Agriculture* (Urbana, 1960), 227–239; Gilbert C. Fite, *George N. Peek and the Fight for Farm Parity* (Norman, 1954), 59–63; Saloutos and Hicks, *Agricultural Discontent*, 380–383; Willard W. Cochrane, *The Development of American Agriculture: A Historical Analysis* (Minneapolis, 1979), 118–119.

[45] Saloutos and Hicks, *Agricultural Discontent*, 373–403; Fite, *George N. Peek*, 93, 173–180, 190–196.

Wisconsin farmers were never as enthusiastic about the McNary-Haugen program as were farmers of the Northern Plains. In October, 1923, Secretary Wallace sent Henry C. Taylor out from Washington to sample rural opinion of the Peek-Johnson proposal. The founder of agricultural economics at the University of Wisconsin, and a professor there before going into government service, Taylor stopped in Madison to visit old friends. He was struck by the relative prosperity of dairy farmers, which he thought explained their lack of interest in plans to aid agriculture by legislative action. Taylor supported the McNary-Haugen Bill, but Benjamin H. Hibbard, his successor as chairman of the department of agricultural economics, thought it an "ill-conceived preposterous bill." It did not meet equally the needs of all farmers and was therefore "woefully inadequate to fit the complexities of the market." Favoring growers of a few crops, argued Hibbard, would lead other producers to demand similar treatment. In the end, the government itself would become the country's principal dealer in agricultural commodities.[46]

Although Wisconsin farmers were eager to improve their economic position and obtain better prices for their products, their experience had taught them to be skeptical of an artificial stimulation of prices. The inflation of 1919–1920 had led some farmers to speculate in land and to increase the size of their operations. Then, when prices collapsed, limited access to further capital and credit prevented their buying the machinery that would permit more intensive cultivation.[47]

The agricultural dilemma of the 1920's was frustrating, and in the end perhaps insoluble. Yet to farmers who detected few benefits for themselves in the McNary-Haugen Bill, marketing co-operatives seemed a better remedy for their economic ills than price-fixing. And to some of them, extending mechanization to marketing as well as production offered greater possibilities for achieving their

[46] Fite, *George N. Peek*, 56–57, 197–198.

[47] John J. Blaine to John D. Jones, January 27, 1926, in the Blaine Papers; *Wisconsin Agriculturist*, May 5, 1923, p. 18; Benjamin H. Hibbard and Guy A. Peterson, *How Wisconsin Farmers Become Farm Owners*, UW Agricultural Experiment Station, *Bulletin*, no. 402 (1928), 34–35; *Wisconsin Farmer*, 49 (April 1, 1920), 699; "Farm Mortgage Debt in the United States and Wisconsin," table compiled by Irene Appuhn, July, 1934, in the LRB; *University of North Carolina News Letter*, February 8, 1928, in the LRB; Oswald H. Brownlee, "State Farm Credit in Wisconsin" (master's thesis, University of Wisconsin, 1939), 2–4; F. M. White, "The Tractor Is Here," in *Wisconsin Country Magazine*, 10 (October, 1915), 13–16; Robert E. Ankli, "Horses vs. Tractors on the Corn Belt," in *Agricultural History*, 54 (January, 1980), 141–147.

objectives than did legislative tinkering. Ever since the Granger protests of the nineteenth century, farmers had believed that they were victims of the railroad companies' manipulation of railroad rates. Acting upon Governor Robert La Follette's recommendations, the state legislature had created the Railroad Commission of Wisconsin in 1905. While touted as a measure that would prevent the gouging of shippers by carriers, however, the effect on rates was negligible. Now at last the technological advance that produced the internal combustion engine had given farmers an alternative to the railroads. By using trucks to transport their products, farmers could gain greater flexibility in marketing and add to the effectiveness of farmer co-operatives. It was neither the first nor the last time that technological innovation appeared to provide at least a partial solution to a problem exacerbated by technology.[48]

"The day is not far distant, in my opinion," predicted the editor of the *Wisconsin Farmer* in 1916, "when the truck and the tractor will be as popular and as prevelant [*sic*] in the country as the automobile is today." Because the motor truck brought a saving of time, it permitted the marketing of produce when it was fresh. It also freed farmers from the necessity of selling at established points along railroad lines. Having a choice, they could sell where prices were highest. Given the development of motor vehicles for hauling, the time when trucks would become indispensable to farmers, as well as popular with them, was rapidly approaching. Meanwhile, the war crisis created the conditions for a dramatic demonstration of the motor truck's utility. To relieve the wartime burden on railroads, convoys of fully loaded trucks were driven from midwestern factories to eastern seaports for shipment to France. Trucks proved their value on the home front as well. The Bureau of Markets in the U.S. Department of Agriculture established a route from rural New Jersey to New York City, and trucks traveled it regularly, picking up eggs from producers and delivering them directly to wholesalers in the metropolis.[49]

[48] Stanley P. Caine, *The Myth of a Progressive Reform: Railroad Regulation in Wisconsin, 1903–1910* (Madison, 1970), 199–201; U.S. Department of Agriculture, *Yearbook of Agriculture, 1960*, p. 303; John B. Rae, *The Road and the Car in American Life* (Cambridge, 1971), 157.

[49] *Wisconsin Farmer*, 45 (July 13, 1916), 899; Rae, *The Road and the Car*, 38; Rae, *The American Automobile*, 71; John B. Rae, "The Internal-Combustion Engine on Wheels," in Kranzberg and Pursell, eds., *Technology in Western Civilization. Volume II*, 129; Benjamin H. Hibbard, *Effects of the Great War upon Agriculture in the United States and Great Britain* (New York, 1919), 96–97.

With the return to peacetime conditions, the *Wisconsin Farmer* welcomed the arrival of "a new helper—the motor truck." Especially useful in hauling livestock, trucks were also proving themselves of great value in milk collection. A farmer might own and operate his own truck, perhaps in partnership with his neighbors. He might also use either a local drayage company that served farmers or one of the trucking lines established after the war for hauling freight to the leading market towns of midwestern agricultural states. Farmers who owned trucks sometimes earned extra income by hauling for their neighbors. Percy Stacey collected about thirty-six cans of milk a day from farmers near Palmyra in Jefferson County. William Arndt, living near Milwaukee, used a two-ton truck for a variety of activities in addition to hauling milk, wood, and grain for himself and other farmers. He reported that his truck served satisfactorily in the field both as a tractor and as a fertilizer spreader. He also sometimes jacked up a rear wheel and used it to run his pump or his grindstone. A. K. Bassett of Baraboo considered his truck a "very necessary adjunct to his farm." He hauled fruit, hogs, and heifers to town, and returned with feed, cement, and other supplies. During the summer he could carry as many as eighteen passengers to family reunions, picnics, and fishing parties.[50]

* * *

Most of the trucks built before the war were used for service and delivery in cities. Because they carried heavier loads, they were far more difficult to operate on country lanes than were passenger cars. Crude and clumsy, they ran on solid tires, and the consequences for both vehicles and roads were ruinous. Clearly, the wartime experience with truck transportation demonstrated the need for improved highways as well as the need for improved trucks. Indeed, by 1918 H. E. Zimmerman, editor of the Burlington *Standard-Democrat*, believed that building better roadways had already become a matter of first importance. New trucks produced for city hauling could carry twenty tons, and "no country road can be made serviceable very long under such traffic." Writing to E. A. Ross shortly before the Armistice, the executive secretary of the Wisconsin Good Roads Association, F. A. Cannon, remarked that "never before was the importance of the highway so brought home as at present."

[50] *Wisconsin Farmer*, 48 (April 24, 1919), 625, 629, 643.

Suggesting that railroad building after the Civil War provided a model, he believed that "highway improvement will be one of the big public efforts after this war."[51]

The postwar period, then, was one of vigorous campaigning for highway improvement, and the arguments for new road construction gave special emphasis to the welfare of farmers. The Burlington *Standard-Democrat* reiterated earlier contentions, pointing out in 1919 that better roads would enable farmers to haul twice the number of loads per day, deliver their products in better condition, use less gasoline, provide children with better schooling, improve social conditions, and keep boys and girls on the farm. But others, too, would benefit. The Bonduel *Times* suggested, for example, that highway building was invaluable as a reconstruction program because it would provide jobs for returning soldiers. Contractors, industrialists, and bankers were all keenly aware of the advantages to be gained from a major new road-building effort. "The automobile owners and the farmers are strongly behind it," asserted *Business and Financial Comment* early in 1921. "Road construction and the increased use of automobiles go hand in hand and help each other. If conditions are made right, therefore, the probability of the expansion of road building will afford a good outlet for industrial activity this year."[52]

The postwar enthusiasm for improved highways was not a new phenomenon, for as early as 1880 the League of American Wheelmen had begun a campaign for better roads to accommodate bicyclists. In 1895 the Wheelmen's efforts in Milwaukee produced the Wisconsin League for Good Roads, and in 1901 the legislature authorized county construction of bicycle side paths along public roads and streets. The efforts of bicyclists anticipated a much stronger movement for good roads that came with the increased use of automobiles. Because the Wisconsin constitution prohibited bonding for internal improvements by the state, a necessary first step in the development of a highway program was a constitutional amendment. In 1905, and again in 1907, the legislature passed a

[51] Rae, *The Road and the Car*, 110; U.S. Department of Agriculture, *Yearbook of Agriculture, 1960*, p. 302; Burlington *Standard-Democrat*, August 9, 1918; F. A. Cannon to E. A. Ross, October 1, 1918, in the Edward A. Ross Papers.

[52] Burlington *Standard-Democrat*, September 5, 1919; Bonduel *Times*, March 6, 1919; *Business and Financial Comment*, January 15, 1921, in the Milwaukee Public Library; Wisconsin Bankers' Association, *Proceedings*, 1916, pp. 203–204.

resolution to permit appropriations for the construction and maintenance of public highways; in the 1908 general election voters approved the amendment by vote of more than two to one. Two highway laws, also enacted in 1907, required that counties of the state help meet the cost of public roads. In 1911, the legislature passed an act known as the State Aid Road Law, which provided for the co-operative development of highways by state, county, and town governments. At the same time, it created the State Highway Commission with supervisory powers and authority over all highway construction undertaken with state assistance. The state aid legislation, with periodic revisions, remained in effect until 1925.[53]

The five years after passage of the State Aid Road Law were years of rapid development of the highway system as more than 5,000 miles of roadway were improved and as the number of motor vehicles registered in Wisconsin increased to nearly 125,000. In 1916, Congress moved to provide assistance to the states. The Federal Aid Road Act, a landmark in the formation of American highway policy, appropriated $75 million for a five-year road-building program placed under the general supervision of the secretary of agriculture. The act stipulated that states were to match federal expenditures, and Wisconsin's share of the appropriation came to $1,913,205.[54]

While supporters of the Federal Aid Road Act pointed out that better roads served the national interest, Congress provided no clear indication of what sort of highway system it hoped to encourage. Opinions were divided throughout the country as well as within the Congress. On the one hand, the nation's railroads recognized the competitive implications of an interstate system, and they lobbied for secondary or farm-to-market roads as a matter of self-preservation. On the other hand, a vocal group of good roads advocates in the cities was fond of pointing out that the only way to build roads was to build them from somewhere to somewhere,

[53] *Laws of Wisconsin*, 1901, pp. 422–426 (Chapter 308); *ibid.*, 1907, pp. 1120–1121 (Chapter 487), 1171–1172 (Chapter 552); *ibid.*, 1911, pp. 353–368 (Chapter 337); M. W. Torkelson, "Wisconsin Highways," in the *Wisconsin Blue Book, 1931*, pp. 10–11; M. W. Torkelson, "State Highway Commission," *ibid., 1923*, p. 178; Ballard Campbell, "The Good Roads Movement in Wisconsin, 1890–1911," in *WMH*, 49 (Summer, 1966), 273–293; *Wisconsin Highway Development*, 21, 24.

[54] *Wisconsin Highway Development*, 77–78; Torkelson, "Wisconsin Highways," *Wisconsin Blue Book, 1931*, p. 13; Torkelson, "State Highway Commission," *ibid., 1923*, p. 181; Rae, *The Road and the Car*, 36–37.

and that urban needs were best served by trunk highways. For their part, farmers wanted a well-developed system of secondary roads, though many of them were uneasy about continued railroad domination of their markets.[55]

Secretary of Agriculture David F. Houston believed that in the allocation of federal funds, farm-to-market roads should receive first consideration. "The roads which the Nation most needs to have improved," he testified before the House committee on roads, "are those that lead from the farm to the nearest railway station." The question of whether improvements were to be made on secondary roads or on trunk highways remained unresolved, however, because the United States entered the Great War before the Federal Aid Road Act could become fully effective. Wartime demands discouraged extensive highway construction, of course, but those very demands demonstrated the importance of a national road system. Logistical problems prevented the efficient delivery of war materiel to American seaports for shipment to Europe, and the difficulties of transporting munitions and supplies added credibility to the argument that the nation's defense depended on a logically planned and well constructed system of national highways, interstate in character.[56]

In the meantime, while railway freight trains and gasoline-powered truck convoys were crawling laboriously towards eastern seaports in 1917–1918, the Wisconsin legislature took a careful look at the state's transportation system with a view towards inaugurating a new network of highways after the war. In 1917, it passed legislation directing the State Highway Commission to plan a trunk system that would interconnect every county seat and every city with a population of 5,000 or more. Following that mandate, the highway commission held public hearings, mapped tentative routes, and on May Day, 1918, took over supervision of 5,000 miles of highway. The State Trunk Highway System so established pene-

[55] Charles L. Dearing, *American Highway Policy* (Brookings Institution, Institute of Economics, *Publication*, no. 88, Washington, 1941), 80–82; Rae, *The Road and the Car*, 36–37; Bloomington *Record*, January 14, 1920; Don S. Kirschner, *City and Country: Rural Responses to Urbanization in the 1920s* (Westport, Connecticut, 1970), 184–186; Saloutos and Hicks, *Agricultural Discontent*, 366.

[56] U.S. House, Roads Committee, *Hearings on Good Roads, December 22, 1913* [statement of David F. Houston], 63 Cong., 2 sess. (1914), part 2, p. 4, as quoted in Dearing, *American Highway Policy*, 261 (see also p. 82); Rae, *The Road and the Car*, 38–39; *United States Statutes at Large*, 42, part 1, p. 212; Frederic L. Paxson, "The Highway Movement, 1916–1935," in the *American Historical Review*, 51 (January, 1946), 245–246.

trated every county and linked 728 of 1,242 towns, 120 of 125 cities, and 157 of 253 incorporated villages. In 1919 the highway commission added another 2,500 miles, and subsequent additions expanded the state trunk and federal aid system to more than 10,000 miles by 1926. In addition to this, there were more than 11,000 miles of county trunk roads, nearly 57,000 miles of roadway that were the direct responsibility of town boards, and nearly 6,000 miles of city and village streets. By 1930, according to the estimate of state highway engineer Martin W. Torkelson, Wisconsin could claim 81,275 miles of roads and highways.[57]

Torkelson's figures indicate that Wisconsin had only 3,660 miles of concrete pavement or its equivalent at the end of the 1920's, and that some 50,000 miles of rural roads remained unsurfaced. It would be a mistake to conclude, however, that dirt roads of the state were little more than cow paths. During the early years of highway construction, the chief problem confronting engineers was the problem of drainage. Roads often flooded during wet seasons, and until adequate control structures could be built, money spent on surfacing would literally have been money drained away. From 1912 to 1917, therefore, the highway commission inspected or installed 2,332 drainage structures before proceeding with grading and surfacing. The abundance of mineral aggregate deposits throughout the state gave Wisconsin an advantage in highway improvement, and between 1912 and 1930, gravel and crushed stone were spread on 28,500 miles of graded roadways.[58]

Although concrete surfacing came much more gradually, the 1920's was a decade of important experimentation in highway design. With its long winters of subfreezing temperatures, together with a substantial amount of melt water from snowfall, Wisconsin presented difficult problems for builders of concrete highways. Frost action, involving freezes and boils, caused loss of bearing power in some soils, and unstable subgrade conditions led to cracking and road damage. The first concrete surfacing of a rural high-

[57] *Wisconsin Highway Development*, 41–43, 46; A. R. Hirst, "Underlying Principles Controlling the Laying Out, Marking and Maintaining of a State Highway Trunk System," in State Highway Commission, *Biennial Report*, 1918, pp. 45–60; Torkelson, "Wisconsin Highways," *Wisconsin Blue Book, 1931*, p. 24. Because the Wisconsin road system overlapped, the sum of mileage in the various categories is greater than the total actual road mileage in the state.

[58] Torkelson, "Wisconsin Highways," *Wisconsin Blue Book, 1931*, p. 24; *Wisconsin Highway Development*, 159.

way in Wisconsin was completed in 1913 on Blue Mound Road in Milwaukee County, and during the next four years a total of 267 miles of similar roadway were constructed in different portions of the state. Varying in width from nine to eighteen feet, the early concrete highways had a thickness of 8 inches at the center and 6½ inches at the edges on a level subgrade. None of this concrete surfacing proved satisfactory, however, and the highway commission continued to experiment with the design. Fortunately, other states were also grappling with the problem, and in the postwar years the Illinois Division of Highways came up with a solution. On an experimental road at Bates, Illinois, engineers found that by thickening the pavement edges rather than the center, and by introducing both a central longitudinal joint and transverse expansion joints, they could greatly reduce cracking from freezes and thaws. From 1926 until after World War II, therefore, nearly all concrete surfacing in Wisconsin followed the Bates pattern. Concrete roads were built twenty feet wide with a cross section of 6½ inches at the center and extending down to 9 inches at the edges.[59]

Such highways, believed residents of Wisconsin, could bring benefits to every community they reached. Village merchants, taking advantage of lower transportation costs, anticipated competing successfully with mail-order houses. Farmers thought that their marketing alternatives might well increase in direct proportion to highway mileage if they could secure easy access to the new roads. Even northern Wisconsin could gain new opportunities. Its timber had been cut, but its lakes remained and they were filled with game fish. Towns in what had once been the North Woods began to advertise themselves as tourist and recreation havens. With the new highways they looked forward to attracting jaded city folk in search of restful vacations. With all the advantages they offered, the new highways were as eagerly sought as railroads had been in the nineteenth century. Aware of the bitterness that had accompanied route selection by railroads, however, legislators and highway commissioners exercised great care to avoid charges of favoritism. The Federal Highway Act of 1921 required that not more than 60 per cent of the federal assistance be allocated by states to primary roads. The State Highway Commission decided to use most of Wisconsin's

[59] *Wisconsin Highway Development*, 159–162; *Concrete Highway Magazine*, 7 (April, 1923), 79–81, in the Center for Research Libraries, Chicago; M. W. Torkelson, "State Highway Commission," *Wisconsin Blue Book, 1927*, pp. 151–152.

primary road allotment for the State Trunk Highway System, which had been thoughtfully planned to serve as many counties, and as many interests, as possible. In 1924, after painstaking investigations and hearings, the commission secured approval from the secretary of agriculture for a layout that included 2,364 miles of primary and 3,152 miles of secondary federal aid highways.[60]

Despite efforts to maintain an even-handed impartiality, controversies did arise. Quarreling and bitterness developed because however statesmanlike the planning, hard choices were unavoidable, particularly in matters of timing and taxation. Proceeding simultaneously with construction in all portions of the state was obviously a physical impossibility; roads in some sections had to be completed before roads in other sections could be started. Many experts advocated concentrating first on the improvement of highways in southeastern Wisconsin, where an existing network provided a base on which to build. Nevertheless, residents of isolated counties resented the early advantages gained by residents of counties lying closer to the Milwaukee-Chicago metropolitan region. Southeastern Wisconsin was already the richest, most densely populated and agriculturally productive portion of the state, and giving more to those who already had much inevitably drew criticism from outlying areas.[61]

Controversy also arose over how to raise the funds necessary to pay for new roads. Until 1925, the main sources of revenue for highways were general property taxes, motor vehicle license fees, proceeds from county bond sales, and appropriations from the state general fund. Farmers of Wisconsin, like those of other states, vehemently opposed taxing rural property in order that city folk might take to the road for "joy rides" with no purposes beyond recreation. State legislators with farm constituencies had already expressed

[60] *Kickapoo Scout* (Soldiers Grove), April 5, 1923; *Taylor County Star News* (Medford), February 14, 1924; *Pierce County Herald* (Ellsworth), April 12, 1923, February 18, 1926; Rhinelander *New North*, December 23, 1926, April 12, 1928; *Wisconsin Highway Development*, 77–79; Torkelson, "Wisconsin Highways," *Wisconsin Blue Book, 1931*, p. 14. Calvin Coolidge helped to publicize the advantages of northern Wisconsin as a resort area when he vacationed on the Brule River in 1928. He not only found there "a privacy which he was unable to enjoy in the Black Hills," but he also had "very good luck fishing, and has landed some beautiful trout." Iron River *Pioneer*, July 12, 1928. That same summer, the Bonduel *Times* (July 5, 1928) noted that in 1927, more than 11,000 people had entered the state by car every day during the tourist season (a total of 4 million or so), spending a total of $124,152,505.

[61] Torkelson, "State Highway Commission," *Wisconsin Blue Book, 1927*, pp. 149–151.

their scorn for property taxes back in 1915 when they had forced a reduction in the annual appropriation for highway construction. Ten years later they still objected to using property taxes for highway construction. Yet by that time an innovative way to raise the money by taxing gasoline at the pump had been tried successfully in several states, and farmers now agitated for adoption of the new tax in Wisconsin.[62]

Oregon had begun levying gasoline taxes in 1919, and the idea gained enormous popularity in rural regions across the country. Farmers favored the measure because it shifted the highway tax burden from property owners to highway users. In other words, it shifted highway taxation from the farm to the city, for city dwellers owned most of the cars and did most of the driving. The Wisconsin legislature approved a gasoline tax in 1923, only to have Governor Blaine veto the bill. In 1925, however, legislators passed a law that completely repealed existing highway revenue regulations and levied a tax of two cents per gallon on all motor vehicle fuel sold or used in the state. Proceeds from the tax were combined with motor vehicle registration fees and federal aid allotments to form a single fund officially known as the State Highway Fund.[63]

Rural counties were pleased with the highway law of 1925, but they began almost immediately to campaign for an increase in the gasoline tax. The Taylor County Board, for example, noted that within ten years farm values had depreciated while taxes on real estate had doubled and in some cases trebled. It therefore passed a resolution petitioning the state legislature to increase the gasoline tax to five cents a gallon and to prohibit using real estate taxes for highway improvement. The State Highway Commission responded to such requests by announcing plans for a new ten-year construction program and recommending an increase in the gasoline tax to pay for it. In 1931, the legislature finally agreed that an increase was in order, and the highway act of that year set the tax at four cents a gallon. Rural counties had won an important victory. The four-cent gasoline tax became, as state treasurer Robert K. Henry

[62] *Wisconsin Highway Development*, 130; Kirschner, *City and Country*, 185–201; Torkelson, "State Highway Commission," *Wisconsin Blue Book, 1923*, pp. 179–180.

[63] Carl Solberg, *Oil Power* (New York, 1976), 110–111; Torkelson, "State Highway Commission," *Wisconsin Blue Book, 1927*, pp. 139–142; Kirschner, *City and Country*, 184–186; *Laws of Wisconsin*, 1925, pp. 149–150 (Chapter 84); *Wisconsin Highway Development*, 37–38.

noted later, "the most productive of all state taxes." The legislature granted yet another favor to farmers in 1931 when it passed a licensing law for trucks. The fee for farm trucks with a gross weight of 1½ tons or less was set at five dollars, half the regular license fee for non-farm trucks of similar weight.[64]

Yet for all the consideration shown to farmers, 1931 was not a year of rejoicing in the Wisconsin countryside. Nor was it a year of rejoicing in towns and cities. The hard times of the Great Depression had arrived, and they brought sobering intimations of misfortunes yet to come. During the troubled thirties, a new congeries of symbols was to surround the nation's roads and highways. For a minority, highways were a means of moving on towards a new beginning, and vagabonds drifted about the country in search of jobs. For others down on their luck, roads and highways meant at least temporary employment as both state and federal governments turned to highway improvement in developing work relief programs. For yet others, especially for the farmers of Wisconsin, good roads continued to promise eventual prosperity. But they meant more than that. Good roads symbolized the tying mechanisms of community, the bonds that united citizens in a common effort to achieve the good society despite hazards and calamities of the modern world. Such, at least, was the message that agricultural extension service director Kirk Hatch delivered at a 1931 American Country Life Association conference in Madison. "Thinking men in every walk of life realize that a democracy like ours cannot well endure with a peasant type of people on the land," asserted Hatch. He then went on to ask rhetorically whether American farmers were becoming peasants because bad roads deprived them of social, educational, and economic opportunities, and he cited letters from farmers who, in writing on the subject, had unburdened their souls. Inadequate roads, he concluded, "eat up the return on the potato crop, force farmers to maintain and use two types of transportation for a single trip to town, keep the family away from neighborhood gatherings, the children away from school, and the mother away from the funeral of her own child!" Although Hatch's line of argument was sentimental and saccharine, his evidence was derived from Depression experiences so traumatic that they made hyperbole

[64] Taylor County Board, *Proceedings*, November 12, 1926, pp. 108–109; Burlington *Standard-Democrat*, November 16, 1928; *Wisconsin Highway Development*, 118; *Wisconsin Blue Book, 1933*, p. 277.

seem credible. It was not the first time an orator had exaggerated to make a point, but Hatch's rhetoric contrasted sharply with confident assertions of the prosperous twenties, when scientific and technological achievements held the promise of a happy future for everyone.[65]

[65] American Country Life Conference, *Proceedings*, 1930, p. 75.

5

Agriculture, Scientific Research, and the Dissemination of Knowledge

THE history of farming in Wisconsin is a record of adaptation to changing market conditions combined with innovation made possible by diligent experimentation and painstaking research. During the pioneer period most farmers raised wheat as their money crop, but the expansion of wheat growing into the trans-Mississippi West greatly increased the competition for Wisconsin farmers. In self-defense they gradually moved towards crop diversification and then to specialization in dairying. The transition, long and difficult as it proved to be, brought a few farm leaders to recognize the need for a more scientific approach towards agricultural activities in the state. Especially receptive to new ideas were members of the Wisconsin Dairymen's Association, founded in 1872.[1]

Yet the primary concerns of most farmers were economic ones, and, confident of their own agricultural skills, they sometimes resented the intrusion of scientists into their domain. Too much learning, they believed, could be a dangerous thing for practical farmers. Thus they did not immediately appreciate the advantages to be gained from the Morrill Act of 1862. The land grant secured by the University of Wisconsin as a result of that legislation provided the means for research and instruction in agricultural science, but it was several years before rural suspicion of "book farming" could be modified. A turning point came during the 1880's and early 1890's, when the regents of the university established the Agricultural Experiment Station and created the College of Agriculture.[2]

[1] Walter H. Ebling, "The Development of Agriculture in Wisconsin," in the *Wisconsin Blue Book, 1929*, pp. 63–65; Eric E. Lampard, *The Rise of the Dairy Industry in Wisconsin: A Study in Agricultural Change, 1820–1920* (Madison, 1963), 115–125; Richard N. Current, *The History of Wisconsin. Volume II: The Civil War Era, 1848–1873* (Madison, 1976), 462–463; Robert C. Nesbit, *Wisconsin: A History* (Madison, 1973), 280–283.

[2] Merle Curti and Vernon Carstensen, *The University of Wisconsin: A History, 1848–*

William A. Henry, who had received an appointment as professor of agriculture in 1880, became the first director of the station and the first dean of the college. Under his leadership, the College of Agriculture developed a program for students pursuing careers in agriculture, while the experiment station searched for scientific solutions to problems in the field. In 1885 the state legislature had approved the creation of a Department of Farmers' Institutes, through which farmers could listen to lectures by professors while remaining in their own communities. It had also approved a new form of study in agricultural subjects: the "Short Course" that later became famous in educating farmers and agriculturalists. Thus from its inception the College of Agriculture was organized to provide teaching, research, and the dissemination of information.[3]

* * *

Adept in dealing with mistrustful rural people, Dean Henry was equally skilled in dealing with his own faculty. A shrewd judge of their abilities, he encouraged research that helped to initiate a golden age for agriculture in the years before World War I. Franklin H. King, appointed in 1888 as the first American professor of agricultural physics, devoted several years to the study of soils and pioneered in the development of silos and barn ventilation. Horticulturist Emmett S. Goff specialized in fruit growing and in the improvement of tomatoes, potatoes, and strawberries. The most widely publicized work was that of Stephen M. Babcock, who devised a quick, easy test for determining the butterfat content of milk. Important as his test was for the emerging dairy industry of Wisconsin, Babcock made many other contributions. Working with Harry L. Russell and other collaborators, he aided in the development of a practical apparatus for pasteurizing milk and in techniques for the cold curing of cheese. Russell, an alumnus of the university who had studied at Robert Koch's institute in Berlin and at the Naples zoological station before completing his doctoral degree at the Johns Hopkins University, joined the faculty as a bac-

---

1925 (2 vols., Madison, 1949), 1:459ff, and 2:374–376; Madison *Capital Times*, January 1, 1927; Wilbur H. Glover, *Farm and College: The College of Agriculture at the University of Wisconsin, a History* (Madison, 1952), 89, 96–97, 111.

[3] Curti and Carstensen, *University of Wisconsin*, 1:467–475, and 2:395–398; E. L. Luther, "Institutes Still Aiding Wisconsin," in the *Wisconsin Agriculturist*, April 3, 1926; Ernest L. Luther, "Farmers' Institutes in Wisconsin, 1885–1933," in *WMH*, 30 (September, 1946), 60–61.

teriologist in 1893. Russell's involvement with pasteurization resulted from his important research on bovine tuberculosis. Henry himself wrote a classic study of feeds and feeding, and along with Babcock and others pursued the study of nutrition. In all, by the time Henry retired in January, 1907, the University of Wisconsin had taken a leading role in the national development of scientific agriculture.[4]

After spending three months in choosing a successor to Dean Henry, President Van Hise and the regents finally settled on Harry L. Russell. Despite some misgivings about his ability to win the support of farmers, they questioned neither his skill in scientific research nor his ability as an administrator. The son of a Poynette physician, Russell lacked practical farm experience, and he never did win the affection that farmers had shown his predecessor. Yet he fundamentally agreed with the direction taken by the College of Agriculture, and he accepted his new post convinced that his principal task was to promote basic agricultural research. His attitude was consistent with the progressive idea of using expert knowledge to resolve practical difficulties. "The ever pressing problem in the development of our agricultural colleges," he wrote in his first report as dean, "is how to correlate the three main lines of agricultural effort, research, teaching at the college, and extension work. . . ." A year later he reaffirmed his belief that the college should "rest on a three-legged foundation—research work of the Experiment Station, teaching work of the College here at Madison, and the extension work throughout the state."[5]

While Russell repeatedly demonstrated his concern for practical application of research, and while he busied himself with the details of academic administration, his primary interest was in theoretical investigations. The fields he most wished to develop were in plant pathology, genetics, entomology, and veterinary science. The first step in building and strengthening those areas was the recruitment

[4] Curti and Carstensen, *University of Wisconsin*, 2:376–378, 384–395; Glover, *Farm and College*, 133–148; Paul de Kruif, *Hunger Fighters* (New York, 1928), 278–280; Edward H. Beardsley, *Harry L. Russell and Agricultural Science in Wisconsin* (Madison, 1969), 5–11, 16, 19, 25–34, 64; Chris L. Christensen, *Wisconsin—Then and Now, 1836–1936: Its Contribution to the Nation's Agriculture*, UW Agricultural Extension Service, *Stencil Circular*, no. 180 (1936), 3.

[5] UW Board of Regents, *Biennial Report*, 1907–1908, p. 123; Russell to Kirk L. Hatch, March 8, 1909, cited in Curti and Carstensen, *University of Wisconsin*, 2:580–581; Glover, *Farm and College*, 216; Beardsley, *Harry L. Russell*, 64, 83.

of qualified scholars; the second involved persuading university officials that the College of Agriculture was the proper place for researchers working to broaden the theoretical foundations of scientific investigation. Much of what passed for science in the United States was still largely empirical and directed towards the solution of practical problems. Scholars with solid grounding in theoretical research were few in number and eagerly sought by other universities. Yet competing with other universities was only a part of the problem Russell faced. A sizable number of administrators and faculty members within the University of Wisconsin agreed with most practical farmers that theoretical research properly belonged in the College of Letters and Science. They tended to regard the dean of the College of Agriculture as an empire builder, and they viewed his actions with the skepticism that university faculties usually reserve for that breed.[6]

To a remarkable degree, however, Russell succeeded in achieving his objectives inside the university. Within two years he had assembled a distinguished group of new faculty members. Lewis Ralph Jones, a respected pathologist, came from Vermont Agricultural College, where he had built a major research center for the study of plant diseases. J. G. Sanders, a young entomologist working in the United States Department of Agriculture, came to head the program in economic entomology. From Yale, Russell recruited Leon J. Cole, a geneticist who was to undertake a detailed study of inheritance in cattle through a series of experiments in cross-breeding. For research in veterinary science, there was F. B. Hadley, who had been specializing in anatomy and pathology at Ohio State University. Through such appointments, activities in the College of Agriculture took on a new vitality. At times a harsh taskmaster, Russell exerted constant pressure to secure results that might contribute to better understanding of scientific theory and scientific principles. The dean's fundamental assumption was that the interests of Wisconsin farmers were better served by basic research than by empirical solutions to immediate problems. In other words, he thought genetic principles more important than stockbreeders' prizes, and an understanding of plant pathology more important than trial-and-error treatment of diseases in plants.[7]

[6] Beardsley, *Harry L. Russell*, 73–74.

[7] *Ibid.*, 70–73; Curti and Carstensen, *University of Wisconsin*, 2:408–410; Glover, *Farm and College*, 306, 313, 323.

Russell's emphasis on theoretical research by no means blinded him to the need for making the applications of that research available to farmers. The agricultural extension program had suffered from inadequate budgets, and even when the legislature funded a new General Extension Division of the University of Wisconsin in 1907, its budget did not include agricultural extension. When Russell succeeded Henry as dean, he knew that he needed an extension program if he was to receive support for the college. Accordingly, he searched for someone who might take over the administration of extension work. In Kirk L. Hatch, principal of the Winnebago County Agricultural School at Winneconne, Russell found his man. Hatch's enthusiasm, organizing skills, and popularity with farmers made him an excellent choice. With a director of the extension service appointed, Russell obtained a special legislative appropriation of $60,000 for 1909–1910, and the extension work gathered momentum.[8]

Hatch and Russell began enlivening the program by promoting a traveling farmers' course, an idea first tried by the Kansas Agricultural College shortly after the Civil War. With support from railroads of the state, trains loaded with produce, livestock, and machinery were sent out to display the achievements of scientific agriculture. Academic departments also became involved in extension work as they set up demonstration plots on the farms of state and county asylums. In 1911 Russell won approval for state support of the county agent system, adapted from the recent experience of other states. Agents were to teach courses during the winter, demonstrate the latest agricultural practices during the summer, and consult with farmers whenever they were requested to do so. Proceeding cautiously with the county agent system, Russell and Hatch approached the state legislature with a bill to make the agents a permanent feature of the university's extension activities. Passed in 1913, the law provided that both the university and the county should contribute towards an agent's salary and other expenses. The system received additional support in 1914 when Congress passed the Smith-Lever Act, which made funds available for county agents and agricultural extension work if the states would agree to match federal expenditures. Having testified before congressional committees, and having worked within the Association of American

[8] Beardsley, *Harry L. Russell*, 85–86.

Agricultural Colleges and Experiment Stations to win approval for the bill, Russell could claim some credit for passage of the act.[9]

Although Russell was always eager to obtain whatever financial support he could for the extension program as well as for research in the College of Agriculture, he scrupulously rejected grants or gifts if they came with strings attached. In 1912 he refused to associate himself with a proposal from the Council of Grain Exchanges, a national association of agricultural suppliers and businessmen. When council representative Bert Ball promised to underwrite the state's county agent program, Russell suspected that the proposal involved exploitation, not philanthropy, and he spurned the offer. On the other hand, the dean approved of assistance from private groups if it did not mean serving those groups at the expense of either the farmers or the university. He had no qualms about a close association that developed between the College of Agriculture and the Wisconsin Bankers' Association (WBA), for example. Indeed, he detected a symbiotic relationship between farming and the financial institutions of the state: if farmers failed, banks would also fail.[10]

The bankers agreed with the dean's point of view, and for several years their association actively promoted scientific agriculture in Wisconsin. In 1913, J. Russell Wheeler, cashier of the Farmers and Merchants Union Bank of Columbus, served on the agriculture committee of the WBA and reported on its activities. Describing the organization's sponsorship of corn contests and agricultural fairs, along with the college bulletins made available through country banks, Wheeler emphasized that bankers were attempting not to teach agriculture but rather to bring scientific knowledge to the farmer. In 1916 the WBA held its annual convention in Madison, where experts from the College of Agriculture could demonstrate

[9] *Ibid.*, 103–109; Alfred C. True, *A History of Agricultural Education in the United States, 1785–1925*, U.S. Department of Agriculture, *Miscellaneous Publication*, no. 36 (1929), 288–289; Willard W. Cochrane, *The Development of American Agriculture: A Historical Analysis* (Minneapolis, 1979), 249–250; U.S. House, Agriculture Committee, *Hearings on H. 7951, Commonly Known as Lever Agricultural Extension Bill, September 23, 1913*, 62 Cong., 2 sess. (1913), 3–14; Andrew W. Hopkins, "Where the County Agent Came From," in the *Wisconsin Agriculturist*, January 7, 1922; *Taylor County Star News* (Medford), April 2, 1925.

[10] Beardsley, *Harry L. Russell*, 87; Russell to J. R. Wheeler, June 10, 1913, in General Subject Files, box 10, "Ag. Ext. Courses" folder, Series 9/1/1/5-1, Papers of Deans Henry and Russell, 1880–1930, College of Agriculture, UW Archives; Harry L. Russell, "Farm Problems of Readjustment," in the *Wisconsin Farmer*, June 24, 1920, p. 1149.

the benefits of good livestock and breeding practices. "In just fifteen to twenty years we could institute in every pasture in the state of Wisconsin a herd which is practically a pure bred herd," Professor A. S. Alexander told the bankers, going on to suggest that bankers would profit from such efforts. "The pure bred sire of Wisconsin is a bank-builder," he noted. "The scrub sire of the state is a bank-wrecker, and you should realize it more and impress the fact upon your clients." J. M. Smith, president of the WBA, conceded that "bankers may indirectly help themselves by aiding the farmers," but he also noted that "the general benefit of greater yields and attendant farm comforts are essentially a help to the whole community."[11]

After the American declaration of war in 1917, both farmers and bankers associated community welfare with victory for the Allies. And, as noted in Chapter 1, food as much as men and munitions became a vital resource. A Malthusian, Dean Russell had always believed that population was increasing more rapidly than were available food supplies, and he had therefore considered improved yields in food production to be the ultimate objective of American agriculture. During the war, the need for greater agricultural productivity was obvious enough to require no merely theoretical Malthusian arguments. At the same time, however, a farm crisis was in the making. The wheat harvest of 1917 was disappointing, and farmers began complaining that the Food Administration favored processors rather than producers.[12]

In Wisconsin, many agricultural leaders urged direct government intervention to provide crop subsidies and assure farmers a larger share in wartime prosperity. Yet such appeals brought from the Wilson administration only an administered price of $2.20 a bushel for wheat and a vigorous campaign to remind farmers of their patriotic duty. Russell, who had gone to Washington to work in the Food Administration as a representative of the Association of Agricultural Colleges, directed the agency's propaganda effort during the spring of 1918. His wartime activities, aimed at increasing ag-

[11] Wisconsin Bankers' Association, *Proceedings*, 1913, pp. 135–141; *ibid.*, 1914, pp. 64–65, 71; *ibid.*, 1916, pp. 94–95; UW Agricultural Experiment Station, *Annual Report*, 1915–1916, published as *Bulletin*, no. 275 (1917), p. 82.

[12] Beardsley, *Harry L. Russell*, 71, 85; UW Board of Regents, *Biennial Report*, 1909–1910, pp. 165–166; John T. Schlebecker and Andrew W. Hopkins, *A History of Dairy Journalism in the United States, 1810–1950* (Madison, 1957), 61–63, 82–84, 106–107, 147–148, 199–200, 222–223.

ricultural production, did little to endear him to Wisconsin farmers in the postwar period. Many a farmer was convinced that the depressed condition of agriculture in the 1920's could be attributed to low prices resulting from expanded production.[13]

While Wisconsin farmers fretted over troublesome economic problems, researchers in the College of Agriculture pursued basic research with a diligence that validated important scientific principles and brought some dramatic discoveries. In the new science of genetics, Leon J. Cole proceeded systematically after joining the faculty in 1910. Knowing that agricultural leaders were exercising common sense in advising farmers to "breed from the best," he also knew that Mendelian principles could be applied in various ways to improve the fundamental traits of cattle. A ten-year study begun in 1912 revealed not only that characteristics such as color and horns were inherited in predictable fashion, but also that cross-breeding could improve livestock. Crossing Holstein cows with Black Angus bulls, Cole produced strong animals that grew rapidly and were meatier than the calves of either breed in their ancestry.[14]

Accomplishments in the experimental breeding of animals were matched by studies of inheritance in plants. Plant breeders were concerned with finding varieties of grain and other crops to produce better yields; they were also involved in a search for strains that were resistant to disease. Ransom A. Moore, who had come to the College of Agriculture to develop the short course, was himself largely self-taught. But he had great determination, and though he received little encouragement from Dean Henry, he began a series of plant-breeding experiments in 1898. Ten years later, Benjamin D. Leith and Edmond J. Delwiche advanced beyond the simple mass breeding techniques of Moore with definite breeding experiments in northern Wisconsin. After working with isolated selections of wheat, Delwiche turned to crosses of selections. The result was a wheat that proved resistant to stem rust, which had hitherto destroyed much of the crop in the state.[15]

Association with the plant-breeding program also led Professor

[13] Beardsley, *Harry L. Russell*, 115–119; David M. Kennedy, *Over Here: The First World War and American Society* (New York, 1980), 119–120.

[14] Glover, *Farm and College*, 313; *Hoard's Dairyman*, 40 (December 24, 1909), 1389; *ibid.*, 41 (February 18, 1910), 80; *ibid.*, 43 (February 9, 1912), 54; Beardsley, *Harry L. Russell*, 147.

[15] Glover, *Farm and College*, 131–132, 204, 316–317.

Leith to work in hybridization, which held far more promise than simple selection. Although the development of hybrid corn was based on theoretical research elsewhere, the University of Wisconsin took part in the process through a broad-scale hybrid field corn program. Initiated in 1924 as a joint enterprise involving the departments of genetics, plant pathology, and agronomy, the program was to have a revolutionary effect on American agriculture by the time of World War II.[16]

Many of the investigations in the College of Agriculture were interdisciplinary and co-operative in character, and the results encouraged the development of teamwork among scientists. After the department of bacteriology had been transferred from the College of Letters and Science to the College of Agriculture, E. B. Fred carried on a study of soils begun in 1906 by Conrad Hoffman. Already well known for his examination of the way bacteria supplied oxygen compounds for plant use, Fred worked with W. H. Peterson, a biochemist, to isolate bacteria for the conversion of corn mash into organic acids. Fermentation chemistry had many commercial applications, and during the decade of the twenties the two scientists provided important technical advice to the chemical industry. Eventually, they were to expand their interests to include the industrial production of acetone and penicillin.[17]

In the years before World War II, the most exciting and best-known research in the College of Agriculture was a study of nutrition begun by Stephen M. Babcock and continued after 1907 by a team of collaborators including Edwin B. Hart, George C. Humphrey, Harry Steenbock, and E. V. McCollum. Babcock's early work on single-grain rations for cows, along with Dean Henry's investigation of feeds, suggested the existence of some unknown dietary factor that was important to growth if not necessary for life itself. Experiment followed experiment as the nutrition team patiently searched for the mysterious substance. At last McCollum isolated a complex of chemicals which he called "fat-soluble A," and which was found to control growth. Announcing his discovery in 1913, McCollum soon identified yet another component which he labeled "water-soluble B." As research proceeded, and as discoveries multiplied both in Europe and in the United States, the term "vitamin"

[16] Curti and Carstensen, *University of Wisconsin*, 2:418–419; A. Richard Crabb, *The Hybrid Corn-Makers: Prophets of Plenty* (New Brunswick, New Jersey, 1947), 199ff.

[17] Beardsley, *Harry L. Russell*, 147; Glover, *Farm and College*, 289.

came to be applied to the organic substances now proven essential for the growth and health of most animals.[18]

McCollum left Wisconsin in 1917 to join the faculty at the Johns Hopkins University, where he discovered vitamin D. Despite his departure, however, nutrition research continued at Wisconsin. Hart and Steenbock found an iodine deficiency to be the cause of goiter among sheep and hairlessness among pigs. Steenbock showed that white corn lacked the vitamin A content of yellow corn and warned farmers of hazards in a white corn diet. Working with James J. Halpin of the poultry husbandry department, Hart demonstrated that the leg weakness of some chickens was the result of insufficient vitamin D in the diet. Steenbock then moved towards an important insight. Having learned that European researchers were curing rickets with treatments of artificial sunlight, he tested the effects of ultraviolet radiation on rachitic rats. They recovered, but so did the rats of a control group that was not exposed. The reason for the astonishing recovery of the unexposed rats was that all rats were kept in the same cage, where they ran about over one another's droppings. In cleaning their feet, the confined but fastidious rats ate the excrement of their sunbathed brethren, and in this way they ingested the antirachitic property, vitamin D. Their restoration to health suggested to Steenbock the possibility of creating vitamin D in food by exposing it to radiation, an experiment that proved successful. The nutrition team further demonstrated that vitamin D made possible the absorption of calcium into the bones of animals, and the importance of vitamins in mineral and protein metabolism was thus established.[19]

By the time the College of Agriculture prepared to celebrate its thirtieth anniversary in 1919, Dean Russell could point with pride to many accomplishments. He also reiterated some of his old concerns. "More and more our work is partaking of a fundamental character, and one in which a better training of investigators is required for its prosecution," he noted in again emphasizing that the best training came with involvement in advanced research rather

[18] Curti and Carstensen, *University of Wisconsin*, 2:414; Glover, *Farm and College*, 301; de Kruif, *Hunger Fighters*, 284–297; Franklin C. Bing and Harry J. Prebluda, "E. V. McCollum: Pathfinder in Nutrition Investigations and World Agriculture," in *Agricultural History*, 54 (January, 1980), 157–159.

[19] Glover, *Farm and College*, 303; Beardsley, *Harry L. Russell*, 148; de Kruif, *Hunger Fighters*, 312–328.

than with acceptance of conventional wisdom. In 1921, when Wisconsin farmers were beginning to experience the pinch of hard times, he warned that "the agricultural college that permits itself to be . . . restricted in its development is ready for the educational junk heap." And in 1923, in recognition of the Experiment Station's fortieth year, he again summarized the achievements for which the College of Agriculture had become famous. Emphasizing the importance of basic research, he encapsulated his general approach to the riddles of Wisconsin agriculture in his comment that "the why of many a knotty problem is often more important than the how."[20]

* * *

Distinguished though its accomplishments were, the College of Agriculture was not immune to criticism. Leading the opponents of Dean Russell and the college was the Wisconsin Society of Equity. Founded by James A. Everett in Indiana in 1902, Equity had soon penetrated Wisconsin in the wheat-growing areas along the Mississippi River, gained a following among tobacco growers in the south-central portion of the state, and expanded northward and eastward into some of the dairy regions. Claiming a paid membership of nearly 30,000 by 1919, the Wisconsin Equity had already far outdistanced the parent organization in size and influence by the time of American involvement in the Great War. Many of the leaders of the organization had come out of the Granger and Alliance movements, and their program was a refinement of earlier efforts at agrarian reform. Stridently antimonopolistic in philosophy, Equity attracted some support among La Follette Progressives. More importantly, the organization urged crop withholding as the best means of obtaining higher prices, although the success of withholding depended on the participation of a great many producers. Later, influenced by a long tradition of co-operative activity in the state, Equity took the lead in promoting the co-operative marketing of agricultural products.[21]

[20] Glover, *Farm and College*, 305; Russell to F. B. Mumford, October 15, 1919, in General Correspondence, box 2, "Russell Correspondence 1915–1921, Press & Public Information File" folder, Series 9/1/1–3, Papers of Deans Henry and Russell, 1880–1930, College of Agriculture, UW Archives; UW Agricultural Experiment Station, *Annual Report*, 1919–1920, published as *Bulletin*, no. 323 (1920), 51; *ibid.*, 1922–1923, published as *Bulletin*, no. 362 (1924), 2, 6.

[21] Theodore Saloutos and John D. Hicks, *Agricultural Discontent in the Middle West,*

To the Wisconsin Society of Equity, sharing the skepticism towards "book farming" that often characterized rural areas, the College of Agriculture stood as a fortress of privilege on the shores of Lake Mendota. Equity members and some of their Progressive allies, in other words, perceived the University of Wisconsin as a "cold storage institution of dead languages and useless learning which costs several millions of bushels of wheat each year." They believed that Dean Russell and his staff were constantly urging efficient farm operation and increased production when they should have been devoting their attention to means by which farmers could secure better incomes. Worse still, the production emphasis of the College of Agriculture had led it to make common cause with bankers and businessmen, grain gamblers and corporations. While the Wisconsin Bankers' Association portrayed its agricultural program as a service to the state, the Equity-Progressive group charged that the bankers were in reality serving only themselves. State library official Matthew S. Dudgeon, for example, sharply criticized bankers for their arrogance in professing support of educational efforts in the College of Agriculture while they stood poised to cram an extortionate loan "down the throat of some farmer patron."[22]

Such criticism had its effect. In 1911 the state legislature enacted, among other Equity-Progressive measures, a law to establish a state board of public affairs—a precursor of the budget department—to study government operations with a view towards improving their efficiency. In 1914, in part because of rural dissatisfaction with Russell's emphasis on basic research, the board began what was intended to be a thorough survey of educational methods employed throughout the university. Under the general supervision of con-

---

1909–1939 (Madison, 1951), 126–127; Theodore Saloutos, "The Wisconsin Society of Equity," in *Agricultural History*, 14 (April, 1940), 81–84; Lampard, *Rise of the Dairy Industry in Wisconsin*, 347–348; Milo K. Swanton, "Cooperatives in Wisconsin: A Historical Summary," in the Wisconsin Council of Agriculture Papers; Writers' Program, Wisconsin, *Wisconsin: A Guide to the Badger State*, compiled by Workers of the Writers' Program of the Works Projects Administration in the State of Wisconsin (New York, 1941), 105–107; *Wisconsin State Journal*, April 1, 1928; Walter H. Ebling, "Recent Farmer Movements in Wisconsin" (master's thesis, University of Wisconsin, 1925), 36–41. Saloutos and Hicks reported an Equity membership of 40,000 in 1920; Ebling's estimate of 28,905 in 1919 is probably more accurate.

[22] Saloutos and Hicks, *Agricultural Discontent*, 128; George D. Bartlett to Russell, March 16, 1914, in General Correspondence Files, box 40, "Russell, Harry L., September 19, 1913–June 14, 1914" folder, Series 4/10/1, President Charles R. Van Hise Papers, UW Archives.

sultant William Harvey Allen, director of the Bureau of Municipal Research of New York City, Eugene C. Branson of the University of North Carolina assumed responsibility for investigating the College of Agriculture.[23]

An early effort to apply principles of scientific management to an educational enterprise, the survey was a disappointment to nearly everyone within the university. Branson's report on the College of Agriculture, inaccurate and filled with inconsistencies, was the product of slipshod research. He made unsubstantiated charges that the University of Wisconsin was unconcerned with the real interests of farmers. Concentrating largely on his own field of agricultural economics, he also condemned the College of Agriculture for being laggard in taking up the study of that field. For all the annoyance it caused, however, the report provided very little information that might have been used in educational planning. After its publication in 1915, George H. Mead, professor of philosophy at the University of Chicago, described it as "an example of how not to survey a university," and Professor Ellwood P. Cubberley of Stanford dismissed it as "outrageous."[24]

Critics of the College of Agriculture did not rely entirely on the board of public affairs to bring about reforms they considered necessary for agricultural prosperity in Wisconsin. While Branson and Allen busied themselves with their survey, sentiment for co-operative marketing associations was gaining strength. Believing that they could expect little help from Russell or the university, members of the Society of Equity discussed the farmers' need to take matters into their own hands. "To buy fairly you farmers must organize," Charles McCarthy told an Equity convention meeting in Madison in December, 1914. "To sell fairly you must do the same thing."[25]

The war proved a great stimulus to organization. Co-operative marketing and purchasing associations increased rapidly in number during the war period, and the Society of Equity did much to

[23] Saloutos and Hicks, *Agricultural Discontent*, 129–131; Curti and Carstensen, *University of Wisconsin*, 2:268–269, 272–273.

[24] Glover, *Farm and College*, 278; Curti and Carstensen, *University of Wisconsin*, 2:273–283 (Mead and Cubberley citations); State Board of Public Affairs, *Report upon the Survey of the University of Wisconsin: Findings of the State Board of Public Affairs and Its Report to the Legislature* (1915). For other criticism of the report, see Observer, "Demos and the Professor," in *The Nation*, 100 (May 27, 1915), 595–597; "A Bull in the Educational China Shop," in *The Dial*, 58 (June 10, 1915), 445–448; *Current Opinion*, 58 (June, 1915), 419–420; and *School Review*, 23 (June, 1915), 417–418.

[25] *Wisconsin State Journal*, December 3, 1914.

advance the cause. By 1920, some 400 of the state's co-operative associations bore the Equity name. The war also brought a flurry of activity among promoters of new ideas for providing economic assistance to farmers. McCarthy took part in those activities as well as in the co-operative movement. On leave from the Legislative Reference Library to work in the Food Administration, he pursued a course markedly different from that followed by Russell in the same agency. He joined Wisconsin Equity leader Charles Holman and other farmer advocates in founding the Federal Board of Farm Organizations, patterned after the American Federation of Labor in structure. At a Chicago convention in February, 1918, the board urged a program of agricultural subsidies, including low-interest loans and the right to buy seed, fertilizer, and machinery at cost. Little came of these proposals, but Russell's opposition to them greatly increased Equity's dislike for the College of Agriculture as Wisconsin farmers entered the postwar period.[26]

The dean also alienated the Wisconsin Farm Bureau, a new organization that developed as an affiliate of the American Farm Bureau Federation (AFBF). Formally organized in 1919–1920, the AFBF grew out of efforts to unite the bureaus created in several states to bring about better co-operation between farmers and county agents. The U.S. Department of Agriculture encouraged the movement as a means of furthering extension classes and programs, and most of the agricultural colleges in northern and western states developed close ties with the AFBF. Russell, however, resisted formal association with the federation as firmly as he resisted affiliation with the Society of Equity. He believed that if the College of Agriculture favored one organization over another it was certain to become entangled in political rivalries. He feared that playing politics would jeopardize federal appropriations and prostitute research programs to political objectives. He therefore held himself aloof from the prosperous, conservative farmers of the Farm Bureau as well as from the progressive agrarians of Equity. The dean paid a price for his determined impartiality. During the postwar recession, when the Wisconsin Society of Equity grew increasingly critical of the College of Agriculture, the Wisconsin Farm Bureau did little to aid either the college or its dean.[27]

[26] Saloutos, "Wisconsin Society of Equity," *Agricultural History*, 14:95; Herbert F. Margulies, *The Decline of the Progressive Movement in Wisconsin, 1890–1920* (Madison, 1968), 216; James H. Shideler, *Farm Crisis, 1919–1923* (Berkeley, 1957; reprinted, Westport, Connecticut, 1976), 10, 23–24; Beardsley, *Harry L. Russell*, 117.

[27] Orville M. Kile, *The Farm Bureau Through Three Decades* (Baltimore, 1948), 40–41,

From the Allen-Branson report of 1914 on through the decade of the twenties, much of the criticism of the College of Agriculture was wide of the mark. Neither Russell nor any of his colleagues ignored the economic needs of Wisconsin farmers; nor was the college indifferent to the hardships wrought by the 1921 depression. Also as early as the 1890's, Richard T. Ely had been interested in developing the study of land economics, and he had encouraged students to investigate the economic problems of agriculture. Responding to Ely's suggestions, Henry C. Taylor in the economics department began teaching courses on the subject after 1902. Three years later, with Ely's editorial assistance, he published the first textbook on agricultural economics. Fascinated by all aspects of rural life, Taylor, together with rural sociologist Charles J. Galpin, initiated a program of social science research. Far from being slow to acknowledge the importance of agricultural economics, as Branson had charged in 1914, the Wisconsin College of Agriculture was in fact among the first in the country to promote the discipline.[28]

As might have been expected, Taylor's early study of the marketing of agricultural produce soon attracted the attention of Charles McCarthy and the Society of Equity. Though McCarthy was not impressed by Taylor's scholarly objectivity, which he found tiresome, he thought the economist to be tractable and open to suggestions about the desirability of co-operative marketing associations. Before long, Taylor became a convert to the co-operative idea. His enthusiasm grew during the war, and by the time peace had returned he was ready to urge that the College of Agriculture assume the initiative in planning a new market strategy for Wisconsin farmers. Thus in 1918, at the very time that the Wisconsin Society of Equity was charging the College with indifference, Taylor persuaded Dean Russell to take a more active part in meeting the problems of agricultural marketing. Having set his hand to the co-operative plow, the dean did not turn back, even though his involvement in the movement drew criticism from various business

44–45, 47–57; Kennedy, *Over Here*, 121–122; Ebling, "Recent Farmer Movements in Wisconsin," 54–70; Beardsley, *Harry L. Russell*, 138–141; "County Agents Plan Year's Work," in the *Wisconsin Farmer*, 49 (April 1, 1920), 707.

[28] Benjamin G. Rader, *The Academic Mind and Reform: The Influence of Richard T. Ely in American Life* (Lexington, Kentucky, 1966), 192–193; Richard T. Ely, *Ground Under Our Feet: An Autobiography* (New York, 1938), 190–192.

interests. He conceded that successful co-operatives might supplant individual enterprises, but he insisted that the college existed to serve farmers, not private business.[29]

In 1919, Benjamin H. Hibbard succeeded Taylor as chairman of the department of agricultural economics. During his tenure from 1919 to 1932, Hibbard continued the market studies begun earlier. Other members of the department followed his lead. Rudolph K. Froker became a specialist in the field of dairy marketing. Henry H. Bakken, who was himself later to write a textbook on fluid milk marketing, concentrated in the twenties on tobacco and potatoes. W. P. Mortenson examined a variety of exchange conditions to develop a complete tabulation of farm prices in Wisconsin from 1841 to 1933. Other investigators, including P. E. McNall, F. B. Morrison, and L. S. Ellis, began the first examination of farm production costs.[30]

In the meantime, even as the College of Agriculture sought to cope with the problems of agricultural economics, the Society of Equity and the Farm Bureau began to lose membership and influence. Some Equity members believed that the organization had been victimized by its own success. J. F. Larson, director of the National Federation of Cooperative Livestock Shippers, for example, thought that the effectiveness of Equity co-operatives had induced independent co-operatives to sprout up all over the state. These unaffiliated associations, he believed, would secure aid from sources other than Equity and "we will then continue to have competition instead of cooperation."[31]

In reality, Equity's problems derived more from internal conflicts than from competition with other farm organizations. James N. Tittemore, who had become president of the Wisconsin Society of Equity in 1917, alienated some members with his efforts to win the Republican gubernatorial nomination in 1918 and 1920. Then, throughout the postwar decade, the poor management of Equity co-operatives exacerbated tensions within the organization. Its declining effectiveness led in 1934 to a merger of Equity with the

[29] Glover, *Farm and College*, 332–334; Beardsley, *Harry L. Russell*, 141–142; Henry C. Taylor and Anne Dewees Taylor, *The Story of Agricultural Economics in the United States, 1840–1932: Men, Services, Ideas* (Ames, 1952), 550–563, 659–662.

[30] Glover, *Farm and College*, 336.

[31] J. F. Larson to George A. Nelson, September 30, 1920, and Edward Swenson to Nelson, December 26, 1921, in the George A. Nelson Papers.

Farmers Union. By that time, Wisconsin farmers were facing economic difficulties of a much greater order of magnitude than they ever confronted in the immediate postwar period. Whatever might be said afterwards about Equity's influence in the twenties, it was the College of Agriculture that took the lead in exploring ways to improve the Wisconsin farmers' economic position.[32]

* * *

The emphasis on scientific investigation in the College of Agriculture aided farmers more than many of them knew, or were willing to admit. At the same time, it raised some important questions about the place of research within the university and about the distribution of profits from discoveries that came out of that research. In a general way, tradition permitted faculty members to reap financial rewards from their scholarly activities. The payment of royalties to authors who published books in the social sciences or the humanities, for example, encountered little resistance. With the scientific investigations of the College of Agriculture, however, it was a different matter. Scientific research was more costly, and the results were more likely to have an impact on the state's economy. Without university sponsorship and assistance, the investigations might not have been carried on or the results promulgated. To many citizens, both rural and urban, it therefore seemed appropriate that rights to scientific discoveries should be controlled by the university or, ultimately, by the state.

For the university to control the returns on scientific research comported well with the widely celebrated "Wisconsin Idea," which assumed that faculty expertise would be used to advance the well-being of Wisconsin's citizens. Nevertheless, the consequences of dedicating scientific discoveries to the public were not always happy ones. Stephen M. Babcock refused to patent his butterfat test for milk because he placed the welfare of citizens ahead of personal gain. He believed that widespread use of the test was important for American society, and he did not wish to limit its application through patent restrictions. Highminded though Babcock had been, he was also naïve in thinking that the dairy industry would prove itself equally highminded. The butterfat test required standardiza-

[32] Theodore Saloutos, "The Decline of the Wisconsin Society of Equity," in *Agricultural History*, 15 (July, 1941), 139–149; Ebling, "Recent Farmer Movements in Wisconsin," 32–33, 36, 40–41.

tion, which Babcock accomplished by setting a uniform size for milk test bottles. Manufacturers of dairy equipment were not so careful, and as handled commercially the butterfat test fell into disrepute. Not until state legislatures imposed adequate manufacturing controls did the test become reliable.[33]

The unforeseen consequences of Babcock's generosity had very nearly negated the good that came from his discovery. Clearly, if the results of research in the College of Agriculture were to benefit humanity, a better means had to be found to make them effective. This was the problem that Harry Steenbock faced in 1924 after his discovery of a way to produce vitamin D through radiation. If he did not apply for a patent, he ran the risk of seeing his process mishandled and abused. On the other hand, if he patented the process he could sell it to the highest bidder and become a wealthy man. But then he would be repudiating the principle of public service to which the University of Wisconsin was committed. If he used his discovery for personal gain, he could not be certain that the children who most needed vitamin D would receive it. Nor could he be certain that his discovery would contribute to the further study of nutrition.[34]

Steenbock's dilemma was one that troubled other researchers as well, for it was part of a much larger problem that accompanied significant scientific advances in the twentieth century. Reaching a balance between the public welfare and commercial advantage involved discriminating calculations. At the heart of the problem were two crucial concerns: first, how to use scientific achievements in a way that would benefit the largest number of people, and second, how to use scientific discoveries to advance further research. Gradually, as scientists, universities, and other interested parties grappled with such questions, a pattern of response began to take shape. Eventually it took the form of an institution that could operate independently of universities, using gifts, endowments, and investments as well as the proceeds of scientific discoveries to support new research.

The evolution of these "research foundations" was an intricate process involving long hours of deliberation and nice legal consid-

[33] Beardsley, *Harry L. Russell*, 157; Robert Taylor, "The Birth of the Wisconsin Alumni Research Foundation" (1956), unpublished manuscript in Wisconsin Alumni Research Foundation (WARF) Manuscripts and Records, WARF Office.

[34] Taylor, "Birth of WARF," 1–2.

erations. One of the first moves towards the creation of modern research foundations came in 1911, when Frederick Gardner Cottrell gave the Smithsonian Institution the rights to an electrostatic precipitation process for controlling air pollution. Trustees of the Smithsonian had then set up the Research Corporation of New York to administer the earnings from patents for the advancement of research. A decade later, T. Brailsford Robertson, a biochemist, donated several patents to the University of California with the understanding that the income they generated would be applied to medical research. While the California regents themselves took over control of the patents instead of establishing an independent foundation, the Robertson gift marked an important step towards liberating research funds from the marketplace. Patent management, it became evident, offered a means of accomplishing the objectives that Steenbock sought. Once that idea had been established, it remained only for Steenbock, university administrators, and benefactors to work out the details.[35]

In 1921 two Chicagoans, William Hoskins and Russell Wiles, developed a plan that was to have a powerful influence on research funding at the University of Wisconsin. Wiles, a patent attorney, and Hoskins, a consulting chemist, were concerned with the general problem of support for research scientists in American universities. Out of that concern came their suggestion for the creation of an independent corporation, managed by friends of a university but not by the university itself. Such a corporation, they believed, would profit from the expert knowledge of the managers, while the university would be required only to distribute the earnings in a manner that might best promote research. Harry Steenbock learned of the Hoskins-Wiles idea for a research foundation in the spring of 1924, seized upon it, and immediately set to work developing a way to implement it.[36]

Taking the matter up first with Harry L. Russell, Steenbock found the dean sympathetic to the foundation idea. A necessary first step, both men agreed, was to secure a patent on the irradiation process.

[35] Frank T. Cameron, *Cottrell, Samaritan of Science* (Garden City, New York, 1952), 149–150, 162–169; T. Brailsford Robertson, "The Utilization of Patents for the Promotion of Research," in *Science*, 46 (1917), 371–379; Beardsley, *Harry L. Russell*, 156. For a discussion of the antecedents of twentieth-century research foundations, see Howard S. Miller, "Science and Private Agencies," in David D. Van Tassel and Michael G. Hall, eds., *Science and Society in the United States* (Homewood, Illinois, 1966), 191–221.

[36] Taylor, "Birth of WARF," 3.

In June, 1924, Steenbock filed with the United States Patent Office an omnibus application covering all phases of his radiation discovery. This was rejected on the grounds that it was "too inclusive" and that "no new products had been produced." Back to his laboratory went Steenbock, and for nearly a year he gathered evidence to amend his application. Finally, in August, 1925, he submitted a second patent application and returned to perfecting plans for a foundation.[37]

By that time several developments had significantly altered the situation in which Steenbock found himself. The Quaker Oats Company, disturbed by findings that indicated a vitamin deficiency in rolled oats, offered to pay the scientist an estimated million dollars for exclusive rights to the patent after it had been obtained. Brooding over the university's apparent lack of enthusiasm for his project—the regents had refused to allocate funds to pay for a patent application—Steenbock had reached the point of accepting the Quaker Oats offer when Dean Charles S. Slichter of the graduate school learned of all that had transpired. In a luncheon conference at the Madison Club, Slichter told Steenbock to set his mind at rest, for he would himself find the money necessary to establish a foundation. As good as his word, the dean called on influential alumni in Chicago and New York, and by the time he returned to Madison he had raised $10,000 as a start. To that sum he added $2,000 of his own.[38]

Steenbock proceeded with caution. The plan he carefully constructed called for a nonprofit corporation managed by trustees who were alumni but had no other official connection with the university. The corporation was to have the power to receive assignments of patents and to utilize them "in a way that will best subserve the interests of this foundation," which was to support research in the university. In August, 1925, the Board of Regents approved the plan. Savoring his triumph, Steenbock held a series of conferences with George I. Haight, a Chicago lawyer who was then serving as president of the Wisconsin Alumni Association. Together they worked out articles of incorporation and then, aware of breaking new ground, they discussed the proposed foundation

[37] *Ibid.*, 10–11; Beardsley, *Harry L. Russell*, 157–158; Glover, *Farm and College*, 294.

[38] Steenbock to George Haight, December 7, 1929, in WARF Manuscripts and Records; Beardsley, *Harry L. Russell*, 158–159; Curti and Carstensen, *University of Wisconsin*, 2:412–414.

with other interested persons including Slichter and Russell as well as prominent alumni Thomas E. Brittingham, Jr., Lucien Hanks, and Timothy Brown. The group called their corporation the Wisconsin Alumni Research Foundation (WARF), and filed papers of incorporation with the secretary of state in Madison on November 14, 1925. It was the final step in creating the foundation that Steenbock had labored five years to establish.[39]

The birth of WARF did not, however, bring to an end the controversy that surrounded discussion of research in the university. Some faculty members in the College of Agriculture feared that the new foundation would induce scientists to concentrate on the development of patentable innovations, diverting them from the main business of assisting farmers. Critics outside the university were more adamant. A. J. Glover, editor of *Hoard's Dairyman*, objected in principle to patenting discoveries financed with public funds and then handing over the patent rights to a private corporation. He especially disliked WARF's policy of licensing particular businesses, a policy that gave licensees an advantage over competitors.[40]

Dean Russell, having played a major role in establishing the foundation, came staunchly to its defense. The corporate structure, he insisted, was not in itself any more prone to abuses than were individuals. Babcock's butterfat test was the prime example of a discovery leading to misuse and fraud because it had been given to the public without restrictions. Furthermore, exclusive licensing might work to the advantage of Wisconsin farmers. Scientists in the College of Agriculture had devoted much time to demonstrating the superiority of butter over oleomargarine, but Steenbock had shown that with irradiation either butter or margarine could be made rich in vitamin D. In one of their first decisions, the trustees of WARF adopted a policy of withholding licenses from oleomargarine manufacturers, and in so doing they were clearly favoring

[39] Taylor, "Birth of WARF," 4, 14–15; *Capital Times*, November 14, 1925; Beardsley, *Harry L. Russell*, 159–160; minutes, May 8, August 22, 1925, in box 20, Series 1/2/2, UW Board of Regents Executive Committee Meetings, 1888–1939, UW Archives. The University of Minnesota had an interest in the thyroid extract found by Edward C. Kendall of the Mayo Clinic. Sir Frederick Grant Banting of the University of Toronto had secured an institute as a result of his success in the development of insulin, and Columbia University had created an administrative board to control one method of producing the concentrated cod liver oil discovered by T. F. Zucker.

[40] F. B. Morrison to Russell, October 28, December 14, 1925, and A. J. Glover to Russell, October 22, 1925, in WARF Manuscripts and Records, WARF Office.

Wisconsin butter producers. Indeed, it was Steenbock's concern for the state's dairy industry that had been a major reason for his patent application in the first place.[41]

Aware of the importance of establishing WARF's good name, the trustees were exceedingly cautious in granting licenses for the use of WARF patents. Except for an agreement that gave Quaker Oats the right to use Steenbock's irradiation process in the manufacture of cereals, they rejected applications from food companies until experimentation proved the value of irradiation. They also rejected contracts with companies manufacturing products such as lipstick and chewing gum, products having no nutritive value. In all, charges that WARF policies hurt Wisconsin farmers were wide of the mark. If the investigation of those policies proves anything, it indicates that WARF trustees not only knew which side of the bread was buttered, but also that they knew how to make certain that the spread was butter and not margarine.[42]

The Wisconsin Alumni Research Foundation managed eventually to quiet the fears of most critics, but it never did entirely escape reproach. In the 1930's, after Russell had resigned as dean to become director of WARF, editor William T. Evjue kept up a running criticism of WARF in the *Capital Times*. The foundation, he insisted, had made common cause with big business to cheat Wisconsin taxpayers of the rewards that should properly have been used for the public welfare instead of a handful of favored researchers. He warned that "the Sacred Cow of Bascom Hall" was responsible to no one and could end up in control of the University of Wisconsin if not contained. Despite such charges, however, WARF won support from the general public as well as from the university faculty. During the Great Depression, the foundation exercised a major influence in maintaining research activities at the university. By the time Russell resigned as director in 1939, WARF's annual contribution had very nearly reached $200,000. While it was true that restrictive licensing had benefited some businesses more than others, trustees of the foundation exercised great care to fulfill the purposes Steenbock had formulated fifteen years earlier. Research

[41] Harry L. Russell to A. J. Glover, January 16, 1926, and to F. B. Morrison, January 22, 1926, in *ibid.*; Beardsley, *Harry L. Russell*, 162; W. S. Kies, "Science Goes to Market," in *Review of Reviews*, 84 (September, 1931), 42–45; Taylor, "Birth of WARF," 19; Glover, *Farm and College*, 296.

[42] Beardsley, *Harry L. Russell*, 162–163.

was itself providing an important portion of the funding for further research at the University of Wisconsin.[43]

* * *

Although scientists and scholars at the University of Wisconsin were committed to basic research, the work of faculty investigators was never carried on in a vacuum. Dissemination of the knowledge obtained in laboratories and libraries often received as much emphasis as did the research itself, and publicizing new findings and discoveries became especially important if they affected a substantial number of the state's citizens. Until 1930, a majority of Wisconsin people lived in rural areas, and the College of Agriculture quite naturally took the lead in demonstrating the practical application of theoretical investigations. As superintendent of farmers' institutes, Ernest L. Luther described his program in 1923 as "education plus." He meant that under his direction the institutes were involved not only in "communicating advanced principles of scientific and practical agriculture," but also in putting those principles to work as quickly as possible.[44]

Of all the scientific and technological achievements of the period, particularly in the field of communication, none exceeded radio broadcasting in leading masses of people, including rural residents of Wisconsin, to perceive themselves as living in a new era. Military exigency placed a premium on both point-to-point and mass communication. The United States mail, the telephone, the telegraph, and cable or wireless services had become commonplace before 1917. So too had newspapers, the only real means of mass communication until the 1920's. Increased use of established media during the war and after was hardly surprising, and it occasioned little comment. Such was not the case with the cinema and radio, both of which had existed before the war but were still novelties at the time of the Armistice. While the social importance of the motion picture cannot be overemphasized, it could scarcely be described as a product of basic scientific research. Radio, however, placed listeners in touch with cosmic forces. Even if audiences did not understand the use of electromagnetic waves of high frequency,

[43] *Ibid.*, 170; *Capital Times*, April 26, May 21, 1931, May 8, October 11, 1934, June 11, July 13, 1937, April 28, 1938.

[44] E. L. Luther, "What Institutes Are Doing," in the *Wisconsin Agriculturist*, March 3, 1923.

By 1923, when H. T. Webster published "The Radio Fan," the new broadcast medium had brought the world into American parlors in both city and country. From an original drawing in the collections of the State Historical Society of Wisconsin.

they did comprehend that scientific investigations had brought them an instrument for establishing contact with all parts of the globe. "Radio is a novel phenomenon, something new under the psychological sun," asserted an early book on the subject. Radio, its authors believed, provoked "*novel* effects in the mental and social life of its devotees." Above all, they claimed, it exerted an influence that was profoundly democratic. "When a million or more people hear the same subject matter, the same arguments and appeals, the same music and humor, when their attention is held in the same way and at the same time to the same stimuli," concluded the study, "it is psychologically inevitable that they should acquire in some degree common interests, common tastes, and common attitudes."[45]

Among the many wireless enthusiasts who initiated experiments with telephony before World War I were University of Wisconsin professors Edward Bennett and Earle M. Terry. As early as 1909 Bennett was using spark transmitters to send messages in code, and by 1915 the United States Department of Commerce had licensed a University of Wisconsin station with the call letters 9XM. Simultaneously, the station initiated daily weather reports in code. By that time, voice transmission had become feasible, and, drawing on current research, Terry set about constructing a transmitter. Obstacles were many, and progress required patience. Because vacuum tubes were difficult to get, Terry and his students learned to make their own. By dint of painstaking experimentation they gradually overcame difficulties and succeeded in transmitting voice and music in their physics department laboratory.[46]

Then came the war. Malcolm Hanson, one of Terry's students on duty at the Great Lakes Naval Training Station in 1917, reported hearing several telephonic broadcasts from Madison. For a short

[45] Harry Barsantee, "The History and Development of the Telephone in Wisconsin," in *WMH*, 10 (December, 1926), 159–163; Malcolm M. Willey and Stuart A. Rice, "The Agencies of Communication," in President's Research Committee on Social Trends, *Recent Social Trends in the United States* (1 vol. edition, New York, 1933), 191–217; John Jewkes, David Sawers, and Richard Stillerman, *The Sources of Invention* (New York, 1969), 286–289; Bernard S. Finn, "Electronic Communications," in Melvin Kranzberg and Carroll W. Pursell, Jr., eds., *Technology in Western Civilization* (2 vols., New York, 1967), 2:293–302; Hadley Cantril and Gordon W. Allport, *The Psychology of Radio* (New York, 1935; reprinted, Salem, New Hampshire, 1971), 4, 18, 20.

[46] S. E. Frost, Jr., *Education's Own Stations: The History of Broadcast Licenses Issued to Educational Institutions* (Chicago, 1937), 464–465; Harold B. McCarty, "WHA, Wisconsin's Radio Pioneer: Twenty Years of Public Service Broadcasting," in the *Wisconsin Blue Book, 1937*, pp. 195–196; Erik Barnouw, *A History of Broadcasting in the United States. Volume I: A Tower in Babel, to 1933* (New York, 1966), 41.

time in 1918 the Navy ordered all stations dismantled for reasons of security, and broadcasting from Madison ceased temporarily. Hanson was placed in charge of wireless communication for all planes patrolling the Atlantic coast. At last returning to Madison in August, 1920, he found 9XM broadcasting daily weather bulletins and market reports. Terry immediately set Hanson to work building a new transmitter for the station, then housed in the basement of Sterling Hall.[47]

Terry and his students were successful with the new transmitter. "Am getting along fine with the wireless telephone," Hanson wrote home in February, 1921, "our concerts are heard in Boston, Texas, North Dakota, and a lot of places." That same year, the station began broadcasting basketball games as well as concerts by remote control from the university armory. Like the technological understanding that made broadcasting possible, the university's program in broadcasting expanded rapidly. In January, 1922, the department of commerce granted a license to operate a broadcast transmitter with 4,000 watts power. To listeners the new call letters, WHA, became symbolic of the university's leadership in radio development; for many students they opened the way to exciting new careers.[48]

Americans became avid radio enthusiasts during the 1920's. Most listeners were satisfied at first merely with hearing another person's voice coming to them over the air, and programming was a simple matter. "Do you live in Wisconsin?" queried J. G. Crownhart in *La Follette's Magazine*. If you did, you could simply turn the switch on your "magic box" during the noon hour and hear Malcolm Hanson tell you what the weather would be for the next twenty-four hours. Then he would provide the latest reports from "every large stock, grain and produce market center in the country." As if that were not enough, "by the time you have had supper Friday night and the table is cleared, just turn that switch again and you will hear all the latest Edison records broadcasted by the University of Wisconsin." Chief credit for such services, noted the *Wisconsin Farmer*,

[47] McCarty, "WHA," *Wisconsin Blue Book, 1937*, pp. 196–197; Barnouw, *Tower in Babel*, 39–41. Hanson went on to a successful career in radio. He served as chief radio engineer with Admiral Richard E. Byrd at the South Pole.

[48] Barnouw, *Tower in Babel*, 41; Frost, *Education's Own Stations*, 464–466; McCarty, "WHA," *Wisconsin Blue Book, 1937*, pp. 199–201. That the letters stood for nothing in particular did not prevent listeners from associating them with excellence.

belonged to the department of markets in the College of Agriculture and to the department of physics in the College of Letters and Science. In all, "no other state has yet done as much toward making the wireless system of economic value to farmers." But farmers were not alone in their devotion to the radio. In 1922 the City Club of Milwaukee installed a "wireless telephone" to accommodate its members. Every evening from 8 to 10 o'clock, a horn and amplifiers carried the sound of music from Westinghouse station KDKA in Pittsburgh to every corner of the dining room, "provided atmospheric and static conditions are favorable." Programs, printed in advance, were posted on the bulletin board for the benefit of club members wishing to attend.[49]

No small part of radio's early popularity is attributable to the ease with which amateurs could construct their own apparatus. Crystal detectors were neither expensive nor difficult to build, and directions for constructing simple transmitters were readily obtained. People came to believe that involvement in radio improved the mind, built character, and provided a perfect outlet for youthful energy. The new means of communication was, in short, also a means by which Americans might preserve traditional virtues while at the same time adapting to the technology of a new era. "When a Chicago boy can sit down at a table in his own house and talk by radio with boys in Iowa, Pennsylvania and other states, and probably in the near future, with other nations," declared the Kewaunee *Enterprise*, "he is pretty likely to be more interested in that than in the pool room down the street."[50]

Clyde S. Van Gorden, who owned and operated WTAQ at Osseo before moving the station to Eau Claire in 1926, began his radio activities as an amateur. Born in 1892 at Hixton, Wisconsin, three

[49] *La Follette's Magazine*, November, 1921; *Wisconsin Farmer*, 50 (November 24, 1921), 1521; City Club of Milwaukee, *City Club News*, March 10, 1922, p. 1. In 1924, farmer witnesses testified in a Milwaukee County circuit court suit that high-tension lines interfered with radio reception. Attorney Carl Hein argued that "the farmer needs the radio not only for pleasure but also for business, as by means of it he receives reports on the current prices of his products." In an advertisement for its Radiola 20, the Radio Corporation of America pointed out in 1926 that "a radio set changes the character of home life, making the evenings more cheerful, and the *business* of farming more profitable." Milwaukee *Journal*, July 24, 1924; *Wisconsin Agriculturist*, November 6, 1926.

[50] Kewaunee *Enterprise*, July 6, 1923. Not everyone responded to radio so affirmatively. Hans H. Swan, who owned a small department store in Stoughton, complained that people had stopped buying pianos because "all they want is radios." By 1925, Swan was reduced to selling "mostly small stuff in music. Ukeleles and such things." Stoughton *Courier-Hub*, July 28, 1925.

years before Guglielmo Marconi sent and received his first wireless signals, Van Gorden grew up as radio was maturing. From reading *Popular Mechanics* and bulletins supplied by the signal corps and the department of commerce, the young man learned enough to build a crystal set, and from a telegraph key, a Ford coil, and a battery he constructed his first transmitter. He passed his amateur operator's examination and for a year operated as a ham before turning to commercial broadcasting in 1923. Van Gorden's experience was not unusual, for most radio enthusiasts demonstrated astonishing resourcefulness.[51]

Businesses as well as ham operators gravitated towards commercial radio. Indeed, department stores wishing to advertise their merchandise, newspaper publishers, or electrical equipment manufacturers were more likely to establish commercial radio stations than were individuals. In 1922 Gimbel Brothers licensed WAAK in Milwaukee, the Northwestern Radio Company experimented with WGAY in Madison, and the Northern States Power Company established WRAL in St. Croix Falls. By June of 1923 Wisconsin had eleven stations, but not all were successful. Within a year WAAK and WGAY had ceased operations. After the intitial excitement of listening to the magic box, audiences began to tire of nothing but recorded music, market reports, and weather bulletins. Yet because budgets were limited and more varied fare was costly, improvement in programming was a gradual process. Revenues from advertising offered a convenient means of increasing the number of radio offerings, and as early as 1922 WEAF began broadcasting sponsored programs in New York. As the idea spread, corporate giants of the industry vied with one another for a national market. Finally, in September, 1926, the Radio Corporation of America, General Electric, and Westinghouse united to establish the National Broadcasting Company.[52]

Until formation of the networks in the late 1920's, educational radio enjoyed an advantage that few commercial stations could match. In Madison, for example, WHA could draw on the faculty

[51] James I. Clark, "Early Broadcasting in Wisconsin: Clyde S. Van Gorden and Station WTAQ," in *WMH*, 41 (Winter, 1957–1958), 90–93.

[52] Clark, "Early Broadcasting in Wisconsin," in *WMH*, 41:90–91; U.S. Bureau of Navigation, *Commerical and Government Radio Stations of the United States*, June 30, 1923, and June 30, 1924; Philip T. Rosen, *The Modern Stentors: Radio Broadcasters and the Federal Government, 1920–1934* (Westport, Connecticut, 1980), 66–69, 88–91, 116–120; Barnouw, *Tower in Babel*, 184–188.

and other resources of the university while commercial stations were relying on recorded music and local amateur talent. The programming opportunities of educational radio along with radio's appeal as an area of vocational specialization led to the licensing of eight college or university stations in Wisconsin during the New Era. Marquette University, the Milwaukee School of Engineering, Superior State Teachers College, and Stout Institute all secured licenses to broadcast. So also did Beloit, Milton, and St. Norbert colleges.[53]

By all odds, however, the most successful of the state's educational stations was WHA. In no small measure responsible for its accomplishments was William H. Lighty of the University of Wisconsin's Extension Division. A social worker in St. Louis before moving to Madison, Lighty had taken charge of the correspondence department of university extension in 1906. His enthusiasm for the improvement of course offerings for nonresident students helped make the extension division a viable branch of the state's educational system before American entry into the war. In the postwar period, sensing that radio offered new possibilities for a further expansion of the university's services, Lighty became WHA's first program director.[54]

As director, Lighty was convinced that programs should serve a variety of interests and that every department of the university should play an active role in program development. The first faculty member to take part in regular broadcasts was Professor Edgar B. Gordon, who had long been promoting community musical activities through the university extension. In 1922 "Pop" Gordon organized and presented a radio course in music appreciation, thereby adding a critical dimension to performances that radio audiences normally heard. Always receptive to new ideas, Lighty found many ways to use the station's system of remote pickups effectively. Through WHA, special events at the university—concerts, lectures by prominent visitors, athletic contests—were broadcast from their points of origin to all sections of the state.[55]

The College of Agriculture, well aware of its mission to supply Wisconsin farmers with useful information, learned to depend upon

[53] Frost, *Education's Own Stations*, 30–31, 193–198, 211, 212–214, 384–386, 421–422, 464–474.

[54] Curti and Carstensen, *University of Wisconsin*, 2:555–562; McCarty, "WHA," *Wisconsin Blue Book, 1937*, p. 198; Frost, *Education's Own Stations*, 466.

[55] McCarty, "WHA," *Wisconsin Blue Book, 1937*, pp. 199–201.

radio as an indispensable medium of communication. In 1922 the Wisconsin Department of Markets built a state transmitter at Waupaca for the specific purpose of providing market reports of interest to farmers. Moved to Stevens Point in 1924 and assigned the call letters WLBL, the station was linked by wire with the U.S. Department of Agriculture, which in turn had direct access to all important markets from coast to coast. The state station in Stevens Point also co-operated with WHA in Madison to offer listeners a rich variety of programs. A wire connection at first, and then a direct pickup using a ground antenna, enabled either station to broadcast programs of the other. A single restriction limited the service thus provided, but it was a serious one: broadcasting was confined to daylight hours.[56]

Functioning effectively during those hours, however, the two stations rendered notable service to the people of Wisconsin. Glenn Frank, president of the university, pointed out in 1932 that by long tradition the state was interested in "the safeguarding and promotion of a free and full discussion" of all problems that affected the commonwealth. He went on to observe that "these state-controlled radio stations may enable Wisconsin to re-create in this machine age the sort of unhampered and intimate and sustained discussion of public issues that marked the New England town meeting and the Lincoln-Douglas debates."[57]

President Frank was speaking at a time when economic depression had blocked the innovative momentum of the postwar decade. "Recreating the New England town meeting with the state for a stage" would, he thought, stimulate the national imagination. While citing pioneer work in radio as an example of Wisconsin's leadership, he might have held up other examples as well. In promoting agriculture as a scientific pursuit, in appropriating the results of scientific research for the benefit of all its citizens, and in linking the work of university researchers and scholars to the welfare of the whole commonwealth, Wisconsin had provided a setting for important and lasting achievements of the New Era.

[56] *Ibid.*, 200, 205–207; Edward Nordman, "Department of Markets," in *ibid., 1923*, pp. 287–288; Edward Nordman, "The Marketing Department," *ibid., 1927*, pp. 336–337; J. H. Vint, "Department of Markets," *ibid., 1929*, p. 323. Radio signals cause interference at greater distances after sundown than they do during daytime hours. Federal regulation required WHA to sign off at local sundown so as to avoid interfering with stations in Fargo, North Dakota, and Louisville, Kentucky.

[57] Cited in Frost, *Education's Own Stations*, 469.

6

City and Hinterland: Tensions of the New Era

ON April 13, 1928, the Kewaunee *Enterprise* noted the passing of Henry Brager, one of the last survivors of the Grand Army of the Republic. More than sixty years earlier he had been among the Union veterans who "came back to their homes in Kewaunee County, strong, sturdy, the flower of our manhood." But Father Time had silently swung his scythe and gathered the veterans one by one. Taps, "the lullaby of the living soldier and in death his requiem," had been sounded for nearly all of Brager's comrades-in-arms, as it had now for Brager himself. The old soldiers of the GAR left behind many people who remembered "the long line of men in Blue on Decoration Day or on the Fourth of July or on other great patriotic occasions." Even after death had also claimed the Kewauneeans who welcomed the return of that long blue line, their children and their children's children remembered, for "the fame of those men will live so long as history is written and so long as patriotism and loyalty are honored among men."[1]

In the same year that Henry Brager died, a trainload of Wisconsin businessmen left the state for a goodwill tour of the Southland, the first of several such junkets. They intended not to dishonor the memory of the Republic's long line of blue but to increase their own prosperity by expanding commercial ties with southern states. Southerners were as patriotic and as loyal as other Americans, the businessmen believed, and everyone stood to gain from overcoming ancient sectional antipathies. Received tentatively at first, the Wisconsin goodwill trains soon captivated southern businessmen. Two years later, as the commercial pilgrims planned their 1930 tour, a

[1] Kewaunee *Enterprise*, April 13, 1928.

flurry of letters and telegrams arrived to assure them of a hearty welcome. The Vicksburg *Evening Post* publicized the venture and extended the keys of the city to men whose grandfathers had helped General Ulysses S. Grant capture the town in 1863. In Jackson, Mississippi, the chamber of commerce offered "real southern hospitality," and the Louisiana chamber expressed regret that the Badger businessmen had time to visit only a few points of interest in the state.[2]

In touring the South, the Wisconsin businessmen were acting on a belief that found frequent expression in commercial pronouncements of the New Era. Chambers of commerce, service clubs, and civic organizations seemed never to tire of elaborating on the beneficent results of co-operative activities undertaken with unity of purpose. At the same time that Wisconsin businessmen sought to gain commercial advantage from establishing cordial ties with the South, they adopted a similar approach to win the support of differing economic interests at home. After the wartime conflicts over patriotism and loyalty, teamwork and harmony became the great desiderata of Wisconsin businessmen in the postwar decade. They believed that prosperity could best be achieved through co-operation, and they went to extraordinary lengths in demonstrating their eagerness to act in concert.

The booster spirit, which Sinclair Lewis attacked with sardonic wit in *Babbitt*, was a crude expression of the co-operative impulse. But George F. Babbitt was a parody, and serious businessmen of the New Era resented the implications of Lewis' novel. They believed they were simply following precepts enunciated far more sincerely by Herbert Clark Hoover. Soon to become secretary of commerce in the Harding administration, Hoover in 1920 condensed his assessment of the postwar mood in America when he addressed the graduating class of Swarthmore College. "The minds of men," he observed, "are groping for readjustments in human relationship that will produce better justice, better equality among men and a higher standard of living to all and greater safety of the civilization we have built up." Later in the year he stressed the need for co-operation—a "solidarity of interest"—among all economic groups in the nation. If it could be secured, he thought, "we should

[2] *Waupaca County Post* (Waupaca), December 12, 1929.

have provided a new economic system, based neither on the capitalism of Adam Smith, nor upon the socialism of Karl Marx."[3]

Hoover never implied that he had developed a new political or economic theory; he claimed only that he was expressing ideas inherent in the American political economy. Business commentaries in Wisconsin newspapers, as well as editorials in the state's commercial publications, expounded similar wisdom. George Bruce, for example, used his position as editor of *Civics and Commerce* to promote the idea of co-operation. "The farm and the factory bear a reciprocal relation," he wrote in 1918. "One is essential to the other." And the following year, in reporting on a promotional trip through northern Wisconsin, he noted that "the gospel which the Milwaukee Association of Commerce carried everywhere was that of state pride and co-operation between the several units of population." In 1922, the year Herbert Hoover published *American Individualism*, "Phil Grau's Page" offered what amounted to a gloss on Hoover's theme for readers of *Milwaukee*, a monthly publication of the city's association of commerce. "*Now* is the time to bring about co-operation between the farmers and the business men," wrote Grau. "*Now* is the time to create a better understanding between the larger and smaller cities. *Now* is the time to develop a more friendly spirit between those who hire and those who are hired."[4]

Co-operation presumably implied a set of values that was in harmony with the highest values of western civilization. It implied respect for one's fellows, fair treatment of the less fortunate among them, and the growth of a community spirit grounded in humanitarian concern. But the principal effect of better social relationships, the advocates of co-operation were fond of suggesting, was certain to be an increase in the prosperity of the American people.

[3] Gary Dean Best, *The Politics of American Individualism: Herbert Hoover in Transition, 1918–1921* (Westport, Connecticut, 1975), 94, 97; Irma H. Herron, *The Small Town in American Literature* (Durham, 1939; reprinted, Brooklyn, New York, 1970), 358–386; *Nation's Business*, 16 (January, 1928), 28–29; James W. Prothro, *The Dollar Decade: Business Ideas in the 1920's* (Baton Rouge, 1954), 63–64; Washington *Herald*, November 20, 1920. For succinct discussions of Hoover's views at the end of the war, see Joan Hoff Wilson, *Herbert Hoover: Forgotten Progressive* (Boston, 1975), 41–43, 51–53, and Richard Norton Smith, *An Uncommon Man: The Triumph of Herbert Hoover* (New York, 1984), 93–98.

[4] *Civics and Commerce*, March, 1918, p. 21, and July, 1919, p. 42; *Milwaukee*, March, 1922, p. 17. See, in addition, *Civics and Commerce*, August, 1916, pp. 9–10, and June, 1918, pp. 14–15, 20.

And prosperity, in turn, had a way of minimizing the inequities that separated one class from another, a way of eliminating social conflict, and a way of strengthening the forces that led to a viable community.

While this argument for co-operation was a circular one, it seemed plausible enough during the prosperous New Era, and it received reinforcement at all points on the circle. Businessmen were not alone in preaching the gospel of co-operation. Carl Russell Fish, who enjoyed a wide reputation as a historian at the University of Wisconsin, thought he was closing the circle when he addressed the City Club of Milwaukee in 1924. Commenting on the effects of business co-operation during the postwar decade, he suggested that "economics and finance are gradually overturning social classes." Three years later, in addressing several hundred Kenosha luncheon club members, Governor Fred Zimmerman outdid the professor in chanting the canons of Wisconsin commerce. "Prosperity comes hand in hand with developed industry and developed agriculture," he proclaimed, adding that "the problem in Wisconsin is to keep prosperity growing. The farmer must have markets. The industries must have markets. Just as we develop industry along the lake shore and in the Fox river valley so will we advance the progress of the farmer around those industrial centers." Then came the plea that by then had become a standard service club canticle: "Live the thought that only by cooperation, by meeting together on common ground can we expect to get anywhere—not by strife and hatred."[5]

The problem with such circular reasoning was that its coherence depended on the prosperity of all citizens, all classes, all sections of the state. And even before the coming of the Great Depression, prosperity was far from universal and certainly far from being equally distributed. Inevitably, therefore, the litany of the New Era was discordant if not actually marred by discontinuities. Northern counties of the poverty-stricken Cutover resented the economic advantages that southern counties enjoyed; advocates of state parks and the conservation of resources struggled with proponents of agricultural expansion; farmers and villagers brooded over the migration of young people to the metropolis, and brows furrowed in contemplation of means to keep them home. In the cities, workers

[5] City Club of Milwaukee, *City Club News*, January 25, 1924; Oshkosh *Northwestern*, March 10, 1927.

fell to bickering as they neglected the goal of solidarity, and organized labor struggled unsuccessfully with advocates of the open shop. Small-town merchants fought a losing battle with chain stores, and independent bankers worried about what might happen if they came under the control of bank groups centered in Chicago or the Twin Cities. In short, the message of co-operation proved to be no more a panacea when preached by the Babbitts of Wisconsin during the twenties than the traditional message of brotherhood had ever been, even when advocated by unselfish men and women of good will throughout history. People who did not fully share in the promised prosperity of the New Era could experience the harmful effects of cupidity as well as the beneficial effects of co-operation; some of them might know only the temporary relief provided by analgesics rather than the permanent relief provided by definitive answers to problems they confronted.[6]

* * *

Early in 1919 the *New North*, one of two newspapers published in Rhinelander, printed an item calling for the collection of photographs and memorabilia from the boom times of timber cutting and logging operations in Wisconsin's pineries. "The picturesque scenes of the early woods operations are fast drawing to a close," lamented the article. "Already the river boys of the spring drive have followed the raftsmen of an early period off the stage of action; they have run the river for the last time." In their red shirts and nail-studded driving boots, those "rugged, big-hearted fellows" had "passed down the old Wisconsin and out of sight never to return."[7]

Not everyone recalled the river boys with such affection. More than a hundred years had gone by since construction of the state's first sawmill at De Pere in 1809, and in that time more than 30 million acres of merchantable timber had dwindled to less than 2 million. Lumber barons had exploited the pineries unstintingly, settlers had slashed away the forests to clear land for crops, and fires had destroyed thousands of acres of timber. Emerson Hough, a popular historian and writer, could not ponder over the devastated

[6] A Janesville *Gazette* editorial, January 11, 1930, suggested the point in commenting on relationships between farmers and businessmen: "The more money that can be made by the farmer the better for all concerned in the business world. He becomes a buyer and not a non-cooperator."

[7] Rhinelander *New North*, January 9, 1919.

landscape without resentment. In 1921 he spoke wistfully of the early days in northern Wisconsin with its abundance of fish and game, and he deplored "the extravagant waste which has resulted in the practical disappearance of our great forests."[8]

While lumbermen had always known that Wisconsin forests were not inexhaustible, they had disliked restriction of their activities and had therefore opposed development of a conservation policy. Nevertheless, a concern for preservation of the state's resources—or at least the prudent use of them—became apparent before the Civil War. And from that time on, conservationists attempted to exert a restraining influence on the lumbermen. By 1897, after hundreds of thousands of acres in the pineries had been reduced to stumpland, the legislature was persuaded of the need for a more rational approach towards the exploitation of Wisconsin timber. The resulting legislation provided for a three-member commission to draft a plan by which the state's forest resources might be protected as well as utilized. In 1903, the commission's recommendations brought further legislation establishing a state forestry commission, revised to become the State Board of Forestry in 1905. Edward Merriam Griffith, who had supervised formulation of the first working plans for the Black Hills reserve in South Dakota, became state forester of Wisconsin in 1904, a position he held until 1915.[9]

Griffith soon demonstrated that he deserved recognition for more than his extraordinary enthusiasm for the advancement of forestry; he also demonstrated an understanding of state needs that led to ten years of productive accomplishment. The state forestry commission had already set aside 40,000 acres of land in northern Wisconsin to provide a nucleus for an integrated forest system, and Griffith immediately set about enlarging that reserve. Within a year he had secured approval for adding another 22,000 acres, and he began dreaming of enlarging the reserve to encompass 2 million acres. With characteristic vigor he regularly persuaded the legislature to approve annual increases in land acquisition, and he urged

[8] Raleigh Barlowe, "Forest Policy in Wisconsin," in *WMH*, 26 (March, 1943), 261; City Club of Milwaukee, *City Club News*, December 2, 1921.

[9] Vernon R. Carstensen, *Farms or Forests: Evolution of a State Land Policy for Northern Wisconsin, 1850–1932* (Madison, 1958), 6–21, 34; *Laws of Wisconsin*, 1897, pp. 438–439 (Chapter 229); *ibid.*, 1903, pp. 744–753 (Chapter 450); *ibid.*, 1905, pp. 383–391 (Chapter 264).

that private persons and the federal government donate lands to the state for forestry projects. Through state purchases, private grants, and federal transfers, the forest reserve increased to 180,000 acres by 1915. Griffith also promoted educational conferences, delivered an annual series of lectures on forestry at the University of Wisconsin, developed a fire patrol and fire-fighting system for the state's forests, launched a reforestation program, urged a detailed study of forest taxation, and assisted in persuading the United States Forestry Service to locate the Forest Products Laboratory in Madison.[10]

Unfortunately for Griffith and for supporters of Wisconsin's forestry program, the state supreme court held the entire forest reserve policy invalid in February, 1915, when it handed down its decision in the case of *State ex rel. Owen v. Donald*. The Wisconsin constitution had originally prohibited the state from contracting debt to pay for internal improvements, but in 1907 the legislature agreed to amend Article VIII, Section 10, in order that it might appropriate funds for the development of water power and forests. In the next session, as required by the constitution, the senate again agreed to the amendment. But the assembly failed to do so and instead simply joined the senate in voting to submit it to popular vote. In the election of November, 1910, the amendment was approved, 62,468 to 45,924, but the vote did not hide the assembly's failure to follow constitutional procedure. In writing the opinion of the court, Justice Roujet D. Marshall noted that the legislature had violated "solemn obligations," and he therefore held the amendment invalid. Without the amendment, the court determined that the forestry program lay "fatally within the 'works of internal improvement,'" borrowing for which had been prohibited when the constitution was adopted in 1848. The court did not rest with invalidating the state forestry program; it also ruled that much of the land placed in the reserve rightfully belonged to the school fund. A referee appointed by the court determined that the general fund of Wisconsin owed the school fund $1,817,514.23, and for several years the state made annual payments of $100,000 to cancel the debt.[11]

[10] Carstensen, *Farms or Forests*, 36; F. G. Wilson, "Forestry in Wisconsin," in the *Wisconsin Blue Book, 1942*, pp. 177–178; Barlowe, "Forest Policy in Wisconsin," in *WMH*, 26:264–265; Conservation Commission, *Biennial Report*, 1915–1916, pp. 76–77.

[11] *Wisconsin Reports*, 160:21, 162:609; *Northwestern Reporter*, 151:377; *Laws of Wisconsin*,

Northern Wisconsin counties applauded the court's decision. The tax base in the north had eroded as lumber companies removed timber and then abandoned the cutover land to become tax delinquent. The only hope for the residents left behind was to find some substitute for logging operations, some revenue-producing activity that would assure continued prosperity. Because northerners perceived a large forest reserve as contributing nothing to tax income, they had vigorously opposed Griffith's forestry program. Instead of withdrawing cutover land from profitable use, they believed the state should make every effort to encourage agricultural settlement of the region.[12]

Was it wise, however, for the plow to follow the axe into northern Wisconsin? Could the northern counties sustain a productive agriculture? Or was the land too sandy, rocky, or swampy and the growing season too short to permit profitable farming? For years the debate over the state's forestry program had centered on such questions. In 1897, through an arrangement with the United States Department of Agriculture, Filibert Roth had conducted a survey of Wisconsin forests and of conditions in the Cutover. Aware of the pressure to extend agriculture into the Cutover, Roth cautioned that at least 40 per cent of the region he had examined—from Jackson and Wood counties to the northern border of the state—was unsuited to farming. "It will be the part of wisdom, therefore," concluded the state forestry commission, "for the state to adopt a policy which will encourage the use of such lands for the purpose of raising timber crops, rather than agricultural crops proper." Here, in a nutshell, was the rationale for the state's forestry program, now blocked by the Wisconsin supreme court's 1915 decision.[13]

In the years following the court's action, the proponents of farming the Cutover pursued their objective without fear of opposition. After 1917, when the United States Food Administration assured

1909, pp. 661–662 (Chapter 514); *Wisconsin Blue Book, 1987–1988*, p. 208; Carstensen, *Farms or Forests*, 38, 83–85; Gilson G. Glasier, ed., *Autobiography of Roujet D. Marshall, Justice of the Supreme Court of the State of Wisconsin, 1895–1918* (2 vols., Madison, 1923, 1931), 2:84–88; Barlowe, "Forest Policy in Wisconsin," in *WMH*, 26:266–267.

[12] Carstensen, *Farms or Forests*, 30, 55, 67; John M. Gaus, "Memorandum on Land Use" (typewritten), July 10, 1931, in the Philip F. La Follette Papers.

[13] Andrew D. Rodgers, *Bernhard Eduard Fernow: A Story of North American Forestry* (Princeton, 1951), 183ff, 245–246; Filibert Roth, *Forestry Conditions and Interests of Wisconsin*, U.S. Division of Forestry, *Bulletin*, no. 16 (1898), 51; Forestry Commission, *Report*, 1898, p. 5.

Americans that food would win the war, patriotism demanded the expansion of agricultural endeavor. And in the postwar period, a citizenry grateful for victory hoped that veterans would find homes on settlements in northern Wisconsin. While skeptics continued to doubt the northern farmers' chances of success, the settlement movement won support throughout the state. Real estate speculators and land companies were happy, of course, to welcome all settlers whether they were veterans or not. Others, believing that the future prosperity of the state required a healthy agricultural economy in the north, also endorsed schemes for converting stumpland to farmland. Even before the Armistice, the Milwaukee Association of Commerce urged the creation of a state development bureau to promote settlement. The Wisconsin Bankers' Association at its annual meeting in 1918 resolved to "encourage under appropriate rural credit methods the development of the unoccupied lands by actual settlers," and to "support such settlers when established on Wisconsin lands." As dean of the university's College of Agriculture, Harry L. Russell threw his influence behind the settlement movement, and even the Wisconsin Society of Equity endorsed it at the society's state convention in 1919.[14]

The postwar labor unrest and the Red Scare of 1919 provided another rationale for the settlement movement. The Milwaukee Association of Commerce had long believed that many urban residents were misplaced, that they were "suffering the inevitable consequences in poverty or dissatisfaction, and would be far better off away from the city." The mounting fear of Bolshevism led banker Henry A. Moehlenpah to emphasize the importance of relieving urban tensions. The best way to circumvent revolution, he thought, was to transfer the discontented from cities out to farms in northern Wisconsin. Dean Russell agreed. Drawing on the ideas of Frederick Jackson Turner, the historian who had been a colleague at the university before leaving for Harvard in 1909, Russell asserted that farm ownership encouraged an independence of mind that served to "stabilize our political and social ideals." The Milwaukee Asso-

[14] Edward H. Beardsley, *Harry L. Russell and Agricultural Science in Wisconsin* (Madison, 1969), 122–124; Madison *Capital Times*, November 21, 1919; Carstensen, *Farms or Forests*, 87; Wilbur H. Glover, *Farm and College: The College of Agriculture of the University of Wisconsin, a History* (Madison, 1952), 281–285; Arlan Helgeson, *Farms in the Cutover: Agricultural Settlement in Northern Wisconsin* (Madison, 1962), 91–92; *Civics and Commerce*, October, 1917, p. 7; Wisconsin Bankers' Association, *Proceedings*, 1918, pp. 144–145.

ciation of Commerce adopted this thesis as a basis for action. "Upper Wisconsin was a new country—a frontier—its future depended upon settlement," suggested an article in *Civics and Commerce*. "It had land, but lacked men to develop it."[15]

No one devoted himself more wholeheartedly to the development of the Cutover than did Harry L. Russell. Certain of the settlement movement's success, he invested $35,000 of his own money in the Wisconsin Colonization Company founded by university regent Ben Faast. Perhaps because the faculty had always been free to participate in such ventures, the dean discerned no conflict of interest so long as he avoided taking part in management decisions. He even encouraged his faculty to join in the enterprise as he led the attack on Cutover problems. Faculty members at the University of Wisconsin and in the Extension did, in fact, become involved as scientists and researchers, if not as investors. Intensive study of the region resulted in analyses of the northern economy, handbooks for new settlers, experiments to develop early-maturing soybeans, peas, and corn, attempts to adapt new crops such as kudzu and sunflowers for silage, and special efforts to refine dairy techniques for northern uses.[16]

The College of Agriculture also assisted in overcoming the most onerous and wearisome problem of all: the problem of clearing the land. "Stumps are the recognized enemy of mankind in upper Wisconsin," noted the *New North*, and clearing them out by primitive mechanical means was arduous, debilitating, discouraging work. One land promoter, exceptional for his candor, recognized the difficulties of the task and conceded that "the waste of human energy, time, and money is terrible." The most efficient method used for stump removal was blasting with dynamite, but dynamite was far too expensive for settlers whose farms were marginal. After

[15] *Civics and Commerce*, October, 1917, p. 7, and October, 1919, pp. 50–52; Beardsley, *Harry L. Russell*, 125; Harry L. Russell, "The Cut-Over Section: An Undeveloped Empire" (mimeographed), in General Subject Files, box 21, Series 9/1/1/5-1, Papers of Deans Henry and Russell, 1880–1930, College of Agriculture, UW Archives. The effort to encourage settlement of the Cutover lands had begun before the turn of the century, when boosters employed traditional land-office promotions. Hyperbolic brochures identified northern Wisconsin as "the great cheese section," "the land of the big, red clover," or the hay and potato belt where, as one poet effused: "Mother Nature's always smiling,/ And the Skies are rarest blue." See Lucile Kane, "Settling the Wisconsin Cutovers," in *WMH*, 40 (Winter, 1956–1957), 94–95.

[16] Beardsley, *Harry L. Russell*, 126–127, 130–131; Harry L. Russell, "The Stability of Wisconsin's Agriculture," in Wisconsin Bankers' Association, *Proceedings*, 1921, p. 131.

the American declaration of war against Germany, however, the war department began stockpiling TNT, and after the Armistice the Wisconsin legislature requested that Governor Philipp find a way to secure some of the surplus for stump removal in the Cutover. Dean Russell was therefore dispatched to Washington, where he conferred with Congressman Adolphus P. Nelson. Together they worked out an arrangement with the war department to secure 200,000 pounds of TNT for land clearing in northern Wisconsin. "The strings of red tape have become unloosed," rejoiced the *Taylor County Star News*, adding that farmers would pay but ten cents a pound for packing and shipping the surplus. When the TNT gave out, Russell obtained picric acid, sodatrol, and pyrotol, and from 1919 to 1928 the College of Agriculture supervised the distribution of nearly 19 million pounds of explosives.[17]

"In the presence of thousands of spectators from city and country alike," reported the *Wisconsin Farmer* in the fall of 1920, "an acre of stumps was sent skyward at one blast in Marinette county. . . . The shattering of a whole acre of stumps in the twinkling of an eye was something unheard of and illustrated most strikingly the superiority of applied science over plodding ways in achievement of practical results." To the people of Wausaukee, the performance marked the "contrast between the old and the new life and practices of the region." They had expected an invasion of spectators, and they were not disappointed as hundreds of automobiles converged on the town. Women and girls provided a free lunch in the public square, and men distributed cigars to the visitors. Then came a plowing exhibition, a musical performance, and a series of speeches including one by Harry L. Russell. Finally, in a natural amphitheater outside the town, the program "culminated in the spectacular blast . . . and when the mighty cloud of earth and stumps and litter shot upward with a deafening explosion amid the delighted shouts and acclamations of the crowd a memorable day in Marinette county history was brought to a happy and triumphant close."[18]

Although the *Wisconsin Farmer* expected the "stimulating effect"

[17] Rhinelander *New North*, April 29, 1920; Beardsley, *Harry L. Russell*, 127–129; Superior *Telegram*, October 20, 29, 1917; Helgeson, *Farms in the Cutover*, 104–110; *Taylor County Star News* (Medford), July 21, 1920. The explosives secured for Wisconsin came to nearly double the amount any other state was able to obtain. Taylor County farmers, according to one estimate, saved $80,000 by using war surpluses. *Taylor County Star News*, November 3, 1927.

[18] *Wisconsin Farmer*, 49 (October 28, 1920), 1828–1829.

of Wausaukee's demonstration to "redound to greater benefits for all northern Wisconsin in the future," the anticipated new era for northern farmers never materialized. Persuasive advertising, expert advice, skillful political manipulation, new methods of land clearing, and prodigious individual effort were not enough to overcome the harsh climate, short growing season, and stingy soils. An increasing number of tax delinquencies in the mid-twenties gave evidence of a profound bitterness and despair that was to remain for years to come. As late as 1968, Hannah O. Gruenwald could still recall how real estate agents and railroad companies had been permitted to sell land for agriculture in Sawyer County. Her parents "had been bamboozled into thinking they could farm up there," and as a child she formed a vivid impression of people immobilized by hunger as well as by cold. Icicles formed on noses and eyelashes, and farmers dried up their cows for lack of forage. Driving over the countryside, one could scarcely fail to observe the great number of abandoned farmsteads. "Their former occupants were the ones lucky enough to have retained some of the money they brought with them. So they could move away."[19]

Farmers in all sections of the country were experiencing difficulties, but none suffered more than did those who attempted to settle the Cutover. In 1928 Benjamin H. Hibbard led a team of investigators in a study of taxation in seventeen northern counties, and their report documented allegations that efforts to farm the Cutover had been ill-advised. In 1921 a million acres had been offered for sale as tax-delinquent in the counties under examination. By 1925 that amount had more than doubled, and in 1927 the land available through tax sales increased to 2.5 million acres, or about a fourth of the total land area in the seventeen counties. In 1921, two-fifths of the tax deeds went unsold, and six years later no takers appeared for more than four-fifths of them. Furthermore, for all the ballyhoo to promote settlement in northern Wisconsin, only about 6 per cent of the total acreage in the seventeen counties was actually under cultivation in 1927.[20]

By the time the Hibbard report was disseminated, Russell had already conceded that the attempt to extend agriculture into the Cutover was a failure, and he warned against "any promotion or

[19] Hannah O. Gruenwald to the Editor, Milwaukee *Journal*, June 9, 1968.

[20] Benjamin H. Hibbard et al., *Tax Delinquency in Northern Wisconsin*, UW Agricultural Experiment Station, *Bulletin*, no. 399 (1928), 9–11, 15–19.

continued effort along lines similar to the past." The dean's volteface signaled a change of heart among his friends in the Wisconsin Bankers' Association. In 1927 J. F. Kettenhofen of Oconomowoc told those in attendance at the association's annual meeting that banks had been financing too much "unsound" agriculture. "Lands in our State recently denuded of timber have been attempting to come back with an agricultural program," he observed, "and that is where the seed fell upon the rock." Clearly, the settlement policy which the WBA had supported required change in the "sections of this State that are not adapted to agriculture," and in 1928 the bankers demonstrated their willingness to change. They expressed their belief that "additional land should only be opened as the needs of the farmers demand, and then only in an orderly development." They also affirmed their recently acquired conviction that "such lands as are best adapted for forestry and game reserves should be under state ownership and supervision."[21]

In the war period after *State ex rel. Owen v. Donald*, the position of the Wisconsin legislature was perforce one that favored agriculture as opposed to forestry in the north. Governor Philipp told the legislature that conservation was a national rather than a state responsibility and that, in any case, forestry could do little to strengthen the state's economy. During the New Era, however, the legislature demonstrated that it could modify its position in much the same manner that bankers had modified theirs. The advocates of a carefully constructed forestry policy never gave up, and when the settlement movement proved a disappointment, the opposition of northern counties gradually diminished.[22]

Amendment of the state constitution was a necessary first step towards a revitalized forestry program. In 1921, state senator William A. Titus of Fond du Lac introduced a joint resolution to readopt the constitutional amendment permitting the state to appropriate funds for forestry and water power. Both houses approved, and the resolution was again passed by both houses in 1923.

[21] Harry L. Russell, "Land Clearing Situation," October 1, 1926, manuscript as cited in Beardsley, *Harry L. Russell*, 135n; Carstensen, *Farms or Forests*, 91; *Wisconsin Blue Book, 1931*, p. 269; Harry L. Russell, *What's New in Farm Science*, comp. Noble Clark, UW Agricultural Experiment Station, *Annual Report*, 1927–1928, published as *Bulletin*, no. 405 (1929), 1–3; Wisconsin Bankers' Association, *Proceedings*, 1927, p. 133; *ibid.*, 1928, pp. 181–182.

[22] *Wisconsin Assembly Journal*, 1915, p. 32; Barlowe, "Forest Policy in Wisconsin," in *WMH*, 26:266.

Titus proposed that the amendment be submitted to popular referendum in the 1924 general election, and at that time voters overwhelmingly approved readoption (336,360 to 173,563).[23]

In the meantime, forestry had once again become a subject of some national discussion. Under the Weeks Act of 1911, the federal government had been buying cutover land in eastern watersheds in order to improve navigation. In 1924 Congress passed the Clarke-McNary bill, which expanded the Weeks law provisions for fighting fires and enlarging federal forests. The following year the Wisconsin legislature authorized federal acquisition of up to 100,000 acres in the state, and by 1933 it had increased that amount to 2 million acres. Federal agencies moved slowly, however, and even by 1935 they had purchased less than 700,000 acres in the state. Nevertheless, northern Wisconsin welcomed the legislation. "Griffith at the head of the Forestry Department years ago told us what we would have to do with this and like areas, but we laughed at him and threw him out of office," remarked Angus MacDonald, owner of a resort at Three Lakes. "Now we are finding Griffith was right, he was far-sighted enough to see just what was going to happen to us. This land as a Federal Forest is going to be worth more to Wisconsin than the few struggling farms that may locate there in years to come."[24]

Enlarging the federal forest reserve was not the only means by which to develop solutions for the problems of northern Wisconsin. In 1925 a legislative committee on administration and taxation began a two-year investigation that won support for amending the uniform tax clause of the state constitution and led to passage of the Forest Crop Law in 1927. Under the terms of that important legislation, the owner of 160 or more acres could declare his land suited for forestry practice. If the state's conservation commission approved, the land was entered under the Forest Crop Law, and such entry constituted a fifty-year renewable contract between the owner and the state. Under its terms the owner was to be relieved of property taxes except for an annual charge of ten cents an acre.

[23] *Laws of Wisconsin*, 1923, pp. 482–483 (Chapter 289); *Wisconsin Blue Book, 1925*, p. 579.

[24] Barlowe, "Forest Policy in Wisconsin," in *WMH*, 26:267; Carstensen, *Farms or Forests*, 92–93; Angus McDonald to Clinton G. Price, April 14, 1926, in vol. 8, "Reports and Proceedings of the Legislature's Interim Committee on Administration and Taxation, 1925–1926" (9 vols.), in the LRB.

In return, he was obliged to pay a severance tax of 10 per cent of the value of the timber when cut. In lieu of the property taxes that a town might have received, the state was to pay ten cents per acre per year for lands entered under the law. Thus everyone benefited. Owners secured tax advantages, towns were compensated for lost taxes, and the state was assured of a new beginning in forestry. During the first year of the law's operation, 160,000 acres were accepted for entry, and large lumber companies as well as individual owners began improving forestry practices in Wisconsin.[25]

The drive for a more rational development of the Cutover did not end with the Forest Crop Law. In December, 1928, representatives from seventeen northern counties met at Rhinelander to consider recommendations for further legislation, and out of that conference came a proposal that each county be given authority to establish land-use zones within county lines. The newly elected governor, Walter J. Kohler, enthusiastically supported county zoning. It would, he thought, serve as "a deterrent against ill-advised location of farms," permit the consolidation of school districts, and avoid unnecessary highway construction. It would also aid in resolving the continuing problem of tax delinquencies in the north. Finally, after much discussion of the proposed legislation, assemblyman Joseph D. Grandine of Forest County submitted a bill in April, 1929, to provide counties with the authority to zone rural land. Both houses passed the measure, and the governor signed it into law in August.[26]

Neither the Forest Crop Law nor county zoning provided instant solutions for problems in the Cutover. Yet a start had been made towards a resolution of economic difficulties in northern Wisconsin by the Depression thirties, when larger and more complex problems engulfed the entire nation. And the experience of the New Era had provided an object lesson in public management of resources. "The cut-over areas of northern Wisconsin speak as eloquently against

[25] Barlowe, "Forest Policy in Wisconsin," in *WMH*, 26:273–276; Gaus, "Memorandum on Land Use," 6, in the Philip F. La Follette Papers; John M. Gaus, "Conservation in Wisconsin," in the *Wisconsin Blue Book, 1933*, p. 79; Wilson, "Forestry in Wisconsin," *Wisconsin Blue Book, 1942*, pp. 179–181. The 1927 legislature also authorized county forests, and in 1928 the attorney general approved entry of county lands under the Forest Tax Law.

[26] Rhinelander *New North*, December 20, 1928; Walter J. Kohler, "Message to the Legislature," in the *Wisconsin Senate Journal*, 1929, p. 23; Carstensen, *Farms or Forests*, 104–105; *Wisconsin Blue Book, 1929*, p. 549.

haphazard development as any city condition," wrote Fred M. Wylie, deputy attorney general of the state in 1931. The establishment of farms in remote areas and "misdirected efforts to farm lands not well-suited to agriculture" had created new difficulties that compounded "the far-reaching economic ill effects of stripping the state of timber." Conditions in northern Wisconsin, in Wylie's view, "all cry out for planning, for social direction of individual effort." He thus found ample reason for predicting that "the judicial tendency is going to be to recognize more and more the great social evil of uncorrelated and unrestrained individual and selfish enterprise and hence to broaden . . . the power of the government to plan the social and economic conditions of the present and the future."[27]

* * *

The ill-fated effort to turn northern Wisconsin into productive farmland was only one of several attempts to find an economic base for that region other than lumber. For many lumbermen the search for alternative economic foundations held few attractions, and they moved on to continue their exploitation of timber in other regions—in the Pacific Northwest, for example, or in the forests of the South. Some of the lumber entrepreneurs, however, remained behind and applied their capital and managerial skills to new industrial and financial enterprises in Wisconsin. These new industries in turn provided steady, year-round jobs for loggers and river boys after the timber had been cut. Indeed, an increase in the labor pool resulting from the disappearance of timber sometimes provided an inducement for industries to move into the state. One reason for the success of the aluminum cookware industry at Manitowoc, Two Rivers, and West Bend, for example, was the availability of cheap labor from the vanishing logging camps.[28]

Marathon County provided the best example of entrepreneurial adaptation to the depletion of timber resources. Located in the north-central highland and bisected by the Wisconsin River, Marathon's place in the lumber industry was secure until the exhaustion

[27] F. M. Wylie to Special Legislative Committee on Forest, Fires, and Delinquent Taxes, September 12, 1931, in Legislature (1931–1932), miscellaneous material (1931–1933) from the Special Committee on Forest, Fires, and Delinquent Taxes, in the LRB.

[28] James M. Rock, "The Wisconsin Aluminum Cookware Industry Prior to World War II" (doctoral dissertation, Northwestern University, 1966), 75–76; James M. Rock, "A Growth Industry: The Wisconsin Aluminum Cookware Industry, 1893–1920," in *WMH*, 55 (Winter, 1971–1972), 87–88.

of timber resources prior to World War I. By then the lumbermen, who co-operated informally to such a degree that they became known as the Wausau Group, turned to other activities. They went into banking, and they organized the Employers Mutual Liability Insurance Company of Wisconsin. They invested in utilities in Marathon and neighboring counties. By 1926 they had consolidated those power interests into the Wisconsin Valley Electric Company, which controlled the generation and distribution of power throughout the northern Wisconsin River Valley. Especially significant for the development of manufacturing in the area was their diversification into wood-processing and paper industries. In 1909 the Wausau Group organized the Marathon Paper Mills Company, and under the creative management of David Clark Everest the firm soon became one of Wisconsin's leading producers of paper specialties.[29]

Important as such adjustments were, it was people residing outside the Cutover who stimulated the growth of the region as a summer playground. At the opening of the postwar decade, the automobile and the highway system had advanced far enough to provide vacationers from Milwaukee or Chicago with easy access to cool northern lakes teeming with fish. During the sweltering months of summer, suggested travel agents and resort owners, nothing could be more refreshing than a few days "away from the hot pavements and busy business centers" of the metropolis. The burgeoning tourist business also taught citizens to view their state with a new sense of wonder. "Of course, the people of Wisconsin have fished and hunted ever since the first pioneer fought his way into the wilderness of this region, but not until recently have we begun to realize how kind the creator really was to us," observed the Rhinelander *New North*; "nor have we given serious consideration to capitalizing this vast natural asset." With much of the timber cut, northerners turned enthusiastically to making the most of the lakes, the fish, and the game that were left. "And the beauty of it all," exulted the *New North*, sensitive to the loss of Oneida County's most valuable natural resource, "is that we can sell our climate and scenery year after year and still retain it forever."[30]

[29] Steven B. Karges, "David Clark Everest and Marathon Paper Mills Company: A Study of a Wisconsin Entrepreneur, 1909–1931" (doctoral dissertation, University of Wisconsin, 1968), 48–49, 56–62.

[30] Burlington *Standard-Democrat*, February 15, 1924; Rhinelander *New North*, February 21, 1924; "Superior, Where It Is Cool, Wisconsin," a brochure published in 1926,

Paved Road Network, 1924

Paved Road Network, 1940

In presenting arguments for a new state park in the spring of 1922, the *Taylor County Star News* contended that "as a commercial proposition alone this undertaking is worthy of the support of Taylor County people." A state park would surely bring thousands of vacationers, "and the tourist leaves money on the road he travels." A highway census disclosed that more than 3,000 automobiles from distant parts passed through Rhinelander during 1922. That fall local businessmen held a meeting to organize the Northern Wisconsin Resort Association. The announced purposes were two: first, to induce tourists to spend their vacations—and their dollars—in northern Wisconsin and, second, to improve both the services for tourists and the outdoor life of the region. Within a year the organization had enlisted 2,000 members from various enterprises including wholesale and retail firms, banks, lumber companies, hotels and resorts, automobile and oil companies, "and many others from business and professional lines." In 1923, to indicate broad participation in its activities, the organization began calling itself the "Wisconsin Land o' Lakes Association."[31]

"Probably never in the history of the state has such an excessive

---

probably by the Superior Public Affairs Committee. Northern newspapers elaborated endlessly on attractions of the region: hunting, fishing, scenic wonders, Indian powwows, lumberjack pageants, and clean, clear air. See, for example, the Iron River *Pioneer*, January 19, 1922, July 24, 1924, and June 13, 1929; Bonduel *Times*, August 27, 1925; *Taylor County Star News* (Medford), March 30, 1922, and July 4, 1929; and the Rhinelander *New North*, August 19, 1926, and July 11, 1929. The account in the Burlington *Standard-Democrat*, February 15, 1924, was typical: "Wisconsin, with her 7,000 lakes, is a great natural playground, offering a diversion [*sic*] of recreation unequaled by many other sections of the country. The big out-doors is still unspoiled and the seeker of the 'wilderness places,' can still, with paddle and canoe, go over the trails of the old French voyagers. The lakes are stocked with game fish; the roads are all-year roads maintained for the comfort and convenience of visiting motorists. The climate of Wisconsin is unsurpassed anywhere in the United States. The days are clear and comfortable and the nights are cool, assuring complete rest. There are very few cloudy days in Wisconsin. Government reports state there is more oxygen in the air in this region than in any other section of the country. An ideal vacationland. . . ."

[31] *Taylor County Star News* (Medford), March 30, 1922; Rhinelander *New North*, October 12, 19, 1922, February 22, 1923; Iron River *Pioneer*, February 1, 1923. The Northern Lakes Park proposal won widespread support, but in 1923 Governor Blaine vetoed a bill for an 8,000-acre park in Price and Sawyer counties. The site was ill-chosen, he argued, for it contained only a few scrub pine, much swampland, and a large amount of hardwood timber that had reached a merchantable point in growth. Furthermore, the governor disliked the tactics employed by the park's promoters. Eventually, in 1925, the legislature established the Northern Forest Park in Vilas County. See Zona Gale to Blaine, May 23, 1923, in the John J. Blaine Papers; "Executive Communication," July 12, 1923, in the Blaine Papers; C. L. Harrington, "The Conservation Commission," in the *Wisconsin Blue Book, 1927*, p. 201.

[*sic*] booster campaign been proposed as that launched by the Wisconsin Land o' Lakes Association," boasted the *New North.* Backers of the campaign made plans to send packets of brochures, road maps, and travel information to cities outside the state. Officers estimated that advertising of the association would reach at least 2 million people a week, and as if that were not enough, tourist bureaus were established in Chicago and Milwaukee as well as at the association headquarters in Rhinelander. The *New North* saw in this campaign "a bigger thing for northern Wisconsin than the summer resort business" alone, for every commercial activity in the region was certain to share in the profits of tourism. If all worked well, the association dared to believe, the tourists might find their experience so enjoyable that they would settle permanently in northern Wisconsin. That possibility, in fact, led the Milwaukee Association of Commerce to pledge $10,000 to "aid the movement to advertise the state not only as a playground second to none in this country, but also to place before the people of the nation the advantages Wisconsin has to offer."[32]

Whether or not the tourists chose to stay in Wisconsin, the Land o' Lakes Association considered its 1923 campaign a resounding success. An automobile census taken by the State Highway Commission revealed that on August 3 there had been 29,409 out-of-state cars in Wisconsin, with an average 3.5 persons per car. More than 15,000 automobiles were from Illinois, but distant states and the Canadian provinces were also represented. Nearly 250 automobiles had come from California, and nearly 350 from New York. Best of all, the 1923 tourists had spent an estimated $100 million in Wisconsin. With such success, the Land o' Lakes Association planned for even greater numbers in the future, and it sought to embellish the natural beauties of the state. Backed by the State Historical Society of Wisconsin and the Indian Pageant Corporation, an Indian celebration at the Apostle Islands was expected "in the first year to rival the Mardi Gras, Frontier Days and other similar entertainments." While plans for festivities in the north were under way, Wisconsin outdoorsmen and businessmen were preparing the state's exhibit at the National Travel and Outdoor Life Exposition to be held at the Chicago Coliseum in May. "Cedar,

[32] Rhinelander *New North,* March 29, 1923; Milwaukee Association of Commerce, *Official Bulletin,* December 20, 1923, p. 2.

pine, balsam and spruce trees, trailing arbutus and ground pine, live game, and fish will convert the Coliseum into a replica of the North Woods in summer," reported the *New North*. "Camps will be reproduced in miniature and live game and fish will be shown against their native background of trees and rocks. Resort men connected with exhibits will dress as trappers and lumber jacks to add realism to the settings."[33]

Providing accommodations for tourists was an undertaking that sometimes proved troublesome during the New Era. In an earlier day, when vacationers customarily took the train from the city to their chosen summer playground, they expected to find a resort or a hotel awaiting their arrival. With increasing numbers of people traveling by automobile, however, a new pattern of vacation behavior began to develop. Tourists called it "gypsying," and it was not entirely unlike the behavior of bohemians living in Greenwich Village, or on the Left Bank in Paris. Freed from railroad timetables, the first automobile vacationers were inclined to indulge their wanderlust, setting up camp at the side of the road when night fell. Enjoying their new freedom, some tourists became downright nuisances. "Farmers have been put to considerable expense in cleaning up after campers and picnickers, and frequently serious damage has been done by the offenders against common decency," grumbled the Burlington *Standard-Democrat* at the height of the vacation season in 1924. The farmers might have thought it obvious enough that "campers should refrain from cutting fences, be careful of fires, return all waste papers, remains of edibles and cans to their own garbage cans." If so, they were disappointed.[34]

The tourists tended to think they had liberated themselves from the strictures of civilization, and they were not easily controlled. Yet Wisconsin towns and cities needed tourist dollars, and they were reluctant to create the impression that vacationers were not welcome. What was to be done? Clearly, communities needed to establish free campgrounds that could be policed, and that is precisely what they did. Beloit, for example, provided a campground with

[33] Rhinelander *New North*, August 2, 1923, January 3, April 3, 17, 1924; Burlington *Standard-Democrat*, February 15, 1924; "Foreign Automobile Census," 1923, in General Correspondence and Subject File, 1918–1983, subject file no. 1863, in folder 18, box 45, Series 918, Records of the Division of Highways, WSA.

[34] Warren J. Belasco, *Americans on the Road: From Autocamp to Motel, 1910–1945* (Cambridge, 1979), 11–13; Burlington *Standard-Democrat*, August 15, 1924.

two wells "of unexcelled spring water," campsites with wooden decks and brick ovens, and a community house with showers, toilets, and lounge. The better the campground, however, the more likely were autocampers to overstay their welcome. In any case, tidiness has never been one of the virtues of tourists, and maintaining the campgrounds could mean considerable municipal expense. By mid-decade, many Wisconsin cities were charging a fee for the use of municipal campgrounds, although when they did the fee was usually minimal. At Prentice Park in Ashland, tourists were required to register and pay twenty-five cents a car for the privilege of stopping overnight to enjoy "nine gushing mineral springs with their crystal clear water, the beautiful lagoon, the fine sand beach a short distance away, the jungle-like foliage casting a deep shade, and the tameness of the squirrels." The point here was not to have the campgrounds turn a profit; it was, rather, to discourage obnoxious tourists who stayed too long. "A reasonable fee system," thought the editor of the Watertown *Daily Times*, attracted "more desirable tourists . . . who are eager to pay for what is prepared for them, rather than to sponge upon public hospitality."[35]

The day of the inexpensive municipal campground, however, was swiftly done. In Rhinelander the *New North*, at one time an advocate of agricultural expansion, never wavered in its conviction that "the tourist crop" was becoming "one of the most profitable crops raised in the state." Most of northern Wisconsin found the metaphor apt. That summer resorts and hotels enlarged their facilities, and that private campgrounds popped up like woodland mushrooms constituted solid evidence that businessmen large and small were taking over the tourist trade. Every summer the vacationers came in increasing number, and as their numbers increased so also did their demands. "Blindly they pour themselves from flivver or Rolls, as the case may be, shrieking for refreshments and a bath," wrote one observer of the incoming hordes. " 'Two hot tubs and a pair of ice cold showers is chapter one of what I want,' remarks the goggled wayfarer, 'and there will be a steak with onions in the second. The story will have a happy ending with a night-long, heartfelt heavenly snore.' "[36]

[35] Belasco, *Americans on the Road*, 78, 124–127; Ashland *Daily Press*, July 17, 1925; Watertown *Daily Times*, June 9, 1925.

[36] Rhinelander *New North*, November 29, 1923; Milwaukee *Journal*, July 6, 1924; *Waupaca County Post* (Waupaca), January 24, 1924.

The summer visitors sometimes expected to find liberation from strict enforcement of the Volstead Act as well as freedom from the demands of the workaday world. "Memories of abolished glory draw the old-time soaks," commented the Milwaukee *Journal*. Along with imbibers came "spinsters with sniffy nostrils" who wanted "to learn how well the constitution is enforced." Spinsters were not alone in finding opportunities to exercise sensitive olfactory organs. In 1926 Albert O. Barton, a Progressive journalist who had once served as the elder La Follette's secretary, congratulated Scott H. Goodnight, dean of men at the University of Wisconsin, for warning students against patronizing roadhouses. Such establishments, thought Barton, had become "a menace of the whole state." On a recent trip to northern counties he had found "moonshine joints often run by high-powered crooks, who boldly defy the law and debauch the neighborhood." The Chicago tourist traffic had brought a curse on Wisconsin: "[N]ot only are large quantities of bootleg liquor brought up from Chicago . . . but a large percentage of men and women in the north are making their living making moonshine and home-brew." Public officials were afraid to act because they did not know but what "their next door neighbor may be in the business himself." Conditions might have been worse during the primitive days of logging, "but with moonshine poison, the auto, good roads and the tourist traffic, a lot of young lives are being ruined."[37]

If there was any truth in Barton's lament and in complaints about the tourists' messiness and lack of respect for private property, one might well ask why Wisconsin welcomed the summer visitors with enthusiasm. The reasons, of course, are obvious: the tourists remained only a short time, they paid their bills, and they returned home. Whatever one thought of their behavior, their money required no laundering to make it acceptable. Besides, tourist behavior was undergoing modification. With the construction of new tourist camps and resorts, the excitement of gypsying tended to

[37] Milwaukee *Journal*, July 6, 1924; Barton to Goodnight, August 6, 1926, in the A. O. Barton Papers; Howard A. Quirt, president, Globe Publishing Company, Ironwood, Michigan, to Fred Zimmerman, January 12, 1927, photocopies in the author's and the History of Wisconsin project files. "Always Hurley officials have looked to the license money from Saloons as one important source of revenue; the more saloons, the more money for the city, hence the saloon business was fostered in pre-Volstead days," wrote Quirt. "With the advent of prohibition [in 1921], it was only natural that city officials would wink at liquor law violations, so long as the violators helped to defray the costs of city government."

diminish. By the end of the decade, vacationers were more likely to plan ahead so as to have a definite idea of where they would be spending their summer holidays. In 1930 the *New North* noted the passing of the chance tourist who "rambled along wherever his fancy . . . might call him, stopping wherever the notion might strike him and seek[ing] shelter wherever he happened to be." Now, "when he leaves behind him the streets of the city he knows just where he is going. It's not a matter of guess work. If he does not own his own lake domicile he has usually made all arrangements and he knows just what particular lake he will visit and just what camp, resort or lodge he intends to take for his woodland home." The only uncertainty about the vacation traffic of 1930, according to Edna Straub, head of the Rhinelander bureau of information, was uncertainty over the volume of business. She thought it would prove to be "a trifle smaller than last year, owing to last fall's slump in the stock market which made ready money a little less available." Even so, the tourists came. And they kept coming during the Depression thirties, though in diminished numbers, to provide at least some hope for economic survival in northern Wisconsin.[38]

* * *

Throughout the postwar decade, northern residents could not avoid ambivalent feelings about the invasion of outsiders during vacation and hunting seasons. On the one hand, by making recreation their business they could enjoy in full measure the natural beauty and the outdoor sports that attracted the visitors. They could also make good use of the money that vacationers left behind. On the other hand, northerners thought that tourists too often made pests of themselves in demanding amenities equivalent to those found in the cities. Furthermore, the tourist business was seasonal, and enterprises catering to vacationers required sizable capital investments. As the promoters of tourism soon learned, rates of failure ran high, and the satisfactions to be derived from maintaining boats and laundering bed linens were few. Yet resort owners and others engaged in the tourist trade could not afford to alienate their patrons. They therefore tended either to suppress resentments they may have felt, or to express their irritations indirectly.

A common tendency in Wisconsin's playground was to draw com-

[38] Rhinelander *New North*, August 21, 1930.

parisons between the wonders of the great outdoors and the restrictive, stultifying environment of metropolitan areas. Northern counties thus shared in some of the anti-urban sentiments that had begun to develop in the state's agricultural hinterland before the war and that reached significant proportions after the coming of the postwar recession. Like the northern regions seeking to attract tourists during the New Era, the farm areas of the state were ambivalent in their attitudes towards the city. The metropolis represented economic opportunities and social activities that attracted the residents of rural villages as well as the sons and daughters of farmers. At the same time, many people believed that by draining off rural population the city represented a serious threat to rural communities. But unlike tourist towns, the villages that depended primarily on agriculture felt no compulsion to soft-pedal their anxieties and resentments. During the postwar decade, therefore, the residents of agricultural communities mounted the ramparts in defense of village and rural ways of life.

A decrease in the percentage of Wisconsin people living in rural areas had been a secular demographic trend from the beginning of settlement, but the rapidity of urbanization at the end of the war drew attention to recent shifts in the state's population. An article in *Civics and Commerce* in 1918 noted that with the many changes taking place in Wisconsin during the previous quarter-century, most of the rural young people had moved away, leaving behind only the remnants of a once-flourishing population in the countryside. Like many later assessments of the twenties, the *Civics and Commerce* piece greatly exaggerated "the drift cityward." Census returns show that while Wisconsin's urban population increased nearly 25 per cent between 1920 and 1930, the state's rural population declined a mere 0.1 per cent. It was a relative and not an absolute decline that caused concern. Those who were optimistic about the future of agriculture correctly pointed out that "with improved machinery less labor is required to produce a bushel of wheat or corn or any other commodity," and that a decrease in the number of farm laborers was not in itself a cause for alarm.[39]

[39] John P. Hume, "How Business Prosperity Depends Upon Agriculture," in *Civics and Commerce*, June, 1918, p. 14; *Sixteenth Census of the United States, 1940: Population: Volume II, Part 7*, p. 549; George L. Leffler, supervised by Harold M. Groves, *Wisconsin Industry and the Wisconsin Tax System*, 2nd ed., UW Bureau of Business and Economic Research, *Bulletin*, no. 3 (1931), 12–13, in the LRB; *Wisconsin Farm Bureau News*, May, 1923, p. 2; "A Declining Agriculture," in *Hoard's Dairyman*, 60 (October 1, 1920), 434.

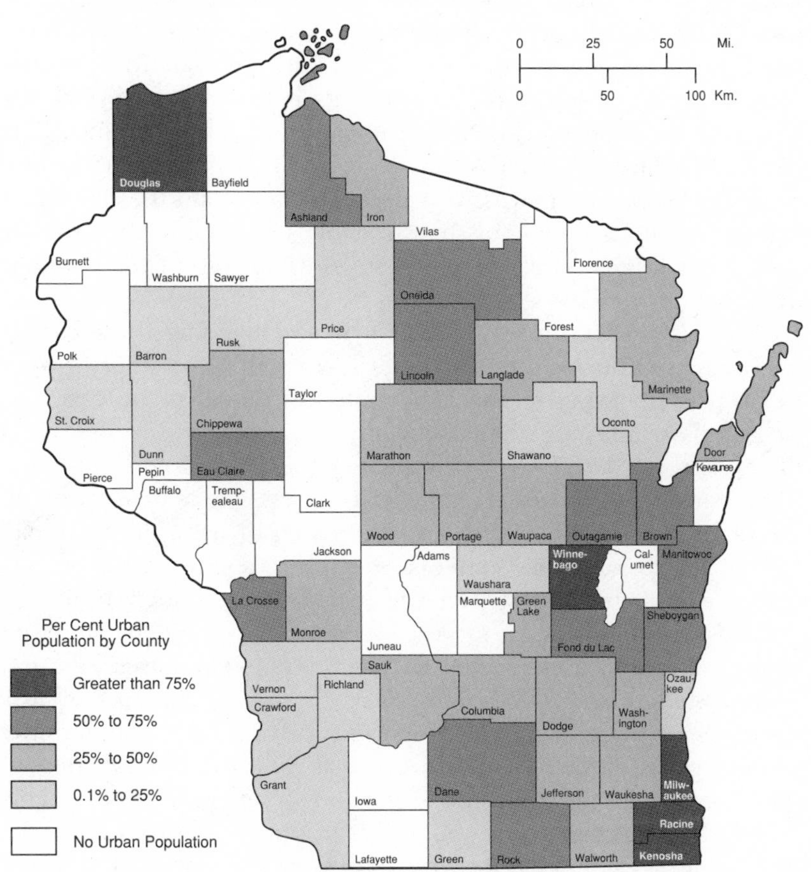

Urban Population, 1930

Yet one of the controlling myths of the 1920's was that rural areas were losers in a great social and economic transformation that followed the war. To the young men and women of isolated farms and rural villages, the well-publicized attractions of the metropolis were often compelling. On the eve of American involvement in the Great War, the *Northwestern Lutheran* reprinted an article from the *Lutheran Witness* that crystalized explanations of the way urban life lured young people from country to city. "To the warm, red blood which pulsates through their veins the city's excitement, movement, and noise appeal with peculiar force," conceded the author of the piece. "The city is the place where honor and fame is obtained. The city is the place of large gatherings. The city is the place of excellent music, bright lights, tempting dishes, beautiful faces, rare gowns, vivacious associates, and the ringing of money constantly changing hands. How natural for the country laddie and lassie to ask the question, Am I to die in the country, or to live in the city?"[40]

The enticements of ready employment and high wages in the cities had increased during the war, and if postwar commentaries were to be trusted, living in the metropolis continued to be easier as well as more exciting than living in the country. "Invention has lifted many burdens," wrote Progressive journalist Fred L. Holmes. "The home is no longer an industrial center. The making of cloth, the tanning of leather for shoes, the curing of ham, the manufacture of soap, once home employments, now are city industries." As urban manufacturing diversified to include the production of such goods, job opportunities increased. And working in the factories of the metropolis, unlike labor on farms and in rural areas, did not require endless toil from dawn to dusk. In June, 1920, the *Wisconsin Agriculturist* suggested that "boys and girls in farm communities were so ground down by hard work that they do not know how to play." Later in the year the *Agriculturist* returned to the same theme, arguing that the country boy would look for work in the metropolis as soon as he became convinced that by moving to the city he could escape the drudgery of incessant toil. In short, "you can't keep the country boy on the farm just by telling him how blue the sky is, if he thinks he can make more money and have more fun in town than he can at home."[41]

How did Wisconsin's rural communities respond to the movement of people from the countryside to the metropolis? One re-

[40] "City and Country," reprinted from the *Lutheran Witness* in the *Northwestern Lutheran*, 3 (November 21, 1916), 174.

[41] Fred L. Holmes, "The Farmer and the Help Problem," in *La Follette's Magazine*, January, 1921, pp. 8–9; *Wisconsin Agriculturist*, June 26, November 6, 1920. *Hoard's Dairyman* consistently held that migration from farm to city was a natural result of coercive economic influences, but that imbalances in favor of the city would eventually correct themselves. See "Is Civilization Passing?" in *Hoard's Dairyman*, 65 (May 4, 1923), 590.

action was to suggest that for all its undeniable advantages, the city could be as dreary and melancholy as any rural village. The same *Lutheran Witness* that observed red-blooded rural youth being drawn to beautiful urban faces and vivacious urban associates also reported a contrasting set of images: "[T]he drawn underlip of the rouged woman in the cafe; the wail of the wife as the verdict-grinding magistrate pronounces sentence; the sodden face of the pawer-over of garbage barrels; the haggard glare of the drug fiend; . . . the man of forty in quest of a job; the teamster, asleep from exhaustion, rolled from his seat, and run over by his own wagon."[42]

Playing variations on the same theme at the close of the New Era, the Burlington *Standard-Democrat* pondered the future of the American people should they continue to swarm into the great centers of population. What was to become of "their power of initiative, their interest in the tasks of citizenship, . . . their personal character?" Visitors to the city could find luxury there, to be sure; and perhaps the metropolis did in fact receive more than its share of the nation's wealth. But if the visitors "would venture down the shabby side streets and dingy alleys where masses of people live, many of them with less sun and air than a horse or dog would get in their home towns, they would obtain a better perspective of real life in such cities." Anyone expecting to attend the big show should also expect to pay the big price. Furthermore, "you get your toes stepped on in the crowd, you get separated from your friends, and then probably have to take a back seat where you can't see much of anything."[43]

Another response to the movement of people from rural areas to cities was far more positive in its emphasis, and it produced a torrent of rhetoric about improving the conditions of life in the small towns. A primary concern here was with a village economy heavily dependent upon farmers who participated in community affairs. Unless the farmers made an adequate living, country towns were certain to experience difficulties. When rural villages confronted hard times, the lure of fabled economic opportunities in

[42] *Northwestern Lutheran*, 3 (November 21, 1916), 174.

[43] Burlington *Standard-Democrat*, February 1, 1929; *Wisconsin Agriculturist*, November 2, 1929. The high cost of living in cities as compared with the countryside was a recurring theme in small-town newspapers. "The rent hogs [of the city] are not satisfied with their pound of flesh. They want the whole carcass, and at the rate they are going they will soon have it devoured." Burlington *Standard-Democrat*, February 4, 1921.

the city was difficult to resist. "There never was a time when the small town, from a commercial standpoint, was being weighed in the balance as in the present era, and this means right now," proclaimed the Bloomington *Record* in 1925. "There never was a time when unanimity of purpose in behalf of the survival of the small town and an impulse of co-operation . . . were of more vital moment than right now." Community prosperity could not be founded on malice and hatred. Prosperity depended instead on fraternal goodwill and co-ordinated efforts to encourage individual ambition and achievement. A notable irony of the New Era was that rural villages drew heavily on the commercial wisdom of cities in order to save themselves from the city. Furthermore, the rhetoric of village business people turned out to be no less vigorous than the promotional enthusiasm of urban chambers of commerce.[44]

In a cultural sense as well as an economic one, rural villages perceived themselves as being weighed in the balance. In 1920, the year Sinclair Lewis published *Main Street*, state school superintendent Charles P. Cary received a letter from a teacher who, like Lewis' character Carol Kennicott, found herself frustrated by the numbing dullness of the small town to which she had moved. "There are no young people here of an acceptable type with whom we can associate," she complained. The retired farmers who controlled the municipal government "do not believe in civic improvement." Twice a week there was a movie, "but generally it is disgusting." Equally disgusting were the advertisements for bimonthly dances: "A good time assured. A lot of nice girls." After all, no self-respecting woman cared to become "a drawing card for a public dance." Left with reading as her only recreation, the teacher became discouraged to the point that she could not do her best work. Obviously, village contentment required more than economic prosperity. "The young people of today will not live in a country district where according to the old saying, the people go to bed when it is dark under the table," warned the Kewaunee *Enterprise*. "They demand an active outlet for their own life, and the community must provide it or lose its active young folks."[45]

The residents of Wisconsin villages well understood the attractions of the metropolis. While they took pains to point out the

[44] Bloomington *Record*, August 26, 1925.

[45] Department of Public Instruction, *Educational News Bulletin*, 12 (April, 1920), 2; Kewaunee *Enterprise*, February 1, 1929.

seamy side of urban life, they also sought to neutralize the lure of the city by developing an agreeable, captivating community life of their own. A speaker at the Delavan community week celebration of 1916 anticipated the postwar effort to improve small-town existence. "Bring some of the city's good things to the farm; modernize and make comfortable your homes with up-to-date heating plant, bathroom, toilet, sanitary plumbing, and supply the women with . . . efficient labor-saving machinery for housekeeping," he advised. He also suggested acquiring telephones, phonographs, and automobiles. And above all, he urged, "be a booster, have pride in your local village and help make it the liveliest, cleanest, most up-to-date place in the county." The *Wisconsin Farmer* echoed this advice, adding that when the farm housewife could "sweep with an electric vacuum cleaner, do her ironing with an electric iron, curl her hair on an electric curler" she would have no reason to envy her friends in the city. "The daughter in the modern, improved country home does not seek to escape it—she is proud of it; she knows there are none better."[46]

The satisfaction of consumer wants provided visible evidence of the small town's ability to keep up with the swift pace of the metropolis. Yet the village resident continued to be haunted by visions of beautiful faces and vivacious associates. Service and community clubs flourished during the New Era, and their popularity was indicative of efforts to fill small-town social needs. Churches became increasingly attentive to recreational and cultural activities. Other traditional organizations—debating societies, lyceums, ladies' aid societies, drama clubs—renewed attempts to provide educational experiences, practical training, and wholesome entertainment.[47]

In the minds of rural residents, the most important social activ-

[46] *Civics and Commerce*, September, 1916, p. 14; *Wisconsin Farmer*, 45 (July 13, 1916), 906. For later expressions of the rural desire for consumer goods, see the Bonduel *Times*, July 8, 1920, the *Kickapoo Scout* (Soldiers Grove), January 10, 1924, and the Burlington *Standard-Democrat*, April 17, 1925.

[47] C. J. Galpin, "Landowning Farmers Backbone of Church," in the *Taylor County Star News* (Medford), November 5, 1919; "Finds New Friendship Village of Substantial, Kindly People," in the *Wisconsin State Journal*, October 14, 1928. See, as well, columns by Elizabeth Clarke Hardy, woman's editor, in the *Wisconsin Agriculturist*, May 8, 1926, p. 12; September 11, 1926, p. 8; and November 20, 1926, p. 8; and, in the same magazine, D. E. Lindstrom, "Stimulating Rural Home Talent," April 13, 1929, p. 5; " 'Book Learnin' ' Grows Popular: County Libraries Would Place Reading Before Thousands of Farm Folks," October 12, 1929, pp. 3, 22; and an editorial, "Community Fellowship," December 7, 1929, p. 4.

ities were those created to interest young people in agricultural pursuits. Farming, rural folk were fond of pointing out, was the nation's most important industry. "Let us then endeavor to aid and interest the boys and girls of the rural communities, not only in those things that pertain to the business or vocation of their parents," urged the *Waupaca County Post*, "but in matters of social and economic interest to the community." Boys' and girls' agricultural clubs began forming shortly after the war, first to provide social activities for rural youth, then to familiarize young people with the latest and most productive agricultural practices. By the end of the New Era, the clubs were organizing as chapters of the Future Farmers of America. The object of the organization was to assure "the best possible farmers" in the years ahead. With such a purpose the clubs were supposed to present farming "in its true light" as a business and as a way of life. In Wisconsin's sixteen chapters, the most important state project in 1929 was a soil-building program carried out with the co-operation of the College of Agriculture in Madison. The Future Farmers also held picnics and banquets, provided programs for community meetings, and conducted project tours as well as poultry and grain shows.[48]

For all their social activities during the New Era, and for all their involvement in community projects, residents of Wisconsin villages required constant reassurance that rural life was indeed happier than life in the metropolis. Throughout the twenties the editors of village newspapers offered their readers a steady diet of rural wisdom and praise for small-town virtues. Country people were told that in rural towns "conditions are more favorable for normal living than they are in large cities, where the living costs are high, where people are crowded into small space." They were told that persons who chose to live in a village environment could be distinguished by the variety of their reading and the clarity of their thinking. They were told to cherish "the warm and free hearted association" among village residents. Unlike the public meetings in cities, where one found "a freezing atmosphere among people who rarely see and care little for each other," small-town social events were "like a jolly family gathering, where everybody knows everyone else, and all act as if they were at home."[49]

[48] Wisconsin Bankers' Association, *Proceedings*, 1922, pp. 95, 97–98, and 1923, pp. 134–142; *Waupaca County Post* (Waupaca), November 15, 1923; Burlington *Standard-Democrat*, July 18, 1919, March 21, 1924; *Wisconsin Agriculturist*, April 27, 1929.

[49] Burlington *Standard-Democrat*, December 1, 1922, August 15, 1924, April 27, 1928, April 12, 1929; *Wisconsin Agriculturist*, November 2, 1929.

The defenders of rural villages were hard put to prove that "free hearted association" was a distinctive village characteristic, especially when friendliness gave rise to gossip and pressure towards conformity. To some small-town residents, "friendliness" was simply a euphemism for prying eyes and wagging tongues, and for such folk the anonymity of the city actually became desirable. In any case, conflicts between the metropolis and the village seemed far more real to rural residents when they fought their battles on economic grounds. One of the great rivalries of the New Era was the competition between village merchants and the chain stores that were busily developing new practices in merchandising. From the rhetoric that accompanied the growth of retail chains one can learn much about the circumstances that essentially troubled Wisconsin's small towns.[50]

An important principle involved in chain-store operations—rapid turnover with a small margin of profit but a large volume of sales—had long been used by mail-order houses such as Sears, Roebuck and Montgomery Ward. During the postwar decade retail chains effectively combined that principle with reductions in the costs of distributing goods. They achieved those reductions in part by doing their own manufacturing and in part by limiting large-scale purchases to single sources. The chains, in short, eliminated duplication of selling effort by taking over much of the wholesale function. Providing a straight-line flow of goods from manufacturers to consumers, they reduced the prices consumers had to pay.[51]

The increasing sophistication of chain-store operations threatened the cohesion of rural communities, for with their lower prices and a diversity of well-advertised products, the chains in large measure succeeded in enticing customers away from village merchants.

[50] Lewis E. Atherton, *Main Street on the Middle Border* (Bloomington, 1954), 182–185.

[51] Victor H. Pelz, "The Development of New Merchandising Standards for the Retail Store," in Conference on Problems of the Small City and Town, *The Small City and Town: A Conference on Community Relations*, ed. Roland S. Vaile (Minneapolis, 1930), 52–53; *Business and Financial Comment*, February 15, 1928, in the Milwaukee Public Library (a monthly publication of the First Wisconsin National Bank). The great popularity of mail-order catalogs among rural people perhaps made them receptive to the coming of retail chains. In his novel *Plowing on Sunday* (New York, 1934), p. 237, Sterling North provided a description of what the arrival of "the Farmer's Bible" (the Sears, Roebuck and Co. catalog) meant to a farm family in southern Wisconsin: "They did not care if the storm was raging outside. They did not care that they were snowbound. They were living in the romantic world of the mail-order catalogue where they were all as rich as kings, where every woman wore a beautiful new dress, and every man was handsome and stylish, where there were bonbons and books and beautiful buggies." Shopping in chain stores added a new dimension to the romance of consumerism.

Small-town merchants did not give up without a struggle. Accustomed to recognition as community benefactors, they drew heavily on community friendliness and goodwill in their battle to retain customer loyalty. The case for patronizing local merchants rather than chain stores or mail-order houses rested on two basic arguments. The first was that village merchants knew their customers personally and could therefore provide goods and services better suited to individual needs than could impersonal mail-order and chain stores. "The mail order house that receives your order doesn't know you from Adam and doesn't care," warned the Burlington *Standard-Democrat* in a typical phrasing of the argument. "The home town merchant knows you as a neighbor and he cares." In 1930, Waupaca merchants organized a rally to oppose the chain-store menace. "Chains of every kind are here," thundered attorney Wendell McHenry to a packed house. "Chain groceries, chain butcher shops, chain banks, chain dry goods stores, chain hardwares and chain drug stores, all with their hearts of steel in Wall Street, what do they care about the individual or the local community?"[52]

The second contention was that money spent locally was money that benefited the community. "CONSIDER these things—before you mail you [*sic*] orders out of town," pleaded the *Pierce County Herald*. "The dollar that you spend out of town is gone forever. The dollar that you spend at home—stays here and works. Whether it goes into civic improvements, taxes, better schools, churches, streets—or whether it simply goes into more merchandise for your next needs—it circulates at home." To deprive the community of consumers' dollars was to close the doors of opportunity for village boys and girls. "The chain store and mail order house [would] be dictators of every opportunity" if rural communities failed to patronize locally owned stores. They would "dictate from their large city offices what your son and daughter shall do,—where and when it shall be done."[53]

[52] Atherton, *Main Street*, 241; J. H. Kolb and Edmund deS. Brunner, "Rural Life," in President's Research Committee on Social Trends, *Recent Social Trends in the United States* (New York, 1933), 525; Kewaunee *Enterprise*, October 10, 1924; Burlington *Standard-Democrat*, August 12, 1921, April 27, 1923, October 1, 1926; *Waupaca County Post* (Waupaca), February 6, October 16, 1930.

[53] *Pierce County Herald* (Ellsworth), August 11, 1921, November 26, 1925; advertisement in the *Taylor County Star News* (Medford), May 8, 1930. For variations of these contentions, see the Bloomington *Record*, May 27, 1925; Kewaunee *Enterprise*, February 3, 1928; Rhinelander *New North*, February 20, 1930; and the *Taylor County Star News* (Medford), April 10, 17, 24, May 1, 15, 22, 29, June 5, 1930.

That local merchants and stores gradually gave way to chain stores is attributable to a number of influences at work in the competitive struggle between the two. For one thing, even though the Wisconsin Bankers' Association vigorously opposed branch banking, it looked more favorably on chain-store operations than did independent merchants. The First Wisconsin National Bank of Milwaukee, for example, took the position that independent merchants were not isolated entrepreneurs and that they must recognize their place in "a system whose object is to route standard goods to the consumer as speedily, smoothly and cheaply as possible." The independent merchants must, if they were to stay in business, "become open-minded students of merchandising." Albert D. Bolens of Port Washington, who identified himself as a "profit engineer," thought that it was precisely at this point that independent retailers had failed. Price alone had been the dominating influence with consumers, but merchants had so neglected to educate themselves on consumer preferences that they were not real merchants at all but "mere dispensers."[54]

Whatever Bolens and the bankers might write about the competition between independent and chain stores, however, price was in fact the basis of the chain stores' success. The chains bought in large lots, usually directly from manufacturers. They carried minimal inventories, and their efficient organizations cut overhead to a minimum. "The chain store represents systematic study of how to distribute goods in the simplest possible way and at the lowest possible cost," was the judgment of *Business and Financial Comment.* "The price differential in its favor is the principal justification for the chain and accounts for its remarkable growth."[55]

One of the proudest boasts of rural villages was that in nurturing a vital community spirit they had reduced the incidence of failure among their inhabitants. Small-town residents listened to countless self-congratulatory sermons, and they read innumerable editorials praising village friendliness and cohesion. Yet, as the *Pierce County Herald* pointed out in 1930, "the competition for growth and pros-

[54] *Business and Financial Comment*, February 15, 1928, in the Milwaukee Public Library; Wisconsin Bankers' Association, *Proceedings*, 1920, p. 152, and 1922, pp. 171–177, and 1924, pp. 173; Burlington *Standard-Democrat*, November 15, 1929; Bolens to A. B. Fontaine, June 15, 1930, in the Albert D. Bolens Papers. See also *La Follette's Magazine*, November, 1922, and the *Kickapoo Scout* (Soldiers Grove), January 11, 1923.

[55] *Business and Financial Comment*, February 15, 1927, July 16, 1928, in the Milwaukee Public Library.

perity between towns and cities everywhere is becoming more intensified each day." In the competition between local retailers and the chain stores, the vaunted community spirit of small towns clearly proved ineffective in assuring the survival of village merchants. Many of them, of course, did survive. But those who stayed in business did so because they managed to remain competitive, not because the citizenry patronized independent stores purely out of a sense of community loyalty. Nonetheless, the rhetoric of village cohesion and boosterism remained vigorous even as the chain stores were capturing small-town markets.[56]

Anomalies abounded in village efforts to promote a community spirit that would foster personal growth and development. The editors of rural newspapers were especially solicitous of village young people, and they devoted themselves to keeping boys and girls at home where they could live happy and productive lives. Yet in contrasting the metropolis and its crowded conditions with the hinterland, "where an elevator is a building to store grain and a siren is a whistle instead of a dangerous female," village editors did more to whet the appetite for a life in the city than they did to subdue it. In making such comparisons, they indicated that they understood neither the youthful desire for advancement to social and economic heights nor the adolescent fondness for living dangerously.[57]

Anomalies abounded, as well, in the way small towns reacted to satire, parody, and literary realism. Although rural people may have read the works of Edgar Lee Masters, Sherwood Anderson, or Sinclair Lewis, the literary criticism of small-town pundits suggests that they never fully comprehended what such writers were up to in their revolt from the village. Zona Gale's relationship with the small towns of Wisconsin is a case in point. Born in Portage in 1874, Gale attended the university in Madison, worked as a journalist in Milwaukee, and in 1901 became a reporter for the New York *World*. After publishing her first short story in 1904, she took to writing saccharine studies of "Friendship Village" and its neighborly residents. Beginning with the publication of *Birth* in 1918, however, she turned to more realistic and sometimes mordant criticism of the society in rural communities. In *Miss Lulu Bett* (1920), the dramatization of which won a Pulitzer Prize, and *Preface to a Life* (1926),

[56] *Pierce County Herald* (Ellsworth), March 6, 1930; Kewaunee *Enterprise*, October 10, 1924.

[57] Rhinelander *New North*, July 12, 1928.

she dealt with frustrated village people struggling to surmount the incessant gossip and uninspiring monotony of country towns. Yet in the Wisconsin countryside, Gale was forever to be identified with Friendship Village. That is, she was always associated with the sweetness, serenity, and neighborliness of idealized rural communities.[58]

Sinclair Lewis never wrote anything comparable to *Friendship Village*, and for the boosters of rural communities he became a favorite whipping boy if not the devil incarnate. The editor of the Kewaunee *Enterprise*, for example, found only paradox in the work of an author who had "made himself famous by punching Main Street in the jaw," but was himself a product of Main Street. After all, so also were Charles A. Lindbergh, Calvin Coolidge, John J. Pershing, Henry Ford, James A. Reed, Charles G. Dawes, and William E. Borah. From the perspective of Kewaunee, "Main Streets are not only charming places, American satirists to the contrary, but they are breeding spots of genius. Our small towns, aided by the little red school-houses, have turned out many men who are shaping the destinies of America today." Yet to the country-bred youth, the message was clear: move to the city if you wish to become rich and famous; move to the city if you wish to take part in shaping the nation's future. This was surely not a message the editor intended to convey, but it was certainly the lesson that village young people learned.[59]

* * *

The rural youth who left Wisconsin's hinterland to find jobs in urban industries often found metropolitan life less exciting and less rewarding than they had been led to believe it would be. Urban workers, in fact, commonly expressed grievances in a way that sounded a contrapuntal theme for rural complaints. In 1925, for example, a Milwaukee industrial laborer grumbled that he had grown sick of the sympathy for farmers he found expressed on every hand. "Why, every farmer I know is better off than us city workers," he fretted. Farmers were their own bosses, they seldom worked during the winter months, and at the end of the year "there's not a farmer but what salts away several hundred at least,

[58] Herron, *Small Town in American Literature*, 345–349; Harold P. Simonson, *Zona Gale* (New York, 1962); August Derleth, *Still Small Voice: The Biography of Zona Gale* (New York, 1940).

[59] Kewaunee *Enterprise*, April 27, 1928.

and that clear." Furthermore, farm families had good food all year round, and while farm children could work at chores to help out, "city kids have got to go to school and are no help at all to their hard working parents." Yet the newspapers constantly urged assistance to farmers, and Congress constantly debated new ways to help them. The agricultural journals, in turn, had come out in favor of the open shop and were supporting a reactionary policy towards organized labor. "Who helps the city workers, I want to know," was the laborer's plaintive cry. "Aren't there more of them? And aren't they worse off?"[60]

Who, indeed, helped the urban laborers? At the dawn of the New Era, the hopes of organized labor had run high despite the Red Scare and the continuation of wartime uncertainties. In Milwaukee, long a focal point for labor activity, the well-established alliance between the Socialist party and organized labor had broken down under the pressure of patriotic opinion. Yet the war had never been popular in Milwaukee itself, and the approach of peace reawakened working-class militancy. Early in 1918 union leaders formed the Labor Forward Movement, a concerted effort to organize workers and increase the power of unions. Distributing thousands of leaflets, and holding several open meetings with representatives of various international unions, leaders of the movement publicized labor's cause. Aided by the wartime labor shortage and the sympathetic attitude of both state and national governments, Milwaukee organizers succeeded in unionizing more than 2,000 workers in the months before the Armistice. With the return of peace, labor leaders had good reason to be optimistic about the future, for the labor movement appeared to be stronger than ever before.[61]

Aside from their organizational accomplishments, Wisconsin unions could find further justification for optimism during the immediate postwar period. University of Wisconsin Professor John R. Commons, who with his best students had just published the first two volumes of the *History of Labour in the United States*, was generating ideas for the settlement of labor disputes and for eliminating the uncertainties that plagued workers. Industrial peace, he told

[60] "A Laborer to the Editor," Milwaukee *Leader*, July 30, 1925; W. C. Roberts to Samuel Gompers, February 6, 1922, in Legislative Reference File, series 2, American Federation of Labor Papers.

[61] Thomas W. Gavett, *Development of the Labor Movement in Milwaukee* (Madison, 1965), 130–134; Wisconsin State Federation of Labor, *Proceedings*, 1919, p. 63.

the National Association of Employment Managers in 1919, could never be secured by crude methods such as injunctions or compulsory arbitration. Neither could misrepresentation—scare tactics intended to link unions with Bolshevism, for example—serve to quiet worker discontent. "We must investigate the conditions which cause this industrial unrest," Commons urged, "and we must prepare in advance to remove the conditions which cause conflict. . . ." Removing the causes of conflict required good will, or reciprocity. Good will, as Commons defined it, "is not government at all, but mutual concession. It yields as much to the prejudices and passions, to the conservatism and even suspicions of patrons as it does to scientific knowledge of what is good for them."[62]

Commons believed that the psychology of labor was "fundamentally the psychology of a class of people whose life is insecure, who are subject to rough methods of discipline." A necessary prerequisite for industrial peace, therefore, was legislation to provide security through compensation for injuries sustained on the job, health insurance, and unemployment insurance. The Wisconsin legislature had already passed a workmen's compensation law in 1911, but much more was required. The pressure for unemployment compensation had not yet become insistent, but workingmen and labor leaders might have derived some satisfaction from the thought that unemployment compensation was at least beginning to receive serious consideration.[63]

For the moment, it was the effort to restrict what Commons called "rough methods" that attracted the attention of labor unions. For years the Wisconsin State Federation of Labor had been working to secure laws to limit the use of injunctions in labor disputes and to prevent industrial espionage. In 1919 the state legislature finally responded with the passage of Wisconsin's first legislation to restrict the issuance of injunctions or restraining orders. It also passed a bill requiring the licensing and registration of private detective

[62] John R. Commons, "Bringing about Industrial Peace," address to the Conference of the National Association of Employment Managers, December 13, 1919, reproduced in John R. Commons, ed., *Trade Unionism and Labor Problems* (second series, Boston, 1921; reprinted, New York, 1967), 2; John R. Commons, *Industrial Goodwill* (New York, 1919; reprinted, Salem, New Hampshire, 1969), 19; Mark Perlman, *Labor Union Theories in America: Background and Development* (Evanston, 1958), 187–188.

[63] Commons, ed., *Trade Unionism*, 7–9; Commons to Matthew S. Dudgeon, January 8, 1919, in the Matthew S. Dudgeon Papers; Gordon M. Haferbecker, *Wisconsin Labor Laws* (Madison, 1958), 122–123.

agencies. Unfortunately for the unions, neither law proved effective. In June, 1920, the Wisconsin supreme court ruled that inasmuch as injunctions had nothing to do with wages or conditions of employment, the anti-injunction law could not be used in strikes for a closed shop. The ruling meant, in other words, that injunctions might be issued if strikers were demanding exclusive recognition of their union. The legislation to license detective agencies also fell short of securing union objectives. It did not provide for licensing individual operatives, and labor organizations continued to worry about the infiltration of spies in the pay of employers.[64]

By the time organized labor began to realize that its legislative efforts were ineffective or had been aborted, the postwar depression had arrived. In Wisconsin, as in other states, wage cuts led to a series of strikes. Most of them were unsuccessful, and when prosperity returned, unions found membership greatly reduced. In the nation as a whole, more than one out of five affiliated workers stopped paying dues, and total membership declined from more than 5 million in 1920 to less than 4 million in 1923. Despite membership drives in Wisconsin during the New Era, organized labor did not recover until long after the coming of the Great Depression. In Milwaukee, trade union membership had been reduced from 35,000 in 1920 to 20,000 by 1932. To put it another way, by the time Philip La Follette was finishing his first term as governor of Wisconsin in 1933, union membership in Milwaukee was down to what it had been when Robert M. La Follette, Sr., won his first gubernatorial election in 1900.[65]

The difficulties of organized labor derived from a variety of interrelated developments occurring after the war. For one thing, migration from rural areas to the metropolis brought an increase in the number of workers whose experience in unions was negligible and whose major concern was with achieving personal objectives

[64] Haferbecker, *Wisconsin Labor Laws*, 159, 176; Gavett, *Development of the Labor Movement in Milwaukee*, 134–135; "The History of the State Federation of Labor Is a Tale of Service to the Workers," in Wisconsin State Federation of Labor, Convention, *Souvenir Program, 50th Annual Convention . . . August 17–21, 1942* (Milwaukee, 1942), 34–35; *A. J. Monday Company v. Automobile, Aircraft & Vehicle Workers of America, Local No. 25*, in *Wisconsin Reports*, 171:532; Gertrude Schmidt, "History of Labor Legislation in Wisconsin" (doctoral dissertation, University of Wisconsin, 1933), 280–285, 309–313; Milwaukee *Leader*, December 4, 1924.

[65] Leo Wolman, "Chapter VI, Labor," in Conference on Unemployment, Committee on Recent Economic Changes, *Recent Economic Changes in the United States* (2 vols., New York, 1929), 2:480; Gavett, *Development of the Labor Movement in Milwaukee*, 137.

rather than working-class solidarity. For another thing, business expansion in the New Era coincided with the emergence of industries hostile to organized labor. Unions encountered resistance, for example, in recruiting members among automobile workers or workers employed in the production of agricultural machinery. The rapidly changing technology of the new industries tended to make traditional crafts obsolete, and unions did not readily adapt themselves to assembly lines and innovative methods of mass production.[66]

In the meantime, employers reacted to labor's postwar militancy by mounting a major offensive to assure the open shop in law and in practice. By the fall of 1920, employers' councils were opposing union activities in almost every manufacturing center in the country. The campaign for the open shop rapidly gathered momentum, and in January, 1921, the manufacturers' associations of twenty-two states met in Chicago to formulate the "American Plan," a euphemistic term for the strategy by which the manufacturers hoped to thwart union organizers. In Wisconsin, the open-shop campaign centered in the Milwaukee Employers Council, established after the defeat of workers' demands for a closed shop at the A. J. Monday plant in 1919. Within two years the Employers Council grew to represent twenty-eight industrial groups that included 602 plants employing 60,000 workers, or more than half the total industry of Milwaukee. The council retained an attorney, Leon B. Lamfrom, who represented the employers in strike cases. It maintained membership in the League for Industrial Rights, an organization that offered advice and legal assistance to employers, and it also published a monthly bulletin to keep members informed of current happenings on the labor front.[67]

The Milwaukee Employers Council was at the cutting edge of the open-shop movement in Wisconsin, but of course it did not exercise a controlling influence over the entire state. Businesses of Wisconsin

[66] Irving Bernstein, *The Lean Years: A History of the American Worker, 1920–1933* (Boston, 1960; reprinted, Jersey City, 1983), 87–89; Mark Perlman, "Labor in Eclipse," in John Braeman, Robert H. Bremner, and David Brody, eds., *Change and Continuity in Twentieth-Century America: The 1920's* (Columbus, Ohio, 1968), 118–119.

[67] Robert H. Zieger, *Republicans and Labor, 1919–1929* (Lexington, Kentucky, 1969), 20, 72–73; Allen M. Wakstein, "The Origins of the Open Shop Movement, 1919–1920," in the *Journal of American History*, 51 (December, 1964), 460–475; Gavett, *Development of the Labor Movement in Milwaukee*, 138–140; Schmidt, "History of Labor Legislation in Wisconsin," 35–39.

might act through one or more of several agencies. The Wisconsin Manufacturers' Association, industrial groups such as the Western Paper Manufacturers Association, and local associations or chambers of commerce all assisted in the cause. Whatever their connections, employers of the state were seldom obliged to act alone in the effort to maintain an open shop. During a paper-mill strike in Port Edwards in 1919, for example, Louis M. Alexander, president of the Nekoosa-Edwards Paper Company, received a pledge of support from Mark C. Ewing, a prominent member of the Wausau Group. "It requires some nerve to face a financial loss and the physical strain of a protracted strike," sympathized Ewing, ". . . but if this Government is to endure[,] this stand must be taken by all, let the costs be whatever they may." Two years later, when workers struck the Northern Paper Mills in Green Bay, the Western Paper Manufacturers Association mobilized for assistance. David Clark Everest of the Marathon Paper Company and Frank J. Sensenbrenner of Kimberly-Clark telephoned other papermakers to persuade them of their common cause and to secure their backing. "If there is anything anyone can do to help you out down there they will be glad to do it," Everest assured W. A. Kelly of the Northern Paper Mills, "and in event you want anything from other manufacturers . . . suggest you telephone Frank Sensenbrenner or C. A. Babcock at Neenah."[68]

In their own minds, Wisconsin employers typically believed the open shop to be consistent with constitutional guarantees as well as necessary for domestic tranquility. Labor agitators, in the words of one employer, were converting "the land of the free and the home of the brave" into a nation "where people have a right to use dynamite and bombs and murder people, burn property, wreck trains, intimidate, bulldoze and bully rag men on their way to and from work." Asserted with conviction, the argument that the American Plan embodied "the American way" won widespread support from businessmen of the New Era. In 1920, the Appleton Chamber of Commerce adopted a resolution declaring the open shop to be "an essential part of the individual right of contract" possessed by both employers and employees, and in 1926 the Milwaukee Asso-

[68] M. C. Ewing to Everest, September 5, 1919, Ewing to L. M. Alexander, September 5, 1919, L. M. Alexander to M. C. Ewing, September 6, 1919 (all in the Wisconsin Valley Electric Company folder), and Everest to W. A. Kelly, March 18, 1921, all in the David Clark Everest Papers.

ciation of Commerce insisted that "the absolute right of the individual to work, if he pleases and is satisfied with the terms of his employment, must be recognized."[69]

Manufacturers and businessmen who subscribed to such views usually considered themselves true friends of the workingman, and they frequently urged understanding between employer and employee. "Labor requires capital and capital requires labor," observed John H. Puelicher, president of the Marshall and Ilsley Bank of Milwaukee. "The antagonism, now so frequent, will disappear when this truth becomes sufficiently understood to result in fair dealing on the part of each; in a greater understanding of the dependence one on the other; in a knowledge of the plain duty of one to the other; in the final handclasp which must come when each serves its own best interest." So spoke the voice of reason, and most employers recognized it as such. Believing themselves to be reasonable men, however, they tended to think it was the trade unions that required lessons in goodwill, reciprocity, and concession.[70]

In 1920, Marvin B. Rosenberry, associate justice of the Wisconsin supreme court, took what he thought might be a step towards the resolution of labor problems by arranging a meeting between John R. Commons and Wausau paper manufacturer David Clark Everest. Little came of it. Everest later wrote Rosenberry that while he was "for almost anything which will eliminate this continual fighting back and forth," he doubted that Commons' ideas on arbitration would ever receive general approval. To implement them would be too time-consuming and too costly, and employers confident of the

[69] M. P. McCollough to D. C. Everest, quoting A. L. Osborn, September 15, 1922, *ibid.*; Appleton Chamber of Commerce, *Proceedings*, 1:38–39, 44, in Appleton Association of Commerce Records, Oshkosh Area Research Center; Milwaukee Association of Commerce, *Official Bulletin*, September 2, 1926, p. 2. The *Salesianum*, the alumni magazine for priests who graduated from the Milwaukee Archdiocese's St. Francis Seminary and a journal not circulated widely among lay Catholics, generally took a pro-labor position and did not hesitate to point out the deception in the rhetoric of employers. See, for example, Francis J. Haas, "Individualism and the Open Shop Campaign," 16 (April, 1921), 2–15, and an editorial, "Freedom of Contract and Legislation," 19 (July, 1924), 51–57. The employers' open-shop campaign, wrote Haas, was "misleading and deceptive, for their activities are aimed not at one of the weapons of the union movement, but against its very vitals, collective bargaining." On the other hand, an active proponent of the open shop thought the week after Easter a good time to run an advertisement including excerpts from a pastoral letter objecting to working-class militancy. See Karl Mathie to D. C. Everest, April 7, 1920, in the Open Shop Association folder, Everest Papers.

[70] *Milwaukee*, February, 1923, p. 7.

correctness of their own views would not find the results satisfactory. On rare occasions union men and employers did meet to discuss common interests, but they almost never reached agreement in matters relating to closed shops. When Frank Sensenbrenner joined laboring men in a conference sponsored by the Catholic church in 1923, he concluded that the workers were not interested in friendly discussion of real problems. He thought, rather, that they had attended the conference "for the sole purpose of making union propaganda and getting as much publicity for it as possible."[71]

For the employers of Wisconsin no less than for George F. Babbitt, the rhetoric of co-operation served as a convenient means of formulating their ideas. Whatever their individual interests and concerns, they exercised that rhetoric to portray themselves as going more than half way to meet workers on the road to industrial peace. They stopped short of recognizing unions they considered unreasonable, but, as if to demonstrate their own reasonableness, they offered company unions or workers' councils instead. They also offered clusters of benefits such as paid vacations for workers, health care, accident and life insurance, and stock purchase plans. Promoted by a new class of personnel managers who took over functions performed in an earlier day by plant managers or foremen, such programs eventually came to be identified as "welfare capitalism."[72]

The Allis-Chalmers benefit program provides an illustration of the way welfare capitalism worked during the postwar decade. Initiated in 1883 with establishment of the Allis Mutual Aid Society, which met social and medical needs of workers, the company's welfare activities multiplied greatly during the 1920's. A new shop hospital, for example, began treating patients at the West Allis Works in 1925. The building provided a laboratory and special rooms for a regular physician, a dentist, and an eye, ear, nose, and throat specialist. Nurses were on hand around the clock. In addition to the hospital, Allis-Chalmers maintained a commissary that sold

[71] Everest to Marvin B. Rosenberry, February 4, 1920, Everest to Frank J. Sensenbrenner, June 28, 1923, and Sensenbrenner to Everest, July 2, 1923, all in the Everest Papers.

[72] Leo Wolman and Gustav Peck, "Labor Groups in the Social Structure," in President's Research Committee on Social Trends, *Recent Social Trends*, 843–846; Bernstein, *Lean Years*, 170–186; David Brody, "The Rise and Decline of Welfare Capitalism," in Braeman, Bremner, and Brody, eds., *Change and Continuity*, 153–156.

shoes and overalls to workers at cost. It also provided refreshments—milk, soup, ice cream, or coffee—at reduced prices. Best of all, the company's prosperity during the twenties made possible a two-week paid vacation for all workers who had been employed for at least a year.[73]

In discussing their labor policies during the New Era, employers usually claimed that they were following humane precepts and that workers became more efficient and productive when they enjoyed the benefits of welfare capitalism. But Sumner H. Slichter, professor of economics at Harvard, argued that neither humanitarian concern nor efficiency was the primary motivation of the employers. Benefit programs, he contended, aimed to prevent employees from "becoming class conscious and from organizing trade unions." Frank J. Weber, the first president of the Wisconsin State Federation of Labor and in 1925 still a powerful influence in the organization, saw clearly that the American Plan coupled with welfare programs was intended "to disrupt and destroy the organizations of labor." Labor leaders in general found the welfare programs threatening, not because their provisions were bad, but because they were a means by which management could gain complete authority over the terms of employment. Once having bribed the workers with a few benefits, and once having destroyed the unions, paternalistic employers could have their way without fear of retaliation.[74]

Despite the vigor of the open-shop campaign, which helped to account for the loss of members during the New Era, Wisconsin unions fought spirited battles for survival on several fronts. Responding immediately to arguments for the open shop, they began lining up in 1920 for what William Coleman, secretary of the Milwaukee Federated Trades Council, thought would be a fight to the finish. "This fight is making a new union spirit," Coleman announced, "and will result in greatly increasing the union memberships." He was wrong about that, but towards the end of the year the Federated Trades Council met to consider proposals for in-

[73] Walter F. Peterson, *An Industrial Heritage: Allis-Chalmers Corporation* (Milwaukee, 1978), 218–220.

[74] Sumner H. Slichter, "The Current Labor Policies of American Industries," in the *Quarterly Journal of Economics*, 43 (May, 1929), 432; Bernstein, *Lean Years*, 186–188; George H. Soule, *Prosperity Decade: From War to Depression, 1917–1929* (New York, 1947), 222–223; Milwaukee *Leader*, June 9, 1920, August 19 ("A Worker" to the editor), and October 23, 1925; Brody, "Rise and Decline of Welfare Capitalism," in Braeman, Bremner, and Brody, eds., *Change and Continuity*, 157–160.

creasing the autonomy of union locals as well as recommendations for "changes that will add to trade union efficiency and leave the unions elbow room to fight." The Wisconsin State Federation of Labor undertook a study of the efficiency of labor and management in unionized plants, and Milwaukee union men initiated a house-to-house campaign to distribute leaflets explaining what organized labor stood for and how it helped to keep "the elements of greed and profiteering from grinding the people down to lower standards of living."[75]

As the American Plan gathered support among employers, organized labor countered with a drive to win acceptance for union labels and to overcome the indifference that led even some workers to buy the products of non-union labor. When the Federal System of Bakeries in Green Bay declared for the open shop, the Federated Trades Council of the city urged working-class families to eat only union-made bread. In 1924 the Trade Union Label Department of the Federated Trades Council in Milwaukee requested that working people send in printed matter that did not bear the label "in order that the secretary can circularize the firms patronizing the nonunion print shops." To the unions, the open shop was the equivalent of a scab shop, and they exerted great pressure to prevent workers from taking jobs in open shops. "All the SUNSHINE in the world is unable to make the life of a MAN or WOMAN, who becomes a SCAB, a happy and contented one," observed Frank Weber in 1922. "He or she may bask in the personal sunshine of a mean and despicable WAGE-REDUCING EMPLOYER, but even that ray of comfort is of little consequence to the man or woman who betrays their fellow workers and becomes branded as a SCAB, for as soon as the WILLING and ASSISTING TOOL of the WAGE-REDUCING EMPLOYER, to enslave their fellow workers is over, then the woe of the SCAB begins, for the SCAB-EMPLOYER is a deceiver and is minus of either heart or feeling, and will speedily dump the

[75] Milwaukee *Leader*, December 13, 1920, January 22, 1921; *Wisconsin News* (Milwaukee), July 23, 1920. Such activities could be costly, but George F. Kull of the Wisconsin Manufacturers' Association alleged that in raising money the union had it "all over" the manufacturers. With evident exaggeration, he reported in 1920 that through a one-dollar monthly assessment on members the International Association of Machinists planned to raise $4 million for the purpose of fighting the open-shop movement. *Weekly Bulletin*, June 21, 1920, in the Wisconsin Manufacturers' Association Records, 1910–1975.

outcasts—the scabs—when their contemptable [*sic*] and DIRTY WORK is no longer needed."[76]

Overcoming indifference became a continuous struggle during the 1920's, and unions experimented with a variety of schemes to sustain interest in union activities. In several cities they formed co-operative purchasing organizations, and in Milwaukee the auto workers, cigar makers, broom and whisk makers, and tailors all initiated efforts to establish co-operative union factories. Union members in Marshfield organized a labor club that met in monthly gatherings of union men and their families. Although the club was primarily a social organization, it increased the workers' sense of solidarity and strengthened "the determination to be union men and women every day of the year, including election day."[77]

The plea for workers to vote as union members on election day was symptomatic of a shift in strategy on the part of labor leaders. After the unrest of 1919, and especially after the failure of the great steel strike of that year, unions tended to abandon use of their ultimate weapon. That only forty strikes occurred in Milwaukee during the decade from 1923 to 1933 led some observers to conclude that the New Era was a period of industrial harmony in Wisconsin. It was, rather, a period when organized labor concentrated more upon legislation and education than it did upon confronting employers directly.

Among the chief items on the agenda of Wisconsin labor were the employers' practice of securing injunctions to halt strikes and the employers' much-criticized use of labor spies. Management frequently resorted to industrial espionage with great effect throughout the twenties, and anti-injunction laws remained subject to legal interpretation during much of the decade. Until the intent of the laws could be carried out, reasoned the unions, the future of organized labor in the state would remain uncertain. And until workers had been educated to think clearly about the place of labor in American society, the effectiveness of trade unions would remain problematical.[78]

[76] Federated Trades Council of Green Bay, Minute Book, August 10, 1920, in the Federated Trades Council Papers, Green Bay Area Research Center; Milwaukee *Leader*, January 11, 1924, December 5, 1925; Federated Trades Council, Milwaukee, *Record of Proceedings*, 1922, microfilm copy in SHSW.

[77] Milwaukee *Leader*, January 16, July 3, August 25, September 11, December 3, 1920, January 21, 1921, April 29, 1924.

[78] Gavett, *Development of the Labor Movement in Milwaukee*, 137–146.

In 1921, as the open-shop movement was building momentum, the detective agencies operating in Wisconsin—Burns, Corporations Auxiliary, Gordon, Ferris, and Pinkerton—sought to obtain greater freedom of action than the 1919 law permitted. Instead of applying for licenses through fire and police commissions, they proposed that licenses be issued by the secretary of state with the approval of five citizens. Despite the efforts of organized labor and the socialists, such a bill to satisfy the detective agencies passed the legislature. Although Governor Blaine vetoed the bill, labor felt threatened and sentiment for stricter regulation of private operatives increased. Again Frank Weber articulated the concerns of the unions. He pointed out that the labor spy, "the most degraded specimen of society," was trained by his agency to apply three tactics in destroying unions: "[F]irst, to attack the honesty and sincerity of the officers; secondly, to present all classes of schemes to deplete the treasury; and thirdly, to advocate radical strikes and criticize the national and international activities so as to disrupt their local organizations." Then, his fury spilling over into characteristic non-stop eloquence, he denounced the labor spies who had been used by the exploiters and enslavers of labor in all ages: "Even Christ, the perfect Man, was crucified by and through the lying evidence of a labor spy—Judas Iscariot—who afterward repented, and to atone his conscience, hung himself, and if the labor spy of today would repent as he did, we would find one hanging from every lamp post in the state."[79]

Labor's mounting concern over industrial espionage led state senator Joseph A. Padway, a Socialist from Milwaukee, to introduce new legislation in 1925. Its essential features required that individual private detectives as well as agencies secure licenses from the

[79] *Ibid.*, 142; Schmidt, "History of Labor Legislation in Wisconsin," 315; Milwaukee *Journal*, June 16, 1921; "Labor Record of the Blaine Administration, 1921–1926" (mimeographed), p. 4, in the Roy Empey Papers; "The History of the State Federation of Labor," in Wisconsin State Federation of Labor, *Souvenir Program*, 34–35; Milwaukee *Leader*, April 20, 1920; Bernstein, *Lean Years*, 149–150; Edwin E. Witte, *The Government in Labor Disputes* (New York, 1932), 184–189. The findings of an inquiry commission authorized by the Interchurch World Movement prompted Richard C. Cabot, professor of social ethics at Harvard, to finance an investigation of industrial espionage. Portions of the study appear in the *New Republic*, but a more extensive account may be found in Sidney Howard, *The Labor Spy* (New York, 1924). See Jerold S. Auerbach, *Labor and Liberty: The La Follette Committee and the New Deal* (Indianapolis, 1966), 20–22, and Darryl Holter, "Labor Spies and Union-Busting in Wisconsin, 1890–1940," in *WMH*, 68 (Summer, 1985), 243–265.

secretary of state; that an application for a license have approval of the local fire and police commission, or, in a locality without such a commission, approval of the chief of police and five citizens; that a detective agency could maintain offices only in the city for which it received a license; and that six persons could petition for revocation of licenses already granted. The bill also required a $10,000 bond for an agency and $2,000 bond for an operative. Senator Bernhard Gettelman, who was also chief deputy sheriff of Milwaukee County, co-operated with lobbyists from the detective agencies in an effort to defeat the bill. He did not succeed, but neither did opponents of the legislation retreat. Almost immediately after passage of the act, the Pinkerton and Corporations Auxiliary agencies attempted to have it declared unconstitutional. Again they failed when the United States Supreme Court upheld the law in 1927. While the measure by no means ended industrial espionage in the state, discussion of it drew attention to the problem. And a decade later, when Robert M. La Follette, Jr., headed an important subcommittee to investigate civil liberties for the United States Senate, labor spies received further publicity that finally ended most of their anti-union activities.[80]

The use of injunctions to halt strikes was another matter of concern to Wisconsin labor unions, even though the number of strikes diminished during the 1920's. Because the 1919 anti-injunction law was narrowly interpreted by the courts to prevent its application in strikes for a closed shop, the unions sought further legislation. They secured it in 1923 with the passage of an amendment restricting the use of injunctions in "any dispute whatsoever concerning employment." The amendment to the law also required that temporary restraining orders could be issued only after giving forty-eight hours' notice to the parties involved. This modification of injunction procedure was intended to provide strikers with an opportunity to make their position clear and to protest the order before it took effect. Another act passed the same year required a jury trial in any case resulting from injunction violations.[81]

[80] "Labor Record of the Blaine Administration, 1921–1926," pp. 1, 3, in the Empey Papers; "The History of the State Federation of Labor," in Wisconsin State Federation of Labor, *Souvenir Program*, 34–35; Witte, *Government in Labor Disputes*, 189–190; Haferbecker, *Wisconsin Labor Laws*, 176–177; Schmidt, "History of Labor Legislation in Wisconsin," 315, 322; Auerbach, *Labor and Liberty*, 97–99, 204.

[81] Haferbecker, *Wisconsin Labor Laws*, 159; Gavett, *Development of the Labor Movement in Milwaukee*, 141.

Wisconsin court cases arising from the issuance of injunctions during the New Era reveal some of the legal uncertainties that surrounded contempt proceedings. A 1921 case involving Peter Christ, a labor organizer from Rhinelander, produced ambiguous results, but it provided a justification for clarifying procedure in litigation resulting from injunction violations. Arrested for picketing in defiance of a court order, Christ was tried without a jury on a criminal contempt charge and sentenced by Circuit Judge A. H. Reid to four months in the county jail. Organized labor protested that the judge had ignored a state statute imposing a maximum of thirty days for criminal contempt. Governor Blaine thereupon pardoned Christ, but on orders from Judge Reid the sheriff refused to release him. Blaine then discharged the sheriff, who appealed his firing to the state supreme court. The court satisfied neither side in the dispute. It held that the sheriff had been discharged without cause and raised questions about the right of the governor to pardon anyone convicted in a criminal contempt case. But the court also questioned the validity of any sentence extending beyond thirty days.[82]

Another contempt case was one involving the Amalgamated Clothing Workers and the David Adler Clothing Company of Milwaukee. In April, 1928, following the death of the senior partner, the company announced that it was an open shop and that Adler workers would be required to sign so-called yellow-dog contracts (meaning that they agreed not to join a union). In the struggle that followed the announcement, some 800 workers were locked out. They then struck the plant, and an injunction was issued against the union. When a striker threw a can of paint, he was arrested and tried for contempt of court. In this case the defendant received a jury trial, but the jury could not agree and did not return a verdict. Protesting the jury's failure to act, the judge questioned the constitutionality of the jury-trial law and referred the question to the Wisconsin supreme court. Because no decision had been reached, the higher court refused to take jurisdiction. It did, how-

[82] Haferbecker, *Wisconsin Labor Laws*, 159–160; Joseph A. Padway, "Memorandum Prepared [for history relating to cases and persons imprisoned or fined for the violation of injunctions issued by the courts of Wisconsin]" (1929), in the LRB. The Wisconsin constitution stipulates that the governor has "power to grant reprieves, commutations and pardons, after conviction, for all offenses, except treason and cases of impeachment." Article V, Section 6.

ever, dissolve the injunction on the grounds that the corporation did not come into court with "clean hands." That is to say, the company was itself guilty of misconduct. With the injunction closed, the contempt proceedings were discontinued with no further action, but the constitutionality of the jury-trial law remained in doubt.[83]

A third labor disturbance was even more confusing, and by demonstrating the complexities of Wisconsin's legal tangle over use of the injunction it helped to create sentiment for reform. The trouble in this instance began early in 1928 at the Allen-A Hosiery Company in Kenosha. With the installation of new knitting machines, the Allen-A management demanded that workers operate two machines rather than one. The knitters rejected the two-machine system and went out on strike. They argued that the new machines were no more efficient than the old ones, and they saw the new system as a way of reducing labor costs by requiring each worker to produce twice as much. The new system, contended the knitters, would place the health of workers in jeopardy and destroy the union by flooding the industry with labor. The company responded to worker unrest by locking its doors. It also secured an injunction against picketing or any act "to obstruct or interfere with the plaintiff . . . in the free and unrestrained control of its property, plant or business."[84]

This strike or lockout—what one called it depended upon one's sympathies and affiliations—attracted national attention, and several prominent labor leaders arrived on the scene to assist the workers. Among them were Harold Steele, vice-president of the American Federation of Full Fashioned Hosiery Workers, and Louis Budenz,

[83] Frederick I. Olson, "The Milwaukee Socialists, 1897–1941" (doctoral dissertation, Harvard University, 1952), 502; Gavett, *Development of the Labor Movement in Milwaukee*, 141; Matthew Josephson, *Sidney Hillman, Statesman of American Labor* (Garden City, 1952), 250; William B. Rubin to John P. Frey, December 9, 1929, in the William B. Rubin Papers. Rubin, a Milwaukee attorney specializing in labor law, had been arguing the "clean hands" doctrine for many years. See Rubin to Samuel Gompers, May 29, 1923, in the Rubin Papers.

[84] Louis F. Budenz, "Conspiracy at Kenosha," in *Labor Age*, 17 (April, 1928), 15; Frank A. Smothers, "Youth Militant Rules Strikers," reprinted from the August 27, 1928, Chicago *Daily News* in Louis F. Budenz, "Headlines and Hunger Strikers," in *Labor Age.*, 17 (October, 1928), 1–4; Leonard Bright, "Judicial Tyranny at Kenosha," *ibid.*, 17 (November, 1928), 15–16; *Weekly Bulletin*, March 19, 1928, in the Wisconsin Manufacturers' Association Records; Leon Applebaum, "Turmoil in Kenosha: The Allen-A Hosiery Dispute of 1928–1929," in *WMH*, 70 (Summer, 1987), 281–303; George W. Taylor, *Significant Post-War Changes in the Full-Fashioned Hosiery Industry* (Philadelphia, 1929), 72–76; George W. Taylor, *The Full-Fashioned Hosiery Worker: His Changing Economic Status* (Philadelphia, 1931), 58–61; Felix Frankfurter and Nathan Greene, *The Labor Injunction* (New York, 1930), 104–105.

editor of *Labor Age*. Although Kenosha's Trades and Labor Council conferred with city manager C. M. Osborn, and although the union leaders consulted Governor Fred Zimmerman, the situation at Allen-A deteriorated rapidly. The company remained adamant in its insistence upon an open shop, and it attempted to coerce the union by offering to restore the jobs of discharged workers if they persuaded others to return on company terms.[85]

With the failure of discussions over a settlement came an outbreak of violence. Although the workers may not have been responsible, bricks and rocks were thrown, guns were fired, and the home of the district attorney was bombed. Kenosha swarmed with private detectives, and the city council voted to enforce the injunction, at the same time adding seven new officers to the police force. The county board also took action. It authorized the sheriff to increase the number of deputies in order to protect the plant.[86]

Yet the violence continued for several months, and lawsuits multiplied. One of the Allen-A buildings was bombed, and a worker was kidnapped and tarred. Budenz brought suit for slander, and the company retaliated with a damage suit against the Dayton Hotel, where Budenz was staying. Two workers, arrested several times for picketing, went on a hunger strike until their case came to trial. They were acquitted, as were twenty-six other workers who had been cited for contempt of court. The jury-trial law, believed union members, was what prevented conviction, for it was a jury that found the defendants innocent.[87]

The industrial violence in Kenosha produced no real winners, but that violence occurred at all provided a powerful argument for reform of Wisconsin's labor laws. Thomas Duncan, a Socialist senator from Milwaukee, introduced a bill embodying a revamped labor code; it received approval of the legislature in 1931; and Governor Philip La Follette signed it into law. The new code made clear that the policy of Wisconsin was to promote the organization of labor and the settlement of disputes through collective bargaining. It again proscribed yellow-dog contracts, and it declared that activities

[85] Carrie Cropley, *Kenosha: From Pioneer Village to Modern City, 1835–1935* (Kenosha, 1958), 153–156; Holter, "Labor Spies and Union-Busting," in *WMH*, 68:252–257.

[86] Cropley, *Kenosha*, 155–156; Smothers, "Youth Militant," in Budenz, "Headlines," in *Labor Age*, October, 1928, pp. 1–4.

[87] Budenz, "Headlines," in *Labor Age*, October, 1928, p. 1; Joseph A. Padway, "Some Reasons Why Wisconsin Is Freer than Other States from Injunction Abuses," in Wisconsin State Federation of Labor, *Wisconsin Labor*, 1930, pp. 71–73.

such as organizing unions, peacefully picketing places of employment, publicizing disputes, and paying strike benefits were not subject to restraint. In sum, the new code followed closely a model anti-injunction bill drafted by the American Federation of Labor. The 1931 legislature also passed a law making jury trial compulsory in all contempt cases, both civil and criminal. The new labor code went into effect just as the Great Depression began to produce its most devastating consequences, and during the troubled thirties organized labor could count on a legal framework to support its activities. In many ways, Wisconsin's labor legislation anticipated that of the New Deal.[88]

[88] "Labor Legislation of the 1931 Session" (carbon copy), in series 1, undated 1931 files, Philip F. La Follette Papers; Haferbecker, *Wisconsin Labor Laws*, 161; Holter, "Labor Spies and Union-Busting," in *WMH*, 68:257. William B. Rubin saw a relationship between the interest in uses of the injunction and concern over enforcement of the Eighteenth Amendment. "People have become interested in the injunction as never before and the reason for it is, not their friendliness for Labor, but that they now see that the injunction may be used to take away their property," wrote Rubin to Chester M. Wright, editor of *International Labor News Service*. "As I put it . . . , very few people concern themselves with the loss of the intangible thing called 'liberty,' but the minute you threaten . . . property—then with pitch-forks, guns and all kinds of arms, they come to its defense." Rubin to Wright, May 14, 1930, in the Rubin Papers.

7

Leisure, Education, and Politics

THE prosperity of the postwar decade was no figment of a Chamber of Commerce secretary's imagination. The value added by manufacture in Wisconsin increased by more than 30 per cent during the twenties, and other economic indicators revealed that the state enjoyed its full measure of industrial prosperity. At the same time, the number of wage earners in manufacturing rose very little. Improvement in plants and machinery, more efficient management, measures to accelerate the speed of workers, and innovations in the use of raw materials brought greater production while reducing the need for labor. Yet during the war period, as Wisconsin industrialists were reducing labor costs, large numbers of people left the Cutover and the agricultural hinterland to search for new jobs in urban, industrial centers. Contrary to the dire predictions of some farm and labor leaders of the state, the increased efficiency of Wisconsin factories and the expanding supply of labor produced neither lower wages nor unemployment. The postwar decade brought, instead, higher wages and a shorter workweek in most industries.[1]

High levels of employment and income were the result of two important influences during the New Era. In the first place, industrialists knew that well-paid workers could become important consumers of goods they helped to produce. Furthermore, a shorter workweek provided workers with more free time to shop for the products of Wisconsin industries. In the second place, as industries devoted more attention to selling their products, they increasingly found themselves relying on the services of experts in banking,

[1] Public Welfare Department, *General Relief in Wisconsin, 1848–1935* (mimeographed, 1939), 15–16, in SHSW with relief agency publications; *Wisconsin Blue Book, 1931*, p. 590; *Fourteenth Census of the United States, 1920: Manufactures, 1919, Volume IX*, 1610–1611; *Fifteenth Census of the United States, 1930: Manufactures, 1929, Volume III*, 561.

advertising, marketing, and business management. The increased efficiency of primary industries, in other words, resulted in the growth of ancillary or secondary institutions. Those institutions helped to maintain high levels of employment, in part by providing new job opportunities themselves, and in part by offering new services and new markets for basic industries.

Developments in Wisconsin were part of a national trend. For the United States as a whole between 1919 and 1929, according to one estimate of the distribution of gainfully occupied persons, the percentage in agriculture declined from 21.3 to 18.3, and the percentage in manufacturing went from 25.4 to 22.3. Patterns of employment during the decade nevertheless suggest not that some farm and industrial workers joined a growing horde of jobless persons, but that a significant segment of the work force changed occupations. Enterprises involved in construction, trade, finance, and services all registered increases in the percentage of gainfully employed. The largest increase was in the service occupations, which went from 12.1 per cent of the gainfully occupied in 1919 to 15.6 per cent in 1929.[2]

The abundance of labor led not only to the creation of new occupations in urban Wisconsin, but also to a shorter workweek in most jobs. Between the Great War and the Great Depression, the average number of Wisconsin wage earners who worked fifty-four hours a week or more declined from nearly 140,000 to less than 85,000, and the number working at least sixty hours went from more than 75,000 to less than 25,000. Related to changes in the nature of work itself, the increase in leisure time may be inferred from Table 7-1, which allows comparison of the prevailing hours for all Wisconsin wage earners in 1914, 1919, and 1929.

Increases in income and leisure throughout the work force were important determinants of the New Era ethos. As incomes increased, wage earners used a part of their free time to find new ways of spending what they earned. Having reduced the hours of labor, industries sought to take advantage of the growing market in consumer goods. American society was rapidly becoming a consumer society in which clever advertisers helped to create new de-

[2] George H. Soule, *Prosperity Decade: From War to Depression, 1917–1929* (New York, 1947), 214–215; Solomon Fabricant, *Employment in Manufacturing, 1899–1939: An Analysis of Its Relation to the Volume of Production* (New York, 1942), 214; Simon Kuznets, *National Income and Its Composition, 1919–1938* (New York, 1941), 346–347.

mands, and credit agencies offered installment plans as a means to satisfy them. Critics of the New Era ethos concentrated on two problems they detected in the trend towards consumerism. First, they thought that people were losing sight of important social virtues in their giddy pursuit of new material possessions and new forms of entertainment. Second, they believed that despite the claims of apologists, postwar prosperity benefited business and industry far more than it benefited middle- and working-class consumers.[3]

Political implications of the emerging new way of life were far more difficult to assess than were the economic changes taking place, and uncertainties of the decade help to explain why political leaders tended to adopt a cautious, tentative approach to problems of the time. Aware of inadequacies in positions formed prior to the social transformations of the twentieth century, politicians nonetheless returned to them for lack of clearer direction. Campaigning as Socialists or Democrats, Progressive Republicans or Stalwart Republicans, they adapted traditional arguments to altered

[3] Public Welfare Department, *General Relief*, 15–16; Industrial Commission, *Wisconsin Labor Statistics*, 1 (May and June, 1923), 8; *Civics and Commerce*, November, 1919, pp. 10–14; "Is the American Home Degenerating?" in *Wisconsin Agriculturist*, March 17, 1923, p. 24; "Proof of Farm Progress," in *ibid.*, January 16, 1926, p. 10, and "Waste of Women in Rural Life," in *ibid.*, July 24, 1920, p. 16; James Fisk to Halbert L. Hoard, February 4, 1928, in the Halbert L. Hoard Papers.

TABLE 7-1
AVERAGE NUMBER OF WAGE EARNERS IN WISCONSIN BY PREVAILING HOURS OF LABOR PER WEEK

	1914		*1919*		*1929*	
Hours of Labor Per Week	*No. of Wage Earners*	*% of Total*	*No. of Wage Earners*	*% of Total*	*No. of Wage Earners*	*% of Total*
48 and under	27,905	14.36	82,574	31.28	67,238	25.47
49–53	9,135	4.70	38,428	14.56	102,916	38.98
54	18,461	9.50	22,582	8.56	11,654	4.41
55–59	62,102	31.96	69,551	26.35	57,546	21.79
60 and over	76,707	39.48	50,814	19.25	24,685	9.35
Wage earners (average for the year)	194,310		263,949		264,039	

SOURCES: *Fourteenth Census of the United States, 1920: Manufactures, Volume IX*, 1617; *Fifteenth Census of the United States, 1930: Manufactures, Volume III*, 563. The figures do not include proprietors, salaried officers, and salaried employees.

conditions. Voters responded in ways that were just as traditional, casting their ballots on the basis of economic, ethnic, religious, or regional interest.[4]

As in the past, reformers tended to identify themselves as Progressives, and when they concentrated their attention on improving the uses of leisure, they generally favored programs of educational reform. In the public schools they found opportunities to assist young people in adjusting to postwar demands through new courses growing out of life experiences, through putting into practice the ideas they developed in classrooms, and through socially desirable extracurricular activities. Educational reformers also sought to broaden the scope of their efforts to include vocational schools that offered practical training to those who sought it.[5]

With the growth of cities and the relative decline in rural population, the Progressives were aware of the need to broaden their programs and their following. Yet the interests of farmers were often at odds with the interests of urban workers, and throughout the twenties and thirties the Progressives confronted a dilemma in appealing to both groups. Under the leadership of Robert M. La Follette and his sons, the Progressives resolved that dilemma by presenting themselves as champions of the people as opposed to the forces of privilege. If the rhetoric of reform had demagogic overtones, it was because Progressive orators dealt mainly in abstract principles to unite divergent interests in a good cause. Spectacularly successful in Wisconsin, Progressives of the state enjoyed great influence among reformers throughout the country. The elder La Follette's independent campaign for the presidency in 1924 served to strengthen that influence, and after his death in 1925 Wisconsin remained a bellwether state for reformers.

* * *

While social justice was the ultimate goal of Progressives, complacent business leaders of the New Era often argued that social justice

[4] David P. Thelen, *Robert M. La Follette and the Insurgent Spirit* (Boston, 1976; reprinted, Madison, 1986), 119, 165; Arthur S. Link and Richard L. McCormick, *Progressivism* (Arlington Heights, Illinois, 1983), 111.

[5] J. T. Giles, "High School Progress and Problems," in Department of Public Instruction, *Biennial Report*, 1928–1930, p. 11. Many people pointed out that the new leisure could be used for home study. See, for example, a prize-winning letter on the subject of how to spend winter evenings, in the *Wisconsin Agriculturist*, February 16, 1929, p. 16. Eugene M. Tobin, *Organize or Perish: America's Independent Progressives, 1913–1933* (New York, 1986) provides a sensitive analysis of the Progressives' thinking in the 1920's.

was certain to result from prolonged economic growth. The business leaders had a point. Prosperity had never seemed more universal, nor had opportunities for self-improvement seemed so readily available to all Americans. Few persons in business doubted the wisdom of Secretary of Commerce Herbert Hoover when he asserted that the "American System" was breaking down the ancient barriers of class and creating a new society based upon equality of opportunity. Wage earners also found merit in the claim. To them, higher individual incomes and a shorter work week justified Hoover's optimistic assertion.[6]

Reducing the hours and increasing the pay of industrial workers have always appeared to some employers as a coddling of labor, but during the postwar decade a shorter workweek and better pay served the needs of primary industries as much as it did the needs of wage earners. Wisconsin manufacturers, anxious to meet wartime requirements, had greatly increased the productive capacity of their plants. As Frank B. Jennings, writing in *Civics and Commerce*, observed after the Armistice, "the war has taught American manhood one supreme business lesson—that the great achievement of business life is to produce." Yet a producer must have buyers; a manufacturer would profit little if increased production served only to increase inventories. Perceptive manufacturers therefore saw advantages in improving the worker's capacity to buy the consumer goods produced by American industry. For the manufacturer, the abbreviated workweek could mean an expanded market for automobiles, radios, refrigerators, vacuum cleaners, and other new products; for the industrial laborer, a shorter workweek meant more time for enjoyment of the goods available to him as a consumer and more time for activities outside the home. Increases in the wages of labor, which accompanied the reduction of hours, improved the worker's capacity to acquire consumer goods.[7]

[6] Joan Hoff Wilson, *Herbert Hoover: Forgotten Progressive* (Boston, 1975), 55–62; David Burner, *Herbert Hoover: The Public Life* (New York, 1979), 138–142.

[7] *Civics and Commerce*, November, 1919, p. 9; Leo Wolman and Gustav Peck, "Labor Groups in the Social Structure," and Robert S. Lynde, "The People as Consumers," in President's Research Committee on Social Trends, *Recent Social Trends in the United States* (New York, 1933), 820–823, 828–829, 861–864. The uses that consumers made of installment buying raises important social questions. John R. Commons believed that by 1930 at least 80 per cent of small loans were contracted to meet emergency needs and that most of the borrowers were "just above the poverty line but not poverty-stricken." Commons, "Small Loans" (typewritten), an address delivered on September 24, 1930, in the John R. Commons Papers.

The results of having more leisure time and more money to spend were not always as salutary as might have been expected. Early in 1922, the editor of the *Waupaca County Post* noted that during the previous year the total amount of money American women had paid for lipstick exceeded the amount spent for furniture. His analysis suggested "the decadence of home spirit compared with [the] growing tendency to doll up for the many occasions that draw members of the family away from the hearthstone." Denouncing the "mistaken idea that young people must be provided with unlimited means of amusement," he warned that "the habit of having always to be amused is an expensive one and is a liability rather than an asset." Cavorting about the countryside from one attraction to another rather than paying close attention to their homework was certain to bring Wisconsin's public school students to no good end. "The need of any community," concluded the editor, "is more furniture and fewer lip sticks; more home life and fewer distractions of young people from the work at hand; more evenings spent around the family circle and fewer evenings spent on the streets; more savings accounts and fewer cigarette bills."[8]

The *County Post* editorial was expressing a judgment that critics were to reiterate time and again during the New Era. Reasons for concern about the American home were many, but the increase in leisure was certainly one of the most important. "In generations farther back than this there was no need for discussing the subject of whether the American home was degenerating," noted the *Wisconsin Agriculturist*, "for the great majority of Americans were too busy getting together the makings of a home to give its degeneration a single thought." They had houses to build and furnish, crops to plant and harvest, foods to prepare and preserve, cloth to weave and clothing to stitch. In short, the home had been "the crystallized center of interest and industry, which precluded any sort of degeneration." But a remarkable transformation had occurred. Tech-

[8] *Waupaca County Post* (Waupaca), February 23, 1922. For the benefit of those who used makeup, the *Pierce County Herald* (Ellsworth), January 22, 1920, offered this beauty tip: "To give the face a good color, get a pot of rouge and a rabbit's foot. Bury them two miles out in the country, and walk out and back once a day to see if they are still there." The use of makeup was common among boys as well as girls. "I know it to be a fact that a great many of the boys carry rouge and powder puffs and openly use them," reported one young woman. "Just watch young men when they enter a restaurant or Ice Cream parlor where there are large mirrors and you will see them continually glancing at themselves and primping up." Miss A. A. R. to Halbert L. Hoard, January 25, 1926, in the Halbert L. Hoard Papers.

nological innovation had eliminated many of the household chores that had made the home a center of bustling activity, and with that transformation people had become preoccupied with matters outside the home. "Today," asserted the *Agriculturist*, "with our ready-to-wear clothing, our commercial household supplies, and labor-saving machinery, both indoors and out, farm people have more leisure for reading and thought on subjects of general interest." It was only natural, then, that they should speculate about the farm family's capacity to survive the momentous changes that had occurred.[9]

To be sure, not all the developments of modern technology threatened the solidarity of the family. People who worried about how technological wonders tended to entice family members away from the hearthstone could take comfort in perfection of the radio. The new means of communication made the home circle more attractive and strengthened family ties. By staying at home, families could grasp a vision of new horizons. "Instead of wandering idly in search of diversion," observed the Kewaunee *Enterprise*, young and old alike could hear "an orchestra, a band, a pipe organ, a religious service or a good play, in their own home, be it in a city, on a farm, or miles away in mountains or desert." Although still in its infancy, radio was "the lustiest youngster of record." By the middle of the decade it had become "a national institution" for education, amusement, and commercial gain. Milwaukee's First Wisconsin National Bank attributed the phenomenal growth of radio to "favorable business conditions" and the capacity of "high average purchasing power to create an unlimited market and put business on a mass production basis." And the end was not yet in sight, for new developments in technology and design were continually creating new opportunities.[10]

To the movies, another form of entertainment that became popular during the twenties, the response was very different. In 1929, Henry Ohl, Jr., of the Wisconsin State Federation of Labor, took a long look at the perfection of the "music machine" in the twentieth century. The first phonograph, he observed, had elicited wonder at "the limitless mechanical genius of man." Further devel-

[9] *Wisconsin Agriculturist*, March 17, 1923, January 16, 1926.

[10] Kewaunee *Enterprise*, April 20, 1923, November 28, 1924, January 16, 1925, September 10, 1926; *Business and Financial Comment*, March 15, 1929, in the Milwaukee Public Library (a monthly publication of the First Wisconsin National Bank).

opment of the phonograph, and then the radio, "had filled a place in many a home." But Ohl thought it quite another matter when the theater, "supposedly an institution established for the promotion and preservation of art, is dehumanized for the sake of commercial advantage." Having entered the realm of music before the war, he argued, the Robot was "now moving upon his victims with rigid precision, aiming to deaden their artistic being."[11]

No one could doubt the popularity of the movies. An article in the entertainment section of the Milwaukee *Journal* anticipated in 1918 that the latest arrival to the theater world, the moving picture, would become a "climber." Having "sloughed off its sans culottes tendencies," it had moved from shabby penny arcades to more fashionable quarters. In sumptuous palaces on the main streets of Wisconsin towns and cities, the cinema had gone a long way towards gaining acceptance among the social elite.[12]

Despite the motion picture's newly acquired respectability, however, opponents joined Ohl in deploring the influence of films, and in their criticism they employed both moral and esthetic arguments. What most aroused churchmen and other pillars of Wisconsin communities was the effect of the cinema on the moral fiber of society. According to one Lutheran pastor, perhaps 50 per cent of the movies were "positively poisonous, not directly and in plain sight, but by innuendo and suggestion." Lust and murder appeared to be the most popular themes, "and as a result men, women, and children are dying morally and spiritually by windrows and in heaps." But churchmen were not alone. Lieutenant-Governor George F. Comings believed in 1921 "that the movies are doing more damage, or I will say as much damage, to our young people, as has been done in the past by the saloon."[13]

A more subtle and perhaps more telling criticism came from those who anticipated Henry Ohl in finding the movies lacking in redeeming esthetic qualities. In her novel *Birth*, Zona Gale described

[11] Henry Ohl, Jr., "The Robotization of Art," in *Wisconsin Labor*, 1929, pp. 11–13.

[12] Milwaukee *Journal*, November 17, 1918.

[13] "The Moving Picture Show," and C. J. Sodergren, "Picture Shows," both in the *Northwestern Lutheran*, 3 (January 21, 1915), 11, and 8 (January 9, 1921), 6, respectively. The criticism of films extended to churches that used films for religious instruction, but an argument for church approval of movies was that it would make for "better and cleaner pictures." See the Burlington *Standard-Democrat*, February 4, 1921. See also George F. Comings to Ada James, February 15, 1921, in the Ada James Papers. An article, "The Perils of Youth," in the *Wisconsin Agriculturist*, November 17, 1923, develops an argument similar to Comings'.

Chicago society as "too weary and unimaginative to inaugurate its own diversions." Yet behind "every sign board, flaming with pale blue women and red devils . . . life could be suspended for one whole evening." The impact of such theater was "artistically negligible," but "socially enormous." Another Wisconsin novelist, Glenway Wescott, agreed. The small-town movie house was "imagination's chapel" and was "dedicated to licentiousness, aspiration, ideals." People flocked there to see themselves "in every foreign and domestic disguise; themselves as they might be, convincingly photographed where they are not—the variable bodies of other Narcissuses on other mesmerizing streams."[14]

The movies seemed to threaten the structure of society by exercising a destructive influence on the family. What might have been a stimulant became instead a narcotic for young and old alike. "The movie is destroying the home influence over the child," asserted one critic. "Would you entrust the important work to mercenary strangers?" Another believed that "if these films had been deliberately planned to rob the individual of moral standards and undermine the family, it could not have been more successfully done." The editor of the *Northwestern Lutheran* hoped "to open the eyes of Christian parents to see that the movies tend to undo their work of bringing their children up in the nurture and admonition of the Lord." And in considering the influence of movies, George Comings urged women's clubs to federate so as to become more effective in "the preservation of good morals and a healthful society."[15]

* * *

Like many other concerned citizens, Comings believed that a better education for the state's young people would do much to strengthen a society confronting the seductive temptations of the modern world. Yet opinions differed on the changes that might be required to produce a better education. Those strongly influenced by the Americanization emphasis of the war years favored the elimination of courses in foreign languages and the use of English as the sole medium for instruction in the schools. The Americanizers also

[14] Zona Gale, *Birth* (New York, 1918), 37; Glenway Wescott, *Good-Bye Wisconsin* (New York, 1928), 24–25.

[15] *Northwestern Lutheran*, 20 (July 16, 1933), 230; "The Moving Picture Show," *ibid.*, 3:11; Sodergren, "Picture Shows," *ibid.*, 8:6; Comings to Ada James, February 15, 1921, in the James Papers.

wanted the schools to propagate American ideals, to warn children against the dangers of Bolshevism, radicalism, and alien ideologies, and to have pupils recite the Pledge of Allegiance as a daily morning ritual. A more common idea among teachers and school administrators was that the schools should appeal to a variety of interests and abilities among young people and become more comprehensive in the programs they offered. When the National Education Association held its convention in Milwaukee in 1919, it adopted a resolution favoring "an American program of education," and it recommended that the states pass laws requiring children to attend school full-time until age sixteen and at least part-time until eighteen.[16]

The convention speakers did not condemn using the schools in the promotion of patriotism, but some of them perceived an economic interest behind the Americanization effort. Suggestions that business influences in public education were not entirely beneficial may have come as a surprise to those teachers who saw nothing unseemly in the schools' reinforcing ideas of the dominant community economic interests. Many educators had in fact welcomed the new involvement of industrial leaders as an awakening of concern for the welfare of education generally. Yet the Wisconsin superintendent of public instruction, Charles P. Cary, charged at the 1919 Milwaukee NEA convention that business leaders had sought to "Prussianize" the schools. That is to say, they had promoted a dual system of education by which students in vocational classes were separated from students in college preparatory classes. Although the advocates of such a system argued for its efficiency, Cary thought that it fostered class distinctions between those looking forward to professional careers and those who could expect to spend a lifetime laboring with their hands. Cary and other prominent educators advocated a different approach, contending that

[16] Edward A. Krug, *The Shaping of the American High School* (2 vols., Madison, 1964–1972), 2:9–17; "The President's Proclamation," in the *Journal of Education*, 94 (December 15, 1921), 597; "Education Week," in *ibid.*, 95 (January 19, 1922), 71; "American Education Week, November 17–23, 1924," in *School Life*, 9 (June, 1924), 245; "Report of the Committee on Resolutions," in National Education Association, *Addresses and Proceedings*, 1919, pp. 22–25. Some of the ways in which American social values were developed in the public schools of Wisconsin are summarized in Maybell G. Bush, "Socialization and Grade Work," in Department of Public Instruction, *Biennial Report*, 1916–1918, pp. 48–56.

the way to true democracy lay in schools where children of all social classes were taught side by side.[17]

The Wisconsin superintendent asserted that at no other time had he detected "a greater tendency to study education in a thorough-going and scientific way than now, and never a time when there was a greater zeal for improvement." The old autocratic management of classrooms was giving way to a democratic spirit, and students were beginning enthusiastically to take part in the exercises and functions of the school. Under the tutelage of "supervising teachers," faculties were developing new methods that involved students in a reciprocal and co-operative relationship with their classmates. To achieve the objectives of promoting initiative, good judgment, and goodwill towards others, schools were emphasizing "life situations and skill in performance." While comprehension of fundamentals in the sciences, social sciences, literature, and mathematics should not suffer from neglect, Cary believed that teaching students to cope with twentieth-century problems meant providing them with "an education in doing as well as in knowing." Such an education was also one that took the individual differences of pupils into account and encouraged each to assume responsibilities appropriate to the child's years, abilities, and training.[18]

As Cary described the schools of Wisconsin, they were powerfully influenced by the "progressive education" associated with philosopher John Dewey and other advocates of a new approach in teaching. Progressive education in fact encompassed so many separate ideas that educators had difficulty in coming up with a succinct description of what it involved. Yet everyone agreed that it had grown out of the early-twentieth-century revolt against formalism; that its purpose was to break down the barriers between school and society; and that it required teachers to be concerned not just with filling young minds with facts, but with development of the whole child. Everyone agreed, too, that the progressive approach involved a rejection of the elitism that had made public school education seem boring and inconsequential to many young people, especially to those who did not expect to go on to college.

A doubling of high school enrollment in the state between 1915

[17] *Wisconsin News* (Milwaukee), July 2, 1919.

[18] Charles P. Cary, "Some Modern Tendencies," in Department of Public Instruction, *Wisconsin Educational News Bulletin*, 11 (November, 1919), 1–2; Department of Public Instruction, *Biennial Report*, 1918–1920, pp. 120–128.

and 1925 no doubt encouraged innovative methods of instruction as faculties sought to employ techniques suitable for educating youngsters from a variety of classes and backgrounds. Abandoning the methods of rote learning, teachers exerted prodigious effort to interest students in affairs of the world as well as activities of the school. Educators in Washington County experimented successfully with a unit plan of instruction developed by Henry C. Morrison of the University of Chicago. Teachers in Beloit, Racine, Watertown, and Oshkosh were among the first in the nation to make extensive use of slides and other visual aids. Schools throughout Wisconsin began offering new courses and increasing the extracurricular activities available to students.[19]

For all the ferment in the schools, however, the philosophy and methods of progressive education never succeeded in winning universal approval from the people of Wisconsin. Economic and demographic development produced in the southeastern counties an environment more conducive to the new approach than one could find in some rural counties, or in counties of the Cutover. Even with provisions to equalize tax burdens throughout the state, citizens of the sparsely settled areas paid a disproportionate share of their local educational costs. The poorest sections of the state were also those with a population density insufficient to justify the programs of educational enrichment adopted in towns and cities of the southeastern section. In the economically disadvantaged counties, then, opposition to new, more elaborate, and more expensive systems of education sometimes became vehement. Residents of the state's poorest counties were most inclined to sing the praises of "the little red schoolhouse," and they were most likely to resist school consolidation. Progressive education encountered resistance in the cities as well. People in the sandstone and Cutover counties found urban allies among the families of some industrial workers who feared middle-class domination of the schools. Thus the new

[19] Krug, *Shaping of the American High School*, 2:163–164, 174–177, 192–196; John Callahan, "The Department of Public Instruction," in the *Wisconsin Blue Book, 1927*, pp. 343–344; Harvey M. Genske, "Washington County's Experience with the Unit Plan," in the *Wisconsin Journal of Education*, 60 (September, 1927), 38–40; Department of Public Instruction, *Biennial Report*, 1916–1918, p. 48; Milwaukee *Sentinel*, January 31, 1922. Morrison's method involved teaching of subject matter in a series of units or segments. In each unit under the Morrison plan, the teaching sequence followed an established formula for mastery: "pre-test, teach, test the result, adapt procedure, teach and test again to the point of actual learning."

progressive education became associated in some minds with privileged young people who were college-bound rather than with children of those farmers and workers who were supposed to derive the greatest rewards from the new approach to learning.[20]

Favoring the compulsory education of all young people, Samuel Gompers observed in 1922 that "knowledge is power and knowledge is culture" and that every child should have an opportunity to obtain knowledge. John J. Blaine, governor of Wisconsin at the time, agreed with Gompers. "The children of the poor do not have a fair chance in Wisconsin today," he told the state teachers' association. Yet when educators sought to reform the schools so as to place power and culture within the grasp of every child, they aroused hostility within the schools as well as in communities of the state. "Every year," grumbled Edgar G. Doudna, superintendent of schools in Wausau, "the schools and teachers are called upon to do more and more and we are by legislation being forced to introduce all sorts of unnecessary subjects in to the curriculum and we find that we have to fight to get down to the job of teaching reading, writing and arithmetic." Parents could also become annoyed, especially when they thought the schools were threatening their beliefs. William Flamm, a veteran member of the Molders' Union in Milwaukee, resented the way "the modern educational system tended to remove all thought of labor solidarity from the minds of the youth of the working class." And in rural communities, observed the *Wisconsin Agriculturist*, the "good enough for me good enough for my son" attitude was difficult to overcome.[21]

"The gospel of work is being neglected today," announced the *Pierce County Herald* through an editorial published early in 1923. "Mother and father are working about as hard as ever, but the young people are loafing as never before." Many of the *Herald*'s subscribers doubtless agreed that a mother who permitted her daughter "to think of nothing but dress and fashion, to play the

[20] *Wisconsin Agriculturist*, April 13, August 31, November 23, 1929; *Pierce County Herald* (Ellsworth), December 9, 1926; Madison *Capital Times*, June 29, 1925; Harley L. Lutz, "The Problem of State Aid, Local Tax Burdens and Tax Delinquency in Wisconsin" (typewritten, November, 1924), in the John J. Blaine Papers; Department of Public Instruction, Biennial Report, 1920–1922, p. 135; Eau Claire *Leader*, April 27, 1916; *Wisconsin Apprentice*, 4 (October, 1921), 2, and 5 (September, 1922), 2.

[21] Samuel Gompers to Frances E. Spaulding, December 5, 1922, in Legislative Reference Files, series 2, American Federation of Labor Papers; Milwaukee *Leader*, November 5, 1921, January 13, 1922, May 7, 1925; *Wood County Tribune* (Wisconsin Rapids), September 14, 1921, typed copy in LRB; *Wisconsin Agriculturist*, November 23, 1929.

piano and use the family automobile when she should be washing dishes and helping to make the beds" was neglecting her parental responsibilities. And who could quarrel with the assertion that "the father who allows his son to grow up a loafer is not a good citizen"? A boy should be set to work cleaning the cellar and bringing up the coal. Such chores would certainly not hurt the lad. "He can wear gloves if he is afraid of ruining his banjo hands. He can wear a skull cap so as not to ruffle his patent leather hair."[22]

Much of the criticism directed at young people during the New Era arose from the impression that public schools were serving the children of privilege and thereby corrupting the sons and daughters of honest toilers. "I have seen children who liked the farm until they attended high school in town," commented one rural mother, "and when they were through with high school they didn't like farming because it was too much work." In Rhinelander, the *New North* regretted the adulation accorded a self-styled "champion hobo" who visited the city in 1927. The young man's boast was that he had traveled through forty-five states and had "never missed a meal or earned a cent." Old-fashioned people who believed in working for their living associated themselves with old-fashioned notions about the virtues of production. During the New Era the emphasis shifted to consumption, and the champion hobo was the ultimate consumer.[23]

People who had grown up believing that work strengthened character could feel uncomfortable about enjoying freedom from drudgery; for their heroes they preferred Henry Ford or Charles A. Lindbergh to champion hoboes. Children of the twenties also admired Lindbergh, but many parents could not entirely escape the feeling that something was amiss. Because young people were malleable, and because they were attending school in increasing numbers, it was easy enough to associate the schools with social change and to see the schools as encouraging a new leisure class composed mainly of the young. People who were uneasy about the direction

[22] *Pierce County Herald* (Ellsworth), February 22, 1923. The editorial first appeared in the Fall River *News* (Massachusetts). After conducting a survey of schoolboys from rural areas, H. W. Schmidt concluded that "most of them indicated short hours of work as one of the prime causes for choosing occupations other than farming." See Schmidt, "Special Subjects in High Schools and Grades," in Department of Public Instruction, *Biennial Report*, 1928–1929, pp. 26–27.

[23] *Wisconsin Agriculturist*, March 23, 1929, p. 10; Rhinelander *New North*, November 17, 1927.

society was taking therefore tended to urge an alternative education that would more adequately train young people for the battles of life. For some this could mean imposing rules to regulate behavior at school functions. Acting on a petition from parents, the teachers of Rhinelander, for example, banned the playing of jazz in the schools and prohibited the dancing of the Charleston at school parties. For others, improvement in education involved expanding the athletic programs of schools, for they believed that competition in sports, like work, served to build character. "Immorality is not found among the athletic boys and girls," contended one school supervisor, "but among the bespectacled bookworms."[24]

A more promising avenue towards an alternative education, however, was one to which Wisconsin had already made a commitment. The legislature of 1911, after considering the report of a blue ribbon committee appointed to study the problem of keeping young people in school, had passed the first of a series of laws creating a state system of vocational education. By 1921, every city with a population of 5,000 or more was compelled to establish a vocational school. Children not attending a full-time school were required to attend a vocational school half-time until they had reached sixteen years of age, and then they were required to spend eight hours a week in classes until they were eighteen. Vocational education received support in matching grants from the federal government after passage of the Smith-Hughes Act of 1917, and by the school year 1925–1926 the State Board of Vocational Education could report a daytime student enrollment of more than 34,000 in the vocational schools of some forty Wisconsin cities. In 1926–1927, the state spent nearly $3 million on vocational schools, or about 4 per cent of its total expenditures for education.[25]

[24] Rhinelander *New North*, April 29, 1926; Kewaunee *Enterprise*, July 8, 1927. In 1928, J. T. Giles raised the question of whether high school athletes were being educated or exploited: "It has been suggested that these boys are being used as a means to advertise the school and the town, to build up local pride and prestige, without considering the educational value to themselves." Giles, "Extra-Curricular Activities in Wisconsin High Schools," in Department of Public Instruction, *Biennial Report*, 1926–1928, p. 42.

[25] State Board of Vocational Education, *Wisconsin Part-Time and Evening Schools for Juvenile and Adult Workers*, published as *Bulletin*, no. 12 (1929), and *Wisconsin Part Time and Evening Schools for Juvenile and Adult Workers*, published as *Bulletin*, no. 18 (1933). George P. Hambrecht published two articles with identical titles, "The Work of the State Board of Vocational Education," the first in the *Wisconsin Blue Book, 1927*, pp. 373–376, and the second in *ibid., 1929*, pp. 415–418. See also Robert J. Spinti, "The Development of Trade and Industrial Education in Wisconsin" (doctoral dissertation, University of Missouri, 1968), 127–136, and Kathleen A. Paris, *A Political History of Voca-*

During the early years of its operation, and especially during the war, the Wisconsin system of vocational education met criticism from educators who believed that separating vocational education from the regular public schools came dangerously close to following a Prussian model. Charles H. Judd, head of the department of education at the University of Chicago, charged that the Wisconsin system was "un-American, undemocratic, unwise, and unheedful of a great deal of experience." He believed that "we are as a nation committed to utter and relentless opposition to the caste system fostered by any such scheme." To offset criticisms such as Judd's, vocational schools in Wisconsin began offering more courses of a general and theoretical character rather than concentrating solely on courses typical of trade schools. Charles McCarthy, who had been a member of the committee that initiated the program in 1911, urged the state's manufacturers to get for their employees "that broad education which will lead to the efficiency which is needed . . . and which will open wide the doors of opportunity for the poorest boy and girl."[26]

Wisconsin's system of vocational education managed to survive the war years, and during the New Era it continued to expand its program for part-time students. Local boards of industrial education received authorization to establish evening classes as well as day classes, and evening enrollments more than kept pace with daytime classes. By the end of the decade, nearly 50,000 Wisconsin people were attending school at night, while daytime enrollments numbered fewer than 37,000. For some of the night students, particularly for recent immigrants, evening classes took the place of elementary school. For others who wished to go on in mathematics, history, language, or literature, the evening classes served the same purposes as undergraduate college courses. For those who wished to develop special skills or a trade, the emphasis was more typically vocational.[27]

---

tional, Technical and Adult Education in Wisconsin, Board of Vocational, Technical and Adult Education (1985), 37–39, 45–46, 56–59.

[26] Department of Public Instruction, *Wisconsin Educational News Bulletin*, 9 (October 1, 1917), 1; Charles McCarthy to Richard T. Cavanaugh, March 26, 1917, mimeographed copy in the LRB.

[27] State Board of Vocational Education, *Wisconsin Part-Time and Evening Schools for Juvenile and Adult Workers*, published as *Bulletin*, no. 12, and *Wisconsin Part Time and Evening Schools for Juvenile and Adult Workers*, published as *Bulletin*, no. 18; Spinti, "Development of Trade and Industrial Education," 136; Hambrecht, "Work of the State Board of Vocational Education," in *Wisconsin Blue Book, 1927*, pp. 376–382, and *ibid.*,

A major reason for the success of the Wisconsin vocational schools during the New Era was the support they received from organized labor. Early in the decade, the Wisconsin State Federation of Labor backed the establishment of labor colleges to provide training in trade-union administration for the workers of several Wisconsin cities. The idea gained support, and by mid-decade labor leaders were urging the expansion of labor college programs. "The greatest enemy of the masses is ignorance," wrote Frank J. Weber in a letter to the Milwaukee *Leader*. "But the time is coming when the workers will realize ignorance is the pillar that upholds wage slavery." As if to fulfill Weber's prediction, the Wisconsin State Federation of Labor held a general conference on education in Milwaukee in 1926. The workers in attendance were quick to respond to the new theories of education then being applied in the public schools. In their discussions they reached a consensus that "education is not a matter of formal instruction for merely a few years, but a process of a lifetime; that it is not enough to send children to school, but it matters much what is done with them while there; . . . that the old way had for its aim the storing of knowledge for future use, while the objective of the new school is the child as the starting point." In general agreement on educational purposes and approaches, the conferees turned to planning for the future education of workers. One conference suggestion was that a labor committee on education be formed in every Wisconsin community. Such a committee could then see to it that every city secured a special college for workers. Ultimately, the practice of according preferential treatment on the basis of social caste could be eliminated, equal opportunities for all could become an accepted rule in the realm of learning, and the new system could produce "a superior citizenry," well qualified to meet its responsibilities in a "permanent democracy."[28]

The labor college idea made modest headway until arrival of the

1929, pp. 419–429. Among the courses offered in the evening schools of Wisconsin were: arithmetic, algebra, geometry, trigonometry, physics, chemistry, civics, modern social conditions, economics, foundations of government, parliamentary law, French, Spanish, German, Latin, and Esperanto.

[28] Frank J. Weber to the editor, Milwaukee *Leader*, July 23, 1925; Henry Ohl, Jr., "Wisconsin's Educational Conference," in the *American Federationist*, 33 (June, 1926), 723–724. John R. Commons believed that labor's co-operation with the University of Wisconsin placed the state in a position "to have as fine a workers' education movement as we can find anywhere in the world." See U.S. Bureau of Labor Statistics, *Monthly Labor Review*, August, 1926, p. 294.

Great Depression and the subsequent expansion of the School for Workers at the University of Wisconsin. In the meantime, the state vocational system bore marks of the workers' demand for courses in liberal as well as technical subjects. When William John Cooper, United States commissioner of education, visited Milwaukee in the summer of 1929, he found the city's vocational school program "the best of its kind in the country." Touring the facility and visiting classes, he thought, led one "to realize that a human being is more than an adjunct to a machine, that to be a resourceful individual he needs music, art, literature as well as mechanical skill." He found the students earnest, and he thought them intent upon getting the most out of what the school had to offer. "In this age of change when you never can tell what moment your job will be wiped out," he concluded on the eve of the stock market crash, "the function of education must be to teach individuals how to adjust themselves to these sudden changes."[29]

The impulses that drove the working classes to demand a practical education for their children also encouraged them to become more assertive in other areas of life. Progressive educational theory held that the schools should serve as "embryonic social communities" in which children might learn to participate in the larger democratic society. Progressive educators argued that they were leading a democratic movement in the schools and that all young people would benefit. Farmers and workers were skeptical, however, for they had heard such arguments before. To them, progressive educational reform often seemed but another excuse to increase taxes in order to pay for the frivolities of the affluent. Instead of ultimate gains for society, they wanted immediate and tangible gains for themselves. The vocational schools sought to meet such demands, and in the process the vocational schools made effective use of new educational theories. As a consequence, the Wisconsin educational system became more democratic than it had been, and it became more responsive to real needs than ever before.[30]

For farmers, responding to needs meant identifying with movements such as those to establish state and co-operative market ex-

[29] Robert W. Ozanne, *The Labor Movement in Wisconsin: A History* (Madison, 1984), 151–155; Ernest E. Schwarztrauber, *Workers' Education: A Wisconsin Experiment* (Madison, 1942); *Capital Times*, June 5, 1929.

[30] John Dewey, *The School and Society* (Chicago, 1899), 43–44; William D. Lewis, *Democracy's High School* (Boston, 1914), 18–21.

changes or to expand credit facilities. For industrial workers, it meant association with labor unions or with the Socialist party. But if anything might be said to have united reformers, radicals, insurgents, and other dissidents, it was opposition to the corrupting influence of privilege. The resentment of privilege helped to exert the pressures needed to bring about educational reforms, and resentment of privilege became important in efforts to reform the politics of the New Era as well.

* * *

While the opposition to privilege of the leveler was not in itself sufficient to bring about reform, it always provided a leitmotiv for dissident rhetoric. In 1908, when Robert M. La Follette had opposed a bill to create an emergency currency backed by state, municipal, and railroad bonds, he delivered a classic statement on the nefarious influence of economic favoritism. Characterizing the panic of 1907 as one perpetrated by the centralized banks of New York for speculative purposes, he charged that fewer than a hundred individuals controlled the entire nation's business. Although he denied that his was a personal attack, he insisted that the Rockefellers, Morgans, and Harrimans were types embodying a great evil in American life. "Back of these men is the THING which we must destroy if we would preserve our free institutions," he warned. "Men are as nothing; the System which we have built up by privileges, which we have allowed to take possession of Government and control legislation, is the real object of my unceasing warfare."[31]

La Follette's combativeness had indeed been unceasing throughout his career in the United States Senate. Although his enemies attempted to smear his reputation with charges of disloyalty during the Great War, he retained his popularity among insurgents across the country. To that following he could now add the support of Germans for whom the war experience had also been traumatic. After defeat of the treaties, La Follette resumed his place among Progressive leaders, and to postwar insurgents he appeared as a logical choice for President in the election of 1920.[32]

[31] *Congressional Record*, 60 Cong., 1 sess., 3793–3795; Belle Case La Follette and Fola La Follette, *Robert M. La Follette* (2 vols., New York, 1953), 1:239–244; Thelen, *Robert M. La Follette*, 62–64.

[32] David L. Brye, *Wisconsin Voting Patterns in the Twentieth Century, 1900 to 1950* (New

Despite the enduring themes of Progressive rhetoric, however, too much had happened to permit a resumption of politics as usual. The nation had moved towards a centralization of political power during the war. To achieve needed efficiencies, industry had become highly organized, and economic interest groups had benefited from wartime contracts. To obtain new contracts, industrial firms had established effective lobbies, and when peace came, major corporations broadened their influence over public policy. Yet the war had also encouraged divisive tendencies in American politics as voters began to insist that politicians meet the needs of other interest groups as well.[33]

The economic problems of the postwar years—inflation and recession—placed a premium on sustaining efficiency, economic rationalization, and acceptance of practices that businessmen and industrialists considered essential for prosperity. In such times, the opposition to privilege lost much of its force. Progressive leaders in search of new unifying principles confronted voters whose primary concern was jobs rather than principles. And after the return of prosperity, reformers continued to encounter great apathy among people who were willing to ignore inequality if they could enjoy at least some measure of affluence. "To a greater degree than ever before . . . ," wrote journalist William Hard, "small business men have identified their interests with the interests of great corporate wealth. To put it lightly but precisely, they think now that a granting of a Rolls-Royce to others is a small price to pay for the getting of a Buick for themselves."[34]

Although powerful influences during the New Era worked against the renewal of reform activities in American society, dissenters and insurgents refused to abandon the effort. To many voters, wartime activities of the Wilson administration represented a denial of the Progressive faith which they now wished to restore. Furthermore, the decline of the Socialist party after 1912 had left a void that

---

York, 1979), 246–247, 264–265, 269–278; Herbert F. Margulies, "The Election of 1920 in Wisconsin: The Return to 'Normalcy' Reappraised," in *WMH*, 41 (Autumn, 1957), 15–22; Samuel Lubell, *The Future of American Politics* (3rd ed., New York, 1965), 142.

[33] Thelen, *Robert M. La Follette*, 160–163; David M. Kennedy, *Over Here: The First World War and American Society* (New York, 1980), 95–98.

[34] Link and McCormick, *Progressivism*, 111; Arthur S. Link, "What Happened to the Progressive Movement in the 1920's?" in the *American Historical Review*, 64 (July, 1959), 833–851; William Hard, "More Conservative and More Radical," in *The Nation*, 118 (May 7, 1924), 525.

reformers sought to fill. After wartime persecution and left-wing defections that led to formation of the Communist and Communist Labor parties, Socialist party membership in the United States dwindled to less than 30,000 by 1920. In only a few cities such as Milwaukee and Seattle did the party retain pockets of strength. As the Socialist party lost its following, independent farmer and labor organizations increased in number and influence, especially in the Middle West. Before long the remaining Socialists were discussing the feasibility of making common cause with farmer and labor organizations in a new political alliance. By the end of 1919, a few of them, such as Duncan McDonald, president of the Illinois Federation of Labor, and Max Hayes, editor of the Cleveland *Citizen*, had gone over to the American Labor party, recently formed to consolidate the working-class vote.[35]

Also alive to the possibilities of a new third party were Progressive survivors of the 1912 Bull Moose campaign, who looked forward to re-establishing a Progressive party in 1920. To that end, J. A. H. Hopkins, who had been national treasurer of the Roosevelt Executive Committee in 1912, organized the Committee of Forty-Eight, so named because Hopkins hoped to establish connections in all forty-eight states. Especially influential in directing the committee's activities were George Record, a New Jersey reformer who had supported La Follette for President before switching to Roosevelt in 1912, and Amos Pinchot, a New Yorker who had also had a hand in forming the Progressive party and nominating TR. A more reliable Forty-Eighter, from La Follette's point of view, was Gilbert Roe, who had for ten years been his law partner before moving from Madison to New York. In Wisconsin, the Committee of Forty-Eight included such middle-class Progressives as C. B. Ballard of Appleton, Ada James of Richland Center, Henry Krumrey of Plymouth, A. J. Schmitz of Milwaukee, and Zona Gale.[36]

[35] Entry for February 14, 1920, Ada James's diary, in the James Papers. James compared Wilson to Kaiser Wilhelm II: "With the Kaiser it was me & Gott, with Wilson it is God and I." See also Herbert F. Margulies, *The Decline of the Progressive Movement in Wisconsin, 1890–1920* (Madison, 1968), 249–250; Kenneth Campbell MacKay, *The Progressive Movement of 1924* (New York, 1947; reprinted, 1966), 54–55; David A. Shannon, *The Socialist Party of America: A History* (New York, 1955), 163; James Weinstein, "Radicalism in the Midst of Normalcy," in the *Journal of American History*, 52 (March, 1966), 773–774. Despite the arguments for consolidation, however, most of the Socialist remnant remained skeptical. See Eugene Staley, *History of the Illinois State Federation of Labor* (Chicago, 1930), 376–378.

[36] La Follette and La Follette, *La Follette*, 2:998–999; Nathan Fine, *Labor and Farmer*

The Committee of Forty-Eight favored political reform under the aegis of a new Progressive party, but Forty-Eighters were always uncomfortable with movements that seemed to emphasize class differences. Instead of forming a new party based on class or economic interest, they wished to form a new party to eliminate such interests. Nonetheless, as wartime gains for economic rationalization and losses for the victims of persecution gave way to postwar uncertainties for farmers and workers, dissidents moved towards organizations pledged to promote the interests of farmers and workers. National unity could become as threatening in peacetime as it had been in wartime; security or even survival might depend upon the ability of interest groups to exercise political power. The prewar Progressives' faith in the innate goodness of man had been found wanting. It had to be replaced by a hard-headed realism and by organizations with programs to assure the survival of groups that did not share the advantages of a privileged class.

The first such organization to gain strength among the farmers and workers of Wisconsin was the Nonpartisan League (NPL), which had originated before the war in North Dakota under the leadership of A. C. Townley. A skilled organizer, Townley had traveled about the North Dakota countryside in his Ford, stopping to urge farmers to take matters into their own hands and reverse the economic trend favoring big business. During the conflict with Germany, which Townley described as a rich man's war, the Nonpartisan League had enlisted the support of La Follette and other reformers. It had then gone on to help elect state officials pledged to support a state-owned grain elevator and milling system, a state-owned bank, state hail insurance, and other reforms to place the North Dakota economy in the hands of agrarian radicals.[37]

Townley dreamed of extending Nonpartisan League influence beyond North Dakota. By the end of World War I the league had gained 20,000 members in Wisconsin and had eighty organizers at work to increase membership in the state. Although for a time it

---

Parties in the United States, 1828–1928 (New York, 1928; reprinted, 1961), 363–364, 389–394; Margulies, *Decline of the Progressive Movement*, 249.

[37] Robert L. Morlan, *Political Prairie Fire: The Nonpartisan League, 1915–1922* (Minneapolis, 1955; reprinted, Westport, Connecticut, 1975, and St. Paul, 1985), 31–34, 79–81, 89–91, 106–108; Charles E. Russell, *The Story of the Nonpartisan League: A Chapter in American Evolution* (New York, 1920; reprinted, Salem, New Hampshire, 1975),193–201, 213–214, 224–228, 238–248, 256–278; Herbert E. Gaston, *The Nonpartisan League* (New York, 1920; reprinted, Westport, Connecticut, 1975), 45–54, 150–155, 189–196.

seemed certain to become the driving force in efforts to unite dissidents in the Upper Midwest behind a program of reform, the league soon met resistance it was unable to overcome. Attacked for its lack of patriotic enthusiasm during the war, as well as for its socialist proclivities, the NPL met defeat in its bid to elect former congressman Charles A. Lindbergh, Sr., as governor of Minnesota in 1918. Stung by the defeat, the league then sought to accommodate demands of interest groups other than farmers. In 1919 it co-operated with the Minnesota Federation of Labor to form the Working People's Nonpartisan League as a political action group for labor. The workers in turn organized similar affiliates in the Dakotas and urged the national Labor party to nominate Lynn Frazier, the Nonpartisan governor of North Dakota, as its presidential candidate. In Wisconsin, where the league was not as strong, the NPL joined Progressive Republicans in support of the La Follette candidates for state offices and for Congress in the elections of 1920. The efforts of the league formed an important base for a farmer-labor-Progressive coalition, but whether the NPL could dominate such a coalition was problematical. What appeared as a more likely and more appealing prospect to labor leaders and many Progressives was a new kind of political organization that might become an American equivalent of the British Labour party.[38]

Progressives in the Committee of Forty-Eight sympathized with the farmers and workers who were using the NPL to eliminate political and economic favoritism. Yet they believed that to emphasize class interests rather than the national interest would serve only to exacerbate the problem of privilege in American life. They sought instead to identify the causes of privilege and eliminate them. In this way they could create a society favoring no particular interest group, a commonwealth in which all classes could benefit from new technologies and new methods of production. To achieve their objectives, however, the Progressives had to secure political power, and to obtain it they had to win support from dissatisfied

[38] Morlan, *Political Prairie Fire*, 262–263; Selig Perlman and Philip Taft, *History of Labor in the United States, 1896–1932. Volume IV: Labor Movements* (New York, 1935), 527; Gaston, *Nonpartisan League*, 260–261, 313–318; Russel B. Nye, *Midwestern Progressive Politics: A Historical Study of Its Origins and Development, 1870–1958* (2nd ed., East Lansing, 1959), 291–294; Theodore Saloutos and John D. Hicks, *Agricultural Discontent in the Middle West, 1900–1939* (Madison, 1951), 342; William E. Walling, *American Labor and American Democracy* (New York, 1926; reprinted, 1971), 63–64, 104.

(X3)45055

ABOVE: Intersection of Port Washington and Silver Spring roads, Milwaukee County, c. 1922. BELOW: Roadside farm market between Delavan and Beloit, c. 1930.

WHi(X3)22748

WHi(G5)1344

ABOVE: Entrance to Island Resort, west of Wisconsin Dells near Mauston, 1929.
BELOW: The Herman Taylor family camping at Devil's Lake, 1919.

WHi(T78)

(X3)22406

ABOVE: Female motorcyclist, c. 1914. BELOW: Mrs. Charles Meade in her modern kitchen, Ripon, c. 1930.

WHi(X3)27492

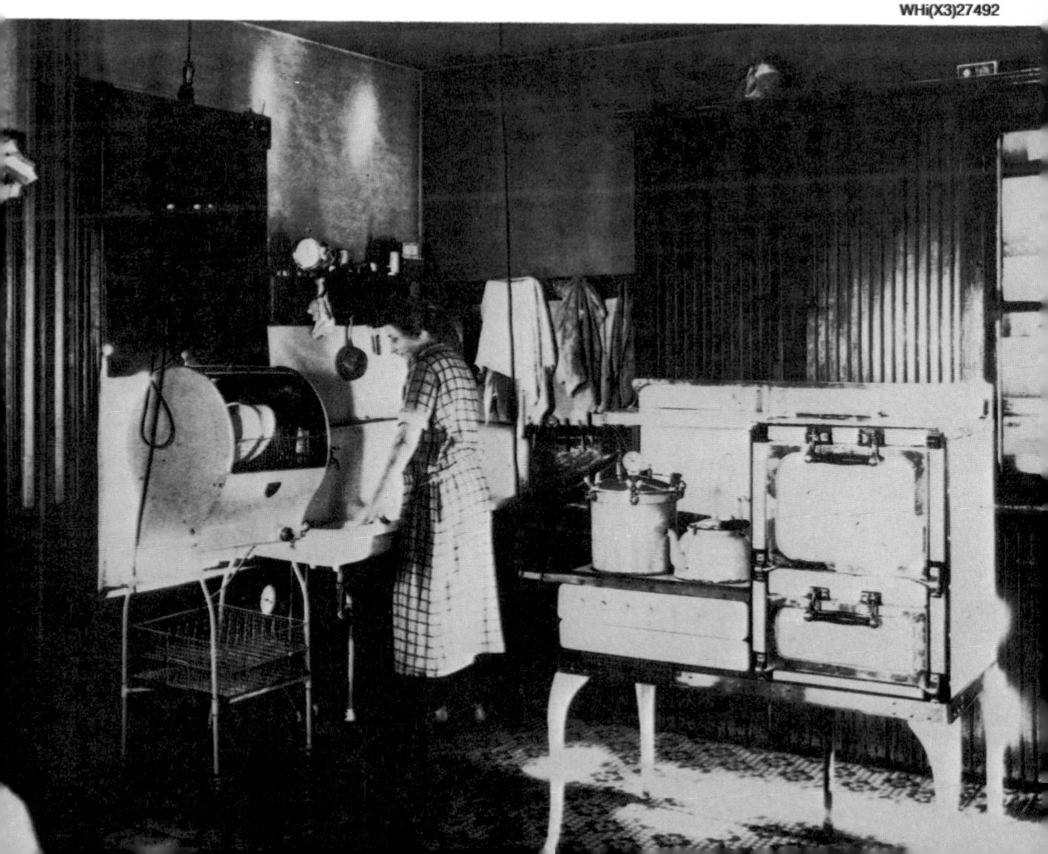

Farm Security Administration photo, Library of Congress

ABOVE: Crawford County school, 1939. BELOW: High school assembly room, Humbird, c. 1910.

WHi(X3)342

WHi(G5)2089

ABOVE: Tennis courts at the Birchcliff Hotel, Wisconsin Dells, 1926. BELOW: Dormitory room at Grafton Hall, Fond du Lac, 1922.

WHi(X3)26018

WHi(X3)28940

ABOVE: Maypole dance on Bascom Hill, University of Wisconsin, 1916. (State capitol on horizon at left center.) BELOW: McKinley Beach, Milwaukee, c. 1910.

Milwaukee Public Museum photo

WHi(G5)1078

ABOVE: Bathers at Squire's Evergreen Retreat, Lake Delton, 1932. BELOW: Bayfield County strawberry festival parade, 1938.

WHi(D749)11314

WHi(W63)6107

ABOVE: Menominee Indian powwow, Keshena, 1929. BELOW: Parlor at resort on Long Lake, New Auburn, 1926.

WHi(G5)1574

farmers and workers. After several organizational conferences and discussions with representatives of farmer and labor organizations, the Committee of Forty-Eight decided to convene in Chicago in July, 1920, at the same time that the Labor party planned to nominate a presidential candidate. The Forty-Eighters hoped that a new Progressive party would emerge from the simultaneous conventions, and most of them favored La Follette as its standard-bearer.[39]

Shortly before the Chicago meetings, when Amos Pinchot believed a La Follette campaign likely, he made bold to write the senator. Admitting that he felt "like a sign painter giving Leonardo advice," Pinchot suggested that "the great issue is no longer that of preventing the abuse of power by the privileged class." As he and George Record saw it, "the great issue now is to take away the power itself." To do that, Pinchot urged, "we must deprive the privileged class of its present control over transportation and the great natural resources, such as coal, iron ore, oil, etc., which are the raw materials of industry and the sources of energy." Control over transportation and the sources of energy had led to monopoly. With competition stifled, the privileged class could fix prices and exploit labor. Determined to eliminate favoritism, Pinchot proposed a short, vigorous platform that called for government ownership and operation of railroads and natural resources.[40]

In the meantime, La Follette was still working within the Republican party, and he had himself written a platform that delegates representing his views could present to the Republican National Convention in Chicago. Much longer than that of Pinchot and Record, and calculated to please farmer, labor, progressive, and German voters, the La Follette platform contained nineteen planks. Among them were provisions for the conclusion of peace and the restoration of trade with all nations, a soldiers' bonus, repeal of the Espionage and Sedition acts, public ownership of the railroads and natural resources, and enactment of legislation to recognize labor and farm organizations "for the purpose of collective bargaining in industry, trade, and commerce." Although the La Fol-

[39] Amos Pinchot to James H. Maurer, February 4, March 23, 1920, in the Amos Pinchot Papers, Library of Congress; MacKay, *Progressive Movement of 1924*, p. 58; Thelen, *Robert M. La Follette*, 164; Nye, *Midwestern Progressive Politics*, 299–300; J. A. H. Hopkins to Mercer Johnston, May 18, 1920, in the Mercer Johnston Papers, Library of Congress.

[40] Amos Pinchot to La Follette, June 25, 1920, and Pinchot to Henry Delbarre, June 28, 1920, in the Pinchot Papers, Library of Congress.

lette delegate slate was successful in the Wisconsin primary, the Wisconsin platform met vehement opposition when offered as a minority report to the Republican convention. The cries "Bolshevik!" and "Socialist!" rose above the cacophony of jeering, but twenty-four of the twenty-six Wisconsin delegates ignored them and voted repeatedly for La Follette's platform.[41]

Recuperating from an operation to remove his gall bladder, La Follette did not attend the Republican convention. When it adjourned after nominating Warren G. Harding, a succession of Forty-Eighters and Labor party members traveled to Madison to urge that La Follette enter the campaign as the head of a new party. The senator did not reject the proposal, and Young Bob and Gilbert Roe traveled to Chicago for the Forty-Eight and Labor conventions. They were to look after La Follette's interests, which included acceptance of a La Follette platform. The Labor party dominated the gatherings and, insisting on maintaining the integrity of its own platform, refused to compromise. As hopes for co-operation dwindled, La Follette began to have second thoughts about becoming a candidate even if a new party were formed. Finally, when the Labor party rejected both his platform and that of the Committee of Forty-Eight, he asked that his name be withdrawn from consideration. Impressed with the futility of the attempt to co-operate with the Labor party, most of the Forty-Eighters abandoned the effort. The victorious Labor delegates and the remaining Forty-Eighters then proceeded to form the Farmer-Labor party and nominate Parley P. Christensen, who had come to Chicago from Utah as a delegate to both conventions.[42]

The postmortems were many following the Chicago fiasco, and for the Committee of Forty-Eight they were bitter. The heart of the problem, grumbled Pinchot, was that "the committee of 48 cannot possibly get anywhere under the leadership of men who don't understand the difference between socialism and individualism and who naturally drift into socialism every time George [Record] and I turn our backs." Other reactions revealed a sense of futility. William B. Rubin, whose sympathies were with organized

[41] La Follette and La Follette, *La Follette*, 2:992–998; *Congressional Record*, 66 Cong., 2 sess., 4665–4666; *La Follette's Magazine*, March, 1920, p. 36.

[42] New York *Times*, June 15, July 13, 14, 15, 16, 1920; La Follette and La Follette, *La Follette*, 2:998–1008; Thelen, *Robert M. La Follette*, 164–165; Fred Greenbaum, *Robert Marion La Follette* (Boston, 1975), 190–191; Tobin, *Organize or Perish*, 114–116.

labor, had spent four days at the conventions believing that the Forty-Eighters and the Labor party could agree on common ground. Yet "it seems as through the extremists at either end pulled away from the middle," he reported to his friend, John P. Frey, president of the International Molders' Union, "and the whole thing is a bubble and a waste of effort." Yet there was hopefulness as well as bitterness and a sense of futility. The Nonpartisan League, for its part, had not formally participated in the Chicago conventions, and, remaining loyal to La Follette, never endorsed Christensen. The *Minnesota Leader*, an NPL newspaper, nonetheless found some reason for optimism in the thought that the activities of 1920 might lead to "the ultimate formation of a truly progressive third political party in the United States."[43]

The lesson to be learned from the 1920 experience, however, was neither that Progressives were difficult to organize nor that they had successfully laid the groundwork for a new party. The lesson to be learned was that the very foundations of Progressivism had shifted. Revolution abroad had increased class consciousness at home. At the same time, technological innovation and industrial efficiency made new products readily available, and Americans increasingly thought of themselves as consumers rather than producers. Businessmen and their allies saw the trend towards an emphasis on consumption as one that demonstrated the superiority of the American system. Secretary of Commerce Herbert Hoover, hailed as a spokesman for business, argued that individual initiative and expanded production were means by which class differences could be overcome. After the war, it seemed, the business community had appropriated Progressive rhetoric about equality of opportunity. For social critics and reformers, on the other hand, the rhetoric had come to have a hollow ring. As Pinchot and other Forty-Eighters discovered, insurgents were ready to forgo discussion of the fundamental principles by which they justified a crusade against privilege. They were prepared to turn instead to the more

[43] Amos Pinchot to A. W. Ricker, January 21, 1921, in the Pinchot Papers, Library of Congress. In the same collection, see also Pinchot to Lincoln Steffens, October 6, 1920; J. A. H. Hopkins to Pinchot, November 20, 1920; Pinchot to Hopkins, November 26, 1920; George Record to Hopkins, December 2, 1920; Arthur Wray to Pinchot, December 10, 1920; and A. W. Ricker to Record, December 16, 1920. See also Rubin to John Frey, July 16, 1920, in the William R. Rubin Papers. The quotation from the *Minnesota Leader* appears in Morlan, *Political Prairie Fire*, 296.

limited and attainable objectives of particular interest groups such as farmers and workers.[44]

* * *

More than most of the other prewar Progressives, La Follette was sensitive to changes that had taken place in American life. He understood that his continued political success depended upon winning the support of farmers and workers, and he knew that to win their votes he would be obliged to advance their interests. Yet he was also aware of the possibility that in fighting interest-group battles, farmers and workers could lose perspective on the fundamental causes of their problems. La Follette himself never abandoned his conviction that equal opportunity for all citizens required the elimination of economic privilege and that the power of large corporations required regulation and control. For the rest of his life he continually sought opportunities to remind his followers of the Progressive tradition while he fought new battles for farmers and workers. He finally waged a campaign for the presidency, not because he hoped to win but because he could not neglect an opportunity to direct the course of Progressivism in a nation that might otherwise forget what the Progressive insurgents hoped to accomplish.

Evidence of La Follette's sensitivity to changes in American life came soon after the arrival of economic depression in 1921, when farmers across the country perceived themselves as having to sustain the major impact of hard times. Agreeing with the rural contention that farmers should receive as much assistance as manufacturers, La Follette joined congressmen and senators from other agricultural states to form a loose but effective association of legislators known as the "farm bloc." With the assistance of the American Farm Bureau Federation, the farm bloc organized in May, 1921, with a view towards introducing legislation to facilitate farm credit, control merchants and middlemen, and promote co-operative marketing at home as well as the sale of agricultural products abroad. Frankly committed to advancing rural causes, the farm bloc enjoyed great success in passing legislation to benefit a particular interest group. Among the measures it supported during the postwar recession were the Packers and Stockyards Act, which provided for reg-

[44] Herbert Hoover, *American Individualism* (Garden City, New York, 1922), 22–25, 41–47; Robert H. Zieger, *Republicans and Labor, 1919–1929* (Lexington, Kentucky, 1969), 60–67.

ulation of the industry to prevent unfair trade practices and assure reasonable rates for stockyard services; the Future Trading Act, which taxed speculative grain transactions; the Capper-Volstead Act, which exempted co-operative marketing associations from prosecution under the antitrust laws; and various provisions authorizing loans to farmers and farm co-operatives through the War Finance Corporation and the Federal Land Bank system. Later, in 1923, the Agricultural Credits Act made further provisions for farm loans. In the same year, Congress passed a filled-milk bill, of special interest to Wisconsin farmers because it outlawed the interstate shipment of milk from which the fat content had been removed and replaced with vegetable oil.[45]

In the meantime, while generally voting with the farm bloc, La Follette was busy with more traditional Progressive activities. Shortly after the election of Warren Harding in 1920, he helped organize a Washington conference of insurgent senators and congressmen, labor leaders, farm leaders, and independent Progressives. Out of that gathering came the People's Legislative Service, ostensibly created to provide information on congressional activities and impending legislation. Basil Manly, who had been co-chairman of the War Labor Board, became director of the service, and La Follette became chairman of its executive committee. Formally launched at a dinner in Washington, the organization quickly became identified, at least rhetorically, with traditional Progressivism. Supporters at the affair heard La Follette denounce "the encroachment of the powerful few upon the rights of the many," and they applauded his assurance that the People's Legislative Service "offers today the best single hope of relief for the people."[46]

While relief for the people remained a consistent theme in La Follette's rhetoric, social and economic conditions of the postwar period created a new setting for the application of his ideas. In that new setting, old ideas sometimes took on features that suggested a shift in the implications of Progressivism. The relationship between La Follette's followers and the railroad brotherhoods pro-

[45] MacKay, *Progressive Movement of 1924*, p. 44; Thelen, *Robert M. La Follette*, 167–168; Saloutos and Hicks, *Agricultural Discontent*, 321–341; Arthur Capper, *The Agricultural Bloc* (New York, 1922).

[46] Edward N. Doan, *The La Follettes and the Wisconsin Idea* (New York, 1947), 98–101; Greenbaum, *Robert Marion La Follette*, 211.

vides an important example of the way a changing political economy could modify the meaning of conventional terminology.

The brotherhoods were a major source of funds for the People's Legislative Service, yet they were also among the least ideological of American labor unions. Behind the apparent contradiction here lay some hardheaded interest group calculations on the part of the unions. At the close of the war, the brotherhoods' general counsel, Glenn E. Plumb, offered a proposal that called for the issuance of government bonds for the purchase of all railroad properties. The railroads might then be leased to a national nonprofit corporation. Having prospered with government operation of the railroads during the war, the brotherhoods supported the plan. In part because of the railroad companies' effective opposition, however, Wilson issued a presidential proclamation in December, 1919, returning the railroads to private ownership.[47]

At the end of the war, then, disposition of the railroads became an issue in interest-group politics. Instead of the Plumb Plan, Congress passed the Esch-Cummins Act, which provided for collective bargaining and set up the Railway Labor Board to supervise the mediation of labor disputes. John J. Esch, co-author of the measure, was a Wisconsin congressman whose closest ties were with the Stalwart faction of the Republican party. La Follette, on the other hand, favored government ownership of the railroads and vigorously opposed the Esch-Cummins legislation. The railway unions, grateful for La Follette's support, demonstrated their appreciation with heavy contributions to his cause and to the People's Legislative Service. Thus even when La Follette sought to promote the general welfare by encouraging an informed public, a particular interest group—in this case the railway workers—intervened to move Progressivism towards interest-group politics and in some measure to increase the class consciousness of American workers.[48]

One reason for La Follette's promoting the People's Legislative Service was that he faced a campaign for re-election to the Senate in 1922, and the PLS could be an effective means of retaining Progressive support. With an impressive re-election victory, he would then be in a good position to carry the Progressive cause

[47] MacKay, *Progressive Movement of 1924*, p. 30; Perlman and Taft, *History of Labor. Volume IV*, p. 408; Zieger, *Republicans and Labor*, 19, 25.

[48] *La Follette's Magazine*, November, 1918, p. 2; La Follette and La Follette, *La Follette*, 2:985–988; Tobin, *Organize or Perish*, 119–120; Thelen, *Robert M. La Follette*, 158–160.

forcefully into the 1924 presidential campaign. There were, as usual, obstacles to be overcome. President Harding had ignored La Follette's recommendations on appointments, in effect depriving him of patronage, and the Republican National Committee opposed his renomination.

Yet the "Old Man" of Wisconsin politics was not to be denied the satisfaction of victory in 1922. After an easy primary win over William Ganfield, president of Carroll College, La Follette traveled outside Wisconsin to identify himself with the cause of farmers and workers in other states. He campaigned in North Dakota for Lynn Frazier, who was running for a seat in the Senate under the auspices of the Nonpartisan League, and in Minnesota he delivered several speeches for Henrik Shipstead, who was running as a Farmer-Labor candidate for the Senate seat of conservative Republican Frank B. Kellogg. Once a supporter of Theodore Roosevelt, Kellogg had become wealthy as a lawyer for corporations in the steel, flour-milling, and lumber industries. It was Kellogg who had introduced a resolution to expel La Follette from the Senate in 1917, and La Follette now proceeded to deal with him as the worst of an evil breed whose members had sold their souls to corporate power. Kellogg did not stand erect, and he walked with a noticeable stoop. "God Almighty through nature writes men's characters on their faces and in their forms," La Follette told a packed house in the St. Paul Auditorium. "Your Senator has bowed obsequiously to wealth and to corporations' orders and to his masters until God Almighty has given him a hump on his back—crouching, cringing, un-American, unmanly."[49]

Although many of La Follette's supporters, including his wife, thought his invective too harsh, it apparently did not produce a negative reaction in the polling places of Wisconsin. His Democratic opponent in the general election was Jessie Jack Hooper, whose opinions on social questions were much like La Follette's own. Whatever her views, however, her party affiliation was a handicap after the peace treaties raised doubts about the purpose of "Wilson's War" and the reliability of Democratic leadership. German voters—whether Catholic or Protestant, urban or rural—deserted

[49] Saloutos and Hicks, *Agricultural Discontent*, 347–348; Chester H. Rowell, "La Follette, Shipstead, and the Embattled Farmers," in *World's Work*, 46 (August, 1923), 415–417; La Follette and La Follette, *La Follette*, 2:1060–1064; St. Paul *Pioneer Press*, November 4, 1922.

the Democratic party in great number between 1912 and 1920. By 1922, many of them were committed to La Follette, and with their help he captured 80.6 per cent of the total vote.[50]

Ethnic voting, important though it was, does not fully explain La Follette's strong showing in 1922, for place of residence could modify ethnic preferences. Among voters who had supported him prior to the war, La Follette either held his ground or gained noticeably with the farmers of Norwegian, Finnish, Belgian, and French Canadian townships. His greatest losses in 1922 as compared with 1916 were among Swedes, Norwegians, and Danes living in cities and villages. Among voters who had not supported him before the war, La Follette made his greatest advances in Swiss, German, and Austrian rural townships as Teutonic farmers joined other farmers in adding greatly to Progressive strength during the New Era.[51]

The importance of the rural vote in 1922 was equally apparent in the gubernatorial race, in which none of the candidates was prominently identified either with opposition to the war or with the ethnic sensitivities to which such opposition appealed. Incumbent governor John J. Blaine, running as a Progressive, defeated William Morgan and A. C. McHenry in the primary and Democrat Arthur Bentley in the general election. Supported by various farm organizations in the state, Blaine won 83 per cent of the total vote in counties with no concentration of population greater than 10,000 and 71.8 per cent of the vote in counties that had at least one city of 10,000 or more. While such a comparison is too crude to mean very much, it does lend credence to the suggestion that La Follette's vote was not entirely a personal one, and that rural areas remained predominantly Progressive after the war.[52]

* * *

The 1922 elections brought encouragement to dissident groups, for La Follette's victory was only one of several in which farmers,

[50] Lawrence L. Graves, "Two Noteworthy Wisconsin Women: Mrs. Ben Hooper and Ada James," in *WMH*, 41 (Spring, 1958), 174–180; James Howell Smith, "Mrs. Ben Hooper of Oshkosh: Peace Worker and Politician," in *WMH*, 46 (Winter, 1962–1963), 124–135; Brye, *Wisconsin Voting Patterns*, 273–280.

[51] Brye, *Wisconsin Voting Patterns*, 269–271.

[52] MacKay, *Progressive Movement of 1924*, pp. 67–68; Saloutos and Hicks, *Agricultural Discontent*, 346–347; Rowell, "La Follette, Shipstead and the Embattled Farmers," *World's Work*, 46:409–412.

laborers, or Progressives exerted an influence. While La Follette and Blaine triumphed in Wisconsin, Frazier emerged a winner in North Dakota, and Shipstead defeated Kellogg in Minnesota. Other successes in Minnesota, Iowa, Oklahoma, Kansas, North Dakota, Colorado, Montana, and Washington, as well as in Wisconsin, added momentum to Progressive and dissident activities already underway. In February, the railroad brotherhoods had held a conference in Chicago, to which they invited "progressive elements in the industrial and political life of our nation." William H. Johnston, president of the International Association of Machinists, chaired the sessions; the Socialists, the Committee of Forty-Eight, the Farmer-Labor party, the Nonpartisan League, the Church League for Industrial Democracy, the Methodist Federation of Social Service, and the National Catholic Welfare Council all sent representatives. From that mélange came an organization known as the Conference for Progressive Political Action, and it was able to claim credit for helping to win the Progressive victories in 1922. Anticipating still more triumphs to come, the CPPA immediately set about formulating a program and organizing for the 1924 presidential campaign.[53]

The CPPA agreed to meet again after the elections in a second convention to be held in Cleveland on December 11 and 12, 1922. In the meantime, La Follette and Manly arranged a more informal gathering at the City Club in Washington on December 2. Sponsored by the People's Legislative Service, and attended by many of the Progressives who were active in the CPPA, the City Club meeting resolved to aid in promoting Progressive co-operation throughout the nation. To further the cause the gathering formed several committees to draft legislation on issues it considered vital for the next session of Congress. La Follette agreed to chair the committee on transportation.[54]

[53] M. M. Hedges, "The Liberal Sweep in the West," in *The Nation*, November 22, 1922, p. 543; Fred E. Haynes, "The Collapse of the Farmer-Labor Bloc," in *Social Forces*, 4 (September, 1925), 153; Rowell, "La Follette, Shipstead and the Embattled Farmers," *World's Work*, 46:412; LeRoy Ashby, *The Spearless Leader: Senator Borah and the Progressive Movement in the 1920's* (Urbana, 1972), 55; MacKay, *Progressive Movement of 1924*, pp. 60–68; Saloutos and Hicks, *Agricultural Discontent*, 345–351; Greenbaum, *Robert Marion La Follette*, 212.

[54] La Follette and George Huddleston to George Norris, November 18, 1922; La Follette to Norris, November 24, 1922; Norris to B. Brewer, December 8, 1922; La Follette to Norris, Edwin F. Ladd, Smith Brookhart, Lynn J. Frazier, Henrik Shipstead, and Magnus Johnson, November 30, 1923, all in the George Norris Papers, Library of

Assured of support from the People's Legislative Service, the second conference of the CPPA convened in Cleveland on schedule. Labor and farm organizations, co-operative societies, the Farmer-Labor party, the Single Taxers, the League for Industrial Democracy, the Nonpartisan League, state and local organizations of the CPPA, and the Socialist party all sent an assigned number of delegates. Votes were apportioned according to a formula providing one vote for every 10,000 members in each participating organization. The Communists were not invited, but they were not reticent about appearing to take part in the proceedings anyway. At the Second Congress of the Communist International in 1920, and at the Third Congress a year later, Lenin had recommended a united front with working-class organizations such as the CPPA. He favored supporting them, he said, "in the same way as a rope supports one who is hanged." The Progressives and the railroad brotherhoods therefore suspected that the Communists were up to no good. Edward Keating, the editor of *Labor*, introduced a motion to eject them on the grounds that their objectives were incompatible with those of the CPPA. The resolution passed easily. In confronting the problem of whether to form a third party—the most important matter to be decided at the Cleveland convention—the delegates were determined to avoid disruption by the Communists.[55]

Two points of view emerged from debates over the third-party question. Morris Hillquit, an influential Socialist from New York, favored a new party. So also did the Socialists of Wisconsin. Socialist leaders Victor Berger, Daniel Hoan, and John Work had all opposed the Progressives before the war, but in 1922 they had urged their Milwaukee comrades to support La Follette in his re-election campaign. The reason for the Socialists' change of heart was that the party's decline after the war led many of them to believe that their political survival depended upon co-operation with the CPPA. In the state legislature, fourteen party members were already working with La Follette Republicans to prevent conservatives from dominating either house. Yet a new party over which they could exercise

---

Congress. See also La Follette and Huddleston to John J. Blaine, November 18, 1922; La Follette to Blaine, telegram, November 23, 1922; and La Follette to Blaine, April 11, 1923, all in the Blaine Papers.

[55] MacKay, *Progressive Movement of 1924*, p. 80; Lowell K. Dyson, *Red Harvest: The Communist Party and American Farmers* (Lincoln, 1982), 17–18; Theodore Draper, *American Communism and Soviet Russia: The Formative Period* (New York, 1960), 31–37.

an influence was a far more appealing prospect for the Socialists than was continued co-operation with another party, however Progressive it might be.[56]

The railroad brotherhoods, the strongest organization within the CPPA, had different ideas about forming a new third party. They believed that they could have greater power to secure their objectives by working within one of the major parties. With some support, they might even have enough strength to determine which of the candidates received major-party presidential nominations in 1924. Among the Republicans, La Follette was their choice, though they were concerned about his age and his health. They also favored William Gibbs McAdoo, wartime administrator of the railroads and a contender for the Democratic nomination. The brotherhoods, therefore, had little patience with third-party arguments. They wanted to use CPPA influence either to win Democratic adoption of a program such as the Plumb Plan or to build within the Republican party an attitude equally favorable to their interests. As for the farm organizations, they preferred the strategy of the Nonpartisan League and were more sympathetic to arguments for using the CPPA as a means of electing candidates in state contests than they were towards talk of a new party.[57]

The strength of the railroad brotherhoods at the Cleveland convention allowed them to defeat a motion to form a third party. Awaiting an indication of what La Follette or McAdoo wished to do, the CPPA rested content with adopting a six-point "postcard" platform with which neither La Follette nor McAdoo could disagree. It called for repeal of the Esch-Cummins Act, constitutional amendments for the direct election of the President and removal of the Supreme Court's power to declare legislation unconstitutional, enactment of the Norris-Sinclair bill to raise prices on farm products while also reducing food prices for consumers, payment of a soldiers' bonus through restoration of an excess profits tax, and equal rights as well as maternity benefits for women. When

[56] Scott D. Johnston, "Wisconsin Socialists and the Conference for Progressive Political Action," in *WMH*, 37 (Winter, 1953–1954), 96; La Follette and La Follette, *La Follette*, 2:1156–1157.

[57] Dyson, *Red Harvest*, 17–18; Fine, *Labor and Farmer Parties*, 402–405; Shannon, *Socialist Party of America*, 170; Tobin, *Organize or Perish*, 142–143; Saloutos and Hicks, *Agricultural Discontent*, 457; MacKay, *Progressive Movement of 1924*, pp. 69–70; Zieger, *Republicans and Labor*, 173–176; Robert H. Zieger, "From Hostility to Moderation: Railroad Labor Policy in the 1920s," in *Labor History*, 9 (Winter, 1968), 23–38.

the convention adjourned it was clear that the CPPA had in effect decided to await further developments before taking action on which candidate or party it would support if it did not reverse its decision against forming a new party.[58]

Despite continuing concern over his health, La Follette fared far better than did McAdoo during the months after the CPPA met in Cleveland. The disposition of oil reserves controlled by the Navy became the issue that brought a victory for one and political ruin for the other. For years La Follette had advocated the general proposition that natural resources should be government-owned. Recognizing that objective as attainable only to a degree, he had become a watchdog over public lands and government reserves to protect them from private exploitation and despoliation. Because of his concern, he was disturbed by reports he received shortly after Harding's election. Secretary of Interior Albert B. Fall, it appeared, had been involved in quiet manipulation to lease naval oil reserves to private companies.[59]

It was not until the fall of 1923, after the elections of 1922, that La Follette was able to persuade Thomas Walsh, a Montana Democrat, to take on the oil investigation for the public lands committee of the Senate. The probe ultimately exposed a series of intricate and far-reaching scandals that affected plans for the 1924 political campaign. Teapot Dome, site of the naval oil reserve in Wyoming, soon became a shorthand term for the corruption that plagued the Harding administration and ruined McAdoo's chances for winning a presidential nomination. Walsh's investigation revealed, among other things, that one of the involved oil producers, Edward L. Doheny, had paid McAdoo an annual legal retainer of $25,000. News of McAdoo's association with the likes of Doheny devastated his supporters in the Democratic party and in the CPPA. The New York *Times* reported that, in the opinion of most political observers, the revelation had taken McAdoo out of the running. While McAdoo had not been implicated in the oil scandal itself, no party that hoped to project an image of moral purity could nominate a man who had accepted a lucrative retainer from one of the corrupt principals.[60]

[58] MacKay, *Progressive Movement of 1924*, pp. 70–71; Greenbaum, *Robert Marion La Follette*, 212.

[59] La Follette and La Follette, *La Follette*, 2:1041–1048; Burl Noggle, *Teapot Dome: Oil and Politics in the 1920's* (Baton Rouge, 1962), 32–40.

[60] Dyson, *Red Harvest*, 18; Robert K. Murray, *The Harding Era: Warren G. Harding and*

La Follette had not intended to eliminate a rival by exposing the manipulations of oil men, but one result of Walsh's investigation was that La Follette himself became the only possible candidate the CPPA could support. Did the old man, at age sixty-nine, seriously wish to run? He had suffered a series of illnesses during 1923, and while few persons doubted either his willingness or his courage, some of his friends wondered if he were capable of undertaking a strenuous campaign. When Magnus Johnson, a Minnesota Farmer-Laborite, asked his help in a special senatorial election hailed as a test of Progressive strength, La Follette was relaxing in the Battle Creek Sanitarium in Michigan. Because he could not travel to Minnesota himself, he sent his son Phil to make a personal appeal for Johnson's election. Interpreting Johnson's victory as a triumph of Progressivism over conservative Republicanism, La Follette was heartened by the results. Encouraging though it may have been, the victory was a more accurate indicator of Progressive support than of La Follette's capacity to conduct a strenuous campaign.[61]

While La Follette was still resting at Battle Creek, he received a letter from his friend William T. Rawleigh, urging him to vacation in Europe and offering to pay his expenses. He accepted the offer and, on August 1, 1923, he left New York for a three-month tour with his wife, his son Bob, and the Manlys. Eager to learn what he could about postwar Europe, La Follette held discussions with prominent persons in the countries he visited. In London he met John Maynard Keynes and Norman Angell. In Berlin he conferred with Chancellor Gustav Stresemann, as well as with business leaders and members of the Reichstag. Then, in the company of journalist Lincoln Steffens and sculptor Jo Davidson, the La Follettes traveled on to the USSR. Denied no interview he requested, La Follette had long talks with Boris Tchitcherin, minister of foreign affairs, and Aleksei Rykov, the acting premier. On their return trip the senator and his wife behaved like ordinary tourists, stopping to visit famous

His Administration (Minneapolis, 1969), 470; J. Leonard Bates, "The Teapot Dome Scandal and the Election of 1924," in the *American Historical Review*, 60 (January, 1955), 303–322; New York *Times*, February 2, 1924. "Surely the oil scandal has created a perfect situation for us," exulted Nonpartisan Leaguer Henry G. Teigan. See Teigan to J. A. H. Hopkins, February 5, 1924, in the Henry G. Teigan Papers, Minnesota Historical Society.

[61] Noggle, *Teapot Dome*, 103; MacKay, *Progressive Movement of 1924*, 74; Greenbaum, *Robert Marion La Follette*, 212–213; Milwaukee *Journal*, April 7, 22, 1924; La Follette to Mercer Johnston, June 19, 1924, in the Johnston Papers, Library of Congress; Saloutos and Hicks, *Agricultural Discontent*, 354; New York *Times*, July 3 and 9, 1923.

sites along the way. In Rome they called on Benito Mussolini, and in Munich they watched soldiers drilling in the streets. La Follette had hoped to visit Ramsay MacDonald, but illness from a cold contracted in Berlin forced cancellation of those plans, and in mid-October he and his wife sailed for home.[62]

Shortly after his return from Europe, La Follette again fell ill, this time with pneumonia. Yet before taking to his sickbed he helped write a Progressive platform to be submitted to the voters of Wisconsin in the primary election on April 1, 1924. Reading between the lines, the New York *Times* reported that La Follette had decided to head a third-party ticket in the fall. Whatever the voters of Wisconsin may have believed about the old man's political future, the Progressive platform received overwhelming approval in the primary, and twenty-eight Progressives won election as delegates to the Republican National Convention scheduled to meet in Cleveland on June 10. In the meantime, La Follette had begun to organize for a campaign before going off to Atlantic City to breathe fresh salt air in hopes of a speedy recovery from his bout with pneumonia.[63]

He was still in Atlantic City when delegates from dissident organizations on the left began preparing for the Farmer-Labor convention called to meet in St. Paul on June 17. The Farmer-Labor party had experienced difficulty in setting the date, for the factions seeking to control the FLP favored different strategies. The western farmers, led by Henry G. Teigan and William Mahoney of the Minnesota organization, hoped to secure a definite commitment from La Follette pledging that he would run for President on the Farmer-Labor ticket. The Teigan-Mahoney faction wished to defer the convention until after the Republican party had named its candidate. Then, when Republicans had adopted a platform La Follette would be compelled to reject, they could proceed with the certainty that he would accept their nomination. Some of the Communists within the FLP, most notably John Pepper, a Hungarian-born journalist

[62] La Follette and La Follette, *La Follette*, 2:1074–1087; *La Follette's Magazine*, November, 1923, pp. 164–166, and January, 1924, pp. 5, 11–12; Joseph Lincoln Steffens, *The Autobiography of Lincoln Steffens* (New York, 1931), 806; Joseph Lincoln Steffens, *The Letters of Lincoln Steffens*, eds. Ella Winter and Granville Hicks (2 vols., New York, 1938), 2:631.

[63] La Follette and La Follette, *La Follette*, 2:1094–1097; New York *Times*, March 18, 1924; New York *World*, March 22, 1924; Doan, *The La Follettes and the Wisconsin Idea*, 117.

who had no stomach for co-operation with bourgeois politicians, preferred an earlier date as one that would be more likely to assure Communist control of the party.[64]

Leaders of organized labor viewed with dismay the prospect of a third party dominated by Communists, and they employed their heavy artillery in attacking the FLP. *Labor*, the railway unions' weekly newspaper, warned against having anything to do with the St. Paul convention because "a small but very active band of communists is in control of the arrangements." Late in April, Samuel Gompers cautioned labor unions against supporting any third party, and he denounced the Farmer-Labor party in particular as an organization controlled by Communists with whom the unions could co-operate only at their own peril. In sympathy with the views of organized labor, Bob La Follette, Jr., grew worried about his father's becoming a catspaw for the Third International, and he hastened to Atlantic City for a family conference with Gilbert Roe and Basil Manly.[65]

Warning his father that the Communists were attempting to use the FLP as a means of taking over the Progressive movement, Young Bob urged him to repudiate the party and insist that his name be withdrawn from consideration for a presidential nomination. La Follette complied with his son's wishes on May 28, when he released a message he had sent to Herman Ekern, attorney general of Wisconsin. Drafted largely by Young Bob, the four-page letter conceded that La Follette's friends in the FLP were motivated "by the purest desire to promote genuine political and economic progress." Yet it also emphasized that they had "committed the fatal error of making the Communists an integral part of their organization." In permitting Communist participation in the St. Paul convention, ran the argument, the Farmer-Labor party was relying on the support of "the mortal enemies of the progressive movement and democratic ideals." Furthermore, that support provided the reactionary

[64] Dyson, *Red Harvest*, 18–20; James Weinstein, *The Decline of Socialism in America, 1912–1925* (New York, 1967), 304–307; Draper, *American Communism and Soviet Russia*, 102–103; Milwaukee *Journal*, May 28, 1924. The problems of the Farmer-Labor party are evident in the papers of Henry G. Teigan of Minnesota in the Minnesota Historical Society. See for example, Teigan to J. A. H. Hopkins, October 1, 1923; Teigan to J. G. Brown, November 8, 1923; Carl D. Thompson to Teigan, December 13, 1923; J. A. H. Hopkins to Teigan, January 22, 1924; J. G. Brown, John Fitzpatrick, and Robert M. Bach to Teigan, February 6, 1924; and J. A. H. Hopkins to Teigan, February 23, 1924.

[65] *Labor*, April 5, 1924; La Follette and La Follette, *La Follette*, 2:1098; Weinstein, *Decline of Socialism*, 310–312.

interests of the two major parties with "the best opportunity to plant their spies and provocatory agents for the purpose of confusing and destroying true Progressive movements." The letter obviously precluded a nomination of La Follette by the Farmer-Labor party, and his supporters withdrew from the convention, which then proceeded to name Duncan MacDonald for president and William Bouck for vice-president.[66]

La Follette's attitude towards Communist participation in the FLP, along with the revelation of McAdoo's involvement with Doheny, made his nomination by the CPPA a virtual certainty. Yet there were problems to be resolved. The senator had not formally announced his candidacy, and he was still at least nominally a Republican. For the CPPA to proceed with a third-party ticket, La Follette would have to break with his party. Calvin Coolidge had become President after Warren Harding's death in 1923, and he perched taciturnly atop an irresistible steamroller when the Republican National Convention met in Cleveland. Henry Allen Cooper, a leader of the Wisconsin delegation, offered the La Follette platform as a minority report, but the convention gave it short shrift. Coolidge won the nomination with 1,065 votes to thirty-four for La Follette. While the party of Coolidge conservatism was one that held no attraction for La Follette, he was still reluctant to run as the nominee of a third party. He feared that doing so would hurt the chances of Progressives in both of the two major parties and reduce whatever possibility remained for Progressive legislation in Congress.[67]

Such were the thoughts running through the senator's mind on June 24, when a delegation from the La Follette for President Committee, headed by William T. Rawleigh, called to present him with a sizable package of petitions from across the country asking that he run for President. That same evening, La Follette received a telegram from William H. Johnston, chairman of the CPPA national committee, urging him to lead Progressive forces in the coming campaign. The Democrats were meeting in New York at the

[66] Milwaukee *Journal*, May 28, 1924; New York *Herald Tribune*, May 29, 1924; MacKay, *Progressive Movement of 1924*, pp. 86–88; Weinstein, *Decline of Socialism*, 313–318; Doan, *The La Follettes and the Wisconsin Idea*, 120–121.

[67] La Follette and La Follette, *La Follette*, 2:1107–1108; Donald R. McCoy, *Calvin Coolidge: The Quiet President* (New York, 1967), 254–256; Republican Party National Convention, *Proceedings*, 1924, pp. 116–124, 154, 164–165; MacKay, *Progressive Movement of 1924*, p. 94.

time, but they were deadlocked and they seemed unlikely to name a candidate more Progressive than Coolidge. The CPPA was scheduled to begin its deliberations on July 4, and La Follette could delay no longer. If there was to be a Progressive candidate at all, the ailing senator would have to act immediately.[68]

Under such pressure, La Follette decided formally to become a candidate. Young Bob, who read to the CPPA convention an announcement of his father's candidacy, stressed that the La Follette race was to be an independent one, and that his father was not running as the candidate of a third party. Furthermore, Old Bob would take no part in selecting a complete ticket that might compete with good Progressives still affiliated with one of the major parties. The unusual procedure was hardly what the Socialist delegates had in mind, for they had anticipated the formation of an entirely new party. Yet they respected La Follette's wishes in the matter, and the next day the Cleveland convention nominated him by acclamation. At the same time, the delegates authorized the CPPA national committee to select a vice-presidential candidate on behalf of the organizations they represented. The Socialist party convention, meeting independently, endorsed La Follette's nomination on July 7.[69]

The selection of a vice-presidential candidate awaited the outcome of the chaotic Democratic deliberations in New York. Progressives of the CPPA hoped to name a Democrat so as to meld the independent insurgents with those of the major parties into a cohesive force for reform. La Follette himself favored Supreme Court Justice Louis D. Brandeis, but Brandeis refused the offer. At that point, shortly after the Democrats nominated as their presidential candidate a conservative New York lawyer, John W. Davis, Senator Burton K. Wheeler of Montana announced that he could not concur in his party's decision to go to Wall Street for its candidate. Wheeler's position was one the Progressives could respect. They had long been impressed with his record in opposing copper interests in Montana and in upholding civil liberties during the war.

[68] La Follette and La Follette, *La Follette*, 2:1109–1110; Greenbaum, *Robert Marion La Follette*, 214; MacKay, *Progressive Movement of 1924*, pp. 118–119; Mercer Johnston to his wife Katherine, July 4, 1924, in the Johnston Papers, Library of Congress.

[69] La Follette and La Follette, *La Follette*, 2:1112–1113; Doan, *The La Follettes and the Wisconsin Idea*, 124–126; New York *Times*, July 5 and 6, 1924; Morris Hillquit, *Loose Leaves from a Busy Life* (New York, 1934), 316–320; Shannon, *Socialist Party of America*, 173–175.

After he entered the Senate in 1923, Wheeler worked assiduously to oppose corruption in the Justice Department, an activity consistent with La Follette Progressivism. Now, after the young Montana senator announced that he would not support the Democratic ticket, he appeared as the logical choice to become La Follette's running mate. The executive committee of the Conference for Progressive Political Action notified Wheeler of his nomination on July 18. After some hesitation he accepted the honor, and the Progressives began developing a strategy for the campaign ahead.[70]

* * *

With enthusiasm for La Follette running high after the Cleveland convention, his candidacy attracted support from New York to California. To be sure, not everyone who had been involved in earlier Progressive efforts approved of this one. Many of the old Bull Moosers still harbored resentment against La Follette for his refusal to back Theodore Roosevelt in 1912, and they thought his encouragement of the Socialists a violation of Progressive principles. James R. Garfield, son of the assassinated President and an admirer of TR, thought the senator "a dangerous man and his followers wild." Yet other Bull Moosers embraced a different, more class-conscious form of Progressivism, and their number included such notables as Harold Ickes, Jane Addams, and Herbert Croly. The Progressives of 1924 had emerged as a new breed; they were progenitors of the New Deal rather than offspring of the Bull Moose. La Follette received support from independent thinkers—Oswald Garrison Villard, W. E. B. Du Bois, Thorstein Veblen, and Louis F. Post, for example—as well as from remnants of Roosevelt's 1912 following.[71]

[70] Louis D. Brandeis, *Letters of Louis D. Brandeis. Volume V (1921–1941): Elder Statesman*, eds. Melvin I. Urofsky and David W. Levy (5 vols., Albany, 1971–1978), 135; Milwaukee *Journal*, April 7, 1924; New York *Times*, July 17, 1924; Burton K. Wheeler with Paul F. Healy, *Yankee from the West* (Garden City, New York, 1962), 247–251; Thelen, *Robert M. La Follette*, 183–184; MacKay, *Progressive Movement of 1924*, pp. 134–136.

[71] Alan R. Havig, "A Disputed Legacy: Roosevelt Progressives and the La Follette Campaign of 1924," in *Mid-America*, 53 (January, 1971), 52–53; La Follette and La Follette, *La Follette*, 2:1120–1121; New York *Times*, September 24, October 24, 1924; Oswald Garrison Villard to La Follette, February 1, 1924, in the Oswald Garrison Villard Papers, Harvard University; Thelen, *Robert M. La Follette*, 184; "Progressivism—1912 and 1924," in the *New Republic*, August 11, 1924, p. 312; New York *Times*, October 24, 1924; Michael Wreszin, *Oswald Garrison Villard: Pacifist at War* (Bloomington, Indiana, 1965), 164–167. Although Ickes defended La Follette during the campaign, he wound up voting for John W. Davis who was a Wall Street lawyer. See Linda J. Lear, *Harold L. Ickes: The Aggressive Progressive, 1874–1933* (New York, 1981), 292–296.

Because the postwar Progressives confronted new and exceedingly complex problems, and because there was only an amorphous political structure within which they could work, La Follette's lieutenants were slow in launching their campaign. Not the least of their difficulties was La Follette's determination to run as an independent with formal ties to no political party. An independent candidacy exacerbated the problem of co-ordinating the activities of several discrete organizations. Without a party mechanism, Progressive leaders held a series of conferences to develop a strategy, and out of those meetings came a joint executive committee that assumed responsibility for guiding the campaign. Most committee members were active in the CPPA, but they tended to identify with the groups from which they had originally come. Thus the direction of the campaign was left to a confederation of farmers, socialists, and the railway brotherhoods. La Follette himself relied most heavily on the men and women who had demonstrated their trustworthiness in his earlier political campaigns in Wisconsin. Representative John M. Nelson, from the Third Congressional District where La Follette maintained his residence, became chairman of the joint executive committee, and Young Bob La Follette became vice-chairman.[72]

The attempt to conduct the campaign through a sharing of responsibilities led to bickering among the factions supporting La Follette and plagued Progressive efforts from the start. Nelson operated out of headquarters in Chicago so as to concentrate on winning the farm vote of the Upper Midwest. At the same time, the Progressives established additional offices in New York and Washington. The division of responsibilities among the Progressive headquarters remained unclear, however, and the campaign received little direction from the top as the senator sought to conserve his strength for a series of campaign speeches in October. As a result, the business of conducting the campaign rested with enthusiastic amateurs who lacked the experience necessary to handle the inevitable crises that arose.[73]

[72] MacKay, *Progressive Movement of 1924*, pp. 148–149; James H. Shideler, "The La Follette Progressive Party Campaign of 1924," in *WMH*, 33 (June, 1950), 450–452. Victor Berger's wife Meta had argued in April that "to organize after July 4th means that we will be ineffective & give up the national election." George Norris, on the other hand, did not believe "that any good can be accomplished by an attempt to organize a third party." See Berger to Ada James, April 10, 1924, in the James Papers; and Norris to J. A. H. Hopkins, January 6, 1924, in the Norris Papers, Library of Congress.

[73] Patrick J. Maney, *"Young Bob" La Follette: A Biography of Robert M. La Follette, Jr.,*

The most serious problem the Progressives faced was that of securing financial support. Rawleigh, who had already given substantial sums to his friend, became national treasurer for the campaign. Disgusted by the absence of business acumen among his colleagues, he dipped ever deeper into his own pocket and in the end contributed $28,000, or 6 per cent of the total amount in the La Follette campaign fund. Because of their great need, the La Follette managers resorted to direct methods of money raising. They sold copies of the campaign textbook, campaign buttons, and other campaign mementos. They passed a plate for contributions at campaign rallies, and they sometimes charged admission to hear campaign speeches. It was all hopelessly inadequate. The national La Follette-Wheeler finance committee, which had hoped to have a $3 million budget for the Progressive canvass, was able to raise only $222,000. The fund-raising effort in the states brought the La Follette total to $460,000, a paltry sum for a national campaign.[74]

The shortage of money made the financial support of organized labor just as important as the votes of workers. The AFL included nearly three million workers, and if they and the voters whom they could influence would contribute both money and votes, labor could determine the outcome of the election. When the AFL broke a long-standing tradition against partisan political support and endorsed La Follette early in August, Progressives were jubilant. But their celebration was premature. Although the AFL announced its support, the member unions were reluctant to contribute in any substantial way to a Progressive victory. Having used nonpartisanship to secure bread-and-butter gains, they had little interest in a movement that could lead to the creation of a new party. Helping to form such a party, after all, could mean a loss of influence with Republicans, who were already showing signs of a commanding lead in the race for the White House. At best, then, the AFL and the railway brotherhoods together contributed only $50,000 to the La Follette campaign.[75]

1895–1953 (Columbia, Missouri, 1978), 35; La Follette and La Follette, *La Follette*, 2:1121–1122; Greenbaum, *Robert Marion La Follette*, 216–217; Oswald Garrison Villard, *Fighting Years: Memoirs of a Liberal Editor* (New York, 1939), 503.

[74] Shideler, "La Follette Progressive Campaign," in *WMH*, 33:452–453; MacKay, *Progressive Movement of 1924*, pp. 184, 188–193; *Senate Reports*, 68 Cong., 2 sess., no. 1100 (serial 8389).

[75] La Follette and La Follette, *La Follette*, 2:1117–1118; New York *World*, August 4, 1924; *American Federationist*, 31 (September, 1924), 708; William B. Rubin to John P.

Old Bob's health and the lack of financial support from the unions were important reasons for the delay in getting La Follette out to address the crowds that awaited his vaunted rhetoric. Not until October 6, when he addressed a gathering at Rochester, New York, did his campaign begin in earnest. He had but a month to make his case before the voters. To reach as many people as possible, and at the same time escape the rigors of traveling about the country by rail, La Follette tried using the radio. Despite the advantages of campaigning via the air waves, results of a Labor Day address delivered over a national hookup were disappointing. Making the arrangements was time-consuming, the costs were beyond expectations, and the response was difficult to determine. La Follette's only alternative was to go out, press flesh, and speak to the folks. Beginning in the East, he headed west and reached Kansas City, Omaha, and Sioux Falls before returning to wind up his campaign in Cleveland. It was an exhausting tour, but the old campaigner seemed to hold up well.[76]

Before La Follette began his campaign tour, Republicans took every advantage of the opportunity to portray him as the head of "a heterogeneous collection of those opposed to the existing order of things, the greatest section of which, the Socialists, flies the red flag." Frequently referring to his lack of patriotism during the war, Republican orators predicted that a calamity would befall the American people if La Follette captured enough votes to deadlock the electoral college. Should that happen, it was constitutionally possible that Charles Bryan, the vice-presidential candidate of the Democratic party, could be selected as vice-president by a majority vote in the United States Senate. Then, if the House failed to agree on a choice for President, Bryan would become the nation's chief executive. Davis' running mate on the Democratic ticket was the younger brother of William Jennings Bryan, and he had been nominated to placate the Great Commoner, who retained a sizable following and whose loyalty to the party was essential for Democratic

---

Frey, June 30, 1924, and Samuel Gompers to Rubin, September 19, 1924, both in the Rubin Papers; Thelen, *Robert M. La Follette*, 188; MacKay, *Progressive Movement of 1924*, pp. 154–155, 188–189.

[76] La Follette and La Follette, *La Follette*, 2:1125–1147; *New Republic*, November 19, 1924, p. 284; MacKay, *Progressive Movement of 1924*, pp. 212–213; New York *Herald Tribune*, October 6, 1924; New York *Times*, October 7, 1924; Shideler, "La Follette Progressive Campaign," in *WMH*, 33:455.

unity. But in using the Bryan name, Republican orators summoned up fears of economic vagaries and stubborn impracticality.[77]

In effect, argued Republicans, voters were faced with a choice of "Coolidge or Chaos," and the President prudently nurtured the statesmanlike image his supporters created. By speaking mainly at ceremonial functions and by avoiding the turmoil of active campaigning, Coolidge managed to reinforce the impression that of the three principal candidates he was the most qualified to be President. The Democratic party was too divided to have much chance of electing Davis, and the Progressives' hopes never materialized. The more La Follette emphasized the evils of monopoly, and the more he attacked the way economic privilege controlled the American government, the more he appeared to fulfill Republican prophecies that he would be a fomenter of revolution and chaos.[78]

In the end, La Follette lost much of the support he had attracted at the beginning of the campaign. After receiving cordial reassurance that labor would be with him, he was forced to watch as labor leaders abandoned the Progressive effort. Except in Wisconsin, a solid rural Progressive vote never developed. None of La Follette's lieutenants had the skill that Arthur C. Townley had shown in organizing agricultural sections of the country for the Nonpartisan League, and during the campaign a sudden increase in agricultural prices mitigated rural discontent. Seduced by the thought of prospering with a Republican President, farmers began to consider the advantages of improvement in their economic well-being as opposed to whatever satisfaction they might derive from losing courageously in a righteous cause.[79]

Among the various political factions and economic interests that supported La Follette, the most unswerving in its faithfulness to

[77] New York *Times*, August 20, September 20, 1924; Havig, "A Disputed Legacy," *Mid-America*, 53:52–53; MacKay, *Progressive Movement of 1924*, pp. 167–169; Shideler, "La Follette Progressive Campaign," in *WMH*, 33:449–450. La Follette's campaign managers defended his wartime position in "La Follette's Record in the World War," Leaflet No. 3, distributed by the La Follette-Wheeler publicity department. Copies of the campaign leaflets are in the Blaine Papers.

[78] MacKay, *Progressive Movement of 1924*, pp. 159–160; McCoy, *Calvin Coolidge*, 262–263.

[79] Thelen, *Robert M. La Follette*, 185–187; Frederick C. Mills, "Price Movements and Related Industrial Changes," in Conference on Unemployment, Committee on Recent Economic Changes, *Recent Economic Changes in the United States* (2 vols., New York, 1929), 2:620, 629, 631; McCoy, *Calvin Coolidge*, 261–262; William Hard, "La Follette's Party—Will It Last?" in *The Nation*, August 6, 1924, pp. 142–143.

the senator was the Socialist party. Though many of the party members had been reluctant to endorse him in the first place, they were persuaded by Victor Berger's argument that the party name meant little. "You can call an elephant a horse, but it does not make it such," observed the Milwaukee editor. "It is the principle of a political movement that counts." Throughout the campaign the Socialists defended La Follette against the charges leveled at him by the "tools of Wall Street" who were seeking only "to safeguard the interests of the big profiteering lords of business who own them." In a fortuitous choice of words, the Milwaukee *Leader* asserted that "the time is ripe for a new deal," but it was one of the few newspapers in the country urging voters to cast their ballots for La Follette and Wheeler. Throughout the campaign it steadfastly contended that a vote for La Follette would aid in bringing about "immediate deliverance from some of the worst evils that surround the people." Yet the Socialist party was itself experiencing hard times and internal dissensions, and its support had little effect except also to lend credence to Republican charges that La Follette was the candidate of radicals and revolutionaries.[80]

What the 1924 election returns portended, then, was not so clear as the Progressives had hoped when they initiated their attempt to create an alternative to the two major parties. The promise of a new party's emerging from the La Follette campaign had stirred the Progressives' imagination, and third-party enthusiasts were to cherish their hopes through two decades of prosperity, depression, and war. Yet the American two-party system survived the Progressive challenge of 1924. While the Democratic party bided its time, the party of Calvin Coolidge and Herbert Hoover became identified with prosperity and with the efficient use of modern technology for the benefit of all social classes.

Coolidge won the election with 54 per cent of the total vote as compared with 28.8 per cent for Davis and 16.5 per cent for La Follette. The distribution of Coolidge's 15,725,016 popular votes resulted in his winning thirty-five of the forty-eight states, and newspapers described the outcome as a Coolidge landslide. La Follette carried only Wisconsin and placed second to Coolidge in eleven other states, all of them west of the Mississippi River. Those twelve

[80] Johnston, "Wisconsin Socialists and the Conference for Progressive Political Action," in *WMH*, 37:98; Milwaukee *Leader*, May 30, 31, July 15, 24, August 2, 5, October 6, 13, 29, 1924.

states accounted for 42 per cent of La Follette's total vote, but to conclude that the Wisconsin senator had a significant following only in western agricultural regions would be a mistake. In eighteen of the nation's twenty-nine cities with a population greater than 250,000, La Follette exceeded his percentage of the national total.[81]

While broad comparisons such as these can be suggestive, they are of limited value in identifying either the specific sources of La Follette's strength or the voting trends into which the returns of 1924 might be placed. A more meaningful analysis requires sharper focus, and for such purposes the voting pattern of Wisconsin offers significant insights into later political developments as well as the politics of the New Era. To be sure, Wisconsin was exceptional in that it was La Follette's home and the one state from which he secured electoral votes. Yet the Progressive victory there cannot be explained solely as the consequence of a favorite son attraction. Wisconsin's importance for analyzing the results of 1924 rests on other, more significant influences: the state's economic diversity, the unusual way in which processes of urbanization occurred without destroying the dairy farming that provided an agricultural base, the years of innovation in agriculture and politics that made Wisconsin a model for Progressive emulation, the number of self-conscious ethnic groups in its population, the profoundly devastating effects that World War I had on several of those ethnic groups, and, finally, the activities of La Follette's two sons in state and national politics from the close of the New Era to World War II.

Analysis of Wisconsin county data reveals that La Follette's 1912 presidential and 1916 senatorial primary votes correlate at .659, while his 1922 and 1924 votes correlate at .748. The correlations suggest that a significant number of the people who voted for La Follette in 1912 also voted for him in 1916; an even larger percentage of those voting for La Follette in 1922 also cast their ballots for him in 1924. Yet just as important is the lack of correlation between the two earlier elections and the two later ones. La Follette's vote in 1922 shows no correlation with his vote in the earlier races; his vote in 1924 correlates with 1912 at only .290 and with 1916 at .341. Obviously the tensions of the war years and the

[81] Thelen, *Robert M. La Follette*, 190–191; MacKay, *Progressive Movement of 1924*, pp. 220–229.

whirling wheels of change had a profound effect on the state's political behavior during the New Era.[82]

After his defeat in 1924, La Follette assured his followers that "the priceless heritage of our free institutions is not to be yielded up because one battle with the enemy of progressive democracy has been lost." Although the senator died of a heart attack on June 18, 1925, his sons were to carry on in the tradition he had established. It was a tradition that brought the younger La Follettes into a close though often unsteady relationship with Franklin D. Roosevelt and the New Deal. Ultimately, in a different social and economic context from that of the the New Era, the bearers of Wisconsin's Progressive tradition were again to engage in a third-party effort. The important transition from the Progressivism of Robert M. La Follette to the Progressivism of his sons provides a central theme for the chapters that follow.[83]

[82] Brye, *Wisconsin Voting Patterns*, 274–276.

[83] Doan, *The La Follettes and the Wisconsin Idea*, 129–130, 134; La Follette and La Follette, *La Follette*, 2:1168–1169; Brye, *Wisconsin Voting Patterns*, 300–301, 320–335; Leon Epstein, *Politics in Wisconsin* (Madison, 1958), 147–148, 153–154.

8

The Progressive Tradition and Political Behavior in Wisconsin

ON Monday, June 22, 1925, people from near and far flocked to Madison to pay their respects to Robert M. La Follette. "We must say farewell, but we shall always remember him," eulogized the University of Chicago's A. E. Haydon in a homily of eloquent simplicity. Yet the people La Follette had championed since his first election to public office in 1880 could do more than remember. "We may give him earthly immortality in our lives," Haydon counseled the mourners. "The old enemies against which he fought still are in the field; the causes which he championed still call for battling, heroic hearts." As the chimes of Grace Episcopal Church sounded "Lead, Kindly Light," the funeral cortege made its way to Forest Hill Cemetery. "Upon few men has Wisconsin bestowed higher honors in life and perhaps to none has she given so impressive a tribute in death," reported the New York *Times*. "Yet there was nothing of pomp or display. It was the outpouring of peoples, high and low, bowing their heads in silent respect."[1]

The passing of the man who had dominated Wisconsin politics for more than a generation raised important questions about the future direction of political activity in Wisconsin as well as the future of the Progressives he had led. The year of La Follette's death was one in which citizens of the state seemed equivocal about their political objectives. Not all the Stalwart Republicans were as reactionary as La Follette had made them out to be. Some of them, in fact, had originally aligned themselves with the Progressive Re-

[1] New York *Times*, June 23, 1925; Philip F. La Follette, *Adventure in Politics: The Memoirs of Philip La Follette*, ed. Donald Young (New York, 1970), 111–113; Belle Case La Follette and Fola La Follette, *Robert M. La Follette* (2 vols., New York, 1953), 2:1170–1174.

publicans. Furthermore, the Progressives were also divided; no more than the Stalwarts did they represent a cohesive political force. As for the Democrats, they had their own problems. The postwar opposition to Woodrow Wilson's foreign policies had greatly reduced the party's following in Wisconsin. Throughout most of the New Era, the Democratic remnant represented the state's most conservative faction on social and economic questions, and not until the close of the decade did some reformers come to regard the Democratic party as a usable instrument for achieving their objectives.[2]

The New Era, then, was a decade of unusual political uncertainty and ambivalence in Wisconsin, and astute observers seemed to sense that a political realignment was underway. Yet despite wartime disruptions and subsequent shifts in voting behavior, the politics of the state also bore the weight of habit and custom. "You and Bob bred true," Lincoln Steffens wrote Belle Case La Follette in 1929. "You have founded an aristocracy; your children repeat." The two La Follette sons, Bob and Phil, in many ways adhered to the Progressivism of their father as they sought to apply the principles they had learned at home. After assuming the responsibilities of political leadership, both sons attempted to steer a course the elder La Follette might have approved even though the political environment in which they functioned did not remain constant. The political history of Wisconsin in the 1920's thus offers several instances of conflict between change and tradition. Ironically, it was the Progressives who represented tradition, even though it was they who always claimed to represent reform.[3]

A major problem for students of Wisconsin's political history is to find some way of measuring the tensions between change and tradition during the years between the wars. Comparing political platforms and opposing positions in political debates can be instructive, as can perusal of the private papers of politicians. And

[2] Roger T. Johnson, *Robert M. La Follette, Jr., and the Decline of the Progressive Party in Wisconsin* (Madison, 1964; reprinted, Hamden, Connecticut, 1970), 3–4; Patrick J. Maney, *"Young Bob" La Follette: A Biography of Robert M. La Follette, Jr., 1895–1953* (Columbia, Missouri, 1978), 37–38; Herbert F. Margulies, *The Decline of the Progressive Movement in Wisconsin, 1890–1920* (Madison, 1968), 286–288; Herbert F. Margulies, *Senator Lenroot of Wisconsin: A Political Biography, 1900–1929* (Columbia, Missouri, 1977), 378–380.

[3] Steffens to Belle Case La Follette, October 2, 1929, in the Philip F. La Follette Papers.

certainly it is important carefully to scrutinize election campaigns. Yet an understanding of the interplay between political tradition and political change requires more than forming impressions from pubic documents and private papers, and then counting the votes. In addition to utilizing traditional sources, therefore, this chapter relies upon statistical techniques to enrich and clarify the relationship between voting behavior and variables such as ethnicity, religious affiliation, place of residence, and economic well-being. Quantitative procedures provide the basis for assessing the strength of the Progressive tradition in Wisconsin as well as the nature of changes that occurred. [See Appendix B for further explanation of methodology.]

From 1914 to 1940 there were, excluding the presidential election of 1924, twenty-one statewide elections in which a La Follette ran for public office. Of that number, eleven were primaries and ten were general elections. As already noted, Old Bob won re-election to the United States Senate in 1916 and 1922. After his death, Young Bob emerged the victor in a special election to fill his vacant seat, and Young Bob was successfully to run again in 1928, 1934, and 1940. Phil, whose zest for political campaigning matched that of his father, was out on the hustings at his first opportunity in 1930, in a campaign to succeed Walter J. Kohler as governor. He won that election, suffered defeat in the primary of 1932, came back into office as governor in 1934, and won re-election in 1936. In seeking yet another term in 1938, Phil lost the election to Julius Heil.

The twenty-one La Follette elections provide electoral data for a quarter-century of Wisconsin politics. Assuming that Lincoln Steffens was correct, and that the La Follettes were all bearers of a Progressive tradition, the La Follette returns can be analyzed to show shifts in the locus and nature of Progressive support during the years from 1914 to 1940. From such analysis one might also make judgments about the way Wisconsin voters, as well as the La Follettes themselves, responded first to the new society that took shape after the Great War, and then to a world that experienced a succession of calamities in the 1930's. To begin, however, this chapter focuses on Progressive leaders of the New Era, their Stalwart opponents, the issues that divided them, and the rise of the brothers La Follette to positions of political power.

* * *

The Progressives of Wisconsin often invoked the name of Robert M. La Follette to suggest the principles they all shared. In point of fact, Wisconsin's reformers had never been noted for unity of mind and purpose. The Progressives had always constituted an uneasy coalition within the Republican party, and their uncertain prospects during the New Era helped to make that coalition far more volatile than invocation of the La Follette name would suggest. The senator himself had contributed to Progressive factionalism by habitually employing a Manichean rhetoric to identify his opponents with "the interests," thereby implying that persons who disagreed with him were in league with the forces of darkness. The implication was offensive, of course, and when advanced in debates among reformers it often had the effect of alienating friends as well as intensifying enmities. "Bob La Follette's biggest weakness has been, and is, his hostility toward his opponents and critics," an astute observer once remarked when La Follette's star was in its ascendancy. Although the Old Man pleaded for Progressive unity in later years, he left an aggregation of followers who quarreled bitterly among themselves while professing loyalty to his principles.[4]

At the time of the elder La Follette's death, the Progressives were deeply involved in one of their sectarian controversies, each group of partisans claiming to be guided by the one true Progressive vision and charging that the others were breaking faith with the cause. Governor John J. Blaine led the dominant faction, and in part for that reason drew fire from all the others. Having entered politics in 1898, when he became mayor of Boscobel, he supported La Follette for governor in 1900 and in every campaign thereafter. Although he never became a member of La Follette's inner circle of advisers, he had served as a state senator, as attorney general of Wisconsin, and since 1921 as governor. On the basis of his record in political campaigns, no one could question his fidelity to La Follette. Yet there was always something about Blaine—perhaps an abrasiveness in his manner, perhaps a hint of opportunism—that seemed to make other Progressives uneasy.[5]

[4] Johnson, *Robert M. La Follette, Jr.*, 3–4; Margulies, *Decline of the Progressive Movement*, 92–96; La Follette, *Adventure in Politics*, 66–67. The person who described La Follette's attitude towards critics was John Strange, a paper manufacturer who ran as a candidate for lieutenant-governor in 1906.

[5] Fred L. Holmes, "Sketch of John J. Blaine" (typewritten), in the John J. Blaine

The struggle for ascendancy among Progressives had its origins in postwar social unrest and economic recession. In 1920, when Wisconsin farmers and workers were beginning to search for political solutions to the problems that troubled them, La Follette supported Blaine for governor. Blaine's principal opponent in the primary was Roy P. Wilcox, whose wartime attacks on Emanuel Philipp as well as on La Follette had alienated potential backers among the Stalwarts and assured Blaine's victory. In the meantime, Blaine was campaigning as the candidate who would be most responsive to the demands of reform-minded farmers, labor unions, and Progressives. In the general election he received the endorsement of all three groups, and he emerged an easy winner over R. B. McCoy, whose wartime hyperpatriotism matched that of Wilcox. Elected lieutenant-governor along with Blaine was George Comings from Eau Claire. Comings had been a breeder of Holsteins, a lecturer for Equity, and a member of the Nonpartisan League.[6]

Only a month after moving into the governor's mansion, Blaine became involved in controversy over prohibition. Never an advocate of sumptuary legislation, he nonetheless faced the task of enforcing state laws enacted in conformity with the Eighteenth Amendment. Like La Follette himself, Blaine believed that prohibition raised issues extraneous to the real problems of an industrial society dominated by special interests, but not all Progressives agreed with Blaine and La Follette. To many of them the Eighteenth Amendment offered a means by which they could begin a Progressive reconstruction of Wisconsin society. George Comings was among those who held such views, and when difficulties with prohibition enforcement became apparent, the lieutenant-governor joined critics of the governor. Comings' dissatisfaction increased, as did that of other dry Progressives, after Blaine vetoed the Matheson Bill, a measure intended to improve the effectiveness of prohibition enforcement in the state. Instead of accepting a bill drafted by the Anti-Saloon League, Blaine preferred to write his own. The resulting legislation, introduced by Senator Herman J. Severson of

---

Papers, n.d., but probably written for but not included in Holmes, *Badger Saints and Sinners* (Milwaukee, 1939); *Wisconsin Blue Book, 1923*, p. 602.

[6] Margulies, *Decline of the Progressive Movement*, 269–278; *Wisconsin Blue Book, 1923*, pp. 602–603; La Follette, *Adventure in Politics*, 66–68; James H. Daffer, "Progressive Profile: John James Blaine from 1873 to 1918" (master's thesis, University of Wisconsin, 1951), 143.

Iola, became effective on July 1, 1921. The new law brought little satisfaction to the Wisconsin drys, however, and they continued to oppose Blaine throughout his tenure as governor.[7]

Both Blaine and Comings won re-election in 1922, but the seeds of distrust planted during the prohibition battle grew into full flower during the 1923 legislative session. The Progressives had won important victories in the 1922 election, and many of them hoped to use their influence to secure reforms for the relief of taxpayers. Several tax bills came up for legislative consideration, but the discussion of tax-reform measures resulted in great resentment of Blaine and produced little of the anticipated reform.

The legislature had passed the first income tax law in Wisconsin in 1911, and most supporters of the measure expected the income tax eventually to replace property taxes as the principal source of revenue for the state. Yet the law included a provision that became a source of irritation and contention among Progressives. In order to assure collection of local taxes on personal property, which were easily evaded, the legislature had agreed to a personal property tax offset. That is, receipts for the payment of personal property taxes might in effect be used to pay taxes on income. The provision reduced state income tax revenues by an estimated 40 per cent, however, and many Progressives wished to eliminate the offset. Transferring tax burdens from property to income was tantamount to a transfer of tax burdens from farms to cities. Most income tax proceeds came from cities, argued proponents of the offset, and if state revenues came primarily from income taxes, the cities would pay far more than they could ever expect to receive in return.[8]

[7] Jeffrey Lucker, "The Politics of Prohibition in Wisconsin, 1917–1933" (master's thesis, University of Wisconsin, 1968), 20–21, 28; *Wisconsin Senate Journal*, 1921, vol. 2, pp. 1037–1039; Madison *Capital Times*, May 27, 1921; Milwaukee *Journal*, June 7, 1921. Also, all in the Blaine Papers: Blaine to O. L. Olen, January 21, 1920; Blaine to the senate and the assembly, May 26, 1921; Blaine to the assembly, May 31, 1921; Blaine to P. W. Gullford, June 4, 1921; Blaine to the Reverend W. J. James, June 7, 1921; Blaine to D. F. Burnham, June 30, 1921; Blaine to the Reverend B. C. Flint, January 14, 1922; George M. Sheldon to Blaine, October 24, 1921; Blaine to Anna T. Helgeland, December 21, 1922; Blaine to Robert M. La Follette, Sr., April 13, 1923; Blaine to W. H. Stayton, December 13, 1923; P— to Robert M. La Follette, Sr., January, 1924; and Blaine to Annie Wyman Warren, February 10, 1925.

[8] John J. Blaine, "Wisconsin Finances and Taxes" (carbon copy), returned to Blaine in E. G. Leander to Blaine, November 13, 1925, in the Blaine Papers; Harold M. Groves, "The Wisconsin State Income Tax," in the *Wisconsin Blue Book, 1933*, pp. 51–52, 62; W. J. Conway, "Taxation in Wisconsin," in *ibid., 1927*, pp. 119–122; Thomas E. Lyons, "The Wisconsin Tax System," in *ibid., 1923*, pp. 85–87; W. Elliot Brownlee, Jr., "Income Taxation and the Political Economy of Wisconsin, 1890–1930," in *WMH*, 59 (Summer,

For his part, Blaine believed that repeal of the property tax offset was essential to an equitable distribution of taxes in Wisconsin. The controversy over taxation during his second term centered on the geographical allocation of the state's tax obligations. Retaining the property tax offset would maintain the importance of property tax revenues and benefit the urban southeastern portion of the state; repealing it, and thus relying more heavily on income taxes, would benefit the agricultural hinterland.

In the discussion of taxation during 1923, Senator Severson, representing Waupaca and Portage counties, and Assemblyman John L. Dahl, from Barron County, took a position that avoided the problem. Instead of confronting the offset, they introduced bills to repeal taxes assessed for education and to pay for education out of a surtax on large incomes. Blaine listened to their arguments, but he finally concluded that he should concentrate on repeal of the property tax offset. He drafted a bill to accomplish that objective, and he turned it over to Charles E. Hansen, chairman of the senate committee on taxation, who introduced it.[9]

In the end, the debates over taxation produced results that proved disappointing to Blaine and to other Progressives as well. The governor insisted that his own tax bill would have provided more tax relief than any other. Yet it failed to attract sufficient support from a conference of Progressive legislators, and the effort to repeal the property tax offset was aborted. On the other hand, the Dahl and Severson bills were no more successful. Blaine believed that both "soaked everybody except the corporations, and relieved no individual materially." The governor's supporters in the legislature therefore united to prevent the passage of either bill. The upshot was that a Progressive legislature found itself unable to come up with the anticipated tax reform.[10]

1976), 300–301; W. Elliot Brownlee, Jr., *Progressivism and Economic Growth: The Wisconsin Income Tax, 1911–1929* (Port Washington, New York, 1974), 78–80.

[9] Arthur J. Sweet to George Comings, September 21, 1923, copy in the Ada James Papers; speech of Senator Herman J. Severson before the Dayton La Follette Club at Waupaca, ca. July, 1923, in the Blaine Papers.

[10] Maney, *"Young Bob" La Follette*, 32; Robert M. La Follette, Jr., to Mother and Dad, June 5, 26, 28, 1923; Robert M. La Follette, Jr., to Robert M. La Follette, Sr., telegrams, June 14, 21, 1923, all in box A-30, the La Follette Family Papers, Library of Congress. Also, in the Blaine Papers: Blaine to Joseph Poss, May 1, 1924; Blaine to Arthur Brisbane, April 21, 1925; and Edwin E. Witte, "Taxation Problems in Wisconsin," address to the Wisconsin Association of Real Estate Brokers, Racine, October 28, 1926. Also, in the James Papers: Arthur J. Sweet to George Comings, September 21, 1923, and Mary Trace to Ada James, January 31, 1924.

Each side in the controversy blamed the other for failure of the reform effort. Severson charged that the governor had actually sought to prevent passage of any tax bill at that session because "it was a good talking point and a good vote getter for the next election." Blaine, on the other hand, believed "the real trouble was that there were too many, some Stalwarts and some so-called Progressives, wanting more taxes instead of less taxes." Ultimately, as Blaine saw it, a "political cabal" composed of "phoney Progressives" had thwarted tax reform.[11]

The bitterness of the struggle over taxation jeopardized the entire Progressive program that La Follette was laboriously putting together in preparation for the state and federal election campaigns of 1924. Much as the Wisconsin Progressives sympathized with his calls for unity, maintaining neutrality in the tax controversy was virtually impossible. Each side had its adherents. Only Senator La Follette seemed able to command respect from both; but even he did not emerge unscathed. When Blaine announced his intention to run for a third term as governor, the Old Man endorsed Blaine's candidacy and stirred the anti-Blaine forces to action. They rejected out of hand the very suggestion of another term for Blaine and backed Comings, who was more than happy to make the race. Prominent Progressives who supported Comings included Senator Severson and Assemblyman Dahl; Secretary of State Fred Zimmerman; Congressmen John Cooper, John Mandt Nelson, and John Schafer; Arthur Sweet and Ada James of the Wisconsin Committee of Forty-Eight; editor William T. Evjue of the Madison *Capital Times*; Chester Platt of the Nonpartisan League; Edward J. Gross, president of the La Follette Progressive Association; and many others who either opposed Blaine's stand against prohibition or deplored his failure to secure tax reform.[12]

[11] Severson speech to the Dayton La Follette Club, Waupaca, ca. July, 1923; George F. Comings Campaign Committee, "Should Governor Blaine Have a Third Term?" ca. January, 1924; George Staudenmayer to Whom It May Concern, ca. April 20, 1924; A. E. Carey to Mrs. O. D. Bates, August 25, 1923; and Blaine to Joseph Poss, May 1, 1924, all in the Blaine Papers.

[12] Robert M. La Follette, Sr., signed editorial, in *La Follette's Magazine*, August, 1924; Milwaukee *Journal*, April 18, 1924; *Capital Times*, August 28, 1924; La Follette and La Follette, *La Follette*, 2:1069–1070; Johnson, *Robert M. La Follette, Jr.*, 4–5, 9; Belle Case La Follette to Ada James, February 27, 1923, in the James Papers. Also, in the Blaine Papers: Blaine to Alfred T. Rogers, February 29, 1924; J. D. Beck to Blaine, June 9, 1923; George M. Sheldon to Blaine, ca. August, 1923; P— to Robert M. La Follette, Sr., typewritten copy, ca. January, 1924; and Comings Campaign Committee, "Should Governor Blaine Have a Third Term?"

Comings was not the only candidate who entered the 1924 primary in an effort to oust Blaine and win the gubernatorial nomination for himself. Arthur R. Hirst, the state highway engineer, was also troubled by Blaine's tax policies, but it was taxation for highway construction that most concerned him. In 1923 the legislature passed a bill to impose a tax of two cents per gallon on all motor fuel sold in the state. Although it was ostensibly a tax requiring users to pay for the construction and maintenance of highways, and thus reduce highway tax obligations of the counties, Blaine doubted that it would benefit farmers in the Wisconsin hinterland. Funds derived from the tax were to be used primarily for improving the state trunk highway system and not for the construction and maintenance of county roads. Blaine therefore vetoed the bill. In his veto message, he pointed out that the state trunk system, or about 10,000 miles of highway, was already "fairly well improved." But Wisconsin also had 60,000 to 70,000 miles of unimproved highway serving rural communities. Proceeds from the tax, Blaine argued, should be distributed in proportion to total mileage, with less going to the state trunk system and more to the unimproved roads on which farmers depended.[13]

Hirst's response to what he thought were Blaine's unwarranted attacks on the state highway commission was to inject himself into the gubernatorial campaign of 1924. Road builders and some county highway commissioners were quick to rally behind Hirst, who thought that as a "Constructive Republican" he could present an attractive alternative to the petulant candidates of quarrelsome Progressive and Stalwart factions. Fred J. Deutsche, of the Wisconsin Municipal and Highway Contractors' Association, sent out a circular letter warning that "our future is at stake" and appealing for contributions to Hirst's campaign. County highway commissioners across the state busied themselves with passing resolutions commending Hirst for his contributions to highway development. Variously describing the engineer as "fair and honest," and "a high-class gentleman" who was "faithful and untiring," the resolutions

[13] "Governor Blaine's Statement on Gasoline Sales Tax," June, 1923; Blaine to the senate, typewritten copy, June 27, 1923; C. B. Ballard to Blaine, June 29, 1923; Blaine to William Mantle, June 30, 1923, all in the Blaine Papers. Blaine's position was explained and defended by George Staudenmayer in a letter to the Reedsburg *Times*, July 18, 1924, a copy of which he enclosed in a letter to Frank Kuehl, July 28, 1924, also in the Blaine Papers.

deplored the baneful influence of a few "misinformed or misguided officials" and "petty politicians" who were threatening to destroy all that Hirst had accomplished. John T. Donaghey, the state highway maintenance engineer, sent a letter to division engineers and department heads suggesting that they contribute towards the purchase of a gift of appreciation for their chief. The gift he suggested was a seven-passenger Buick, to be paid for with contributions amounting to 8 per cent of each employee's salary for the month of May. Those who contributed perhaps had a vision of Hirst mounting his Buick, driving out to campaign on the highways he had built, and slaying political dragons on the way.[14]

Although Hirst received support from some disgruntled Progressives as well as from persons who stood to gain from his highway program, the rural communities of Wisconsin remained loyal to Governor Blaine. "The authorities have gone state road crazy," asserted Philip Lehner, a lawyer from Princeton. "I have forgotten the name of the bird who is at the head of this state road work, but I have for several years thought, that if he were fired, it would be a positive gain." E. S. Pattison, a Durand attorney, warned that "Hirst seems to have quite a strong foothold on the gasoline question" and that "this tax question has a great undercurrent." He recommended drafting a half-dozen good speakers who could "simply pulverize Hirst and his entire machine." Lawrence J. Brody, a Blaine supporter in La Crosse, also urged the governor to attack Hirst, who he said was misleading the farmers of western Wisconsin with tax figures that were "as false as hell itself."[15]

Annoyed by Hirst's tactics, Blaine assumed the offensive with vigor, and his backers were soon lending their assistance. L. P. Gaillardet, a physician and health officer of Black River Falls, contributed a piece of wretched doggerel on Hirst's motives and supporters:[16]

[14] Hirst to Ada James, June 30, 1924, in the James Papers; Hirst to Members of the County Boards of 1923, June 24, 1924; political advertisement signed by Fred J. Deutsche for the La Follette-Blaine Club of Western Wisconsin, June 23, 1924; Donaghey to Division Engineers and Department Heads, May 29, 1924, all in the Blaine Papers. The Blaine Papers also contain resolutions in support of Hirst passed in 1924 by the highway committees for the following counties: Taylor, February 29; Wood, March 6; Milwaukee, March 11; Washburn, March 24; Iron and Walworth, March 27; Richland, March 31; and Eau Claire in April.

[15] Lehner to Blaine, May 6, 1924; Pattison to Blaine, August 1, 1924; and Brody to Blaine, August 15, 1924, all in the Blaine Papers.

[16] Gaillardet to Blaine, ca. August 12, 1924, *ibid.*

I'll never play at politics,
Said little Artie Hirst
Of the mean and horrid game,
I think it is the worst[.]
Ther[e]'s Johnnie Blaine who spoiled my fun
At making highways grand[,]
I'd used a lot of trust cement
And some Wisconsin sand.
So now I'm out to get his goat,
I'll get him if I can[,]
The stalwarts they will back me up
And mighty KU KLUX KLAN.

Rumors that Klansmen were working for Hirst's election led C. J. Schoenfeld, a Beaver Dam Progressive, to ask Hirst if he did not, in fact, "expect the support of the big corporations and the Ku Klux Klan?" In the same letter Schoenfeldt went on to suggest that Hirst's highway program "was a wrong system to the farmers as they pay most of the taxes, and less than twenty per cent are directly benefited by them."[17]

Aside from attacking Hirst's arguments for highway expansion on their merits, Blaine supporters began emphasizing charges that the highway commission was rife with corruption. Noting the gift from Hirst's subordinates, they implied that commission employees had been assessed a percentage of their May salaries in order that Hirst might secure a campaign limousine. There were other charges as well. Frank H. Hanson of Mauston wrote Blaine to point out that some years earlier Hirst had attempted to prevent any municipality or county from buying cement without approval of the commission. Because this could mean controlling the purchase of as much as a million barrels of cement a year, the possibilities for graft were enormous. W. H. Shons, a contractor from Freeport, Illinois, the town where La Follette patron William T. Rawleigh maintained his residence, offered to provide Blaine with information on specific instances of waste in the construction of Wisconsin highways "if the campaign gets strong enough or you need anything of this kind."[18]

[17] Schoenfeld to Hirst, copy, August 23, 1924, *ibid.*

[18] "Something to Think About," paid Blaine advertisement, sponsored by the Farmers & Merchants Club of Alma Center, in G. W. Griswold to Frank W. Kuehl, September 9, 1924; W. H. Shons to Blaine, June 10, 1924; George Staudenmayer to Blaine, June 13, 1924; Hanson to Blaine, July 5, 1924, all in *ibid.* A few months earlier, Blaine had written to Hirst complaining of "a ruthless and arrogant attitude on the part of the cement bidding companies," as well as "monopolistic control of cement." See Blaine to

A similar condemnation of Hirst appeared in a letter to the Madison *Capital Times* from the village of Whitehall in Trempealeau County. The writer, J. P. Hanson, charged that Hirst had been responsible for spending $127 million of the taxpayers' money on what "from an engineering and financial standpoint has been a gigantic blunder." Although the highway commission had failed to discover a method of building highways that would outlast the bonded indebtedness incurred to pay for them, Hirst remained unabashed. Apparently oblivious to the waste involved, he proposed to continue "this mad experimenting with the public funds." Hanson concluded that the only beneficiaries of the highway commission's schemes were Hirst himself and the construction firms that were illegally meeting the expenses of his race for the governorship.[19]

Because the campaign against Hirst succeeded in enhancing Blaine's reputation in the rural areas of Wisconsin, it helped him in his campaign against Comings as well. Blaine emerged as the choice of voters in the Republican primary, and he went on to a comfortable victory over Martin Lueck in the general election. A former circuit court judge, Lueck had, according to Blaine, "dragged the judicial ermine in the mud by joining and leading a riot to prevent free speech and free assembly, during the war." In Blaine's view, Lueck's one demonstration of judicial perspicacity had been to resign from the bench rather than confront "an outraged constituency" in another election. Despite Progressive defections, then, Blaine retained enough of his following to capture 51.8 per cent of the vote as opposed to 39.9 per cent for Lueck. He had accomplished his objective with tough, no-holds-barred campaign tactics. Although he claimed that his election marked a triumph for Progressive principles, he never succeeded in establishing his Progressive credentials among those who had been alienated by his stands on prohibition and tax reform.[20]

* * *

Hirst, February 12, 1924, *ibid.* As for Hirst, George M. Sheldon thought him "the biggest Czar in the State of Wisconsin." Sheldon to Blaine, May 5, 1924, *ibid.*

[19] Hanson to William T. Evjue, copy, August 23, 1924, *ibid.*

[20] Blaine, statement released October 28, 1924, *ibid.*; David L. Brye, *Wisconsin Voting Patterns in the Twentieth Century, 1900 to 1950* (New York, 1979), 372. The Socialist candidate, William J. Quick of Milwaukee, polled 5.7 per cent of the vote; the remainder went to other minor party candidates.

Wisconsin Progressives were still waging internecine warfare when they gathered in Madison to attend La Follette's funeral and to discuss the selection of a candidate to complete his term. Most of the Progressives, fearful of the disintegration of their forces, believed that only the La Follette name could unite them in a common effort. For that reason, Belle was their first choice to succeed her husband. The senator's widow was indeed an extraordinary woman. Holder of a law degree from the University of Wisconsin, a gifted writer and an effective public speaker, she was, Old Bob had often remarked, his "wisest and best counsellor." Yet she was sixty-six years old, had never acquired a taste for political combat and its attendant uncertainties, and simply did not wish to run. "It would be against nature for me to undertake the responsibilities of political leadership," she remarked in rejecting the appeal of her supporters. Her second son, Phil, on the other hand, would have been happy to make the race, for he was a skilled campaigner and politically ambitious. But at twenty-eight he was too young to meet the constitutional age requirement for the United States Senate.[21]

That left Young Bob—two years older than Phil—as the only available La Follette, who six weeks after his father's death announced that he would become a candidate in the special election to be held in September. Like Belle, Bob disliked the indignities of stump politics. Troubled by illness much of his life, he had contemplated a career in journalism, banking, or commerce rather than in the political arena. But filial loyalty led him to accept a position as an assistant clerk in his father's office in 1916, and from that point on he became increasingly preoccupied with the intricacies of Progressive politics. Although inexperienced in conducting a national political campaign, he more than any other adviser had brought a measure of credibility to his father's quest for the presidency. Now, aspiring to succeed Old Bob, he won support from Progressives across the country. Ernest Gruening, later to become a senator himself, noted in *The Nation* that during the recent presidential campaign the young man had been "prodigiously energetic, unfalteringly enthusiastic, sound in reasoning yet quick in decision." Managing somehow to maintain unity among "a host of hetero-

[21] Johnson, *Robert M. La Follette, Jr.*, 6; Maney, *"Young Bob" La Follette*, 38–39; La Follette, *Adventure in Politics*, 113. Oswald Garrison Villard, perhaps unaware of Phil's age, sent a telegram to Governor Blaine urging temporary appointment of Phil to succeed his father. Villard to Blaine, June 18, 1925, in the Blaine Papers.

geneous and disparate elements," he had demonstrated remarkable perception and understanding of "Washington's problems and pitfalls." In Gruening's opinion, "none other in the Progressive group of Wisconsin could speak both for the State and for the nation as effectively" as could Young Bob.[22]

Although the Wisconsin Progressives welcomed Bob's candidacy with enthusiasm, not everyone who had supported the La Follette-Wheeler ticket in 1924 could agree with Gruening. To many of the Socialists, having the son succeed the father suggested monarchy rather than democracy. "I believe young Bobbie ought to take time to earn his spurs," commented Victor Berger. "Why should we have to take a crown prince?" Yet the Progressives had more to fear from the Stalwarts than from anyone in the coalition of 1924. In the spring of 1925, just before the Old Man's death, conservatives had organized the Republican Voluntary Committee (RVC) to bring leadership and provide heavy funding for the forces opposing the Progressives. Meeting in Oshkosh, they selected Roy P. Wilcox to carry the Stalwart banner in their attempt to defeat La Follette in September.[23]

Wilcox and the Republican Voluntary Committee campaigned on a platform that identified the Stalwarts with Coolidge Republicanism. Their principal tool in asserting their fealty to the President who believed that the "chief business of the American people is business" was an extensive survey of taxation in Wisconsin. During the winter of 1923–1924, the Wisconsin Manufacturers' Association had financed an inquiry undertaken by the National Industrial Conference Board with Laurence R. Gottlieb, a New York University economist, as chief investigator. The report of the study suggested that taxes, especially income taxes, had inhibited economic growth in Wisconsin. In fact, it asserted, the corporate tax burden was so great that manufacturers were driven to seek refuge in states more favorably disposed to industrial development.[24]

Completed in the summer of 1924, the WMA-sponsored report

[22] "Young Bob," in *The Nation*, July 8, 1925, p. 59; Frank W. Kuehl to Lewis S. Gannett, July 3, 1925, in the Blaine Papers.

[23] New York *Times*, July 27, 1925; Johnson, *Robert M. La Follette, Jr.*, 12. On the RVC, see Francis J. Sorauf, Jr., "The Voluntary Committee System in Wisconsin: An Effort to Achieve Party Responsibility" (doctoral dissertation, University of Wisconsin, 1953).

[24] Brownlee, *Progressivism and Economic Growth*, 82; Edwin E. Witte, "Chronology of the Activities of the Wisconsin Manufacturers Association to Defeat Increases in Income Taxes," enclosed in Witte to Blaine, March 3, 1925, in the Blaine Papers.

on taxation in Wisconsin was intended for use against La Follette in the presidential campaign. The effort obviously backfired, for La Follette had captured Wisconsin's electoral votes. More importantly, the Gottlieb investigation galvanized the Progressives, who set about disproving its findings and preparing for passage of the tax reform that had failed to win legislative approval in 1923–1924. Edwin E. Witte, chief of the Wisconsin Legislative Reference Library, compiled a detailed refutation of the charge that taxes were forcing manufacturers to seek refuge elsewhere. He cited claims made about specific firms and then systematically demolished the notion that any had left Wisconsin because of taxes. Indeed, he noted, a survey conducted in the fall of 1924 had found that in sixteen cities there were 138 new manufacturing plants representing an increase of $34,500,000 in manufacturing investment. Despite a decline in the manufacture of lumber and timber products that followed depletion of timber resources, and despite a sharp decline in the production of malt liquors after adoption of the Eighteenth Amendment, the rate of growth in manufacturing had been greater in Wisconsin than in the nation as a whole.[25]

When the legislature convened in 1925, it turned to a consideration of proposals for amending the tax laws of the state, and the WMA renewed its efforts to prevent their passage. The propaganda of the manufacturers, Witte observed in a communique to Governor Blaine, "abounds in falsehoods," and "has reached volumes never before known since the committee tax bill was introduced." To discredit the tax bill, opponents of the measure produced newspaper articles, letters, telegrams, statements, and petitions without end. "Perhaps never before have so many downright lies been circulated in connection with any bill before the legislature," Witte observed, "and all to the end that those best able to pay shall continue to escape their just share of the tax burden."[26]

The WMA and its allies apparently had failed to learn a lesson from the campaign of 1924. Legislators responded to the hyperbole of the manufacturers by moving ahead with income tax reform. The new law increased exemptions from $1,200 to $1,600 for a husband and wife, from $800 to $1,600 for the head of a family

[25] Edwin E. Witte, "Effect of the So-called 'Progressive Legislation' of Wisconsin upon Its Industrial Development," August, 1925, in the Blaine Papers.

[26] Witte to Blaine, March 3, 1925, *ibid.*

who was neither a husband nor a wife, and from $200 to $300 for each child or total dependent. It also repealed the personal property tax offset, which in Blaine's words enabled "some taxpayers to escape all or a part of their income taxes while their neighbors with the same income had to pay their taxes in full." Finally, in addition to closing loopholes, the legislation provided that the projected increase in revenue be used to reduce property taxes. For the WMA the meaning of the legislation was clear: the Progressives of Wisconsin intended to continue their policy of aiding the state's farmers by means of taxation. In raising public consciousness of the tax issue, however, the manufacturers had simply broadened support for legislation to increase their own tax obligations.[27]

This, then, was the context of the special elections to choose a successor to Senator La Follette. Postwar disillusionment had left the Democrats discredited and ineffective. The Socialists could muster significant support only in Milwaukee, and even there the Socialist candidate could not expect to win. Given the weakness of other parties, the election hinged on the outcome of the Republican primary, which came down to a contest between Roy Wilcox and Young Bob. In that duel, Stalwart efforts to link the Wilcox candidacy with Coolidge prosperity became tangled in the negative arguments of the income tax debate. Defeated in their attempt to prevent Progressive tax reforms, the Stalwarts were reduced to carping criticism of the "Madison ring" (their term for the La Follettes), Governor Blaine, and tax reformers. The Progressives, on the other hand, could draw on the magic of the La Follette name and the appeal of principles which, as the tax battle had just demonstrated, seemed as cogent as ever.

When Young Bob opened his campaign in Stoughton, it was ob-

[27] Edwin E. Witte, "Summary of the Provisions of Bill No. 122, S, as Passed by the Senate," March, 1925, *ibid.*; John J. Blaine, "Wisconsin Finances and Taxes," in *National Income Tax Magazine*, December, 1925, p. 431. Despite the arguments of Witte and Blaine, the WMA and its supporters continued their opposition to the Progressive tax program. A good summary of the manufacturers' contentions may be found in a series of articles by R. A. Kennedy, city editor of the Green Bay *Press-Gazette*. Published under the title "What's Happening to Wisconsin?" the articles appeared in the *Press-Gazette* in August and September of 1925. (Copies also appear in the Blaine Papers.)

Later scholarly studies by W. Elliot Brownlee support the position that Wisconsin's manufacturing growth would have proceeded more rapidly if tax conditions had been more favorable to capital formation. See Brownlee, *Progressivism and Economic Growth*; Brownlee, "Income Taxation and Capital Formation in Wisconsin, 1911–1929," in *Explorations in Economic History*, new series 8 (Fall, 1970), 77–102; and Brownlee, "Income Taxation and the Political Economy of Wisconsin," in *WMH*, 59:299–324.

vious that he lacked the oratorical skills of his father. Yet after he had hit his stride, speaking four times a day across the state, he became more relaxed and more effective. Young Bob impressed his audiences with his seriousness of purpose and command of the issues rather than with fustian fervor or passionate rhetoric. In substance the speeches left little doubt that he was his father's son. He spoke in favor of economy and efficiency in government, a graduated reduction in income taxes, and an increase in inheritance taxes to prevent the perpetuation of large fortunes. Emphasizing the need to control big business, the young candidate urged strict enforcement of antitrust laws, an investigation of the Federal Trade Commission's ineffectiveness, and government operation of the Muscle Shoals nitrate and electric power plants. He promised to work for repeal of the Esch-Cummins Act, which had imposed high freight rates on agricultural products, and he promised to introduce legislation preventing the use of injunctions in labor disputes. While opposing American entry into the World Court, he favored a reduction of military expenditures and a treaty to outlaw war.[28]

The results of the Republican primary were predictable. La Follette received 178,031 votes to 81,834 for Wilcox. In the general election two weeks later, with Wilcox out of the race, former Lieutenant-Governor Edward F. Dithmar filed as an independent candidate. Receiving the support of anti-La Follette Republicans, he continued the campaign Wilcox had waged in the primary, and the results of the general election were similar. Bob emerged victorious in every county save Rock. "La Follettism swept Wisconsin off the Republican map today," announced the New York *Times*. Bob himself believed that his victory "gives the answer of the people of this state to the nation that they stand solidly behind the movement founded by Robert M. La Follette during his forty years of public service to bring Government back to the people." The son's senatorial style, like his manner on the stump, turned out to be different from that of his father, but the evidence indicates that a majority of Wisconsin's voters were pleased with his election in 1925. Young Bob was to remain in the Senate until 1947.[29]

[28] La Follette, *Adventure in Politics*, 115; *La Follette's Magazine*, September, 1925; Maney, *"Young Bob" La Follette*, 39–40.

[29] Johnson, *Robert M. La Follette, Jr.*, 14–17; *Capital Times*, September 18, 24, 30, 1925; New York *Times*, September 30, October 1, 1925.

* * *

Although the Wisconsin Progressives had won an important victory that allowed them to plot a course for the future, the lessons of 1925 were not lost on conservative Republicans. The Stalwarts knew that continuing to present themselves as the spokesmen for special economic interests would strengthen the Progressives. They, too, would have to appeal to moderate reform sentiment, and after Young Bob's victory a shift in the Stalwart approach soon became apparent.

Before the special election, Young Bob had held earnest conversations with Governor Blaine to discuss his prospects and the future of Wisconsin Progressivism. Having successfully waged three gubernatorial campaigns, Blaine was himself ready to move on to other responsibilities. His admirers had been suggesting that he enter the 1926 race for the United States Senate seat held by Irvine Lenroot, and Blaine was amenable to the idea. To see that the situation contained opportunities for a bargain required no unusual political sensitivity. Bob wanted Blaine's support in the special election, and if Blaine chose to run against Lenroot, Bob's endorsement would be invaluable. Yet Blaine's involvement in disputes over prohibition, taxation, and other matters could also make his support a liability with some of the Progressives, especially if rumors of a bargain between the two men proved accurate. Bob did not deny meeting with Blaine, but he did deny the rumors. Conferring with several Wisconsin congressmen, he assured them that he had no intention of forcing his will on the state's congressional delegation. With that assurance, he won the support of the anti-Blaine faction, but Blaine took no offense at Bob's courting of his opponents. The governor required no certificate of political indebtedness to understand that defeating Lenroot in 1926 depended on maintaining friendly relations with the La Follette family.[30]

After Bob won the contest to succeed his father, Progressives began the process of selecting candidates for the 1926 election. Blaine announced his readiness to enter the lists against Lenroot,

[30] Johnson, *Robert M. La Follette, Jr.*, 9; Patrick G. O'Brien, "Senator John J. Blaine: An Independent Progressive During 'Normalcy,' " in *WMH*, 60 (Autumn, 1976), 28. For examples of letters encouraging Blaine's candidacy, see in the Blaine Papers: E. B. Gennrich to Blaine, July 22, 1925; W. B. McCabe to Blaine, July 22, 1925; George Staudenmayer to Blaine, August 21, 1925; and William B. Rubin to William Green, March 24, 1926.

and having campaigned for Bob, he received La Follette's endorsement. With Blaine running for the Senate, the Progressives chose Herman Ekern as their candidate for governor. Ekern had been as faithful to Old Bob as anyone in Wisconsin, and it was with the Old Man's blessing that he won election as attorney general of the state in 1922. An acknowledged legal expert in the field of insurance, Ekern was a conscientious attorney general, but he proved to be an ineffective gubernatorial candidate in 1926. With a home in Madison, law offices in Chicago, and his knowledge of mutual insurance in demand throughout the country, Ekern found waging a political campaign to be all but impossible.[31]

Ekern's candidacy gave the Stalwarts an opportunity, and this time they acted with a political sagacity not evident in the fight against Progressive income-tax reform. Prominent businessmen such as W. H. Alford of Nash Motors and Otto Falk of Allis-Chalmers agreed with WMA secretary George Kull that the lobbying efforts of the manufacturers had been a mistake. A far better course, they now argued, would be to support a gubernatorial candidate who could win and who, once elected, would recognize the legitimacy of their concerns. The person they had in mind was Secretary of State Fred Zimmerman, a skilled campaigner who possessed the credentials that Stalwarts were seeking. As a member of the Wisconsin Assembly, he had voted with the Progressives and had been a La Follette delegate to the Republican National Conventions in 1916, 1920, and 1924. Elected secretary of state in 1922, he had won re-election in 1924 with a half-million votes, more than two-thirds of the votes cast in a five-person race. Progressives and Stalwarts alike tended to see Zimmerman as a glad-hander whose convictions did not run deep and whose knowledge of the issues was superficial. Although that assessment led the Progressives to prefer Ekern, the Stalwarts found Zimmerman's qualities appealing. Here was a candidate who could win the race for governor but was unlikely to risk dying on the ramparts for Progressive principles. Bending with prevailing political sentiment in Wisconsin and rejecting an authentic conservative, the Stalwarts overwhelmingly embraced Zimmerman.[32]

[31] La Follette, *Adventure in Politics*, 123–125; Maney, "*Young Bob*" *La Follette*, 46.

[32] *Wisconsin Blue Book, 1927*, p. 669; Brownlee, *Progressivism and Economic Growth*, 85–86; Brownlee, "Income Taxation and the Political Economy of Wisconsin," in *WMH*, 59:320. One of Zimmerman's campaign handouts in 1926 quoted Old Bob: "I have

Taken in combination, the 1926 primary election results represented a convincing triumph for neither the Progressives nor the Stalwarts. Blaine defeated Lenroot, and with his victory came the promise of increased strength for Wisconsin's Progressive representation in Congress. Back home, the Progressives retained control of the assembly and most state offices. On the other hand, the new Stalwart strategy resulted in victory for Zimmerman, and Stalwarts backed by the Republican Voluntary Committee became a dominant force in the state senate. For each faction, the mixed results of the 1926 election demonstrated the need for greater unity of purpose and a larger role in activities of the national Republican party. Looking towards the future after the general elections, the RVC first sought control of the state organization, and with RVC support A. B. Fontaine of Green Bay became state party chairman. Then, expanding their operation, RVC Stalwarts defeated Progressives in contests for seats on the Republican National Committee. In the meantime, the Progressives were becoming increasingly sensitive to the need for more effective organization. Their only equivalent of the RVC was the La Follette family, but for all its brilliance, the house of La Follette failed in the end to provide a structure through which Progressives could cogently operate. The quest for an effective competitor to the RVC was not to conclude satisfactorily until after World War II.[33]

* * *

The sons of Robert M. La Follette had been weaned on politics, and after Young Bob's victory in 1925 they were ready to assert leadership of reform forces in the nation as well as in Wisconsin. Differing in temperament and character, they were equally intelligent and equally committed to principles they inherited from their father. Friends and acquaintances considered Bob the more reserved and contemplative of the two, while Phil seemed more ebullient, energetic, and politically ambitious. Both sons had attended the University of Wisconsin, but Bob, beset by illness, had never completed the requirements for a baccalaureate degree. Phil had

known Fred Zimmerman for twenty years, and he has always been right." A copy may be found enclosed in Robert S. Cowie to Blaine, August 15, 1926, in the Blaine Papers.

[33] Richard C. Haney, *A Concise History of the Modern Republican Party of Wisconsin, 1925–1975* (Madison, 1976), 4; Brownlee, *Progressivism and Economic Growth*, 86–87; Maney, *"Young Bob" La Follette*, 46–47; Johnson, *Robert M. La Follette, Jr.*, 25–26.

been an enthusiastic student, excited by the intellectual challenge of his classes and the variety of opportunity in extracurricular activities.[34]

The United States declared war on Germany when Phil was a junior, and he enlisted in the army. After a brief tour of duty with the Student Army Training Corps at the University of Oklahoma, he returned to Wisconsin to complete his senior year. He went on to earn his law degree in 1922. That was the year of his father's last campaign for the Senate, and Phil devoted his prodigious energies to stumping the state. Delivering more than 200 speeches, he developed a vigorous oratorical style much like his father's. Unlike Bob, Phil delighted in the give-and-take of political combat, and two years later he became a candidate for district attorney of Dane County. Already a seasoned campaigner, he worked for the La Follette-Wheeler presidential ticket as well as for his own election. He succeeded in becoming district attorney, and had he been eligible he would gladly have entered the race to succeed his father the following year. But with Bob in the Senate, Phil instead began thinking about running for governor.[35]

After the special election of 1925, neither of the La Follette brothers could afford to mark time. Bob faced re-election in 1928, and he needed to keep his political fences in good repair. Phil's future was less certain. With his experience as district attorney behind him, he was tempted to pursue an academic career. He lectured in criminal law at the University of Wisconsin during the academic year 1926–1927. He then received two inquiries about his interest in becoming the dean of a law school, one at the University of Wisconsin and the other at the University of Chicago. Although Phil found both positions attractive, he turned them down. He chose instead to practice law, lecture on the Chautauqua circuit, and travel to Europe to learn what he could about the drift of affairs in other countries.[36]

In the meantime, Bob was concerning himself with affairs in the Senate and with the uncertain condition of the Progressive faction

[34] John E. Miller, *Governor Philip F. La Follette, the Wisconsin Progressives, and the New Deal* (Columbia, Missouri, 1982), 4–7; Maney, *"Young Bob" La Follette*, 31.

[35] Summaries of interviews with Isabel Bacon La Follette, March 11, 1969, and October 16, 1972, copies in both the author's and the History of Wisconsin project files.

[36] La Follette, *Adventure in Politics*, 116–118; Maney, *"Young Bob" La Follette*, 31; Philip F. La Follette to Robert M. La Follette, Jr., Fola La Follette, and Ralph and Mary Sucher, May 7, 1929, in box A-38, La Follette Family Papers, Library of Congress.

back home. The young senator's loyalties had become apparent almost immediately upon his arrival in Washington, when he strode into the midst of a controversy over his party affiliation. Having read Old Bob out of the party at the time he ran for President, Republican leaders now had to decide whether the son was truly a Republican. It was a matter of some importance because it involved committee assignments. Furthermore, coming up for re-election in 1928, Bob would be campaigning during a presidential year. To have him run as a Republican might turn out to be helpful in securing Wisconsin's electoral votes for the party's presidential nominee. After backing and filling on the question of Bob's party membership, the Senate Committee on Committees finally voted unanimously to recognize the young senator as a Republican and to assign him to the committees on mines and mining, Indian affairs, and manufacturing. Bob accepted the assignments, but in an open letter to the chair of the committee, he announced that his loyalty belonged not to the party of Calvin Coolidge but to "progressive principles and policies of government as interpreted and applied by the late Robert M. La Follette."[37]

Bob was amused by the discomfiture of Republican leaders, but he found no humor in the situation confronting the Progressives at home. He observed that in Wisconsin "many of the leaders upon whom daddy depended have become aged and infirm," and he believed that the younger Progressives lacked the experience to provide them with an understanding of the causes that had guided his father. Weak and irresolute leadership, he thought, was also in part attributable to the New Era prosperity which "appears to have completely anaesthetized the rank and file." Bob found insurgent leadership in the Senate to be just as weak and divided as Progressive leadership in Wisconsin. Many of the Progressives expected George Norris of Nebraska to take Old Bob's place, but Norris was too independent a thinker to care much for heading any organization. His commitment was to nonpartisan action, not to the leadership of a Progressive group or party.[38]

[37] Edward N. Doan, *The La Follettes and the Wisconsin Idea* (New York, 1947), 147–148; New York *Times*, December 2, 16, 1925.

[38] Robert M. La Follette, Jr., to Philip and Isabel La Follette, January 11, 1925, in the Philip F. La Follette Papers; New York *Times*, September 9, 1926; Robert M. La Follette, Jr., to William T. Rawleigh, February 12, 1927, in box C-6, La Follette Family Papers, Library of Congress; Maney, *"Young Bob" La Follette*, 47–48; Richard Lowitt, *George W. Norris: The Persistence of a Progressive, 1913–1933* (Urbana, 1971), 400–401.

Young Bob saw things differently. Before the close of his first year in the Senate, he set to work on a plan to unite the Progressives into a more effective senatorial bloc. Borrowing from ideas advanced during his father's presidential campaign, he urged the Progressives to focus their vision on "two or three constructive bills dealing with transportation, hydro-electric power and credit." By concentrating their energies, he believed, the Progressives could coerce recognition from Republican leaders and force accommodation to Progressive demands. By the time the Senate convened in December, 1927, however, Bob had been able to secure cooperation only from Lynn Frazier and Gerald Nye of North Dakota, Henrik Shipstead of Minnesota, and John Blaine, his colleague from Wisconsin. Without the endorsement of Norris and William E. Borah of Idaho, little came of his efforts.[39]

Despite the lack of support, Bob remained on good terms with his colleagues. The way he responded to the neglect of his program for concerted Progressive action was not only characteristic of the man, but also indicative of a political style that differed markedly from that of Old Bob. In substance, the speeches and the point of view of the son closely resembled those of the father, but Young Bob never allowed his convictions to interfere with personal relationships or with friendships. Even old guard senators found him a congenial colleague, and they in turn treated him with an affection they could not bring themselves to extend to his father. Bob recognized that there were more ways of killing a cat than by choking it with cream, but for him it seemed the best way. He thus quickly took his place as one of the most respected members of the Senate; yet with the respect went an awareness that he remained staunch in his convictions.[40]

Because Bob's campaign for re-election came during a presidential year, he had an opportunity to attract attention to his beliefs and the Progressive cause. When Calvin Coolidge chose not to run in 1928, Herbert Hoover entered the race for the Republican presidential nomination as the favorite of most party members. An early

[39] Robert M. La Follette, Jr., to William T. Rawleigh, February 12, 1927, in box C-6, La Follette Family Papers, Library of Congress; LeRoy Ashby, *The Spearless Leader: Senator Borah and the Progressive Movement in the 1920's* (Urbana, 1972), 235–236; Washington *Post*, December 1, 1927; New York *Sun*, December 1, 1927.

[40] Maney, *"Young Bob" La Follette*, 44–45; Chicago *Tribune*, January 23, 1926; Johnson, *Robert M. La Follette, Jr.*, 20–21.

test of Hoover's strength, believed political observers, would come in the Wisconsin presidential primary on April 3. If a Progressive could defeat Hoover in Wisconsin, the victory would indicate that there, at least, insurgency retained its attraction for voters. Immediately prior to the primary, therefore, a group of eight Progressive senators issued statements endorsing George Norris, who consented to have his name entered in competition with those of Hoover and a scattering of other candidates. The results of the election were immensely gratifying to Progressives, for Norris won overwhelmingly with 162,822 votes to Hoover's 17,659. La Follette and Blaine, who had been among the senators endorsing Norris, easily won election as delegates-at-large to the Republican National Convention in June.[41]

Despite Norris' showing in Wisconsin, Hoover's nomination was assured by the time the convention opened, and the proceedings offered little to excite either the delegates or the general public. The only real fireworks came when La Follette presented the minority platform of the Wisconsin delegation. Highly critical of the Republican administrations and policies of the last eight years, Bob spoke with such grace and good humor that even Secretary of the Treasury Andrew Mellon applauded his effort. In H. L. Mencken's opinion, Bob's speech was a "pleasant oasis in a desert of blather." But it had no effect on the outcome of the convention. While "La Follette got the cheers," observed a reporter from the New York *Telegram*, "Hoover got the votes."[42]

The comment was accurate in the context of the convention, but in the context of Bob's campaign for re-election, there was little question that his performance enhanced his standing among Wisconsin voters. Indeed, the La Follette name had never been more highly regarded; so great was Bob's popularity that the Stalwarts were hard put to find someone to run against him in the primary election on September 4. At last George Mead, a banker and paper mill owner who was also mayor of Wisconsin Rapids, consented to undertake what every knowledgeable person in the state knew was a futile campaign. Conceding that Bob was certain to win, the Stal-

[41] Lowitt, *George W. Norris: The Persistence of a Progressive*, 403–404; *Wisconsin Blue Book, 1929*, pp. 720–721.

[42] New York *Times*, June 15, 1928; Maney, *"Young Bob" La Follette*, 58–60; H. L. Mencken in the Baltimore *Sun*, June 22, 1928; Ludwell Denny, quoted in the *Literary Digest*, 97 (June 30, 1928), 40.

warts chose to concentrate on the governorship instead. The Republican Voluntary Committee had gained its objectives with the Zimmerman victory in 1926 and had become an effective political force in the state. Now those Stalwarts who had supported Zimmerman were ready to abandon him if they could find a bona fide conservative. When Walter J. Kohler, the well-known manufacturer of plumbing ware, indicated his willingness to run, the Stalwarts knew they had their man.[43]

In considering possible candidates for governor in 1928, the Progressives momentarily found themselves in a quandary. Herman Ekern remained a favorite of many of them, but he had run so poorly in 1926 that the La Follette brothers opposed his candidacy. They decided to throw their influence to the congressman from the Seventh District in the western portion of the state, Joseph Beck, who very much wanted to be governor. Beck was a farmer by profession, but he had served eight years as commissioner of labor and industrial statistics, and six years as a member of the Wisconsin Industrial Commission before his election to Congress in 1920. Careless in dress, plebeian in manner, and an inveterate chewer of tobacco, he was highly intelligent and devoted to the La Follettes. Unfortunately for the Progressives, Beck proved unable to overcome the appeal of Kohler. Carefully nurturing recognition as an enlightened businessman who had built an industrial city to house his employees, the plumbing-ware magnate added to his reputation for doing the unusual by campaigning throughout the state in his private airplane. In addition to the attractiveness of his opponent, Beck confronted a more effective organization in the Republican Voluntary Committee than any he was able to establish.[44]

For all the talk about convictions and principles in 1928, the outcome of the Wisconsin elections appear in retrospect to have had as much to do with the personal magnetism of candidates as

[43] Belle Case La Follette to Mary La Follette, June 30, 1928, in box A-36, La Follette Family Papers, Library of Congress; Maney, *"Young Bob" La Follette*, 60; Brownlee, *Progressivism and Economic Growth*, 86; Brownlee, "Income Taxation and the Political Economy of Wisconsin," in *WMH*, 59:320–321. "Somebody ought to run for the United States senate in Wisconsin against Bob," wrote the editor of the Janesville *Daily Gazette* to Albert D. Bolens. "If they do not, there will be nothing to keep him from being on the stump for Al Smith after the primary." Stephen Bolles to Bolens, July 22, 1928, in the Albert D. Bolens Papers.

[44] La Follette, *Adventure in Politics*, 125–128; Miller, *Governor Philip F. La Follette*, 10; *Wisconsin Blue Book, 1929*, p. 135; Haney, *Concise History of the Modern Republican Party of Wisconsin*, 4.

it did with the platforms on which they campaigned. Young Bob easily defeated Mead in the primary, and in the general election he carried every county in the state while receiving 635,376 of the 716,678 votes cast for senator. On the other hand, La Follette's support was insufficient to carry the day for Beck, who lost the primary by a little more than 20,000 votes. In the general election, despite the opposition of the La Follettes, Blaine, and other Progressives, Walter Kohler defeated his Democratic opponent, Albert Schmedeman, with 58 per cent of the total vote. The ambivalence of the Wisconsin electorate was puzzling, and the presidential returns added to the enigma. Blaine and Phil La Follette followed George Norris in endorsing the Democratic nominee, Al Smith. While Bob could not bring himself to go that far, he specifically refused to support Hoover. He believed that as secretary of commerce the Republican candidate had tied himself to a big-business kite, and in Bob's view that association made him anathema. Hoover nevertheless secured 54 per cent of the votes cast for President in Wisconsin. Thus, even though more citizens of the state voted for Young Bob La Follette than at any other time before or after 1928, it was evident that popular support for the man did not prevent voters from casting their presidential ballots for Hoover.[45]

Taking pleasure in Young Bob's personal triumph, his followers did not think themselves justified in celebrating it with categorical jubilation. After all, a successful industrialist sat in the governor's mansion, and in Washington, President Hoover was affirming the wisdom of policies that Republicans had followed for the past eight years. It was no reflection on Bob La Follette to believe that the Progressives needed a state leader who could successfully challenge Kohler in 1930, yet they were reluctant to take up the challenge. The new governor appeared to be popular, and potential candidates seemed unwilling to risk their political reputations in what was likely to be an unsuccessful campaign against him.

Most Progressives believed that Phil La Follette had long ago planned to run for governor, but Phil was still young and still being courted by the law faculty at the University of Wisconsin. Active in politics though he was, the time for challenging Kohler did not seem favorable until after the stock market crash in 1929 signaled

[45] Maney, "*Young Bob*" *La Follette*, 61; Johnson, *Robert M. La Follette, Jr.*, 19–20; James R. Donoghue, *How Wisconsin Voted, 1848–1972* (Madison, 1974), 111–128; New York *Times*, November 7, 8, 1928; *Wisconsin Blue Book, 1929*, pp. 815–817.

the onset of the Great Depression. Even then, Phil waited in the wings until he was sure that no other Progressive wished to take on the Stalwarts in 1930.[46]

In the end, the developing economic crisis strengthened Phil's determination to enter the race against Kohler. To his mind—as to Progressives' for as long as he could remember—the central consideration was the need to limit the concentration of economic power. Selfish economic interests, he believed, had been responsible for the disaster on Wall Street. And Phil blamed kindred interests for dangerous trends in the political economy of Wisconsin. The spread of chain banking and chain stores in the state was, he thought, symptomatic of a more general evil, and on that issue he believed he could defeat Kohler and the Stalwarts. He discussed the matter with members of his family and with trusted friends such as Charles Crownhart and Alf Rogers. As economic troubles in the state increased, sentiment for Phil's candidacy waxed stronger by the day, and in April he met with Bob and his mother in Atlantic City, New Jersey, for a quiet weekend of deliberation. He returned to Madison committed to making the race.[47]

When Phil announced his candidacy late in June, astute political observers were reluctant to concede that he had much chance of defeating Kohler. Despite the deepening economic crisis and the support he received from Progressives, he still had problems to overcome. Having just celebrated his thirty-third birthday, he seemed very young to be entrusted with the highest office of the state during a time of economic peril. He was also a La Follette, and though the name had enormous appeal, no one could tell how voters might react to placing another member of the family in a position of political power. Would they shy away from voting for him because in so doing they might contribute to the creation of a La Follette fiefdom in Wisconsin? No one could tell. Nor could anyone tell, despite his obvious familiarity with the stump, how

[46] Miller, *Governor Philip F. La Follette*, 10–11; Belle Case La Follette to Mrs. Glenn Frank, October 3, 1930, in the Philip F. La Follette Papers. Also: Philip F. La Follette to Belle Case La Follette, August 8, 1929; Philip F. La Follette to Robert M. La Follette, Jr., May 13, November 18, 1929; and Robert M. La Follette, Jr., to Philip F. La Follette, December 10, 1929, all in box A-38, La Follette Family Papers, Library of Congress.

[47] La Follette, *Adventure in Politics*, 135–139; Miller, *Governor Philip F. La Follette*, 10–11; Philip F. La Follette to Dear Ones, June 26, 1930, in box A-39, La Follette Family Papers, Library of Congress.

effective he would be in confronting the Republican Voluntary Committee.[48]

In a well-conceived and well-conducted campaign, Phil soon put all doubts to rest. He consulted Progressives in the legislature and on the university faculty in drafting his platform; he enlisted the rhetorical skills of his wife, his brother, and John Blaine; and he shrewdly set his timetable so as to allow an opportunity for speaking engagements in every county before committing ten days to Milwaukee, Racine, and Kenosha. By his own count, Phil delivered 261 speeches in the two months before voters went to the polls in the September primary, and by that time he had pressed so much flesh that his right hand was swollen to nearly half again its normal size. An overconfident Kohler, spending scarcely a month on his re-election campaign, attempted to belittle Phil by calling him an "upstart" and a "whippersnapper."[49]

The campaign speeches Phil delivered during that summer of anxiety represented no startling departure from the themes Progressives had been rehearsing for years. Neither he nor Bob commented extensively on the stock market crash, business failures, or growing unemployment. Yet what Phil said to the voters sounded fresh, exciting, and above all, accurate in its implications. Again and again he hammered away at the evils of the chains, the high rates charged by the "power trust," and a possible Stalwart infringement of the state's corrupt practices act. Again and again he asserted that by controlling choices, monopoly interests threatened to control even trivial daily decisions. He implied that in the end, ordinary citizens always lost their freedom of action whenever the state government entered into full partnership with "powerful and selfish monopoly interests." Finally, Phil emphasized that it was those very interests that had elected Herbert Hoover and Walter J. Kohler, and he argued that only if the voters once again asserted themselves could they confound their oppressors.[50]

[48] Maney, *"Young Bob" La Follette*, 78; Philip F. La Follette to Isen La Follette, March 18, 1944, in the Philip F. La Follette Papers; New York *Times*, December 8, 1929.

[49] Robert M. La Follette, Jr., to Philip F. La Follette and Alfred T. Rogers, May 24, 1930; Ralph Sucher to Isen La Follette, July 30, 1930; E. G. Littel to Jack Kyle, telegram, August 26, 1930; E. G. Littel to Jack Kyle, September 7, 1930; and "PFL Itinerary," June 26 to September 16, 1930, filed as September 13, 1930, in series 1, all in the Philip F. La Follette Papers. Also Philip F. La Follette to Fola and George Middleton, September 26, 1930, in box A-39, La Follette Family Papers, Library of Congress; La Follette, *Adventure in Politics*, 138–143.

[50] Maney, *"Young Bob" La Follette*, 78–79; Miller, *Governor Philip F. La Follette*, 11;

"When Wisconsin falls for an idol, she does a thorough job of it." John T. McCutcheon's homage to the La Follette dynasty was published in the Chicago *Tribune* in 1930 following Phil La Follette's election to the governorship. From an original drawing, courtesy La Follette, Sinykin, Anderson & Munson of Madison, Wisconsin.

When voters went to the polls on September 16, 1930, they asserted themselves with vigor to give Phil a decisive primary victory and drive Kohler out of the race. The vote in other contests was also convincingly Progressive. Friends of the La Follettes won nominations for all the remaining state offices and for all the seats in Congress except one. In the aftermath of the primary, in which victory was tantamount to election in November, Phil sought to heal the wounds his campaign had inflicted and to mollify the Stalwarts whose help he would need in governing the state. The results of the general election were gratifying. Phil won 70 per cent of the total vote and soundly defeated Charles Hammersley, his Democratic opponent. Progressivism had apparently passed though a time of trouble reflected in the ambivalence of voters and in the shifting election returns at the end of the New Era.[51]

* * *

Since early in the twentieth century, legislation establishing procedures in Wisconsin elections had distinguished between partisan elections held in the fall, and nonpartisan spring elections of all judges, municipal councils and administrators, town officials, county board members, and the state superintendent of public instruction. Political activity in the state had acquired some its unusual character from the partisan election regulations approved in a referendum submitted to voters in 1904. Under terms of the statute enacted the following year, all nominations for all offices came through a direct primary by which voters selected candidates to compete in a subsequent general election. Wisconsin primaries were "open"; that is, there was no registration of party affiliation, and the voter had no obligation to reveal membership in a particular party. In the September partisan primaries, voters received two or more party ballots, but only one of them could be tallied. From election to election, therefore, voters could change the party in which they voted depending upon which candidates they wished to support.

Alfred T. Rogers to Philip F. La Follette, September 20, 1930, in the Philip F. La Follette Papers; Philip F. La Follette to Dear Ones, September 11, 1930, in box A-39, La Follette Family Papers, Library of Congress. During Phil's campaign, Progressives distributed copies of his platform with the slogan "The People Must Resume Control of Their Government If It Is to Serve Them Instead of Monopoly," on p. 2 of the campaign handout, September, 1930, in the Blaine Papers.

[51] Belle Case La Follette to Philip F. La Follette, September 16, 1930, in the Philip F. La Follette Papers; *Wisconsin Blue Book, 1931*, pp. 462–467.

Although party organizations could endorse candidates, the ballots in primary elections could not indicate such endorsement. Furthermore, anyone obtaining the requisite number of signatures on nomination papers could be listed on one—though only one—of the primary election ballots.[52]

As the electoral system developed after adoption of the open primary, Wisconsin became to all intents and purposes a one-party state with the Republicans predominating. In most elections, a victory on the Republican ballot in the primary became a guarantee of victory in the general election. Yet, as is evident from the struggles between Stalwarts and Progressives during the New Era, the two Republican factions acquired many of the characteristics of discrete political parties. The kinds of decisions reached in the general elections of most states were decisions that Wisconsin voters made when they chose the Republican ballot in the open primary.

Only when major national problems transcended the problems of Wisconsin, as they did during the Great War, were Democrats likely to have much of a following. Even then, it was not Democrats but Stalwart and Progressive Republicans who struggled for control of the state. With widespread Progressive opposition to Herbert Hoover and strong Progressive support of Al Smith in 1928, with the beginning of the Great Depression at the end of the New Era, and with the election of Franklin D. Roosevelt in 1932, Progressive and Stalwart Republicans alike found cohabitation in the Grand Old Party increasingly difficult. Eventually, during the New Deal decade, the Progressives withdrew to pursue an independent course, and with that development—to be examined in the chapters that follow—Wisconsin began to assume some of the features of a two-party political system.[53]

As the political history of Wisconsin unfolded after the Great War, the fortunes of the La Follette family depended on the strength of the Progressive faction of the Republican party. That association proved to be one of immense importance to the state, and the twenty-one state elections involving the candidacy of a La Follette between 1916 and 1940 provide a peculiarly valuable insight into the gradual political transformation of Wisconsin during

[52] Leon D. Epstein, *Politics in Wisconsin* (Madison, 1958), 24–26.

[53] *Ibid.*, 36–56; Harold F. Gosnell and Morris H. Cohen, "Progressive Politics: Wisconsin an Example," in the *American Political Science Review*, 34 (October, 1940), 920–935.

those years. Like the private papers of Progressive partisans, data from the La Follette elections refute the notion that the Progressives were a homogeneous body of voters guided by the La Follettes' rhetoric and ideology into a pattern of political behavior that remained consistent from 1916 to 1940. What the twenty-one elections do indicate are shifts in the locus of Progressive strength. By relating those shifts to factors such as ethnicity, religion, place of residence, or economic well-being, it is possible to discern some of the underlying causes of political change in Wisconsin.[54]

Two series of bivariate correlations, one for the primaries and one for the general elections, provide a starting point for the analysis of voting behavior in Wisconsin from 1916 to 1940. A coefficient of correlation is simply a measure of the strength of relationship between two variables, or sets of data. The value of the coefficient varies from zero (indicating no relationship) to 1.00 (indicating a perfect relationship). The coefficients of correlation between every possible pair of La Follette primary elections and every pair of La Follette general elections from 1916 to 1938 are shown in the matrices, Tables 8–1 and 8–2.

The tables indicate two major shifts in support for the La Follettes. The first occurred between 1916 and 1922, and it is readily apparent in both the primary and the general election correlations. In the primary as well as in the general election of 1922, the La Follette vote differed markedly from the La Follette vote of 1916. The shift in Old Bob's support was so great, in fact, that the coef-

[54] Data for this analysis came from four main sources. The most important is the collection, "Wisconsin Historical County-Level Data, 1840–1960," compiled in seven files by the Research Division of the State Historical Society of Wisconsin. These files, in machine-readable form, are organized into two series, one demographic and the other economic. The Demographic Series includes a General Demography File, an Age File, an Incorporated Cities and Villages File, and a Country of Origin File. The Economic Series includes an Agricultural file, a Banking File, and a Manufacturing File. The second principal source of data, "Historical Election Returns, 1788–1976," was obtained in machine-readable form from the Inter-University Consortium for Political and Social Research (ICPSR), Ann Arbor, Michigan. Third, the ICPSR also provided information on religious bodies and affiliations in the collection, "Historical Census Data for United States Religious Bodies." Finally, the data for every Wisconsin primary election came from the relevant *Wisconsin Blue Book*, compiled by the Wisconsin Legislative Reference Bureau and published biennially.

These sources provided the data for the maps generated by the Calform Map Programs, as presented in Craig A. Latham and Denis White, *Calform Manual* (Cambridge, 1978). Duncan Aldrich of the University of Oklahoma applied the appropriate regression and other equations, using the OSIRIS III programming manual and software. Mr. Aldrich's help throughout the entire investigation was indispensable.

ficient of correlation between the primary elections of 1916 and 1922 was a minuscule .07. That the 1925 primary correlation with the 1916 primary was even less suggests a continuation of the wartime trend into the early twenties. The shift at the close of the decade is less obvious, however, because it appears earlier (1928) in the primary than in the general election (1930). The apparent reason for the difference is the Norwegian vote, which did not reverse trends until 1930 in the general election. Nonetheless, the shift was a significant one. The coefficient of correlation between the general election of 1928 and that of 1930 was even less than that between 1916 and 1922. Indeed, it was smaller than the coefficient of correlation for any other pair of successive general elections during the period.

In other respects, the two tables are similar. Both matrices indicate that during the mid-twenties the electorate became ambivalent in its response to La Follette Progressivism. Between 1925

TABLE 8-1
CORRELATION MATRIX: THE LA FOLLETTE PRIMARY ELECTIONS

	RML Sen. 1916	*RML Sen. 1922*	*RML Jr. Sen. 1925*	*RML Jr. Sen. 1928*	*PFL Gov. 1930*	*PFL Gov. 1932*	*RML Jr. Sen. 1934*	*PFL Gov. 1934*	*PFL Gov. 1936*	*PFL Gov. 1938*
RML, Sen. 1922	.07									
RML Jr., Sen. 1925	.03	.71								
RML Jr., Sen. 1928	.47	.59	.53							
PFL, Gov. 1930	.36	.47	.43	.67						
PFL, Gov. 1932	.66	.36	.28	.69	.73					
RML Jr., Sen. 1934	.44	.37	.38	.55	.64	.69				
PFL, Gov. 1934	.44	.37	.38	.55	.65	.70	1.00			
PFL, Gov. 1936	.63	.43	.43	.59	.62	.71	.79	.79		
PFL, Gov. 1938	.65	.42	.29	.57	.52	.79	.67	.67	.83	
RML Jr., Sen. 1940	.57	.40	.28	.50	.43	.61	.68	.68	.77	.86

and 1928, the coefficient of correlation dropped to .53 in the primary elections, and between 1925 and 1930 it fell to .31 in the general elections. During the next decade, however, the correlations between successive La Follette primary and general elections were relatively high and relatively constant. In other words, the years of the Great Depression were years in which support for the La Follettes appeared to stabilize. The lowest correlation between any two La Follette general elections during the thirties was between Bob's vote in 1934 and Phil's vote in 1938; returns in those elections generated a coefficient of .51.

Another way to view the shifts in voter support of La Follette Progressivism is by examining maps portraying patterns of voting in Wisconsin. Maps for all La Follette elections between 1916 and 1940 are reproduced on the following pages so as to display as fully as possible the loci of La Follette strength and weakness. The quantiles of each map are grouped according to the percentage of voters favoring the La Follette candidacy in each county, but the reader should note that the percentages in each quantile vary from map to map.

TABLE 8-2
CORRELATION MATRIX: THE LA FOLLETTE GENERAL ELECTIONS

	RML Sen. 1916	*RML Sen. 1922*	*RML Jr. Sen. 1925*	*RML Jr. Sen. 1928*	*PFL Gov. 1930*	*RML Jr. Sen. 1934*	*PFL Gov. 1934*	*PFL Gov. 1936*	*PFL Gov. 1938*
RML, Sen. 1922	.20								
RML Jr., Sen. 1925	.06	.62							
RML Jr., Sen. 1928	.01	.49	.64						
PFL, Gov. 1930	.63	.52	.31	.19					
RML Jr., Sen. 1934	.39	.57	.51	.32	.63				
PFL, Gov. 1934	.46	.58	.52	.27	.69	.96			
PFL, Gov. 1936	.36	.53	.37	.13	.66	.75	.76		
PFL, Gov. 1938	.43	.45	.21	.04	.66	.51	.58	.83	
RML Jr., Sen. 1940	.27	.53	.33	.10	.61	.65	.66	.85	.86

La Follette Elections, 1916–1940

This map serves as a guide to the twenty-two election maps that follow on pages 331–341, portraying the distribution of votes in elections between 1916 and 1940 involving a member of the La Follette family. Note that the percentages in the five quantiles on each map vary from map to map.

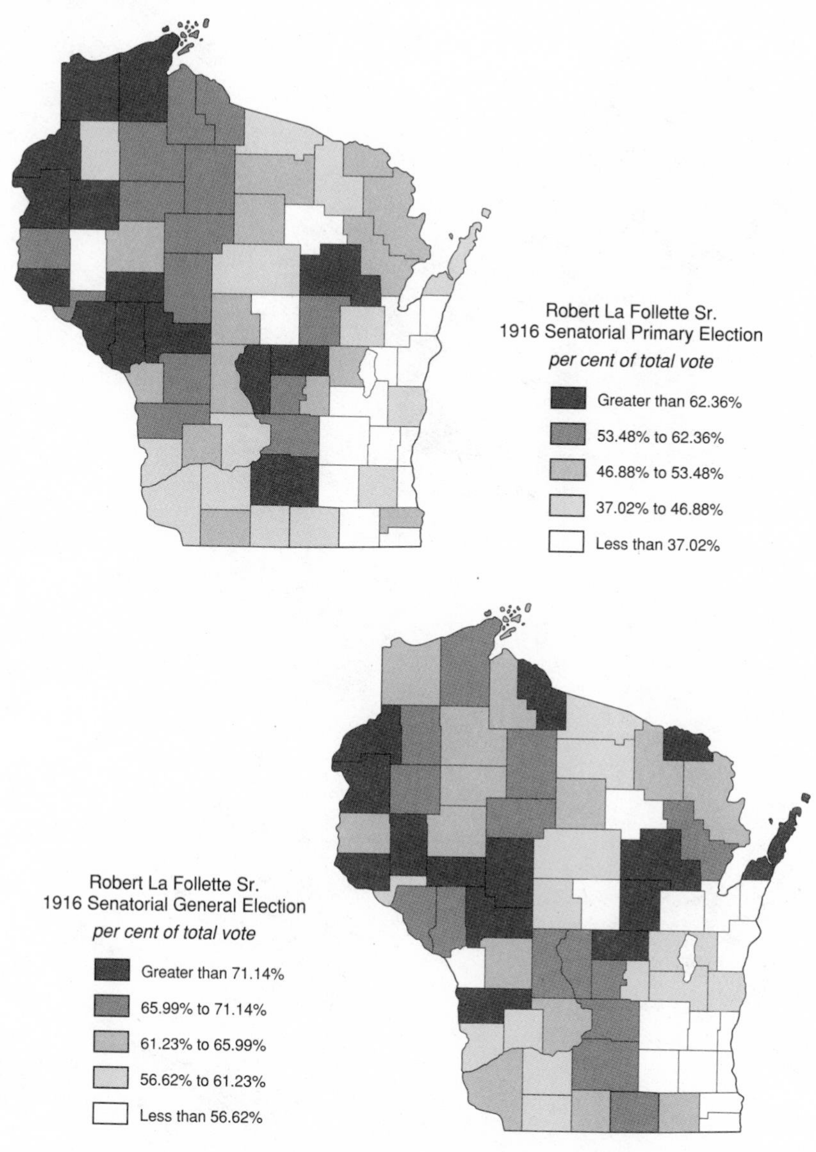

Senatorial Primary and General Elections, 1916

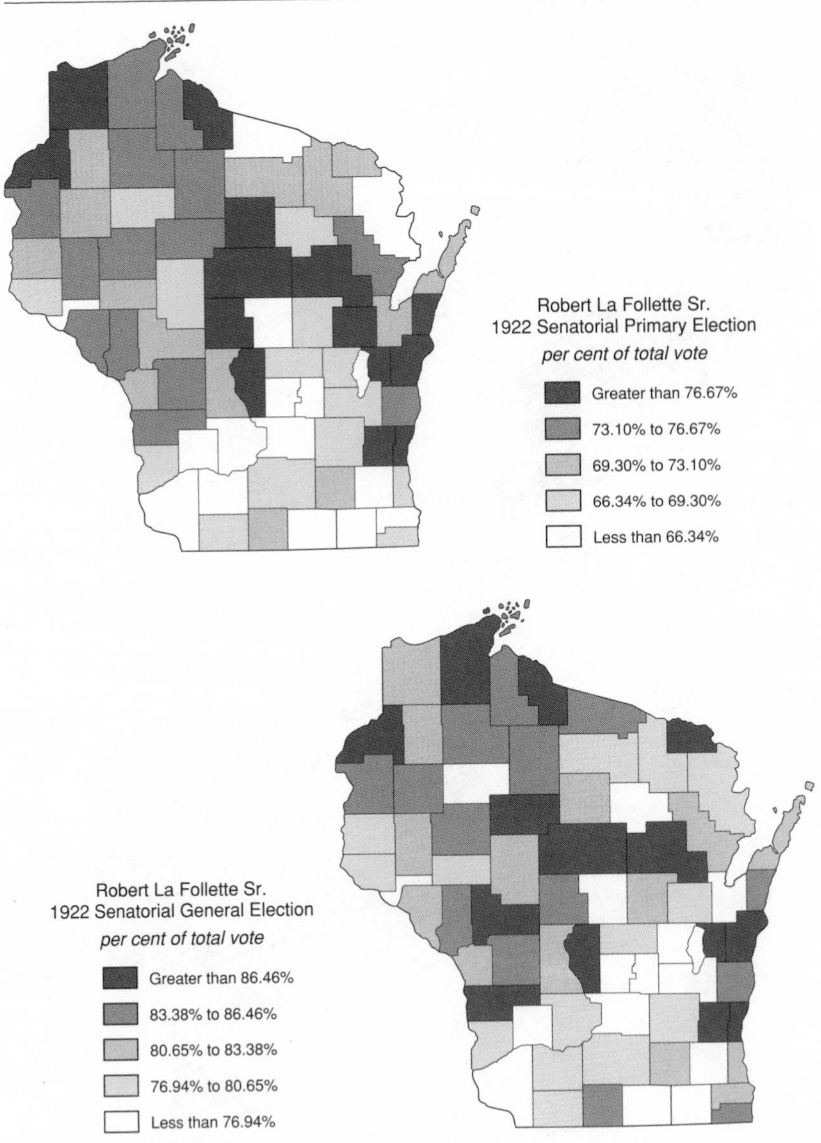

Senatorial Primary and General Elections, 1922

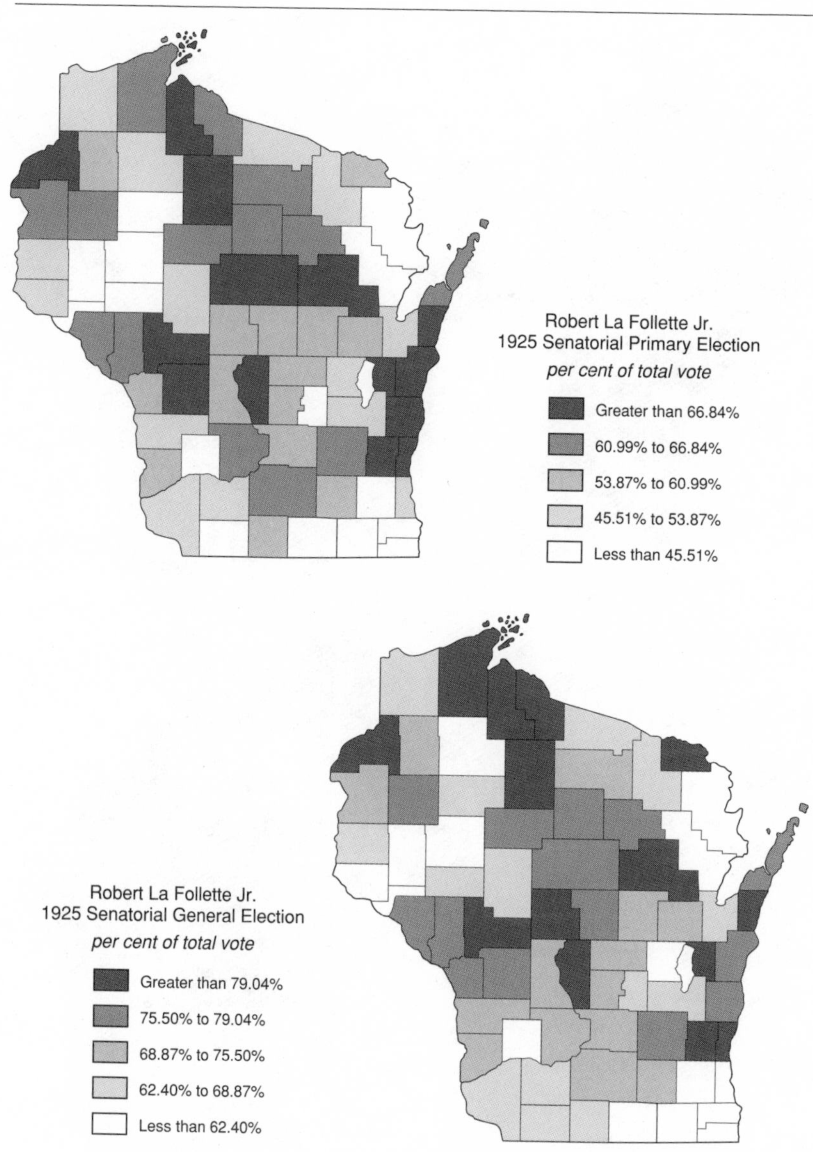

Senatorial Primary and General Elections, 1925

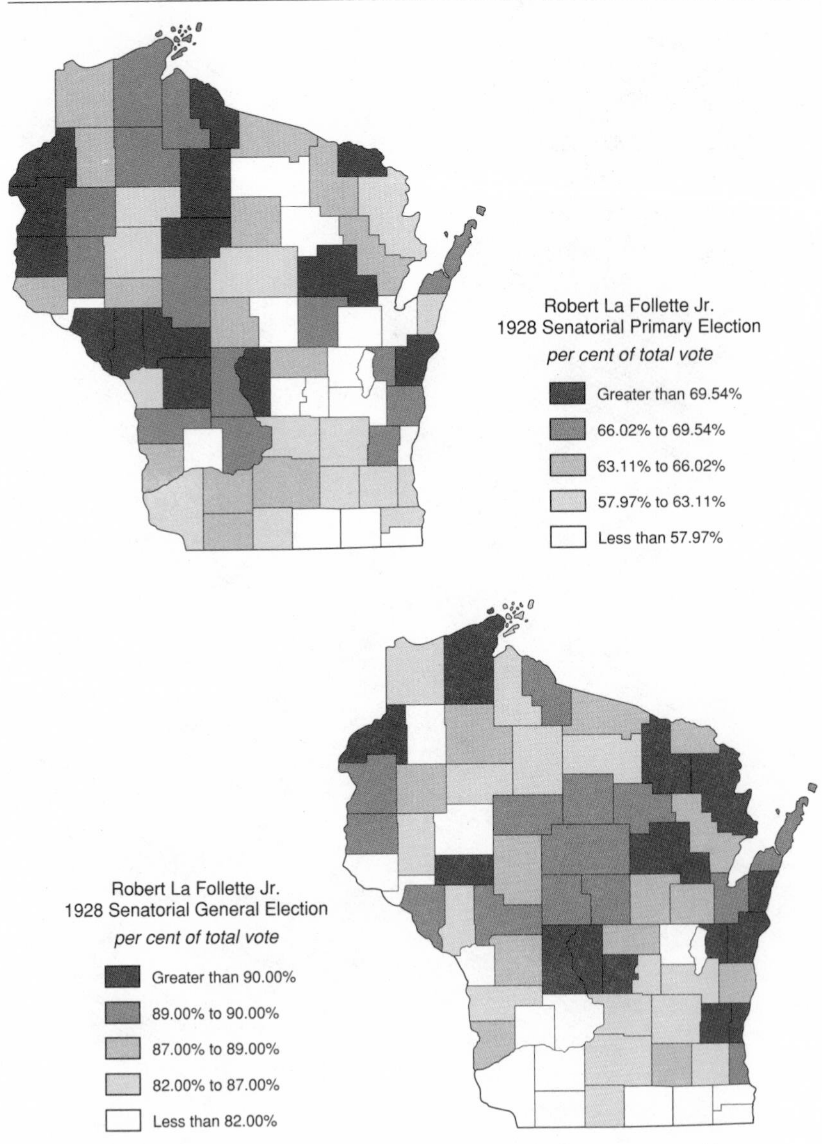

Senatorial Primary and General Elections, 1928

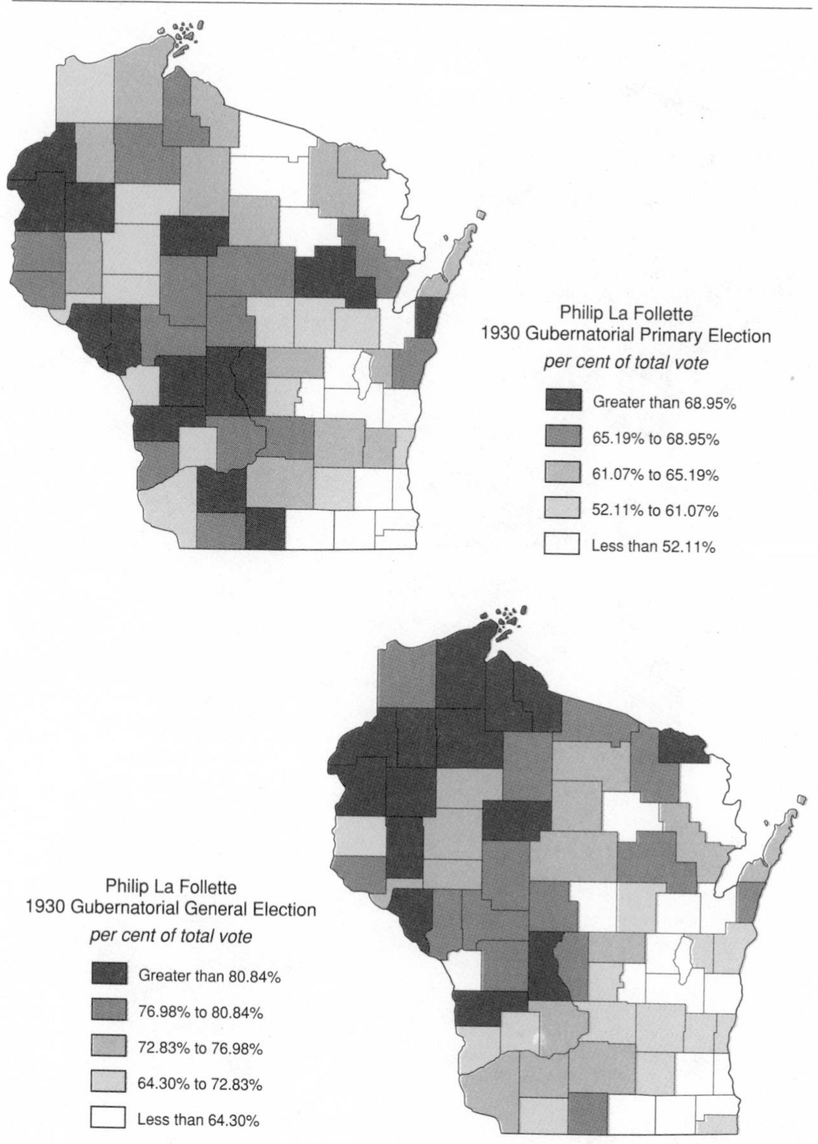

Gubernatorial Primary and General Elections, 1930

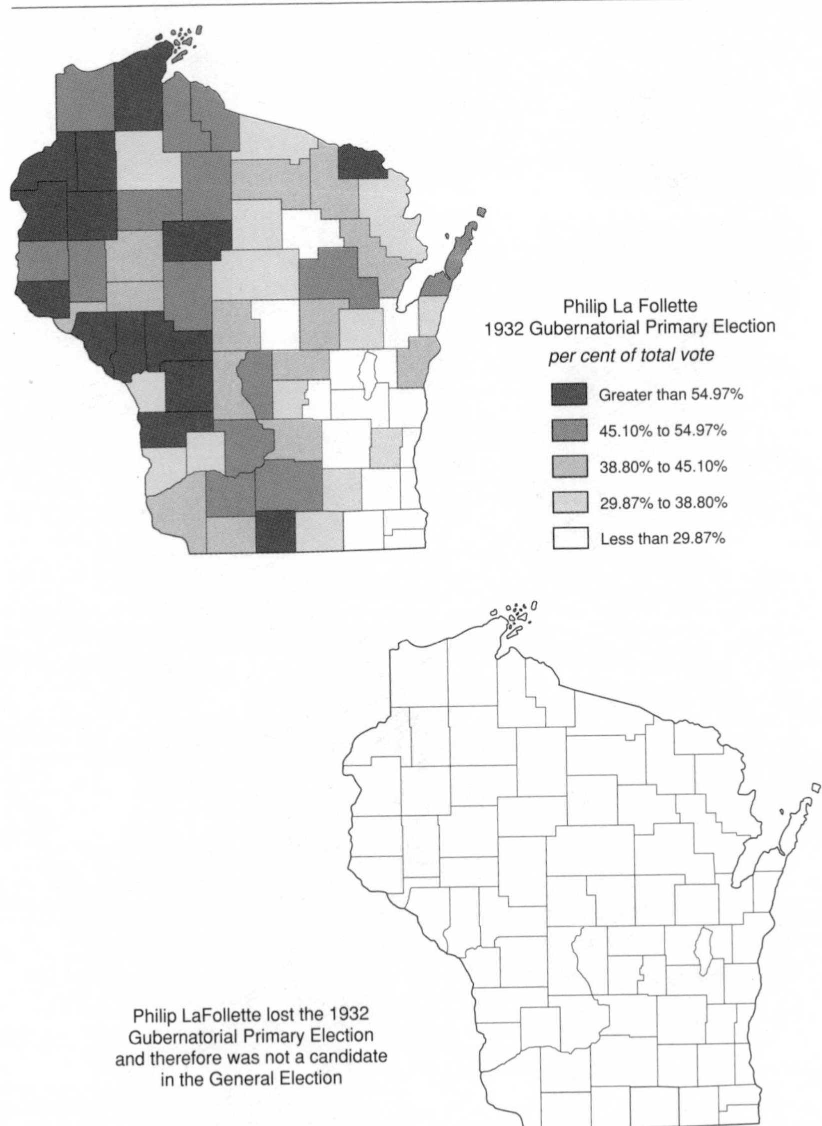

Gubernatorial Primary and General Elections, 1932

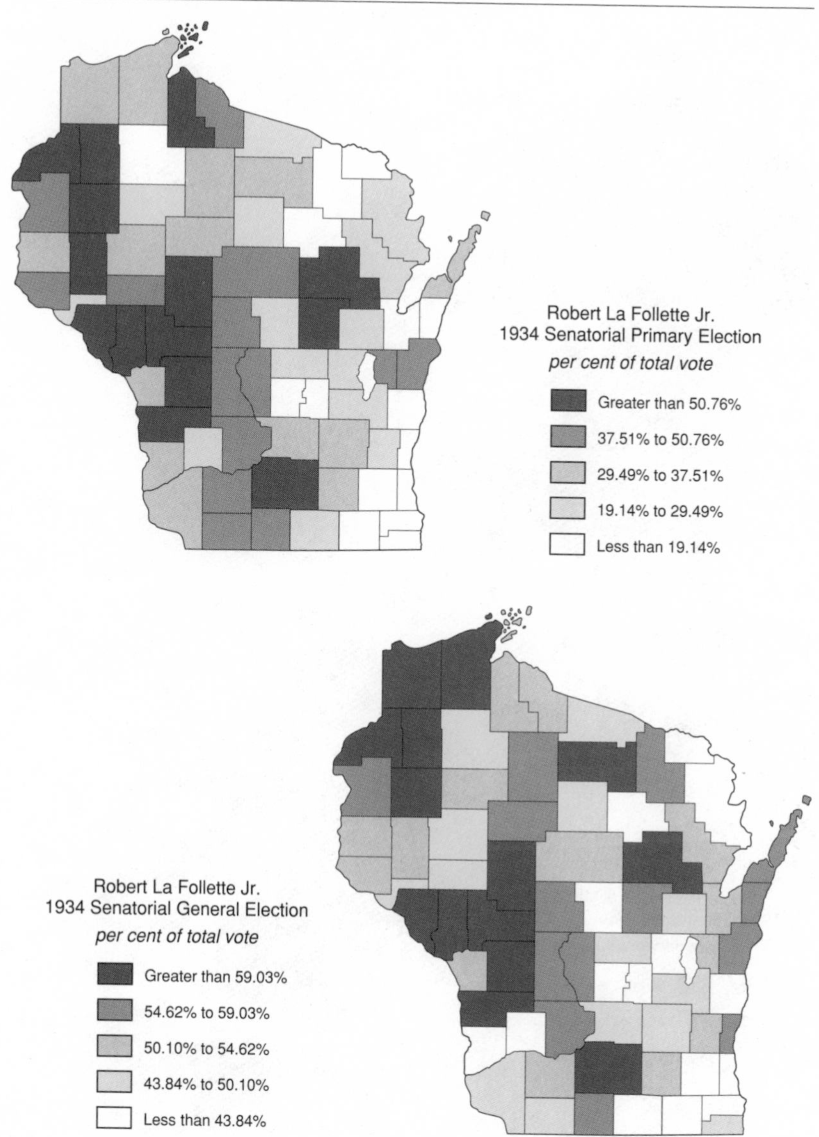

Senatorial Primary and General Elections, 1934

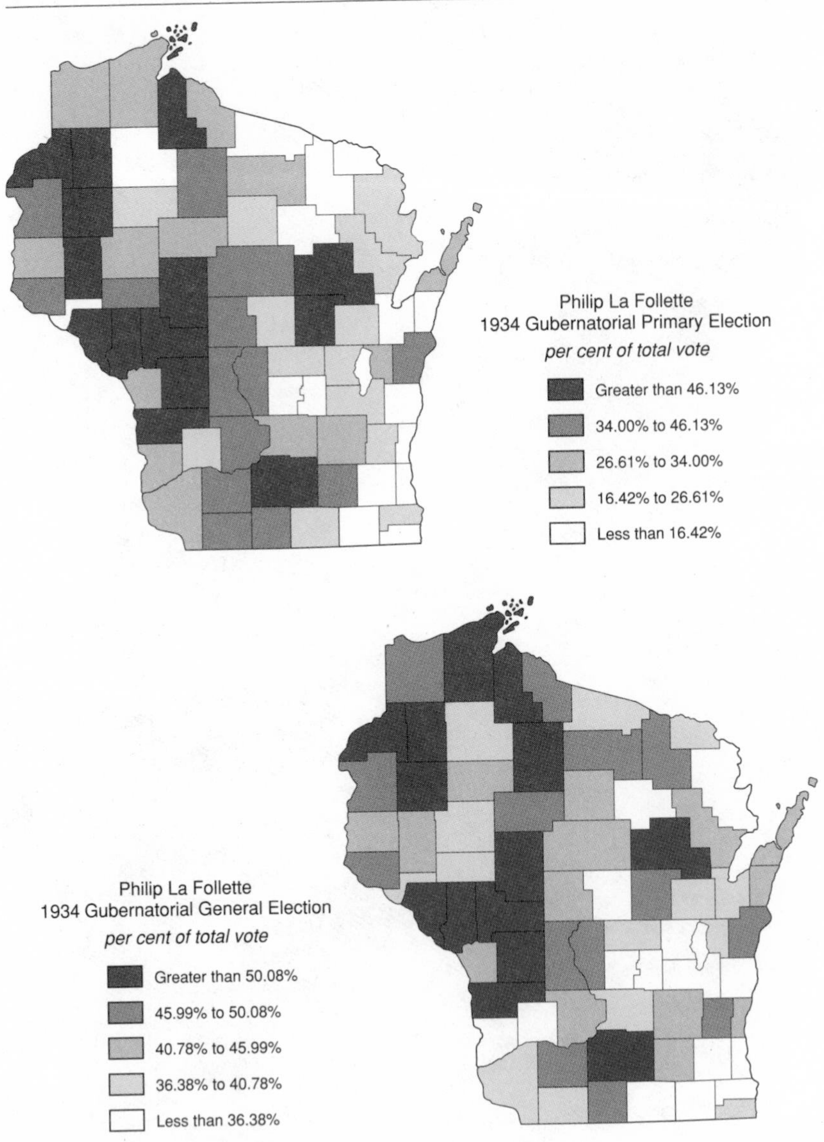

Gubernatorial Primary and General Elections, 1934

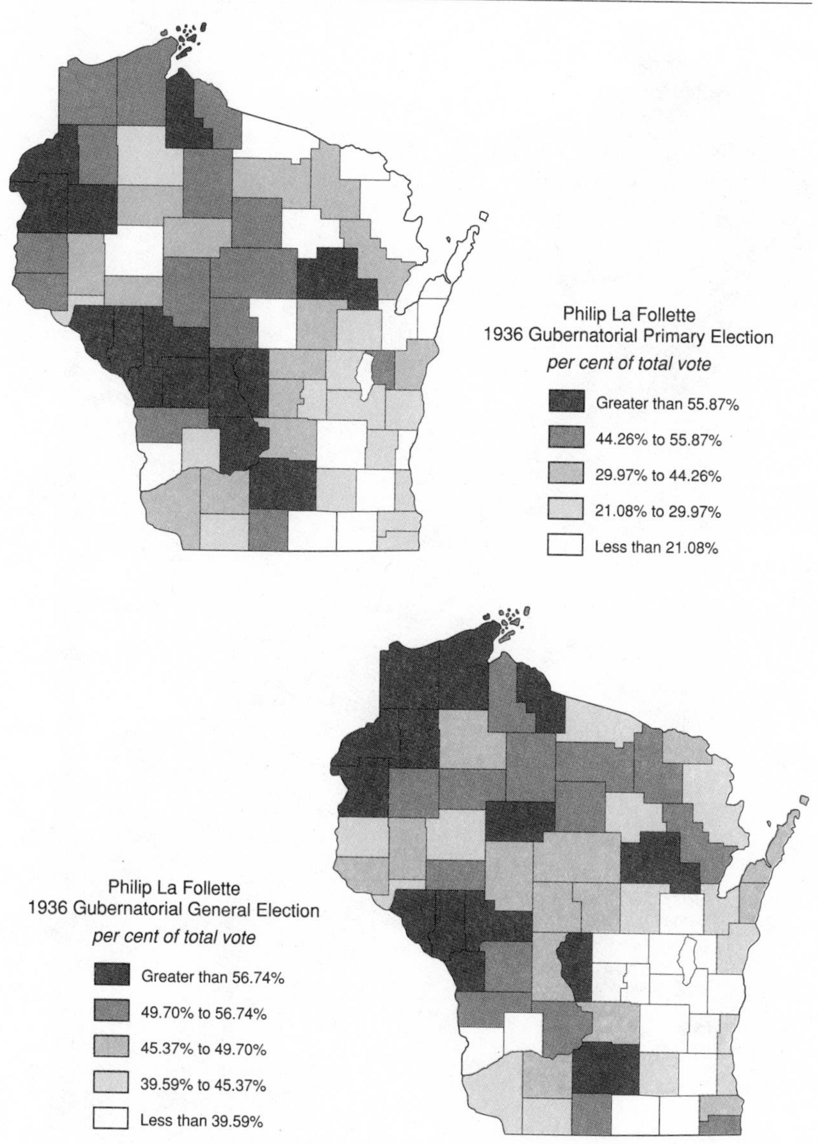

Gubernatorial Primary and General Elections, 1936

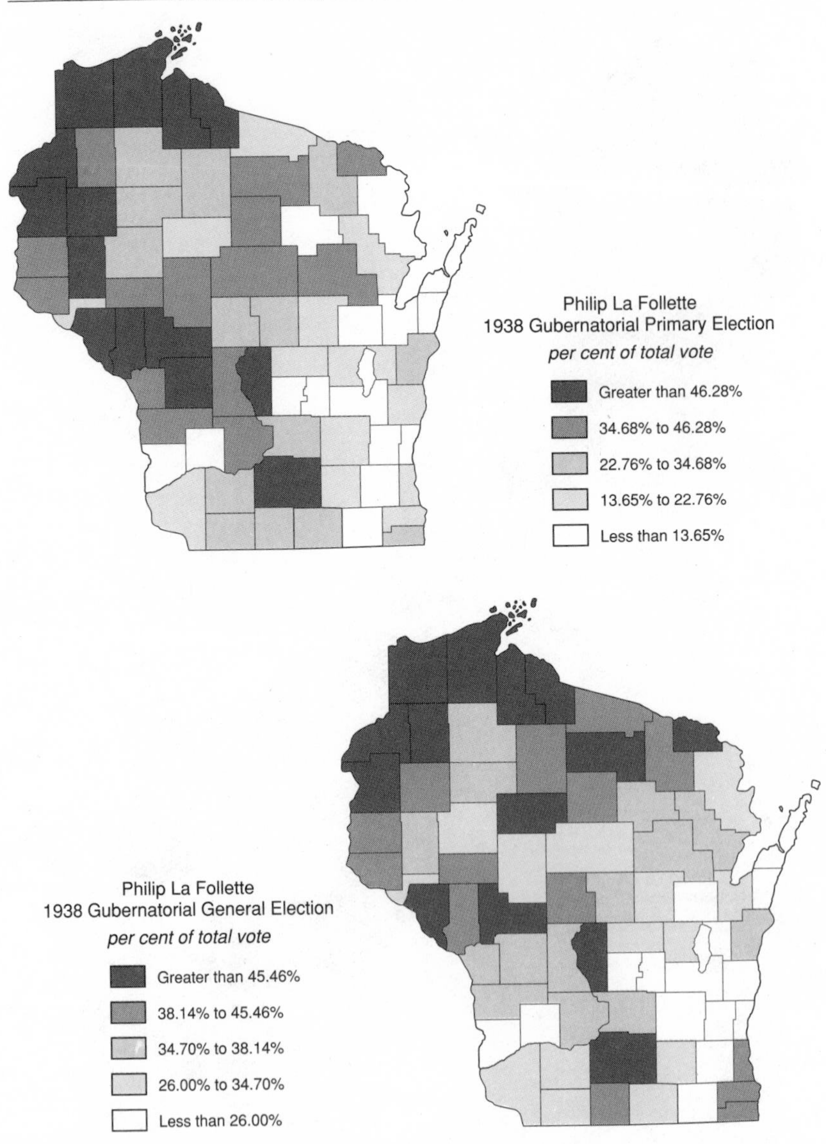

Gubernatorial Primary and General Elections, 1938

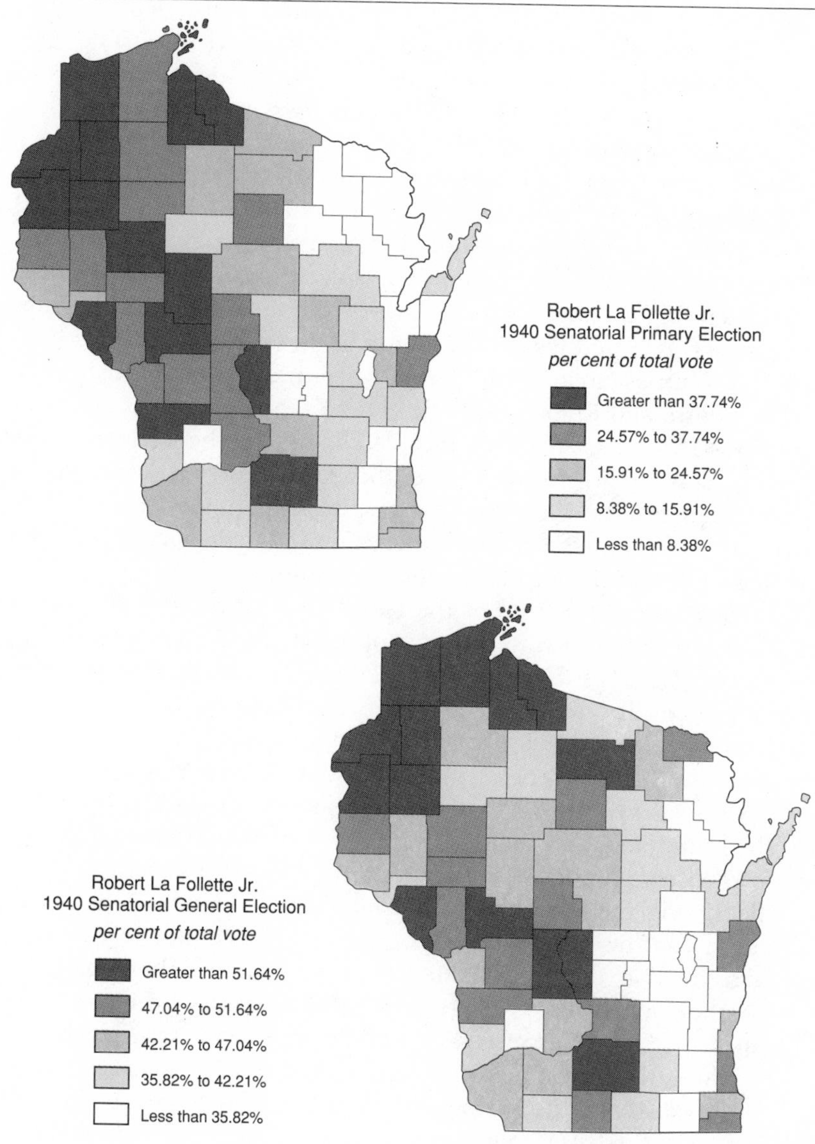

Senatorial Primary and General Elections, 1940

Like the correlation matrices, the election maps depict broad trends in the size and importance of the support given Old Bob and his sons by the voters. And like the correlation matrices, the maps depict the shifts and changes that perhaps made some elections more memorable than others. Especially noteworthy are the maps for the years 1916 and 1922, and those for 1925 to 1934. The maps for Old Bob's re-election campaigns of 1916 and 1922 clearly reflect the major shift in alignment that coincided with the Great War and its aftermath. That shift produced a geographic movement of La Follette support away from the northwestern counties (a heavily Scandinavian, Lutheran area) to the central and east-central counties (an area with large concentrations of German, Austrian, Polish, and Roman Catholic voters). The postwar realignment continued to have an effect into 1925, but in the 1928 primary Young Bob began to recapture the northwestern Scandinavian stronghold for the La Follettes. Despite some losses there in the primary of 1930, Phil made the area a well-nigh impregnable La Follette fortress during the general election.

Throughout the decade of the Great Depression, the portion of the state that most consistently supported the La Follettes lay in the west. Although both Phil and Young Bob were able to make some inroads into Milwaukee, Racine, and Kenosha during the late thirties, the election map of 1940 is more decidedly western than is the map of 1916. Generalizing about the entire period from 1916 to 1940, it is safe to say that the La Follettes' greatest support lay in the hinterland, and that their greatest opposition came from the more densely populated southeastern portion of the state.

Identifying the Wisconsin hinterland as the principal region of strength for the La Follette Progressives should not lead to the conclusion that the La Follettes attracted support there only because they appealed to village and rural interests. Ethnic and religious associations also weighed heavily with voters, particularly in the 1920's, when wartime disruptions were still influencing behavior at the polls. While the various ethnic and religious groups in Wisconsin were far from unanimous in the way they cast their ballots, the ethnic alignment from election to election does much to explain important shifts in the La Follettes' support during the postwar decade. The voting behavior of citizens having Norwegian and German antecedents merits elaboration.

In the senatorial race of 1916, the elder La Follette received strong endorsement from Wisconsin citizens of Norwegian ancestry. They in fact constituted the most important single influence in bringing about the senator's re-election victory. From that campaign, completed on the eve of American entry into World War I, Norwegian support of the La Follettes declined for more than a decade. Then, in the first general election following the stock market crash of 1929, the Norwegian Progressives reasserted themselves. They influenced the La Follette vote more significantly in 1930 than in any of the earlier elections under investigation. Throughout the years of the Great Depression, Norwegians remained the most important ethnic force in Wisconsin Progressivism.

The pattern of political behavior among Wisconsin Germans was strikingly different from that of the Norwegians. In the 1916 senatorial election, German support for Old Bob was minimal. After the war, however, election returns indicate an important change in tendency among German voters, and by 1925 the positive association of Germans with the La Follette vote reached statistical significance. Germans exerted more influence to secure the victory of Young Bob in the special election to replace the elder La Follette than did any other ethnic group. Yet the 1925 election was the last one in which the Wisconsin Germans voted in sizable numbers for the Progressives. Their support of the Progressives declined in 1928, became negative in 1930, inconsistent during the early thirties, and negative again towards the close of the decade.

The major religious affiliations among voters of German and Scandinavian heritage reinforced trends in the political behavior of Wisconsin. Of the various denominations with ethnic ties, the Lutherans were particularly important. Although committed to the separation of church and state, the Lutheran synods predominating in Wisconsin had organized largely along lines of national origin. Patterns of voting among Lutherans therefore bore a strong relationship to patterns of voting among immigrants and their descendants. Exerting an influence beyond that of the individual synods were three associations established to promote co-operation among independent Lutheran bodies.

The three inter-synodical associations were the National Lutheran Council (NLC), the American Lutheran Conference (ALC), and the Lutheran Synodical Conference (LSC). The National Lutheran Council represented some German Lutherans, but officers of the council came from the Norwegian Lutheran Church and the General Synod, which had always opposed what it regarded as the rigidity of the German synods. The American Lutheran Conference was a smaller group, and though not formally organized until 1930, it grew out of discussions carried on in the mid-twenties by the Swedish Lutherans of the Augustana Synod, the Norwegian Lutheran Church in America, the United Danish Evangelical Lutheran Church, and the Lutheran Free Church (which emphasized congregational independence). The third group, the Lutheran Synodical Conference, was theologically the most traditional of the Lutheran associations; it was also the one most strongly identified with the synods of Wisconsin, Missouri, and other states that attracted a sizable number of immigrants from Germany.[55]

In general, Lutherans affiliated with the American Lutheran Conference tended to follow the pattern of Norwegian voters in Wisconsin. That is, they supported the La Follettes with greater consistency than did other Lutheran associations. Voters affiliated with the Lutheran Synodical Conference, the most Germanic of the three Lutheran associations, tended to cast their ballots much as did other Germans. In other words, Wisconsin Lutherans associated with the LSC were inclined to support Old Bob La Follette during the postwar period, but after 1925 they tended to move back towards a Stalwart position. Lutherans affiliated with the National Lutheran Council, coming from diversified backgrounds, were more ambivalent in their response to the La Follettes than were affiliates of the other two associations. Yet the voting behavior of Lutherans associated with the NLC was closer to that of Norwegians than to that of Germans.

Despite the efforts of Americanizers during the Great War and the New Era, analysis of the La Follette elections suggests the continuing importance of ethnic associations during the years between the two world wars. After the arrival of the Great Depression, to be sure, agricultural productivity became an important determinant of the Progressive vote. Yet even then the La Follettes and their Progressive followers were justified in considering the Norwegian voters their most reliable supporters. In part because those loyal Norwegians constituted a significant proportion of the electorate in the hinterland, the Wisconsin Progressives tended to shape their

[55] E. Clifford Nelson, ed., *The Lutherans in North America* (Philadelphia, 1975), 247–251, 380–382, 399–400, 403–404, 443–445.

programs with a view towards meeting needs of the state's rural areas.

Nevertheless, during the troubled years of the Great Depression, many Progressives began to question the continued suitability of a rural orientation. Cities were expanding, and critics of the La Follettes sometimes argued that prosperity depended more on urban industry than on agriculture. This was a point the state's manufacturers had attempted to make in the debates over taxation during the 1920's, and the argument gained credibility after 1929. With the arrival of the Great Depression, the La Follettes themselves were to seek solutions for economic problems that affected urban as well as rural areas. The remaining chapters of this volume deal with the coming of hard times and with efforts to restore prosperity in Wisconsin.

PART III

The Great Depression

WITH the stock market crash of 1929, a creative period of economic growth and prosperity came to an end. In Wisconsin, as elsewhere, the attention of citizens turned to devising means of surviving the worst depression in the nation's history. So harsh did conditions become that old formulas for prosperity seemed effective neither in meeting the economic emergency nor in establishing a basis for the return of good times. Under the leadership of Robert M. La Follette's sons, Wisconsin Progressives committed themselves to the development of new programs in response to new needs. Even before the coming of the New Deal, the Wisconsin legislature passed a measure to provide unemployment compensation for workers who lost their jobs. As governor, Phil La Follette exerted a major influence in securing relief legislation, and in his three gubernatorial terms during the 1930's, he worked incessantly to restore prosperity.

Attempts to overcome the economic stagnation took place in an atmosphere of acute social tension. In 1933, violence broke out in several Wisconsin counties as embattled farmers sought to halt the delivery of milk until they received better prices. In industrial plants of the state, workers renewed organizational efforts quiescent during the twenties, and labor organizers began to anticipate an increase in union influence. In Milwaukee, the number of strikes increased sevenfold in 1933–1934.

Clearly, a national calamity as serious as the Great Depression called for a national recovery program. The New Deal, formulated in a flurry of frenzied activity after Franklin D. Roosevelt took office as President in 1933, provided programs that won overwhelming support from the American people. Throughout FDR's first term, the President and the Wisconsin Progressives worked harmoniously in tandem. Some of the La Follette followers— notably Edwin Witte and Arthur Altmeyer—contributed greatly to the New Deal's program of Social Security. And programs developed under Progressive auspices in Wisconsin usually received favorable treatment from New Deal agencies in Washington.

Still, the relationship between the Wisconsin Progressives and the New Dealers did not lead to a melding of forces within either party. The Wisconsin Democrats constituted by-and-large the most conservative political organization in the state. The Progressives of the thirties could no more think of moving into the Democratic party than Roosevelt could consider associating himself with a Progressive coalition. Aspiring to national leadership, Phil La Follette in the end saw no alternative to forming a new party, the National Progressives of America.

The governor began his move for national power in 1938, a year of mounting international tension. Economic difficulties of the 1930's decade were confined neither to Wisconsin nor even to the United States. The Great Depression had a devastating effect throughout the world, and the crisis exacerbated problems in other countries. The Depression became a global concern, and as nations of the world experimented with new theories and formulas, international peace again became tenuous. Fascist control of Italy, National Socialist control of Germany, and Communist control of the Soviet Union all influenced the way Americans thought about national economic difficulties. Citizens of Wisconsin did not live in a vacuum, and their awareness of international affairs shaped the way they dealt with affairs at home.

9

The Challenge of Economic Depression

IN the fall of 1927, the Milwaukee Federated Trades Council (FTC) debated a resolution to promote public works projects for the employment of workers who had lost their jobs. Economic conditions in Wisconsin were reasonably good at the time, and few people were taking precautions either to avert a depression or to cope with a depression should it come. Yet the general secretary of the council, Frank J. Weber, read alarming handwriting on the wall as he spoke in favor of the FTC resolution. Conceding that jobs would be plentiful until after the 1928 presidential election, he predicted that unemployment would become a problem towards the end of 1929 and then become "quite severe" for a two-year period. In 1931–1932, he believed, a few factories would again commence operations. "Prosperity has returned" would become the slogan of the political party in power, but the factories would be running with fewer workers than before. In Weber's vision, the unemployed would be "walking the highways and biways [*sic*] seeking work but finding none." The labor leader saw little hope that conditions for the workers would improve "as long as the people permit this system of private profits to rule us like despots."[1]

In the spring of 1929, after Herbert Hoover had moved into the White House, Reedsburg attorney James A. Stone wrote his congressman as if to verify Weber's predictions. Having just learned that his neighbor had been laid off his job at the woolen mill, Stone admitted to "getting quite disturbed over conditions" in Wisconsin. The employees who remained at the mill were working half time at a 10 per cent reduction in wages, and inasmuch as Reedsburg had no other industries worth mentioning, the possibility of finding

[1] The December 19, 1930, *Union Laborer* of Marinette cites Weber's prescient 1927 forecast.

another job was illusory. While the situation in Sauk County was "not conducive to a happy outlook," other parts of the state seemed to be faring no better. Stone reported that over in Kenosha the Nash Motors Company had just dismissed 800 employees, and that conditions in Racine resembled those in Kenosha. Despite all the indications of impending hard times, Stone remarked bitterly, the newspapers continued to reiterate their cry of "Prosperity, prosperity!"[2]

The newspapers were not alone in repeating incantations that had resounded throughout the New Era. Merle Thorpe, editor of *Nation's Business,* addressed the Milwaukee Association of Industrial Advertisers at the Hotel Schroeder on the evening of October 9, 1929. The alternating cycle of depression and prosperity in America was a thing of the past, he informed his audience. Business had become so flexible, and commercial innovation so frequent, that the nation simply did not have the time for a period of depression. Thorpe confidently predicted that throughout the autumn American business would continue to progress.[3]

A few days after the industrial advertisers listened to Thorpe's reassuring remarks, the First Wisconsin National Bank's monthly *Business and Financial Comment* presented a more realistic assessment of the business outlook for the last quarter of 1929. Iron and steel production had decreased moderately, noted the newsletter, and automobile output was lagging more than it should. There were "plain indications that long-continued tensions in the money market" had brought about a severe setback in building construction financed with borrowed money. A decline in foreign borrowings could mean reduced sale of American wheat in England and other wheat-importing countries. High interest rates were also creating "a weak technical situation in the stock market itself." The rapid rise in brokers' loans, which coincided with indications of a business recession, had clearly made for uneasiness on Wall Street. Yet *Business and Financial Comment* also reported a bright side to current conditions. After all, it was "a healthy thing that there should be a slowing down in certain over-expanded lines of business and even more desirable that there should be some moderation introduced into the speculative situation." Whistling a happy tune

[2] James A. Stone to Merlin Hull, May 16, 1929, in the James A. Stone Papers.
[3] Milwaukee *Journal,* October 10, 1929.

as the nation's economy sped towards disaster, the blithe spirits writing for *Business and Financial Comment* assured their readers that "it is hardly probable that either business recession or stock market liquidation will go to any serious lengths."[4]

Business people and investors had scarcely had an opportunity to digest the First Wisconsin's confident report on the economic outlook when they confronted the much more difficult task of explaining the extraordinary stock market collapse of October 24, 1929. On that "Black Thursday" nearly thirteen million shares traded hands, the ticker ran four hours behind the frenzied trading activity, and prices dropped precipitously. The Crash proved to be more devastating than even the gloomiest of the Jeremiahs had anticipated, and bad as it was, the worst was yet to come. Despite strenuous efforts of bankers and financiers to support prices, and despite the appearance of a rally in the first months of 1930, the market quickly fell back into a dismal trough. By the summer of 1932, stock prices were 72 per cent below the lowest levels of 1929.[5]

Whatever the precise relationship between the market decline on Wall Street and the economic distress soon to become evident on the Main Streets of Wisconsin, the Great Depression of the 1930's became the cardinal preoccupation of the state's residents. It was a preoccupation they shared with the residents of other states, of course, and like the Great War, the Great Depression had the effect of forcing attention on national affairs. While Wisconsin citizens often took pride in their ability to cope with hard times, none of them doubted that recovery was necessarily a national undertaking. Having witnessed an increase in the exercise of power by the federal government during the war, the people of Wisconsin joined those of other states to demand nationwide solutions. Still, not many believed the government in Washington fully competent to resolve all problems. Their experience during the war perhaps made them wary of nationalist solutions at the same time that they recognized the Depression as a national problem. Thus the decade of the thirties was one in which the state's people felt themselves drawn in

[4] *Business and Financial Comment*, October 15, 1929, in the Milwaukee Public Library.

[5] Lester V. Chandler, *America's Greatest Depression, 1929–1941* (New York, 1970), 18–19; John Kenneth Galbraith, *The Great Crash, 1929* (Boston, 1955), 103–118; George H. Soule, *Prosperity Decade: From War to Depression, 1917–1929* (New York, 1947), 306–311.

two directions. Sometimes they called for federal aid to counteract economic deprivation; at other times they recalled Wisconsin's distinctive accomplishments in the past and proudly offered the Wisconsin experience as a guide to survival and recovery.

The complex relationship between the New Deal and Wisconsin Progressivism provides a leitmotiv for the history of the state during the Great Depression, but the theme had begun to resonate even before there was a New Deal. While Hoover still occupied the White House, the Roosevelt administration in New York state and the La Follette administration in Wisconsin were both attempting to counter the calamitous consequences of depression. The manner in which FDR responded to economic disaster helped prepare the way for his presidential candidacy and subsequent election. In Wisconsin, the Progressives' reaction to adversity helped to increase popular acceptance of the New Deal. In contributing to a political realignment in the state, the Progressives were moving towards independent political action, towards the formation of a new party, and towards the ultimate migration of the younger leaders into the Democratic party.

* * *

The stock market crash that in retrospect became a symbol for the onset of the worst economic depression in American history seemed at the time to be a matter of serious but not devastating proportions. After Black Thursday, the editor of the Appleton *Post-Crescent* acknowledged that the frenzied trading activity "might come the nearest to a financial panic the country has experienced since the inauguration of the Federal Reserve system." Yet the perhaps instinctive reaction in financial circles was to look on the bright side of the stock market debacle. "No buildings have burned down, no industries have died, no mines, railroads, steel plants have vanished," soothed Arthur Brisbane in his syndicated column, and other journalists joined in the effort to allay popular anxieties. The Antigo *Daily Journal* predicted that "thanks to the Federal Reserve system and the fundamental soundness of the country's business structure there will be no panic," and it asserted that "there should be no confusing of Wall Street with 'Main Street.' " After sounding an initial alarm, the Appleton *Post-Crescent* sought to correct whatever misconceptions it might have encouraged. It quickly took the position that many Americans, "not only on Wall and Broad streets, but on Main Street" as well, were wrong in assuming that American prosperity depended on the vagaries of the stock exchange. The profits of speculators, suggested the *Post-Crescent*, had as little to do with the nation's real prosperity as did bridge game winnings. "After a card game, there is just as much money in the room as there was before," ran the argument. "It is merely distributed differently. It is the same with operations on the stock exchange."[6]

On Capitol Square and in downtown Madison, business people responded calmly to the furor on Wall Street that October. Realtor Stanley C. Hanks thought the most important lesson it taught was that investments should be made in real estate rather than in stocks and bonds. T. R. Hefty, president of the First National Bank-Central Wisconsin Trust Company, believed that while drastic readjustment was unfortunate, "it will bring the public back to legitimate lines of investments, instead of gambling." Harry S. Manchester was confident that his department store would not be harmed even though "the whole country has gone stark crazy over stocks." Leo T. Crowley, president of the State Bank of Wisconsin, thought that "this decline is merely a natural reaction to the speculative buying that has prevailed," and that "the market will right itself" and "people buying for investment will be able to go in on a sound basis." L. L. Pidcoe of Burdick and Murray, a dry goods and women's ready-to-wear company, saw "nothing wrong with business conditions," and though "some people's knees may be knocking together now," he was certain that they would "straighten up." A. O. Paunack, president of the Commercial National Bank, and H. L. Garner, secretary of the Anchor Building, Savings, and Loan Association, believed that after the wave of speculation a "general cleaning up of the market was necessary to get things back to a sound basis."[7]

Again and again during the first few weeks after the market debacle in October, Wisconsin newspaper editors parroted the economic opinions of Main Street in a monotonous refrain. Too many people, reiterated the newsmen, had risked too much in hopes of making a killing. While speculators had lost heavily with the collapse

[6] Appleton *Post-Crescent*, October 25, 28, 1929; Milwaukee *Journal*, October 28, 1929; Arthur Brisbane, "Today," in the Madison *Capital Times*, October 26, 1929; Antigo *Daily Journal*, October 30, 1929.

[7] *Capital Times*, October 29, 1929. The unanimity of Madison business people seemed almost to persuade editor William T. Evjue himself. The day after publishing these interviews, the *Capital Times* (October 30, 1929) printed an editorial under the heading, "The Stock Market Convulsion a Good Thing."

of the boom, their get-rich-quick schemes had never had much chance anyway. In the meantime, the consensus interpretation of market behavior held that real investment would not be jeopardized by what had taken place. Indeed, the Crash would prove a good thing in the long run because it had purged the stock exchange of speculators who knew little of what they were about. Now, directed by cooler and wiser heads, the market was in a position to carry on normal activity.[8]

Variations on the standard initial explanation of the Crash added little to economic understanding, but concentrated instead on the psychology of speculation and the irrationality of speculators. "The speculative world does not pause to reflect, nor are its actions governed by sober thought," was the editorial opinion of the Racine *Journal-News.* "It will be impossible to prevent the blowing of speculative soap bubbles," argued the Beloit *Daily News,* "so long as people see other people apparently making 'easy money' out of speculation." Elaborating on the consequences of mass hysteria, the editor regarded the Crash as "a thumping rebuke to speculative mania." In summarizing the causes of the catastrophe, *Business and Financial Comment* emphasized in November, 1929, that "the market had been nervous and irregular for some time." Then, in going to excess "both in point of prices and volume of credit," and in attracting "many people of little experience," it became susceptible to the psychology of fear.[9]

The self-serving analyses of amateur psychologists on both Wall Street and Main Street could be misleading. When people thought the Crash only a psychological phenomenon, they could too readily accept assurances that the business of the country remained sound and required application of no economic correctives. The La Crosse *Tribune,* for example, emphasized the "largely psychological" nature of Wall Street behavior and argued that there was no economic justification for "either a business panic or a business depression." In fact, according to the *Tribune*'s editorial writer, the economy stood to gain from what had happened because there was certain

[8] Janesville *Gazette,* October 25, 1929; Marshfield *News-Herald,* October 26, 1929; Beloit *Daily News,* October 27, 1929; Merrill *Daily Herald,* October 29, 1929; Antigo *Daily Journal,* November 7, 1929; *Business and Financial Comment,* November 15, December 16, 1929, in the Milwaukee Public Library; *Capital Times,* December 17, 1929.

[9] Racine *Journal-News,* October 30, 1929; Beloit *Daily News,* November 15, 1929; *Business and Financial Comment,* November 15, 1929, in the Milwaukee Public Library.

to be a "diversion of cash reserves from speculative to sound industrial and commercial development." Neither in La Crosse, nor in Wisconsin, nor in the entire nation, ran the argument, could anyone find a person of standing or substance "who does not see in the immediate future a substantial benefit to society and business in this deflation of a balloon that could soar only because it carried no substantial weight of earned revenue or permanent responsibility."[10]

Other newspapers of the state published similar analyses. The Beloit *Daily News* deplored the effects of the Crash on "innumerable pocketbooks," but it believed that in broad perspective the decline in stock prices would "come as a stimulus rather than as a damper." The *Daily News* editor thought that "capital that has been absorbed in speculation will flow back in large quantities into productive channels." Arguing that "no legitimate business" had suffered serious damage, the Racine *Journal-News* discerned a solid basis for recovery. Echoing Arthur Brisbane's optimism, the paper emphasized that railroads continued to run, industrial concerns were carrying on, and public service corporations maintained their operations in the public interest. Contemplating the promise of economic growth, the *Journal-News* analyst apparently became so excited by the possibilities that he lost all control over his imagery: "the entire fabric of business is only somewhat shaken by the rustle of stock markets as a cooling wind fans the heated brow." The clarity if not the substance of an assessment in *Business and Financial Comment* inspired more confidence. "Nearly always before a recession gets far along," the newsletter assured its readers, "constructive factors assert themselves." The obvious response to the market activity of 1929, then, was to sit tight and wait for the economy to right itself.[11]

While most citizens of Wisconsin were willing at first to follow the advice of experts, the state was never without its skeptics. The Superior *Evening Telegram* was caustic in its assessment of "our financial and industrial overlords," who seemed so relieved to find that small investors had been wiped out. "One high commentator says that the market got out of kilter because the small investor persisted in putting in his money," noted the *Evening Telegram*. Another blamed the small investor because he suddenly stopped

[10] La Crosse *Tribune and Leader Press*, October 31, 1929.

[11] Beloit *Daily News*, November 15, 1929; Racine *Journal-News*, November 12, 1929; *Business and Financial Comment*, November 15, 1929, in the Milwaukee Public Library.

buying. "It was reprehensible for the little fellow to start and it was reprehensible for him to stop. He caused trouble both ways." If one listened to such pronouncements, suggested the editorial, one could only conclude that standards for little fellows were different from the standards for millionaires. When the "big fellow" buys a thousand shares of U.S. Steel, "he is investing, he is helping to maintain the flow of credit and financial support that sustain our prosperity," but when a shoe salesman buys fifty shares "he is gambling, and his activities hurt the market, discommode business and lower the moral tone of the nation." Such reasoning, though typical "of the fuzzy way in which our mental processes always seem to work where Wall Street is involved," struck the editor as "harder to understand than the stock market crash itself."[12]

* * *

While critics took a somber view of the future, a steady economic decline in Wisconsin and in the nation justified their pessimism. After Phil La Follette became governor in 1931, each day's mail brought letters commenting on the economic crisis in the state. Taken together, they convey an impression of discomfiture, distress, and even desperation. Pleading deliverance, some correspondents solicited aid; others offered suggestions for overcoming persistent economic tribulation. "It seems that there never was a time when it required as much effort to do business as at the present time," wrote auto maker Charles W. Nash early in 1931. Troubled by the way economic conditions were affecting his work force and eroding profits, Nash was persuaded that "every employer's effort should be put in the direction of furnishing more employment." To that end, his firm made plans to produce parts ready for assembly into automobiles. By increasing his parts inventory, Nash could maintain employment and at the same time prepare for a return to full production. In the fall of 1931, with the nation still languishing in financial and commercial doldrums, Janesville pen manufacturer George S. Parker informed the governor that his firm was $66,000 in the red, "a condition that has never before confronted this company in its entire history." He had already cut expenses and salaries, even to the extent of reducing his own salary by 40 per cent. Yet with no end to hard times in sight, Parker was inclined to favor a

[12] Superior *Evening Telegram*, November 8, 1929.

surtax on incomes of $2,000 or more to be used for unemployment relief. After all, "people who have employment are so much better off than those that have no employment that they ought to contribute to an extent for those not so fortunate."[13]

The communications from Nash, Parker, and many others suggest that by 1931 the seriousness of the Depression was becoming apparent to all. At the opening of the year, in fact, *Bankshares Review* provided its readers with a summary of the damages inflicted on Wisconsin's economy after the Crash on Wall Street. From August, 1929, to November, 1930, employment in manufacturing industries fell by almost a fourth, and payrolls declined 37 per cent. During August, 1929, every hundred jobs available in the state had attracted 117 applicants; in October, 1930, employers received 178 applications for every hundred job openings. After recovery from the 1921 recession, employment in Wisconsin industry had leveled off at approximately 248,000 workers until 1929, when New Era prosperity provided jobs for 265,000 of them. Then, following the Crash, the number of wage earners declined to 184,000 in 1931, and to 159,000 by 1933.[14]

Terrifying increases in the rate of unemployment across the country came as aftershocks of devastation in the nation's industrial plants, especially in those producing durable goods. Personal consumption of durable goods, at current prices, declined from $9.2 billion in 1929 to $3.5 billion in 1933, while domestic investment in producers' durable equipment went from $5.9 billion to $1.6 billion. Investment in new residential nonfarm construction declined from $3.6 billion in 1929 to $0.5 billion in 1933. National income in current prices fell from $87.8 billion to $40.2 billion, and the gross national product from $104.4 billion to $56 billion.[15]

In Wisconsin, reported *Bankshares Review*, the industries hardest hit were metalworking, machinery, automobile, and lumber and wood-products industries. New automobile and truck registrations in Wisconsin declined from 118,397 in 1929 to only 30,039 in

[13] Nash to La Follette, January 5, 1931, and Parker to La Follette, June 8, October 6, 1931, all in the Philip F. La Follette Papers.

[14] *Bankshares Review*, January 20, 1931, in the Milwaukee Public Library; *Fifteenth Census of the United States, 1930: Manufactures, 1929, Volume III*, 561; U.S. Bureau of the Census, *Biennial Census of Manufactures, 1931*, pp. 20–21.

[15] U.S. Bureau of the Census, *Historical Statistics of the United States: Colonial Times to 1957* (1960), which also appears as *House Documents*, 86 Cong., 1 sess., no. 33 (serial 12216), 139–142.

1932. In 1930, total building and construction contracts were but 13.4 per cent lower in value than in the previous year. In 1931, however, total construction contracts amounted to only $76,036,400, a decrease of 46 per cent compared with 1929. Value added by manufacture, a broader and more revealing measure of problems in nearly all Wisconsin factories, declined from $950 million in 1929 to $530 million in 1931. Continuing the downward trend without a reversal, the state's value added fell to $370 million in 1933. In the Milwaukee industrial area, which included Kenosha and Racine counties as well as Milwaukee County, the value added went from $550.3 million in 1929 to $295 million in 1935.[16]

The manufacturers of Wisconsin and the workers employed in the factories of the state were not alone in experiencing economic difficulties after 1929. At the time of the Crash, nearly half of the state's total population of 2,939,000 people lived in rural areas, and a fourth of the state's work force was engaged in agricultural pursuits. In surveying the impact of hard times on farmers in 1930, *Bankshares Review* noted that about 85 per cent of Wisconsin's gross farm income derived from livestock. Taking a characteristically optimistic view of the agricultural situation, the review pointed out that because income from livestock products had declined less than other farm income, Wisconsin farmers were better off than farmers in other regions of the country. The newsletter estimated that gross farm income for the year would be about $61 million less than during the previous year—a severe cutback in agricultural income, to be sure. Even so, *Bankshares Review* proved unduly sanguine. As it turned out, the gross farm income of Wisconsin fell from $438 million in 1929 to $357 million in 1930, and eventually to a low of $186 million in 1932.[17]

In the meantime, Wisconsin farmers confronted a cluster of related problems. Farm prices fell sharply during the early years of

[16] *Bankshares Review*, January 20, 1931, January 20, 1932, and January 20, 1933, in the Milwaukee Public Library; *Fifteenth Census of the United States, 1930: Manufactures, 1929, Volume III*, 561; U.S. Bureau of the Census, *Biennial Census of Manufactures, 1931*, 20; *ibid., 1933*, p. 20; *ibid., 1935*, pp. 20, 39.

[17] *Bankshares Review*, January 20, 1930, in the Milwaukee Public Library; Walter H. Ebling, "Changes in Wisconsin Agriculture Since the Last Census," in the *Wisconsin Blue Book, 1933*, p. 139; Chris L. Christensen, "The Future of Agriculture in Wisconsin," in *ibid., 1937*, p. 156. Except for 1932, the gross farm income of Wisconsin reported by the U.S. Department of Agriculture was higher than the figures used by Ebling. See the U.S. Department of Agriculture, *Yearbook of Agriculture, 1933*, p. 700, and *ibid., 1935*, p. 670.

the Depression as hard-pressed consumers reduced expenses by cutting grocery bills. In 1928 the Wisconsin farm price index had risen to 56 per cent above the prewar level; after the Crash, farm prices declined rapidly, and by 1932 they were more than 30 per cent below the prewar level. To maintain income, farmers were faced with a need to increase production, but expanding output was not always a simple matter. To increase milk production, dairy farmers had either to expand the size of their herds or to increase the production of their cows. Both means of achieving larger quantities of milk meant using a greater quantity of hay and other feed. Unfortunately, the weather was unusually dry in Wisconsin during the early thirties, and unfavorable growing conditions imposed limits on available feed. Thus milk production in the state declined from 1929 to 1933, a time when, in the absence of other controls, falling farm prices required greater production if dairy farmers were to maintain incomes.[18]

Along with falling prices for agricultural products went a decline in the estimated value of agricultural real estate. Having reached a peak average of $69.38 per acre in 1920, the value of all Wisconsin farmland had fallen steadily throughout the New Era. By 1932 the state's farmland had sunk to an estimated average value of $36 an acre. The average value of land and buildings per farm went from $9,526 in 1930 to $6,238 in 1935. Farmers and economists were concerned not only with the decline in land values but

[18] Ebling, "Changes in Wisconsin Agriculture," *Wisconsin Blue Book, 1933*, p. 139; *Bankshares Review*, January 20, 1932, January 20, 1933, in the Milwaukee Public Library; U.S. Department of Agriculture, *Yearbook of Agriculture, 1934*, p. 628. Wisconsin milk production decreased from 11,305 million pounds in 1931 to 10,825 million in 1933, owing to several factors. Cost-conscious consumers tended to use inexpensive substitutes, like oleomargarine, for higher-priced products of Wisconsin agriculture, like butter. On January 23, 1930, the Iron River *Pioneer* argued that the consumption of butter substitutes was a major cause of distress in dairyland Wisconsin.

Rainfall in 1930 and 1932 was less than twenty-six inches in Wisconsin, more than six inches below the annual mean for the state. Although precipitation in 1931 and 1933 was greater, it was still below average. Some areas of the state were, to be sure, more fortunate than others. In 1930 Madison received 29.88 inches of precipitation, a fraction less than the normal amount. Green Bay, on the other hand, received only 16.31 inches in 1930 and 19.61 inches in 1932. See U.S. Department of Agriculture, *Yearbook of Agriculture, 1932*, p. 922; *ibid., 1933*, pp. 742, 746; and *ibid., 1934*, pp. 732–733. To improve the feeding of dairy herds, experts in the University of Wisconsin College of Agriculture urged using lime and phosphates on pasture land. Spreading commercial fertilizer on pastures would increase yield and would also increase the lime and phosphorus required by dairy stock for bone development and milk production. See A. R. Whitson, *Fertilizers for the Dairy Farm*, UW Agricultural Extension Service, *Radio Circular*, November, 1930; and Ebling's *Wisconsin Blue Book, 1933*, article, p. 137.

Changes in Farm Value, 1910–1920

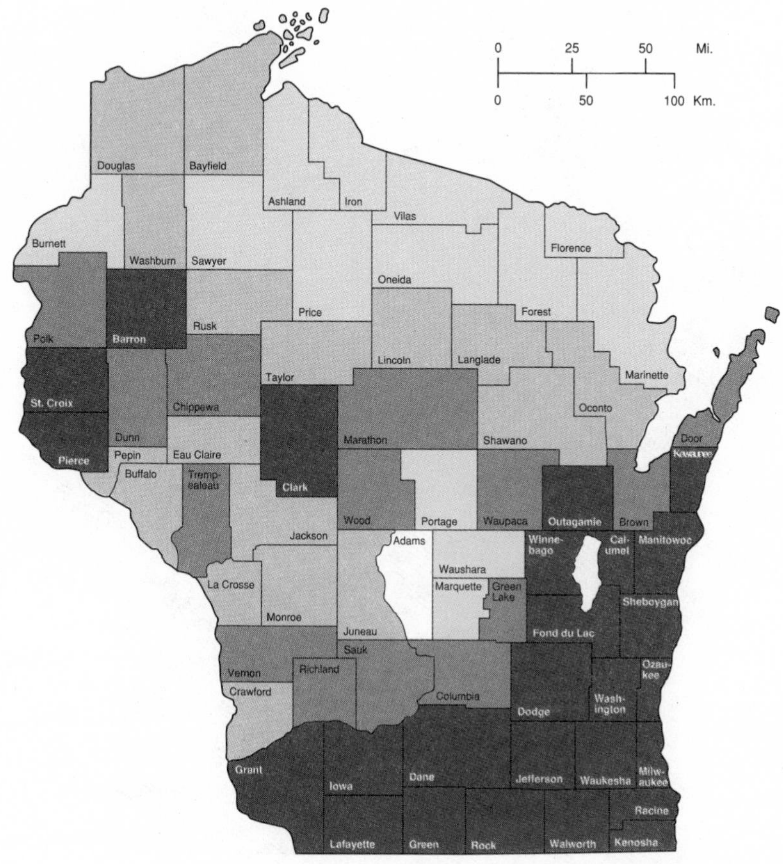

Change in Average Value Per Acre of Farm Land, Buildings, and Implements and Machinery
(In Constant 1926 Dollars)

Larger Increase (Over $125)	Large Increase ($100–$125)	Moderate Increase ($75–$100)	Small Increase ($50–$75)	Smaller Increase (Less than $50)

Changes in Farm Value, 1920–1930

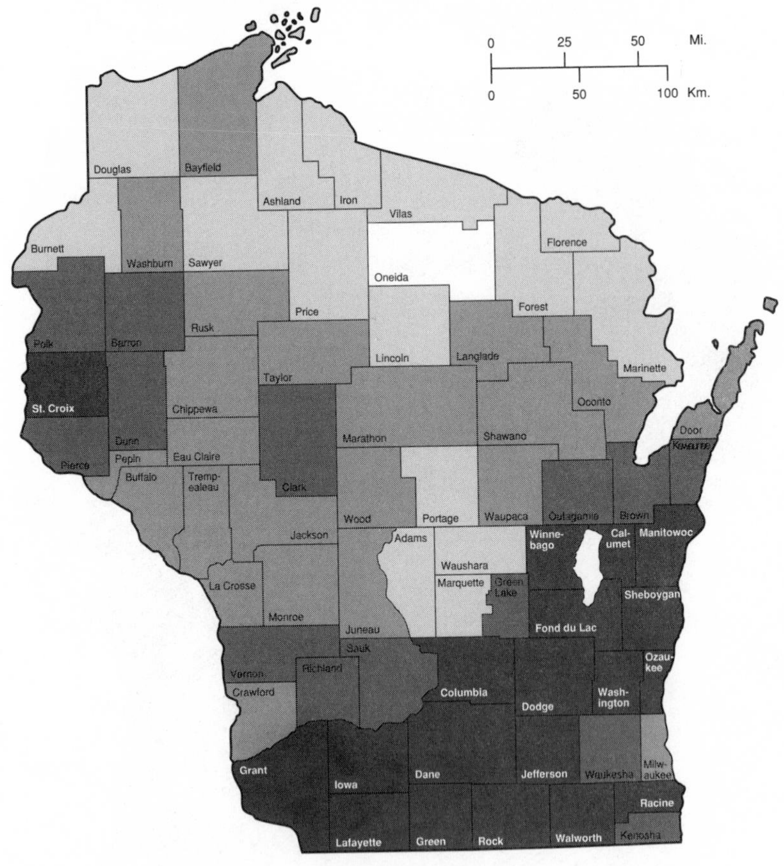

Change in Average Value Per Acre of Farm Land, Buildings, and Implements and Machinery
(In Constant 1926 Dollars)

Larger Decrease (Over $100)
Large Decrease ($75–$100)
Moderate Decrease ($50–$75)
Small Decrease ($25–$50)
Smaller Decrease (Less than $25)

Changes in Farm Value, 1930–1940

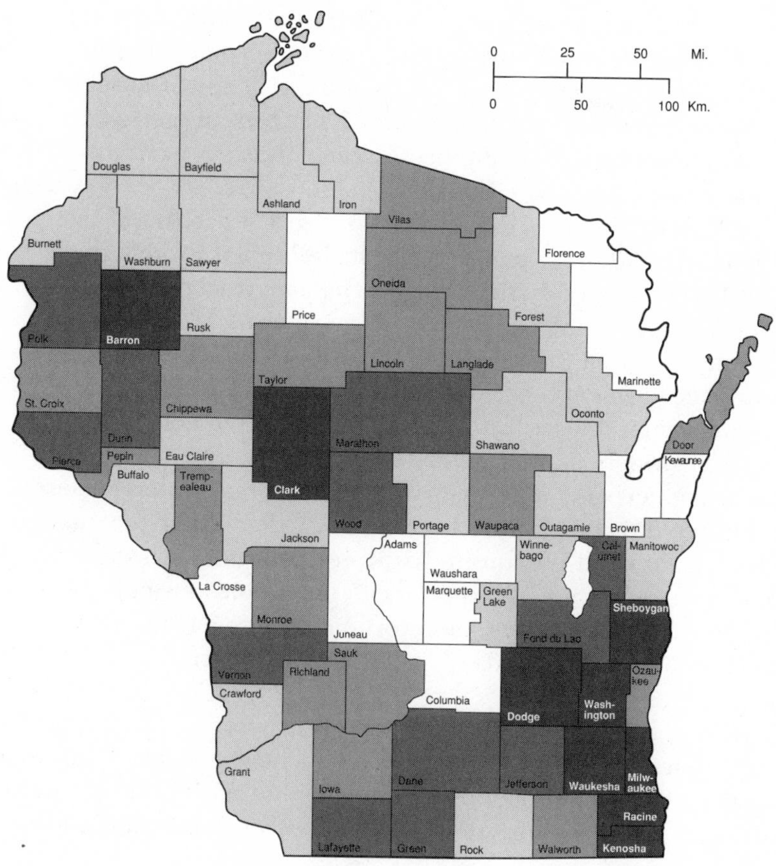

Change in Average Value Per Acre of Farm Land, Buildings, and Implements and Machinery
(In Constant 1926 Dollars)

Larger Decrease (Over $35) | Large Decrease ($30–$35) | Moderate Decrease ($25–$30) | Small Decrease ($20–$25) | Smaller Decrease (Less than $20)

also with the extent to which land was encumbered. According to a survey conducted by John R. Commons, fifty-nine of every hundred Wisconsin farms were mortgaged in 1930. That percentage was not in itself unusual, inasmuch as farmers of the state had always made extensive use of credit facilities; but under duress of hard times, insurance, trust, and mortgage companies, as well as banks, were becoming increasingly wary of loans to farmers.[19]

At the beginning of 1933, about 17 per cent of mortgaged farms in Wisconsin had encumbrances greater than 75 per cent of their value, and it was those farms that were most likely to be lost through foreclosure. The U.S. Department of Agriculture found that from 1925 to 1929 farmer bankruptcies had declined steadily in the East North Central states. Then, in 1933, failures reached the 1925 level, with a farmer bankruptcy rate of more than 13 per cent in the region. Although the record of Wisconsin farmers in meeting their mortgage payments excelled that of neighboring states, the decline in land values and in farm prices brought reductions in the equity of farm owners as well as losses in farm income. "Farmers have been agitated and unsettled as never before," observed farmers' institutes director Ernest L. Luther in describing the mounting concerns of rural Wisconsin. As protest movements began to form, he detected "an air of expectancy" that could portend social disruption if "foreclosures, moratoriums, tax relief, milk strike possibilities and 'farm holidays' " diverted attention away from "constructive enterprises."[20]

During the years after 1929, with nearly everyone experiencing hard times, no escape from distress seemed possible. Those who sought relief in the nation's cities encountered legions of laborers who had lost their jobs or faced curtailed work schedules. Most of

[19] U.S. Department of Agriculture, *Yearbook of Agriculture, 1934*, p. 276; *Bankshares Review*, January 20, 1932, in the Milwaukee Public Library; "Here's Badger Farm Credit Situation," UW, *Press Bulletin*, March 9, 1933, clipping in LRB; "Farm Credit in Wisconsin" (typewritten), ca. 1936, in box 6, Wisconsin Council of Agriculture Papers; John R. Commons, "Statistical Survey of an Economic Survey of Wisconsin, 1931–1932" (mimeographed), in the John R. Commons Papers; Oswald H. Brownlee, "State Farm Credit in Wisconsin" (master's thesis, University of Wisconsin, 1939), 2–4.

[20] *Bankshares Review*, January 20, 1933, in the Milwaukee Public Library; U.S. Department of Agriculture, *Yearbook of Agriculture, 1934*, p. 5; John D. Black, "The Agricultural Situation, January, 1933," in the *Review of Economic Statistics*, 15 (February 15, 1933), 34; U.S. Department of Agriculture, *Agricultural Statistics*, 1936, p. 354; "Annual Report of the Department of Farmers' Institutes, 1932–1933," in the E. L. Luther Papers; *Waupaca County Post* (Waupaca), November 19, 1931.

the unemployed were far from lazy; many, in fact, were obsessed with the need to find "constructive enterprise." It was that very need, along with Wisconsin's reputation for relative prosperity even in hard times, that quickly attracted job seekers to the state. Lucina G. Irish, executive secretary of the Milwaukee Travelers' Aid Society, noted that as early as mid-November of 1929 her agency had in one week received fifty frantic petitions for employment. "We heard there was a lot of work to be had in Milwaukee," ran a common refrain of the petitioners.[21]

Wisconsin, of course, could not provide jobs for all who sought them. "The unemployment situation is very bad here," wrote John J. Handley, secretary-treasurer of the Wisconsin State Federation of Labor to his counterpart in Iowa. In Milwaukee alone, he estimated, 20,000 unemployed were looking for work by March, 1930. The Milwaukee Family Welfare Association and other eleemosynary agencies were hard-pressed to provide assistance, and the unemployed often became desperate. Some of the jobless pawned what possessions they could, but by the end of the year 1930 many of them had nothing more to pawn. "People think we have good business, now," reported the owner of a Milwaukee buy-and-sell shop. "They think that many come here, hock stuff, and then can't get it back. But working people ain't got nothing to hock anymore." Early in 1930 police arrested a father of six for stealing four loaves of bread from a grocery store.[22]

Because of university and state government payrolls, Madison was more fortunate than most of the towns and cities of Wisconsin. In December, 1930, the *Capital Times* pointed out that state treasurer Sol Levitan was paying $300,000 monthly in salaries and wages to 2,200 state employees, most of whom lived in Madison. "You don't know what the depression is," a chain-store executive told editor William T. Evjue. "You should see the situation in such factory

[21] Press release issued by Roy Empey, state director of employment, May 21, 1931, in the Philip F. La Follette Papers; Milwaukee *Leader*, November 21, 1931.

[22] Handley to Michael E. Sherman, March 14, 1930, in the Wisconsin State Federation of Labor Papers; Milwaukee *Journal*, January 15, 1930; Milwaukee *Leader*, November 14, 1930. With thousands of Wisconsin families denied the opportunity to earn a living, the federation in a meeting on January 3, 1930, urged that the state at least keep accurate records of unemployment, records that were as important as reports on the production of cattle and other livestock. Speaking in favor of establishing a shelter for the unemployed in Milwaukee, William Flamm of the Molders' Union told the Milwaukee Federated Trades Council that unemployment was becoming more and more unbearable. Milwaukee *Leader*, March 6, 1930.

towns as Akron and Ft. Wayne." Yet even in Madison the unemployment rate had risen to 16 per cent, near the national average, during the year ending April 1, 1931. Out of a work force of 21,698 men and women, 3,466 were unemployed. In discussing the plight of 195 families that had applied for municipal welfare aid, labor leader William L. Forrest argued that only the most extreme need drove breadwinners to accept public charity.[23]

Reports of people barely scratching out a subsistence came from all parts of the state, and they provided only a hint of the magnitude of the disaster that had paralyzed Wisconsin. In La Crosse a citizens' survey of a hundred families revealed that twenty-three of them earned far less than $1,499.88, the average annual income of those surveyed. Through intermittent employment, twelve of the most destitute earned but $200. The Iron River *Pioneer* found that in northern forested areas a surprising number of "shackers" had taken to the woods after losing their jobs. Building shanties for themselves, they had laid in whatever supplies they could afford, and with some hunting and trapping they expected to survive the cold winter months.[24]

A life in the wilds of northern Wisconsin, however rational an alternative it may have been for some of the unemployed, was neither attractive nor possible for most of the destitute. "I am a laboring man through and through," a Kenosha worker told the Wisconsin Legislative Interim Committee on Unemployment in 1931. "I raised a family of nine children. Two of them are working a half day a week over to Nash Motors. And I am about to lose my home. I had it twenty-seven years. Haven't worked for two years. Who is going to [do] anything for me? . . . My children can't help me. They can't even pay their board." What he wanted was "a good law that will protect the laboring man." Like many of his co-workers, he probably never even dreamed of retreating to the north woods.[25]

[23] *Capital Times*, March 20, August 13, December 17, 1930; Kimball Young, John L. Gillin, and Calvert L. Dedrick, *The Madison Community*, UW, *Studies in the Social Sciences and History*, no. 21 (1934), 55.

[24] La Crosse County Community Council and the Wisconsin Conference of Social Work, *The La Crosse Citizens' Survey* (La Crosse, 1930), 19–20; Iron River *Pioneer*, December 10, 1931. In 1932 a group of South Dakota farmers wrote the Wisconsin Department of Agriculture and Markets to ask, "Would your state not donate a tract of land to a good class of farmers in the cutover lands or similar place that could be developed into a good agricultural and dairy section?" See the *Taylor County Star News* (Medford), March 3, 1932.

[25] "Hearing Held by the Wisconsin Legislative Interim Committee on Unemployment, 1931" (typewritten), 2 vols., 2:33, in the Wisconsin State Federation of Labor Papers.

The substance of his dreams was surely as far removed from the rhetoric of Main Street merchants as it was from the lonely self-sufficiency of the shackers in Bayfield County. In the summer of 1930, the *Waupaca County Post* printed an editorial parable that, had he read it, would have been meaningless to the Kenosha workingman. In attempting to approach the ninth green on the Waupaca golf course, the editor had been so intimidated by the hazards along the way that he sank three balls in the Waupaca River. His difficulties on the golf course reminded him of the way the mental hazards of the Depression were sinking the sales of businessmen. Recovery, for him, was a matter of approaching objectives with confidence. "Keep your sunny side up, keep buying, advertise, go after business," he counseled fellow townsmen. "Forget that mental hazard and it will disappear."[26]

Business people in Wisconsin could no longer deny the seriousness of the Depression during the summer after the Crash, but many of them, like the Waupaca editor, continued to insist upon the need for confidence. Wisconsin was "on the upgrade following the pessimism engendered by the stockmarket break of October," Charles W. Nash told dealers and distributors at the annual banquet of the Nash Motors Company in 1930. It took no prompting for businessmen and editors to contribute their own variations on that theme as they strove valiantly to keep their sunny side up. Early that year, *Business and Financial Comment* reported that "the most important thing that happened in January was the re-establishment of confidence." One of the most persistent sounds in the state during the months that followed was the steady drumbeat of optimism hailing the anticipated return of confidence and prosperity.[27]

The great fear haunting Main Street early in the Depression was not a fear that the free market might prove itself unable to restore prosperity. Rather, the great anxiety of many business leaders was that elected officials might become too zealous in promoting their own schemes for recovery and so create a bureaucracy that would

[26] *Waupaca County Post* (Waupaca), August 21, 1930. In a more typical comment, *Bankshares Review* on November 15, 1930 (in the Milwaukee Public Library), emphasized that "the most depressing thing about the depression is the way people lost their perspective."

[27] Milwaukee *Sentinel*, January 17, 1930; *Business and Financial Comment*, February 15, 1930, and *Bankshares Review*, June 15, 1930, both in the Milwaukee Public Library. For other expressions of optimism, see the Kewaunee *Enterprise*, February 14, 1930; Antigo *Daily Journal*, October 2, 25, 1930; Appleton *Post-Crescent*, November 18, 1930; Rhinelander *New North*, January 1, 1931; and *Kickapoo Scout* (Soldiers Grove), August 4, 1931.

serve only to prolong depression. The canny engineer in the White House, businessmen assured themselves, had succeeded in reversing the downturn in the economic cycle by gaining the co-operation of business leaders. Ralph S. Kingsley, publisher of the Kenosha *Evening News* and president of the Wisconsin State Chamber of Commerce, asserted the importance of maintaining the influence of businessmen when he addressed the second annual meeting of the state chamber in 1930. "In all of our deliberations we have consistently followed the policy of discouraging the encroachment by government upon business," he told his audience. "We believe that a policy of self-regulation of business is better than governmental regulation of business." Some businessmen saw their most urgent battle as a fight to maintain autonomy over their own affairs. "If you were to make a list of the legislative mandates of this State you would begin to wonder who was really running your business, the State Government or you," remarked H. W. Story, chairman of the legislative committee of the Milwaukee Association of Commerce (MAC). "When you think of your taxes you might naturally wonder whether you are really working for the State or for yourself."[28]

Lest anyone should think that Wisconsin entrepreneurs were concerned only with lining their own pockets, commercial associations expended great effort to demonstrate civic responsibility. Involvement in community affairs reflected a major premise of the Main Street creed: that business prosperity served the public good. "No community can have cultural progress or community happiness except as the private business within that community succeeds and prospers," asserted Harry B. Hall, retiring president of the Milwaukee Association of Commerce, in 1933. "In the last analysis, the welfare of every man, woman and child in Milwaukee depends on the success of Milwaukee business."[29]

During Hall's term as president, the MAC had considered its first concern to be the adoption and implementation of "*some* tangible

[28] Ralph S. Kingsley, "The Wisconsin State Chamber of Commerce" (typewritten), address to the State Chamber of Commerce, November 24, 1930, in the Wisconsin State Chamber of Commerce Papers. Wisconsin businessmen responded positively to Hoover's countercyclical measures. See *Business and Financial Comment*, February 15, 1930, and *Bankshares Review*, March 21, 1932, both in the Milwaukee Public Library; and Merrill *Daily Herald*, January 6, 1930. Story's remarks appear in the Milwaukee Association of Commerce, *Milwaukee Commerce*, March 12, 1931, p. 1.

[29] Harry B. Hall, "Fare of Community and Individual Depend on Commerce and Industry," in Milwaukee Association of Commerce, *Milwaukee Commerce*, February 16, 1933, pp. 2–3.

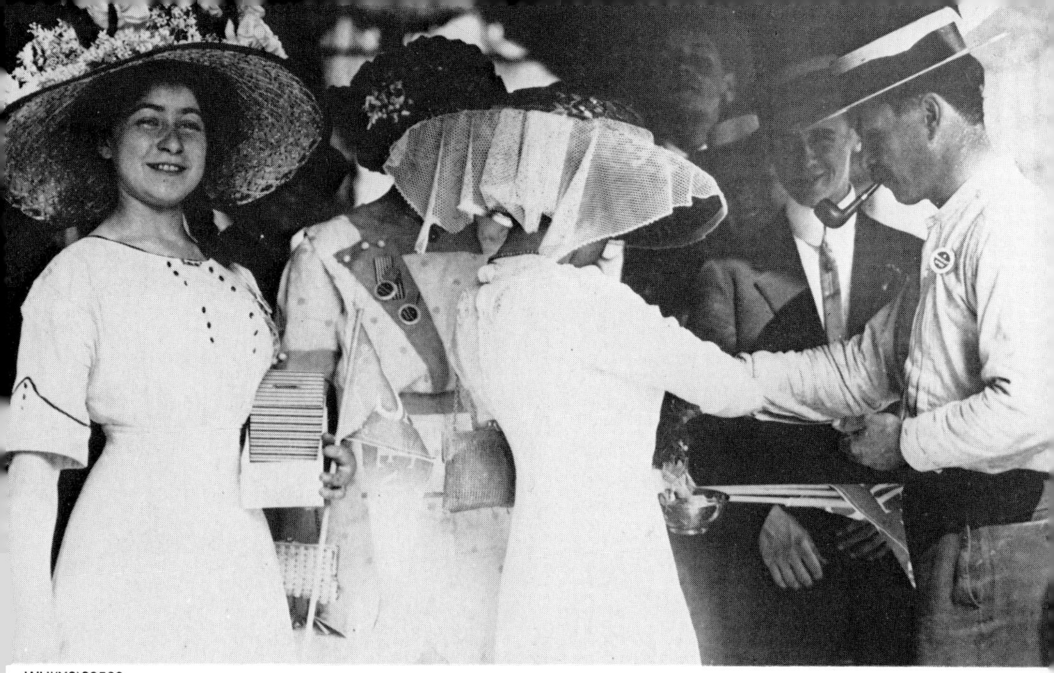

WHi(X3)29509

ABOVE: Milwaukee suffragists hand out literature on a downtown street, c. 1910.
BELOW: Wisconsin women vote for the first time in a primary election, Racine, 1920.

WHi(X3)2289

RIGHT: Gen. Otto H. Falk of Allis-Chalmers. BELOW: Winding motors and generators at the Allis-Chalmers plant in West Allis, c. 1922.

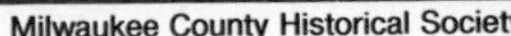

Milwaukee County Historical Society

WHi(W6)1957

WHi(G5)2157

ABOVE: Construction crew on the Wisconsin River bridge at Bridgeport, 1930.
BELOW: Machine operators at the Nash Motors shop in Kenosha, c. 1918.

WHi(X3)15456

WHi(X3)27813

ABOVE: Postal employees march in Milwaukee to demand higher wages, 1919. BELOW: 200 Klansmen attend the funeral of a slain policeman, Madison, 1924.

WHi(X3)31277

Hi(X3)27919

ABOVE: Farmers dump seven carloads of milk on the Soo Line tracks near Burlington, 1934. BELOW: National Guardsmen, sworn in as deputies, rout striking dairy farmers with tear gas and clubs, near Shawano, 1933.

WHi(X3)31243

WHi(X3)10581

ABOVE: Gov. Emanuel Philipp (left) and entourage, 1917. BELOW: George Clarke Sellery (left) and UW president Glenn Frank, c. 1930. RIGHT: Gov. John J. Blaine at the state fair, 1923.

UW Archives

WHi(X3)3127

WHi(X2)14550

ABOVE: Old Bob La Follette at the polls, 1924. BELOW: The La Follette dynasty listening to election returns on the radio, 1924. (Left to right: Isen La Follette; Mrs. John J. Blaine; Phil; Gov. John J. Blaine; Old Bob; Young Bob.)

WHi(X3)18807

WHi(X3)17646

ABOVE: Old Bob La Follette's funeral procession, Madison, 1925. BELOW: Progressive party rally for Young Bob La Follette, Mauston, 1936.

WHi(X3)22749

WHi(D487)24651

ABOVE: Wisconsin senate chamber, 1934. BELOW: State employment service office, Green Bay, c. 1935.

WHi(X3)33734

WHi(X3)33891

ABOVE: Civilian Conservation Corpsmen, Devil's Lake State Park, c. 1936.

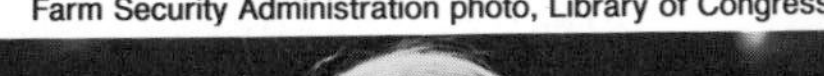
Farm Security Administration photo, Library of Congress

BELOW: Phil La Follette and supporters, c. 1930. RIGHT: Mrs. Hale of rural Black River Falls, 1937. (Her husband and home are pictured opposite.)

WHi(X3)22371

WHi(X3)14584

ABOVE: Distribution of rough fish to the poor at the Winnebago County relief station, 1935. BELOW: The Hale farmstead in Jackson County, 1937.

Farm Security Administration photo, Library of Congress

WHi(X3)45180

ABOVE: Wisconsin Civil Works Administration sewer project, Green Bay, 1934.
BELOW: Another CWA project: renovating the interior of the Lincoln County courthouse, Merrill, 1934.

WHi(X3)22734

WHi(X3)33375

ABOVE: Gov. Phil La Follette signs Wisconsin's pioneer unemployment compensation law, January 28, 1932. (Left to right: Henry Ohl, Jr.; Elizabeth Brandeis; Paul Raushenbush; John R. Commons; the governor; Henry A. Huber; Harold M. Groves; Robert A. Nixon.) BELOW: Neils B. Rudd (left) of Madison receives the first unemployment compensation check issued in Wisconsin. To Rudd's left are Voyta Wrabetz, chairman of the state industrial commission, and professors Edwin E. Witte and John R. Commons.

WHi(X3)43008

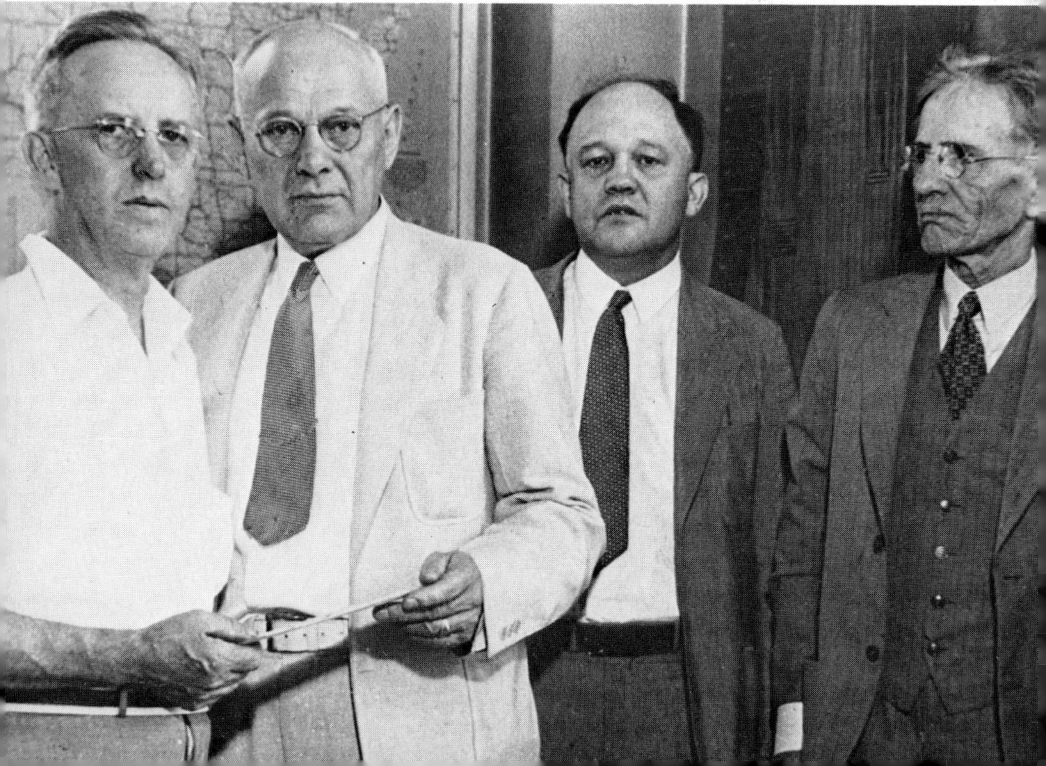

WHi(X3)27389

ABOVE: Prosperous-looking dairy farm near New Glarus, c. 1939. BELOW: County agent consulting with unidentified Wisconsin farm family during the Great Depression.

Farm Security Administration photo, Library of Congress

WHi(C741)2013

ABOVE: Residential street in Whitehall, Trempealeau County, 1936. BELOW: Intersection of North 7th and Galena streets, Milwaukee, c. 1939.

WHi(W821)562

WHi(X3)14473

ABOVE: Phil La Follette delivering his speech at the National Progressives of America rally in the UW Stock Pavilion, 1938. BELOW: Phil La Follette campaigning for governor in the fall of 1938.

WHi(X3)45

program . . . designed specifically to break the almost complete present deadlock between consumption, production and employment and to restore public confidence." The organization urged that businesses first conduct a consumer survey and then a campaign to secure from their customers specific commitments to purchase Milwaukee products. Despite good intentions, however, the MAC plan and others fell short of bringing about added employment, and far short of stimulating enough spending to initiate recovery. Herbert Hoover likewise failed to restore national prosperity, and the persistence of depression called for some explanation. Confusing cause and effect, community leaders across Wisconsin sometimes pointed to the hunger marches and protests that shocked substantial citizens during the early thirties. "The most serious aspect of the unemployment situation," argued the Merrill *Daily Herald* in an editorial that typified the solid citizens' point of view, "is the attacks made on the government by the radical press and radical speakers." The editor thought that "these so-called insurgents . . . have contributed more to the unemployment situation than the collapse of the stock market."[30]

* * *

On the afternoon of February 5, 1930, a group of 400 shabbily dressed men paraded through the streets of Milwaukee to City Hall. They carried a petition they were intent on presenting to Mayor Daniel Hoan on behalf of unemployed workers. Along with other requests, the petition asked for the use of public funds for the jobless, the transfer of funds from the community chest to welfare programs for the destitute, and free food, clothing, shelter, and medical services for the unemployed. When the demonstrators arrived at City Hall, Mayor Hoan told their representatives that he was sorry the city had no money available for relief, and he advised them to apply to the county. In the meantime, the demonstrators outside were blocking traffic. Although they were far from being an unruly mob, police officers dispersed them and herded several to the central police station a block away, where three of them were arrested and jailed. Later in the day, Hoan asked Police Chief Jacob Laubenheimer to release the three. "There is no question that there is a greater unemployment problem facing us now than in several

[30] Milwaukee Association of Commerce, *Milwaukee Commerce*, July 28, 1932, pp. 1–2, November 3, 1932, p. 3; Merrill *Daily Herald*, January 6, March 15, 1930.

years," he observed, adding that "men out of work are likely to make such demonstrations as this."[31]

Three weeks later, a smaller group marched into Madison's City Hall and confronted Mayor Albert G. Schmedeman. Lottie Blumenthal, a member of the Young Communist League, spoke for the unemployed laborers and zealous university students. Responding to her query about what he intended to do for 3,000 jobless workers in Madison, Schmedeman replied that he did not know there were that many. But, he asked, even if there were, "What can I do? . . . What power do you think I have to create work?"[32]

Dissatisfied with official responses to unemployment, the Madison council of the National Trade Union Unity League staged another demonstration the following week. It was March 6, a day the Communists had designated as International Unemployment Day. When the protesters began their march around Capitol Square, they encountered an irate crowd of students who threw Lottie Blumenthal to the pavement, manhandled other radical leaders, destroyed banners and signs demanding work, and seized bundles of radical pamphlets, which they scattered over the streets. The violence resulted in the arrest of five university athletes, who had led the attack. Commenting on events of the day, one of them later remarked that "the United States at large considers the University of Wisconsin an I.W.W. institution, and since there is no way of stopping these half-baked, un-dry behind the ears kids . . . from giving us a bad name, a group of us decided to take the matter in hand." The fundamental ugliness of the melee became even more evident in the remark of another participant: "We are getting so damned many radical Jews here that something must be done."[33]

The press usually characterized such incidents as having been instigated by the Communist party and other radical organizations. The press also tended to exaggerate the influence of the Communist party by associating the Socialists, the Industrial Workers of the World, and other radical groups in what many people perceived as

[31] Milwaukee *Journal*, February 5, 1930; *Capital Times*, February 6, 1930.

[32] *Capital Times*, March 1, 1930.

[33] *Ibid.*, March 6, 7, 1930. For the relationship between the Trade Union Unity League and the Communist party, see Irving Howe and Lewis Coser, *The American Communist Party: A Critical History, 1919–1957* (Boston, 1957), 255–257. The Communist hunger marches and unemployment demonstrations of the early Depression are discussed in Irving Bernstein, *The Lean Years: A History of the American Worker, 1920–1933* (Boston, 1960; reprinted, Jersey City, 1983), 425–435.

a united effort of all organizations on the left. To young Bob La Follette, blaming the demonstrations on radicals and then suggesting that radicals were also responsible for the Depression's severity seemed both inaccurate and illogical. In the senator's opinion, the influence of the Communist party was negligible, and to identify the hunger marches with communism was to do "a great injustice" to millions of Americans who through no fault of their own were out of work.[34]

The best way to reduce the number and violence of demonstrations, suggested the Kewaunee *Enterprise*, was for employers to restore prosperity so that people could go back to work. Other moderates believed, as well, that rhetorical bromides about the need for a restoration of confidence and the importance of courage and character did more harm than good. "Wouldn't it be better if we could hear a little more about the need for brains and unprejudiced study, and a little less about courage and character?" queried the Superior *Evening Telegram*. Presenting similar arguments, the Marshfield *News-Herald* emphasized that it was time to give serious consideration to real conditions. If business leaders did that, they would come to realize that substantiating their leadership required them to work for "an era [when] employment can be stabilized and . . . dire want can be eliminated in proportion to man's willingness to labor."[35]

Knowing that the return of full employment might be far distant, the communities of Wisconsin recognized the immediate importance of providing relief for the needy and as many jobs as they could find for the unemployed. The impulse behind community

[34] Frank Weber was annoyed at the way the Socialist party was thus linked with the Communists, who were in fact enemies of the Socialists. "Are thinking people making any mistake when they reach the conclusion that there is no difference in the agitation program of big business and the Communist party?" he asked. "Both endeavor to destroy the Socialist party, as well as the trade union movement." Michael Sherman to J. J. Handley, February 27, 1930, Wisconsin State Federation of Labor Papers; Milwaukee *Leader*, March 8, 1930. For an incident involving differences of opinion among radical groups, see the Milwaukee *Journal*, February 22, 1930. "The trouble with the American people today," wrote one staunch opponent of communism, "is that they do not know what bolshevism realy [*sic*] is." A. W. Larson to Halbert L. Hoard, December 20, 1932, in the Halbert L. Hoard Papers. Also *Capital Times*, March 3, 1930.

[35] Kewaunee *Enterprise*, August 7, 1931; Superior *Evening Telegram*, December 26, 1930; Marshfield *News-Herald*, December 16, 1930. "For every effort of President Hoover to lighten conditions, we have the fullest sympathy and even applause," noted a Milwaukee *Journal* editorial writer (May 4, 1930) in attacking the President's rhetorical clichés. "But he must not talk nonsense about causes."

welfare and job programs was in part humanitarian. Such programs were also in part a matter of self-interest, a means of preventing the spread of dissatisfaction that could bring social upheaval and even revolution to the state. Thus the community assistance programs that burgeoned in the early 1930's drew support from all groups and classes, irrespective of their economic interests, their political views, or their social concerns. And community effort produced an astonishing variety of programs intended to meet the needs of the time.[36]

During the early months of the Depression, limited funds prevented relief agencies from coping systematically with the problems of massive unemployment. Fortuitously, odd jobs and temporary employment occasionally became available, as they did in Madison when a midwinter blizzard in 1930 provided street-clearing jobs for eighty men. But for the most part, established municipal agencies found themselves unable to respond adequately to the growing number of requests for work. By year's end, 1929, the Milwaukee Welfare Association had overdrawn by more than $6,000 its allowance from the Community Fund, and welfare agencies in cities throughout Wisconsin struggled with similar budgetary problems.[37]

Addressing the annual Wisconsin Bankers' Association convention in Milwaukee in 1930, Mayor Hoan described having watched "men walking the streets, led by communists, being urged to go in the stores and help themselves." If good men could be persuaded to become thieves, he believed, it was because of basic problems they confronted, and in his opinion none was more pressing than unemployment. Carefully avoiding any temptation he might have had to blame bankers and other businessmen for hard times, the mayor suggested that a principal cause of joblessness was the technological proficiency of American industry. "Now, you know that with the improved methods of production and with the throwing of men out of employment, there must be some attention given to this problem," asserted Hoan, "and I plead with you, the Bankers' Association, the advisers of industry, to give it some thought."[38]

Business leaders and industrialists were, in fact, already giving

[36] Janesville *Gazette*, March 10, 1930; Marshfield *News-Herald*, November 14, 1930.

[37] *Capital Times*, January 10, April 2, 1930; Milwaukee *Leader*, February 11, 1930; Milwaukee County, Citizens Committee on Unemployment, and Public Employment Office of Milwaukee, *Annual Report*, 1932, p. 9; Kewaunee *Enterprise*, February 10, 1933.

[38] Remarks of Hoan, in Wisconsin Bankers' Association, *Proceedings*, 1930, pp. 62–64.

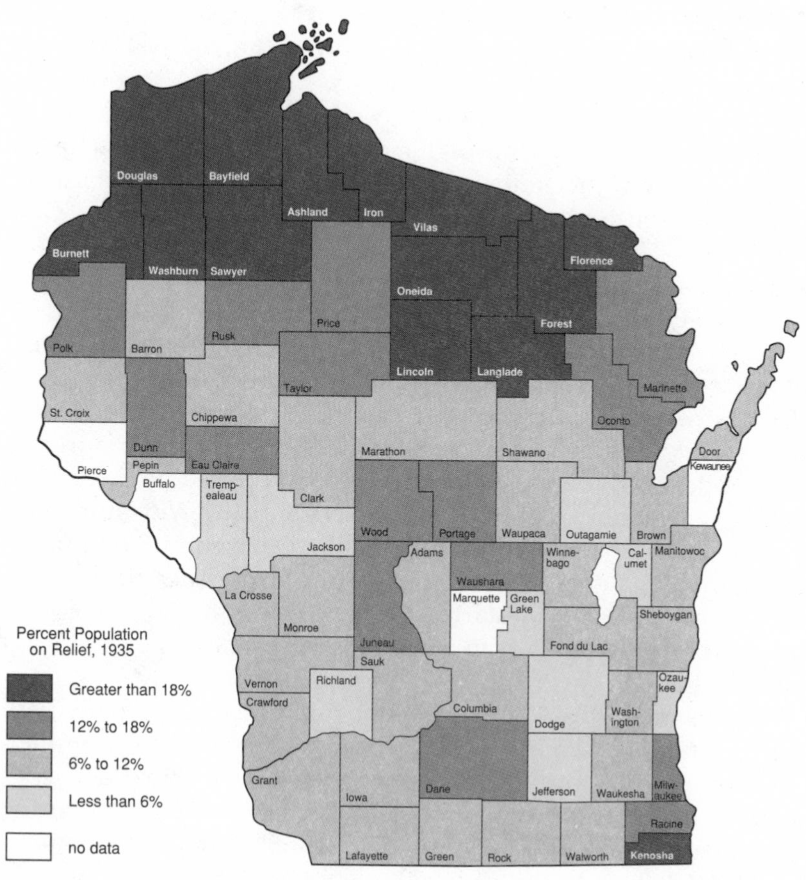

Impact of the Great Depression, 1935

thought to the problem. Many of those associated with seasonal industries believed it necessary to plan production in a way that might eliminate alternating cycles of intensive employment and no employment. "The business which seeks to operate only on seasonal schedules has an obligation to organize or extend itself [so] as to afford continuous employment," asserted the Appleton *Post-Crescent*. A more common reaction was to reduce the hours for labor in order to increase the number of jobs. The automobile industry in Detroit, noted the *Capital Times*, "seeks to meet the specter of unemployment not by creating more work, but by making more jobs out of the work that already exists." The five-day work week, once written off as the fantasy of "a woozy theorist" or "an outright bolshevik, under suspicion of lugging Moscow gold about in his pockets," now attracted the support of sober, conservative business people. The idea also attracted support from Progressives. Governor La Follette thought that "no single thing will contribute more to providing employment, and thereby restoring normal conditions in this country, than the reduction of the hours of labor."[39]

Yet proposals to divide less work among more employees had limited appeal for both workers and employers. Laborers feared the loss of income that seemed certain to follow a reduction of hours, and some employers resisted personnel increases during a time of depression even if more employees required no increase in payroll expenditures. Community leaders in many Wisconsin cities were therefore persuaded that they should concentrate on providing more jobs rather than reducing work loads. They thus redoubled their efforts, begun during the New Era, either to attract new industries to Wisconsin or to encourage the expansion of industries already there.[40]

The city of Hartford, a small Washington County community with a population of 3,754 in 1930, provides an example of a promotional effort that proved highly successful. Few Wisconsin cities suffered more serious economic setbacks than did Hartford during the months following the Crash. The Kissel Motor Car Company failed in 1930, and shortly after that the Bear Brand Hosiery Company and the Luick Ice Cream Company both moved their plants. Taken together, the three firms had provided employment for a majority of the town's industrial workers, who thus faced the dif-

[39] Appleton *Post-Crescent*, January 8, 1930; *Capital Times*, March 29, October 14, 1930; La Crosse *Tribune and Leader-Press*, November 5, 1930; Superior *Evening Telegram*, November 27, 1930; Milwaukee Association of Commerce, *Milwaukee Commerce*, June 9, 1932. Also Don D. Lescohier to La Follette, February 24, 1931; La Follette to W. K. Kellogg, May 2, 1931; and C. W. Nash to La Follette, November 12, 1931, all in the Philip F. La Follette Papers. "Wouldn't it be just to give heed to some means to shorten the hours of work of those engaged in agriculture?" queried the *Waupaca County Post* (Waupaca) on February 12, 1931. "Under present conditions is it any wonder that many farmers look with a wistful eye on proposals for six hour days and five day weeks?"

[40] Lewis E. Atherton, *Main Street on the Middle Border* (Bloomington, Indiana, 1954), 338–345.

ficult choice of searching for employment elsewhere or remaining jobless at home. To meet the crisis, a group of local businessmen and industrial workers organized themselves to raise $25,000 in cash and at least an additional $5,000 in free labor and free use of equipment to attract another industry.

The Rich Vogel Shoe Company, manufacturers of women's shoes, responded to Hartford's blandishments, but the firm remained in business there for less than two years. Refusing to admit defeat, the Hartford group then persuaded the Weyenberg Shoe Manufacturing Company to open a plant in return for $40,000, to be paid in five annual installments. Some workers later encountered difficulty in making their contributions to the company, and some residents resented further requests for assistance. Yet throughout the thirties the firm maintained its operations in Hartford, employing about 225 workers and meeting an annual payroll of $300,000 to $350,000.

Despite some resistance to Weyenberg's demands, the Hartford group did not cease its promotional efforts. In 1933, citizens of the community approved a referendum calling for a $2,000 annual municipal appropriation for commercial and industrial development. Kissel Industries, organized to manufacture outboard motors for Sears, Roebuck and Company, purchased the old Kissel motor car plant at a receivership sale in 1934. Assisted by a $2,000 grant from the Hartford municipal industrial fund, it began operations. Starting with only a hundred employees, the firm expanded its operations, and by 1933, when it sold out to the West Bend Aluminum Company, it was employing about 300.

Other industries were also attracted to Hartford. In 1936, the Kraft Cheese Company moved into the old Luick building and received $500 from the industrial fund. The International Stamping Company began producing automobile mufflers that same year with a donation of $1,500, and two years later it received another $2,000 for expansion. In 1937, the Hebenstreits Furniture Company and the Truck Equipment Company both moved to Hartford with assistance from the industrial fund. Although the furniture company remained in business less than a year, the Truck Equipment Company did better, and by the end of World War II it was developing plans for expansion. Overall, despite some failures and some criticism from residents, Hartford thus achieved considerable success with its program of subsidization during the Depression decade.

Considering the city's grim prospects in 1930, when the program began, the success was in fact remarkable.[41]

Hartford was by no means the only city in Wisconsin that demonstrated great imagination in dealing with problems that accompanied the Depression. In municipalities across the state, volunteer committees went about soliciting food and funds, which they turned over to commissaries where the destitute could obtain a share of what had been collected. A citizens' committee in Milwaukee proposed dividing the city into sections in which householders could pledge to hire a jobless person for at least an hour of work every week. The Marshfield *News-Herald* announced that it would publish free of charge the names of farmers willing to donate waste wood to anyone willing to cut it. A citizens' relief committee in Oneida County collected donations in cash or farm products for distribution to the unemployed. The Lions Club of Ellsworth sponsored a charity show at the local theater and contributed the proceeds to a relief fund. The Rhinelander *New North* urged that all persons with jobs take at least one sandwich a day to a central point for distribution to the hungry. The city council of Rice Lake purchased a five-acre tract of timber, paid unemployed persons a dollar a cord for cutting it, sold the wood, and gave the proceeds to persons in need. Delavan placed coin boxes in several places of business and asked residents to deposit a coin a week. Racine set up a barter exchange where certificates were issued in return for anything a person might bring in; the scrip currency could then be used to purchase other goods deposited with the exchange. Taylor County hired crews to gravel country roads and paid the men in delinquent tax lands, presumably with the understanding that they could scratch out an existence on cutover land. Oshkosh developed a "Loan Your Job for a Week" plan whereby ninety-six jobless men earned two weeks' wages as substitutes for city workers who volunteered to take time off.[42]

[41] This sketch of Hartford's efforts during the 1930's summarizes the more extended discussion in William D. Knight, *Subsidization of Industry in Forty Selected Cities in Wisconsin, 1930–1946*, UW Bureau of Business Research and Service, *Wisconsin Commerce Studies*, vol. 1, no. 2 (1947), 67–76.

[42] Milwaukee *Leader*, March 3, 1930; Superior *Evening Telegram*, December 13–14, 1930; Milwaukee *Journal*, November 27, 1930; Marshfield *News-Herald*, November 3, 1930; *Pierce County Herald* (Ellsworth), December 3, 1931; Rhinelander *New North*, November 6, 1930, October 29, 1931; *Taylor County Star News* (Medford), January 29, 1931, July 14, 1932; Burlington *Standard-Democrat*, January 20, 1933; Racine *New Day*,

Several state and national organizations provided assistance to communities in which they were represented. Chambers of commerce were active in setting up employment offices, and some of them offered financial advice to those who sought help. In 1930, Wisconsin posts of the American Legion co-operated in conducting a detailed economic survey of towns and cities. Two years later, the Legion concentrated on a survey of the unemployed. Working on a national basis with Matthew Woll, vice-president of the American Federation of Labor, the Legion hoped to find jobs for a million men. In Wisconsin the survey won enthusiastic endorsement. "There has been some criticism of the Legion in the past, because some of its spokesmen have given the impression that they were more concerned with bonuses and beer than with unselfish public service," noted the Kewaunee *Enterprise*. "We hope that this movement for the relief of unemployment will not only put [an] end to that criticism, but that it will turn out to be the beginning of a broad, continuing policy of public service which may make the American Legion the most powerful influence in the United States for the betterment . . . of social and economic conditions."[43]

Volunteer efforts to provide relief and employment during the early years of the Depression sometimes contained more than a hint of patronizing smugness. A few of the municipal projects were silly, and most of them achieved limited success at best. Nonetheless, they filled a profound psychological need for people who had worried about the way New Era prosperity seemed to undermine the spirit of community. "The social instinct of . . . the country has developed more noticeably during the past few years than ever before," observed the Burlington *Standard-Democrat*. For all the hardships and anxieties that clouded Wisconsin during the Depression, inveterate seekers after a silver lining could usually find one in the zeal for co-operation that accompanied attempts to care for the needy. "Americans have learned that there is something more important, finer and far more worthwhile than the pursuit of the almighty dollar," concluded the *Standard-Democrat*. Yet some of

---

April 14, 1933; George F. Oaks, "Oshkosh Helps Unemployment Situation," in *The Municipality*, 26 (January, 1931), 12.

[43] Appleton *Post-Crescent*, December 16, 1930; Janesville *Gazette*, November 4, 1930; Milwaukee Association of Commerce, *Milwaukee Commerce*, September 28, 1933; "Wisconsin Community Survey," in *The Municipality*, 25 (April, 1930), 70; Kewaunee *Enterprise*, February 19, 26, 1932; *Pierce County Herald* (Ellsworth), February 25, 1932.

those whose bellies ached for real sustenance found such self-righteous truisms unpalatable.[44]

* * *

Overcoming unemployment and other difficulties that came with the Depression obviously required money. Whether costs were to be borne by government agencies or by private enterprise, the unemployed and the destitute needed assistance. If the assistance came from government sources, it was likely to be opposed by citizens unwilling to increase taxes at a time when their own incomes were declining. If resolution of the problems associated with unemployment were left to business and industrial organizations, there would always be doubts about the adequacy of the assistance extended. Touching on the dilemma, the editor of the Marshfield *News-Herald* applauded President Hoover's efforts to stimulate new construction and municipal improvements, but he also expressed his belief that "governmental bodies are in a far better position to do things of this kind than are private industries."[45]

Eventually it was the argument for government responsibility rather than voluntary private action that proved persuasive, and the main reason people turned to government agencies for help was simply that such agencies seemed more effective (because better-funded) than voluntary associations. The goodwill and imagination of Wisconsin residents were everywhere manifest after the Crash, but in most cities the laying of sewers, the surfacing of streets, the construction of bridges, or the erection of municipal

[44] Burlington *Standard-Democrat*, April 21, 1933.

[45] John R. Commons et al., *History of Labor in the United States, 1896–1932. Volume III: Working Conditions and Labor Legislation*, written by Don D. Lescohier ("Working Conditions") and Elizabeth Brandeis ("Labor Legislation") (New York, 1935), 183; Don D. Lescohier and Florence Peterson, *The Alleviation of Unemployment in Wisconsin*, Industrial Commission, Bureau of Unemployment, *Research Series*, no. 1 (1931), 55–56; Marshfield *News-Herald*, November 29, 1929. Although willing to have municipalities and counties assume responsibilities for relief, commercial organizations generally opposed state or federal aid to the unemployed. The advisory council of the Wisconsin State Chamber of Commerce objected to having "charity made the football of politics." See Wisconsin State Chamber of Commerce to Vice-President Charles Curtis as president of the Senate (telegram), February 10, 1932, in Report of Advisory Council Meeting sent to all members of the Wisconsin State Chamber of Commerce, February 15, 1932, in the Chamber Papers; and Appleton Chamber of Commerce, board of directors' minutes, December 4, 1931, in the Appleton Chamber of Commerce Papers in the Oshkosh Area Research Center.

buildings provided far more jobs and economic assistance than did the volunteer efforts of concerned private citizens.[46]

Like Herbert Hoover, Governor Walter Kohler was troubled by nightmares of an authoritarian state; and like Hoover, he sought to encourage co-operative solutions for problems of the Depression. He therefore created the Wisconsin Citizens' Committee on Employment, and to head the committee he chose Don D. Lescohier, one of John R. Commons' students who had become a professor of labor economics at the University of Wisconsin. Kohler also asked George Kull, secretary of the Wisconsin Manufacturers' Association, to conduct a survey of the state to determine where jobs were plentiful and where they were scarce.[47]

The citizens' committee began its labors enthusiastically. Its initial move was to urge county boards and city councils first to increase their budgets for relief and then to proceed with public works that had been scheduled but not begun. Because the committee could not compel action, however, it experienced repeated frustrations. Hoping to develop a program for the retraining and guidance of adult workers, Professor Lescohier had to admit in 1931 that "thus far we have not been able to get beyond the formulation of plans." Equally disappointing was the committee's effort to increase the effectiveness of public employment services. Hoover's pocket veto of an unemployment compensation bill introduced by Senator Robert Wagner of New York cut off anticipated federal assistance, and as a result the hope of improving state employment services went aglimmering. The best the citizens' committee could do in developing a program of unemployment insurance was to carry on "a good deal of educational work." And so it went throughout Kohler's remaining months in office. Whether or not he might eventually have developed a more cogent agenda, he lost his chance in 1930 when he failed to win re-election.[48]

Having defeated Kohler, Phil La Follette's first responsibility was

[46] "Wisconsin Municipalities and the Unemployment Situation," in *The Municipality*, 25 (December, 1930), 263–264. Superior departed from the standard for municipal construction projects when it built a municipal golf course. See *The Municipality*, 26 (June, 1931), 101.

[47] *Wisconsin State Journal*, April 11, 1930. For a sample of letters sent to city and county officials, see Kohler to Fred Hermann, county clerk, in Taylor County Board, *Proceedings*, November 11, 1930, pp. 23–24, and the La Crosse *Tribune and Leader-Press*, November 1, 1930.

[48] "Report of Wisconsin Citizens' Committee on Employment," June 19, 1931, in the Philip F. La Follette Papers.

to hold hearings on the state budget. Stalwarts, along with others the governor-elect had identified as "reactionaries" during the campaign, worried about how the young man might attack the state's economic problems. They were pleasantly surprised. La Follette was aware of business people's concerns, and throughout the budget hearings and after, he took great pains to solicit their ideas on the resolution of difficulties that came with the Depression. He consulted bankers, presidents of the principal railroads, farm leaders, and representatives of the Wisconsin State Federation of Labor and other interest groups. Proceeding with caution and taking care to disarm those most likely to criticize his actions, he gradually worked out his agenda with the help of academicians affiliated with the university.[49]

Among the faculty members who formed an advisory group close to La Follette were John Gaus, professor of political science, Lloyd Garrison, dean of the Law School, and Max Otto, professor of philosophy. But the most important of Phil's academic consultants were John R. Commons and the economists who had acquired their training in Commons' seminar. The Commons students who were to exert the strongest influence during Governor La Follette's first term were Harold Groves (who also sat in the state assembly), Elizabeth Brandeis, Paul A. Raushenbush, and Edwin E. Witte. This academic "kitchen cabinet" worked closely with Progressive legislators who assumed responsibility for guiding a Progressive program through both the senate and the assembly.[50]

In the upper house, the young governor relied heavily on Glenn D. Roberts, his law partner; Orland S. Loomis of Mauston, a graduate of Ripon College and the University of Wisconsin Law School who had just won election to the senate after serving one term in

[49] Philip F. La Follette, *Adventure in Politics: The Memoirs of Philip La Follette*, ed. Donald Young (New York, 1970), 146–148; John E. Miller, *Governor Philip F. La Follette, the Wisconsin Progressives, and the New Deal* (Columbia, Missouri, 1982), 12–13; John L. Borchard to E. H. Krueger, November 6, 1930, in the Philip F. La Follette Papers.

[50] Philip F. La Follette to Dear Ones, December 20, 1930, in box A-39, La Follette Family Papers, Library of Congress; summary of interview with Isabel Bacon La Follette, October 9, 1969, copy in both the author's and History of Wisconsin project files; Paul A. Raushenbush, "Starting Unemployment Compensation in Wisconsin," in U.S. Department of Labor, *Unemployment Insurance Review*, 4 (April–May, 1967), 17–24; summary of interview with Elizabeth Brandeis and Paul Raushenbush, November 16, 1969, copy in both the author's and project files. Elizabeth Brandeis was the daughter of Justice Louis D. Brandeis. Her husband, Paul Raushenbush, was the son of theologian Walter Rauschenbusch, a prominent advocate of the Social Gospel.

the assembly; Leonard Fons, a Milwaukee lawyer; and Thomas M. Duncan, a graduate of Yale University who had served as Daniel Hoan's secretary before winning election to the senate from Milwaukee. Although a member of the Socialist party, Duncan was to become Phil's executive secretary and, until 1938, his right-hand man. The assemblymen on whom the governor most depended were, in addition to Groves, floor leader Robert A. Nixon of Washburn, E. Myrwyn Rowlands of Cambria, John Grobschmidt of Milwaukee, Stanley Slagg of Edgerton, and Carlton Mauthe of Fond du Lac.[51]

In his first address to the legislature on January 15, 1931, Phil relied upon what he had learned as a student majoring in history at the university. Drawing upon the frontier thesis of Frederick Jackson Turner, he argued that with the disappearance of unoccupied land the American people confronted a need to find new social and economic opportunities. Wisconsin, he argued, could lead the way towards a new "vertical frontier," and he left no doubt about his intention to use the instrumentalities of government to achieve that objective. Moving towards the vertical frontier required taking steps to increase markets for the abundance of goods that Wisconsin industries were capable of producing, and that in turn required improving consumers' capacity to buy. The central problem, La Follette reiterated again and again, was to increase the "purchasing power" of people who suffered from an inequitable distribution of income. "As a state and a nation we have astounded the world in production," he had asserted in his inaugural address. "Unless we can solve the problem of the distribution of this abundance—unless we can stop hunger and hardship in all this plenty, we will be actors in the greatest tragedy in history."[52]

According to Lescohier of the Wisconsin Citizens' Committee on Employment, joblessness in the state had risen to more than 150,000 by May, 1931. He estimated that unemployment had in-

[51] La Follette, *Adventure in Politics*, 154–155; *Wisconsin Blue Book, 1929*, pp. 525, 533, 540, 544, 548, 553, 565, 572; *ibid., 1931*, pp. 198–210; *ibid., 1933*, p. 217; Miller, *Governor Philip F. La Follette*, 15–16.

[52] La Follette, *Adventure in Politics*, 149, 152–153; John E. Miller, "Governor Philip F. La Follette's Shifting Priorities from Redistribution to Expansion," in *Mid-America*, 58 (April–July, 1976), 120–121; *Wisconsin Senate Journal*, 1931, pp. 13–14. In emphasizing a redistribution of income as a means of increasing consumption, Governor La Follette took a position very close to that of other Progressives. See Theodore Rosenof, *Dogma, Depression, and the New Deal: The Debate of Political Leaders over Economic Recovery* (Port Washington, New York, 1975), 39–43.

creased by 136,000 persons during the previous year and a half. Attempting to compile meaningful data on unemployment in Wisconsin, Arthur J. Altmeyer, secretary of the industrial commission, concentrated on a sample of fourteen cities and counties having a combined population of slightly over a million persons. He found that 18,000 families in the study were receiving public assistance, but he thought the future even gloomier. He predicted that the number of families receiving aid would double within a year. With consequences of the Depression approaching monumental proportions, the young governor turned his attention to measures for the employment and relief of the jobless. John Donaghey, chief engineer of the highway commission, suggested that a program for the improvement of railroad crossings could be accelerated to provide a form of work relief for 10,000 or more of the unemployed, and La Follette found the idea attractive.[53]

During the month before Phil took office, he held a conference with presidents of the seven railroads operating in Wisconsin and proposed that the railroad corporations meet a fourth of the grade-crossing improvement costs. The state's contributions to the project, the remaining three-fourths, would come from a two-cent increase in the gasoline tax. After the project had been completed, the governor told the presidents, the gasoline tax increase would be returned to local jurisdictions in order to reduce property taxes. The railroad presidents accepted the proposal, and a bill for the improvement of crossings became the first major enactment of the 1931 legislature. The Emergency Highway Act also provided for the creation of a five-member unemployment commission to supervise the grade-crossing program. By the end of 1932, forty-six overhead and sixteen underpass structures had been completed.[54]

Although the grade-crossing project provided employment for some 8,000 men during 1931, it was clearly inadequate to meet the needs of all state residents who were without work. Recognizing

[53] Altmeyer to Philip F. La Follette, September 12, 1931, Lescohier to Edward G. Littel, May 18, 1931, and La Follette to Roy Empey, May 14, 1931, all in the Philip F. La Follette Papers; La Follette, *Adventure in Politics*, 147–148; Wisconsin State Highway Commission and United States Public Roads Administration, *A History of Wisconsin Highway Development, 1835–1945* (1947), 110.

[54] La Follette to John J. Blaine, February 6, 1931; Blaine to La Follette, February 11, 1931; La Follette to L. Ray Smith, telegram, March 27, 1931; governor's press release, April 2, 1931; Chief Engineer, Unemployment Commission, to Senate of the State of Wisconsin, June 27, 1931, all in the Philip F. La Follette Papers.

the necessity for more comprehensive legislation even before he took office, the governor had asked Elizabeth Brandeis, Paul Raushenbush, and Harold Groves to draft an unemployment compensation and relief bill that the legislature could approve. They had set to work with enthusiasm, and Groves submitted their proposal to the assembly on February 6, 1931. Other bills directed towards the same end had been placed in the hopper, however, and it became evident that enacting a viable program for unemployment compensation would require time. La Follette therefore encouraged the legislature to approve a joint resolution creating an interim committee to study unemployment relief and compensation over the summer and to report its findings to a special session later in the year. The resolution passed, and a committee began preparation of a new bill for that session.[55]

In the meantime, following recommendations of the Wisconsin State Federation of Labor, the legislature enacted several other measures to improve the lot of workers. It extended the coverage and increased the benefits of the existing workmen's compensation law. It provided that any public building contract include a clause requiring the contractor to pay a minimum wage equal to the prevailing wage of the county in which the structure was to be erected. It passed a measure giving the state industrial commission authority to assist workers in collecting wages due them and to prosecute employers failing to meet their payroll obligations. It approved a bill to make state and local jurisdictions subject to safety laws of the state. Finally, it enacted a labor code that recognized the legitimacy of union membership and permitted payment of strike benefits, publication of the facts in a labor dispute, peaceful assembly and picketing, and new measures to restrict the use of injunctions in labor disputes.[56]

The labor legislation of 1931 suggests that the Wisconsin Progressives were prepared to move in a new direction. While they

[55] Paul A. Raushenbush and Elizabeth Brandeis Raushenbush, *Our "U.C." Story, 1930–1967* (Madison, 1979), 55–74; Paul A. Raushenbush, "The Wisconsin Idea: Unemployment Reserves," in American Academy of Political and Social Sciences, *Annals*, 170 (November, 1933), 65–75.

[56] "Labor Legislation of the 1931 Session" (carbon copy), in series 1, undated 1931 files, Philip F. La Follette Papers; La Follette, *Adventure in Politics*, 159; Gordon M. Haferbecker, *Wisconsin Labor Laws* (Madison, 1958), 161; Theron F. Schlabach, *Edwin E. Witte: Cautious Reformer* (Madison, 1969), 70–71; Thomas W. Gavett, *Development of the Labor Movement in Milwaukee* (Madison, 1965), 141–142, 154.

continued to attract support from rural areas of the state, they were obviously ready to devote increased attention to the urban centers. In reaching out to the cities, however, they found themselves compelled to intervene in matters that were of minimal concern to the countryside. Even unemployment seemed largely an urban problem during the early years of the Depression. Farmers were less troubled by joblessness than they were by agricultural prices, tax burdens, and the cultural costs of rural life.[57]

As the analysis of voting behavior in Chapter 8 has revealed, the most loyal Progressive support came from counties in Wisconsin's agricultural hinterland. And while Phil La Follette wished to gain the votes of urban workers, he had no intention of losing the backing of Wisconsin's rural areas. From his perspective, expanding the state's program for development of hydroelectric power seemed a logical way to retain rural support. After the war, Wisconsin farmers had rapidly come to believe that the benefits of electrification outweighed the costs, and many of them began employing electric power in their operations and in their homes. The number of rural customers served by central power stations in the state increased from less than 7,000 in 1920 to 35,000 in 1930. If La Follette and the Progressives could develop a feasible plan for the production, distribution, and regulation of hydroelectric power, they might thereby achieve a statewide community of interest.[58]

The governor placed great emphasis on the need for a power program in his opening message to the legislature on January 15, 1931. Taking his stand with the advocates of public power, he reiterated time-tested Progressive arguments that private control of power production and distribution had resulted in "high prices to the consumer with high profits to financial manipulators." Following closely the advice of Carl D. Thompson, secretary of the Public Ownership League of America, La Follette offered three recommendations. He asked first that the legislature approve a referendum on amending the constitution so as to allow municipal financing of public utilities by mortgage rather than by taxation. Second, he called for the organization of "power districts" by municipal utility plants wishing to expand their services. The third

[57] Miller, *Governor Philip F. La Follette*, 16.

[58] Forrest McDonald, *Let There Be Light: The Electric Utility Industry in Wisconsin, 1881–1955* (Madison, 1957), 281–284, 294, 320; Samuel Mermin, *Jurisprudence and Statecraft: The Wisconsin Development Authority and Its Implications* (Madison, 1963), 3–6.

recommendation, which the governor considered the most important, was that the constitution be amended to permit establishment of "a state-wide publicly owned power system."[59]

Phil La Follette made a good case for a co-ordinated system of power production, transmission, and distribution. It would, he argued, raise rural standards of living, increase the stability of rural populations, create new opportunities for economic development, and open new markets for business. The legislature endorsed much, but not all, of what he requested. Legislators took the necessary steps to assure mortgage financing of public utilities, and their action was approved in a 1932 referendum. They also passed legislation for the organization of power districts. Only the attempt to create a state power system encountered difficulties. The legislature passed a joint resolution for a constitutional amendment authorizing the state to engage in the production, transmission, and distribution of power, but not until creation of the Wisconsin Development Authority in 1937 did La Follette achieve his objective. By that time the concert of interests he envisioned was beginning to break apart.[60]

Whatever hopes the governor might have had for the future, and whatever disappointments he was later to experience, he could take satisfaction in his achievements during the legislative session that closed at the end of June, 1931. In addition to victories for highway improvement, labor relations, and power development, there was a long list of new measures for which Progressives claimed credit. The railroad commission had been reorganized as the public service commission, and under its new name it had received additional regulatory powers. The legislature had also enacted measures to reduce personal property taxes, to impose a tax on chain retail stores, and to establish a state old-age pension system for the elderly. Finally, an executive council had been created to advise and assist the governor on problems associated with relief, banking,

[59] *Wisconsin Blue Book, 1931*, pp. 447–448; *Wisconsin Senate Journal*, 1931, pp. 31–32; McDonald, *Let There Be Light*, 316–318; Mermin, *Jurisprudence and Statecraft*, 5–6. Also Thompson to La Follette, January 9, February 5, 1931; La Follette to Donald R. Richberg, January 26, 1931; James C. Bonbright to La Follette, February 2, 1931; and Orland S. Loomis, "Wisconsin's Public Power Program," address (mimeographed) to the Public Ownership Conference of the Public Ownership League of America, Los Angeles, September 28, 1931, all in the Philip F. La Follette Papers.

[60] Mermin, *Jurisprudence and Statecraft*, 5–6; McDonald, *Let There Be Light*, 320–321; Miller, *Governor Philip F. La Follette*, 111–112. For details on the WDA, see Chapter 12 *infra*.

transportation, the stabilization of industry, and similar matters of concern. "I am amazed and pleased beyond expression by the success with which your legislative program is going through the legislature," Bob La Follette had written his brother before the session ended. "It is a great tribute to your industry, ability and wonderful capacity for leadership."[61]

* * *

The five-month recess between the regular and special legislative sessions of 1931 was a time of intense investigation of means to meliorate effects of the Depression in Wisconsin. The interim committee on unemployment relief and compensation, stimulated by the efforts of Groves, Raushenbush, and Brandeis, worked hard at developing a program the legislature could approve in the fall. "A way will be found to meet unemployment," the governor told a reporter from the New York *Times*. "I am sure of it. We merely need organization, determination." The Progressives needed understanding as well, and despite Phil's zest for political action, he seemed little more certain of the measures necessary for recovery than did the man on the street.[62]

Groping for solutions to the problems of economic stagnation, the Wisconsin Progressives sought enlightenment from the experience of other states and countries. Characteristically, Phil held conferences with economists and industrialists, and he eagerly solicited information on relief and recovery programs initiated at home and abroad. While listening to a variety of opinions, however, he still held fast to the position he had taken during his election campaign and throughout the regular legislative session. That is, he continued to insist that the fundamental economic problem was a maldistribution of income. Noting that 504 of the nation's wealthiest families enjoyed a combined income equal to the combined average income of four million American farmers, he argued that a return to prosperity demanded the reversal of policies by which the rich became richer while the poor became poorer.[63]

[61] McDonald, *Let There Be Light*, 321–322; La Follette, *Adventure in Politics*, 159–160; Miller, *Governor Philip F. La Follette*, 18–19; Robert M. La Follette, Jr., to Philip F. La Follette, April 15, 1931, in the Philip F. La Follette Papers.

[62] New York *Times*, September 27, 1931.

[63] F. J. Sensenbrenner to La Follette, October 6, 1931; La Follette to various Wisconsin manufacturers, October 20, 1931; La Follette to C. W. Nash, November 9, 1931; rough draft of remarks prepared for the Governor's Conference of Mayors, September 22,

In the meantime, the rapidly increasing unemployment in the state was creating problems that demanded immediate attention. Following his practice of examining the experiences of others, the young governor found the evolution of unemployment relief in Britain to be particularly instructive. During that summer of 1931, Edwin Witte had joined a team of experts sent abroad by the Carnegie Endowment for International Peace to study responses to the Depression in European countries. Focusing on the British system of unemployment insurance, Witte wrote La Follette a long letter in which he outlined the history of the British program and speculated on some of its implications for the legislation about to be considered in Wisconsin.

Witte's letter made three points that reinforced La Follette's own thinking on the matter of unemployment compensation. The economist, who was to help draft the federal Social Security Act, noted first that any unemployment insurance system enacted in 1931 would have little effect on people recently thrown out of work. While he favored such a system, he emphasized that it would serve as "a protection for future periods of unemployment, rather than a measure for immediate relief." Second, in elaborating on the need for immediate relief, he discerned but two possibilities: public works and direct financial assistance. Of the two approaches, Witte favored direct assistance similar to the system known in Britain as the dole. His reasons were economic ones. "Cash or food given the unemployed goes back in toto into the channels of trade," he observed, whereas "only a small part of the expenditure for public works goes directly to labor and it is a long time before the part going to profits gets back into consumption." Finally, Witte argued, a major cause of the Depression had been rapid technological advance, particularly in the design and production of labor-saving capital goods. The remedy, as he saw it, was a permanent reduction in the hours of labor. Conceding that unemployment insurance was justified because in the long run it would assure workers a regular income, Witte emphasized the practical importance of other measures more likely to provide immediate relief.[64]

1931; account of meeting of chairmen of county boards in senate chamber, September 22, 1931, all in the Philip F. La Follette Papers. Also Miller, "Governor Philip F. La Follette's Shifting Priorities," *Mid-America*, 58:120–121, and Miller, *Governor Philip F. La Follette*, 17.

[64] Schlabach, *Edwin E. Witte*, 87; Witte to La Follette, July 27, 1931, in the Philip F. La Follette Papers.

While La Follette rejected a system of doles, he accepted Witte's argument for providing relief as quickly as possible. Calling legislators into special session on November 24, 1931, the governor emphasized measures for immediate relief and unemployment compensation. The nation, he declared in opening the session, was confronting the greatest difficulties it had encountered since the Civil War. He attributed the sense of crisis in part to a fundamental difference between those who favored collective solutions for problems of the day and those who held out for the efficacy of individual effort. Taking his stand with the advocates of collective action, Phil was careful to point out that co-ordinated programs did not entail a loss of individuality. On the contrary, he argued, the state had a responsibility to provide the fullest possible opportunity for the development of all citizens great and small, rich and poor. In sum, he advocated legislation to encourage what he called "collective individualism."

Presenting a formula that amounted to a synthesis of many ideas then under discussion across the country, Phil described several programs appropriate for meeting needs of the time. He suggested, first, an extension of electric power projects begun during the regular session. Perhaps recalling the platform favored by the Committee of Forty-Eight during his father's campaign for the presidency in 1924, Phil offered a justification for government ownership of public utilities. In modern times the utilities had become instruments of common necessity, he argued, and citizens had every right to control them through municipal, state, and national governments. With state ownership, the people of Wisconsin could secure efficient service, protect themselves from extortionate rates, and bring about a more equitable distribution of profits.

Moving on to appeal for support from business interests and from Stalwarts loyal to Herbert Hoover, the governor argued that the state should provide machinery and incentives for private businesses to conduct their own affairs. The success of business self-government depended upon shaping public policies that business people could readily find advantageous. When public policies coincided with private interest, La Follette believed, compulsive legislation became unnecessary. The drafting of such policies, however, necessarily required research, planning, and consultation, an extension of the celebrated "Wisconsin Idea." Agencies of the state could boast of long experience in gathering information that private interests were able to use to their advantage. During hard times the need for planning had become more apparent than ever, and Phil urged the legislature to consider expanding the research upon which wise policy formation depended.

Finally, concluding his remarks, the governor returned to an old Progressive refrain, decrying the inequitable distribution of income in the state. The power to tax, he believed, was "an effective instrument with which to redistribute money to enable farmers and workers to trade with one another." In its regular session earlier in the year, the legislature had passed a measure to tax corporate dividends during 1931, and the governor now made clear his intention to use taxation as the primary means of correcting problems of income distribution.[65]

Phil's address to the legislature received nationwide acclaim. Here, it seemed, was a fresh approach that neither repudiated the past nor relied upon conventional wisdom in formulating responses to unprecedented problems. Letters of praise poured in from across the country, and editorial writers conferred accolades on the young man for his intelligence and understanding. George Norris secured permission to print the address in the *Congressional Record* immediately after President Hoover's annual message to Congress. Felix Frankfurter wrote from the Harvard Law School to congratulate his young friend for having produced "the most heartening state paper that has come out of the depression." The well-known historian, Charles A. Beard, was less restrained. "In all the history of American public documents," he asserted, "there has not appeared a more important or more reasoned state paper."[66]

The positive response to Phil's speech was in part attributable to his having tapped a growing belief among businessmen and reformers alike that the Depression crisis demanded a restructuring of American capitalism. In Washington, Bob La Follette was proceeding along similar lines. As the Wisconsin legislature deliberated

[65] La Follette, "A Proclamation," November 16 (filed as November 17), 1931, in the Philip F. La Follette Papers. The governor's address to the legislature was printed in the *Wisconsin Senate Journal*, 1931, pp. 23–25.

[66] David E. Lilienthal to La Follette, December 11, 1931; Ernest Gruening to La Follette, December 16, 1931; Frank Latenser to La Follette, December 9, 1931; Frankfurter to "Young Friend" (La Follette), December 10, 1931; Roy Nash to La Follette, November 30, 1931; and Beard to Roy Nash, December 9, 1931, all in the Philip F. La Follette Papers. Also *Congressional Record*, 72 Cong., 1 sess., vol. 75, part 1, pp. 27–33.

in special session, Bob introduced bills in the United States Senate to create a national economic council, to provide relief for the jobless, and to expand public works. All three bills failed to win the necessary support in the Senate, but they nevertheless attracted considerable public attention. "This piece of legislation," Senator La Follette observed in speaking for a national economic council, "is a challenge to the fixed belief that hard times and good times alternate in cycles." In his view, "the only sound approach to the problem of unemployment and business instability is the creation of the necessary public machinery of planning and control."[67]

A particularly interested reader of Phil's address to the special session was Gerard Swope, president of General Electric, who had been working on a program that went beyond the economic council that Bob advocated. Swope proposed stabilizing American industry by creating powerful trade associations that would eliminate waste and inefficiency through co-operation and planning. For the workers, there would be pensions, workmen's compensation, and unemployment insurance. While the La Follette brothers found much to admire here, neither supported the Swope plan in its entirety. Favoring trade associations and unemployment compensation, they worried over the possible consequences of the cartelization of business.[68]

For his part, Swope could not conceal his reservations about Phil's program for Wisconsin. "I am going to watch with the greatest interest to see what voluntary action is taken by the industries of Wisconsin to forestall the necessity of any action by the Legislature," he wrote the governor. "As you say, I suppose there always will be some companies where the compulsion of the law will be necessary, but I am sure you also will appreciate that if Wisconsin does this and some other states do not, you will be placing a burden on the industries of Wisconsin [in] that it is going to be harder for them to compete with similar industries in other states." It was because of just such difficulties with separate state action that

[67] Patrick J. Maney, *"Young Bob" La Follette: A Biography of Robert M. La Follette, Jr., 1895–1953* (Columbia, Missouri, 1978), 91–100; Edward N. Doan, *The La Follettes and the Wisconsin Idea* (New York, 1947), 164–165; New York *Times*, November 2, 1931; "Congress Considering National Economic Planning," in *Congressional Digest*, 11 (April, 1932), 97–118.

[68] R. Alan Lawson, *The Failure of Independent Liberalism, 1930–1941* (New York, 1971), 63; Daniel Nelson, *Unemployment Insurance: The American Experience, 1915–1935* (Madison, 1969), 141–142.

Swope favored a new industrial structure through the formation of trade associations.[69]

As Swope expected, many Wisconsin business and industrial leaders were disappointed in Phil's program. F. J. Sensenbrenner, president of Kimberly-Clark Company, wrote to express his regret that the speech to the legislature seemed to have dampened "a fine spirit of cooperation" that Phil had aroused through nearly a year of conferences with a variety of interest groups. Rejecting the governor's proposals, some of the state's manufacturers made clear that they did not share the La Follette brothers' enthusiasm for planning and control. "If the bills proposed are enacted into law," warned John H. Bartlett, Jr., vice-president of Oshkosh Trunks, Inc., "it will be necessary for this company to 'stabilize employment' by the only method open to it, that is *downward*." And lumber manufacturer William A. Holt of Oconto agreed that the "immediate effect of Unemployment Insurance will be to reduce the number of employees to the lowest possible number."[70]

Yet the business community was not monolithic, and La Follette heard from supporters as well as critics. "I notice that there is quite an opposition to your proposed legislation for the benefit of the unemployed on the part of manufacturers and many prominent business men," wrote H. L. Nunn, president of the Nunn, Bush and Weldon Shoe Company of Milwaukee. "Personally, I do not want to be classed with this group that seems to be always opposed to anything that puts additional burdens on them, regardless of the necessity for help to others." By the time a revised version of the Groves Bill came up for consideration, there were other straws in the wind to indicate that employers were not beyond reason. The United States Chamber of Commerce and the National Association of Manufacturers had both advocated unemployment insurance as a means of stabilizing employment, and the Wisconsin Manufacturers' Association had begun to consider a voluntary plan of in-

[69] Swope to La Follette, December 10, 1931, in the Philip F. La Follette Papers. Swope did not, however, close the door on possibilities of reaching some accommodation with the Wisconsin Progressives. See, for example, Swope to La Follette, December 16, 1931, April 7, 1932; La Follette to Swope, May 19, June 8, 1932; and Robert E. Wood to La Follette, May 20, 1932, all in *ibid.*

[70] F. J. Sensenbrenner to La Follette, November 30, 1931; La Follette to F. J. Sensenbrenner, December 8, 1931; John H. Bartlett, Jr., to La Follette, December 16, 1931; and William Arthur Holt to La Follette, December 22, 1931, all in *ibid.*

surance that seemed less threatening than anything the Progressives envisioned.[71]

At the beginning of 1932, perceptions of what was needed to restore prosperity had changed significantly since the days immediately following the Crash on Wall Street. Herbert Hoover had lost credibility with people who were hardest hit, and he was rapidly losing support among Progressive business leaders. Now, with the young Wisconsin governor's special session address setting the parameters for an enlightened discussion of relief, unemployment compensation, and other means of dealing with consequences of the Depression, the legislature settled down to business in a way that suggested liberation from White House pronouncements.[72]

* * *

Discussion and debate in the special session centered on the report submitted by the interim committee that had been investigating problems of unemployment. The committee membership included Assemblymen Harold Groves and Robert Nixon, who had both introduced unemployment compensation bills during the regular session. On the other side of the question were Frederick H. Clausen, president of the Van Brunt Manufacturing Company in Horicon, who served as a representative of the state's employers, and Ira E. Burtis, a conservative assemblyman from Dodge County. John J. Handley, secretary of the Wisconsin State Federation of Labor, represented the workers. Having co-operated with John R. Commons in drafting an unemployment compensation bill in 1921, the Huber Bill, he had supported its principles for a decade. The two committee members from the senate were Anton M. Miller, a member of the Wisconsin Society of Equity, and Peter J. Smith, a Danish-born resident of Eau Claire who had served on the Wisconsin Board of Normal School Regents. Except for Burtis and Clausen, the committee members were Progressive in viewpoint and favorably disposed towards the idea of unemployment compensation.[73]

[71] H. L. Nunn to La Follette, December 5, 1931, in *ibid*; Nelson, *Unemployment Insurance*, 122, 126, 142–144; *Wisconsin State Journal*, November 17, 1931; Charles A. Beard, ed., *America Faces the Future* (Boston, 1932), 225, 259.

[72] Nelson, *Unemployment Insurance*, 144; Joan Hoff Wilson, *Herbert Hoover: Forgotten Progressive* (Boston, 1975), 151–153; David Burner, *Herbert Hoover: A Public Life* (New York, 1979), 234.

[73] Raushenbush and Raushenbush, *Our "U.C." Story*, 94, 98–99; Nelson, *Unemployment Insurance*, 122–123.

While Commons was no longer directly concerned with developing such legislation, a number of his students made important contributions to the work of the committee. Elizabeth Brandeis and Paul Raushenbush played a key role in the investigation, as did Arthur Altmeyer, Merrill Murray, Harry Weiss, and John B. Andrews. As secretary of the Wisconsin Industrial Commission, Altmeyer became involved in the staff work of the committee. Andrews, who had long been active in promoting labor reform as secretary of the American Association for Labor Legislation, used the resources of the AALL to provide advice and assistance. Murray and Weiss, who belonged to a younger generation of Commons students, worked effectively to promote public interest in committee hearings. The sixty-nine-year-old Commons stood on the sidelines, cheering his students on and urging them to "stir up as much discussion throughout the state . . . as possible and see to it that the interim committee is kept on its toes." Stir up discussion they did, organizing a Wisconsin Committee for Unemployment Reserves Legislation to inform citizens of their efforts and win them to the cause.[74]

The enthusiasm of the Commons students inspired confidence, but the scent of victory did not in itself overcome the possibility of defeat. Differences even among the supporters of unemployment compensation could hamper their combined effort to get a bill through. Such differences arose largely from proposed modification of the original unemployment compensation provisions in the Huber Bill of 1921. Along with other bills submitted during the twenties, the Huber Bill called for the creation of an employer-controlled mutual insurance company that would collect and administer employer contributions. Unemployed workers would thus receive benefits from a pooled fund. At the same time, firms maintaining a record of steady employment would receive a reduction in their assigned contributions to the fund. While the AALL and the Wisconsin State Federation of Labor supported the Huber Bill, the Wisconsin Manufacturers' Association opposed it on grounds that it was both costly and "socialistic." If employers approved any form of unemployment compensation, they generally preferred a

[74] Paul Raushenbush, "Wisconsin's Unemployment Compensation Act," in *American Labor Legislation Review*, 22 (March, 1932), 11–12; Raushenbush and Raushenbush, *Our "U.C." Story*, 94–95; Bernstein, *Lean Years*, 498–499; Nelson, *Unemployment Insurance*, 123; Commons to John B. Andrews, July 20, 1931, in the John R. Commons Papers.

voluntary plan. And with the state's business people courting the state's farmers throughout the 1920's, the Huber Bill never succeeded in winning legislative approval.[75]

In working out legislation on unemployment compensation, Groves, Brandeis, and Raushenbush had quickly adopted a fresh approach. First incorporating their ideas into the Groves Bill presented in January during the regular session, they hoped that a new version prepared for the special session would win the support of business interests. Instead of calling for a pooled fund of employers' contributions to be administered by a mutual insurance company, they proposed a system of individual accounts for all employers. Each would contribute a percentage of payroll only to the employer's own account until it reached a predetermined level. Then contributions would cease, and as long as the employer maintained payroll and avoided depleting the account, further payments would not be required. On the other hand, should workers become unemployed, they could draw compensation from the accumulated reserves in their employer's account.[76]

The new plan drafted by La Follette's advisers had grown out of Commons' idea that the goal was to prevent unemployment, and that the best way to achieve the goal was to make full employment profitable for firms hiring workers. Yet to Andrews, the AALL, and the Wisconsin Federation of Labor, the reserves plan seemed to concede too much to the employers. Workers were wary of depending only on their own employers' funds for benefits, and they much preferred a pooling of employer contributions. Always one to prefer half a loaf to none, however, Commons came out in favor of the Groves Bill, and the resistance of labor interests declined.[77]

[75] Edwin E. Witte to Harry A. Millis, October 26, 1938, in the Edwin E. Witte Papers; "Summary of the Principal Provisions of the Last Huber Unemployment Insurance Bill," January 25, 1924, in the Commons Papers; Daniel Nelson, "The Origins of Unemployment Insurance in Wisconsin," in *WMH*, 51 (Winter, 1967–1968), 118–119; *Capital Times*, June 2, 1921; Milwaukee *Leader*, November 17, 1922; Milwaukee *Sentinel*, February 24, 1923; *Wisconsin Agriculturist*, March 10, 1923; *Wisconsin State Journal*, March 27, April 5, 1923; *Wisconsin Farmer*, May 3, 1923; *Wisconsin Farmers Union News*, February 15, 1925.

[76] John R. Commons, "The Groves Unemployment Reserves Law," in the *American Labor Legislation Review*, 22 (March, 1932), 8–10; Harold M. Groves, "Unemployment Compensation in Wisconsin" (speech, December 6, 1932), in University of Wisconsin, Department of Economics, "Unemployment Compensation in Wisconsin, Articles by Harold M. Groves," in the LRB; Edwin E. Witte to Abraham Epstein, June 29, 1933, in the Witte Papers.

[77] Nelson, *Unemployment Insurance*, 120–121; Milwaukee *Leader*, June 19, 1931; *Capital*

In the meantime, some employers were reacting negatively to proposals that seemed inconsistent with their own view of what the times required. The Groves Bill and other schemes for compensating the unemployed were, suggested Oshkosh lumberman A. L. Osborne, "irridescent [*sic*] dreams." Because unemployment resulted from wars, embargoes, emotions, and other influences over which most business people had no control, he argued, employers should not be asked to meet costs of unemployment. It was not the intention of the Founding Fathers "to take property from one in order to give it to another," asserted a Milwaukee critic. If the legislature acceded to that principle, it would be "but a short step to the communistic principle of leveling all financial inequality." Rather than adopting schemes to reward the "shiftless and lazy," schemes promoted by "theoretical economists with little or no practical experience," it would be far better to rely on the voluntary efforts of employers who were as anxious as anyone to keep their workers busy.[78]

As employers refurbished old arguments against a government-sponsored scheme of unemployment compensation, the Commons students countered by soliciting the endorsement of other groups, particularly those associated with agriculture. They also made sure that their proposal received adequate attention in hearings conducted by the interim committee. Supporters who testified for the Groves Bill or some other system of unemployment reserves included former governor Francis McGovern, Fond du Lac manufacturer William Mauthe, Wisconsin Society of Equity president Barney Gehrman, and Albert G. Schmedeman, the mayor of Madison.[79]

Just before the special session began, state farm organizations held a "Farmers Get Together" at Shawano. Supporters of unemployment compensation appeared at the gathering armed with well-developed arguments to persuade the delegates that farmers

---

Times, January 21, February 19, 20, 1931; John R. Commons, "Permanent Prevention of Unemployment" (typescript of address), May 9, 1931, in the Commons Papers.

[78] Milwaukee *Journal*, March 5, 1931; Milwaukee Association of Commerce, *Milwaukee Commerce*, March 26, 1931; Chicago *Tribune*, January 4, 8, 1931; *Capital Times*, January 8, 1932.

[79] Wisconsin Committee for Unemployment Reserves Legislation to members of the Wisconsin legislature, November 24, 1931, reprinted in Raushenbush and Raushenbush, *Our "U.C." Story*, 108–111 (also pp. 27–28, 31–32); *Wisconsin Farmers Union News*, November 15, December 1, 1931; Nelson, *Unemployment Insurance*, 124–125.

as well as urban workers would benefit from an unemployment reserves program. Contending that urban workers were consumers of farm products, and that without a reserves program farmers would be taxed more heavily for relief, the reformers succeeded in securing approval of an unemployment compensation resolution. Shortly thereafter, the Wisconsin Pure Milk Products Cooperative Association, the Wisconsin State Union of the American Society of Equity, and the Wisconsin Farm Bureau Federation all endorsed the action taken at Shawano.[80]

In winning support from the state's farm organizations as well as from organized labor, the advocates of unemployment compensation effectively neutralized employer opposition. The legislative interim committee released its report on November 16, 1931. With Burtis and Clausen submitting a minority report, the majority recommended enactment of a law to carry out the essential provisions of the Groves Bill as one of several measures dealing with the Depression. The report set July 1, 1933, as the date for employers to begin making contributions to their accounts. All that remained to assure victory for the proposed bill was for a few independent senators and some of the state's employers to accept its provisions.[81]

With a deft treatment of the subject in his address of November 24, the governor cleverly outmaneuvered the employers who were still insisting upon a voluntary plan as preferable to the Groves Bill. Assuring the employers that he did not doubt their sincerity, Phil proposed taking them at their word. "The fairest method of procedure for us at this time is to adopt a just and sound compulsory unemployment compensation program for Wisconsin," he suggested, "but to make the taking effect of such legislation conditional upon industry's failure to establish a fair voluntary system in Wisconsin within a reasonable time." In essence, Phil was calling the employers' bluff. If the legislature enacted a bill that included his proviso, employers would be compelled either to develop a volunteer unemployment compensation program of their own within a specific period or to accept the plan embodied in the Groves Bill. Supporters of the Groves-interim committee bill agreed to incorporate the governor's proviso, and Edwin Witte drafted an amend-

[80] *Capital Times*, October 23, 28, 1931; Elizabeth Brandeis, "Wisconsin Tackles Job Security," in *The Survey*, 67 (December 15, 1931), 295–296; Milwaukee *Leader*, November 4, 1931.

[81] Legislature, Interim Committee on Unemployment, *Report* (1931), 53–70.

ment stipulating that the compulsory sections would not go into effect if employers established voluntary plans covering 200,000 workers by June 1, 1933. The senate reduced the number, and in its final form the bill required that voluntary plans covering 175,000 workers be approved by the Industrial Commission.[82]

With very little debate the assembly passed the amended unemployment compensation bill on December 21, 1931, and the senate approved its version of an amended bill early in the new year. After the two houses had reconciled their differences, Governor La Follette signed into law the first unemployment compensation act in American history. The terms of the new legislation required any employer of ten or more persons to deposit 2 per cent of the payroll in the employer's own state-controlled account. After accumulated deposits reached $55 per employee, employer contributions would be reduced to 1 per cent of the payroll. They would continue at that level until the individual reserve reached $75 per employee. At that point, if there were no withdrawals to provide compensation for unemployed workers, the employer contributions would cease. As for the workers, they could draw benefits up to a maximum of ten weeks a year at a rate of 50 per cent of their average weekly wage. Their compensation, however, could not exceed $10 in a given week.[83]

Climaxing a decade of reform effort, the Wisconsin Unemployment Compensation Act was the most notable piece of legislation to come out of the special session, but it was not the only one. Late in January, 1932, the legislature enacted a companion bill, the Emergency Relief Act, which had also received endorsement from the legislative interim committee. At the opening of the session the governor requested an appropriation of $17 million to be used for direct relief and public works projects, for a reduction in property taxes, and for a forestry program in northern Wisconsin. The conservative legislators of Wisconsin, like those elsewhere, were ada-

[82] Thomas M. Duncan to H. C. Rassmann, February 3, 1932, in the Philip F. La Follette Papers; Raushenbush, "The Wisconsin Idea," American Academy of Political and Social Sciences, *Annals*, 170:2; Raushenbush and Raushenbush, *Our "U.C." Story*, 111–113; Manitowoc *Herald-News*, January 27, 1932.

[83] Major provisions of the Wisconsin Unemployment Compensation Act are reprinted in Nelson, *Unemployment Insurance*, 225–231. A summary of the act appeared in *Congressional Digest*, 14 (February, 1935), 33–37. Newspapers in Wisconsin and elsewhere also provided summaries of the act. See, for example, the Manitowoc *Herald-News*, January 27, 1932, and the St. Louis *Post-Dispatch*, February 21, 1932.

mantly opposed to such programs because they believed that work relief would not only involve great expenditures and heavier taxes, but would also set a pattern of state intervention. To avert as much of the work relief program as possible, opponents of the relief bill cut the appropriation to $8 million. Having staked his reputation on securing unemployment compensation, the governor shied away from further testing of his influence and took what he could get. The costs of the Emergency Relief Act were to be met through a surtax on incomes, a dividends tax, and a tax on chain stores—an indication that while the Progressives were forced to compromise on the size of the relief program, they could still take pride in their fidelity to principle.[84]

The Progressive legislators of the special session also demonstrated that they were as consistent as the conservatives in keeping faith with one of the state's most important economic interest groups: the dairy farmers. By an overwhelming majority both houses passed a bill imposing a tax of six cents a pound on all oleomargarine sold in the state. The legislation also required licenses for all dealers in the product and for all bakeries and boardinghouses using it. After ten weeks of strenuous deliberation, the legislature adjourned to prepare for the crucial political campaign of 1932.[85]

* * *

During the depths of the Depression the sons of Robert M. La Follette appeared to offer a new vision and a new hope. In March, 1932, the brothers joined in speaking to the nation through facilities of the National Broadcasting Company. Viewing the problems confronting the American people from their own state and national perspectives, the governor and the senator developed their theme,

[84] La Follette, *Adventure in Politics*, 165–166. Also "Roll Call on Important Progressive Measures—Regular and Special Sessions, 1931" (typewritten, in box 24), 2–3; Philip F. La Follette to Clarence D. Coe, January 18, 1932; Edwin E. Witte to La Follette, December 31, 1931; Aubrey Williams to La Follette, January 5, 1932; Edward G. Littel to C. J. Petretic, January 14, 1932; La Follette to Mr. and Mrs. John A. Stress, January 15, 1932; and Thomas M. Duncan to Mrs. John Henry Moore, February 19, 1932, all in the Philip F. La Follette Papers. For a critical assessment of the governor's role in the special session, see Bernhard Gettelman to La Follette, May 16, 1932, in *ibid*.

[85] "Roll Call on Important Progressive Measures—Regular and Special Sessions, 1931" (typewritten, in box 24), 4, in the Philip F. La Follette Papers. During the regular session the legislature had enacted a law prohibiting the distribution of oleomargarine to persons on relief. La Follette to County, Town, Village, and City Clerks, February 15, 1932, in *ibid*.

"Progressive Government," as a contribution to the NBC National Radio Forum.

Phil spoke first. Recalling once again the images of a primeval continent, he compared the American people to travelers whose guide had lost his way. "The forest looms about, its stillness intensifying the terror that lurks within you," he told his listeners. Yet responding to uncertainties of the Depression with irrational despair and panic was "not worthy of our heritage." Americans should rely on past experience; they should blaze the trail towards a new "economic government." Wisconsin, Phil suggested, was showing the way with its development of public power, its economic and social planning, its encouragement of business self-government, and its programs for relief and public works. While "the reactionaries will still continue to call the Progressives of Wisconsin radical and destructive," the reactionaries were wrong. The governor closed his remarks by emphasizing that "in the true meaning of the word 'conservative'—to conserve and preserve—the only real conservatives in America today are the Progressives."

When it was Young Bob's turn to speak, he cited several economic indicators to demonstrate the folly of "speculative control of industry and finance." After describing his own efforts to secure a national economic council, a program of public works, and a relief program for "human victims of economic calamities and governmental mistakes," Bob argued for national adoption of Wisconsin's new system of unemployment compensation. Urging Americans to reject dictatorship from both left and right—the dictatorship of Russia as well as that of Italy—the senator reinforced his brother's plea for a sensitive appreciation of the American experience. "If we apply the same fundamental principles to the control of our economic life that our forebears applied to the problems of government," Bob concluded, "we can and we will solve the problems of this generation and build for the future economic security of all the people."[86]

At the time of the National Radio Forum broadcast, the brothers La Follette had reached the height of their influence. How they would use that influence in the years ahead remained to be seen.

[86] "Progressive Government," the speeches of Philip and Robert La Follette on the National Radio Forum, March 14, 1932, brochure in *ibid*. Later in the year, Phil reiterated his praise of Wisconsin's relief and unemployment compensation programs in an article for *The Exchangite*, October, 1932, in *ibid*.

10

Cries of Protest, Murmurs of Discontent, and Formation of the Progressive Party of Wisconsin

THE Wisconsin Progressives derived great satisfaction from their initial accomplishments in responding to the Depression that ended the New Era. Confronting continued economic uncertainty, however, they could not be sure of further political rewards for their efforts. The economic upheaval that had disrupted patterns of everyday life among the American people seemed certain to bring changes in the patterns of politics as well. Throughout the postwar decade, the Republican party had claimed ascendancy. Now, as the Depression deepened and attacks on the Hoover administration multiplied in volume and intensity, Democratic party leaders optimistically calculated their chances of once again placing a Democrat in the White House.

Preparing for the presidential election of 1932, Democrats centered their attention on the search for a candidate who could not only win but could also unite a party badly torn by dissension during the decade after the Great War. As a transfer of political power appeared more and more likely, voters as well as political leaders found themselves increasingly drawn to the candidacy of Franklin D. Roosevelt. The New York governor had shown no profound understanding of what had brought on the economic calamities that plagued the American people, but he had certainly shown a capacity for responding to their distress with imagination and compassion. He was not the sort of man to satisfy conservative ideologues, but his skillful courting of rank-and-file Democrats might well overcome opposition within the party.[1]

[1] John E. Miller, *Governor Philip F. La Follette, the Wisconsin Progressives, and the New*

When Wisconsin held its presidential preference primary on April 5, 1932, Roosevelt's name was the only one to appear on the Democratic ballot. His vote exceeded by a hundred thousand the vote of George Norris, the state's Republican favorite, and he won twenty-four of twenty-six Wisconsin delegates to the Democratic National Convention in Chicago. FDR's victory in the Wisconsin primary, followed by his success in capturing the Democratic presidential nomination, raised serious questions about the direction of political trends in Wisconsin. For nearly eighty years the Republican party had dominated the state, and since the turn of the century most political contests had come down to a struggle between Progressive and Stalwart factions of the party. Not since Woodrow Wilson's victory in 1912 had Wisconsin's electoral vote gone to a Democrat. Not since George W. Peck won successive elections in 1890 and 1892 had a Democrat occupied the governor's mansion. And not since 1894 had Democrats won control over either house of the state legislature. Now, in 1932, the voters' endorsement of FDR suggested that Wisconsin's political profile was beginning to change.[2]

Might the economic frustrations of the Depression lead to a permanent revival of the moribund Democratic party of Wisconsin? If Roosevelt were to revitalize the national party, would the voters of Wisconsin join a nationwide movement into Democratic ranks? If Roosevelt became President, would he employ his political proficiency and tactical skill to build a productive partnership with the sons of Robert M. La Follette? In 1932 the answers to these and other questions were by no means self-evident. With long-established political affiliations undergoing rapid change, there was no guarantee that the process would stop short of truly radical alteration of Wisconsin society. People talked of revolution as a real possibility, and should a revolution occur, traditional questions

Deal (Columbia, Missouri, 1982), 26; *Pierce County Herald* (Ellsworth), February 11, 1932; William B. Rubin to August Rehwinkle, March 11, 1930, and William B. Rubin to Jacob Rubin, July 5, 1932, both in the William B. Rubin Papers; Arthur M. Schlesinger, Jr., *The Crisis of the Old Order, 1919–1933* (Boston, 1957), 393, 396–398; Raymond Moley, *The First New Deal* (New York, 1966), 4–5; William E. Leuchtenburg, *Franklin D. Roosevelt and the New Deal, 1932–1940* (New York, 1963), 4–5; Burton K. Wheeler to Philip F. La Follette, February 23, 1932, in the Philip F. La Follette Papers.

[2] *Wisconsin Blue Book, 1933*, pp. 526–530; Miller, *Governor Philip F. La Follette*, 25; James R. Donoghue, *How Wisconsin Voted, 1848–1972* (Madison, 1974), 81–83, 102–112; David L. Brye, *Wisconsin Voting Patterns in the Twentieth Century, 1900 to 1950* (New York, 1979), 375.

about the state's political future could quickly become inane. While no such radical change took place, the stresses of the Depression produced protests and demonstrations that seemed at times to threaten orderly political processes in Wisconsin.

* * *

Roosevelt's growing popularity in 1932, arising in large part from his attractiveness to a people desperately hoping for an economic messiah, placed the Democratic party of Wisconsin in an awkward position. To be sure, the state party included some liberals who would have been comfortable with their own version of a Progressive platform. Yet the dominant faction within the state organization succeeded in preserving the party as a haven for cautious conservatives. It was not in character for Democratic wheelhorses to look either for new ideas or towards new approaches to economic problems. Endorsing Roosevelt was as far as they would go, and that endorsement simply meant that they wished to support a winner; it did not necessarily imply that they wished to support an affirmative program.[3]

As the political campaign of 1932 began, then, it seemed to signal no significant departure from state campaigns of earlier years. Once again Republicans took to the hustings in a manner suggesting that they alone were discussing live options. Once again Stalwarts and Progressives fought battles within the Republican party as if settling political questions for everyone else. And once again, most voters expected the primary and not the general election to be decisive. Without questioning long-accepted standards of the Wisconsin political ethos, they believed that Phil La Follette could win a second term as governor simply by defeating his Stalwart opponent, Walter J. Kohler, in the primary.[4]

With characteristic vigor, Phil began his re-election campaign in May, and he soon realized that 1932 differed from previous election years. Traveling about the state, mending fences and attempting to stimulate enthusiasm for his candidacy, he was one of the first to sense the extent of Roosevelt's support. New Democratic leaders

[3] William T. Evjue, *A Fighting Editor* (Madison, 1968), 510–551; Philip F. La Follette, *Adventure in Politics: The Memoirs of Philip La Follette*, ed. Donald Young (New York, 1970), 178; Miller, *Governor Philip F. La Follette*, 26.

[4] Philip F. La Follette to Robert M. La Follette, Jr., May 15, 1932, in box A-42, the La Follette Family Papers, Library of Congress; *Wisconsin State Journal*, July 20, 1932.

were beginning to assert themselves, and they appeared to be moving away from the Democratic old guard. F. Ryan Duffy, a lawyer from Fond du Lac who was soon to become a candidate for Blaine's seat in the Senate, had come out for Roosevelt. So had Sheboygan *Press* editor Charles E. Broughton, Milwaukee labor attorney William B. Rubin, and several others who had never seemed entirely at ease with the party's conservative leadership. More importantly, as the presidential preference primary indicated, FDR was gaining steadily in popular support and luring voters away from the Progressives.[5]

Despite the continued confidence of many Progressives that La Follette would defeat Kohler, Phil himself became increasingly doubtful of his chances. Yet he held to his initial campaign strategy. It had always been effective before, and he could come up with no good way to adapt to the unusual circumstance of 1932. Avoiding mention of Roosevelt and the Democrats, he emphasized his own achievements while linking the Stalwarts with Hoover's failed efforts to restore prosperity. Kohler, for his part, carried on a dignified campaign that left Stalwart fireworks up to John B. Chapple, editor of the Ashland *Press*, who was challenging John Blaine for his seat in the United States Senate. The editor was anything but dignified as he fired a series of vituperative charges against the Progressives, alleging among other things that they were corrupting students at the University of Wisconsin with their radicalism, atheism, and immorality. Chapple apparently did his campaign no damage with his wild fulminations. When the primary returns came in, the Progressives were dismayed to learn that he had defeated Blaine. Worse yet, with 57 per cent of the vote, Kohler had decisively beaten La Follette. In 1932, the time-tested formulas of Progressive Republicans obviously failed to win sufficient support in the primaries; the Stalwart Republicans might well experience just as convincing

[5] *The Progressive*, April 9, 1932; Arthur Hitt to Philip F. La Follette, June 5, 1932, in the Philip F. La Follette Papers; Elmer Davis, "Wisconsin Is Different," in *Harper's Magazine*, 165 (October, 1932), 613–614. Rubin was one of FDR's early supporters in Wisconsin, but in running against Albert Schmedeman for the Democratic gubernatorial nomination in 1932, he tended to modify his views. William T. Evjue chided him for "voicing an anti-liberal tone" in his campaign, but there was more here than met the eye. After his defeat, Rubin confessed, "I cannot erase from my memory the fact that some people within the party have through selfish motives, spread the gospel of racial hatred toward me." See the following in the Rubin Papers: Rubin to Franklin D. Roosevelt, November 6, 1930; Franklin D. Roosevelt to Rubin, November 14, 1930; Evjue to Rubin, December 5, 1932; and Rubin to C. W. Henney, September 28, 1932.

a defeat in the general election. Wisconsin Democrats began sniffing victory in the air.[6]

In the meantime, from across the country letters and telegrams of commiseration poured in to La Follette headquarters. Closer to the Progressive campaign, however, and more directly involved in the accomplishments of 1931–1932 than were most of Phil's supporters, Elizabeth Brandeis sent a note of appreciation. "It was a thrilling experience," she wrote, "to live in Wisconsin in these years, to feel that there was a program under way, that government was playing a constructive part, that real things were being planned and done."[7]

Others who expressed their disappointment were more interested in the political future of Wisconsin—and its Democratic party—than they were in the Progressive record. From Maine, Ernest Gruening wrote that he found Phil's defeat "particularly ironic" because "there has never been a time in our history when the stand-pat and reactionary policies have been more thoroughly discredited." How Wisconsin voters could nominate "such an utter ass and blatherskite as Chapple" was difficult for Gruening to understand. As for the election of other candidates, however, he believed that "the chance to vote against the Hoover administration in November and join the Democrats was an important factor." Andrew Furuseth, president of the International Seamen's Union and an old friend of the La Follettes, agreed with Gruening that now with Phil's defeat, the La Follettes should make common cause with those who had voted Democratic in the primary. It was, he believed, "the way to defeat Kohler and all the other stand patters."[8]

After the primary election, the La Follettes' thinking ran parallel to that of Gruening and Furuseth. Early in October, Phil told a rally of his followers that their objective should be to elect Progressives, and that they need not feel compelled to support Stal-

[6] Miller, *Governor Philip F. La Follette*, 28; Madison *Capital Times*, September 20, 1931, September 21, 1932; Washington *Post*, April 24, 1932; *Wisconsin State Journal*, August 20, 1932; *The Progressive*, September 17, 1932; C. P. Thorne to John B. Chapple, April 24, 1932, copy in the John J. Blaine Papers; *Wisconsin Blue Book, 1933*, pp. 515, 597–606. In Milwaukee County, where Progressives hoped to make last-minute gains, Kohler more than doubled La Follette's vote. The final returns showed him winning 89,304 to 41,281 in the county.

[7] Elizabeth Brandeis to Philip F. La Follette, September 21, 1932, in the Philip F. La Follette Papers.

[8] Ernest Gruening to Philip F. La Follette, received September 24, 1932, and Andrew Furuseth to La Follette, September 23, 1932, both in *ibid.*

warts. Shortly thereafter, editor William T. Evjue announced in the *Capital Times* his intention to back FDR. "We are at the crossroads," he pointed out. The road on the left led to "the sound, constructive liberalism of Franklin D. Roosevelt." On the road to the right, "the forces of special privilege and organized wealth were directing traffic towards 'a form of fascism behind which stands a dictatorship of wealth.' " The following day, Bob La Follette came out for FDR even though he still regarded the Wisconsin Democratic party as "an adjunct of the reactionary Republican organization." In a contest between Roosevelt and Hoover, neither Bob nor his brother had qualms about supporting FDR.[9]

With the Progressives falling into line behind Roosevelt's candidacy, the Democrats swept to victory in November. Roosevelt won with 22.5 million popular votes nationally, as against less than 16 million for Hoover. The winner's 472 electoral votes included twelve from Wisconsin. Albert G. Schmedeman defeated Kohler in the gubernatorial race, and F. Ryan Duffy overwhelmed Chapple in the senatorial contest. Other state Democratic victories occurred in the elections for lieutenant-governor, attorney general, and state treasurer. Electing fifty-nine assemblymen, the Democrats gained control over the lower house of the state legislature. Eugene A. Clifford of Juneau, who had been the one lonely Democrat in the senate, acquired seven new Democratic colleagues.[10]

The Democratic sweep of Wisconsin in 1932 did not represent a long-term triumph for New Deal liberalism; most of the state's Democrats of that year never changed their conservative spots. Analysis of election returns, not only in 1932 but in 1924 as well, provides a basis for understanding the peculiar relationship that developed between Wisconsin Democrats and the New Deal coalition. FDR achieved his overwhelming victory in Wisconsin with the backing of Progressives. Comparing his support in 1932 with that of Robert M. La Follette, Sr., and John W. Davis in 1924 suggests that FDR's vote was roughly equivalent to Old Bob's vote combined with that of Davis. La Follette and Davis together won 62.6 per cent of the total vote in 1924; FDR captured 63.5 per cent in 1932. More refined analysis indicates that the combined La

[9] Milwaukee *Journal*, October 4, 1932; *Capital Times*, October 18, 1932; Patrick J. Maney, *"Young Bob" La Follette: A Biography of Robert M. La Follette, Jr., 1895–1953* (Columbia, Missouri, 1978), 105.

[10] *Wisconsin Blue Book, 1933*, pp. 531–534, 536–537, 540–541, 552–556.

Follette and Davis returns correlate at .732 with the vote for Roosevelt in 1932.[11]

Roosevelt achieved his 1932 victory in Wisconsin by attracting support from two very different if not antithetical traditions represented by the Progressives and the regular Democrats. But if Progressives and Democrats united to provide FDR with his margin of victory, why did they not also unite in supporting New Deal liberalism? During the New Deal era, Wisconsin Democrats never fully understood Roosevelt's obligations to the Wisconsin Progressives. They often complained that while the President ignored members of his own party, he frequently consulted with the La Follettes and just as frequently bestowed favors on friends of the La Follettes. The complaints of Democratic regulars were well-founded, to be sure, but they placed far greater emphasis on party loyalty than FDR ever wished to encourage. The Progressives, on the other hand, could never quite get over the idea that the state Democratic party was composed of stand-patters and reactionaries who simply reinforced the Stalwart Republican foes of Progressivism. Neither Democrats nor Progressives seemed to understand the President's need to walk a fine line in Wisconsin and to avoid alienating either of two factions that found working in tandem almost impossible. Democrats failed to appreciate the usefulness of FDR's alliance with the La Follettes, however tenuous it might become; the Progressives, for their part, tended to believe that working too closely with Democrats would compromise their own high principles.[12]

Another factor that shaped the often uneasy relationship between the President and Wisconsin's political factions was the desire of some Progressives to extend their influence beyond state borders. Phil La Follette often conveyed the impression that he was consumed by a driving ambition to succeed FDR as President, and he seemed at times compelled to instruct New Dealers on the lessons of Wisconsin Progressivism. The idea that Wisconsin might serve

[11] Brye, *Wisconsin Voting Patterns*, 295—301, 309–321. Brye corrects some of the findings of Harold F. Gosnell and Morris H. Cohen reported in "Progressive Politics: Wisconsin an Example," in the *American Political Science Review*, 34 (October, 1940), 920–935.

[12] Miller, *Governor Philip F. La Follette*, 33–34, 39–40, 55–57, 64–65, 90–92; Richard C. Haney, "The Rise of Wisconsin's New Democrats: A Political Realignment in the Mid-Twentieth Century," in *WMH*, 58 (Winter, 1974–1975), 91–92; Robert M. La Follette, Jr., to John F. Sinclair, January 17, 1933, and Robert M. La Follette, Jr., to Philip F. La Follette, January 20, 1933, both in the Philip F. La Follette Papers.

as an example for other states became firmly fixed in his mind. Bob was more diffident, more reluctant to strike out on paths of political conquest, and far more willing to subordinate his own ambitions to FDR's larger objectives. Thus Roosevelt, sensing no threat in Bob, believed that through him he could retain the support of Wisconsin Progressives, and through him could perhaps curb Phil's ambitions.

With Roosevelt gracefully expressing his gratitude to the La Follettes after his election, political observers began to speculate about the possibility of Phil's being asked to join the new administration in Washington. Rumors that FDR was planning to offer cabinet appointments to Progressive Republicans were in the air, and during Phil's last days in office he wrote his brother to indicate that he would consider an appointment if it met with the approval of congressional Progressives. Hearing nothing by the end of the year, Phil and Isabel, his wife, decided on an alternative plan. James Causey, a wealthy New York investment broker, suggested that with momentous events occurring abroad it would be a good time for another trip to Europe. Phil liked the idea, and when Causey offered to help finance the expedition he responded enthusiastically. The day after Schmedeman took the oath of office as governor, Phil and Isen left New York on the French liner *La Fayette*. Their itinerary included visits to London, Brussels, Berlin, Moscow, Warsaw, Budapest, Vienna, Rome, and Paris.[13]

While abroad, Phil hoped to learn how other nations were coping with the world depression and what their experiences might mean for the United States. In London, he conferred with several British leaders; he was most impressed with Sir Josiah Stamp, a director of the Bank of England, and Sir Robert Vansittart, permanent undersecretary for foreign affairs. Over tea, he and Stamp talked about consequences of the closing of frontiers and the need to provide for economic needs without resorting to communism or fascism. And shortly before the La Follettes crossed over to the continent, Vansittart warned Phil of dreadful consequences should Adolf Hitler come to power in Germany.

Phil and Isen arrived in Berlin on January 28, 1933, and so the

[13] Philip F. La Follette to Robert M. La Follette, Jr., December 9, 1932, in box A-42, La Follette Family Papers, Library of Congress; La Follette, *Adventure in Politics*, 183–184; New York *American*, April 23, 30, May 7, 14, 21, 28, 1933. Among friends and family members, Isabel La Follette used a familiar form of her name: "Isen."

two of them were present at the creation of a new order that was supposed to last a thousand years. "The Nazis are everywhere, very cocky and noisy in their kakhi [*sic*] uniforms," Isen recorded in her diary. A few days later she commented on Nazi anti-Semitism and added that "one distinguished man told Phil that he had no doubt but what the intellectual class—scientists, scholars, etc. would all leave the country if America would let down our immigration bars." Fully warned of mounting tensions as they headed eastward towards Moscow, and then towards Rome, Phil and Isen saw for themselves how the nations of Europe appeared to be taking steps that could lead to war.[14]

Back home, Roosevelt was still working at putting his cabinet together and making other appointments. Senator Bronson Cutting, a progressive Republican from New Mexico, was FDR's first choice for the Department of the Interior, but he told the President that he would not consider the position unless Phil or some other Progressive were also in the cabinet. "I want Phil in my official family," Roosevelt remarked to Bob in mid-January. "I do not know just where yet, but he must come in." A few days later he invited Bob to join Cutting in a visit to his retreat at Warm Springs, Georgia, where he said that if Senator Thomas J. Walsh of Montana declined the position of attorney general, he intended to ask Phil if he would take it. Walsh accepted the position, however, and the chances of a La Follette appointment seemed remote. Then the Montana senator died two days before the inauguration, and Bob wired Phil in Rome to urge that he return home.[15]

Back in the United States, Phil accompanied his brother to the White House for an hour's conference with the President. FDR had asked to see them in order to discuss three matters: the problem of relief, Phil's impressions of events taking place in Europe, and the possibility of Phil's joining his administration. Relief was to be a continuing concern, of course, and Bob pointed out that inad-

[14] La Follette, *Adventure in Politics*, 186–189; Philip F. La Follette to Dear Ones, February 5, 18, 1933, in box A-43, La Follette Family Papers, Library of Congress; entries for January 30, February 4, 1933, in Isabel Bacon La Follette diary, "Journal of Our Trip," Philip F. La Follette Papers.

[15] Robert M. La Follette, Jr., to John F. Sinclair, January 17, 1933; Robert M. La Follette, Jr., to Philip F. La Follette, January 20, 24, 1933; and Robert M. La Follette, Jr., to Philip F. and Isen La Follette, February 7, 1933, all in the Philip F. La Follette Papers. Also Ronald L. Feinman, *Twilight of Progressivism: The Western Republican Senators and the New Deal* (Baltimore, 1981), 51–53.

equate measures to deal with it would disappoint millions of Americans. Having earlier discussed the subject with FDR, the senator urged him to act quickly if he expected co-operation from the states. The President had already prepared a message to Congress outlining his wishes, and he sent it on to Capitol Hill the following day.[16]

Turning to Phil, Roosevelt asked what he had learned on his European tour. In response, Phil expressed his concern over the imminent danger of war, adding that the European "war psychology was a by-product of the economic process . . . going on in every country." FDR said he thought fear was a factor producing the war scare, but Phil insisted on making his point: "unless the economic process that makes these people self-sustaining can be reversed so that their economic livelihood comes from exchange of goods and services, they are going to continue to think in terms of self-sufficiency and nationalism—which are things leading to war."

Responding to a query about Russia, Phil told the President that he thought the USSR more important relative to American foreign policy than to any economic lessons the Russians could teach the United States. He believed that, if asked, the Russians would say their greatest need was for heavy machinery, but that far more than machinery they needed foodstuffs. He suggested a prompt recognition of the Soviet Union, and he urged the President to extend recognition as part of a program to dispose of the American agricultural surplus. Any assistance the United States could provide, he thought, could be repaid through the Red Army. A deterrent to German military expansionism, that army made Russia "the key to the peace of Europe."[17]

Towards the end of the conversation, FDR reiterated his desire to have Phil join other Progressives in his administration. In a general way, he mentioned four positions that might be of interest: one as head of the power program, one involving transportation

[16] Copies of Philip F. La Follette's notes on the conference with FDR, March 20, 1933, in both the Philip F. La Follette Papers and in box A-43, La Follette Family Papers, Library of Congress; Moley, *First New Deal*, 269–271. Congress passed the Emergency Relief Bill, and Roosevelt signed it on May 12, 1933. The legislation created the Federal Emergency Relief Administration and provided it with $500 million in relief money to be distributed by state and local agencies. See Leuchtenburg, *Franklin D. Roosevelt and the New Deal*, 120, and Arthur M. Schlesinger, Jr., *The Coming of the New Deal* (Boston, 1958), 264–265.

[17] Copies of Philip F. La Follette's notes on the conference with FDR, March 20, 1933, in both the Philip F. La Follette Papers and in box A-43, La Follette Family Papers, Library of Congress; Feinman, *Twilight of Progressivism*, 54.

and communication, one with the Federal Trade Commission, and finally, a position as head of public works and relief. Perhaps doubting Roosevelt's seriousness, and aware of FDR's skill in dropping hints without making commitments, Phil turned him down. Pleading that his roots were in Wisconsin, La Follette suggested that he could be of greater service "on the firing line" at home. He promised, however, "that when the contest got bitter and [Roosevelt] thought there was no one to do a particular task as well as I could do it, that then I would be glad to do it." Having pledged to support the President, Phil left for home, and Bob turned his attention to legislation.[18]

The senator had mixed feelings about the programs approved during the hectic Hundred Days of the Roosevelt administration. He supported abandonment of the international gold standard, creation of the Tennessee Valley Authority, and, in a more qualified way, the Agricultural Adjustment Act (AAA). He welcomed creation of the Civilian Conservation Corps, and like most Wisconsin Progressives he credited Phil with having first developed the idea for such a program. His position on the National Industrial Recovery Act was ambivalent. He approved of establishing the Public Works Administration, but he believed its $3.3 billion allotment insufficient to meet either employment or recovery needs. He, Cutting, and Edward P. Costigan of Colorado had introduced a public works bill providing $6 billion, and he disliked reducing the amount. As for the other new agency in the NIRA, the National Recovery Administration, it seemed to Bob a risky business to suspend antitrust laws and encourage business consolidation. He strongly favored Section 7(a) which guaranteed labor's right to bargain collectively, but in the end he could not bring himself to vote for the bill in its final form.[19]

[18] Copies of Philip F. La Follette's notes on the conference with FDR, March 20, 1933, in both the Philip F. La Follette Papers and in box A-43, La Follette Family Papers, Library of Congress; Miller, *Governor Philip F. La Follette*, 37–38. Phil's reluctance to go into the Roosevelt administration may be in part attributable to the advice of Thomas M. Duncan. "I think first Bob and you must decide whether to unite with R. if you feel . . . that he has a program and that he really wants to construct a Progressive party," wrote Duncan, who went on to add that "if Bob and you feel that you cannot aid R then I think the new party is the thing." See Duncan to Philip F. La Follette, March 15, 1933, in the Philip F. La Follette Papers.

[19] Maney, *"Young Bob" La Follette*, 116–117; *Congressional Record*, 73 Cong., 1 sess., 2966; La Follette, *Adventure in Politics*, 165; Miller, *Governor Philip F. La Follette*, 58; Robert M. La Follette, Jr., to Fola La Follette and George Middleton, June 6, 1933, in box A-43, La Follette Family Papers, Library of Congress.

Roosevelt bore no grudges against Bob for opposing the NIRA. Indeed, during the summer he assured the senator that he would carry through on the public works program, and then he appointed Wisconsin Progressive David E. Lilienthal as a director of the Tennessee Valley Authority, and John J. Blaine as a director of the Reconstruction Finance Corporation. Senator La Follette, for his part, generally supported New Deal programs. When he differed with FDR, it was as a friendly critic.[20]

* * *

Traveling by train from Berlin to Moscow in February, 1933, Phil and Isen La Follette had been impressed by deteriorating conditions they observed in the Russian countryside. "There is evidence of building everywhere," Isen noted in her diary, "but things are not 'kept up.'" Later, after they had reached their destination, they checked the accuracy of their observations with New York *Times* correspondent Walter Duranty. The policy of collectivization begun in 1928, he told them, had resulted in the elimination of skilled farmers, thus leaving actual farm production in the hands of large numbers of rural folk who had little understanding of scientific agriculture. Production declined as a consequence of the change, and resulting food shortages created problems throughout Soviet society. "There is no doubt that the people one sees are badly nourished," wrote Isen, conscientiously taking notes. "We are told they still get bread, but that it is practically impossible to get butter, meat, vegetables, etc."[21]

At the very time the La Follettes were chatting with Duranty about Russian agricultural problems, the dairy farmers of Wisconsin were going on strike. That is, they were withholding their milk from markets in order to secure higher prices. Three strikes occurred that year, and the violence that accompanied them seriously threatened the peace in Wisconsin's normally tranquil dairyland. The central problem confronting the state's dairy farmers was not one of production, as in the USSR, but of marketing. Although the cooperative movement had made some headway during the 1920's,

[20] Thomas K. McCraw, *TVA and the Power Fight, 1933–1939* (Philadelphia, 1971), 43; Robert M. La Follette, Jr., "Address at the Funeral Services of John J. Blaine, April 19, 1934" (typewritten), in the Blaine Papers.

[21] Entry for February 13–14, 1933, in Isabel Bacon La Follette diary, "Journal of Our Trip," Philip F. La Follette Papers; La Follette, *Adventure in Politics*, 194–195.

farmers had gained little control over the prices they received for their milk. They suffered from declining prices throughout the New Era, and with the arrival of the Great Depression the milk price index dropped precipitously. After receiving almost three dollars per hundredweight in 1919 and about two dollars in 1929, dairy farmers were getting less than a dollar by 1932. At a time when Wisconsin farmers were already concerned over making mortgage payments and meeting other obligations incurred during the prosperous war years, low milk prices threatened disaster.[22]

Many difficulties confronted dairy farmers seeking adequate returns on their labor and investment, and in a complex market relationship each difficulty increased the magnitude of all the others. For years, milk sold for fluid use had brought a higher price than had milk that went to condenseries or milk manufactured into products such as cheese, butter, and ice cream. The difference between the two prices was attributable to the stable market demand for fluid milk in the cities, the reduced spoilage of milk products as compared with fluid milk, and the feasibility of using substitutes such as oleomargarine in place of process milk. The two-price system encouraged increased production of fluid milk, and with the increase, city markets received more fluid milk than consumers could use. The surplus had to be converted into manufactured products, but doing so further reduced the price of milk sent to condenseries and processing plants.[23]

After consumers had begun to feel the pinch of hard times during the early thirties, they cut down on fluid milk purchases and milk prices continued to drop. Distressed producers tended to believe that large dairy companies had been responsible for bringing about price reductions, and their belief was not entirely wrong. Such companies had benefited far more from technological innovations of the New Era than had smaller companies. Through acquisitions and mergers by which large companies grew larger, and through

[22] Harry L. Russell, *Forward Steps in Farm Science*, UW Agricultural Experiment Station, *Annual Report*, 1926–1927, published as *Bulletin*, no. 396 (1927), 3–4; A. William Hoglund, "Wisconsin Dairy Farmers on Strike," in *Agricultural History*, 35 (January, 1961), 24, 28; Herbert Jacobs, "The Wisconsin Milk Strikes," *WMH*, 35 (Autumn, 1951), 30, 32–35.

[23] Hoglund, "Wisconsin Dairy Farmers on Strike," *Agricultural History*, 35:24; and two publications by W. P. Mortenson: *An Economic Study of the Milwaukee Milk Market*, UW Agricultural Experiment Station, *Research Bulletin*, no. 113 (1932), 38–39, and *Economic Considerations in Fluid Milk Marketing*, UW Agricultural Experiment Station, *Research Bulletin*, no. 125 (1934), 40, 53.

capital investments in efficient equipment that smaller companies could ill afford, the large companies reduced labor costs, improved their methods of distribution, cut prices for consumers when necessary, and drove smaller dairies out of business or into consolidation with other dairies.[24]

As large dairies gained power over markets, they instituted practices that were eventually to cause resentment among milk producers. Particularly annoying to farmers was the way dairies used the two-price system to reduce what they paid for milk, whatever its intended use. Sometimes dairy companies simply set a flat price for all milk, which was of course lower than the price they would have had to pay for fluid milk alone. Sometimes they calculated a composite price that reflected the proportion between fluid and manufactured milk usage. In either case, the dairies were able to reduce what they paid for Class I, or fluid milk, and they were able to continue making profits. Dairy farmers, on the other hand, became frustrated. The more milk they produced, the more they increased the amount going into condenseries and cheese factories. And the greater the volume of milk used for manufacture, the lower the price for all milk became. By 1933, about three-fourths of the milk produced in Wisconsin went into the manufacture of dairy products, and dairy farmers began contemplating a concerted drive to raise the prices they received for their milk.[25]

During 1931, organizers Ivan M. Wright and Harvey Holmes set about creating the Central Co-operative Association to promote cooperative marketing and to co-ordinate the activities of all groups seeking to improve farm income. Before the end of the year, disagreement over tactics led to formation of the Wisconsin Cooperative Milk Pool, which withdrew from the parent association in 1932.[26]

[24] Mortenson, *Economic Considerations in Fluid Milk Marketing*, UW Agricultural Experiment Station, *Research Bulletin*, no. 125, pp. 36–39, 53–55; R. K. Froker, "Some Recent Developments in the Marketing of Dairy Products," address presented to the Central State Extension Conference, Purdue University, April 24–26, 1929, in LRB clipping file; John R. Randall, "The Geography of the North-Central Dairy Region of Wisconsin" (doctoral dissertation, University of Wisconsin, 1934), 313–315; Sheboygan *Times*, November 11, 1937.

[25] Hoglund, "Wisconsin Dairy Farmers on Strike," *Agricultural History*, 35:24–25; Mortenson, *Economic Study of the Milwaukee Milk Market*, UW Agricultural Experiment Station, *Research Bulletin*, no. 113, pp. 4–5.

[26] Hoglund, "Wisconsin Dairy Farmers on Strike," *Agricultural History*, 35:26; unidentified newspaper clipping, June 4, 1932, in the Wisconsin Cooperative Milk Pool Records; Milwaukee *Journal*, November 11, 1932.

The feuding among farmers brought Walter M. Singler to the fore as president of the Milk Pool, and by early 1933 he exerted a power to be reckoned with in Wisconsin's dairyland. Singler was a physical giant with a goatee and mustache who affected outlandish accouterments consisting of a fancy wool vest, red blazer, spats, and a ten-gallon hat. So attired, he skillfully exercised his persuasive talents wherever farmers gathered to discuss means of increasing agricultural income. The program he urged upon them was neither new nor complicated. Borrowing ideas developed in other organizations, especially the Farmers Union, he adopted a "cost-of-production" argument. That is, he proposed that farmers should receive a larger return on what they had invested in producing and processing the commodities they sold. Singler often played upon resentment of bureaucracy, as he did when he enjoined farmers against relying on the Wisconsin Department of Agriculture and Markets. Farmers had long complained about state officials who were, in the words of one farm leader, "pussyfooting and side-stepping on marketing." Now, argued Singler, it was up to the farmers themselves to put a price tag on milk and hogs and then make sure they received full payment; if they did not get what they were asking, their recourse was to go on strike, withholding their products from distribution.[27]

"Farmers by uniting can turn this nation upside down," thundered Singler shortly after Roosevelt's election. "We must prove that it is not money, not gold, but food that is essential." He assured his followers that by closing down markets they could secure their demands without much hardship or sacrifice to themselves: "Farmers of this country must bond together without regard to political party to take what we have and get what we want." Farmers packed the meetings at which he spoke and responded clamorously to his attacks on dairy "trusts" and his demands for "cost of production plus" payments to producers. Membership of the Wisconsin Cooperative Milk Pool grew from less than 3,500 in July, 1932, to more than 11,000 a year later. The Milk Pool's greatest support was among the poorest dairy farmers in the eastern sections of the state, especially in the Fox River area. Singler came from Shiocton

[27] Jacobs, "Wisconsin Milk Strikes," *WMH*, 35:31; Milwaukee *Journal*, February 19, 1933; John L. Shover, *Cornbelt Rebellion: The Farmers' Holiday Association* (Urbana, 1965), 21–23; *Capital Times*, November 6, 1930; W. P. Tucker, "Populism Up to Date: The Story of the Farmers' Union," in *Agricultural History*, 21 (October, 1947), 198–208.

in Outagamie County, and he well understood how to use the courage that desperation engendered among his neighbors.[28]

Neither the Milk Pool nor the eastern Wisconsin dairy region operated in a vacuum. In the neighboring state of Iowa, farmers under the leadership of Milo Reno were working to build a National Farmers' Holiday Association. Acting on the cost-of-production-plus formula, they had already carried out a strike during the summer of 1932, and they were eager to extend their influence into Wisconsin. Reno traveled to Ladysmith that summer, and together with local Farmers Union leaders arranged for a mass meeting to be held at Marshfield on September 2. Over 5,000 farmers attended the fall meeting, and they elected Arnold Gilberts of Dunn County to head a new Wisconsin Farmers' Holiday Association. Of gentle personal demeanor, Gilberts rose to the occasion with an inflammatory speech warning that "we'll solve our problems with bayonets, and I don't mean maybe." The rhetoric turned out to be inconsistent with Wisconsin Farm Holiday actions. Although claiming a membership of 130,000 farmers in the state, the organization never seemed able to carry out its threats. At best the Farm Holiday stirred producers to action; at worst it repeatedly betrayed the Wisconsin Milk Pool, and in the end left the Pool holding little but empty milk cans.[29]

At the start of 1933, however, no one knew where the constant discussion of a farm strike in the Middle West might lead. Stung by charges that he was bluffing, Walter Singler finally decided it was time to act. "Call a strike or quit," he told directors of the Milk Pool on February 8, and with their support he announced that within a week the members of his organization would begin

[28] Milwaukee *Journal*, November 21, 1932; Hoglund, "Wisconsin Dairy Farmers on Strike," *Agricultural History*, 35:26; Jacobs, "Wisconsin Milk Strikes," *WMH*, 35:31–32. Despite Singler's persuasiveness, the press tended to be skeptical. See, for example, the *Waupaca County Post* (Waupaca), September 29, 1932, and "Farm Strikes," in *Hoard's Dairyman*, 77 (September, 1932), 436.

[29] In the Olin Swenson Papers, see Emma Swenson to William Sanderson, August 31, 1932; Sanderson to Swenson, September 2, 1932; A. W. Ricker to Fritz Schultheiss, August 21, 1932; and Wisconsin Farmer Holiday Association, "Resolutions Adopted by the First Annual State Directors' Meeting, Held at Marshfield, November 26, 1932." See also Jacobs, "Wisconsin Milk Strikes," in *WMH*, 35:30–31. In correspondence and publications, leaders of the Wisconsin Farmers' Holiday used several forms in referring to the organization. Among the most common were the following: Wisconsin Farm Holiday Association; Wisconsin Division, National Holiday Association; Farm Holiday Association; Farmers' Holiday Association; Wisconsin Division, Farmers' National Holiday Association. See the Arnold Gilberts Papers, Eau Claire Area Research Center.

withholding milk until prices reached $1.40 a hundredweight. Although representing only a minority of farmers, Milk Pool members turned out on the appointed day, February 15, to close the small cheese and butter factories in the Fox River Valley. When they attempted to barricade the roads leading to city markets, however, they quickly learned that striking successfully was more difficult than Singler had led them to believe.[30]

Even though Milk Pool pickets patrolled the highways day and night, they could not prevent shippers from using alternate routes. Nor could they prevent sheriff's deputies from using tear gas and clubs to disperse striking farmers. The inadequacy of strike preparations soon became evident. "This sudden, over-night attempt to organize and strike is not what it is 'cracked up to be,' " observed William Rubin, who had become counsel for the Milk Pool. Having received assistance from neither the Farm Holiday nor any other farm organization, Singler called a truce on February 22, after Governor Schmedeman agreed to study the problem that had led to the disturbances.[31]

The six weeks after the truce were uneasy ones in rural Wisconsin. Singler became a whipping boy as the press and public officials alike charged him with radicalism and self-aggrandizement. Rubin warned him of the "strong undercurrent" against strike tactics, but despite the mobilization of hostile opinion, the Milk Pool membership stood firm. When the National Farm Holiday Association announced its intention to strike in May, milk producers welcomed the news. They could detect little progress resulting from the governor's study, and some of them felt betrayed. Furthermore, while legislators in Washington seemed only too eager to pass measures such as the National Industrial Recovery Act, no farm legislation had reached the President's desk. Carl Oman, a director of the Milk Pool, complained to Rubin that Congress was dallying with a bill to provide mortgage relief and that it refused even to consider cost-of-production as a desirable objective. If farmers were to get what

[30] Milwaukee *Journal*, February 19, 1933; minutes of the February 9, 1933, executive committee meeting, Wisconsin Cooperative Milk Pool Records.

[31] Unidentified clippings, in the Wisconsin Cooperative Milk Pool Records; Milwaukee *Journal*, February 22, March 15, 1933; Burlington *Standard-Democrat*, February 24, 1933; William B. Rubin to Milo Reno, February 24, 1933, and Rubin to Ed Nockels, February 23, 1933, both in the Rubin Papers.

they wanted, therefore, Oman could see no alternative to another strike.[32]

In the meantime, Gilberts was stirring up support for the scheduled Farm Holiday strike. "We have used up all of our resources, begging, pleading and praying for legislation," he bellowed. "Now we are through. . . . The legislation proposed at Washington, with all due respect to the president, is not proposed by agriculture." The nation's churches were soon to observe Passion Week, "the week Christ was nailed to the cross to save the world." It was a time of suffering and sacrifice, and Gilberts wanted Wisconsin farmers to know that he, too, was prepared to permit sacrifices for the sake of humanity: "I want to see a holiday so terrible that it will darken the sky and go down as the greatest tragedy in history, so your children and mine can read what happened in 1933 when agriculture went on a rampage, and won't let it happen again."[33]

At last, it seemed, the dissident farm organizations stood united. Milk Pool representatives met in Madison the second week in May to co-ordinate strike policies with farmers from Michigan, Minnesota, South Dakota, and Illinois. As the discussions were reaching a conclusion, however, a telephone call came in from a similar conference of the National Farm Holiday Association in St. Paul. Milo Reno had postponed the strike for thirty days! What were the Milk Pool militants to do? Having already determined to strike, they refused to turn back. Reasoning that postponement would "kill all our farm organizations," they voted unanimously to carry on towards their objective. They resolved to hold their products at their farms; they would sell nothing, buy nothing, and pay nothing. Thus the second strike got underway, and again the Milk Pool was on its own.[34]

The second strike was, if anything, more difficult to carry out than the first had been because this time Governor Schmedeman had made plans for dealing with the strikers. If farmers simply

[32] William B. Rubin to Walter Singler, April 28, 1933, and Carl Oman to Rubin, April 29, May 8, 1933, all in the Rubin Papers; "What Then?" and "More What Then?" in *Hoard's Dairyman*, 78 (March 25, 1933), 124, and 78 (April 25, 1933), 162; *Taylor County Star News* (Medford), April 20, 1933; Burlington *Standard-Democrat*, April 28, 1933.

[33] Undated Milwaukee *Journal* clipping, ca. April 16, 1933, in the Wisconsin Cooperative Milk Pool Records.

[34] Minutes of the May 11, 1933, executive committee meeting, and minutes of the Milk Producers' Conference, May 12, 1933, both in the Wisconsin Cooperative Milk Pool Records; Albert Schmedeman to F. Ryan Duffy, May 12, 1933, in the Albert Schmedeman Papers; Milwaukee *Journal*, May 13, 1933; Shover, *Cornbelt Rebellion*, 130.

withheld their products from market, he promised, there would be no difficulty. But if strikers threatened or attempted to intimidate anyone, he intended to use his authority to prevent violence. To protect property, he proposed closing all creameries, condenseries, cheese factories, and distributing plants. To protect the defenseless, he gave sheriffs and district attorneys authority to assure milk deliveries to children and hospitals. And most importantly, to protect access to markets, the governor prepared to use any means necessary to keep highways open for anyone wishing to transport milk or any other farm product.[35]

When the Milk Pool announced that members intended to carry out their strike after May 13, Adjutant General Ralph Immell of the Wisconsin National Guard placed 2,500 men under the command of local sheriffs. The employment of thousands of special deputies added strength to the forces of peace and order. Shipments of tear gas arrived from Washington, along with a cathartic gas certain to keep strikers off the roadways and in the woods attending to other business. The preparations brought back memories of the Great War, and for six days a quasi-war did in fact come to eastern Wisconsin. No longer able to use pickets effectively in some areas, farmers adopted guerrilla tactics. Finding an unprotected truck, they would dump the milk and quickly scatter in cars before Guardsmen arrived.[36]

Under such circumstances, violence was difficult to avoid. One Waukesha County farmer, discouraged by the size of forces arrayed against milk producers, described the misfortunes of a gang of strikers engaged in stopping and dumping milk trucks. "Yesterday they went thru Richfield," he reported to Rubin, "and there they ran into a bunch of Nat. Guard & deputies [who] . . . surrounded the truck while one man with a gun lined them up and the rest pounded the hell out of them & I mean pounded. One man has a fractured skull."[37]

[35] Albert Schmedeman address (typewritten), ca. May, 1933, Schmedeman Papers; minutes of the May 16, 1933, executive committee meeting, Wisconsin Cooperative Milk Pool Records; Charles W. Taylor, "On the Farm Front," in *The Nation*, 136 (May 17, 1933), 559.

[36] Undated and/or unidentified clippings, and clippings from the Milwaukee *Journal*, Milwaukee *Sentinel*, Sheboygan *Press*, and other newspapers, May 13–18, 1933, in the Wisconsin Cooperative Milk Pool Records; Jacobs, "Wisconsin Milk Strikes," *WMH*, 35:33–34; Hoglund, "Wisconsin Dairy Farmers on Strike," *Agricultural History*, 35:29.

[37] L. D. Dempsey to William B. Rubin, May 17, 1933, in the Rubin Papers.

More dramatic, but also more contrived, was the "Battle of Durham Hill" in southeastern Waukesha County. Eager to demonstrate his control of the area, Sheriff Arthur J. Moran orchestrated the affair, timing it to attract as many reporters and photographers as possible. Confronting a small group of farmers, Moran's forces first laid down a barrage of gas. Then about seventy-five Guardsmen charged with fixed bayonets, driving the strikers over a hill to their rear. Surviving photographs of the incident are reminiscent of the treatment accorded veterans who marched to Washington in hopes of receiving bonuses in 1932. And a Wisconsin farm wife asked the question that people were asking before Roosevelt's election: "Is this America?"[38]

Unable to surmount problems of communication and support, and finding the press increasingly critical of its tactics, the Milk Pool quickly ended the strike on May 19, 1933. The organization's arbitration committee, which did not include Singler, issued a statement that was defensive in tone. Though it continued to insist on "the right of the farmer to withhold his products in order to gain his just demands," it deplored "the fact that in his making such demands, outside and undesirable elements have entered upon unlawful activities and violence."[39]

After the second strike had failed to bring higher prices, Milk Pool leaders resolved to redouble their efforts to influence farm legislation. To be effective, they needed to expand membership, and they therefore sought to bring about affiliation with the Farmers Union. The attempt to join forces proved disappointing. The Department of Agriculture in Washington, determined to stick with the AAA program of domestic allotment and production control, rejected cost-of-production schemes. Governor Schmedeman, who had always believed in the need for national solutions to the farm problem, delayed taking action in Wisconsin on the assumption that with the success of New Deal programs no action would be necessary. Thus the Milk Pool farmers once again grew restive, and once again their leaders came under attack. "They promise the millenium," charged Schmedeman, "and they leave only chaos."[40]

[38] Jacobs, "Wisconsin Milk Strikes," *WMH*, 35:34; Milwaukee *Journal*, May 18, 1933.

[39] Minutes of May 18, 1933, arbitration committee meeting, Wisconsin Cooperative Milk Pool Records; Hoglund, "Wisconsin Dairy Farmers on Strike," *Agricultural History*, 35:29–30.

[40] Carl Oman to William B. Rubin, May 26, 1933, Rubin to Oman, July 7, 1933, and

During the summer of 1933 the citizens of Wisconsin began to experience *déjà vu* as they read newspaper accounts of disillusioned milk producers calling for still another strike. Congressional passage of the Agricultural Adjustment Act in May had nevertheless altered the circumstances confronting Wisconsin farmers, and they adapted their rhetoric to new conditions. Now it was the AAA, rather than the "dairy trust" or the "milk trust," that became the villain for cost-of-production prophets. When Milo Reno realized that his panacea was not to become part of FDR's program, he began attacking both FDR and Secretary of Agriculture Henry A. Wallace. Following Reno's example, Gilberts warned that while Roosevelt was a "highly humanitarian president," it was "only a step from commendable humanitarianism to selfish, blighting, radical socialism and communism." Apparently unable to resist religious allusions, he warned that "the people of this country are today being NAILED TO THE CROSS by Politicians and Labor Union Officials, and there is no one going to suffer more from this FOOLISH NRA-AAA PROGRAM than the Farmer himself."[41]

With tensions increasing, and with completion of the summer's harvest freeing farmers for one last effort, the National Farm Holiday Association proclaimed another strike to begin on October 21. The Wisconsin Cooperative Milk Pool, twice deserted, bided its time until it could be certain that the Farm Holiday would carry out its promises. Reno gave his solemn assurance that the Milk Pool would be consulted both during and after the strike, and the milk producers voted to cast their lot with the Holiday. The united effort lasted two days. Then Gilberts withdrew the Wisconsin Holiday from the strike to await results of a five-state midwestern governor's conference. At that point, leaders of the two associations met in the assembly chamber of the state capitol to work out their differences. In the end they simply decided that each should pursue its own course and leave co-operation up to their respective executive committees. The Wisconsin Farm Holiday then rejoined the strike.[42]

Rubin to James Moriarity, July 1, 1933, all in the Rubin Papers; Albert Schmedeman address (typewritten), n.d., in the Schmedeman Papers; minutes of July 11–12, 1933, executive committee meetings, Wisconsin Cooperative Milk Pool Records.

[41] Shover, *Cornbelt Rebellion*, 141, 144–145, 149–151; Arnold Gilberts addresses (typewritten), October 10, 30, 1933, in the Arnold Gilberts Papers, Eau Claire Area Research Center.

[42] Proclamation of the National Farmers' Holiday Association, October 19, 1933, and proclamation by Arnold Gilberts, November 4, 1933, in the Arnold Gilberts Papers, Eau

Like the previous strikes, the third was short-lived. Yet the level of violence increased markedly during the first three turbulent weeks of that final effort. Strikers, strike sympathizers, or unaffiliated vandals dumped milk whenever they had an opportunity, poured oil and kerosene into the vats of condenseries, forced the closing of milk-processing plants, and bombed at least seven cheese factories. Someone in an automobile fired on pickets who were stopping traffic near Madison, and one striker was killed. Enough was enough. Citizens on both sides began calling for domestic tranquility. Assemblyman Arthur Hitt, a war veteran and a leader of the Buffalo County Farm Holiday, expressed majority sentiment across the state when he wrote Gilberts to point out that "there are many people in our county who are in favor of going on a peaceful strike but who are opposed to picketing and similar tactics that might lead to violence." The strike petered out, and after several days of inactivity, farm leaders officially called it off on November 18.[43]

Both the Wisconsin Farm Holiday and the Wisconsin Cooperative Milk Pool survived the strikes of 1933, but their influence withered. Milo Reno died in 1936, and with his passing, death came to the Wisconsin Farm Holiday as well. Always more concerned with the economics of cost-of-production than were Reno's followers, farmers in the Milk Pool concentrated increasingly on co-operative marketing. Eventually, with insufficient capital, the co-ops were also to fail. Nevertheless, farmers of the Milk Pool and the Farm Holiday could take satisfaction in having drawn attention to serious problems in rural Wisconsin in 1933. Overall, the year's events there testified to the sense of desperation prevailing in many communities, to the inadequacy of government actions in meeting the farmers' demands and proposals, and to political threats inhering in the extralegal activities that produced violence.[44]

Claire Area Research Center; minutes of October 25 and November 3, 1933, emergency special board of directors' meeting, Wisconsin Cooperative Milk Pool Records; Shover, *Cornbelt Rebellion*, 156–162.

[43] Undated and/or unidentified clippings, and clipping from the Sheboygan *Press*, October 31, 1933, in the Wisconsin Cooperative Milk Pool Records; Arthur Hitt to Arnold Gilberts, November 7, 1933, in the Gilberts Papers, Eau Claire Area Research Center.

[44] Charles H. Backstrom, "The Progressive Party of Wisconsin, 1934–1946" (doctoral dissertation, University of Wisconsin, 1957), 115; Miller, *Governor Philip F. La Follette*, 47, 49, 53, 85; Shover, *Cornbelt Rebellion*, 204–205, 209; Hoglund, "Wisconsin Dairy Farmers on Strike," *Agricultural History*, 35:30; Green Bay *Press-Gazette*, September 3, 8, 1940.

* * *

Early in 1932, long before the milk strikes, a dairy farmer from Hartland wrote Charles L. Hill, chairman of the state's department of agriculture and markets, to express his concern about the future of agriculture in Wisconsin. He saw two alternatives: "we must have lower taxes & higher prices for our commodities, or lower taxes & very much lower prices on the articles we buy." Yet he despaired of achieving necessary increases in farm income for the simple reason that he could see "little or no community of interest between the farmers & the laboring classes." If farmers achieved a reduction in their tax burdens, he elaborated, the state would be forced to cut services which urban workers desired. And if agricultural prices increased, the food costs would take a larger proportion of workers' wages. Indeed, should farmers obtain the prices they were demanding, not much would be left for either the laboring classes or the industrialists. "So where in hell is the money going to come from?" queried the Hartland dairyman.[45]

The dilemma was one that John R. Commons had confronted many years before when he arrived in Wisconsin to begin compiling his magisterial *Documentary History of American Industrial Society*, a collection that established a solid foundation for the investigation of American labor. Not content merely to present the source materials for an understanding of workers, their problems, and the evolution of their organizations, the professor and his students turned to the preparation of the equally ambitious *History of Labour in the United States*. In the first volume (1918) of that seminal study, Commons emphasized that he and his collaborators intended to show how laborers had gradually separated themselves from farmers, merchants, and employers. After three centuries in an environment far different from Europe, he argued, American workers had come to understand that their position and progress in society derived from wages and not from prices, rents, or profits. Adhering to objectives that differed from those of other interest groups, laborers became involved in a complex transactional mechanism (or

[45] C. E. Dempsey to Charles L. Hill, January 24, 1932, in the Philip F. La Follette Papers. Some farmers were less sympathetic to urban labor than was Dempsey. Arnold Gilberts, for example, urged farmers to "go after the common enemy—POLITICIANS and LABOR UNION LEADERS—and bring them into line." Address (typewritten), October 20, 1933, in the Gilberts Papers, Eau Claire Area Research Center.

institutional framework) through which the American political economy was able to function.[46]

Commons suggested several influences that accounted for the disjoined nature of American working-class movements and turned labor away from broad, revolutionary class consciousness. The condition that most clearly distinguished the American from the European labor experience was, first, the existence of a vast area of free land. Drawing on the ideas of his colleague at the university, Frederick Jackson Turner, he regarded the frontier as offering an escape from conditions that subjected workers to the domination of others. Even more fundamental was the provision for universal white manhood suffrage. Granted a share in the political process from the beginning, American workers did not experience struggles that had shaped the class consciousness of their European counterparts.[47]

Within the United States a vast system of markets had developed across state lines. The complexity of varying state laws, combined with a court system that protected established interests, forced labor leaders to concentrate on gaining by trade-union action the objectives that workers in other countries sought through political processes. The problem was compounded by the influx of immigrants from many lands, "for immigrants and races come first as wage-earners, and it is only by the assimilating power of labour organizations that they can be brought together in a movement that depends for success on their willingness to stop competition and espouse co-operation." The tendency of employers to play off one ethnic group against another led some workers to become more conscious of racial or ethnic interests than they were of class interests.

Finally, the extremes of American business cycles, characteristic of a fluid society, increased the instability of American trade-union influence. In good times, when business prospered and labor was in demand, union activities expanded over industrial sections of the

[46] John R. Commons, "Introduction," in John R. Commons et al., *History of Labour in the United States* (4 vols., New York, 1918–1935), 1:3–4; Maurice Isserman, " 'God Bless Our American Institutions': The Labor History of John R. Commons," in *Labor History*, 17 (Summer, 1976), 321–324; Neil W. Chamberlain, "The Institutional Economics of John R. Commons," in *Institutional Economics: Veblen, Commons, and Mitchell Reconsidered, a Series of Lectures by Joseph Dorfman and Others* (Berkeley, 1963), 63–94.

[47] Commons, "Introduction," in Commons et al., *History of Labour in the United States*, 1:4–11.

country. In bad times, when unemployment reduced workers to helplessness and defensive strikes failed, labor turned to "politics, panaceas, or schemes of universal reform, while class struggle has dissolved in humanitarianism." Fluctuations of the business cycle, in sum, brought into perspective the distinctive features of labor organizations and movements in the United States. The flexibility and plasticity of American society worked against the development of a class-conscious labor perspective. During periods of prosperity, labor unions sought to deal with employers as equals in working out wage bargains that were essentially a form of trade agreement. During periods of economic stagnation, with their influence diminished, the unions sought a return to prosperity in order that their bargaining effectiveness might be restored. In either case, Commons insisted, the American working class never became "class conscious" in a revolutionary sense. The singular conditions of the American environment made American labor " 'wage conscious' in the sense of separation from, but partnership with, the employing class."[48]

Commons had been groping for an explanation of differences between American labor movements and labor movements in Europe. Like Frederick Jackson Turner, he found in the peculiar conditions of the American environment the basis for American uniqueness. From his perspective, European workers' movements, especially those influenced by Karl Marx, tended to regard labor as a mass, and they looked to the solidarity of the working class as vital to the overthrow of capitalism. In the United States, however, conditions had brought workers into the economic system where they competed for higher wages and better working conditions but not for replacement of the system itself. Commons' analysis of the American labor movement drew heavily from his investigations prior to the Great War. During the 1920's and 1930's, changing circumstances forced a modification of some of the generalizations he had advanced in 1918, when the first two volumes of his *History of Labour* appeared. The prosperity of the twenties turned out to be no guarantee of labor union expansion; nor did the Depression of the thirties lead to a decline in the influence of unions.

Commons himself was never one to hold unvalidated theories in high esteem, nor did he ever approve of scholarship that amounted

[48] *Ibid.*, 1:9–11, 15.

to little more than a gloss on received wisdom. His method was to proceed inductively towards the development of hypotheses which could then be tested in practical application, and in his seminar at the University of Wisconsin he expected students to base theoretical constructs on a solid foundation of factual information. To be sure, that approach was one that could lead simply to the accumulation of vast amounts of undigested data. Yet the Commons seminar also engaged in theoretical discussion and analysis.

One of Commons' students whose background and intellectual curiosity made him an especially valued associate in the developing Wisconsin school of labor historians was Selig Perlman. Born in Russia, Perlman arrived in Madison in 1909 as a twenty-year-old refugee from czarist pogroms. An enthusiastic Marxist, he had taken part in the revolution of 1905; and, once enrolled at the University of Wisconsin, he did his best to convert Commons to socialism. Instead, Commons turned the tables on him. While studying labor history, Perlman found himself completely persuaded by his mentor's wisdom, and he went on to become an extraordinarily articulate spokesman for the Commons approach. He served as a collaborator in writing the *History of Labour in the United States*, and after becoming a professor of economics at the University of Wisconsin he added refinements to the interpretation of the workers' experience in America. In 1928, Perlman published *A Theory of the Labor Movement*, which incorporated his ideas along with those of Commons and served as a model of analysis for reformist labor historians.[49]

A major contribution of Perlman's study derived from his interest in the psychology of workers and the way they perceived themselves relative to their employers. It was Perlman's contention that the mentality of both manual laborers and entrepreneurs derived from the way they assessed their chances for economic success. The entrepreneur, he observed, was an eternal optimist who saw the world as "brimful of opportunities . . . to be made his own." The "manualist," on the other hand, tended to see that same world as one of limited economic alternatives in which competition increased the odds against his reaching objectives he set for himself. The manual

[49] Selig Perlman, *Selig Perlman's Lectures on Capitalism and Socialism*, ed. A. L. Reisch Owen (Madison, 1976), xv–xvii; John R. Commons, *Myself* (New York, 1934; reprinted, Madison, 1963), 81; Isserman, "Labor History of John R. Commons," *Labor History*, 17:312–313.

worker's scarcity consciousness resulted from two main influences, one intensely personal and the other deriving from the way he perceived the economic order. The typical manualist was acutely aware of his limited capacity to make the most of circumstances in the United States, for "he knows himself neither for a born taker of risks nor for the possessor of a sufficiently agile mind even to feel at home in the midst of the uncertain game of competitive business." Furthermore, while the entrepreneur saw possibilities everywhere, the manualist perceived opportunities limited either by nature or by social institutions that allocated the choicest openings to privileged groups.[50]

Lacking the obsessive drive of the entrepreneur, and easily intimidated by an environment that led him to doubt his competitive abilities, the American worker became passive. Pessimistic about his chances for success as an individual, he sought job security through organization. Trade unions therefore became the principal means by which workers learned to protect themselves and assure their survival in a fiercely competitive economy.

By the time Perlman's *A Theory of the Labor Movement* appeared, employers across the nation were effectively discouraging the growth of unions, not by the old methods of force and intimidation, but by offering "welfare capitalism" as an alternative. The chief strength of management's labor policies during the New Era, Perlman believed, was that they could so easily be presented from the workers' point of view. Apparently benign employers promised workers fair wages, reasonable working days, security from unemployment and injury, profit-sharing and stock-distribution plans, life insurance, and old-age pensions. In short, welfare capitalism offered workers nearly all they might have expected to receive through the bargaining power of their unions. And by the end of the 1920's, the humane policies of welfare capitalists had greatly reduced both the impulse to organize and the ability of unions to hold their membership.[51]

[50] Selig Perlman, *A Theory of the Labor Movement* (New York, 1928; reprinted, New York, 1966, and Philadelphia, 1979), 237–253; Robert Ozanne, "The Labor History and Labor Theory of John R. Commons: An Evaluation in the Light of Recent Trends and Criticism," in Gerald G. Somers, ed., *Labor, Management, and Social Policy* (Madison, 1963), 29–34.

[51] Perlman, *A Theory of the Labor Movement*, 208–213; John R. Commons et al., *History of Labor in the United States, 1896–1932. Volume IV: Labor Movements*, written by Selig Perlman and Philip Taft (New York, 1935), 580–581; David Brody, "Labor and the

For all the humane features of welfare capitalism, and despite its apparent success during the New Era, the system contained inherent weaknesses that did not escape Perlman's notice. The central problem, as he saw it, was that workers had become dependent on the goodwill of a single employer. Under the stress of increased competition or business depression, that employer might be driven to renege on promises he had made to his workers. And with the arrival of business depression, workers might well face the uncertainties of joblessness along with the loss of benefits they had accumulated.[52]

That unexpected development became a disastrous reality after 1929, of course, and during the early years of the Depression workers were hard-pressed to regain the sense of security they had lost. Some of them never did regain it. Nevertheless, as the Depression exposed the flaws in company welfare programs, workers renewed their efforts to organize themselves and to achieve their objectives through stronger and more effective unions than they had ever before established. When Roosevelt signed the National Industrial Recovery Act on June 16, 1933, labor leaders hailed it as their official authorization to proceed with their plans. The much-debated Section 7(a) of Title I stipulated that employees should have the right to organize and bargain collectively through representatives of their own choosing, and that they should be free from the restraint or coercion of employers. Employers were, on the other hand, forbidden to require that workers join company unions, and the law called for compliance with approved hours and wage standards.[53]

Although William Green, president of the American Federation of Labor, described 7(a) as a "Magna Carta" for labor, his jubilation was premature. Employer opposition to unions by no means diminished after passage of the legislation, and the National Association of Manufacturers led the way in a nationwide assault on its

---

Great Depression: The Interpretative Prospects," in *Labor History*, 13 (Spring, 1972), 242; James O. Morris, *Conflict Within the AFL: A Study of Craft Versus Industrial Unionism, 1901–1938* (Ithaca, 1958), 40–41.

[52] Perlman, *A Theory of the Labor Movement*, 211–215; Irving Bernstein, *The New Deal Collective Bargaining Policy* (Berkeley, 1950; reprinted, Jersey City, 1975), 14–15.

[53] Irving Bernstein, *Turbulent Years: A History of the American Worker, 1933–1941* (Boston, 1970), 29–31; John R. Commons and John B. Andrews, *Principles of Labor Legislation* (4th ed., New York, 1936; reprinted, 1967), 421–424; Schlesinger, *Coming of the New Deal*, 136–137.

provisions. As NAM lawyers carefully examined the language of the law, they were gratified to discover that it did not prohibit company unions. All that was new was the provision that employers could neither require workers to join one nor demand that they refrain from joining organizations of their own choosing. Acting on NAM advice, industries redoubled their efforts to promote their own unions, or "kiss me clubs" in the cynical argot of labor organizers. Coinciding with the intensified activities of resurgent labor unions, the employers' drive to create their own workers' associations increased industrial unrest in Wisconsin and helped to bring about a series of strikes that began during the summer of 1933. The strikes of that year also offered a means of measuring the impact of the Depression on management-worker relationships as Commons and Perlman described them during the New Era.[54]

* * *

Until the summer of 1933, labor had been remarkably quiescent throughout the country. In July, however, worker-days lost because of strikes increased to 1,375,000, more than double the time lost in any previous month of 1933. And the end was not in sight. In Milwaukee, the number of strikes increased from only six in 1933 to forty-two in 1934, and worker-days lost in Wisconsin's largest industrial city went from 8,489 in 1933 to 307,002 in 1934. In the state's iron-and-steel products industry, idle worker-days increased from 1,385 to 109,678; in the transportation-equipment industry the increase was from 25,588 to 148,903; and lost worker-days in textiles and textile products jumped from 7,524 to 43,312.[55]

The overriding issue in the industrial strife of the New Deal's first year was labor's right to organize and bargain collectively. The National Industrial Recovery Act was supposed to guarantee that right, argued John J. Handley, secretary of the Wisconsin State Federation of Labor. "But what happens?" he asked rhetorically at the height of the labor troubles of 1934. "Did those in control of

[54] Bernstein, *Turbulent Years*, 34–36, 38–40; Schlesinger, *Coming of the New Deal*, 144–145; Robben W. Fleming, "The Significance of the Wagner Act," in Milton Derber and Edwin Young, eds., *Labor and the New Deal* (Madison, 1957; reprinted, Jersey City, 1972), 126–127; Bernstein, *New Deal Collective Bargaining Policy*, 34–35, 38–39, 57–58; Maney, *"Young Bob" La Follette*, 126.

[55] Bernstein, *Turbulent Years*, 172–173; Florence Peterson, *Strikes in the United States, 1830–1936*, U.S. Bureau of Labor Statistics, *Bulletin*, no. 651 (1938), which also appears as *House Reports*, 75 Cong., 2 sess., no. 444 (serial 10213), 83, 121–122; Thomas W. Gavett, *Development of the Labor Movement in Milwaukee* (Madison, 1965), 155.

the large industries of the country cooperate with the government?" The answer was clear. They most assuredly did not! They discouraged unionization by discharging union members and by dominating agencies of control from the National Labor Board to local boards of compliance. Most importantly, "they used coercion and intimidation through company unions to compel workers to work for wages below a subsistence level." Handley warned that if workers failed to resist the employers' tactics, they might never have another opportunity to secure their rights.[56]

In the strikes that occurred in Wisconsin during 1934, however, the determination of workers' rights was clouded in ambiguity because of uncertainty about the intent of labor legislation drafted during the New Deal's hectic first months. And the confusion resulting from ambiguity sometimes prevented an easy settlement of disputes. A struggle that took place in and around the village of Kohler near Sheboygan became, for example, one of the most protracted in American history. The village had been widely hailed as a model community, and it seemed an unlikely place for one of the bitterest, most mean-tempered battles of the decade. Yet Kohler was to become a microcosm of industrial America in 1934. Events surrounding the struggle there provide dramatic evidence of the seriousness of labor's intention to obtain recognition and to bargain collectively. The strike at Kohler also reveals how the lack of clarity in early New Deal legislation increased the difficulties confronting both employers and employees.

The Kohler Company had its origins in the entrepreneurial skills of an Austrian immigrant's son, John M. Kohler, Jr., who had settled in Sheboygan in 1871 and established a foundry for the manufacture of agricultural implements. By 1888 the firm had turned to the production of enameled bathtubs and kitchenware, and Kohler himself had become a leading citizen of Sheboygan. In 1898 the Kohler Company moved to a new plant four miles out in the country. There, Walter J. Kohler took over the presidency of the

[56] *The New Deal* (Sheboygan), August 31, 1934. The National Labor Board was created to resolve labor disputes arising under the NRA; it should not be confused with the National Labor Relations Board, which came into being with the passage of the Wagner Act in 1935. The press committee of the Wisconsin State Federation of Labor in 1933 presented a statement expressing its interpretation of employers' activities: "The whole profit system now stands out in all its sinister ghoulishness preying on humanity from the cradle to the grave." See the minutes of the January 6, 1933, general executive board meeting, Wisconsin State Federation of Labor Papers.

firm after his father and an older brother died. There, too, the young executive planned the residential area that he expected to become a model community for his staff, his workers, and his family. Kohler village was to have no company houses, and Walter Kohler never intended that it should become a typical company town. The site was to be administered by the Kohler Improvement Company, a nonprofit organization with no formal ties to the Kohler plant, and residents were expected to own their own homes. The village was supposed to be a self-governing community free of paternalism and exploitation. Although fewer than half of the rank-and-file Kohler workers had actually established residences there by 1934, the idea behind it was that it should provide an atmosphere in which labor and management could live together in mutual respect. Whatever the rationale, Kohler village came to stand as the epitome of benign efforts to assure industrial peace and an open shop.[57]

So long as New Era prosperity encouraged new housing construction—and consequently the installation of new plumbing—the Kohler Company flourished, and peace prevailed in the village. But when hard times came to the construction industry, the company suffered along with housing contractors and builders. The Kohler plant nevertheless continued to operate full-time without cutting back on wages, and company inventories piled up. In the third year of the Depression the firm began to reduce wage rates and to spread the work by reducing hours, hoping that it could in that way survive until prosperity returned. But the Depression continued. Having satisfied himself that he had done his best to maintain employment, and confronting heavy financial obligations, Kohler finally resorted to laying off workers.[58]

Overall, affairs were going very badly for Walter Kohler. In 1930 and 1932 he lost in attempts to win another term as governor, and with the coming of the New Deal, labor leaders began considering a drive to organize the Kohler plant. Kohler scrupulously followed recommendations of his legal advisers so as to avoid violating the laws enacted during FDR's first Hundred Days. In July, 1933, after creation of the NRA, the plumbing-fixtures industry reached an

[57] Walter H. Uphoff, *Kohler on Strike: Thirty Years of Conflict* (Boston, 1966), 2–10; Garet Garrett, "Section Seven-A at Sheboygan," in the *Saturday Evening Post*, October 27, 1934, pp. 5–6.

[58] Uphoff, *Kohler on Strike*, 14–15; Garrett, "Section Seven-A," *Saturday Evening Post*, October 27, 1934, pp. 6–7.

agreement to set a minimum wage standard of forty cents an hour with a maximum work week of forty hours. Without waiting for NRA approval, the Kohler Company applied the wages and hours agreement immediately. Again, from management's point of view, the company was going out of its way to be generous towards employees despite the tribulations it had suffered. From the labor leaders' point of view, however, the company was simply continuing its paternalistic policies in order to maintain an open shop. While Walter Kohler sought industrial goodwill, in other words, his name was becoming anathema among labor organizers.[59]

Ironically, if Selig Perlman had correctly assessed the "manualist mentality," Kohler's approach to industrial management should have succeeded. Both the company and the Kohler family treated workers with great personal respect and demonstrated deep concern for their welfare. So long as the company prospered, Kohler's methods were in fact successful. Yet Perlman had also foreseen that New Era welfare capitalism might well prove inadequate during periods of economic depression. As hard times eroded job security at the Kohler plant, and as Section 7(a) opened the way for union membership drives, organizers came to regard the conquest of Kohler as an objective of the first importance. The plumbing-ware company had maintained its commitment to an open shop while at the same time nourishing its reputation as a good employer. An AFL victory at Kohler, thought union leaders, would therefore have great symbolic significance for the future of labor relations in Wisconsin and the nation. It would represent a triumph of organized labor over paternalistic welfare capitalism in the workers' continuing struggle to control their own destiny.

With AFL organizers signing up new members daily, Walter Kohler and his employees appeared to be on a collision course. Because of their differing points of view, the company's managers and AFL leaders adopted differing interpretations of Section 7(a). Kohler's position was substantially that of the National Association of Manufacturers. Scrupulously following the assessment of the law advanced by NAM lawyers, he insisted that employees might join whatever organization they chose, or that they might join no organization at all. He repeatedly promised that he would deal with

[59] Garrett, "Section Seven-A," *Saturday Evening Post*, October 27, 1934, pp. 77–78; New York *Times*, July 16, 1934.

any organization of workers, or with workers individually. Reluctant to encourage labor solidarity, however, he refused to yield on one important point: no union should have *exclusive* bargaining power for all workers. Both state and national federations of labor interpreted the law differently. Their position was that the majority of workers should prevail. That is, should a majority accept membership in the AFL, the AFL would become the bargaining agent for all workers in the plant.[60]

It was obvious that industrial peace at Kohler required definitive guidelines for the interpretation of 7(a), but neither the National Recovery Administration nor FDR provided much help. General Hugh S. Johnson, appointed to head the NRA, set up a National Labor Board in August, 1933, to deal with labor disputes. Although the NLB's powers and responsibilities were never clearly stated, it set to work developing a "common law" on 7(a), and during a strike by the Full Fashioned Hosiery Workers, it came up with an agreement known as the Reading Formula. One of the formula's implicit provisions was that the board should hold elections in which workers could vote for representatives to bargain collectively and exclusively with management. But Roosevelt himself helped to undermine the Reading agreement when he assisted in mediating a strike involving automobile workers. Requiring only that employees bargain "with the freely chosen representatives of groups," the automobile settlement repudiated the AFL demand for majority rule and exclusive representation. The way was thus left open for the formation of company unions. One such union, the Kohler Workers' Association, became an instrument for maintaining an open shop at the Kohler plant.[61]

In the meantime, the AFL Union of Kohler Workers No. 18545 was claiming a membership of at least 1,200 employees in a force numbering more than 2,000, and it was ready to open negotiations with the company's management. Preparing a list of fourteen demands, the union stressed the importance of three: a minimum wage rate of sixty-five cents an hour, a thirty-hour work week, and the right to bargain collectively for all Kohler workers. On July 11,

[60] Garrett, "Section Seven-A," *Saturday Evening Post*, October 27, 1934, pp. 78, 80–81; Uphoff, *Kohler on Strike*, 26–27.

[61] Schlesinger, *Coming of the New Deal*, 136–137, 144–151; Bernstein, *Turbulent Years*, 173–177; Bernstein, *New Deal Collective Bargaining Policy*, 59–60; Fleming, "Significance of the Wagner Act," in Derber and Young, eds., *Labor and the New Deal*, 126–127.

Walter Kohler returned a written rejection in which he pointed out that his company was paying the NRA code rate of forty cents and maintaining a forty-hour work week. Most importantly, he remained adamant in his refusal to recognize the right of any organization to exercise sole and supreme bargaining power. With Kohler's denial of their demands, the AFL workers decided to strike the plant beginning on the morning of July 16, 1934.[62]

The attitude of most strikers seemed amiable as they set up their picket lines. One of their leaders, Arthur Kuhn, told a reporter that he held no grudges against the boss. He had known Walter Kohler for forty-five years and considered him a "fine man" of admirable character. "But there is a principle at stake in this controversy," Kuhn added. "We have taken our course and we intend to stand by it." When Kohler appeared the first day, intent upon crossing the line to walk to his office, some of the strikers lifted the rope so that he could pass. The plumbing-ware manufacturer was soon conferring with the Reverend J. W. Maguire, a Catholic priest assigned by the Chicago regional labor board to mediate the strike, but Kohler proved intractable. After all, he had a reputation to defend. He cherished his celebrity as the employer of happy and contented workers in an open shop, and he would not budge. "In every other case I've been able to beat the table with my fist and say to the employer, 'Here, now, settle this thing. Sign and be done with it,' " Maguire later recalled. Pride and stubbornness made this employer exceptional, however, and the mediator "couldn't do that to Kohler." For his part, Kohler issued a statement alleging that the strike was inspired by "outside labor agitators" who had not set foot inside his plant. "How," he asked, "can there be any bargaining with law violators who have never even worked for us?"[63]

There were other complications. Forecasts of what was to take place had circulated on the eve of the strike, and for reasons best known to themselves, about 200 employees loyal to Kohler had entered the plant. There they remained besieged the next day, with neither food nor supplies, and anxious about what might become of them. Someone finally thought of using the U.S. mail, and so by parcel post there arrived regular deliveries of life's necessities. Another series of problems resulted from the strikers' cutting off

[62] New York *Times*, July 15, 16, 1934; Uphoff, *Kohler on Strike*, 30–34, 92–93.

[63] Uphoff, *Kohler on Strike*, 37–40; Garrett, "Section Seven-A," *Saturday Evening Post*, October 27, 1934, p. 81; New York *Times*, July 18, 1934.

coal deliveries to the Kohler power plant. Without coal the plant would be shut down, and the entire village would be without water, sewerage, or fire protection. Fortunately, Father Maguire managed to persuade strikers to pass one coal car every other day, enough to keep the power plant in operation.[64]

It was all peaceful enough, but village authorities had been preparing for trouble. They had placed machine guns and caches of arms at strategic points, wrapped several trucks in sheet iron to serve as armored cars, and deputized volunteers to keep order. The strikers, too, were preparing for violence by collecting clubs, blackjacks, slingshots, and other weapons. The trouble finally came on July 27, 1934, after a hundred special deputies broke through the picket lines to escort a coal car the strikers had turned back. Both sides called for reinforcements, and that night a battle occurred along a mile-long front outside the plant. Strikers and strike sympathizers began throwing bricks and stones, smashing windows, and causing as much damage as possible. The special forces responded with tear gas and, ultimately, with bullets. Two strikers were killed and some forty of them wounded before the battle came to an end.[65]

"Much has been said of the sincere interest felt by Walter Kohler in the welfare of his workers," observed labor organizer Gunnar Mickelsen after calm had returned to the village. But he added that "when it came to a final question of Kohler property or Kohler workers, it was gas, cracked heads, gunshot wounds, and death to the workers for the sake of the property." His bitter conclusion was that "the crash of windows shattered on that sacred property was reason enough to loose a stream of lead into the well-loved employees." The next day Governor Schmedeman called out the National Guard. To the relief of both sides, the Guardsmen restored order, but there was little the governor could do to hasten union negotiations with Kohler towards a satisfactory conclusion. The strikers buried their dead, Kohler talked of moving his plant to another state, and the strike continued.[66]

[64] Uphoff, *Kohler on Strike*, 43–46; Garrett, "Section Seven-A," *Saturday Evening Post*, October 27, 1934, pp. 81–82; New York *Times*, July 21, 1934.

[65] Sheboygan *Press*, July 28, 1934; New York *Times*, July 28, 29, 1934; "Revolt in Utopia," in *The Nation*, 139 (August 8, 1934), 162–163.

[66] Gunnar Mickelsen, "The Kohler Myth Dies," in *The Nation*, 139 (August 15, 1934), 187–188; New York *Times*, July 29, 30, 31, August 6, 1934; Uphoff, *Kohler on Strike*, 73–83.

While Sheboygan and Kohler counted the costs of violence, the Roosevelt administration was coming to the realization that steps had to be taken to prevent such disturbances not only in Wisconsin but throughout the country. At a White House conference with concerned party and administration leaders, the President formulated what became know as Public Resolution No. 44, and Senator Robert Wagner of New York persuaded Congress to adopt it on June 19. Acting on the joint resolution, FDR quickly replaced the powerless NLB with the new National Labor Relations Board (NRLB) under the temporary chairmanship of Lloyd K. Garrison, dean of the Law School at the University of Wisconsin. The new agency immediately confronted the problem of employee representation in negotiations with management, and it affirmed majority rule as "the keystone of any sound, workable system of industrial relationships by collective bargaining."[67]

Because the regional labor relations office in Chicago found itself unable to settle the Kohler strike, the case came before the National Labor Relations Board in Washington. The NLRB heard testimony from Federal Labor Union No. 18545, the Kohler Company, and the management-sanctioned Kohler Workers' Association. Joseph Padway, attorney for the AFL, brought three complaints against the company: that it had fired employees for union activity, that it had refused to bargain collectively with representatives of the union, and that it had interfered with workers' efforts to organize themselves. The NLRB's findings substantiated the accuracy of AFL complaints, but they did so in a way that brought little satisfaction to the union. The board agreed that the Kohler Company had participated in forming its own employees' association. It agreed, as well, that such an association represented a deliberate effort to interfere with the "free and unhampered self-organization which Section 7(a) guarantees." Nevertheless, the board asserted that "the wrong done by the company can . . . be remedied by an election." Employees, in other words, could now choose between the AFL and the company union.[68]

Labor leaders reacted to the NLRB ruling with anger and disgust. If the Kohler Workers' Association had been formed in violation

[67] Bernstein, *Turbulent Years*, 200–205, 318–322; Bernstein, *New Deal Collective Bargaining Policy*, 84–87; Schlesinger, *Coming of the New Deal*, 149–151.

[68] Uphoff, *Kohler on Strike*, 83–85; Garrett, "Section Seven-A," *Saturday Evening Post*, October 27, 1934, pp. 81; New York *Times*, September 16, 1934.

of the law, argued Padway, it made no sense to permit its campaigning for the support of the workers. Yet the NLRB would not reverse its decision, and it scheduled an election for September 27. Although both sides did all they could to win votes, it was soon evident that the company's campaign was better-organized and better-financed than the union's effort. "When you are alone in the polling booth to vote for your representation, you will be alone with your conscience and your God," asserted an AFL circular. "Vote as you think, and not as the Kohler Company wants you to vote." The company countered this appeal to principle by distributing sandwiches, candy, and cigarettes to workers on the job. It also served free meals at the company cafeteria. Most importantly, it circulated rumors that if Local 18545 won the election, the company would either fire union members or move to another state. The AFL later charged that irregularities had occurred on the day of the election as well as during the campaign. Although each side had four poll watchers, the number was insufficient for a thorough check of credentials, and the union was convinced that supervisors, foremen, company chauffeurs, village employees, and other unqualified voters had cast ballots for the company union. Whatever irregularities there may have been, the final count showed that 1,063 employees had voted for the Kohler Workers' Association as opposed to 643 for Local 18545.[69]

Unwilling simply to concede defeat and reluctant to accept the reality of an open shop at the Kohler plant, the Wisconsin State Federation of Labor decided to continue the strike. Local 18545 officially approved a boycott of Kohler products in October, 1934, and it asked the AFL to place the Kohler name on a "We Don't Patronize" list. The union accomplished very little through its recalcitrance, however, and the strike continued in a desultory manner through the remainder of the Depression. Many of the strikers drifted away to search for jobs elsewhere, and with rates of unemployment diminishing but slightly, the company encountered little difficulty in filling its limited need for new workers. Happy to have jobs at all, most Kohler employees appeared content with the company union, which sustained itself through nominal dues and the income from vending machines in the plant. KWA members

[69] Uphoff, *Kohler on Strike*, 85–90; Hans Christian, "Kohler Wins," in *The Nation*, 139 (November 7, 1934), 540.

seldom asked questions about wages and working conditions, and except for a lonely handful of pickets outside the plant, few evidences of the strike remained. As World War II increased the demand for Kohler products, the strike itself finally came to an end in 1941.[70]

The long, anticlimactic story of the Kohler strike in the 1930's suggests that, despite the Great Depression, Kohler workers could not bring themselves to break sharply with their tradition of wage-conscious unionism. Encouraged by the bright promise of Section 7(a), and confident of support from New Dealers, they attempted to organize the Kohler plant only to meet defeat at the hands of a stubborn defender of the open shop. Eventually, nearly all the members of Federal Labor Union No. 18545 either relocated to an environment more hospitable to organized labor, or they accepted the blandishments and the material rewards of Kohler paternalism. In neither case did any but a committed remnant of union activists follow radical leaders who hoped to use the economic depression to build a class-conscious labor movement in Wisconsin.

* * *

In volume four of the *History of Labor in the United States*, published together with volume three in 1935, Selig Perlman and Philip Taft predicted that if the Depression continued, wage-conscious American unions would be inclined to favor national economic planning and government management of the economy. At the very least, they argued, "as long as government is kept in the center of the industrial arena by general depression and other economic problems, labor will hardly revert back to the 'economism' of the twenties." To the two labor historians it seemed far more likely that wage-conscious unionism would "exercise unremitting pressure on government, even if no great success may be anticipated." That pressure, they believed, would become apparent in efforts to manipulate Congress, in strike movements, and in "close agreements with other dissatisfied groups."[71]

An attempt to work out such an agreement was already under way at the time of Roosevelt's victory in 1932. Paul Douglas, an economist at the University of Chicago, Sherwood Eddy, a reform

[70] Uphoff, *Kohler on Strike*, 93–95, 99–101.

[71] Commons et al., *History of Labor in the United States, 1896–1932. Volume IV*, written by Perlman and Taft, 580–582, 614–620, 625–626.

clergyman who had long been active in social causes, and Norman Thomas, the leader of the Socialist party, had for several years been attempting to bring about a new political party that might accomplish for the United States what the Labour party had achieved in Great Britain. After the election of 1928 they organized the League for Independent Political Action, enlisting Progressives from across the nation in their effort. John Dewey, an old hand at reform, became national chairman of the LIPA, and prominent members of the organization included Zona Gale, W. E. B. Du Bois, Robert Morss Lovett, Oswald Garrison Villard, A. J. Muste, and Reinhold Niebuhr. Howard Y. Williams, a Congregational clergyman from St. Paul, became executive secretary.[72]

The League for Independent Political Action never gained the influence its founders envisioned. Dominated by university intellectuals and reform journalists, it was candidly elitist in orientation. Thus for years the league enjoyed little success in winning the endorsement of farmers and workers despite a deliberate effort to organize grass-roots support for a rationalized, planned economy. Presuming to save voters from themselves and from American society's cultural and economic myopia, the LIPA leaders failed to understand why they sometimes appeared arrogant. Conceived not as a new political party, but as a radical interest group that might aid in the creation of a new party, the league also failed to recruit prominent politicians such as George Norris or William E. Borah, who might have provided the political credibility it sorely needed. In Wisconsin, the brothers La Follette were careful to avoid offending the organization, but they tended to regard it more as a nuisance than as a contributor to the Progressive cause.[73]

[72] Karel D. Bicha, "Liberalism Frustrated: The League for Independent Political Action, 1928–1933," in *Mid-America*, 48 (January, 1966), 19–20; Paul H. Douglas, Sherwood Eddy, and Norman Thomas to the persons invited to the meeting called for December 15, 1928, tentative statement, and also Kirby Page to the National Committee and the Executive Committee of the League for Independent Political Action, May 29, 1929, both in the Howard Y. Williams Papers, Minnesota Historical Society, St. Paul.

[73] See the Williams Papers in the Minnesota Historical Society for the following: John Dewey to Devere Allen, October 2, [1929]; John Fitzpatrick to Williams, December 6, 1929; Norman Thomas to Williams, December 26, 1930; and James D. Staver to Williams, May 30, 1932. "The people who were generals in the La Follette movement in 1924 do not respond," wrote one frustrated member of the LIPA, Norman Studer, to Edgar Nixon on July 14, 1930. "Perhaps they are tired and we will have to develop some new leadership." W. E. B. DuBois had his own reasons for becoming dissatisfied with the LIPA effort. On January 10, 1929, he wrote to Kirby Page: "[S]o long as the wholesale disfranchisement of both black and white voters is allowed to continue without

The only important Wisconsin politician to take the league seriously was Thomas R. Amlie, who had served a term in Congress as representative from the state's First District. Amlie had grown up in rural North Dakota, graduated from the University of Wisconsin Law School, and settled in Elkhorn where he practiced law before his election to Congress as a La Follette Republican. Defeated in 1932, and by then in his mid-thirties, he soon became a critic of the New Deal. The Roosevelt administration, he asserted in 1933, was proving no more adept than the Hoover administration in solving economic problems. Persuaded that the times required a far more radical program than anything Roosevelt was offering, Amlie looked to the LIPA as a means of achieving the cooperative commonwealth he sought for America. Perhaps by linking the LIPA with Wisconsin Progressivism, he reasoned, he might achieve his radical goal. Working with Amlie were Alfred Bingham and Selden Rodman, recent Yale University graduates and editors of *Common Sense*, a journal that took up the LIPA cause and became an instrument for propagation of the league's objectives.[74]

In July, 1933, Bingham asked Phil La Follette to write an article for an issue of the magazine he and Rodman planned to publish in conjunction with a LIPA conference called to meet in Chicago in September. "If you could discuss the formation of a national farmer-labor party from the perspective of the Wisconsin experiments and also in light of the experience of your father in running on a third-party ticket," wrote the youthful editor, "it would be of tremendous value to us." Although Phil discussed chances of a third-party movement with Howard Y. Williams when the LIPA director visited Wisconsin that summer, he did not write the article Bingham requested. Neither did he attend the league's conference in Chicago. Yet the independent radicals did not give up on an alliance with the Wisconsin Progressives. Amlie, who served as conference chairman, sent Phil a report on the proceedings in Chicago and pointedly noted that the LIPA program "follows quite closely many of the ideas expressed by yourself."[75]

---

public criticism in the South, or without any attempt to supply legal remedies, a Third Party movement is predestined to failure."

[74] Miller, *Governor Philip F. La Follette*, 40–42; Theodore Rosenof, "The Political Education of an American Radical: Thomas R. Amlie in the 1930's," in *WMH*, 58 (Autumn 1974), 19–22; Donald L. Miller, *The New American Radicalism: Alfred M. Bingham and Non-Marxian Insurgency in the New Deal Era* (Port Washington, New York, 1979), 112–116.

[75] Alfred M. Bingham to Philip F. La Follette, July 13, August 3, 1933, and Thomas

Phil was not, in fact, averse to the general idea of forming a new party. Indeed, as he surveyed the options available to the Wisconsin Progressives, he gradually came to regard a new party as essential for people who took their Progressivism seriously. He was reluctant only to associate himself with the LIPA as the best means for bringing it about. Writing to his sister Mary and her husband Ralph Sucher during the summer of 1933, Phil summed up his thinking on the matter. Noting first that "people generally feel Roosevelt is trying, and want him given a fair chance," he confessed that he could see but three choices for Wisconsin Progressives: "the old Republican route, going into the Democratic party, or a third party." His fundamental concern in considering those choices, he insisted, must be the likely effect of each upon his brother's campaign for re-election to the Senate in 1934.

Inasmuch as Phil could see no chance of a Republican victory, he believed that continuing even nominal association with the Republican party would result in Bob's defeat. While the senator could probably win re-election as a Democrat, Phil had doubts about "the ultimate result in going to bed with that organization." That left only the third-party alternative. Forming a new party was risky, Phil admitted, but "it would have the advantage that the nomination would be certain, and in the election people can scratch their tickets."[76]

In his letter to the Suchers, Phil made no mention of his own political ambitions, although it must have been apparent that he badly wanted to reclaim the office of governor. One reason for his third-party enthusiasm was his calculation that running as the gubernatorial candidate of a new party might improve his chances of election in November. Bob, on the other hand, remained cool to the idea of forming a new party. He was temperamentally more cautious than Phil, he had learned in 1924 how frustrating third-party activities could become, and he feared that running on a third-party ticket would diminish the likelihood of his own election. For the first time since the La Follette brothers entered public life,

R. Amlie to Philip F. La Follette, September 6, 1933, all in the Philip F. La Follette Papers.

[76] Philip F. La Follette to Ralph and Mary Sucher, July 8, 1933, in the Philip F. La Follette Papers; Roger T. Johnson, *Robert M. La Follette, Jr., and the Decline of the Progressive Party in Wisconsin* (Madison, 1964; reprinted, Hamden, Connecticut, 1970), 30.

evidence of rivalry pointed to a possible rift in what had always been a harmonious relationship.[77]

During the fall and winter of 1933–1934, as Progressives throughout Wisconsin debated the pros and cons of forming a new party, two developments moved them portentously towards an irreversible break with the Republican party. For one thing, Tom Amlie was proving himself an effective advocate of a new radical political organization, and his success in winning converts to the idea threatened the La Follettes' domination of Wisconsin Progressivism. For another thing, Roosevelt was having problems with conservative Wisconsin Democrats. He very much wanted Bob La Follette to win re-election, he told the senator, but he could not publicly endorse a Republican without offending members of his own party. Because FDR believed supporting an independent created fewer problems than endorsing a Republican, he suggested that Bob run as an independent party candidate.[78]

Reluctant to follow the President's advice for fear that he might be surrendering Wisconsin to the New Deal Democrats, and dubious about forming a third party, Bob consulted his advisers both in Washington and at home. He finally agreed that early in March the Wisconsin Progressives should hold a conference in Madison to discuss the immediate problem of his re-election as well as the larger problem of establishing a new party. Together with his old supporters, Theodore Dammann and Herman Ekern, the senator sent out invitations to county leaders throughout Wisconsin, and on March 3 more than 400 Progressives joined the brothers La Follette in the ballroom of the Park Hotel to decide their future course. "We have before us one of the most momentous decisions Progressives in this state have ever been called upon to make," Bob told the audience. "I appeal to you not to consider your decision on the basis of the political fortunes of any individual." In effect, he was telling the conference that he would accept whatever the delegates wished to do about forming a new party.[79]

That most of the delegates were prepared to enter the 1934

[77] Maney, *"Young Bob" La Follette*, 134–136; Miller, *Governor Philip F. La Follette*, 45.

[78] Maney, *"Young Bob" La Follette*, 138–139; Robert M. La Follette, Jr., to Alfred T. Rogers, February 15, 1934, in box C-12, and Robert M. La Follette, Jr., to Philip F. La Follette, February 27, 1934, in box A-43, La Follette Family Papers, Library of Congress.

[79] *Capital Times*, February 25, March 3, 4, 1934; Evjue, *Fighting Editor*, 530–532; Johnson, *Robert M. La Follette, Jr.*, 32–33.

campaign under a new party banner was obvious, but they required a declaratory judgment from the Wisconsin supreme court before they could be certain that a new party name could legally appear on the ballot in the fall. With the court's approval, the Progressives arranged for another convention to meet in Fond du Lac on May 19. There, at the second important gathering of Wisconsin reformers in 1934, convention chairman William T. Evjue directed attention to the question of forming a new party. After the seemingly endless discussions of the previous months, the response of the delegates was almost an anticlimax. By a vote of 252 to 44 they endorsed the proposed new party.[80]

The lopsided vote was by no means an indication that the delegates were of one mind about what their ultimate objectives should be. Representing various organizations of farmers and workers, the Socialists, Tom Amlie's radicals, faithful followers of Old Bob La Follette, supporters of Young Bob's re-election, and advocates of Phil's attempting a comeback, the Fond du Lac convention agreed on neither the nature nor the purpose of the new party they created. In part because time was short, in part because arguments of the principal groups were already well-known, the most vigorous debate of the convention centered on the apparently trivial question of the new party's name.

Yet party nomenclature was not as unimportant as it may have seemed to casual observers. While discussion in Fond du Lac concentrated on the name, participants understood that there was more at stake in that discussion than was immediately obvious. Representatives of farmer and labor organizations, the Socialists, and the radicals favored calling their new political association the Farmer-Labor party. The name symbolized a class-conscious departure from the consensus politics of the past. It symbolized, as well, the objectives they shared with similar organizations in Minnesota and other states. The La Follettes and their followers, on the other

[80] Maney, *"Young Bob" La Follette*, 140–141; minutes of May 4, 1934, Third Party Committee Meeting, Madison, in the Thomas R. Amlie Papers; O. F. Christenson to Fellow Progressives, May 7, 1934, Emil Markee to Philip F. La Follette, May 10, 1934, Herbert L. Mount to Philip F. La Follette, May 14, 1934, and transcript of the Fond du Lac Progressive Conference, May 19, 1934, pp. 53–59, all in the Philip F. La Follette Papers. Evjue was unanimously elected to chair the conference, in part because he had long advocated the creation of a new party. See Howard Y. Williams to William T. Evjue, August 21, 1931, in the Williams Papers, Minnesota Historical Society, and the *Capital Times*, February 25, 1934.

hand, favored using the time-honored Progressive label. In presenting arguments for the class-conscious factions, labor leader John J. Handley contended that including the terms "farmer" and "labor" could mean thousands of votes from members of the Farm Holiday, the Wisconsin Milk Pool, the Farmers Union, and other agricultural associations, as well as thousands more from organized labor. The advocates of holding to a simple "Progressive" designation just as adamantly insisted that if the party emphasized class differences, it would unnecessarily limit its appeal. In a fervent closing argument, Phil La Follette maintained that for the new party to win mass support it must attract voters "as Americans and not by reason of their occupation."[81]

In the end, the delegates voted to call their new organization the Progressive party. Yet the debate had revealed the depth of feeling that separated the radicals from the old Progressives. Phil La Follette had earlier hoped to obtain a statement of principles as well as a party name, but rather than risk greater alienation of the radicals he gave up the attempt. After all, were he to become a candidate for governor, he would need to maintain peace within the new party. Amlie, Handley, and others among the farmer-labor-radical groups were sorely disappointed in the outcome of the convention, and it took all of Phil's persuasive skill to retain their support. With the Progressive party established, the dissidents formed the Farmer-Labor and Progressive League under the leadership of Samuel Sigman, an Appleton attorney who had strongly favored a farmer-labor alliance. On June 30 they held their own convention, again in Fond du Lac, for the purpose of drafting a platform and endorsing candidates. Phil La Follette appeared before the group and managed to prevent a party split. For the moment, at least, the farmer-labor faction agreed to accede to the wishes of the Progressive party's founding convention.[82]

No one was completely satisfied with the establishment of the new Progressive party. Bob La Follette had never been an enthusiastic supporter of a third party and had accepted the decision

[81] Transcript of the Fond du Lac Progressive Conference, May 19, 1934, pp. 59–82, in the Philip F. La Follette Papers.

[82] Miller, *Governor Philip F. La Follette*, 53–54; Farmer, Labor and Progressive League of Wisconsin, *Progressive Party Platform* (1934) and the Wisconsin Farmer, Labor, and Progressive League, *Statement of Principles* (1934), both pamphlets in the Philip F. La Follette Papers.

because it seemed the only way to avoid turning the state over to permanent Democratic control. The radical faction of the new party agreed that allowing conservative Democrats to ride FDR's coattails to another victory could mean the loss of their last chance to shape policies favorable to the class interests they represented. Yet the radicals also resented the way old Progressives gained ascendancy over the party that radicals were helping to create. Phil La Follette had more to gain from the new party than did anyone else because it provided a vehicle for his again becoming a candidate for governor. Nevertheless the thoughts of most Progressives centered on Bob's re-election, not on the problems confronting Phil. Indeed, Phil was not even invited to take part in a series of political discussions that Bob held with his advisers at Maple Bluff Farm, the longtime family seat, during the summer of 1934.

One of the matters to which Progressive party leaders devoted considerable attention was the advisability of Phil's becoming candidate for governor at the same time his brother was running for re-election to the Senate. Bob quite frankly opposed the idea because he believed that voters might react unfavorably to "too much La Follette." Nor did other members of the La Follette family favor Phil's entering the race. Yet Bob's consultants agreed that the younger brother should have a chance. They reasoned that he too possessed the magic name, he had been unstintingly loyal to the Progressive cause, and no better candidate could be found. Bob finally agreed that his brother should again seek the office of governor, and Phil announced his candidacy on the last day for filing.[83]

With Phil in the race, the campaign tactics of the La Follette brothers followed a pattern established long before either of them had entered the political arena. Meeting incessantly with local leaders throughout the campaign, they planned for contingencies that might arise and permitted no detail to escape their attention. They of course took to the stump themselves, and asked prominent Progressives from other states to speak in their behalf. Gerald Nye, Henrik Shipstead, Edward P. Costigan, Burton K. Wheeler, George W. Norris, Frank P. Walsh, Lynn Frazier, and Fiorello La Guardia all visited Wisconsin to extol the virtues of the La Follettes and to

[83] La Follette, *Adventure in Politics*, 212–213; Maney, *"Young Bob" La Follette*, 143; Miller, *Governor Philip F. La Follette*, 55.

welcome the formation of the new Progressive party as a harbinger of better times to come.[84]

Yet despite the familiar tactics and rhetoric, the contest of 1934 differed from previous La Follette campaigns. For years, winning the Republican primary had assured victory in the general election. Now, with the Progressives declaring their political independence, the primary lost its importance, and the general election became a triangular contest pitting the Progressives against both Republicans and Democrats. How well the Progressives might fare depended in part on how seriously Roosevelt took his implied promise to endorse Bob's re-election. As it turned out, FDR provided very effective assistance indeed, but it was support for the senator and not his brother. And he formally endorsed neither. The President visited Wisconsin on August 9, and in Green Bay he warmly praised "your two senators, Bob La Follette and Ryan Duffy, both old friends of mine." He also thanked Governor Schmedeman "for his patriotic cooperation with the national administration." For Phil La Follette and for other Progressive candidates there was nary a word.[85]

The Wisconsin Democrats were sorely disappointed with Roosevelt's kind words for Bob La Follette. Though they may have had no liking for the New Deal, they believed that the President had committed a serious political sin in failing to stand behind a Democrat for the Senate seat. In an effort to counteract the effect of FDR's remarks in Green Bay, they stoutly insisted that the President had not actually endorsed Bob, and they tried to claim that Phil was working to defeat New Deal programs. Their tactics backfired, for in drawing attention to what FDR had said about Bob, conservative Democrats encouraged co-operation between liberal Democrats and the Progressives. Then John M. Callahan, a supporter of Al Smith but not of Roosevelt, won the Democratic senatorial nomination in the September primary, and his victory drove the New Dealers and the Progressives towards an even closer alliance.

[84] Several letters in the Philip F. La Follette Papers attest to the La Follettes' efforts to obtain endorsement from prominent Progressives. See especially Selden Rodman to Philip F. La Follette, October 31, 1934; Lynn J. Frazier, endorsement of Robert M. La Follette, Jr., October 4, 1934; Peter Norbeck to Robert M. La Follette, Jr., September 11, 1934; Gerald P. Nye to Robert M. La Follette, Jr., September 11, 1934; Burton K. Wheeler to Robert M. La Follette, Jr., September 12, 1934; Henrik Shipstead to Robert M. La Follette, Jr., September 12, 1934; Gerald Nye to Gordon Sinykin, October 18, 1934; and Gordon Sinykin to Harry V. Carlson, October 9, 1934.

[85] Maney, *"Young Bob" La Follette*, 145; Johnson, *Robert M. La Follette, Jr.*, 38; Miller, *Governor Philip F. La Follette*, 57.

In the meantime, Progressives countered Democratic charges by suggesting that many of the New Deal programs had their origins in measures enacted by the Progressives during Phil's tenure as governor and earlier. This claim exaggerated the Progressive influence, but it nevertheless reinforced New Deal-Progressive co-operation.[86]

After the primary, Callahan campaigned against entanglements abroad and for balancing the budget at home, but few voters found his formula an adequate prescription for peace and prosperity. Bob's Republican opponent, John B. Chapple, refurbished the vituperative charges he had used in his 1932 primary campaign, and added a few new ones, in an effort to link the La Follettes with international communism. Clearly, Bob had as little to fear from Chapple's absurd allegations as he did from Callahan's stale bromides, and during the last month of the campaign he dedicated much of his time to securing his brother's election.[87]

Phil La Follette was unquestionably the underdog in his effort to defeat Albert Schmedeman. To Progressives and New Dealers alike, the Democratic governor was personally more attractive than were most other candidates of his party. As the American minister to Norway during the Wilson administration, and as the American representative to the international conference that established Norwegian sovereignty over Spitzbergen, Schmedeman enjoyed a special relationship with the Norwegians of Wisconsin. The gratitude of other American Norwegians also influenced some of the prominent figures Phil had hoped to enlist in his own campaign. Neither Minnesota Governor Floyd B. Olson nor Minnesota Senator Henrik Shipstead, for example, wished to speak publicly in opposition to the incumbent. Then, shortly before his seventieth birthday, Schmedeman experienced a terrible accident when he fell and injured his leg during the campaign. Infection set in, and an amputation became necessary. The La Follettes were distressed, in part because they wished Schmedeman no personal misfortune, but mainly because they feared that sympathetic voters might tip the scales in his favor.[88]

[86] *The Progressive*, August 11, October 6, 1934; Miller, *Governor Philip F. La Follette*, 57–58.

[87] Maney, *"Young Bob" La Follette*, 146–147; Johnson, *Robert M. La Follette, Jr.*, 38; *Capital Times*, October 11, 1934.

[88] *Wisconsin Blue Book, 1933*, p. 268; Floyd B. Olson to Philip F. La Follette, October

Political savants generally agreed that Bob would win re-election, and their predictions proved accurate. The senator polled 48 per cent of the total vote compared with 24 per cent for Callahan and 23 per cent for Chapple. Close observers did not believe, however, that Phil could succeed in his comeback attempt. Phil himself did not believe it, and he prepared a concession statement so as to have it ready should the returns indicate a Schmedeman victory. Much to everyone's surprise, he had no need to use it. When the votes were tallied, Phil learned that he had defeated Schmedeman, 373,093 to 359,467. Howard Greene, the Republican, secured but 172,980 votes.[89]

The election of 1934, with the brothers La Follette both emerging as victors, was one of the most notable in Wisconsin's political history. In its first campaign the new Progressive organization had won a seat in the United States Senate and in the governor's office, as well as other important positions. Tom Amlie had been elected to Congress from the First District, and he was joined by Harry Sauthoff from the Second, Gardner Withrow from the Third, Gerald Boileau from the Seventh, George Schneider from the Eighth, Merlin Hull from the Ninth, and Bernhard Gettelman from the Tenth. Seven of the state's ten congressmen elected in 1934 thus identified themselves as Progressives. In the Wisconsin state senate the Progressives had captured twelve of thirty-three seats, and in the assembly forty-five of 100. The Democrats had won three of the five state offices, but Theodore Dammann succeeded in his campaign to become secretary of state. Even after giving due weight to the Progressives' years of preparation and experience, pundits agreed that it was an impressive achievement for a party that had come into being less that six months before the election.[90]

Analysts assessing the 1934 election in Wisconsin generally saw it as a triumph for the distinctive Progressivism of the state. Successes in the La Follette campaigns could also be attributed to the continuing power of the La Follette name. It was the voters' perception of Bob and Phil as worthy political heirs of the elder La Follette that best explained voting behavior. The votes for Young Bob and Phil in 1934 correlate at .708 and .664 respectively with

6, 1934, and Henrik Shipstead to Robert M. La Follette, Jr., October 6, 1934, both in the Philip F. La Follette Papers; La Follette, *Adventure in Politics*, 215–216.

[89] Maney, *"Young Bob" La Follette*, 147; Miller, *Governor Philip F. La Follette*, 59–60.

[90] *Wisconsin Blue Book, 1935*, pp. 613, 615, 618–621.

Old Bob's 1924 presidential vote. Some observers thought that the Wisconsin returns of 1934 represented, as well, a triumph of liberalism over reaction, and they predicted a new political alignment of New Deal liberals with the La Follette Progressives. Whatever influence Roosevelt may have had on the way people voted, however, the correlation of the 1934 La Follette votes with the Roosevelt votes in either 1932 or 1936 diminishes to insignificance. Wisconsin Progressives of the 1930's, it is safe to assert, were a species different from New Deal liberals.[91]

The Progressive party victories of 1934, in fact, reveal much more about factional struggles among Progressives than they do about new alignments. Early in 1935, free-lance writer Louis Adamic published two articles on Phil La Follette in *The Nation*. In them he summarized Progressive speculations about the political future of reform in the United States. According to the most sanguine of the Progressive scenarios, an overwhelming Roosevelt victory in 1936 would result in the demise of the Republican party. Then Roosevelt would reveal himself in his true colors as a conservative, leaving the way open for the culminating triumph of Progressivism over reaction in 1940. After publication of his articles, Adamic received a note from Freda Kirchwey, who sat on *The Nation*'s board of editors. Informing him that he held the Wisconsin Progressives in higher regard than did eastern liberals, she remarked that the La Follettes had really not wanted a separate party, and that "their hands were forced by the strength of the left movement and the Farmer-Labor group."[92]

Upon receipt of Kirchwey's letter, Adamic promptly fired off a copy to Tom Duncan, Phil La Follette's closest adviser, and requested a response. Duncan replied with succinct clarity. "The problem that Phil and Bob faced was that of the mythical western character who conducted a swarm of bees across the Rocky Mountains without losing a bee." Progressive critics of the La Follettes thought during the campaign that the brothers had not been "sufficiently argumentative and dictatorial." Yet Duncan believed that with patient consultation of "all the elements of the La Follette

[91] Brye, *Wisconsin Voting Patterns*, 321–323; *Capital Times*, November 8, 9, 1934.

[92] Freda Kirchwey to Adamic, February 15, 1935, enclosed in Adamic to Thomas M. Duncan, February 16, 1935, in the Philip F. La Follette Papers; and Adamic's two articles in *The Nation*: "La Follette Progressives Face the Future," 140 (February 20, 1935), 213–215, and "A Talk with Phil La Follette," 140 (February 27, 1935), 242–245.

movement," Old Bob's sons had avoided a serious split with faithful supporters. They had lost a few bees, but they had won an impressive victory for Wisconsin Progressivism.[93]

Although the Progressives had good reason to celebrate, their success did not bring peace and contentment to the politics of Wisconsin. Instead, after their hard-won triumph, the La Follettes encountered extraordinary resentments and jealousies exacerbated by the Depression, the dream of extending the influence of Wisconsin Progressives far beyond the borders of the state, and finally, the effort to avoid American involvement in a second world war. Phil La Follette was to serve another four years as governor, and Bob was to remain in the United States Senate until after World War II. How far the sons of Robert M. La Follette might go towards achieving their objectives—if they could define what their objectives were—depended on a variety of contingencies, many of them unpredictable. Yet an influence of overpowering importance had already become apparent, and that was the enormous prestige of Franklin D. Roosevelt. Whatever course the Progressives might wish to take, their future and that of their new party depended heavily upon their relationship with FDR and the programs initiated under his leadership to provide a New Deal for the American people.

[93] Duncan to Adamic, February 25, 1935, and Gordon Sinykin to Robert M. La Follette, Jr., February 18, 1935, both in the Philip F. La Follette Papers.

11

Wisconsin and the New Deal

THE Great Depression set the context for important modifications in relationships that had prevailed among federal, state, and local governments during the 1920's. At the onset of hard times, the Hoover administration seemed reluctant to interfere with an economy that appeared to have functioned well during the New Era. Believing the economic downturn to be temporary, the President and his advisers took the position that providing relief to persons in need was essentially a local responsibility. Yet with revenues steadily declining, municipalities and local jurisdictions found themselves unable to meet rising welfare costs, and they began turning to the states for assistance. Unfortunately, state governments were no more prepared to meet welfare needs than the municipalities. Even when they adopted programs for relieving the distressed, as Wisconsin did in establishing a system of unemployment compensation, they confronted economic problems that extended far beyond their capacity to resolve.

After Roosevelt's victory in the election of 1932, and as the New Deal took shape, advocates of national solutions for national economic difficulties welcomed an opportunity to centralize the American political economy. On the other hand, the promise of political and economic centralization held little appeal for persons who feared the consequences of an unlimited concentration of power. Roosevelt himself believed that to confer on the national government all responsibility for developing relief or recovery programs might compound the disaster.

Even so, the federal government greatly increased its power during the Depression thirties. By the end of the decade, it was exerting an influence over the American people that even some enthusiastic nationalists had thought impossible without revolution. A major reason for the federal government's growth in influence was its advantage over the states in the collection of revenue. The Sixteenth Amendment, ratified in 1913, had given Congress the power to tax personal incomes from whatever source derived and without an apportionment of those revenues among the states. Grant-in-aid programs for agricultural extension, highways, vocational education, and public health had received congressional approval shortly after ratification of the income tax amendment. During the Great Depression, federal grants-in-aid for still other purposes became important instruments for implementing New Deal programs.

Nothing in the Constitution gave Congress the power to regulate welfare activities directly. But Congress could appropriate money for welfare purposes, and it could require the states to meet federal standards in implementing welfare programs for which they received federal assistance. Thus the New Deal developed in large part as a system of grant-in-aid programs to alleviate economic distress in states and communities. This was no violent revolution of the sort that many Americans had feared. What emerged instead was a new co-operative federalism in which national and state governments shared costs and responsibilities. The central government expanded its influence during the Depression thirties, to be sure, but that was because in sharing federal revenues with the states, New Dealers sought to control and direct the expenditure of funds. The relationship between federalism and localism that developed during the 1930's was neither tranquil nor entirely happy, but it worked well enough to meet some of the most pressing needs of the states as well as the nation.[1]

* * *

"It is one of the happy incidents of the federal system," wrote Justice Louis D. Brandeis in 1932, "that a single courageous State

[1] Two particularly thoughtful historical essays that treat the tensions between the states and the federal government are James T. Patterson's *The New Deal and the States: Federalism in Transition* (Princeton, 1969; reprinted, Westport, Connecticut, 1981) and Barry D. Karl's *The Uneasy State: The United States from 1915 to 1945* (Chicago, 1983). The American federal system has long been a subject of particular interest to political scientists. Of the many books written from a constitutional or social science perspective, the following have provided especially valuable insights: Jane Perry Clark [Carey], *The Rise of a New Federalism: Federal-State Cooperation in the United States* (New York, 1938; reprinted, 1966); Morton Grodzins, *The American System: A New View of Government in the United States*, ed. Daniel J. Elazar (Chicago, 1966); and Thomas R. Dye, *Politics in States and Communities* (Englewood Cliffs, New Jersey, 1969; 6th ed., 1980).

may, if its citizens choose, serve as a laboratory; and try novel social and economic experiments without risk to the rest of the country." The justice's observation appeared in an opinion that did not directly concern Wisconsin, but he may well have had recent events in Wisconsin at the back of his mind. His daughter, Elizabeth, had been deeply involved in the drafting and passage of the state's unemployment compensation law, and he himself had served as an informal consultant on its provisions. Although unemployment compensation became a familiar topic of discussion across the country that year, Wisconsin was the first state to enact such a law, and that law was to exert a profound national influence.[2]

The 1932 Democratic platform had endorsed old-age insurance as well as unemployment insurance, but as the New Deal took shape, Wisconsin's plan became the focal point for discussion of both forms of compensation. The provisions of the Wisconsin law attracting the most attention were those that required separate employer accounts and a system of merit ratings by which companies with good employment records could reduce contributions to their compensation reserves. The principal rival of the Wisconsin plan was one developed in Ohio, where the state commission on unemployment insurance proposed that workers as well as employers contribute to a single state fund. Critics of the Wisconsin system, which supporters labeled the "American Plan," tended to favor some form of pooled reserves. The chief argument against the American Plan, advanced by Paul Douglas of the University of Chicago and Abraham Epstein of the American Association for Old Age Security, emphasized that its system of rewarding individual employers was inappropriate because individual firms had little control over economic conditions or general employment.[3]

Rallying to defend their handiwork, the Wisconsin reformers followed the lead of Elizabeth Brandeis and Paul Raushenbush in an

[2] *New York State Ice Co. v. Liebmann*, in *U.S. Reports*, 285:262, 311; Patterson, *New Deal and the States*, 3.

[3] Arthur M. Schlesinger, Jr., *The Coming of the New Deal* (Boston, 1958), 301–302; Paul A. Raushenbush and Elizabeth Brandeis Raushenbush, *Our "U.C." Story, 1930–1967* (Madison, 1979), 130–135; Daniel Nelson, *Unemployment Insurance: The American Experience, 1915–1935* (Madison, 1969), 184–195, 195–197; Paul H. Douglas, *Social Security in the United States: An Analysis and Appraisal of the Federal Social Security Act* (New York, 1936; reprinted, Salem, New Hampshire, 1971, and Westport, Connecticut, 1972), 12–21, 29–44; Abraham Epstein, *Insecurity, a Challenge to America: A Study of Social Insurance in the United States and Abroad* (New York, 1936; 3rd ed., New York, 1968).

effort to persuade legislators, New Deal administrators, and liberal business people of the merits of the American Plan. From Justice Brandeis came the idea of using the federal tax system as leverage to secure state co-operation. Informally, he suggested to associates that a law might be written to reduce an employer's federal taxes by the amount paid in state taxes levied for unemployment benefits. On a visit to Washington during the 1933 Christmas holidays, Elizabeth attended a dinner at which Lincoln Filene, a Boston merchant and friend of the Brandeis family, outlined the tax-offset idea. Other dinner guests, especially Secretary of Labor Frances Perkins and New York Senator Robert Wagner, found merit in the Brandeis suggestion as Filene explained it. Elizabeth immediately telephoned her husband Paul, who had remained in Madison, to ask that he draw up a bill incorporating the offset. He set to work without delay, and when he had finished he sent off a night letter containing the rough draft of a bill that Senator Wagner promised to introduce.[4]

With Wagner's acceptance of the offset principle, Raushenbush traveled to Washington, where he and Thomas H. Eliot, assistant solicitor in the Department of Labor, hammered out the details of a national unemployment compensation bill. Wagner kept his promise to sponsor the measure in the Senate, and Representative David J. Lewis of Maryland introduced it in the House. Secretary Perkins strongly endorsed the proposed legislation, and a few days later the President himself urged its enactment. Yet there were some critics who feared that scattering vast unemployment insurance funds to the states might have an unfortunate effect on an already disrupted economy. Furthermore, an old-age pension bill which had been introduced by Senator Clarence C. Dill of Washington and Representative William P. Connery, Jr., of Massachusetts added to the difficulty of formulating satisfactory unemployment legislation.[5]

Reflecting upon both forms of compensation and considering advice he received from Rexford Tugwell, a member of the President's "Brains Trust," Roosevelt finally decided in June, 1934, that

[4] Raushenbush and Raushenbush, *Our "U.C." Story*, 174–179. The account of the Washington dinner in Schlesinger, *Coming of the New Deal*, 302–303, is substantially correct but inaccurate in some details.

[5] J. Joseph Huthmacher, *Senator Robert F. Wagner and the Rise of Urban Liberalism* (New York, 1968), 174–176; Frances Perkins, *The Roosevelt I Knew* (New York, 1946), 278–279; Thomas H. Eliot, "The Advent of Social Security," in Katie Louchheim, ed., *The Making of the New Deal: The Insiders Speak* (Cambridge, 1983), 161–162.

instead of dealing with the two measures separately he should seek a comprehensive law that would encompass his entire social security program. Stipulating that he wanted the states to work with the federal government in a unified system, he appointed the cabinet Committee on Economic Security (COES) to develop specific provisions under the direction of his secretary of labor.[6]

Frances Perkins did not minimize the task confronting the COES. "As I see it," she observed with some apprehension, "we shall have to establish in this country substantially all of the social-insurance measures which the western European countries have set up in the last generation." Furthermore, she was aware of economic arguments against such a comprehensive program. Inasmuch as the nation was in the midst of a deflationary cycle, she warned the President, the placing of large sums of money in reserves, by whatever method, could reduce investment and increase economic problems. "We can't help that," Roosevelt responded. "We have to get it started or it will never start." Thus the COES began its labors with the understanding that there was no perfect solution to the problem it faced, and that some compromises would be necessary if it was to develop even a partial solution.[7]

Arthur Altmeyer, who had left his position as secretary of the Wisconsin Industrial Commission to become assistant secretary of labor, drafted the President's executive order creating the cabinet committee. He included provision for consultation and administration. There was to be an advisory council to represent workers, employers, and the public; a technical board of experts selected by committee members from their departments; and an executive director who was to supervise staff investigations and develop proposals for COES consideration. The structure appeared cumbersome—and indeed there proved to be problems of co-ordination—but Roosevelt accepted it on the condition that the committee "steered clear of people who were too theoretical and who would take months of research before they could write a report."[8]

[6] Theron F. Schlabach, *Edwin E. Witte: Cautious Reformer* (Madison, 1969), 95–96; Edwin E. Witte, *The Development of the Social Security Act: A Memorandum on the History of the Committee on Economic Security and Drafting and Legislative History of the Social Security Act* (Madison, 1962), 4–5; Perkins, *The Roosevelt I Knew*, 279–280; Arthur J. Altmeyer, *The Formative Years of Social Security* (Madison, 1966), 7.

[7] Schlesinger, *Coming of the New Deal*, 304; Frances Perkins, "The Way of Security," in *Survey Graphic*, 23 (December, 1934), 620–622, 629; Perkins, *The Roosevelt I Knew*, 281.

[8] Altmeyer, *Formative Years of Social Security*, 7–9; Perkins, *The Roosevelt I Knew*, 285; Witte, *Development of the Social Security Act*, 7–9.

The search for a director was easy; Perkins and Altmeyer both knew a person with all the qualities Roosevelt wanted. From the University of Wisconsin economics department, they chose another Commons student, Edwin E. Witte, who earlier, as head of the state Legislative Reference Library, had worked closely with Altmeyer. Both Perkins and Altmeyer knew Witte to be a down-to-earth, practical reformer, a supporter of unemployment and old-age compensation, and a skilled draftsman of desired legislation. He had never in his life tilted with windmills, and his study with Commons had reinforced a natural inclination to forsake ideal objectives in order to accomplish realizable goals.

Notified of his selection on July 24, Witte left Madison for Washington and set to work immediately. In co-operation with Perkins and Altmeyer, he quickly determined that his staff should concentrate on problems associated with unemployment insurance and old-age security. While he was willing at first to consider the related problems of health insurance, he did not wish to risk jeopardizing the whole program by challenging the powerful American Medical Association, which adamantly opposed compulsory, government-subsidized health insurance. Thus the COES carefully avoided the subject, and recommendations on health insurance were not included in its final report.[9]

Even in concentrating on old age and unemployment, Witte, his staff, and the committee encountered difficulties in determining the limits of their responsibilities. Here and there, especially in the Treasury Department, economists of Keynesian persuasion saw in social insurance a means of restoring the economy by channeling federal funds to people in need. Alvin Hansen and other Keynesians on the COES technical board believed that the committee's report should, at the very least, provide some assessment of how its recommendations might affect the entire economy. Neither Witte nor the majority of his colleagues was taken with Keynesian devices for

[9] Arthur J. Altmeyer, "The Wisconsin Idea and Social Security," in *WMH*, 42 (Autumn, 1958), 23; Raushenbush and Raushenbush, *Our "U.C." Story*, 190–191; Schlabach, *Edwin E. Witte*, 112–114. Wilbur J. Cohen, a graduate student in economics at the University of Wisconsin, became one of Witte's research assistants in developing the Social Security Act. After its passage, he joined the staff of the Social Security Board where he remained until 1956. During the 1960's he became assistant secretary, undersecretary, and then secretary of the Department of Health, Education and Welfare. He was instrumental in securing passage of a Medicare bill in 1965, three decades after his experience with Witte in drafting the Social Security Act. For his account of that experience, see Eliot, "Advent of Social Security," in Louchheim, ed., *Making of the New Deal*.

stimulating aggregate demand, however, and throughout his directorship Witte insisted that the principal concern of the cabinet committee must be the welfare of the aged and the unemployed. Overall economic recovery was a desirable objective, of course, but the Wisconsin economist never believed that promoting recovery was a part of the COES mission.[10]

Another policy debate among Witte's colleagues centered on the question of whether to emphasize immediate relief for the distressed or, on the other hand, to concentrate on developing a long-term program of social insurance. As might have been expected, close associates of Harry Hopkins, who headed the Federal Emergency Relief Administration, thought the immediate need more important than the long-term goal, however desirable a program of social insurance might be. Witte recognized the merit in the relief advocates' argument, but in the end he used his influence to promote social insurance rather than relief. His preferences in the matter were consistent with his conviction that with many New Deal agencies concentrating on economic recovery, his responsibility was to help create a program of permanent utility through good times and bad. Contributing to the welfare of American workers by establishing some form of social insurance was always uppermost in his mind.[11]

By far the most heated policy discussions within the COES structure concerned federal-state relationships in proposals for a system of unemployment compensation. With his experience in shaping the state program in Wisconsin, Witte was inclined to emphasize the President's desire for an unemployment insurance system "under state laws," and for "a maximum of cooperation between States and the Federal Government." COES counsel Thomas Eliot, who had helped draft the Wagner-Lewis unemployment compensation bill, became an ally in urging extensive state involvement. Drawing on the advice of Justice Brandeis and Harvard law professor Felix Frankfurter, Eliot argued that a national system of social insurance could encounter legal problems if seen as an unconstitutional in-

[10] Schlabach, *Edwin E. Witte*, 104–105; Edwin E. Witte, "The Objectives of Social Security," in Edwin E. Witte, *Social Security Perspectives, Essays*, ed. Robert J. Lampman (Madison, 1962), 101–111.

[11] Witte, *Development of the Social Security Act*, 11–12, 20–22, 30, 70–71; Schlabach, *Edwin E. Witte*, 106–107.

trusion upon the powers of the states. There were those, however, who strongly favored an exclusively national system.[12]

Neither Witte's research staff nor the technical board that Altmeyer chaired was able to resolve the disagreement over state participation. Witte finally drafted a report which he submitted first to the technical board for correction and approval, and then to the cabinet committee for consideration and action. The report outlined three alternative programs that Witte's staff and the technical board had discussed, and it implied that the cabinet committee should decide which of the three it preferred.[13]

The first alternative was a national system in which the states would have no administrative responsibilities. The major advantages of such a system were the uniformity of benefits it could provide, its reduction of risks through extension of the program over a broad area, and the relative ease with which it could protect workers in high unemployment areas or workers who moved from one state to another. The principal hazard in a national system was that its constitutionality remained open to question, and at a time when the U.S. Supreme Court appeared to be casting a critical eye over New Deal programs, constitutional considerations loomed large. If a national system were enacted and the courts set it aside, the COES would be left with little to show for its efforts—and workers would be left with nothing. It was anxiety over the constitutional question that had led many of Witte's associates to join him in support of a federal-state system.[14]

The two remaining alternatives outlined in the report were variations of the federal-state pattern. One of them was essentially the plan embodied in the Wagner-Lewis Bill. That is, it adopted the tax-offset principle. States would collect unemployment contributions directly, and employers would be permitted to deduct state unemployment contributions from their federal taxes. The other federal-state alternative, the so-called "subsidy plan," would impose a federal tax on employers. The revenues collected in each state

[12] Altmeyer, *Formative Years of Social Security*, 14–15, 21–23; Nelson, *Unemployment Insurance*, 206–207; Perkins, *The Roosevelt I Knew*, 286; Schlabach, *Edwin E. Witte*, 115–116; Schlesinger, *Coming of the New Deal*, 305.

[13] Schlabach, *Edwin E. Witte*, 118–119; Altmeyer, *Formative Years of Social Security*, 17–18.

[14] Altmeyer, *Formative Years of Social Security*, 19–20; Schlesinger, *Coming of the New Deal*, 305–306; Nelson, *Unemployment Insurance*, 207–208; Perkins, *The Roosevelt I Knew*, 291.

would then be returned to that state for use in unemployment compensation if state authorities could demonstrate compliance with federal regulations. The idea for the subsidy plan had come out of technical discussions with the board, and to some members it represented a compromise between the Wagner-Lewis proposal and a strictly national scheme. It would obviously permit greater national control over the system than would the offset device, but it also seemed more likely to encounter difficulties in the courts.[15]

While the cabinet committee deliberated the three proposals, Witte and his staff were completing plans for the National Conference on Economic Security. Scheduled to meet on November 14, after the 1934 elections, the conference was supposed to provide information about old-age and employment security as well as an opportunity for interested outsiders to make suggestions for COES consideration. The conference also presented Roosevelt with a chance to make his views a matter of record. Shortly before the conference began, the cabinet committee decided to base the new unemployment compensation program on a system of federal-state co-operation. With that decision in mind, Witte drafted the President's address, and Roosevelt told the conference that he would recommend "a cooperative federal-state undertaking." While the unemployment reserve funds should be held and invested by the federal government, he declared, the states were "the most logical units" for the administration of benefits.[16]

Inasmuch as Witte had drafted the speech, the President's endorsement of his views was scarcely surprising. Yet the reaction of experts and interested persons attending the conference was unexpected. In roundtable discussions following Roosevelt's address, the conferees made clear their overwhelming preference for a national system. Newspaper accounts of the conference conveyed the impression that despite the President's urging, an influential body of expert opinion stood opposed to a program such as the one embodied in the Wagner-Lewis Bill. And in the aftermath of the conference, opponents of the tax-offset device campaigned vigorously against it. The subsidy plan, they believed, more nearly rep-

[15] Schlabach, *Edwin E. Witte*, 119; Altmeyer, *Formative Years of Social Security*, 18; Witte, *Development of the Social Security Act*, 115–118; Edwin E. Witte, "Major Issues in Unemployment Compensation," in Witte, *Social Security Perspectives*, ed. Lampman, 241–245.

[16] Witte, *Development of the Social Security Act*, 41–45; Schlabach, *Edwin E. Witte*, 119–120; Altmeyer, *Formative Years of Social Security*, 19.

resented the views of persons who had studied unemployment compensation problems.[17]

Witte later concluded that holding the National Conference on Economic Security had been a mistake—or at least that the conference had been badly handled—and that its net effect was to hinder his efforts to secure an acceptable program. Opposing Witte, and claiming to speak for a majority of social insurance experts, the proponents of a national system sought to influence public opinion. They also sought to influence members of the COES advisory council, which began to meet in mid-November. As a lay body with no special knowledge of welfare, old-age pensions, or unemployment compensation, the advisory council reviewed the findings of Witte's staff and those of the technical board, as well as various proposals discussed at the national conference.[18]

Efforts to win the day for a subsidy plan came to naught. The cabinet committee once again reviewed proposed unemployment compensation programs, but in the end it returned to the tax-offset plan that Witte, Altmeyer, and Perkins favored. In the meantime, the President had asked Rexford Tugwell to make independent inquiries about the subsidy plan. FDR read arguments for it, listened to its advocates urge a more centralized system than the cabinet committee was willing to recommend, and then he, too, reasserted his preference for the more cautious tax-offset law. With the President's support, Witte looked forward to the successful conclusion of his efforts.[19]

In the meantime, developing a program of old-age insurance was proving almost as difficult as securing agreement on a program of unemployment compensation. A particularly troublesome question concerned using a system of reserves to finance old-age annuities. Another involved the size of annuities to be awarded older workers who were expected to retire before making contributions equivalent to the contributions younger workers might be expected to make. Several experienced actuaries, whose advice the committee solicited, suggested paying for old-age pensions with government subsidies

[17] Schlesinger, *Coming of the New Deal*, 306; Witte, *Development of the Social Security Act*, 119–121; Perkins, *The Roosevelt I Knew*, 288–291.

[18] Witte, *Development of the Social Security Act*, 41–47, 54–61; Witte, "Major Issues in Unemployment Compensation," in Witte, *Social Security Perspectives*, ed. Lampman, 235–256; Nelson, *Unemployment Insurance*, 209–211.

[19] Schlabach, *Edwin E. Witte*, 126; Witte, *Development of the Social Security Act*, 126.

as well as contributions. Subsidies, they pointed out, would eliminate the need to employ reserve financing. Another possibility was to place employee and employer contributions in a reserve and to pay workers only the benefits their contributions merited on an actuarial basis. This second approach would place reserve funds in a government agency, and it would provide minimal benefits to workers who retired before making significant contributions.[20]

Both plans presented problems. Basing the program on a full actuarial reserve would be tantamount to reducing aggregate income by $50 to $60 billion through a system of forced saving, and then placing the vast sum in a government agency. On the other hand, subsidizing the pensions of workers nearing retirement would impose stresses on the general treasury and increase the size of national deficits. After examining the alternatives, Witte's staff and the technical board under Altmeyer's guidance worked out a compromise. Maintaining the principle of separating old-age insurance from old-age assistance, they proposed making an exception so as to provide extra insurance credits to older workers and thereby increase their annuities. At the appropriate time, younger workers were to receive benefits calculated as if the system were operating entirely on actuarial principles.[21]

Witte had at first opposed giving a government agency control over reserve funds. Favoring "pay-as-you-go financing," he helped stir up a controversy over the emphasis on unemployment compensation as opposed to old-age insurance. When he drafted Roosevelt's speech for the National Conference on Economic Security, he included only an ambiguous reference to old-age insurance and raised questions about the appropriateness of immediate legislation for the elderly. In editing Witte's draft, Roosevelt inserted a sentence in which he expressed the hope "that in time we may be able to provide security for the aged." The phrasing of FDR's national conference speech greatly disturbed Witte's critics and older workers who read newspaper accounts alleging that the COES intended to scrap old-age assistance measures in order to concentrate on unemployment insurance. With California's Dr. Francis E. Townsend and other advocates of old-age assistance winning converts daily, it was no time to suggest that New Dealers were laggard in

[20] Schlabach, *Edwin E. Witte*, 126–127; Perkins, *The Roosevelt I Knew*, 292–294.

[21] Perkins, *The Roosevelt I Knew*, 294; Schlesinger, *Coming of the New Deal*, 309; Altmeyer, *Formative Years of Social Security*, 26.

providing for the nation's elderly. Witte, pulling in his horns, joined his staff in recommending the compromise plan for old-age insurance.[22]

Although the technical board and the cabinet committee approved the compromise plan, Witte's difficulties were by no means over. The compromise program required eventual payment of subsidies from the general treasury, and when the COES recommendation reached the President, Secretary of the Treasury Henry Morgenthau, Jr., objected. FDR shared a distaste for the final deficits that were certain to result from subsidies, and at the last minute he asked for changes in the program. Witte, Altmeyer, and their associates complied by increasing the schedule for contributions and by decreasing benefits. The changes eliminated deficits, to be sure, but increasing the size of the reserve fund could also increase the program's deflationary impact.[23]

At last, after seemingly endless discussion, debate, and controversy, the final COES report went to the President, and on January 17, 1935, he sent it on to Congress with a special message urging that it "be brought forward with a minimum of delay." After consulting various agencies and departments, Thomas Eliot drafted a bill to carry out the committee's recommendations, and upon its introduction it went to the Senate Finance Committee and the House Ways and Means Committee. Witte appeared before both, and in characteristic fashion he presented a wealth of detailed explanation of the bill's provisions.[24]

The introduction of rival measures complicated the already tangled history of the economic security bill. The Townsend Plan, developed by a sixty-six-year-old physician from Long Beach, California, was proving enormously appealing to old-timers across the country; and in part because of pressure from constituents, it attracted congressional support. Urging that all persons over sixty receive a monthly allotment of $200, Townsend proposed but one condition: that beneficiaries of the government bounty spend their allotments within the month. Even so experienced a legislator as

[22] Witte, *Development of the Social Security Act*, 45–47; Altmeyer, *Formative Years of Social Security*, 13; Schlabach, *Edwin E. Witte*, 127; Edwin E. Witte, "Old Age Security in the Social Security Act," in Witte, *Social Security Perspectives*, ed. Lampman, 143–147.

[23] Witte, *Development of the Social Security Act*, 74, 148–151; Perkins, *The Roosevelt I Knew*, 293–294; Altmeyer, *Formative Years of Social Security*, 29.

[24] Eliot, "Advent of Social Security," in Louchheim, ed., *Making of the New Deal*, 162, 164; Schlabach, *Edwin E. Witte*, 133, 223.

Idaho Senator William E. Borah endorsed the Townsend Plan, probably in order to assure his re-election in 1936. Another competing proposal was Louisiana Senator Huey Long's "Share Our Wealth." Playing the catchy tunes of a political pied piper with extraordinary skill, the Louisiana Kingfish attracted a devoted following among people who thought they would benefit from a program to confiscate the fortunes of the wealthy. Less flamboyant than Long, and less demagogic, Minnesota Farmer-Labor Representative Ernest Lundeen introduced a bill to create programs of social insurance operated by the beneficiaries themselves. Neither Lundeen nor anyone else worked out technical details in the bill, but it won support from Earl Browder, general secretary of the American Communist party.[25]

To Witte, his colleagues, and most members of Congress, rivals of the COES bill scarcely merited serious consideration, and debate focused on the measure that Eliot had drafted. After prolonged hearings and meticulous rephrasing of the bill, the House Ways and Means Committee finally filed a favorable report on April 5, 1935. Until the Ways and Means Committee began its tinkering, the measure had been the "Economic Security Act"; it now became the "Social Security Act." Debate in the House produced several motions to amend, but all were rejected, and on April 19 the House passed the measure by a vote of 371 to 33.[26]

On May 20, having completed its own investigation and hearings, the Senate Finance Committee also filed a report favoring passage. Like the bill approved in the House, the Senate committee's version introduced few changes in substance. The principal modification was an amendment offered by Senator La Follette to permit in each state the type of unemployment insurance it desired, including a system of company reserves as provided in the Wisconsin law of

[25] Charles McKinley and Robert W. Frase, *Launching Social Security: A Capture-and-Record Account, 1935–1937* (Madison, 1970), 11; Arthur M. Schlesinger, Jr., *The Politics of Upheaval* (Boston, 1960), 35–36, 59–63; T. Harry Williams, *Huey Long* (New York, 1969), 696–701; Alan Brinkley, *Voices of Protest: Huey Long, Father Coughlin, and the Great Depression* (New York, 1982), 79–80, 222–224; Schlesinger, *Coming of the New Deal*, 295–296; Altmeyer, *Formative Years of Social Security*, 30–31; Witte, *Development of the Social Security Act*, 85–86.

[26] U.S. House, Committee on Ways and Means, *Economic Security Act, Hearings on H.R. 4120, to Alleviate Hazards of Old Age, Unemployment, Illness, and Dependency, to Establish a Social Insurance Board in Department of Labor, to Raise Revenue, and for Other Purposes, Jan. 21–Feb. 12, 1935*, 74 Cong., 1 sess. (1935), 1–172; Witte, *Development of the Social Security Act*, 91–99; Altmeyer, *Formative Years of Social Security*, 35–38.

1932. In a brief prepared by Paul Raushenbush, Young Bob argued that a new social security law should not penalize "those who have pioneered" in the effort to achieve social progress.[27]

Debate in the Senate focused largely on an amendment introduced by Senator Bennett Champ Clark of Missouri that had the support of conservative interests. It stipulated that employees of companies with private annuity plans be exempt from compulsory old-age insurance. Roosevelt opposed the amendment, and so did Witte and La Follette. Although La Follette failed to prevent inclusion of the Clark Amendment, the Senate passed the Social Security Bill on June 17, and it went to the conference committee. Debate over the Clark Amendment delayed final passage, but with the amendment deleted and the differences between House and Senate versions finally ironed out, the Social Security Bill received approval of both houses. Roosevelt signed it on August 14, 1935, and it became the law of the land.[28]

The Social Security Act was an omnibus measure that included a national system of old-age annuities, a state-administered unemployment insurance program under federal supervision, and federal subsidies for state programs established to provide assistance for the elderly, the blind, and children deprived of parental support. Without creating a system of compulsory health insurance, the act also sought to enhance health services in the states by encouraging research, improving state health staffs, and providing special assistance for crippled and disadvantaged children. An independent administrative agency, the Society Security Board, was to supervise the programs encompassed by the act.[29]

The old-age insurance program was the only portion of the new welfare system that was to be exclusively national in character. Congress followed the cabinet committee's recommendation that it should be a contributory program, with funds for old-age annuities coming from the contributions of workers as well as employers.

[27] Raushenbush and Raushenbush, *Our "U.C." Story*, 208–209; Patrick J. Maney, *"Young Bob" La Follette: A Biography of Robert M. La Follette, Jr., 1895–1953* (Columbia, Missouri, 1978), 163; Edwin E. Witte to Robert M. La Follette, Jr., July 5, 1935, in the Edwin E. Witte Papers.

[28] Eliot, "Advent of Social Security," in Louchheim, ed., *Making of the New Deal*, 166–167; Witte, *Development of the Social Security Act*, 105–108, 157–159; Schlesinger, *Coming of the New Deal*, 312; Nelson, *Unemployment Insurance*, 218.

[29] McKinley and Frase, *Launching Social Security*, 12–17; Edwin E. Witte, "Social Security: A Wild Dream or a Practical Plan?" in Witte, *Social Security Perspectives*, ed. Lampman, 6–7.

President Roosevelt himself strongly favored worker contributions because of their political and moral implications. Taxing employees was "politics all the way through," he later recalled. "We put those payroll contributions there so as to give the contributors a legal, moral, and political right to collect their pensions and their unemployment benefits." In fact, however, the act itself excluded large numbers of people from the program. Agricultural workers, domestic servants, casual laborers, maritime workers, government employees, and employees of philanthropic or educational institutions could not qualify for old-age pensions under the 1935 act, and only after World War II did such workers gain entry into the old-age insurance system.[30]

Other programs included in the Social Security Act all involved joint action with the states. The act provided, for example, that the federal government should pay for "the proper and efficient administration" of state unemployment compensation laws. Similarly, federal funds could be used in support of state programs created to assist the needy aged. Yet federal participation in state unemployment compensation and old-age assistance programs required federal approval, and to receive it, state programs had to meet federal standards. Accepting an administration grant meant that a state unemployment compensation agency placed itself under obligation to pay no benefits until two years after receiving its first unemployment contributions, to deposit the contributions in an unemployment trust fund under the supervision of the United States Treasury, and to pay benefits through public employment offices. The financial foundation of state unemployment compensation programs was a payroll tax levied by the United States Treasury, but in exchange a taxpayer under an approved state law could receive a credit against his federal taxes. State old-age assistance programs also had to accept federal regulations if they wished to secure federal help. To qualify for aid, a state old-age assistance program had to show that it operated in all sections of the state, that the state could pay a part of the program's costs, that any applicant denied assistance could obtain a fair hearing of his case,

[30] Witte, "Old Age Security in the Social Security Act," in Witte, *Social Security Perspectives*, ed. Lampman, 32–34, 115–125; Schlesinger, *Coming of the New Deal*, 308–309; Altmeyer, *Formative Years of Social Security*, 25–26; Witte, *Development of the Social Security Act*, 152–157; Eliot, "Advent of Social Security," in Louchheim, ed., *Making of the New Deal*, 165.

that the state could provide the Social Security Board with adequate reports and information, and that the state would employ appropriate methods in administering the program.[31]

The patchwork system that Congress approved when it passed the Social Security Act satisfied no one entirely. Witte, Altmeyer, Perkins, and Roosevelt were all aware of its limitations. Yet they worked diligently for its implementation, defending the vast program not as a perfect welfare system, but as the best system attainable under conditions and attitudes that prevailed in 1935. They reasoned that rather than wait for a more propitious moment, they should take what they could and work to improve the program in the years ahead. The improvements were in some areas slow in coming—it took more than a decade to extend coverage of the old-age and survivors' insurance system—but from the very beginning the program worked better than its critics expected. The early successes of the system were in part attributable to the extraordinary skill and patience of the newly created Social Security Board.

Edwin Witte did not remain in the federal bureaucracy after passage of the Social Security Act. Returning to Madison and the university he loved, he spent the next twenty years as a faculty member, including twelve as chairman of the department of economics. Witte's students and colleagues, as well as fellow citizens of the state, often spoke of him as "the Father of Social Security," but he always insisted that Arthur Altmeyer better deserved the title. Altmeyer had been largely responsible for organizing the COES, and he had assumed a major role in its investigations and deliberations. From 1935 to 1945 he sat as a member of the Social Security Board. In 1937 he became chairman, and from 1946 to 1953, after termination of the board through administrative reorganization, he held the position of commissioner for social security.[32]

Shortly after Altmeyer's retirement, when Arthur Schlesinger, Jr., wrote the second volume of his monumental study, *The Age of Roosevelt*, he credited Altmeyer with "prodigious achievement" in carrying out his assignments. "No government bureau," asserted

[31] McKinley and Frase, *Launching Social Security*, 13–14; Edwin E. Witte, "The Federal Government's Role in Unemployment Insurance in 1938," in Witte, *Social Security Perspectives*, ed. Lampman, 257–262.

[32] Schlabach, *Edwin E. Witte*, 220–222; McKinley and Frase, *Launching Social Security*, 30, 285–390; Altmeyer, *Formative Years of Social Security*, 220–221.

Schlesinger, "ever directly touched the lives of so many Americans—the old, the jobless, the sick, the needy, the blind, the mothers, the children—with so little confusion or complaint." Like Witte, Schlesinger attributed the success of Social Security largely to Altmeyer. Altmeyer himself was more modest. "I have been called the 'father of social security,' " he once noted, "but what really happened was that I was the man on whose doorstep Ed Witte left the bastard." Perhaps Witte thought of the strapping infant as a Wisconsin family responsibility.[33]

* * *

As one who had helped secure passage of Wisconsin's unemployment compensation law in 1932, Phil La Follette gladly claimed some credit for federal social welfare legislation during the Depression decade. Like Justice Brandeis, he believed that a single state could serve as an admirable laboratory for social and economic experiments that might prove valuable to the nation. And in the development of Social Security, he believed that Wisconsin had served as such a laboratory. Praised for his innovative accomplishments during his first term, Phil fretted over his defeat in 1932, and he eagerly sought once more to lead Wisconsin and the nation in new directions. With his victory in the election of 1934, he won another opportunity, and he intended to make the most of it. Thus, at the time Witte, Altmeyer, and their associates in Washington were working out details of the federal Social Security Act, the governor of Wisconsin was proposing a new agenda for restoring prosperity to his state.

The nation was entering its sixth year of depression, and for all the efforts to relieve distress, prosperity seemed as far away as in 1929–1930. Yet very important changes had taken place. One great difference between Phil's second term and his first was that by the time of his second inauguration, New Dealers had taken the nation a considerable distance towards co-operative federalism. The Social Security Act was but one measure that channeled federal funds out to the states and, in the process, influenced state activities. Another was the Federal Emergency Relief Act, passed much earlier during the New Deal's first Hundred Days. The act had created the Federal Emergency Relief Administration (FERA), which received an ap-

[33] Schlesinger, *Coming of the New Deal*, 314–315; Schlabach, *Edwin E. Witte*, 157.

propriation of $500 million for distribution to the states. Half that sum was for matching grants, with the states contributing three dollars for every one they received in federal money. The other half was to be spent in the states at the discretion of FERA administrator Harry Hopkins.[34]

How well a state fared in its relationship with the FERA depended on the adequacy of its relief appropriations, the efficiency with which it administered the grants it received, and the readiness of state officials to follow FERA regulations and guidelines. In Wisconsin, Hopkins and his subordinates found the Schmedeman administration unwilling to provide sufficient funding for relief, inefficient and given to political favoritism in its supervision of relief projects, and resentful of FERA bureaucrats. Lorena Hickock, a keen-eyed, sharp-tongued social worker who served Hopkins as a field agent, visited Madison late in 1933 and called on Governor Schmedeman. She found his timidity appalling. According to her report, he was so fearful of being attacked by radicals that he was "afraid to go home." When she told him that she would protect him, the governor's only response was "a dirty look."[35]

While Schmedeman never received high marks for derring-do, it was his administrative incompetence that troubled Hopkins. Falling behind in making state contributions for relief, Wisconsin had rapidly lost the FERA administrator's goodwill. After the 1934 election, La Follette learned that it would take a state appropriation of $5 million to meet Wisconsin's relief obligations and maintain the state's eligibility for further aid. When Phil assumed office, he promptly urged the legislature to take appropriate action. Over the opposition of disgruntled Democrats, a relief bill easily passed both houses, clearing the way for bolder, more imaginative moves.[36]

During the transition period after his election, Phil had worked hard at fashioning an agenda for his second term as governor. He

[34] Patterson, *New Deal and the States*, 50–52; Robert S. McElvaine, *The Great Depression: America, 1929–1941* (New York, 1984), 151–152; William E. Leuchtenburg, *Franklin D. Roosevelt and the New Deal, 1932–1940* (New York, 1963), 120–121.

[35] Patterson, *New Deal and the States*, 177; Schlesinger, *Coming of the New Deal*, 271–273.

[36] Harry Hopkins to Philip F. La Follette, January 14, March 11, 1935; La Follette to Harry Hopkins, March 1, 1935; La Follette, message to the legislature, January 21, 1935; and Herman M. Somers to Thomas M. Duncan, June 29, 1935, all in the Philip F. La Follette Papers. Also Milwaukee *Journal*, December 17, 1934; *Wisconsin State Journal*, January 22, February 26, 1935; and John E. Miller, *Governor Philip F. La Follette, the Wisconsin Progressives, and the New Deal* (Columbia, Missouri, 1982), 62.

had always thought that relief measures, though necessary during hard times, had little to do with meeting the fundamental problems of the economy. After 1929 he echoed other Progressives in contending that the most basic problem was a maldistribution of wealth and income. With the elimination of economic privilege and the regulation of special interests, ran the argument, all citizens would live happier, richer lives. Incidentally, they would also consume more of the products of American industry and thus increase the market demand that nearly everyone thought essential for the restoration of prosperity. Phil refurbished traditional Progressive arguments during his 1934 campaign, but he was beginning to modify his ideas about the causes and cures of the Depression. The longer he thought about needs of the times, the more he came to believe that his emphasis should be on economic expansion and the production of goods rather than on the redistribution of income and relief for the unemployed.[37]

In December, 1934, before taking over the reins of government in the state, Phil traveled to Washington, where he and Bob conferred with FDR at the White House. Knowing that Roosevelt intended to propose replacing the FERA with a new work-relief program, the governor-elect wisely sought presidential approval of his own plans for Wisconsin. He believed that his program might well become a pilot project for other states, and he wanted to be sure that Roosevelt had no objection to his taking independent action. Listening attentively to the explanation of Phil's bold proposal, the President urged him to proceed. FDR was sensitive to the political threat of visionary leaders—Huey Long, Francis Townsend, Upton Sinclair, and others—who might persuade voters to forsake the New Deal for attractive but dangerous alternatives. Eager to retain not only the support of his party but also that of Progressives who had often made common cause with radical groups, Roosevelt asked only that Phil keep him informed of developments in Wisconsin. It seemed a small price to pay for the endorsement of La Follette Progressives.[38]

The governor returned to Madison from the first of several sim-

[37] John E. Miller, "Governor Philip F. La Follette's Shifting Priorities from Redistribution to Expansion," in *Mid-America*, 58 (April–July, 1976), 120–123; "The New La Follette," an editorial in the Two Rivers *Reporter*, September 3, 1935.

[38] Miller, *Governor Philip F. La Follette*, 63; Philip F. La Follette to Isabel La Follette, December 7, 8, 1934, in the Philip F. La Follette Papers.

ilar missions, and he set about his business with characteristic determination. In 1931 he had helped establish the State Regional Planning Committee, a body that included citizen and university representatives as well as members from various state boards, departments, and commissions. Charged with collecting data and developing plans for the economic and social improvement of Wisconsin, the planning committee had worked first with the Civil Works Administration and then with the FERA. Phil now asked it to draw up an inventory of projects appropriate for inclusion in a public works program. The committee also compiled information on Wisconsin's population, its transportation and industry, and its educational and health-care institutions. Gradually, the plan that Phil had discussed with the President began to take shape.[39]

In the meantime, Roosevelt and his advisers were continuing their discussion of the need for new measures to replace the FERA. Like Phil, FDR had come to believe that relief programs for the distressed did not get to the heart of their problems. "Continued dependence upon relief induces a spiritual and moral disintegration fundamentally destructive to the national fibre," he asserted in his message to Congress on January 4. "The Federal Government must and shall quit this business of relief." To restore the self-respect of the jobless he proposed employment in useful, important work, and to carry out his objective he suggested an appropriation of $4 billion. Combining that amount with $880 million not expended from previous appropriations, the President envisioned providing work for 3.5 million persons. Introduced as a joint resolution, the measure easily passed the House. The Senate moved more slowly, but with amendments to restrict and regulate the allocation of funds, it too voted in favor of the resolution. Roosevelt signed the Emergency Relief Appropriation Act on April 8, 1935.[40]

Within limits imposed by the Senate, the act gave Roosevelt power to spend as he saw fit one of the largest single appropriations in American history to that time, and Wisconsin's governor was quick to suggest allocations to his program for the state. Phil had taken

[39] *Wisconsin Blue Book, 1935*, pp. 337–338; Philip F. La Follette, *Adventure in Politics: The Memoirs of Philip La Follette*, ed. Donald Young (New York, 1970), 219; *A Study of Wisconsin: Its Resources, Its Physical, Social, and Economic Background*, Regional Planning Committee, *Annual Report*, 1934; Philip F. La Follette to Robert M. La Follette, Jr., February 8, 1935, in the Philip F. La Follette Papers.

[40] Leuchtenburg, *Franklin D. Roosevelt and the New Deal*, 124–125; Schlesinger, *Politics of Upheaval*, 267–270; Patterson, *New Deal and the States*, 74–75.

great pains to keep the President apprised of his thinking about work-relief, and Roosevelt had indicated his approval. In addition, while the Senate was debating the bill, the governor had broadcast a national radio appeal for a program of work rather than doles. He reminded his listeners that while billions of dollars had been spent on relief, "practically nothing has been spent to create more wealth." Phil promised that he would recommend a plan for putting Wisconsin citizens back to work "increasing our own individual incomes and thereby increasing the income of the whole community."[41]

With passage of the Emergency Relief Appropriation Act, Phil put the finishing touches on his program and went to Washington, where he spent the first ten days of May explaining his plan to the President and to administration officials. He proposed that Wisconsin receive a lump-sum grant of $100 million from the federal appropriation; in return, the governor would assume responsibility for carrying out work-relief activities to provide employment for a hundred thousand persons in the state. The amount Phil requested was sizable, to be sure, but he calculated that it still would not be enough to complete the contemplated projects. There were other problems as well. Article VIII of the Wisconsin Constitution prohibited the state government from contracting any debts for works of internal improvement.[42]

To circumvent constitutional limitations, La Follette proposed that the legislature charter a new corporation, which he called the Wisconsin Finance Authority. Although modeled on the Reconstruction Finance Corporation, it was not, like RFC, to be used in assisting banks, insurance companies, railroads and other business organizations. Its purpose was, rather, to make possible a rapid turnover of the $100 million grant. Operating as a bank, it would also control funds from the sale of municipal bonds and revenues from an income surtax, a dividends tax, a chain-store tax, and an increase in inheritance taxes. With the assets from grants, bonds, and taxes as backing, the corporation would have power to issue notes or warrants in denominations of $1 and $5 to circulate within

[41] A. W. Zeratsky to Richard Patterson, telegram, February 27, 1935, and Philip F. La Follette, "Work or Doles—Wisconsin's Answer," NBC radio address, March 8, 1935, both in the Philip F. La Follette Papers.

[42] *Wisconsin Blue Book, 1935*, pp. 126–127; "Data on the Wisconsin Plan, May 21, 1935," in the Philip F. La Follette Papers; La Follette, *Adventure in Politics*, 220–221.

the borders of the state. Inasmuch as the holders of warrants might at any time exchange them for U.S. currency, Phil refused to concede that they could be considered scrip—a fine point that few people understood. More importantly, argued the governor, the use of Finance Authority warrants in work-relief projects would help support Wisconsin enterprise and increase investments in Wisconsin business.[43]

Roosevelt found the Wisconsin proposal intriguing, and he invited his advisory committee on allotments to hear the La Follettes present their arguments for it. Harold Ickes later noted in his diary that "it looks like a well-thought-out and intelligent plan and we were all favorably disposed toward it." Of the New Dealers who learned of the proposal, Tugwell appeared the most skeptical. While he admired Phil's intelligence and administrative abilities, he worried about how the Wisconsin proposal served the national interest. Conjuring with thoughts of what might happen if Huey Long of Louisiana or Eugene Talmadge of Georgia made a similar proposal, he urged caution. Nonetheless the three members of the allotments committee—Frank Walker, Harry Hopkins, and Harold Ickes—approved the proposal, and so did Roosevelt. On May 16 Phil learned that Wisconsin had received the requested grant; it was now up to the state legislature to accept it.[44]

"This is a matter of great public importance," the governor asserted in sending his proposal to the legislature. "May I again respectfully urge that the State take prompt action." Within a week Phil went on the radio in the first of a series of broadcasts designed to explain how projects in soil conservation and erosion control, fish and game management, tree planting and forestry, urban renewal and highway construction would provide jobs and increase wealth in Wisconsin. He left little doubt that the program was skillfully prepared, but he could not entirely satisfy skeptics who doubted that it would indeed accomplish its objectives.[45]

[43] "Articles of Organization" (carbon copy), May 22, 1935, for the Wisconsin Finance Authority; Ralph M. Hoyt to Philip F. La Follette, May 14, 1935; and Thomas M. Duncan, speech at hearing on Bill No. 443-S, May 29, 1935, all in the Philip F. La Follette Papers.

[44] Harold L. Ickes, *The Secret Diary of Harold L. Ickes* (3 vols., New York, 1953–1954; reprinted, Jersey City, 1974), 2:355–356; La Follette, *Adventure in Politics*, 222–223; Miller, *Governor Philip F. La Follette*, 64–65; Philip F. La Follette to Marguerite Le Hand, night letter, May 15, 1935, in the Philip F. La Follette Papers; *Wisconsin State Journal*, May 17, 1935.

[45] Philip F. La Follette to the senate and the assembly, May 22, 1935, and La Follette,

Opposition to the works bill surfaced almost immediately. The measure included so many innovations that citizens had difficulty understanding what the governor was proposing. The complexity of the measure gave critics an opportunity to charge that it would encourage an extravagant expansion of the Wisconsin bureaucracy. The Milwaukee *Journal* repeatedly warned that through the Wisconsin Finance Authority the governor might either bankrupt the state or gain dictatorial control over it. Milwaukee lawyer Raymond J. Cannon, the Democratic representative from Wisconsin's Fourth Congressional District, summarized the doubts that troubled many of the state's citizens. "The Wisconsin Finance Authority is practically another government set up for the State of Wisconsin and paralleling in many ways the government of the state created by our constitution," he observed. "The fundamental difference is, that the Government, by means of this private corporation, is beyond the control of the legislature or the people." Businessmen were concerned about the additional taxes the program would require. Some bankers asserted that they would not accept the warrants of the Finance Authority. And the Wisconsin League of Municipalities, headed by Daniel Hoan, had questions about the program's effectiveness in the larger cities where the problem of unemployment was most acute.[46]

The works bill dominated political discussions throughout the state as the senate began its deliberation of the measure. Compounding the problems confronting the governor in that chamber were the senators' political concerns, which had little to do with the substance of the bill. Governor La Follette could count on the support of thirteen Progressive senators, but to secure a majority he needed to gain four additional votes. To win them he sought to show that his bill was a measure that Roosevelt strongly supported. But that tactic, in turn, placed the Democratic senators on the horns of a dilemma. If they supported the works bill because it had FDR's approval, they would strengthen La Follette politically and reduce the strength of their own party on the eve of an election campaign.

---

radio address on the Wisconsin Plan for Employment, May 24, 1935, both in the Philip F. La Follette Papers; *The Progressive*, June 1, 1935.

[46] Milwaukee *Journal*, May 21, 23, June 4, 5, 6, 10, 1935; Edwin Witte to Francis D. Tyson, April 8, 1936, in the Witte Papers. Also Raymond J. Cannon, comment on Bill No. 443-S, May 30, 1935; Daniel W. Hoan to Philip La Follette, two letters both dated May 31, 1935; and La Follette to Daniel W. Hoan, June 1, 1935, all in the Philip F. La Follette Papers.

On the other hand, if they opposed the bill they would seem to be repudiating a Democratic President and handing the Progressive governor an issue that could help re-elect him in 1936. Furthermore, their opposition to the bill would help cement an alliance between the Wisconsin Progressives and FDR, and that could mean surrendering to Progressives the patronage that they thought rightfully belonged to the Democratic party.

Whatever the implications, the opposition lines held firm, and on June 13, 1935, the senate defeated the works bill. The governor refused to abandon his plan, however, and after making several modifications he sent a revised bill to the assembly. Responding to public and senate criticism, Phil eliminated some of the taxes included in the original bill, and he dropped the most controversial of all its provisions, the one permitting the Wisconsin Finance Authority to issue warrants. Having made those concessions, the governor resolved "to open both barrels" to salvage his program. Directing his fire at the most unyielding of his opponents, he decided to appeal directly to voters in the districts of those senators who had voted against the bill. After holding meetings in Milwaukee, Racine, Kenosha, Oshkosh, and Appleton, however, he began to sense that his efforts might prove counterproductive. With the controversy his speeches stirred up, it was just possible that he would alienate Roosevelt and the New Dealers whose support he needed whether the legislature passed a revised bill or not. Thus, despite his skill in political repartee and his zest for the fight, the governor withdrew and returned to Madison, hoping for the best.[47]

He was disappointed. The assembly passed a revised bill as expected on June 26, but two days later the senate turned it down by a single vote, 17 to 16. Without the La Follette works plan, Wisconsin had to rely on the federal program, the Works Progress Administration. Fortunately, WPA administrator Harry Hopkins seemed partial to proposals from Wisconsin, and he appointed La Follette's old friend, Ralph Immell, as head of the state program. Overall, in the long struggle over the state works bill, it was the

[47] New York *Times*, June 2, 1935; Milwaukee *Journal*, June 18, 1935; *The Progressive*, June 15, 1935; Miller, *Governor Philip F. La Follette*, 68–70. Also, in the Philip F. La Follette Papers: Claire B. Bird to La Follette, Rogers and Roberts, June 10, 1935; Robert McCarthy to Frank S. Durham, June 18, 1935; Philip Morrissey to Gordon Sinykin, night letter, June 20, 1935; Frank S. Durham to Robert M. La Follette, Jr., telegram, June 22, 1935; and Philip F. La Follette to the senate and the assembly, June 25, 1935.

conservative Democrats who seemed to have lost the most. Their actions had strengthened the ties between Roosevelt and the Wisconsin Progressives, and they had little to show for their successful campaign against the bill.[48]

For the remainder of the 1935 session, which continued for another three months, senators moved ponderously through one acrimonious debate after another. In addition to defeating the works bill, the senate also killed a farm-mortgage moratorium bill, a labor-disputes bill modeled on the Wagner Act, and a bill to promote public power development. The only important measures to pass were a budget bill and revenue bills to provide a part of the state's share of old-age pensions and school aids. The governor was predictably unimpressed with the legislative record, and he said so repeatedly. Yet his biggest disappointment remained the defeat of his works program. With that defeat, he remarked in one of his radio broadcasts, it became his "regrettable duty" to call on the President and report the action of senators who had refused "to enable Wisconsin to carry out this magnificent program."

In another broadcast just before the end of the session, he told listeners that he could find but two redeeming features in the year's political activities. First, the legislative session had given citizens of the state "a vivid demonstration of the proposition that we cannot have progressive government without a progressive legislature." And second, the legislative debates had "again proved that there is no difference whatever between a reactionary Democrat and a reactionary Republican." The governor scarcely needed to point out that "the reactionary Democrats in the Wisconsin legislature repeatedly have repudiated every liberal principle advocated by the national government." The lessons of 1935, he believed, should guide the state's voters in deciding the fundamental question of the coming election: "Shall your government be controlled and used by those who believe in reaction, or those who believe in progress?"[49]

* * *

[48] Milwaukee *Journal*, June 25, 29, July 1, 2, 7, 1935; La Follette, *Adventure in Politics*, 224–226.

[49] Philip F. La Follette, radio addresses, July 12, September 24, 1935, in the Philip F. La Follette Papers; Edwin E. Witte to Janet Austriana, February 5, 1937, in the Witte Papers.

Roosevelt's first-term relationship with the La Follettes, and that between New Dealers and Wisconsin Progressives, squared with the new relationship developing between the federal government and the states. The President's exceptional cordiality towards the Progressives and his willingness to support social and economic experimentation in Wisconsin were in part attributable to the meshing of his objectives with those of the La Follettes. FDR sensed that he need have no concern about the senator's becoming a competitor, and while he had no such confidence that the governor's ambition could be contained, he was pleased to have Phil fighting his battles in the trenches of Wisconsin. Furthermore, with potential rivals emerging on both the right and the left, the President needed the La Follettes. He supported their ideas and programs because he found in them an acceptable alternative to the distasteful prospect of association with the state's conservative Democrats. More importantly, he saw in the Progressive party of Wisconsin a viable means of checking the thrust of radical forces on the national left.

The close co-operation of Wisconsin Progressives with FDR and the New Dealers disappointed both the conservative Democrats of the state and the independent reformers who were hoping to build a new third party through the Farmer Labor Political Federation. In the fall of 1935, Philip La Follette's adviser and legal counsel, Gordon Sinykin, issued a press release commenting on arguments the Democrats had advanced in support of Albert Schmedeman during the 1934 election campaign. They had alleged that "the cooperation existing between the state and federal governments . . . would break down, and that the state would not receive its share of money for relief, for a works program, and for other recovery projects." But Sinykin pointed out that, contrary to dire Democratic predictions, the Progressive state administration had "demonstrated that it could get more assistance and cooperation from Washington than could the Democratic Schmedeman administration or Democratic administrations in other states of the Union." It was an achievement that might have been expected to please reformers generally, but some of those who hoped for the establishment of a new national party were wary of selling their Progressive souls. Alfred Bingham grumbled about the difficulty of establishing a new party in co-operation "with such a time-server as Phil La Follette," and Howard Y. Williams thought the governor was "making a mistake in playing so closely with Roosevelt." If the La Follettes did not show more interest in building a national party, warned Williams, "the leadership in Wisconsin might pass on into other hands."[50]

Of course the brothers La Follette were aware of the opinions of third-party advocates, but they saw no reason for acrimonious response. Phil was especially careful to avoid criticizing independent political activities. At the Wisconsin Progressive party's first anniversary celebration in Fond du Lac on May 19, 1935, he came out in favor of a national political realignment; at the same time, he warned that building a national party demanded more than flag-waving and ballyhoo. Creating a new national organization necessarily required long hours of hard work to build a solid foundation in the states. Only with strong state organizations, Phil cautioned, could the Progressives proceed to the formation of a national party.[51]

Again and again during 1935, the governor offered the same advice. In July, New York *Times* reporter Fred C. Kelly traveled through several states by automobile, talking politics with people he met along the way. Having listened to differing opinions on the formation of a third party, and having determined that the position of the La Follette brothers was crucial, he stopped in Madison to interview Phil. Responding to Kelly's observation that some people had been disappointed in the La Follettes' reluctance to promote a national third-party movement, the governor repeated his argument that building a new party required prodigious effort and that the American people would not be ready for fundamental political changes in 1936. Even though there were voters in every state who were "disgusted with the two major parties," he told Kelly, the third-party enthusiasts were "not altogether realistic." As for himself, Phil left no doubt that, faced with a choice between Roosevelt and some reactionary Republican, he intended to support Roosevelt.[52]

[50] Gordon Sinykin, "The Week's Fact," September 3, 1935, and Howard Y. Williams to Philip F. La Follette, April 2, 1936, both in the Philip F. La Follette Papers; Alfred Bingham to Thomas R. Amlie, February 13, March 15, 1935, both in the Thomas R. Amlie Papers; Miller, *Governor Philip F. La Follette*, 80.

[51] Milwaukee *Journal*, May 19, 1936; Robert Morss Lovett, "Progressive Birthday," in the *New Republic*, 83 (June 5, 1935), 95–96.

[52] New York *Times*, July 28, 1935. Phil La Follette held to his position, and his aides elaborated on it, in correspondence with third-party supporters. See Aldric Revell to A. W. Rees, May 17, 1935; Gordon Sinykin to Rees, August 19, 1935; and La Follette to

Unwilling to join the La Follettes in backing FDR, and persuaded that the work of organizing a new party must begin at once, leaders of the Farmer Labor Political Federation called for a conference to meet in Chicago on July 5 and 6, 1935. Tom Amlie was one of the organizers of the gathering, and delegates from Wisconsin included Andrew Biemiller, Samuel Sigman, Walter Graunke, William Sommers, and Harold Groves. Although neither Bob nor Phil La Follette attended the conference, it was clear that many of those who did shared the La Follettes' opinion that it was premature. In the end, the delegates took no significant action. They satisfied themselves merely with changing the name of the sponsoring organization from the Farmer Labor Political Federation to the American Commonwealth Federation. They also pledged to continue working towards a national political realignment.[53]

The "chief obstacle to the formation of a national third party," observed University of Chicago Professor Robert Morss Lovett after the conference had adjourned, "is the success that its natural leaders have achieved in several states." He was suggesting that a new party required a leader of prominence, but no such person was willing to risk losing the political power he had acquired at home. Lovett might well have been describing the governor of Wisconsin. Late in July, Phil wrote Selden Rodman to offer the same "realistic" advice he had given the Wisconsin Progressives in May: establishing a new party required "a tremendous amount of hard and long work." Confiding that he had been doing what he could "to promote the building of a new party strength . . . from the bottom upward," he asserted that to develop strong organizations in the states would be far more effective than "to call a national conference out of a clear sky and expect that to pave the way."[54]

In the meantime, the dismal record of the 1935 legislature in Wisconsin was enough to persuade reform organizations of the need for united action if the state was to do better in the future.

Charles W. Ownby, September 24, 1935, all in the Philip F. La Follette Papers. See also Newman Jeffrey to Thomas Duncan, May 11, 1936, *ibid.*

[53] Schlesinger, *Politics of Upheaval*, 150–151; Donald L. Miller, *The New American Radicalism: Alfred M. Bingham and Non-Marxian Insurgency in the New Deal Era* (Port Washington, New York, 1979), 126–128; *Wisconsin State Journal*, July 5–8, 1935.

[54] Robert Morss Lovett, "A Party in Embryo," in the *New Republic*, 83 (July 24, 1935), 295–297; Philip F. La Follette to Selden Rodman, July 25, 1935, in the Philip F. La Follette Papers. In his article, Lovett was drawing in part on the ideas contained in a speech that New York Congressman Vito Marcantonio had made at the conference.

During the annual convention of the Wisconsin State Federation of Labor in July, the advocates of concerted action succeeded in winning approval for a conference of various interest groups supporting change. The conference met in Milwaukee at the end of November, and representatives of the Progressive party, the Socialist party, the Farmer-Labor and Progressive League, the Wisconsin State Federation of Labor, the railroad brotherhoods, the Workers Alliance, the Farm Holiday Association, the Farmers' Equity Union, and the Wisconsin Cooperative Milk Pool agreed to coordinate their efforts through a single agency. Hoping to unite the state's various radical and liberal splinter groups, they chose to call their new agency the Farmer-Labor Progressive Federation.[55]

The proponents of political realignment hailed the creation of the Wisconsin FLPF as a victory for those who favored a radical coalition as a first step towards the foundation of a new national party, and for a time it seemed to be fulfilling their hopes for unity on the left. The governor's most trusted associate, Tom Duncan, helped draft the platform adopted at the Milwaukee conference, and it differed little from the platform of the Progressive party. The Socialists agreed to forgo using their own party's name on the ballot if they could run some of their candidates on the Progressive ticket. Despite successes for the unity movement, however, the governor remained cool towards efforts to bring about political realignment in 1936. He had obviously concluded that he stood to gain far more from supporting FDR than he could ever hope to

[55] Wisconsin State Federation of Labor, *Proceedings*, 1935, pp. 97–98, 212, 232. Also, in the Philip F. La Follette Papers: minutes for the November 2, 1935, session of the Third Conference on Political Action, November 2, 1935; J. J. Handley to Thomas M. Duncan, November 4, 1935; Duncan to B. C. Vladeck, December 4, 1935; and Farmer-Labor and Progressive Federation Principles, Platform, and Constitution adopted at Milwaukee, November 30–December 1, 1935. Nomenclature is a source of confusion about the relationships among reform groups in Wisconsin during the 1930's. The national Farmer Labor Political Federation (FLPF) developed out of the Chicago Conference of the League for Independent Political Action in 1933. Thomas R. Amlie became its chairman, and Alfred Bingham served as executive secretary. After 1935 it functioned nationally as the American Commonwealth Federation, but in midwestern states, including Wisconsin, some units retained the old designation. The Farmer-Labor and Progressive League (FLPL) came into existence in 1934, and it included among its members the radicals who were dissatisfied with proceedings at the Fond du Lac convention that created the Progressive party of Wisconsin. Both the Wisconsin FLPF and the FLPL participated in the Milwaukee conference of 1935, and nearly all the state's members of the two organizations affiliated with the Farmer-Labor Progressive Federation. Creating another FLPF was supposed to help unite the Wisconsin associations pledged to bring about fundamental change and political realignment.

achieve by identifying himself with farmer-labor organizations. In continuing to back Roosevelt he portrayed himself as a rational leader who refused to heed the siren call of the radicals. At the same time, he did not reject the possibility of fundamental realignment in the future if economic conditions did not improve.[56]

As the campaign approached, then, the farmer-labor hopes for a third-party effort in 1936 went aglimmering. In the Wisconsin presidential preference primary early in April, Roosevelt scored an overwhelming victory with more than 400,000 votes. In the Republican column, William E. Borah defeated Alfred E. Landon 187,334 to 3,360. "We had an election out here in Wisconsin which was not at all disappointing to us," Phil wrote his friend Francis Brown of the New York *Times*. Noting that FDR had run "two hundred thousand votes ahead of his delegates," and that "the Old Guard Republicans took a licking at the hands of Mr. Borah's friends," he added that "all in all there was no moaning around here as a result of the balloting." At the end of the month Tom Amlie wrote the governor that "it would seem now that President Roosevelt had everything buttoned up," and Alfred Bingham conceded that "Roosevelt is *it* this year."[57]

Pleased with the results of the Wisconsin preferential primary, FDR conferred with both La Follettes at the White House early in May. The President made clear his reliance on the Wisconsin Progressives, and he later asked Bob to head a national committee of political independents who favored his re-election. In September, with the campaign under way, the senator organized and chaired a conference of Progressives meeting at the Morrison Hotel in Chicago. On hand were several delegates who had taken part in Old Bob's 1924 campaign, and the large Wisconsin delegation played a major role in the proceedings. New York's Mayor Fiorello La Guardia introduced a statement of principles taken from the

[56] Milwaukee *Leader*, December 3, 1935; Milwaukee *Journal*, December 3, 1935; Lester F. Schmidt, "The Farmer-Labor Progressive Federation: The Study of a 'United Front' Movement Among Wisconsin Liberals, 1934–1941" (doctoral dissertation, University of Wisconsin, 1955), 55–64; Miller, *Governor Philip F. La Follette*, 86–87. Also, in the Philip F. La Follette Papers: Thomas R. Amlie to La Follette, December 22, 1935; La Follette to William H. Mielke, January 23, 1936; Thomas M. Duncan to Edward Kinney, February 29, 1936; Gordon Sinykin to Edward L. McKenzie, May 29, 1936; and La Follette to Edward L. McKenzie, June 19, 1936.

[57] *Wisconsin Blue Book, 1937*, pp. 299–300; Miller, *Governor Philip F. La Follette*, 90–91; Philip F. La Follette to Francis Brown, April 14, 1936, and Thomas R. Amlie to La Follette, April 30, 1936, both in the Philip F. La Follette Papers.

Wisconsin Progressive platform of 1934, and he then proposed a resolution urging "all progressive-minded citizens in every walk of life to vote for Franklin D. Roosevelt for president of the United States." The motion carried unanimously, and the chair appointed a committee that included Amlie and Phil La Follette to draft a telegram to Roosevelt informing him of the action.[58]

The unity of reformers was to become a prominent theme during the 1936 election campaign, but neither the La Follette Progressives nor the Wisconsin Farmer-Labor Progressive Federation welcomed the participation of all those who wished to take part in their activities. In 1935, the Seventh Congress of the Communist International had issued a call for a Popular Front to unite all Progressives against fascism. While the farmer, labor, and Progressive groups searched for common ground, the Communist party in Wisconsin and elsewhere sought to join the effort. Few persons in the Wisconsin PLPF welcomed the idea of working with Communists, however, and the American Commonwealth Federation stoutly opposed including Communist party members in Progressive deliberations.

Speaking at the Milwaukee Auditorium in September, Eugene Dennis, state secretary of the Communist party in Wisconsin, warned that "either a united front of struggle will be forged, or reaction will win." He called for putting an end to "the red-baiting, labor-splitting, anti-unity tactics" of such persons as Milwaukee Socialist Andrew Biemiller and Madison Progressive Harold Groves. And he asked that the Wisconsin FLPF "shall become neither anti-Communist nor anti-Socialist, but shall be anti-fascist." Although Popular Front arguments were to gain a sympathetic response from liberals who were troubled by the success of Italian fascism and German national socialism during the late thirties, Wisconsin Progressives were too deeply involved in state politics to allow the Communists to divert their attention. From a broader perspective, the American Commonwealth Federation was even more hostile to a Popular Front alliance. A linkage with the Communist party, ar-

[58] Donald R. McCoy, "The Progressive National Committee of 1936," in the *Western Political Quarterly*, 9 (June, 1956), 454–469; Maney, "*Young Bob*" *La Follette*, 190–191. Also, in the Philip F. La Follette Papers: Thomas R. Amlie to La Follette, July 2, 1936; La Follette to Floyd B. Olson, telegram, August 18, 1936; Floyd B. Olson to La Follette, August 19, 1936; George W. Norris et al. to La Follette, night letter, August 31, 1936; and minutes for September 11, 1936, sessions of the National Progressive Conference, Chicago.

gued Amlie and Bingham, would hinder co-operation with "many far more important groups" and would impede "a broad popular movement for a new social order of abundance." As Bingham viewed it, the Popular Front posed a real threat to the third-party movement, and he wrote Phil La Follette that "if this is not countered by vigorous action on our part it is likely to do incalculable damage." The Communist party was not strong enough in Wisconsin to take over direction of liberal or Progressive organizations, however, and the La Follettes largely ignored the Popular Front.[59]

With Wisconsin's Progressive and farmer-labor organizations holding third-party activities in abeyance, and with Senator La Follette working to carry out Progressive pledges to Roosevelt, the governor turned attention to his own campaign for re-election. Following traditional practice, Phil stumped every part of the state and delivered more than 200 speeches in appealing for votes. Yet the emergence of the Progressive party and the extraordinary independent political ferment throughout the state in 1936 precluded the possibility of conducting a campaign entirely along traditional lines. Wisconsin no longer remained predominantly Republican, and the primary election had lost much of its significance. The governor now had to encourage voters of all parties to cast their ballots for Progressive candidates in both the primary and the general elections; at the same time, he was committed to campaigning for Roosevelt in the general election.[60]

In his speeches Phil identified both of his principal opponents, Republican Alexander Wiley and Democrat Albert Lueck, with outmoded policies. The central issue of the campaign, he argued repeatedly, was whether the people of Wisconsin wanted reaction or progress. He made much of the legislature's refusal to approve his works bill in 1935, and he attributed the defeat to an unholy alliance

[59] Irving Howe and Lewis Coser, *The American Communist Party: A Critical History, 1919–1957* (Boston, 1957), 319–332; Lowell K. Dyson, *Red Harvest: The Communist Party and American Farmers* (Lincoln, Nebraska, 1982), 122–126; Communist Party, U.S.A., Wisconsin, *The Communists and the Farmer-Labor Progressive Federation, 1936* ([Milwaukee, 1936]). Also, in the Philip F. La Follette Papers: Thomas R. Amlie and Alfred Bingham to State Committee, Farmer Labor Association, St. Paul, Minnesota, May 18, 1936, enclosed in Nathan Fine to Thomas Duncan, May 18, 1936; Amlie to La Follette, May 18, 1936; Bingham to La Follette, June 17, 1936; and Walter D. Corrigan, Sr., to La Follette, June 24, 1936.

[60] Leon D. Epstein, *Politics in Wisconsin* (Madison, 1958), 40–43; Gary D. Wekkin, *Democrat Versus Democrat: The National Party's Campaign to Close the Wisconsin Primary* (Columbia, Missouri, 1984), 51–54; Miller, *Governor Philip F. La Follette*, 96–97.

of reactionary Republican and Democratic senators. In a Labor Day address, and in speeches to working-class audiences, the governor pointed out that the same reactionary senators had also blocked a bill to complement the National Labor Relations Act. On the positive side, he claimed credit for balancing the state budget while at the same time increasing state highway construction and school aid. He also made much of his support for a variety of state programs: advertising the state's recreational, hunting, and fishing attractions; promoting Wisconsin dairy products; protecting the state's remaining forests from the ravages of fire; and improving the working conditions in state institutions.[61]

"We live in a harassed and changing world," Phil told the voters of Wisconsin in a radio campaign address. "Political upheavals, violence, civil war and colossal preparations for another world war confront us daily in the newspapers." The greatest task of government, he argued, was "to restore and maintain the right of every able-bodied citizen to earn his living from useful work." But reactionary leaders myopically refused to meet that challenge. Without a program for providing the unemployed with jobs on "constructive things that will build a better life," the reactionaries were drifting towards a condition in which they would be setting people "to work at the business of war." Progressives, on the other hand, had accommodated themselves to the passing of "the rugged frontier when men went it alone." They knew that in modern times "the welfare of each of us depends on the welfare of all of us." To avert the disaster of another war, American voters should elect Progressive leaders who were pressing forward on a new frontier "where mankind is battling to solve the problems of the machine age."[62]

Supporters of the President and the governor responded to Phil La Follette's plea: "Close ranks! Stand united!" FDR secured 802,984 votes in Wisconsin to Landon's 380,828. Governor La

[61] Philip Morrissey to *The Progressive*, telegram reports on La Follette's speeches, September 18, 24, 25, 26, October 3, 4, 1936; and *The Progressive Campaigner*, a campaign textbook issued by the Progressive party in 1936, pp. 6–10, 23–27, 29–32, 39–42, all in the Philip F. La Follette Papers. The papers also contain other speeches delivered by the governor and the senator in 1936. See especially Philip F. La Follette, "Can We Pay As We Go?" delivered at Town Hall, New York City, January 9, 1936, and Robert M. La Follette, Jr., radio address, Columbia Broadcasting System, September 28, 1936.

[62] Philip F. La Follette, radio address, WTMJ, Milwaukee, November 1, 1936, in the Philip F. La Follette Papers.

Follette won re-election with 573,724 votes while Wiley received 363,973 and Lueck 268,530. Phil's share of the total vote increased from 41 per cent in 1934 to 48 per cent in 1936. His greatest gains were in Milwaukee, Racine, and Kenosha counties, an indication that Progressive appeals for unity had been effective among members of the Wisconsin FLPF and the Socialists. Progressives also elected Henry A. Gunderson as lieutenant-governor, Theodore Dammann as secretary of state, Solomon Levitan as state treasurer, and Orland S. Loomis as attorney general. Progressives won seven of the ten Wisconsin seats in Congress. Of the sixteen contested seats in the state senate, Progressives captured eight to give them a total of sixteen as compared with nine for the Democrats and eight for the Republicans. Returns showed that the Progressives were victorious in forty-eight contests for places in the assembly, while the Democrats won thirty-one and the Republicans won twenty-one. Although the Progressives had failed to elect an absolute majority in either house, they had gained working control of both. The governor therefore anticipated greater success for his legislative program in 1937 than he had been able to achieve in 1935.[63]

The election brought rejoicing in the Progressive party's Madison headquarters. Messages of felicitation poured in from across the country. Fiorello La Guardia, Sidney Hillman, Donald Richberg, Felix Frankfurter, Alfred Bingham, and Harry Hopkins all sent congratulatory telegrams. On the eve of the election Bob and Phil La Follette had wired Roosevelt a message praising him for the "MAGNIFICENT JOB" he had performed in his quest for a second term. "EVERY PROGRESSIVE IN AMERICA IS PROUD OF YOU," they assured the President, and they promised that every Progressive "WILL BE AT THE POLLS TOMORROW WITH HIS COAT OFF TO GIVE THE REACTIONARIES THE LICKING THEY SO RICHLY DESERVE FOR THEIR ROTTEN CAMPAIGN." After the votes had been tallied, and the proportions of Roosevelt's victory over Landon had become evident (FDR had carried every state except Maine and Vermont), the President responded with a graceful note to Phil. "As you know, I am a strong believer in close cooperation between Washington and the various states," he wrote, "and I look forward to a very pleasant associa-

[63] *Wisconsin Blue Book, 1987–1988*, p. 716.

tion." Then he scribbled an addendum: "Let's keep up the good work!"[64]

In the euphoria of his own victory, Phil La Follette perhaps exaggerated both his influence in bringing about Roosevelt's more stunning triumph and the extent to which the President felt obliged to return Progressive favors. Confident of Wisconsin's eminence as an innovative commonwealth, the La Follette Progressives had worked effectively to implement state and national programs. The governor justifiably believed that the Progressives would continue to benefit from Roosevelt's goodwill and that Wisconsin would continue to share in the co-operative federalism that had developed during Roosevelt's first term. Yet as FDR sensed from the beginning, Phil was never one to bridle his own ambition. When the governor permitted his imagination to gallop towards the trophies of national leadership, he became impatient to establish himself as a political leader of national stature. And the more zealously Phil La Follette pursued his goal, the more cautious Roosevelt became in associations with his Progressive allies in Wisconsin.

[64] Robert M. La Follette, Jr., and Philip F. La Follette to Franklin D. Roosevelt, day letter, November 2, 1936, and Roosevelt to Philip F. La Follette, November 21, 1936, both in the Philip F. La Follette Papers.

12

Controversies Along the Middle Way

THE Great Depression was global in its ramifications, and the social turbulence that accompanied it produced political behavior abroad that threatened traditional values at home. Following the victory of the National Socialists in Germany and the emergence of Adolf Hitler as chancellor in January of 1933, a succession of international crises gradually moved the world towards a second great war. Citizens of Wisconsin, despite their reputation as isolationists, could not remain aloof from events in Europe. Anxieties mounted as the German Führer withdrew from disarmament talks and took Germany out of the League of Nations in 1933, encouraged Austrian Nazis to agitate for unification with Germany in 1934, gained control of the Saar basin in 1935, reoccupied the Rhineland in the spring of 1936, and formed the Rome-Berlin Axis with Mussolini in that autumn.

In 1935, Sinclair Lewis published *It Can't Happen Here*, a novel suggesting that the United States was not immune to fascist terrors. As readers in Wisconsin and the nation contemplated its message, they might have given thought to American demagogues who were promising salvation. Yet for all the uncertainties abroad, and for all the thunder on the right and the left at home, calmer voices were calling for reason, moderation, and the avoidance of extremes.

During the spring before the election of 1936, at a time when Hitler's new Wehrmacht was establishing German military power in the Rhineland, Senator Robert M. La Follette reviewed a book that was causing a flurry of excitement among Wisconsin Progressives. The author, Marquis Childs, had attended the University of Wisconsin, where he had been a contributor to the *Wisconsin Literary Magazine* and to other student publications. Later, he had become a political reporter and had developed a particular interest in the northernmost nations of Europe. With the world in turmoil, and with concerned citizens hoping for rescue from political and economic disruption, the young journalist came to believe that experiences in the Scandinavian countries suggested solutions to problems that vexed the United States. Focusing most of his attention on Sweden, he gave his book the title *Sweden: The Middle Way*. When La Follette published his review in the Madison *Capital Times*, he advised careful consideration of the Swedish experience.[1]

Childs's study traced Sweden's economic evolution from struggles against monopoly power to the creation of a mixed economy. The Swedes, thought the author, had always paid less attention to ideological purity than to negotiating the adjustments and compromises necessary for meeting realities. Such an approach had important consequences. State-owned industries competed with private firms. Public hydroelectric power plants served both private and public users. State agencies engaged in economic planning to provide low-cost housing, social services, and economic stability. The Swedes, concluded Childs, were "the ultimate pragmatists, interested only in the workability of the social order."[2]

The senator's review noted that "the cooperative movement and the government's program have made Sweden's economy an outstanding success in a depression-weary world." Although he recognized differences between economic conditions in the United States as compared with conditions in Scandinavia, he asserted that "every nation can profit by a study of Sweden's example." Like his brother, Phil La Follette found Childs's book compelling. Traveling in Europe after the election of 1936, Phil scheduled a tour of Scandinavia to confirm what he had read. Observing Sweden's advance towards recovery, he verified the feasibility of his works program. From Swedish successes with economic planning and budgeting, he gained confidence in his own plans for Wisconsin's future.[3]

The La Follettes' enthusiasm over Childs's book is understand-

[1] Marquis W. Childs, *Sweden: The Middle Way* (New Haven, 1936); Merle Curti and Vernon Carstensen, *The University of Wisconsin: A History, 1848–1925* (2 vols., Madison, 1949), 2:513; Madison *Capital Times*, April 23, 1936.

[2] Childs, *Sweden*, 160–161.

[3] *Capital Times*, April 23, 1936; John E. Miller, *Governor Philip F. La Follette, the Wisconsin Progressives, and the New Deal* (Columbia, Missouri, 1982), 101–102; Philip F. La Follette, *Adventure in Politics: The Memoirs of Philip La Follette*, ed. Donald Young (New York, 1970), 228–230; Isabel La Follette, "A Room of Our Own," in *The Progressive*, January 9, 1937.

able, for the Swedish experience provided a paradigm that seemed more usable in Wisconsin than in the United States as a whole. As one of the far northern states, Wisconsin had impressed Scandinavian immigrants who settled there as a region to which they could easily adapt their customary practices. Indeed, the forested portions of the state reminded them of home, and the climate presented no special difficulties for Scandinavians. Stockholm lies a thousand miles closer to the North Pole than does Milwaukee, but the moderating influence of Sweden's greater water surface and of the Gulf Stream-North Atlantic Current has the effect of placing the two cities in the same isothermal band.

The similarity in physical features of the two areas helps to account for analogous economic development. Lumbermen who led the assault on the timber resources of Wisconsin employed techniques first developed in the Baltic area. From Sweden, Finland, and Norway came the lumberjack's axe, the practice of using snow roads for ease of skidding or hauling by ox team, and, most importantly, the lumber raft. To the La Follettes, the parallels seemed striking. The Wisconsin lumber industry had adopted Baltic methods in harvesting timber and in floating it to sawmills down the Wisconsin and other rivers. Now that timber resources no longer provided a base for the state's economic prosperity, the Wisconsin Progressives believed that they might again profit from studying the way Swedes were coping with their economic problems.[4]

In celebrating the Scandinavian middle way, Childs emphasized a Swedish consensus that avoided ideological extremes. Hoping to find a middle way for Wisconsin, Phil La Follette sought to establish an undogmatic consensus such as the one that Childs discovered in Scandinavia. The governor had no wish to lead his Progressive followers down the road that Hitler was taking in Germany. The La Follette brothers did not envision the middle way as an autobahn.

[4] Arthur R. M. Lower, *Great Britain's Woodyard: British America and the Timber Trade, 1763–1867* (Montreal, 1973), 13–15, 27–28; William G. Rector, *Log Transportation in the Lake States Lumber Industry, 1840–1918: The Movement of Logs and Its Relationship to Land Settlement, Waterway Development, Railroad Construction, Lumber Production, and Prices* (Glendale, California, 1953), 63–64; William G. Robbins, *Lumberjacks and Legislators: Political Economy of the U.S. Lumber Industry, 1890–1941* (College Station, Texas, 1982), 3–7, 32–33; Axel H. Oxholm, *Swedish Forests, Lumber Industry, and Lumber Export Trade*, U.S. Bureau of Foreign and Domestic Commerce, *Special Agents Series*, no. 195 (1921), 16–20, 73–74, 81–88.

* * *

Phil La Follette was not the only advocate of cultural and economic consensus to gain influence in Wisconsin between the two world wars. During the first great conflict, patriots of the Loyalty Legion and other such groups had devoted prodigious effort to uniting Americans against the Hun. During the New Era, the Wisconsin Chamber of Commerce and other champions of business had sought to throttle criticism with promises of continued prosperity. Yet the people of Wisconsin had never entirely submitted to prevailing fashion, and an important reason for the persistence of pluralism was the dispersion of various ethnic groups throughout the state.

Of all the ethnic minorities in Wisconsin, the state's Indians—who numbered approximately 11,500 in 1930—had for a century been the most pressured to conform to majority patterns of thought and behavior. Even before the nineteenth century drew to a close, Indian ways appeared doomed. In 1887, Congress passed the Dawes Severalty Act as a means of hastening the integration of Indians into white society. The measure allowed Indians who elected to do so to divide their reservations into individual parcels of land, or allotments, from which they were expected to make their living as agriculturists. While the program may have been well-intentioned, it opened the way for land-hungry whites to secure title to reservation lands. As a result, the assimilation policy threatened the cohesion and even the existence of tribal associations, deprived individual Indians of close tribal affiliations and identity, and jeopardized the economic well-being of tribes that engaged in lumbering and other enterprises.[5]

The shortcomings of the Dawes Act become increasingly apparent in Wisconsin and the nation as hard-pressed Indians lost their allotments through nonpayment of taxes or through distress sales. Even though government agencies in Wisconsin offered some help through farmers' institutes and the like, the assistance that came from the Bureau of Indian Affairs (BIA) in Washington was entirely inadequate. Long before the Great Depression brought hard times for everyone, many Indians of Wisconsin had reached dire straits.

[5] *Wisconsin Blue Book, 1987–1988*, p. 765; Delos S. Otis, *The Dawes Act and the Allotment of Indian Lands*, ed. Francis Paul Prucha (Norman, 1973), a reprint of Otis' 1934 presentation, *History of the Allotment Policy*, to the U.S. House, Committee on Indian Affairs, part 9 of *Hearings on H.R. 7902*, 73rd Cong., 2 sess. (1934).

Those who tried to become farmers often failed or sold their allotments. For the Chippewa bands scattered throughout northern portions of the state, government policies were especially damaging. In the forested areas attractive to lumber companies, the BIA encouraged Chippewa allottees to cut and sell their timber in order that they might undertake agricultural pursuits. Unfortunately for the Chippewa, as for others, farming the Cutover proved extraordinarily difficult, and with poverty came a deterioration of living conditions. Smallpox, tuberculosis, and venereal infection took a heavy toll, alcoholism became endemic, and teachers in Indian schools faced monumental problems in their classrooms. Children could not avoid consequences of the anomie that followed upon white society's destruction of their ancestors' way of life. Day school students, reported one teacher, not only suffered from inadequate diet and health care, but "would return each evening to homes of vice and immorality, where the law is ignored or evaded."[6]

The experience of the Menominee people differed from that of other Wisconsin Indians, in part because their land was never divided into individual allotments. While conditions of existence on their reservation in Shawano and Oconto counties were as deplorable as on other Indian lands, the Menominee managed to maintain a consolidated economic base that other tribes lost through allotment and alienation of tribal land. The Menominee were thus in a better position to take advantage of opportunities that appeared when the federal government abandoned its efforts to encourage assimilation.[7]

BIA attempts to eradicate the distinctive features of tribal cul-

[6] J. F. Wojta, "Indian Farm Institutes in Wisconsin," in *WMH*, 29 (June, 1946), 423–434; Graham D. Taylor, *The New Deal and American Indian Tribalism: The Administration of the Indian Reorganization Act, 1934–45* (Lincoln, Nebraska, 1980), 6, 53–55; Nancy O. Lurie, "Wisconsin: A Natural Laboratory for North American Indian Studies," in *WMH*, 53 (Autumn, 1969), 13–14, which has been revised and expanded as Nancy O. Lurie, *Wisconsin Indians* (Madison, 1980; reprinted, 1982 and 1987); Edmund J. Danziger, Jr., *The Chippewas of Lake Superior* (Norman, 1978), 100–102, 119–126; Milwaukee *Journal*, November 10, 1926, July 8, 1929; *Wisconsin State Journal*, July 8, 9, 1929; *Capital Times*, July 12, 1929; Milwaukee *Sentinel*, June 10, 1929, March 22, 1930; Superior *Evening Telegram*, April 9, 1930; Ashland *Daily Press*, January 3, 1931; Edwin E. Witte, "Claim of the La Point [*sic*] Band of the Chippewa Indians of the Bad River Indian Reservation Against the State of Wisconsin" (1927), in "Indians in Wisconsin" clipping file, LRB.

[7] Patricia K. Ourada, *The Menominee Indians: A History* (Norman, 1979), 179–180; Frank Christy, U.S. Office of Indian Affairs, to Leone G. Bryhan, LRL, November 5, 1940, in "Indians in Wisconsin" clipping file, LRB; Milwaukee *Sentinel*, August 12, 1930.

tures and to encourage the entry of Indian peoples into the mainstream of white society came under increasingly pungent criticism after World War I. The manifest failures of policy led to demands for reform, and in 1926 Secretary of Interior Hubert Work asked the Brookings Institution to conduct a detailed investigation of Indian problems. Completed in 1928 under the direction of Lewis Meriam, the Brookings report emphasized the need for development rather than annihilation of tribal cultures. To accomplish that objective it recommended better planning for use of Indian resources, government loans to Indians, the elimination of boarding schools, and decentralization of the BIA. "Both the government and the missionaries have often failed to study, understand, and take a sympathetic attitude toward the Indian ways, Indian ethics, and Indian religion," concluded the report. "The exceptional government worker and the exceptional missionary have demonstrated what can be done by building what is sound and good in the Indian's own life."[8]

By the time Franklin D. Roosevelt succeeded Herbert Hoover, criticisms of the assimilation policy had prepared the way for an "Indian New Deal" to accompany other reforms sponsored by the new administration. FDR appointed John Collier to the position of Indian commissioner, and in so doing he demonstrated his support for reform of the BIA. Collier had been working with the Indian Defense Association to bring about changes in policy. After his appointment as commissioner, he wasted no time in implementing his ideas. His first annual report argued for the abandonment of allotments and for the management of Indian resources by tribal corporations, and in June, 1934, Congress passed the Indian Reorganization Act. The measure ended the allotment system, provided means for the return of reservation lands to the tribes, set up procedures by which the tribes might secure charters of incorporation and manage their own affairs, and established a $10 million fund for loans to chartered tribal corporations.[9]

[8] Taylor, *New Deal and American Indian Tribalism*, 13–14; Brookings Institution, Institute for Government Research, *The Problem of Indian Administration*, comp. Lewis Meriam et al. (Baltimore, 1928); Randolph C. Downes, "A Crusade for Indian Reform, 1922–1934," in the *Mississippi Valley Historical Review*, 32 (December, 1945), 351–354; Danziger, *Chippewas of Lake Superior*, 128–131.

[9] Lawrence C. Kelly, *The Assault on Assimilation: John Collier and the Origins of Indian Policy Reform* (Albuquerque, 1983), 355–377; S. Lyman Tyler, *A History of Indian Policy*, U.S. Bureau of Indian Affairs (1974), 125–131; Kenneth R. Philp, "John Collier and

Critics accused Collier of wishing to rewrite American Indian history, but even though he may have wanted to correct mistakes of the past, he and other reformers knew they would have to set realizable objectives. "We have tried to energize the individual Indian and the group," Collier later told the House Appropriations Subcommittee, "and to equip individual and group with knowledge and skills to enable them to go into the white world successfully if they want to or to hold their own and make their way where they are if they want to." Even so, the task was fraught with difficulties. The Winnebago of Wisconsin, who held no land in common, were suspicious of the new policy. Unwilling to risk participation in any program that might prevent their collecting unpaid monetary commitments, they decided against tribal incorporation. The Wisconsin bands of Lake Superior Chippewa, the Menominee, and other state tribes all voted in favor of the new policy, but the Indian Reorganization Act proved an inadequate instrument for fulfilling the promise of a new day. In areas of the state attractive to vacationers and tourists, whites had gained title to reservation lands and surrounded the most desirable lakes with cottages and resorts, and in agricultural areas white farmers had secured control of the best land. The Wisconsin tribes that voted to incorporate were thus left with swampy, cutover tracts of little value either for recreation or farming. The Chippewa bands, for example, received scattered parcels of land in several northern counties. Of the 128,132 acres in the Bad River Reservation east of Ashland, more than 50,000 had been alienated and only about 400 were under cultivation. Such circumstances brought great difficulties in maintaining Chippewa tribal cohesion and establishing an economic base for tribal activities.[10]

the American Indian," in Leon B. Blair, ed., *Essays on Radicalism in Contemporary America* (Austin, 1972), 63–67; U.S. Commissioner of Indian Affairs, *Annual Report*, 1933–1934; Kenneth R. Philp, *John Collier's Crusade for Indian Reform, 1920–1954* (Tucson, 1977); Charles J. Kappler, comp., *Indian Affairs: Laws and Treaties. Vol. 5*, published as *Senate Document*, 76 Cong., 3 sess., no. 194 (serial 10458), 381–382 (or see Chapter 576 in *United States Statutes at Large*, 48, part 1, pp. 984–988); Michael T. Smith, "The Wheeler-Howard Act of 1934: The Indian New Deal," in *Journal of the West*, 10 (July, 1971), 521–534; William H. Kelly, ed., *Indian Affairs and the Indian Reorganization Act: The Twenty Year Record* (Tucson, 1954); Theodore W. Taylor, *The Bureau of Indian Affairs* (Boulder, 1984), 20–22; John J. Blaine to Nicholas Longworth, April 12, 1926, and James A. Frear to Blaine, April 14, 1926, both in the John J. Blaine Papers; Milwaukee *Leader*, February 26, 1926; *United States Daily* (Washington), June 5, 1931; Milwaukee *Sentinel*, November 15, 1933.

[10] Collier is quoted in William Zimmerman, Jr., "The Role of the Bureau of Indian

The Menominee were exceptional among Wisconsin Indians in that they had held on to their reservation land in toto. And instead of attempting to farm individual tracts, they had gone into business as lumber producers. Back in 1908, Old Bob La Follette had persuaded Congress to pass an act providing for the construction of a sawmill at Neopit and for the annual harvesting of 20 million feet of timber. A tribal fund established from the sale of Menominee lumber was to be kept in the United States Treasury and used for the benefit of the tribe.[11]

Despite a promising beginning, neither Congress nor the BIA seemed willing to free Menominee enterprise from government supervision and control. A succession of problems, including a costly fire at the mill and the cutting of timber by outsiders in violation of the 1908 legislation, led the tribe formally to charge government agents with mismanagement. Only after tangled litigation in the United States Court of Claims were the Menominee finally to receive an award of $8.5 million in 1951. In the meantime, despite a recommendation in the 1928 Brookings report that the Menominee receive training to operate the lumber business by themselves, tribal affairs changed little as a result of the Indian Reorganization Act. Voting members agreed in 1935 to accept the act, but they kept their elected Advisory Council of ten and the General Tribal Council as their official governing bodies.[12]

At the end of the 1920's, Chief Reginald Oshkosh had envisioned an expansion of Menominee business activities to include more than the production of lumber. Employing the sanguine rhetoric that characterized chamber of commerce pronouncements of the New

---

Affairs Since 1933," in American Academy of Political and Social Science, *Annals*, 311 (May, 1957), 34, and in Danziger, *Chippewas of Lake Superior*, 134 (in which see also pp. 145–150). See also James A. Frear, "Indian Bureau Oppression a Disgrace," in *La Follette's Magazine*, February, 1927; Lurie, "Wisconsin: A Natural Laboratory," in *WMH*, 53:16; Lurie, *Wisconsin Indians*, 26, 41–42; and A. Irving Hallowell, *Culture and Experience* (Philadelphia, 1955), 339.

[11] Jay P. Kinney, *Indian Forest and Range: A History of the Administration and Conservation of the Redman's Heritage* (Washington, 1950), 120; Robert M. La Follette, *Cutting Timber on Indian Reservations in Wisconsin*, published as *Senate Report*, 60 Cong., 1 sess., no. 110 (serial 5218); Milwaukee *Journal*, December 5, 1937; "Wisconsin Indians" (typewritten memo), November 30, 1932, in "Indians in Wisconsin" clipping file, LRB.

[12] Brookings Institution, *Problem of Indian Administration*, comp. Meriam et al., 515–516; Nancy O. Lurie, "Menominee Termination: From Reservation to Colony," in *Human Organization*, 31 (Fall, 1972), 260 (reprinted as article no. 11 with original pagination in Paul W. Gates, ed., *The Rape of Indian Lands* [New York, 1979]); Ourada, *Menominee Indians*, 182–185; Milwaukee *Journal*, September 9, December 5, 1937.

Era, he predicted that "the Indians with their own money will open highways in the reservation. . . . They will establish camps for the Boy Scouts. They will build log camp homes with [their] timber. They will build fish hatcheries and stock the streams with trout." But the Great Depression drastically reduced the demand for lumber, and tourism or recreation could at best cushion the shock.[13]

During the hard times of the 1930's, the Menominee people, along with other Indians, found New Deal programs to be of some assistance. The Office of Indian Affairs in the Civilian Conservation Corps (CCC) provided employment for a total of 2,190 Wisconsin Indians during the Depression, and young men of the Menominee tribe assisted in various Wisconsin CCC projects. Government funding enabled the Menominee to construct a community center at Keshena, and in 1937 government money paid for a roller rink and eighty pairs of roller skates. An adult education program of the WPA supported pageants at the annual tribal fair. Appealing mainly to tourists, the pageants of the Depression years were not sufficiently profitable to help establish a stable economy for Menominee enterprise, and the roller skates perhaps suggested something about white perceptions of Indian people.

The Menominee Indians thus encountered many of the same problems that confronted other tribes during the Great Depression, but after World War II they were persuaded to terminate their status as wards of the BIA and to convert their reservation into Menominee County. Intended to liberate the Menominee people, termination served mainly to establish the new county as a kind of colonial dependency within the structure of Wisconsin state government. The creation of Menominee County was to diminish rather than enhance tribal autonomy and economic initiative. For no one were the frustrations of the Great Depression and its aftermath more bitter than for the Menominee. That they fared far better than did many minority groups elsewhere neither justified failures of policy nor meliorated the conditions that imposed extraordinary hardships on the tribes of Wisconsin.[14]

[13] Shawano *Leader Advocate*, October 3, 1929; Milwaukee *Journal*, September 26, 1929.

[14] Perry H. Merrill, *Roosevelt's Forest Army: A History of the Civilian Conservation Corps, 1933–1942* (Montpelier, 1981), 190; Ourada, *Menominee Indians*, 186; David Ames and Burton R. Fisher, "The Menominee Termination Crisis: Barriers in the Way of a Rapid Cultural Transition," in *Human Organization*, 18 (October, 1959), 101–110; Donald L. Parman, "The Indian and the Civilian Conservation Corps," in the *Pacific Historical Review*, 40 (February, 1971), 39–56; Lurie, "Menominee Termination," *Human Organization*, 31:261–269; Taylor, *Bureau of Indian Affairs*, 20–24, 120.

* * *

Like supporters of the Indian Reorganization Act, other critics of American social and economic trends during the New Era later saw in the calamities of the 1930's an opportunity to bring about a needed change of direction. New Dealers talked of relief, recovery, and reform, but for those who looked beyond the economic Depression itself, reform was always the most important of Roosevelt's three R's. Among reformers, none were more sensitive to the need for long-term planning than those concerned with the natural environment. In a decade of drought and dust storms in the West and ravaging floods in the Ohio and Mississippi valleys, ecologists and environmentalists found themselves drawn towards the argument that never again should national policy encourage the rape of a continent for the short-term benefit of a privileged few.

In April, 1935, Wisconsin WPA administrator Ralph Immell delivered an address over the Columbia Broadcasting System to promote the conservation of natural resources nationally and to explain the conservation achievements in Wisconsin. "Responsible government plans in terms of centuries," he explained. "We who live today are but temporary tenants of the resources of the state or nation." Noting that Wisconsin had for years regulated hunting and fishing, he observed that the decline in the lumber industry added new economic dimensions to the need for an effective conservation program. With increased tax delinquency and unemployment in northern Wisconsin, forest restoration had become a practical concern. But it was not only the forests that required attention, for intensive cropping had led to soil erosion and loss of fertility in agricultural sections of the state. "While the loss of our forest and wild life was to be deplored," conceded Immell, "the threatened loss of our basic agricultural resources foreboded disaster."[15]

Happily, Wisconsin's need for restoration of soil and forests offered a means of providing unemployment relief during hard times. State and local agencies had moved towards conservation measures even before initiation of New Deal programs. By 1935, the Civil Works Administration, the Works Progress Administration, the Civilian Conservation Corps, and other federal programs had also taken up the cause. Their combined efforts were helping to preserve the state's natural resources and the scenic attractions that made

[15] Ralph Immell, "Conservation of Our Outdoor Resources" (typewritten), CBS radio address, April 22, 1935, in the Philip F. La Follette Papers.

tourism one of Wisconsin's most important industries. Of all the federal agencies involved in conservation, however, the Civilian Conservation Corps had the broadest appeal. The CCC attracted support from people who worried about the restlessness of unemployed youth as well as from those who hoped to preserve Wisconsin's resources. Others wished to see young men employed in useful work that was far removed from competition in industrial labor markets.[16]

A gentleman farmer whose love for his Hyde Park estate became legendary, Franklin Roosevelt had always taken an interest in conservation. As governor he had used the New York Temporary Emergency Relief Administration to create jobs in state conservation programs. After becoming President, he had drawn up a plan for placing an army of young men in reforestation and other conservation projects across the country. Congress enacted a refinement of the President's proposal when it established the Civilian Conservation Corps on March 31, 1933. A week later FDR issued an executive order appointing Robert Fechner, a vice-president of the American Federation of Labor, as director of emergency conservation work.[17]

The departments of war, agriculture, interior, and labor had already co-operated in developing a structure for the CCC. The new agency immediately set about establishing procedures for selecting enrollees, organizing training programs, and deciding on campsites and projects. As was the case with many of the New Deal agencies created during the Hundred Days, disorder and confusion at first hampered CCC efforts. The Army quickly moved to exert a controlling influence, however, and within three months' time, the Civilian Conservation Corps developed into the largest peacetime government labor force in American history. By early July, the CCC had assigned 250,000 enrollees and 25,000 administrative and service personnel to 1,300 camps throughout the nation.[18]

[16] Barry D. Karl, *The Uneasy State: The United States from 1915 to 1945* (Chicago, 1983), 122–123; Arthur M. Schlesinger, Jr., *The Coming of the New Deal* (Boston, 1958), 335–340.

[17] John A. Salmond, *The Civilian Conservation Corps, 1933–1942: A New Deal Case Study* (Durham, 1967), 6–25; Frank Freidel, *Franklin D. Roosevelt. Volume 3: The Triumph* (Boston, 1956), 224–225; George P. Rawick, "The New Deal and Youth: The Civilian Conservation Corps, the National Youth Administration, and the American Youth Congress" (doctoral dissertation, University of Wisconsin, 1957), 56–58.

[18] Alfred B. Rollins, *Roosevelt and Howe* (New York, 1962), 403; Salmond, *Civilian Conservation Corps*, 40–42; Schlesinger, *Coming of the New Deal*, 338–340.

During its first five years, the CCC employed more than 60,000 persons in Wisconsin, and by the end of its nine-year existence it had provided work for more than 92,000. At the peak of its operations during the summer of 1938, it was carrying on the work of conservation at forty-five camps in the state. Thirteen of the camps, run by the Soil Conservation Service, were primarily concerned with preventing soil erosion through terracing, drainage control, tree planting, and other such measures. By far the most important activities, however, involved the parks and forests of Wisconsin; the CCC had placed twelve of its camps in national forests, twelve in state forests, and eight in state parks.[19]

The young men of the CCC, sometimes identified as "Roosevelt's forest army," found abundant opportunities to become skilled foresters in the Wisconsin camps. They learned how to develop and maintain nurseries, how to plant seed and seedlings, how to control pests and diseases of forested areas, how to prevent and fight forest fires, and how to use trees and forest products in landscaping and buildings. Throughout the state, CCC boys constructed nearly 500 bridges and more than 4,000 miles of fire lanes, truck trails, roads, and telephone lines. When they were not engaged in such activities, they devoted their energies to fish and game management, stocking the streams of Wisconsin with more than a half-billion fish and helping take a census of the state's deer population.[20]

Contemporary assessments of CCC programs in Wisconsin were for the most part positive, and so also were enrollees' responses to their conservation experience. Fed, clothed, and housed at government expense, the CCC boys received $5 a month for themselves and $25 for their families back home. With fresh air, exercise, and adequate health care, they improved in body and spirit. Yet they did not minimize the disagreeable features of life with Roosevelt's forest army. Some of them complained of the military discipline, and nearly all disliked the cold winters and the hard work of combating fires in the fall. In later years they remembered winter

[19] "A Brief Summary of Certain Phases of the Program in Wisconsin, April 1933–June 30, 1938," enclosed in Robert Fechner to Philip F. La Follette, October 28, 1938, in the Philip F. La Follette Papers; Merrill, *Roosevelt's Forest Army*, 190–191.

[20] Salmond, *Civilian Conservation Corps*, 121–128; Leslie Alexander Lacy, *The Soil Soldiers: The Civilian Conservation Corps in the Great Depression* (Radnor, Pennsylvania, 1976), 139–141; A. L. Riesch Owen, *Conservation Under F.D.R.* (New York, 1983), 129–135; Guy D. McKinney, "An Army in the Forests," in *Natural History*, 34 (March–April, 1934), 145–149.

months when it was too cold to leave camp, and months during the fire season when they were so busy fighting fires that they scarcely had time to return to camp. Ed Norman, an enrollee who served in northern Wisconsin, never forgot the hardships; but after a career in the Marine Corps and his retirement in California, he noted that "few of us would deny that character building was a great part of our inheritance from the C-Cs."[21]

Educators were concerned that the CCC administrators too often allowed character building to take the place of more formal training. U.S. Commissioner of Education J. W. Studebaker urged a reduction of the CCC workweek in order that enrollees might attend vocational and other classes on Wednesday afternoons and Saturdays. But Roosevelt opposed the idea, and the CCC never achieved all that it might have accomplished in education of enrollees. Despite inadequacies in the training program, there were some significant accomplishments. Jack Vincent, who served as an educational adviser at a camp in Richland Center, took great pride in aiding more than 150 boys to become literate. He later recalled that "they had to write a letter home and read a newspaper before they got the coveted reading and writing certificate."[22]

Conservation efforts in Wisconsin were certainly noteworthy, but some facets of the CCC programs drew criticism from persons long identified with conservation. One such critic was Aldo Leopold, the Iowa-born ecologist who was working towards a new philosophy encompassing the subtle and often misunderstood relationships existing in nature. Educated at Yale University, Leopold had joined the U.S. Forest Service in 1909. Assigned to the Southwest, he had held several positions, first as supervisor of the Carson National Forest in northern New Mexico, then as acting head of the office of grazing in Albuquerque, and finally as assistant district forester. In all his assignments he had made careful observations of the fragile southwestern environment, and he fretted over disrupting the natural articulation of its interacting parts.[23]

[21] Frances Perkins, *The Roosevelt I Knew* (New York, 1946), 179; W. Frank Persons to P. D. Flanner, November 3, 1938, copy enclosed in Persons to Philip F. La Follette, November 3, 1938, in the Philip F. La Follette Papers; Salmond, *Civilian Conservation Corps*, 121–124; Lacy, *Soil Soldiers*, 177–192; Merrill, *Roosevelt's Forest Army*, 103–104.

[22] Rawick, "The New Deal and Youth," 117–131; Merrill, *Roosevelt's Forest Army*, 66.

[23] Susan L. Flader, *Thinking Like a Mountain: Aldo Leopold and the Evolution of an Ecological Attitude Toward Deer, Wolves, and Forests* (Columbia, Missouri, 1974), 7–14; Roderick Nash, *Wilderness and the American Mind* (New Haven, 1967), 182–187.

In 1924, with a record as a skilled administrator behind him, Leopold became associate director of the Forest Products Laboratory in Madison. Far more interested in the forest itself than in the uses made of its products, he left the laboratory after four years and become deeply involved in producing his *Report on a Game Survey of the North Central States*. This study established his reputation as a leader of wildlife management in America; and in 1933 the Wisconsin Alumni Research Foundation created a chair for him in the department of agricultural economics at the University of Wisconsin. As a member of the faculty, Leopold found his metier. He initiated a graduate training program, set up a group of demonstration farms for co-operative experimentation among farmers and sportsmen, and served as research director of the University Arboretum in Madison. Most importantly, he found the time to publish books and articles in which he elaborated on the need for an ecologically based conservation ethic. He helped reorganize the Wisconsin Conservation Commission in 1927, and he became a member himself in 1943.[24]

As an adviser on many conservation programs in Wisconsin, Leopold took a dim view of the CCC. For one thing, he favored state rather than federal planning. He thought the state management of the Central Wisconsin Conservation District, for example, ought to avoid CCC practices he considered detrimental to the area: excessive clearing and burning of underbrush, planting of jack pines, and cutting of fire lanes. He believed that CCC administrators failed to appreciate the need for an approach to game management and reforestation that took into account the carrying capacity of the environment and the optimum balance between wildlife and forests. Given the overall economic situation, however—desperate men still searching for jobs—Leopold despaired of the possibility that he could persuade CCC administrators to look beyond the immediate need for unemployment relief and towards the restoration of a natural balance in the environment.[25]

In questioning CCC activities, Leopold was (almost literally) a

[24] Flader, *Thinking Like a Mountain*, 18–35. Leopold's most influential works, in addition to his game survey report, include *Game Management* (New York, 1933), and *A Sand County Almanac: And Sketches Here and There* (New York, 1949).

[25] Flader, *Thinking Like a Mountain*, 133–134; Anthony Wolff, ed., *The Sand Country of Aldo Leopold: A Photographic Interpretation by Charles Steinhacker; Essay by Susan Flader; Selections from Writings of Aldo Leopold* (San Francisco, 1973).

voice crying in the wilderness. When other critics expressed doubts about the CCC, they tended to emphasize not its efforts at conservation but its social and political implications. And in assessing the program, they drew upon experience abroad. Bulgaria, the Netherlands, Norway, Sweden, Denmark, Austria, and Germany had also established conservation camps to provide work for unemployed young people. The youth camps operating under the German *Arbeitsdienst*, or Labor Service, aroused the greatest anxieties about the direction of CCC activities. The German labor camps, a creation of the Weimar Republic, had at first been entirely voluntary. Young men enrolled for six months, and they received token wages for their work in conservation. After Hitler and his Nazi followers came to power, however, the *Arbeitsdienst* underwent transformation. Enrollment became compulsory for all young men between the ages of eighteen and twenty-six, and their training in the camps included thorough indoctrination in Nazi ideology as well as basic military training.[26]

The CCC never emulated the program of Hitler's Germany, but the U.S. Army's control of the camps, its involvement in CCC activities, the uniforms of the enrollees, the strict regimen imposed upon participants, and the efforts of camp commanders to build esprit de corps all led to doubts about the real purposes of the agency. In 1936, Socialist presidential candidate Norman Thomas compared the CCC with forced labor programs, and the Socialist party platform called for abandonment of the agency. Carl Minkley, state secretary of the Socialist party in Wisconsin, accepted Thomas' assessment and cautioned that the CCC was "a breeding spot for militarism or Fascism." Jonathan Mitchell, a contributing editor to the *New Republic*, argued that "at least in theory, it is impossible to take 300,000, or 600,000, young men out of the traditional American family system, and organize them on a basis of loyalty to each other and their camp leaders, without by the same act creating a political instrument of unknown potentialities."[27]

[26] Salmond, *Civilian Conservation Corps*, 5–6, 86; Kenneth Holland, *Youth in European Labor Camps: A Report to the American Youth Commission* (Washington, 1939); Stephen H. Roberts, *The House That Hitler Built* (London, 1937), 211–218; Walter Thacher Winslow and Frank P. Davidson, eds., *American Youth: An Enforced Reconnaissance* (Cambridge, 1940), 82–103.

[27] Salmond, *Civilian Conservation Corps*, 114; James MacGregor Burns, *Roosevelt: The Lion and the Fox* (New York, 1956), 242; *Capital Times*, May 1, 1937; Jonathan Mitchell, "Roosevelt's Tree Army," in the *New Republic*, 83 (May 29 [part 1], June 12, 1935 [part

Roosevelt was quick to reject the suggestion that German labor camps had provided a model, and defenders pointed out that the CCC avoided overt indoctrination, military drill, and training for combat. Nevertheless, the critics persisted. The agency was also vulnerable to denunciations of the treatment accorded to young Negro men who managed to enroll in the program. CCC Director Fechner noted that "there is hardly a locality in this country that looks favorably, or even with indifference, on the location of a Negro CCC camp in their vicinity." Yet neither he nor Roosevelt attempted to modify community opinion.

Phil La Follette, who generally opposed discriminatory practices, asked in 1938 that the CCC establish integrated camps in Wisconsin rather that send the state's Negroes to a segregated camp in Illinois. Both La Follette brothers had strongly supported the CCC, and the governor might have expected a favorable response. Fechner nevertheless rejected the request—arguing that integrated camps were contrary to policy—and little came of Phil's entreaties. William Kelly, executive secretary of the Milwaukee Urban League, pointed out that inasmuch as Wisconsin had no units exclusively for Italians, Poles, Germans, or Jews, Negro enrollees were justified in asking why they were shunted aside into "so-called Negro units." The question never received a satisfactory answer; until the end of its existence in 1942, the CCC enrolled a smaller proportion of Negro than of white applicants, and integrated camps remained a rarity.[28]

Defenders of the CCC and its activities often responded to criticism by arguing that the program was consistent with the American ethos, and that it represented an extension of the processes by which a national unity of purpose had come to transcend ethnic diversity. *Happy Days*, the authorized CCC newspaper published in Washington and distributed to all the camps, frequently printed communications suggesting that enrollees themselves were conscious of their part in preserving cherished traditions. "America has often been called the melting pot," wrote enrollee C. W. Kirkpatrick from Finley, Wisconsin. "It is now a double-boiler. The Civilian Conservation Corps is a smaller melting pot within the big

---

2]), 129; George R. Leighton and Richard Hellman, "Half Slave, Half Free: Unemployment, the Depression, and American Young People," in *Harper's Magazine*, 171 (June–November, 1935), 342–353.

[28] Salmond, *Civilian Conservation Corps*, 5–6, 88–96, 189; Rawick, "The New Deal and Youth," 137–170.

one." He pointed out that in the CCC camps "rustic farm lads" mingled with "Polish and Italian boys from back of the [railroad] yards," and he thought that "this process many times results in the elimination of traditional prejudices based on ignorance and misinformation."[29]

* * *

While popular approval of the CCC far outweighed objections, criticism of the agency represented a concern for principles that sometimes seemed threatened by the creation of other programs as well. Political leaders of the thirties felt compelled to develop innovative measures to meet unusual needs. Yet as New Dealers discovered, creativity and innovation often brought disapproval, much of it based upon constitutional considerations. At a time when national socialism in Germany presented an unacceptable alternative to American political traditions, political disputes in the United States sometimes raised questions about an innovator's fidelity to American democracy. During his third term as governor, Phil La Follette faced one such dispute at the University of Wisconsin. Simultaneously, he participated in a second controversy after President Roosevelt sought to reform the Supreme Court.

The controversy at the University of Wisconsin was approaching a climax when Governor La Follette and his wife returned from their European travels early in 1937. They found the university community in an uproar. Glenn Frank, the president, had alienated influential members of the board of regents, and a confrontation was in the making. As students, faculty, and alumni took sides, the university reached a state of turbulence unequaled since the unrest of 1918.[30]

The dispute over the university's administration had actually been fermenting for years. Upon the death of Charles R. Van Hise in 1918, the dean of the College of Letters and Science, Edward A. Birge, had assumed the presidency. At sixty-seven, Birge was approaching the end of his career, and everyone (including Birge) anticipated a short, caretaker term. Yet he remained on the job for

[29] Lacy, *Soil Soldiers*, 88–89, 115–116.

[30] La Follette, *Adventure in Politics*, 230; Miller, *Governor Philip F. La Follette*, 102; Mark H. Ingraham, "The University of Wisconsin, 1925–1950," in Allan G. Bogue and Robert Taylor, eds., *The University of Wisconsin: One Hundred and Twenty-Five Years* (Madison, 1975), 59, 62–63.

seven years, and while he provided continuity with the past, he proved unable to satisfy critics who perceived a process of deterioration taking place within the university. In 1925, Birge's fiftieth year of service, it was clear that the time for appointing a new president had arrived. The regents, after failing to attract Dean Roscoe Pound of the Harvard Law School, turned to Glenn Frank.[31]

The choice was a questionable one, and Frank's credentials raised doubts among academicians. Graduating from Northwestern University in 1912, he had remained another three years in Evanston as alumni secretary. Then, on the recommendation of a former professor, he had accepted a position as private secretary to Edward A. Filene, a prominent philanthropist who had made his fortune as the innovative owner and manager of Boston's largest department store. Filene's involvement with the League to Enforce Peace provided Frank with important connections, and through his speeches and writing he gained prominence as an advocate of reform causes. In 1921, he became editor of *Century Magazine*, which he refurbished in form and substance to increase its appeal for readers who believed that in the New Era the United States was approaching a "Spiritual Renaissance."[32]

Moving confidently into New York literary circles, Frank met Zona Gale. The celebrated author from Portage, still a spinster at the time, became a regular contributor to the *Century Magazine* and one of Frank's most enthusiastic supporters. After the Progressives had firmly re-established their control of Wisconsin in the elections of 1922, Governor John J. Blaine appointed Gale to the university's board of regents. When Dean Pound withdrew his name from consideration for the presidency, she successfully campaigned for the appointment of Frank, arguing that his oratorical and literary skills might resuscitate that languishing university. It was the second time in history, Professor Carl Russell Fish remarked with his notorious causticity, that a virgin had brought forth a savior.[33]

[31] Curti and Carstensen, *University of Wisconsin*, 2:123–158; Merle Curti and Vernon Carstensen, "The University of Wisconsin to 1925," in Bogue and Taylor, eds., *University of Wisconsin: One Hundred and Twenty-Five Years*, 34–37.

[32] Lawrence H. Larsen, *The President Wore Spats: A Biography of Glenn Frank* (Madison, 1965), 15–36; Steven D. Zink, "Glenn Frank of the University of Wisconsin: A Reinterpretation," in *WMH*, 62 (Winter, 1978–1979), 91.

[33] Larsen, *The President Wore Spats*, 47, 49–52; Curti and Carstensen, *University of Wisconsin*, 2:157–158; Thomas R. Amlie to Bruce Bliven, December 15, 1936, in the Thomas R. Amlie Papers.

Although the regents had consulted none of the La Follettes in making the appointment, the Wisconsin Progressives at first seemed willing to co-operate with the new president. Initially they raised no objections when Frank sought to revolutionize higher learning in America through establishment of an experimental college. Furthermore, they recognized that with his rhetorical skills Frank had the ability to counteract the reiterated charges of Ashland editor John Chapple and others that the University of Wisconsin was a hotbed of radicalism and free love. Yet Frank disliked controversy of any sort, and as much as anything it was Frank's uncertainty when faced with difficult decisions that alienated Phil La Follette. Such diffidence, concluded the governor, indicated that Frank lacked the intellectual depth necessary for leadership of a great university.[34]

La Follette's dissatisfaction began to mount soon after he became governor. He was offended by what he took to be Frank's social pretensions, his avarice in augmenting his income with fees for lectures and writing, and his lack of interest in university administration. La Follette also became convinced that Frank had been careless with legislative appropriations. In 1931, Progressives in the legislature led an investigation that turned out to be critical of the university's financial management, and during the two years of La Follette's first term Progressives voted to reduce the university's operating budget by more than $1.5 million. Adding to Frank's problems was a series of disputes over his conduct as an administrator. His opponents charged him with favoritism in the determination of salaries; attempting to replace George Sellery as dean of the College of Letters and Science; overlooking unethical and dictatorial behavior on the part of Chester D. Snell, director of the extension division; and ineffectiveness in dealing with wrongdoing in the university's athletic program.[35]

The developing dispute over Frank's administration of the university soon became a matter of national attention. Early in 1934,

[34] La Follette, *Adventure in Politics*, 232–233; Miller, *Governor Philip F. La Follette*, 102–103; Larsen, *The President Wore Spats*, 84–87; Alexander Meiklejohn, "A New College: Notes on Next Steps in Higher Education," in *Century Magazine*, 109 (January, 1925), 312–320.

[35] Zink, "Glenn Frank," in *WMH*, 62:107, 114–116; George C. Sellery, *Some Ferments at Wisconsin, 1901–1947: Memories and Reflections* (Madison, 1960), 73–84; Gordon Shorney to Philip F. La Follette, February 5, 1936, and J. R. Richards to La Follette, March 3, 1936, both in the Philip F. La Follette Papers.

the *American Mercury* published an article by Ernest Meyer, a reporter for the Madison *Capital Times*. Summarizing complaints against the university's operations, Meyer stirred Frank's supporters to a spirited defense. For his part, Frank became disillusioned with the Progressives, and in his newspaper column he began to direct criticism at President Roosevelt, the Progressives' ally in the White House. In the fall of 1934 he published *America's Hour of Decision*, in which he elaborated on the reasons for his mounting skepticism of the New Deal and all its works. He castigated FDR's growing bureaucracy, which he thought represented "not so much a national plan as a medley of divergent and mutually contradictory plans." He argued that the New Deal was "playing fast and loose with the values of private initiative." Republicans of course welcomed Frank's criticism of the New Deal, and the moderate wing of the party began to talk of nominating Frank for President in 1936.[36]

Little came of such talk, in part because Frank himself did not wish to create the impression that he lusted for political office. He would doubtless have responded to a call from the people, but the call never came. Ultimately, Frank's flirtation with FDR's opponents damaged his reputation in Wisconsin and weakened his hold on the presidency of the university. To Phil La Follette and his Progressive followers, any suggestion that a political rival might be emerging from the University of Wisconsin campus was a suggestion to be nipped in the bud. Before the year 1935 came to an end, therefore, the governor had reached the conclusion that he must bring to an end Frank's association with higher education in the state.[37]

La Follette hoped to avoid an open confrontation that might damage his own chances for re-election, but he knew that there was scant possibility of Frank's leaving quietly. The governor therefore found himself constrained to act indirectly. His first move was to make certain that the board of regents would back the ouster

[36] Ernest Meyer, "Glenn Frank: Journalist on Parole," in the *American Mercury*, 31 (January, 1934), 149–159; Zona Gale, "Some Achievements of Glenn Frank," in the *American Mercury*, 31 (March, 1934), 381–383; Larsen, *The President Wore Spats*, 135–136, 158–159; Glenn Frank, *America's Hour of Decision: Crisis Points in National Policy* (New York, 1934), 9, 43, 45, 49, 51, 83–84, 175; Newark, New Jersey, *Ledger*, n.d., clipping enclosed in J. R. Frawley to Philip F. La Follette, March 30, 1936, in the Philip F. La Follette Papers; Zink, "Glenn Frank," in *WMH*, 62:111.

[37] Larsen, *The President Wore Spats*, 159–161; *Wisconsin State Journal*, May 23, August 28, 1935, February 9, March 12, 1936; Thomas R. Amlie to Bruce Bliven, December 17, 1936, in the Amlie Papers; Harold M. Wilkie to Thomas Duncan, October 7, 1936, in the Philip F. La Follette Papers.

of Frank, and he went to great lengths to secure regent support. The governor's opportunity came in January, 1936, when he found a way to appoint five new regents and at the same time to reduce the size of the board from fifteen to fourteen members. Phil pointed out that Wisconsin statutes required that there be one regent from each congressional district and four regents-at-large. Two regents were to represent agriculture, and two were to represent labor. Compliance with the statutory requirements, explained the governor, made necessary his dismissal of Leonard Kleczka, whose term had not yet expired. Kleczka did not live in the district he was suppose to represent, and furthermore, La Follette insisted that labor interests were entitled to his seat on the board. He did not mention the fact that the departing regent happened to oppose him politically. The governor also eliminated another opponent by insisting that because of congressional redistricting he was obliged to reduce the size of the board. What all of La Follette's maneuvering meant was that by 1936 he had appointed eleven of the fourteen regents.[38]

After naming the new regents, the governor met with Harold M. Wilkie, a Progressive lawyer from Madison who served as president of the board. He also consulted Regent Daniel Grady and State Superintendent of Public Instruction John Callahan. They agreed that Frank should be told of their dissatisfaction with his administration of the university. Frank's response to reports of the regents' attitudes was to prepare an elaborate defense, which he presented to the regents' meeting on March 10. Once again Frank's friends came to his aid, and rather than have the university's administration become a political issue, La Follette asked Wilkie to hold the matter in abeyance until after the 1936 election. Although controversy continued to surround the university during the summer, it apparently had little effect on Wisconsin voters. With the Progressives' electoral victory in November, the governor and the anti-Frank regents decided to act.[39]

[38] Walter D. Corrigan to Philip F. La Follette, January 28, 1935; W. Wade Boardman to La Follette, January 28, 1935; La Follette to Leonard Kleczka, January 3, 1936; and La Follette to Fred H. Clausen, January 3, 1936, all in the Philip F. La Follette Papers. See also Zink, "Glenn Frank," in *WMH*, 62:116.

[39] La Follette, *Adventure in Politics*, 237–238; "Frank Under Fire," in the *Wisconsin Alumni Magazine*, April, 1936, p. 204; *Wisconsin State Journal*, March 14, 15, 1936; "Statement by Harold M. Wilkie, President, Board of Regents of University at Meeting of December 16, 1936 in Reference to University President" (typewritten), in the Philip F. La Follette Papers; Larsen, *The President Wore Spats*, 140–142.

Wilkie and another regent called on Frank to request his resignation, but the substance of their conversation with the president became a matter of dispute. The regents believed that Frank had agreed to resign quietly, but Frank insisted that he made no such promise. In any case, the issue came up before the entire board at its regular monthly meeting on December 16. Before a crowd of interested students and other observers, Wilkie presented a list of charges against Frank. He asserted that the president had lost support in the university community, that he had been indecisive in handling problems of the athletic department and the extension division, that his lecturing and writing not only drew his attention away from concerns of the university but also brought a handsome supplementary income, and that in spite of his sizable salary he had charged personal and household expenses to the university.[40]

Holding firm and standing on his record, Frank refused to resign and asked that he be allowed to defend himself against Wilkie's charges. The regents' executive committee set January 6, 1937, as the date for Frank's presentation of his case and the regents' determination of his fate. In the interim, Frank's friends and foes across the nation debated questions of academic freedom, political interference in the affairs of the university, and the president's extravagance and administrative ineptitude. In the circus atmosphere of the hearings, Wilkie and Frank both elaborated on contentions already advanced, but their extended arguments changed few opinions. In the end, it was a question of which side had the votes, and Frank lost. The regents voted 8 to 7 for his dismissal.[41]

On the other hand, La Follette's supporters had difficulty in contending that the governor had won. At the height of the controversy, Walter Lippmann had written in his regular column for the New York *Herald Tribune* that "the Wisconsin affair is a startling example of one of the many kinds of outside interference against which education has to be protected." He went on to add that

[40] "Statement by Harold M. Wilkie . . . December 16, 1936," in the Philip F. La Follette Papers; Sellery, *Some Ferments*, 80; Zink, "Glenn Frank," in *WMH*, 62:118–119.

[41] Among those who wrote or wired the governor to caution against political interference with the university were: Frank A. Vanderlip, December 14, 1936; Oswald Garrison Villard, December 15, 1936; Abraham Flexner, December 15, 1936; James R. Angell, December 18, 1936; Frank Aydelotte, December 19, 1936; and Paul H. Douglas, December 29, 1936, all in the Philip F. La Follette Papers. For newspaper coverage of Frank's confrontation with the regents, see the Milwaukee *Journal*, December 17, 23, 1936; Minneapolis *Star*, January 2, 1937; New York *Times*, January 4, 1937; and the *Capital Times*, January 6, 1937.

"nothing can be more destructive of the freedom of education than the notion that the regents ought to carry out the will of the governor who appointed them, or that the Governor, because he was elected by the people, should run the university." Such a notion, argued Lippmann, "is a caricature of the democratic principle."[42]

Other prominent Americans also expressed their views on the struggle taking place in Madison. Lacking knowledge of the details, they generally confined their remarks to venerated principles of academic freedom and the democratic need to prevent powerful political interests from interfering with educational processes. Abraham Flexner, director of the Institute for Advanced Study at Princeton, wrote Gordon Sinykin, the governor's secretary, no doubt assuming that Sinykin would pass the message on. "In this day of intolerance, when the universities of Germany, Russia, and Italy have been utilized as mere political tools, nothing affecting the welfare of institutions must be done in the dark," Flexner warned. If Glenn Frank was unwilling to resign, he added, "the whole academic world is entitled to know the 'pros and cons' of the situation."[43]

Even old friends of the La Follette family were concerned. Oswald Garrison Villard, editor of *The Nation*, wrote his cousin, Lloyd K. Garrison of the University of Wisconsin Law School, to ask for information on the reality behind the headlines. "I am much depressed by the character of the stories appearing here in the East in regard to the probable termination of Glenn Frank's relationship to the U. of W.," he confessed. He went on to remark that he hated "to have the Herald-Tribune insisting that only politics are behind it and hinting that Phil La Follette is trying for the job himself."[44]

[42] Walter Lippmann, "Today and Tomorrow," in the New York *Herald Tribune*, December 17, 1936.

[43] Abraham Flexner to Gordon Sinykin, December 18, 1936, in the Philip F. La Follette Papers.

[44] Oswald Garrison Villard to Lloyd K. Garrison, March 19, 1936, in the Oswald Garrison Villard Papers, Houghton Library, Harvard University. On December 15, 1936, Villard telegraphed La Follette (telegram in the Philip F. La Follette Papers) to warn him against precipitous action against Frank (punctuation and capitalization added): "As one of your father's most devoted supporters and friends I urge you most earnestly to go slow . . . I believe that if President Frank is forced out without public hearing and publication of charges in advance, it will have a profoundly serious effect upon your political future and that of Progressive party and [will] alienate many in the East who have supported you and it."

Harry Woodburn Chase, president of New York University, summarized the belief that inspired La Follette's critics: "One test of whether democratic institutions can be maintained in America is our ability to keep our Universities free from partisan political control." To many people during the troubled thirties the "Wisconsin Idea," in which Progressives took great pride, seemed to contain elements of an alien concept. Positing a close relationship between the state government and the state university, the Wisconsin Idea seemed somehow to appear dangerously similar to fascist notions about the proper relationship between the university and society.[45]

Fortunately, the appointment of Clarence Dykstra to succeed Frank calmed the fears of many of the governor's critics. Dykstra had been a professor at the University of Kansas and at UCLA. At the time of his selection as president of the University of Wisconsin he was employed as city manager of Cincinnati. Bob La Follette, who had strongly supported his brother throughout the Frank affair, first suggested Dykstra as a possible successor, and the appointment met with general approval. "I have known him for a number of years and have held him in great admiration," wrote Oswald Garrison Villard in a gracious note to Phil. "I have always found him on the liberal side of things, modest and unassuming, an excellent administrator, and well able to deal with complex situations. . . . So I congratulate you and the University upon the choice, all the more so as I was unable to see eye to eye with you in the matter of the procedure in the case of Glenn Frank." The future of the university seemed assured with the new administration in place, but the crisis left lingering doubts about the course that Phil La Follette intended to pursue in Wisconsin.[46]

With the Frank episode behind him, the governor turned his attention to other problems. Concerned with the continuing Depression in Wisconsin, he sought to obtain increased federal funds for the state, and he went to Washington to assess Roosevelt's reaction to the possibility of his reintroducing his works program. Roosevelt was noncommittal. Later, while the festivities surround-

[45] Quoted in Zink, "Glenn Frank," in *WMH*, 62:122.

[46] Oswald Garrison Villard to Philip F. La Follette, March 23, 1937, in the Philip F. La Follette Papers. In the same collection, see also Helene (Mrs. Howard E.) Wurlitzer to La Follette, March 15, 1937, and George Banta, Jr., to La Follette, March 15, 1937. For an assessment of Dykstra, see Ingraham, "University of Wisconsin, 1925–1950," in Bogue and Taylor, eds., *University of Wisconsin: One Hundred and Twenty-Five Years*, 64.

ing FDR's second inaugural were under way, La Follette talked with New York Governor Herbert H. Lehman, who invited the Wisconsin governor to meet with Roosevelt and with governors Henry Horner of Illinois, Elmer Benson of Minnesota, Charles Hurley of Massachusetts, and Robert Quinn of Rhode Island. Hoping to increase federal subsidies to the states, the governors urged upon the President the need for an expanded federal relief program. They proved unsuccessful. Persuaded that he had already done what he could to restore prosperity, and hankering for a balanced budget, FDR was determined to cut spending rather than to increase federal appropriations. The abrupt reduction of New Deal "pump-priming" efforts helped bring on a recession, the very thing the governors had hoped to avoid. Of necessity, La Follette began in 1937 to consider other measures for counteracting effects of the Depression in Wisconsin.[47]

In the meantime, Roosevelt had become convinced that he was obliged to deal with recalcitrant justices on the Supreme Court who had blocked innovative efforts for relief, recovery, and reform. Arguing that the court was overworked and that several of its members had passed the age when they could deal effectively with the many problems they faced, FDR outlined his plans in February, 1937. He proposed that he be given the power to appoint a new justice for every justice who failed to resign or retire within six months after his seventieth birthday. The President envisioned appointing as many as six new justices to the Supreme Court and forty-four new judges to lower federal courts. Few persons were privy to Roosevelt's plan, and the "court packing" scheme shocked both the Congress and the country. With only one exception, the bloc of Progressive senators who had consistently supported New Deal measures either refused comment on the measure or openly opposed it. George Norris, who for years had been a Progressive bellwether, voiced his disapproval immediately, and other Progressives followed his lead.[48]

[47] *The Progressive*, December 12, 1936; *Wisconsin State Journal*, March 5, 7, April 10, 16, 20, May 21, 1937; Miller, *Governor Philip F. La Follette*, 105–106.

[48] New York *Times*, February 6, 1937; William E. Leuchtenburg, *Franklin D. Roosevelt and the New Deal, 1932–1940* (New York, 1963), 232–233; Samuel I. Rosenman, comp., *The Public Papers and Addresses of Franklin D. Roosevelt* (13 vols., New York, 1938–1950), 6:51–66; Ronald L. Feinman, *Twilight of Progressivism: The Western Republican Senators and the New Deal* (Baltimore, 1981), 122–127; Joseph Alsop and Turner Catledge, *The 168 Days* (Garden City, New York, 1938), 97; Richard Lowitt, *George W. Norris: The Triumph of a Progressive, 1933–1944* (Urbana, 1978), 185.

Among the Senate Progressives, only Bob La Follette staunchly supported the President. On February 13, 1937, the senator took to the air waves to urge that the American people join him in backing the court reorganization bill. "The founding fathers never dreamed that legislative policies adopted by the Congress in carrying out powers clearly delegated to it were to be subject to a rigid review amounting to a judicial veto," he argued. But when the court placed its own will ahead of the will of the people, and when it decreed that the Constitution prevented the American people from taking action necessary to meet their own needs, "then it has become a dictator and we have succumbed to a Fascist system of control." The issue, as the senator saw it, was "between special vested interests represented by an economic theory of days gone by, on the one hand, and the will of the people to govern themselves, on the other." Suggesting that "smart Liberty League lawyers" were portraying FDR as a President who intended to "destroy the Court as an institution," he viewed the reorganization proposal as a measure that would actually save the court, not destroy it. The charge that FDR intended to "pack" the court, thought Senator La Follette, was a red herring. For years the tribunal had been " 'packed' for the benefit of the Liberty Leaguers, 'packed' in the cause of reaction and laissez-faire." The President's measure embodied a plan to "unpack" it.[49]

Phil La Follette joined his brother in supporting the court reform bill. Conscious of similarities between charges that Roosevelt had resorted to dictatorial methods and the charges leveled against himself during the Frank hearings, the governor also delivered a national radio address in defense of Roosevelt's proposal. Reiterating some of the same arguments his brother had made, the governor emphasized that "the principal difficulty blocking the progress of the people of this country is not our great Constitution. It is a majority of the Justices of the Supreme Court of the United States." In far too many decisions involving New Deal legislation, Phil argued, a majority of the justices did not confront a point of law at all. Instead, they debated questions of opinion and cases of prejudice. The governor contended that a basic problem with reactionary jurists was their belief "that the Constitution and the Su-

[49] Robert M. La Follette, Jr., radio address (printed), February 13, 1937, in the Philip F. La Follette Papers; *The Progressive*, February 20, 1937.

preme Court guaranteed in perpetuity a particular economic system" and "that five men can preserve by judicial decree the outworn economic and social beliefs of a favored few." Clearly the economic problems of the Great Depression called for measures never before considered. "Let us not be afraid to use such measure if they are needed for the well-being of the people," Phil pleaded. Only in promoting the general welfare might the American people "prove loyal, in the truest sense, to our traditions."[50]

The La Follettes' speeches in favor of the court reorganization bill brought a mixed reaction. Phil's friend James Causey wrote that he found the governor's address "about the best you ever made." William H. Lighty, director of extension teaching at the university, compared it favorably to "the memorable Cooper Union speech of Abraham Lincoln in another and earlier crisis." John M. Denney, state president of the Oklahoma Southern Tenant Farmers Union, asked Phil for a hundred copies of the address for use in a campaign "to get the truth about the Supreme Court to the people," and Texas Congressman Maury Maverick wired to let the governor know that he thought the speech "SINCERE CLEAR AND BEST MADE SO FAR."[51]

On the other hand, another Texan charged Phil with "trying to arouse the prejudice of the masses," and critics throughout the country saw a basic consistency between the speech and the governor's role in the Frank case. "Coming from one who had successfully 'fixed' the Board of Regents of his own state, it was quite in form," wrote one unsympathetic listener. Another thought it "logical that a governor who would, thru his henchmen, depose a great university president because the university president differed from him politically should applaud the attempt . . . to depose members of the Supreme Court of the United States whose opinions he does not like."[52]

When Justices Owen Roberts and Charles Evans Hughes, the swing votes on the court, began supporting the New Deal position

[50] Edwin E. Witte to Philip F. La Follette, February 26, 1937, and La Follette, radio address (typewritten), n.d., both in the Philip F. La Follette Papers; New York *Times*, February 28, 1937; *The Progressive*, March 6, 1937.

[51] All of the following to Philip F. La Follette in the Philip F. La Follette Papers: Causey, March 1, 1937; Lighty, March 2, 1937; Denney, February 28, 1937; Maverick, telegram, February 27, 1937.

[52] Melville J. France to La Follette, February 28, 1937, and Lloyd M. Cosgrove to La Follette, February 27, 1937, both *ibid.*

in cases involving the Wagner Act and a Washington minimum-wage law, the need for the reorganization bill seemed less urgent. Yet for five months in mid-1937, FDR continued to press for it. Eventually, with support crumbling and with Justice Willis Van Devanter's resignation creating an opening for a Roosevelt appointment, the President abandoned court packing and settled for an innocuous measure involving minor procedural reforms. Phil La Follette deplored FDR's capitulation. In June he had written his brother to argue that backing down on the court reorganization bill would be the equivalent of "our giving up in the midst of the Frank case." He took great satisfaction in the appointment of Hugo Black to replace Van Devanter, however, and his disappointment in the results of the court fight for the time being had no effect on his relationship with the President.[53]

* * *

With Glenn Frank's dismissal and the court fight arousing national concern, Phil La Follette began concentrating his attention on a legislative program for Wisconsin. Progressives again controlled the assembly; in the upper house they could rely on assistance from Philip E. Nelson, a Douglas County Republican, and Arthur Zinmey, a Milwaukee Democrat. Having achieved a working majority in both houses, the Progressives were cautiously optimistic as the governor prepared recommendations for their consideration. Of primary importance, Phil asserted, were a new labor law, a state power program, and the state budget. In formulating his agenda, the governor was sensitive to the influence exerted by the Wisconsin Farmer-Labor Progressive Federation. Twenty-seven Progressive members of the assembly and eight Progressive senators held memberships in the organization, and all of them favored legislation to meet the demands of labor. Wishing to remain on good terms with the FLPF, La Follette made the enactment of a labor bill his first objective.[54]

[53] Miller, *Governor Philip F. La Follette*, 107; Feinman, *Twilight of Progressivism*, 133–135.

[54] Charles H. Backstrom, "The Progressive Party of Wisconsin, 1934–1946" (doctoral dissertation, University of Wisconsin, 1957), 343–347, 354–356; Lester F. Schmidt, "The Farmer-Labor Progressive Federation: The Study of a 'United Front' Movement Among Wisconsin Liberals, 1934–1941" (doctoral dissertation, University of Wisconsin, 1955), 178–179; *Wisconsin State Journal*, April 2, 1937; minutes of January 8, 1937, executive board meeting, Wisconsin State Federation of Labor Papers.

In drafting the bill, advisers to the governor consulted labor leaders as well as legislators sympathetic to the farmer-labor program. Finding strong support for a state labor law, they came up with a bill duplicating the one that had met defeat in 1935. This time they were successful, despite vigorous opposition in the senate. A coalition of Democratic and Republican senators sought to thwart the purposes of a labor disputes bill, but in large part through the efforts of Senator Herman Severson, the Progressives held firm. After offering fifty-six amendments, all of which went down to defeat, the anti-labor forces accepted the inevitable. By a vote of 30 to 3, the senate passed the Wisconsin Labor Relations Act that the Progressives wanted.[55]

Like the national legislation of 1935, Wisconsin's "Little Wagner Act" of 1937 outlawed specific employer practices it identified as unfair. Such practices included interfering with the workers' right to organize, discriminating against union members in the employment and promotion of workers, refusing to bargain with union representatives, and spying on employees or distributing blacklists. The statute also created a three-member state labor relations board. With broad powers to recognize appropriate bargaining agents for employees, the board could hold hearings, conduct investigations, and serve as an agency for the arbitration of labor disputes. Developed in part through a series of compromises, the legislation won general approval throughout the state. Yet both labor and management offered criticism of specific features of the law. Employers complained, for example, that while it identified unfair management practices, it offered no comparable listing of unfair union practices. Labor, on the other hand, pointed out that unlike the National Labor Relations Act, the Wisconsin statute permitted an employer to reach a closed-shop agreement with *any* union, even if it did not represent a majority of workers.[56]

Governor La Follette, who like his rural supporters had some

[55] Gordon Sinykin to Joseph A. Padway, February 17, 1937, in the Philip F. La Follette Papers; *Capital Times*, April 2, 1937; Milwaukee *Journal*, April 2, 1937; Oshkosh *Northwestern*, April 6, 1937; Gordon M. Haferbecker, *Wisconsin Labor Laws* (Madison, 1958), 162.

[56] Nathan P. Feinsinger and William Gorham Rice, Jr., *The Wisconsin Labor Relations Act*, UW, *General Series Bulletin*, no. 2038 (1937); Haferbecker, *Wisconsin Labor Laws*, 162–165; Nathan P. Feinsinger, "The Wisconsin Labor Relations Act," radio address, November 17, 1937, and Gordon Sinykin to W. D. Kyle, November 19, 1937, both in the Philip F. La Follette Papers.

misgivings over the growing strength of organized labor, nevertheless described the new law as "the most comprehensive and far-sighted measure ever taken by any state to safeguard the rights of labor and promote industrial peace." In discussing the legislation, Phil repeatedly stressed the peaceful settlement of industrial disputes. "We cannot have progress without order," he cautioned, "and we cannot have order without progress." Labor partisans had no objection to the aphorism, but they did not underestimate the craftiness of employers. Labor spokesman Edward Keating wanted to be sure that "all jokers have been eliminated and that the measure represents a real gain for workers." Martin Boerner, publisher of the Niagara *Journal* in Marinette County, had similar doubts. He was certain that employers "will seek out every possible loop-hole in the act they can find to maintain the iron hand over the workers."[57]

The second measure to receive legislative approval was a bill providing for a budget the governor described as "self-balancing." In his message introducing it, La Follette explained what he meant. Like the budget the senate had defeated in 1935, he proposed three schedules with the one to be followed depending on state revenues. Budget "A," based on a 15 per cent reduction in appropriations of the previous biennium, provided for minimum expenditures; Budget "B" made possible an increase in appropriations if "warranted and necessary"; and Budget "C" increased expenditures even more if state revenues and federal assistance to the state exceeded expectations. The power to determine which of the three was to become effective rested with the Emergency Board chaired by the governor.

Again adopting tactics of amendment and delay, opponents of the plan argued that this was not actually a budget at all because its sliding scale prevented a determination of how much the legislature was actually appropriating. Furthermore, they argued, the measure would grant too much power to the governor. As ex officio chairman of the Emergency Board, he would have a controlling influence over expenditures. The Progressives again defeated the

[57] "Statement by Governor La Follette about the Wisconsin Labor Relations Act" (typewritten), n.d.; Philip F. La Follette to Edward Keating, night letter, April 6, 1937; Philip F. La Follette, "Democracy Functions in Wisconsin," radio address, October 16, 1937; Edward Keating to La Follette, telegram, April 5, 1937; and Martin Boerner to La Follette, July 2, 1937, all in the Philip F. La Follette Papers.

opposition, however, and La Follette signed the bill into law on May 27, 1937. Having already achieved an increase in tax revenues, he then secured approval for renewing the emergency tax of the previous session so as to justify a budget increase of $10 million. According to Wisconsin Secretary of State Theodore Dammann, the expanded budget held out "more to the needy aged, the needy blind, dependent widows and children, low paid employes of state departments and state institutions, and to the field of education than any previous budget." Proud of his record, Governor La Follette observed that the 1937 budget legislation prohibited the state from spending more than it had on hand. And he promised that his administration would adhere to the principle that if a government "must spend money, it must first find where that money is coming from."[58]

The third measure to which La Follette and his advisers attached great importance was a bill to make possible the development of electric power through means that invited comparison with the Tennessee Valley Authority. Yet the program Phil envisioned was his own, formulated out of his experience with the new federalism of the Depression decade. In May, 1935, Roosevelt had created the Rural Electrification Administration, and the following year Congress had given it power to make self-liquidating loans. Although the Republican-Democratic coalition in the 1935 legislature had defeated the governor's plan to secure REA funds for Wisconsin, Phil had been able to obtain an emergency grant of $300,000 from the Works Progress Administration. The Progressives had then established an agency they called the Wisconsin Rural Electrification Coordination, and under the direction of John A. Becker and Orland S. Loomis the REC had carried on a campaign to promote electrical co-operatives and the use of electricity in rural Wisconsin. By 1937, however, the REC funds were running out. Furthermore, supporters of the program recognized a need for some agency that could provide technical and legal assistance as well as promotional campaigns.[59]

[58] Philip F. La Follette, executive budget message, January, 1937; Theodore Dammann, "20th Century Legislation in Wisconsin" (typewritten), radio address, November 10, 1937; and La Follette, "Democracy Functions in Wisconsin" (printed), radio address, October 16, 1937, all in the Philip F. La Follette Papers; *Wisconsin State Journal*, April 30, June 18, 1937; *Capital Times*, May 6, 1937; Backstrom, "Progressive Party of Wisconsin," 354–355; Miller, *Governor Philip F. La Follette*, 110–111.

[59] Samuel Mermin, *Jurisprudence and Statecraft: The Wisconsin Development Authority and Its Implications* (Madison, 1963), 8–9; Miller, *Governor Philip F. La Follette*, 111.

To avoid constitutional limitations on the state's financing internal improvements, the Progressives had established a private corporation to carry out their objectives. Chartered in March, 1937, the Wisconsin Development Authority (WDA) relied on the same reasoning the Progressives had used to justify the Wisconsin Finance Authority during the 1935 legislative session. That is, the Progressives proposed neither to issue stock nor to seek profits for the WDA corporation. They intended, instead, to use the WDA rather than a state agency as the instrument to carry out state objectives in electrification. As Phil La Follette and his followers planned it, the WDA could carry on the promotional activities of the REC. It could also provide technical and supervisory assistance for electrical co-operatives, municipal utilities, and even private plants. Where existing facilities were inadequate, the WDA might even construct and operate its own utility plants.[60]

Securing a charter for the Wisconsin Development Authority did not require the legislature's approval, but obtaining state funds for its operation obviously necessitated legislative action. Roland E. Kannenberg, a Progressive from Wausau, introduced the governor's WDA bill in the senate; Andrew Biemiller, a labor leader from Milwaukee's Second District and a member of the Farmer-Labor Progressive Federation, sponsored the measure in the assembly. Providing an initial sum of $10,000 and an annual appropriation of $60,000 after July 1, 1937, the bill projected modest expenditures. Yet it touched off a bitter debate that led to noxious behavior in both houses.[61]

In hearings before the joint committee on finance and the assembly committee on state affairs, conducted on April 22, Kannenberg argued that lower rates from public power would aid the state's industries and serve to maintain Wisconsin's industrial leadership. While Kannenberg's presentation was restrained, Biemiller's testimony proved more abrasive. The bill, he declared, brought to a climax "the fight that has been going on for years in this state

[60] Andrew J. Biemiller, "Wisconsin Acts in the Fields of Power and Agriculture" (typewritten), radio address, November 12, 1937, and Philip F. La Follette to Carl D. Thompson, April 22, 1937, both in the Philip F. La Follette Papers; Wisconsin Development Authority's articles of organization as reproduced in Development Authority, *Wisconsin Gets a Power Program: A Story of the WDA* (1938).

[61] Mermin, *Jurisprudence and Statecraft*, 14; Milwaukee *Leader*, March 29, 1937; "State Corporation Planned for Promotion of 'Little TVA,' " n.p., n.d., in the Philip F. La Follette Papers.

between the people on one hand and the power trusts on the other." In Biemiller's view, passage of the bill would allow Wisconsin citizens to develop their own resources; it would prevent holding companies from extracting "huge sums" from the state and transporting them to Wall Street.[62]

In rebuttal, opponents of the bill played upon fears that if the legislature opened the way for the WDA, little could be done to prevent its expanding into the coal business, the oil business, and beyond. They also emphasized that the private utilities of the state were already producing adequate power, and that in any case it was high taxes and not lack of power that drove industries from Wisconsin. Speaking for a group of taxpayers from Racine, Dr. R. J. Miller contended that if legislators were to talk with people who had lost their homes, they would have second thoughts about voting for a "pernicious bill" that might lead to further state expenditures and private losses. Ultimately, he believed, the WDA would "actually create communism" because taxes to support the program would far exceed the capacity of citizens to pay. "With the Christmas tree still in Washington, D.C., with money hanging on every needle," commented R. O. Wipperman in presenting the position of the Wisconsin Manufacturers' Association, it was natural to ask "why should not Wisconsin get a little?" His response was that passage of the bill would involve "burning the candle at both ends." An expanded public utilities program would mean "narrowing the tax base, and . . . when the tax base had been narrowed too much, then property pays the bill or you don't carry on the particular public function." If property could not pay, or if legitimate functions of government were eliminated, "then you may expect a collapse of your state government."[63]

A week after the hearings, the WDA bill came up for consideration in both houses. Again a Republican-Democratic coalition fought the Progressive program with tactics of delay and amendment. The governor responded to criticism by reassuring his opponents that he did not intend to challenge legitimate business. The

[62] "Complete Record of Proceedings of the Joint Hearing by the Joint Committee on Finance and the Assembly Committee on State Affairs," April 22, 1937, in the Philip F. La Follette Papers; Mermin, *Jurisprudence and Statecraft*, 16–20.

[63] "Complete Record of Proceedings of the Joint Hearing," April 22, 1937, in the Philip F. La Follette Papers; Mermin, *Jurisprudence and Statecraft*, 20–22. On April 23, 1937, the *Wisconsin State Journal*, Milwaukee *Journal*, *Capital Times*, and Milwaukee *Sentinel* all provided summaries of the hearings.

WDA, he insisted, was a necessary device for obtaining federal funds. His critics remained skeptical, and extraordinary rancor marred the legislators' discussion of power development.

After amendments limiting WDA activities to those specified in the bill, the measure passed the assembly by a margin of 55 to 36. Senate opponents were more resourceful than their assembly colleagues, however, and with skillful parliamentary maneuvering they forestalled action until June 16. On that day of pandemonium in the upper house, Republicans and Democrats favoring private power twice fled the chamber with unseemly haste in order to prevent a quorum. After the second walkout, Lieutenant-Governor Henry A. Gunderson and Chief Clerk Lawrence Larson signed ten subpoenas requiring recalcitrant senators to return, but the absentee solons were nowhere to be found. When they finally reappeared, the Progressives secured a call of the senate, which required locking the doors to prevent another escape. The senate then proceeded to pass the bill by a vote of 17 to 15; but minority members were in no mood gracefully to accept defeat. Though the hour was already late, they closed the day with a series of blistering attacks on the Progressive party and the governor for employing dictatorial methods to achieve victory.[64]

The assembly concurred in the senate bill on June 25, but the Progressives' triumph actually amounted to very little. Less than a week after the governor signed the measure, the United Taxpayers Cooperative Association of Wisconsin formally demanded that Secretary of State Theodore Dammann and State Treasurer Solomon Levitan withhold the appropriation because the constitutionality of the act was open to question. That move precipitated a year-long legal battle, and by the time the state supreme court upheld the law during the summer of 1938, La Follette was immersed in a campaign for re-election. After 1938, the WDA lost its access to public funds, and while the agency continued to provide technical services on a nonprofit basis, it gradually withered away to insignificance. The Wisconsin Development Authority was finally dissolved in 1954.[65]

[64] Mermin, *Jurisprudence and Statecraft*, 22–31; *Wisconsin State Journal*, June 17, 1937; *Capital Times*, June 17, 1937.

[65] Mermin, *Jurisprudence and Statecraft*, 32–57, 61–62; *Capital Times*, July 16, 1939; Development Authority, [*A Report of the Authority's Activities as a Public Instrumentality from July 1, 1938 Through Mar. 21, 1939*] (1939), in the LRB. The following letters, all

The demise of the Wisconsin Development Authority was not an eventuality the Progressives seriously contemplated in 1937. On the contrary, they celebrated passage of the WDA bill as the successful completion of the program Phil La Follette had set as his goal at the beginning of the legislative session. He and his allies had secured a labor-relations law, a new state budget with the sliding scale that he thought would give him flexibility, and then a power program to benefit both agriculture and industry. Having attained his objectives, he was ready to end the session and send the lawmakers home.[66]

To secure the legislation he sought, however, the governor had relied on help from the Farmer-Labor Progressive Federation, and the FLPF was by no means prepared for adjournment. Its members expected a quid pro quo. They thought themselves entitled to Phil's support for some of their own measures. Among these were bills calling for state-supported medical care, state housing corporations to improve the living conditions of cities, liberalized old-age pensions, more effective control of utilities, protection of consumers from fraudulent advertising, free milk for schoolchildren, and several other novel measures. Favoring a more comprehensive social program than old-line Progressives were inclined to accept, the FLPF exerted such pressure as to threaten the delicate alliances that produced Progressive majorities in the legislature. With the FLPF agitation, the governor's supporters worried about disruption in the ranks, as did La Follette himself.[67]

The locus of FLPF strength was the state assembly. There the Progressive party's radicals—Sturgeon Bay Republican Frank H. Graass later identified them as "left-wingers"—included Andy Biemiller, John Grobschmidt from Milwaukee's Tenth District, David Sigman from Two Rivers, and Paul Alfonsi from the hamlet of Pence

---

in the Philip F. La Follette Papers, provide perspective on the WDA's court fight: David E. Lilienthal to La Follette, November 26, 1937; La Follette to David E. Lilienthal, December 1, 1937; Gordon Sinykin to Henry Zinder, January 15, 1938; H. O. Melby to La Follette, January 21, 1938; La Follette to Ralph Hoyt, day letter, January 23, 1938; La Follette to Claire Bird, day letter, January 27, 1938; John Ernest Roe to La Follette, February 1, 1938; Edward G. Littel to John P. Ferris, February 7, 1938; Raymond L. Breese to La Follette, March 2, 1938; and John A. Becker to A. E. Grassby, September 28, 1938.

[66] Miller, *Governor Philip F. La Follette*, 112, 114; Theodore Dammann, "20th Century Legislation in Wisconsin" (typewritten), radio address, November 10, 1937, in the Philip F. La Follette Papers.

[67] *Capital Times*, July 4, 10, 29, 1937; Chicago *Tribune*, July 4, 1937.

in Iron County. None of the "Four Horsemen of the Federation" maintained strong ties with the Wisconsin farmers who had consistently supported the La Follettes. Biemiller, who had served as a national organizer of the Socialist party and as its educational director in Milwaukee, and Sigman, who was a member of the executive board of the Wisconsin State Federation of Labor, were more responsive to the interests of workers than to the interests of farmers. Even Alfonsi, whose district encompassed sparsely settled Iron and Vilas counties, maintained closer associations with miners and lumber workers than with farmers.[68]

One of Phil's most persistent problems as governor was finding a way to persuade the FLPF to operate in tandem with Progressives from agricultural sections of the state. Securing the passage of the labor-disputes law, which the FLPF strongly supported, seemed a less impressive accomplishment in rural areas than in industrialized eastern and southeastern Wisconsin. At the same time, though the legislature had passed measures for soil conservation, the inspection of cattle, and drought relief, it had enacted no comprehensive farm program.

The governor's decision to bring the regular session to an end, then, was only in part attributable to his having achieved his major objectives; it was also a move dictated by the need to prevent internecine feuding within the Progressive party. Supporting Herman Severson's motion to adjourn the legislature sine die on July 2, he believed that the Progressives would have an opportunity to regroup, resolve differences, and complete a coherent program in a special session. A special session would at least have the advantage of limiting discussion and action to matters indicated in his proclamation calling it together. "The 1937 legislature revealed a startling fact," observed political reporter Aldric Revell after Severson's motion had passed and legislators had departed Madison, "that the concrete unity of the Progressive party is beginning to split; that a Milwaukee bloc of Farmer-Labor Progressive Federationists is getting under the skin of 'regular' Progressives."[69]

* * *

[68] *Capital Times*, July 10, 1937; *Wisconsin Blue Book, 1937*, pp. 47, 51, 53, 56. Graass is quoted in Backstrom, "Progressive Party of Wisconsin," 392.

[69] Miller, *Governor Philip F. La Follette*, 114–115; Schmidt, "Farmer-Labor Progressive Federation," 225–227; La Follette, *Adventure in Politics*, 247–248; *Capital Times*, July 4, 10, 1937.

Following adjournment of the 1937 regular session, Phil La Follette held conferences with representatives of interest groups upon whose support the success of his administration depended. He consulted both farmer and labor spokesmen, and he listened to the demands of FLPF leaders. He also conferred with businessmen such as shoe manufacturers R. E. Freeman of Beloit and H. L. Nunn of Milwaukee, motor company executives J. E. DeLong of Waukesha and C. H. Bliss of Kenosha, and papermakers William Ashe of Kaukauna and D. C. Everest of Rothschild. While he listened to various ideas about how to achieve economic recovery, he also traveled about the country disseminating ideas of his own. Before the end of the regular legislative session he addressed the alumni association of the Harvard Business School, and during the next two months he met forty speaking engagements. After the Harvard address, the most important were at Northwestern University on July 22, at a meeting of the Progressive League of Iowa in Des Moines on July 31, and at a Labor Day rally in Omaha on September 6.[70]

Everywhere he went the Wisconsin governor spoke as the messiah of political realignment. Perhaps thinking of Sweden's middle way, he told his Harvard Business School audience that there was "no need for Americans to choose between communism and Fascism, capitalism and socialism nor individualism and collectivism." The central problem facing the American people, as he saw it, was finding a means of adjusting "economic and political institutions to meet changes in environment without sacrificing the essence of individual initiative." Wisconsin, he thought, had long shown the way: the state's workmen's compensation law, passed in 1911, had provided compensation for injured workers while stimulating employers to assume responsibility for safety in industry; the state's unemployment compensation act of 1931 had provided aid for workers who lost their jobs while encouraging management to stabilize employment; the state's labor-relations law just enacted established the principle of collective bargaining, but it granted nei-

[70] See the following documents in the Philip F. La Follette Papers: List of persons invited to Employers' Conference, July 29, 1937; list of Governor La Follette's speeches, 1936, 1937, and 1938; Philip F. La Follette, "Orderly Progress," speech at Harvard University, June 18, 1937; Helen Rogers Reid to La Follette, July 8, 1937; La Follette, speech at Northwestern University, July 22, 1937; George F. Buresh to Gordon Sinykin, July 6, 1937; H. P. Fagan to Gordon Sinykin, July 29, September 7, 12, 1937; Omaha *World-Herald*, clipping, September 7, 1937; and Edwin Hadfield, Jr., to La Follette, September 12, 1937.

ther workers nor employers the right to use coercion and intimidation.

La Follette urged his Harvard audience to avoid labeling a new program as "radical or communistic or Fascistic merely because it is based on collective action." In the difficult years of the Great Depression, insisted the governor, some form of collective action was inescapable. The question to ask about any new program, he argued, was whether "it encourages or discourages the American spirit." The speeches Phil delivered in 1937 represented variations on the theme of his Harvard address, and in most of the places he visited he perceived sentiment for a political realignment along the middle way he advocated. To take advantage of that vaguely articulated sentiment, however, he would need to provide a sharper focus for third-party efforts. He would also need to establish his credentials as a state executive capable of accomplishing Progressive goals.[71]

By the end of the summer, the governor was more than ever convinced of the need for a special session. On the other hand, his discussions with prominent citizens of Wisconsin made him wary of announcing a comprehensive reform program for legislative consideration. Plunging recklessly ahead could increase tensions among the Progressive factions in Wisconsin and thus strengthen the Democratic-Republican coalition that opposed him. Fearful of another defeat such as the one he had encountered in pressing for his works bill in 1935, Phil sought instead to finesse his opponents. His proclamation calling for a special session to convene on September 15 did not ask for comprehensive legislation, but only for action on highway safety, taxation, and relief funding. At the same time, he promised that if the legislature acted speedily to meet his initial request, he would issue a supplementary proclamation to allow consideration of an expanded program.[72]

The opposition did not give up without a fight, nor did FLPF legislators content themselves with limited objectives. As a result, the legislature took three weeks to pass a relief bill the governor could accept. La Follette then agreed to expand the agenda on the condition that legislators adopt rules to prevent further procras-

[71] La Follette, "Orderly Progress," speech at Harvard University, June 18, 1937, in the Philip F. La Follette Papers; New York *Herald Tribune*, June 19, 1937.

[72] Philip F. La Follette, "A Proclamation," September 12, 1937, in the Philip F. La Follette Papers; *Wisconsin State Journal*, September 11, 13, 1937.

tination. Specifically, they would have to meet eight hours a day for six days a week, waive all rules on public hearings and rules permitting delays, and adjourn on October 16. Meeting the governor's conditions, and accepting rigid discipline for themselves, Progressive legislators also agreed to caucus on every bill and vote as a unit. The unusual procedures did not make for a harmonious session, but they did produce the legislation La Follette sought.

The special session lasted four and a half weeks, but the governor proudly asserted that in its last five days the legislature "did more real work and achieved greater results" that any previous legislature had accomplished in five months. It provided an appropriation of $150,000 to support activities of the Wisconsin Agricultural Authority, an independent nonprofit corporation created to improve the quality of state agricultural products and expand existing markets for them. It established the Department of Commerce "to assist in promoting the welfare of business and industry . . . and to assist our businessmen in finding constructive solutions for their problems." It passed important social legislation to liberalize old-age pensions, to facilitate municipal participation in federal housing programs, to increase state aid for high schools, and to prevent child labor and the economic exploitation of children.[73]

Most importantly, in La Follette's opinion, he secured a bill to reorganize the state government. Pondering problems associated with the exercise of political power, Phil had been impressed with the way constitutional limitations often prevented his taking the action required for efficient administration of programs enacted to meet the needs of citizens. In a day when science and technology had wrought a profound revolution in the way people lived, he thought it important that the executive branch of government have the power to cope effectively with the problems of modern society. In a flash of inspiration, he thought he discerned a solution to a basic dilemma of the Depression years, a dilemma that lay at the heart of difficulties he had faced since his 1934 election victory. "How," he asked, "could we permit the Executive to act without making him a dictator?" The answer, he believed, was to reverse the functions of the executive and legislative branches of government in the state. In his mind, such a reversal meant that the

[73] Philip F. La Follette, "Democracy Functions in Wisconsin," radio address, October 16, 1937, in the Philip F. La Follette Papers; Miller, *Governor Philip F. La Follette*, 115–117.

governor would propose measures he thought necessary, and the legislature would either approve them or reject them by what amounted to a legislative veto.[74]

Insofar as La Follette's Government Reorganization Bill marked a departure from practices already followed, it represented a step in the direction of a cabinet form of government. Whatever the merits of that form, the legislature passed the Government Reorganization Act, and La Follette praised the measure as one "to modernize the administration of our state government." The legislation created a special committee composed of eight members of the legislature, the secretary of state, the state treasurer, the attorney general, the superintendent of public instruction, and the chairman of the state civil service commission. Acting only with the approval of the special committee, the governor was to have power to issue executive orders requiring a reconstruction of state agencies. Each house of the legislature received the power to veto any modification the governor proposed.[75]

Under provisions of the Government Reorganization Act, La Follette juggled several departments and agencies during the winter of 1937–1938 to achieve the more orderly structure he had in mind. The changes, observed John M. Gaus, professor of political science at the university, were inspired not by a desire for power, but by the obvious need to adjust the functions of government to changes that had taken place in society. Gaus believed that as a consequence of La Follette's efforts, the human energies of Wisconsin might "be released and focused for the improvement of the standard way of living." Improving the economic well-being of Wisconsin citizens had, in fact, been the goal of the "little New Deal" the governor had secured for the state as a result of his efforts with the 1937 legislature.[76]

After enacting the comprehensive program La Follette wanted, the legislature had adjourned on schedule amid boos and catcalls from disgruntled Democrats and Republicans. It was a raucous

[74] La Follette, *Adventure in Politics*, 248–249; *Christian Science Monitor*, March 31, 1938.

[75] La Follette, "Democracy Functions in Wisconsin," and Edward G. Littel, "Reorganization of the State Government," clipping from *Forward*, 17 (May, 1938), both in the Philip F. La Follette Papers.

[76] John M. Gaus, "Reorganization in Our State Governments," press abstract of address before Wisconsin League of Women Voters, Memorial Union, Madison, February 1, 1938, and a speech by John A. Thiel to the Wisconsin Federation of Women's Clubs, Second District, Fort Atkinson, May 6, 1938, both in the Philip F. La Follette Papers.

conclusion to a special session that revealed, thought the governor's critics, too great a tendency to emulate the techniques of Adolf Hitler. Arms raised in mimicry of the Nazi salute and chanting "Heil!" in disdainful chorus, opposition legislators had stalked from the chambers of the capitol to prepare for the political campaign ahead. Phil La Follette of course saw the 1937 sessions differently. On October 16, as the lawmakers headed for home, he took to the air with a radio broadcast proclaiming that "democracy functions in Wisconsin."[77]

Yet the means by which Phil La Follette won his legislative victories, coming so soon after the dismissal of Glenn Frank, aroused anxieties even among some of his most committed supporters. The most prominent among Phil's Progressive critics was William T. Evjue, editor of the Madison *Capital Times* and of the *Progressive*, the La Follettes' own journal. The last week of the special session, Evjue remarked, was "a week in which democratic processes were abandoned and an executive dictatorship was in the saddle." Joining the governor's chorus of detractors, he summed up the whole legislative process of the 1937 sessions as one that "smacked of Hitler and Mussolini." Had the governor in fact lost sight of the middle way? Sometimes openly articulated, the question haunted the mind of many a citizen of Wisconsin as La Follette contemplated his next move.[78]

[77] Theodore Dammann, "20th Century Legislation in Wisconsin," radio address, November 10, 1937, in the Philip F. La Follette Papers; Backstrom, "Progressive Party of Wisconsin," 356–363.

[78] *Capital Times*, October 19, 1937; William T. Evjue, *A Fighting Editor* (Madison, 1968), 562; Philip F. La Follette, *Adventure in Politics*, 250.

13

Man CAN Have Work AND Be Free

IN July, 1937, after adjournment of the regular legislative session, Phil La Follette traveled by rail to Washington. There he conferred with his brother on the future of the Progressive party in Wisconsin and on the chances for a political realignment in the nation. President Roosevelt had invited the brothers to join him and Senator Alben Barkley of Kentucky for a weekend cruise on the presidential yacht, and shipboard conversations that weekend of course focused on politics. With his characteristic assertiveness, Phil told FDR that he planned a series of speeches during the months ahead to establish a basis for concerted action by liberal forces throughout the country. The President seemed to approve. "You fellows out West can do things I can't do," he told the governor. "My hands are tied. I have the reactionary South on my hands and I cannot go into my own state, New York, and make the same appeal that you can make out West."[1]

Believing that Roosevelt had grown weary of the effort to keep the Democratic party headed in a liberal direction, Phil proceeded with his plans. If the President followed tradition and did not seek a third term, the opportunity to unite liberal factions of all parties under a Progressive banner offered promising possibilities. Roosevelt had, in fact, already hinted that Bob La Follette might become his successor. If that happened, it was not unreasonable to assume that Phil might look forward to occupying a seat in the Senate and perhaps eventually to running for President himself.[2]

[1] Entry for August 19, 1937, in Isabel Bacon La Follette, Political Diary, and Franklin D. Roosevelt to Philip F. La Follette, August 16, 1937, both in the Philip F. La Follette Papers; Philip F. La Follette, *Adventure in Politics: The Memoirs of Philip La Follette*, ed. Donald Young (New York, 1970), 251–252.

[2] John E. Miller, *Governor Philip F. La Follette, the Wisconsin Progressives, and the New Deal* (Columbia, Missouri, 1982), 122; Madison *Capital Times*, July 24, 27, September

In fulfilling his speaking engagements during the summer of 1937, Phil sampled opinion among reform-minded politicians in Illinois, Iowa, and Nebraska as well as Wisconsin. Visiting George Norris at the senator's summer home on Rainbow Lake in Waupaca County, the governor found the old Progressive warhorse sympathetic. And Phil's audiences elsewhere generally seemed receptive to his prediction that a new party would come into being by 1940. He was forty years old, and he was brimming with confidence as his imagination impelled him towards a national stage for the dramatic culmination of his political career. The only question that remained was one of timing. If he were to launch a drive for national office, Phil believed, he should announce his intentions at a critical moment when his ideas might have a telling effect on potential supporters.

At the conclusion of the special legislative session in October, 1937, Phil and Isen left Madison for a cruise in the Caribbean. Unfortunately, the governor fell ill with the flu and had to spend much of his vacation in the hospital at Colon, Panama. By the time he returned home in late November, Roosevelt's effort to balance the budget by abandoning deficit financing had brought about a serious recession. Private investments were declining, and unemployment rates rising. From the spring of 1937 to the spring of 1938, American industrial production fell by a third, and the Gross National Product in 1938 dropped to 5 per cent below that of the previous year. The governor decided it was time to act. Still feeling the effects of the ailment that had sent him to the hospital in Panama, he canceled his speaking engagements, and while recuperating he formulated his plans.[3]

The decision to create a new party was one that Phil reached largely on his own. Yet he always believed that he followed faithfully the Progressive tradition his father had established. He remained convinced that embedded within the Progressive tradition of Wisconsin rested the principles necessary for judging men and events. In assessing a rapidly changing world, Phil constantly sought to

---

2, 1937; *Wisconsin State Journal*, July 31, September 17, 1937; Stanley High, *Roosevelt—And Then?* (New York, 1937), 273–274, 310.

[3] Lester V. Chandler, *America's Greatest Depression, 1929–1941* (New York, 1970), 130, 140–141; George H. Soule, "The Present Industrial Depression," in the *New Republic*, 93 (November 24, 1937), 62; Kenneth D. Roose, "The Recession of 1937–38," in the *Journal of Political Economy*, 56 (June, 1948), 241; Henry H. Villard, *Deficit Spending and the National Income* (New York, 1941), 323.

apply those principles, and to his way of thinking, that meant drawing on his own experience, first as Old Bob's son, and later as the Progressive governor of a state noted for its Progressive achievements. Wise policy, he thought, required an application to the present of lessons he had learned from the past.

Franklin D. Roosevelt had also identified himself with a Progressive point of view, and until 1937 the President and the governor worked in harmony. Yet from the beginning it had been an uneasy association. While both men valued historical perspective, Roosevelt's less precise intellectual commitment allowed him to act flexibly in the present and to draw his lessons from the course of events rather than from an idealized past. His broad humanitarian instincts provided him the freedom to interpret events without resort to Progressive dogmatism. La Follette was a fundamentalist believer in the Progressive tradition, and like others who profess abiding adherence to received truth, he sometimes found himself stumbling over inconsistencies. Before American entry into World War II, he had parted company with the President.

After the 1938 election, as had become his practice, Phil arranged a tour of Europe to gain insight into whatever the future might hold. His visit to Germany impressed him with the imminence of conflict, and he glimpsed a chilling vision of the troubles ahead. Yet he found himself driven not towards a confrontation of international problems, but towards avoidance of them. Recalling his father's attitude two decades earlier, he managed to persuade himself that the United States could escape war and that the American people would be better off for refusing to become involved.

"Nazism must be smashed," Phil announced upon his return home; but he insisted that Americans could best aid in accomplishing that objective by strengthening the nation's economy. Making his case before the Economic Club of New York in April, 1939, he used arguments similar to those he had used four years earlier in his effort to secure passage of his public works bill. Circumstances had changed, to be sure. With Hitler's success in building up the Nazi war machine, Phil argued, the United States now confronted not just an economic depression but "a totalitarian Europe, allied with a Japan-ized Far East, aggressively bent on dominating the Western hemisphere." Yet after seeing German industrial plants humming with activity, and after observing the German people, Phil thought he discerned the weakness in Hitler's program. "The foundation of Nazism in Germany and Italy is the simple proposition that today men cannot have both work and freedom," he asserted. Thus he could conclude that "nothing would more certainly smash Hitler and Mussolini from within than our demonstration of the counter-proposition that man CAN have work AND be free."[4]

Many of those in La Follette's audience found his message reassuring that April evening in New York. Throughout the nation's history Americans had believed work and freedom compatible, and during the Great Depression they had come to believe them inseparable. Nevertheless something seemed amiss. In the context of international events occurring in the late 1930's, pronouncements such as La Follette's became identified with the America First Committee and its isolationist perspective. Liberals of both major political parties were contending that the survival of democracy at home might well require responsible involvement in the struggle against fascism abroad. To persons urging international commitments, isolationism was beginning to betray ties with self-serving domestic interests and with advocates of a foreign policy that bore scant relationship to international realities.

* * *

As a politician who aspired to national leadership, Phil La Follette knew that he required support from dissimilar and sometimes antagonistic sections, classes, and interests. Striving to form a working partnership with them was a task fraught with difficulties, but it was also a task for which his position as governor of Wisconsin provided valuable experience. From the time Old Bob established his name as a dominant influence in the state, the strength of the Progressives had rested on a rural, Scandinavian base. Yet in confronting business stagnation and unemployment during the Great Depression, Phil found himself grappling with the problems of urban, industrial southeastern Wisconsin as well as with those of the agricultural hinterland.[5]

[4] La Follette, *Adventure in Politics*, 257–263; New York *Times*, April 22, 1939; New York *Herald Tribune*, April 22, 1939; *Capital Times*, April 19, 1939; Philip F. La Follette, "Wide Unrest in Germany Is Described," in *The Progressive*, July 15, 1939, reprinted from *The Commentator*, 5 (July, 1939), 70–75.

[5] John E. Miller, "Governor Philip F. La Follette's Shifting Priorities from Redistribution to Expansion," in *Mid-America*, 58 (April–July, 1976), 125–126; Gordon M. Haferbecker, *Wisconsin Labor Laws* (Madison, 1958), 163–165; Eugene M. Tobin, *Organize or Perish: America's Independent Progressives, 1913–1933* (New York, 1986), 248; David L. Brye, *Wisconsin Voting Patterns in the Twentieth Century, 1900 to 1950* (New York,

Creation of the Progressive party of Wisconsin in 1934 opened the way for co-operation between the traditional La Follette Progressives and new reformers whose sympathies led them towards an alliance of farmers and workers. Some of the new reformers, such as Thomas R. Amlie, Walter Graunke, and David and Samuel Sigman—with the assistance of farmer and labor organizers from outside Wisconsin—actively promoted the urban-rural co-operation that culminated in 1935 in formation of the Wisconsin Farmer-Labor Progressive Federation. Yet like the informal alliance of New Dealers and Wisconsin Progressives that grew out of FDR's associations with the brothers La Follette, the farmer-labor coalition proved tenuous. Phil La Follette had great difficulty with the farmer-labor meld, just as he eventually did in his associations with Roosevelt. He never wholeheartedly identified himself with the FLPF except on a high level of abstraction. On that lofty plane he reiterated principles that placed the Progressives on the side of the angels in their eternal struggle with the forces of darkness.[6]

Both the La Follettes and members of the Wisconsin FLPF took seriously the traditional rhetoric that deplored the deleterious influence of "special interests"; both accepted as fundamentally accurate the charge that reactionary businessmen and industrialists exploited farmers and workers as they pursued their own selfish ends. So far as workers were concerned, the charges were no figment of the radical imagination. Industrial laborers and their Progressive allies could agree that they must oppose employers determined to preserve the open shop. In the Wagner Act they gained legal support for collective bargaining and for their contention that employer interference with the organization of unions violated a fundamental right. Labor secured further support in June, 1936, when Bob La Follette became chairman of the Senate Civil Liberties Committee. Under his leadership, the committee compiled massive amounts of testimony on the way employers used industrial espionage, strikebreaking tactics, private detective agencies, and even

1979), 321–326; Gordon Sinykin to W. D. Kyle, November 19, 1937, in the Philip F. La Follette Papers.

[6] Lester F. Schmidt, "The Farmer-Labor Progressive Federation: The Study of a 'United Front' Movement Among Wisconsin Liberals, 1934–1941" (doctoral dissertation, University of Wisconsin, 1955), 120–121, 390–391; Miller, *Governor Philip F. La Follette*, 17, 84–87; Donald L. Miller, *The New American Radicalism: Alfred M. Bingham and Non-Marxian Insurgency in the New Deal Era* (Port Washington, New York, 1979), 116–118, 131.

munitions and poison gas to prevent the formation of unions. The inquiry continued for four years, and the senator's thoroughness won unstinting praise from the friends of organized labor. After the committee completed its investigations, Norman Thomas remarked that "the country owes Bob La Follette a debt comparable to the debt owed his father."[7]

Neither workers nor their leaders were inclined to disagree with that assessment. Nevertheless, when Progressives attempted to strengthen ties with organized labor, they found that lack of unity among workers themselves compounded problems of co-ordination. The most basic difficulty became apparent in disagreements over the organizational strategies that labor should follow. During the long presidency of Samuel Gompers, the American Federation of Labor had provided a means of uniting skilled workers who formed discrete, closely disciplined craft unions. Because their skills and training increased their bargaining power, the AFL unions had managed to achieve a status in the American work force that unskilled laborers did not enjoy. Competing with cheap immigrant labor during the nineteenth century, the unskilled workers Selig Perlman identified as "manualists" remained unorganized, passive, and subject to the whims of their employers.[8]

The Great Depression obviously changed drastically the conditions of labor in American industry. So long as the AFL adhered to its elitist philosophy and its exclusive principles of organization, it could do little to meet the needs of unorganized workers in the mass production industries. Yet in those years of widespread unemployment, federal and state labor legislation created new opportunities for establishing unions outside the AFL structure. As demands for a new form of organization increased, advocates of industrial unions sought to explain their point of view. At the annual convention of the AFL in Atlantic City in October, 1935, they went further than that. Accepting the leadership of the United Mine

[7] Milwaukee *Leader*, December 6, 1935; Irving Bernstein, *Turbulent Years: A History of the American Worker, 1933–1941* (Boston, 1971), 448–451. Jerold S. Auerbach, *Labor and Liberty: The La Follette Committee and the New Deal* (Indianapolis, 1966) provides a detailed account of the activities and findings of the committee. The senator himself summarized some of the committee's conclusions in a Labor Day speech (copy in the Philip F. La Follette Papers) in Madison on September 5, 1938.

[8] Foster Rhea Dulles, *Labor in America: A History* (3rd ed., New York, 1966), 288–289; Edward Levinson, *Labor on the March* (New York, 1938), 24–48; Henry Pelling, *American Labor* (Chicago, 1960), 146–149; John Higham, *Send These to Me: Immigrants in Urban America* (2nd ed., Baltimore, 1984), 23–25, 38–39.

Workers' John L. Lewis, the most colorful and persuasive advocate of industrial unions, they introduced twenty-two resolutions calling for the establishment of industry-wide union structures. Although the convention rejected the resolutions by a vote of 18,024 to 10,933, Lewis did not turn back; on the contrary, he took the lead in forming the Committee for Industrial Organization.[9]

Lewis and his associates in the CIO announced their intention to promote industrial unions within the AFL, but old-guard champions of the craft union philosophy opposed the idea. In their view, the CIO was engaged in promoting a form of dual unionism that could ultimately bring the AFL to ruin. Unskilled workers in the steel, rubber, automobile, and mass-production industries, they thought, had no real commitment to organized labor. Furthermore, they had little understanding of the insidious influence of radicals and self-serving politicians who were forever appealing to workers in hopes of winning support for their own peculiar causes. For such reasons, the AFL executive council ordered the Committee for Industrial Organization to dissolve. The unions that had affiliated with it thereupon launched an aggressive organizing campaign, to which the AFL responded with organizing efforts of its own. Because workers and labor leaders across the country at first saw dissension in the ranks as destructive, moderates sought to work out a compromise. They did not succeed, however, and late in 1938 the dissident unions formed an independent alliance they named the Congress of Industrial Organizations.[10]

The labor strife of 1935–1938 had its effect on Wisconsin, although workers in the state were no strangers to the concept of industrial unionism. For years the Socialists had been urging an industrial form of organization, and the Milwaukee Federated Trades Council had supported the idea. When the AFL-CIO struggle began, therefore, Wisconsin labor sought to moderate the dispute so as to minimize the damage. At the 1936 annual convention of the Wisconsin State Federation of Labor in Beaver Dam, delegates listened to several resolutions on the subject and eventually

[9] Bernstein, *Turbulent Years*, 360–368, 386–395; Walter Galenson, *The CIO Challenge to the AFL: A History of the American Labor Movement, 1935–1941* (Cambridge, 1960), 3–9.

[10] Robert H. Zieger, *American Workers, American Unions, 1920–1985* (Baltimore, 1986), 41–45, 55–58; Bernstein, *Turbulent Years*, 400–431, 688–695; Kenosha *Labor*, January 7, March 4, 1938; Racine *Day*, April 22, 1938; Henry Ohl, Jr., to Philip F. La Follette, January 3, 1938, in the Philip F. La Follette Papers.

adopted a compromise plan that they hoped might satisfy both sides. The WSFL urged that the AFL drop its charges against the CIO as well as its plans for dismissing or expelling CIO unions. It proposed, further, that the AFL and CIO co-operate in organizing the steel and rubber industries on an industrial basis with the understanding that the CIO should confine its activities to those industries. Finally, it called for the creation of a committee representing both factions to study the problems of organization preparatory to further action. Exhorting the AFL to adopt the Wisconsin Plan at its upcoming national convention, the WSFL then elected two CIO supporters, Emil Costello and John Banachowicz, to its executive board.[11]

The Wisconsin Plan and similar proposals made little headway in the national organization or, indeed, in the state. Although the AFL endorsed expulsion of the CIO unions at its national convention in 1936, leaders of the state organization for a time entertained hopes of avoiding the strife that plagued other parts of the country. CIO organizers were enjoying considerable success, and CIO locals in Milwaukee were gaining acceptance as members of the Federated Trades Council. Despite the hopes for labor peace, however, the AFL-CIO conflict caused tremors in Wisconsin when an organizational dispute broke out at the Allis-Chalmers plant in West Allis early in 1937. Harold Christoffel, a young militant who two years earlier had helped to secure a federal union charter from the AFL to organize Allis-Chalmers workers not eligible for membership in a craft union, began a campaign to change affiliation.[12]

In short order, Christoffel's organization left the AFL to become Local 248 of the United Auto Workers, a CIO union. Fearing a secession movement and determined to hold fast, the AFL ordered the Milwaukee Federated Trades Council to expel UAW delegates.

[11] "The History of the State Federation of Labor Is a Tale of Service to the Workers," in Wisconsin State Federation of Labor, Convention, *Souvenir Program, 50th Annual Convention . . . August 17–21, 1942* (Milwaukee, 1942), 28–53, which duplicates *History of the Wisconsin State Federation of Labor* (mimeographed, 1942), in box 10, Wisconsin State Federation of Labor Papers; Thomas W. Gavett, *Development of the Labor Movement in Milwaukee* (Madison, 1965), 160–161; Paul Krakowski, "Press Treatment of Wisconsin Labor Issues, 1936–38" (master's thesis, University of Wisconsin, 1947), 40–45; Kenosha *Labor*, June 5, September 18, 1936.

[12] Gavett, *Development of the Labor Movement in Milwaukee*, 161–162; Walter F. Peterson, *An Industrial Heritage: Allis-Chalmers Corporation* (Milwaukee, 1978), 322. Robert H. Zieger discusses the importance of Federal Labor Unions (FLU's) in *Madison's Battery Workers, 1934–1952: A History of Federal Labor Union 19587* (Ithaca, 1977), 34–38.

Henry Ohl, Jr., president of the Wisconsin State Federation of labor, charged that in conspiring with Communists and other radicals, the CIO had undermined AFL efforts to secure favorable labor legislation and had also hampered efforts to maintain friendly relations with farmers. After bitter debate, the FTC proceeded to expel Allis-Chalmers representatives. The CIO unions thereupon withdrew from the FTC, and in August, the officers of sixty-two locals formed a new city central with Christoffel as president. "The AFL no longer can claim the right to speak for organized labor," he asserted. "Its leaders are turning the organization into company union channels and responsibility for a genuine labor movement now falls upon the CIO."[13]

The troubles in West Allis had repercussions throughout the state. After the Allis-Chalmers workers withdrew from the AFL, the general executive board of the Wisconsin State Federation of Labor met to consider what action it should take with respect to Costello and Banachowicz, the two CIO members on the board. Banachowicz had resigned, and AFL partisans believed that Costello should also withdraw. At a hearing on April 29, 1937, the board reviewed charges that Costello had sought to "ridicule and discredit" the WSFL and had attempted to "build up rival or dual organizations." Costello himself did not appear at the hearing; instead, he sent a letter replete with charges of his own. "The worst violators of the A. F. of L. Constitution," he argued, "have been Green and the Executive Council, Ohl, Handley and the GEB [General Executive Board]." Furthermore, he continued, "expelling the biggest local union in the state from the Milwaukee Trades Council (Allis-Chalmers local of the United Auto Workers)" was only one of several actions for which the AFL must bear responsibility. Indeed, "treachery, scabbing, sabotage, splitting and disruption—these are the crimes [for] which the Executive Council of the A. F. of L. stands convicted before the working people of America."[14]

Obviously, Costello did not write his letter in an effort to ingratiate himself with the board, which now voted unanimously to dis-

[13] Gavett, *Development of the Labor Movement in Milwaukee*, 162–166; Janesville *Gazette*, April 9, 1937; Milwaukee *Leader*, July 8, 30, 1937.

[14] Henry Ohl, Jr., and J. J. Handley, statement issued by the general executive board of the Wisconsin State Federation of Labor, March 8, 1937, enclosed in Henry Ohl, Jr., to Philip F. La Follette, January 3, 1938, in the Philip F. La Follette Papers; minutes of the April 29, 1937, general executive board meeting, Milwaukee, in the Wisconsin State Federation of Labor Papers.

miss him. Costello, according to a resolution the board members adopted, had been "irresponsible and untrustworthy." He had, in particular, "employed methods and tactics consistent with those used and fostered by the Communist party." In so doing, they might have added, he had offended the sensibilities of Socialists as well as conservatives within the AFL. With Costello's dismissal, the break in the ranks of Wisconsin labor was all but complete. The state CIO crossed the Rubicon on May 8, 1937, when it held a meeting in Milwaukee to form the Wisconsin State Industrial Union Conference. Electing Costello president of the new organization, the conference set itself to the task of winning Wisconsin workers for the CIO.[15]

The Wisconsin State Federation of Labor sought to match the organizational campaign of the CIO, and competition led to a rapid increase in union membership. In March, 1938, the *Wisconsin CIO News* boasted that had it not been for the AFL-CIO rivalry, at least 125,000 men and women in the state would have continued working without union protection. And had it not been for vigorous organizing campaigns, the industrial plants of Wisconsin would have remained bastions of the open shop. Unions of the WSFL doubled their membership, and those of the state CIO counted their gains in tens of thousands. Employers who had never before dealt with unions suddenly found themselves confronting workers who, zealous in their enthusiasm, also proved assiduous in presenting demands. It was a state of affairs in which labor controversies multiplied.[16]

During 1937, with the national and state labor relations acts guaranteeing labor's right to organize, with the CIO and AFL competing for the support of workers, and with many employers hankering for the "good old days" of the open shop, Wisconsin experienced more strikes than in any previous year of its history. There were 190 strikes, nearly four times as many as in 1936, and they entailed a loss of more than 850,000 person-days of work. The Wisconsin Labor Relations Board had its hands full in me-

[15] Minutes of the April 29, 1937, general executive board meeting, Wisconsin State Federation of Labor Papers; Gavett, *Development of the Labor Movement in Milwaukee*, 165–166; Miller, *Governor Philip F. La Follette*, 113–114.

[16] *Wisconsin CIO News*, March 26, 1938, cited in Gavett, *Development of the Labor Movement in Milwaukee*, 167; Zieger, *American Workers, American Unions*, 50; Wisconsin Labor Relations Board, "Report Covering the Period from April 28, 1937, to November 30, 1938," in the Philip F. La Follette Papers.

diating the disputes that came before it. Phil La Follette's appointees to the board—Voyta Wrabetz, chairman of the industrial commission; Edwin Witte of the University of Wisconsin; and Monsignor Francis J. Haas, rector of St. Francis Seminary in Milwaukee—enjoyed widespread public support. Nevertheless, their stature as labor mediators notwithstanding, they were sometimes hard-pressed to achieve settlement of labor disputes.[17]

Despite the difficulties it confronted, the Wisconsin Labor Relations Board worked effectively during the two years of its existence. It intervened in nearly every strike that occurred in the state, and it settled 680 controversies through mediation. Building a solid reputation for fairness, it acted with scrupulous adherence to the law in identifying employers guilty of unfair labor practices, in approving the listing of unions, and in conducting elections to assure the legitimate selection of bargaining agents. To be sure, the labor relations board could not satisfy everyone, but Milwaukee labor lawyer Max Geline surely exaggerated when he wrote Phil La Follette that the board was "so afraid that it might offend somebody that it winds up getting abuse and offense from everybody." A more balanced assessment was that of Monsignor Haas. Tendering his resignation in the fall of 1937 to allow time for new responsibilities as dean of the School of Social Science at Catholic University in Washington, he wrote the governor that the Wisconsin Labor Relations Act had "conspicuously advanced industrial good will and understanding in Wisconsin." Employers and employees alike, he believed, "recognize in the Act an effective instrument to protect the legitimate interests of management and labor."[18]

* * *

[17] Wisconsin Labor Relations Board, "Report Covering the Period from April 28, 1937, to November 30, 1938," in the Philip F. La Follette Papers; Haferbecker, *Wisconsin Labor Laws*, 163–164; Stevens Point *Journal*, April 9, 1937; Oshkosh *Northwestern*, April 13, 16, 1937; Milwaukee *Journal*, April 23, 1937; Janesville *Gazette*, April 24, 1937; Sheboygan *Press*, April 24, 1937; Milwaukee *Sentinel*, April 25, 1937. The following correspondence may be found in the Philip F. La Follette Papers: La Follette to Voyta Wrabetz, day letter, April 21, 1937; B. E. Buckman to La Follette, April 24, 1937; and La Follette to the Right Reverend Monsignor Francis J. Haas, October 4, 1938.

[18] Haferbecker, *Wisconsin Labor Laws*, 164–165, and the following documents, all in the Philip F. La Follette Papers: "Annual Report of the Wisconsin Labor Relations Board, Fiscal Year Ending July 1, 1937"; "Report of Activities of the Wisconsin Labor Relations Board as of December 15, 1937"; Wisconsin Labor Relations Board, "Report Covering the Period from April 28, 1937, to November 30, 1938"; Max E. Geline to La Follette, May 17, 1938; and Francis J. Haas to La Follette, September 17, 1937.

The state and national labor relations acts helped reduce industrial injustice and were essential for union development and growth. Yet the economic recession of 1937–1938 created new difficulties for labor organizers as employers cut back on production and unemployment increased. Struggling with problems of the continuing Depression, many Americans lost sight of the high hopes that had carried FDR to his overwhelming victory in the election of 1936. The recession brought disillusionment. Critics of the President became strident in their denunciation of New Deal policies, and as disenchantment spread throughout the land, the advocates of political realignment gave thought to the next presidential election. Few of them expected Roosevelt to seek a third term, but in neither of the two major parties could they find an obvious successor. With the New Deal coalition apparently coming apart, and the Republicans unable to provide an attractive alternative, the times were unusually auspicious for the formation of a new party. Or so they seemed to Phil La Follette.

Although Wisconsin's Progressive governor had supported the President—even during the fight over reform of the Supreme Court—he had long predicted that a national political realignment would come about. Indeed, his rhetoric seemed to suggest that he planned and built his entire career on the assumption that, irrespective of the Depression, politics as usual could not meet the needs of modern America. As far back as the election of 1928, he had urged his brother to create a new party before another election found Progressives pitted against Stalwarts in a contest for control of the Republican party. Although little came of his suggestion at the time, the Wisconsin Progressive party had come into being by 1934, and Phil looked forward to its soon becoming a national organization. "The failure of our economic system should be obvious to all," he told Wisconsin voters that year. "We must have a political realignment that will put the exploiting reactionary on the one side and the producer and consumer on the other." During his second term, the governor's speeches became increasingly sanguine about political realignment at the same time that he strengthened his ties with the New Deal. A third party could not be created without adequate preparation, he warned, and preparation required time. Nevertheless, he was convinced that a new national party could become a major political vehicle for Progressive reformers during the election of 1940 or 1944. Adhering to that timetable,

Phil initiated a more aggressive drive for a new party. During his third term as governor, he began to exchange ideas with persons on whom he could rely for advice on how to develop the machinery for carrying out his objectives.[19]

The thought that he might have waited too long must have crossed Phil La Follette's mind more than once during 1937 and 1938 as he sought to build the apparatus for a new party. The organizational drives of the AFL and CIO were beginning to penetrate rural Wisconsin, and farmers were having second thoughts about linking themselves with the interests of industrial workers. Touring the state in 1937 to recruit new members for the Wisconsin Farmer-Labor Political Federation, organizer Henry Rutz encountered great resentment towards labor unions in rural areas. A year later, that resentment found a specific target in Richland Center, where workers in a co-operative creamery formed a union. Hostile farmers forced the organized creamery workers to resign from the union or forfeit their jobs, a move that brought the National Labor Relations Board into the fracas. Although the co-operative finally agreed to recognize the union, farmer patrons came away from the settlement convinced that labor laws required revision. A second incident at Franksville, in Racine County, became an even greater irritant. There, striking workers forced the shutdown of a spinach cannery. The action of course infuriated farmers unable to sell their harvest.[20]

The growing hostility towards organized labor had its effect on attitudes within the Wisconsin Farmer-Labor Progressive Federation. Although the governor had always had difficulty in working with the organization, he depended heavily on its support within the state. Beyond that, he recognized the importance of strengthening his ties with the American Commonwealth Political Federation—the national organization most closely linked with the Wisconsin FLPF—if he was to secure backing for a national third party. Unhappily for him, the farmers of Wisconsin became wary of the

[19] Miller, *Governor Philip F. La Follette*, 43–44; *The Progressive*, April 4, August 1, 1931; *Capital Times*, November 8, 1934; New York *Times*, May 19, July 28, October 13, 27, November 2, 1935; Ronald L. Feinman, *Twilight of Progressivism: The Western Republican Senators and the New Deal* (Baltimore, 1981), 145.

[20] Miller, *Governor Philip F. La Follette*, 113–114; Henry Rutz to Thomas R. Amlie, July 13, 1937, in the Thomas R. Amlie Papers; Gavett, *Development of the Labor Movement in Milwaukee*, 168–169; Haferbecker, *Wisconsin Labor Laws*, 165–166; Milwaukee *Journal*, August 7, 8, 1938.

FLPF just at the time when Phil most needed farmer-labor cooperation and support.[21]

Several key persons associated with the American Commonwealth Political Federation had also tempered their enthusiasm for a third party. During the 1936 presidential campaign, Tom Amlie, Alfred Bingham, Selden Rodman, and other members of the organization had finally thrown their support to Roosevelt. In the aftermath of FDR's stunning victory, they concluded that the best hope for Progressives rested in a revitalized New Deal. Fearful of the growing power of Hitler's Germany and Mussolini's Italy, and disturbed by the purge trials in Moscow, the farmer-labor radicals began to develop a new respect for the American two-party system. Whatever its shortcomings, it had at least shown itself capable of adapting to change without going to dangerous extremes. Even as Phil La Follette prepared to launch a new party, Amlie offered his own view that the important political struggles of the immediate future would take place within the Democratic party. The only reasonable Progressive course, it seemed to him, was to support New Dealers in their efforts to prevent conservative Democrats from taking control. Rodman agreed. Conceding that for more than five years he had urged the formation of a new party, he recognized that the circumstances of 1937 differed from those of 1932. "Today," he wrote Oswald Garrison Villard, "the chance of building a really effective political movement, able to challenge the existing order, lies far more in a close alliance of all progressive forces with Roosevelt than their uniting against him." Writing to Phil La Follette, Bingham emphasized the same point: "The way to achieving what we believe in lies through an alliance of the Progressive and Farmer-Labor forces with the New Deal, leaving the old line Democrats to line up with the Republicans."[22]

[21] Charles H. Backstrom, "The Progressive Party of Wisconsin, 1934–1946" (doctoral dissertation, University of Wisconsin, 1957), 405–408; Miller, *Governor Philip F. La Follette*, 151; New York *Herald Tribune*, October 10, 1937; Hugh T. Lovin, "The Persistence of Third Party Dreams in the American Labor Movement, 1930–1938," in *Mid-America*, 58 (October, 1976), 148–149, 152–154; *The Progressive*, October 2, November 20, December 4, 1937.

[22] Miller, *New American Radicalism*, 141–147; Stuart L. Weiss, "Thomas Amlie and the New Deal," in *Mid-America*, 59 (January, 1977), 31; Thomas R. Amlie to Howard Y. Williams, August 30, 1937, in the Thomas R. Amlie Papers; Selden Rodman to Oswald Garrison Villard, August 24, 1937, and Alfred M. Bingham to Villard, August 30, 1937 (misdated July 30, 1937), in the Oswald Garrison Villard Papers, Houghton Library, Harvard University; Alfred M. Bingham to Philip F. La Follette, July 28, 1937, and La Follette to Bingham, August 7, 1937, both in the Philip F. La Follette Papers.

While Phil encountered opposition to the third-party idea in other parts of the country, problems were beginning to develop closer to home. Progressives of Wisconsin were unhappy with the governor's reliance on Ralph Immell, his old college friend, who had served as adjutant general of the Wisconsin National Guard and as state administrator of the WPA. Rumors that the La Follettes were grooming Immell to succeed Phil as governor stirred an angry reaction among Wisconsin Progressives, and criticism of the governor's judgment mounted. Again the chief critic was William T. Evjue, whose admiration for FDR had led him to believe that the President rather than the governor or the senator was the real champion of Progressive principles. While Phil was still considering the formation of a new party, Evjue, in a speech to Madison's East Side Progressive Club, warned against people who believed that "the Progressive ship should sail out into more modern waters and anchor in a more modern setting." It was, argued the editor, a sad delusion that could mean piloting the faithful old vessel out of its serviceable harbor and into the treacherous shoals of political expediency.[23]

Despite many warnings and expressions of doubt, Phil La Follette proceeded implacably with his plans. He did, after all, receive encouragement from some friends and followers. Confident of his skills in the art of persuasion, he believed that he could overcome both critics and doubters. As insurance, he established a friendly relationship with William Benton, who had resigned from the advertising agency he had founded with Chester Bowles to become a vice-president at the University of Chicago. An admirer of Old Bob La Follette, Benton found Phil's ideas worthy of serious consideration. Drawing upon his experience in advertising, he devoted considerable time to providing the Wisconsin governor with expert advice on how to make his case for a new party.[24]

After years of toying with the idea of forming a national third party, then, Phil finally prepared to act early in 1938. Meeting with the Progressive state central committee on February 24, he dis-

[23] See the following letters to Philip F. La Follette in the Philip F. La Follette Papers: George J. Reid, April 10, 1937; Robert M. La Follette, Jr., April 26, 28, 1937; and Walter D. Corrigan, Sr., June 17, 1937. Also, *Capital Times*, January 13, 24, 27, 1938; *The Progressive*, May 1, 1937, January 22, 1938.

[24] Sidney Hyman, *The Lives of William Benton* (Chicago, 1969), 204–205; William Benton to Philip F. La Follette, February 7, March 18, 1938, in the Philip F. La Follette Papers.

cussed his own political future as well as the future of the state party. It was up to the party itself, he told the committee, to decide whether he should seek re-election or run for some other office. A matter he considered more important was whether the Progressives should attempt national realignment by forming a new party or by attempting to gain control of one of the old parties. During the next two months he held several conferences to discuss the Progressives' options with party members representing all parts of the state and every important economic interest and occupation. While he took care to avoid dominating the conversations at such conferences, he left little doubt that he thought the time had come for a bold move to extend Progressive influence. On April 15 he announced that during the following week he planned to deliver a series of four speeches over the state radio network.[25]

The four fifteen-minute addresses, broadcast on consecutive evenings from April 19 to 22, 1938, marked the governor's break with Roosevelt and the New Deal. "We have not been successful in meeting the problems of the depression," he argued, and the reason for failures in policy had been failures in thinking. After nearly a decade of tinkering and patching, Phil asserted, national leaders still seemed unable to recognize one simple but important fact: The way out of the Depression was to provide men and women with the opportunity to work, not at unproductive tasks such as many of those the WPA and other New Deal agencies had undertaken, but "at the kind of work that adds to the total annual production of real wealth."[26]

In his final broadcast, the governor argued that "freedom and prosperity depend upon each other," for dictatorships arose when there was not enough to go around. The greatest achievement of the Roosevelt administration, he thought, had been its recognition of the fact that government must take responsibility for the solution

[25] See the following letters to Philip F. La Follette in the Philip F. La Follette Papers: Gerald J. Boileau, April 12, 1938; O. L. Brownlee, April 18, 1938; Leon Green, April 18, 1938; Paul Hutchinson, April 18, 1938; James H. Causey, April 20, 1938; Arthur H. Harlow, April 20, 1938; T. V. Smith, April 20, 1938; John F. Wirds, April 21, 1938; and Arthur P. McNulty, April 26, 1938.

[26] *Capital Times*, April 20–23, 1938; New York *Times*, April 21–24, 1938. Copies of all four addresses may be found in the Philip F. La Follette Papers. For a variety of responses to the four radio broadcasts, see the following letters to La Follette in the Philip F. La Follette Papers: Harry Sauthoff, April 22, 1938; Henry G. Teigan, April 22, 1938; C. William Duncan, April 22, 1938; Morrison Sharp, April 22, 1938; Ernest Lundeen, telegram, April 22, 1938; and James T. Drought, April 25, 1938.

of social and economic problems. But instead of taking action to produce more, it had been satisfied with producing less. On the one hand, the New Deal had restricted production on the farm and in the factory, and on the other hand it had kept people from productive work through relief, make-work, and doles. Developing a program to meet the fundamental need, Phil admitted, would require organization and planning, and he asked his audience to make suggestions on how to set Americans back to productive work. In the meantime, he announced, he would outline his own plans at a rally in Madison on April 28.[27]

Keeping to himself and refusing to talk with reporters during the few days before his planned rally in the Stock Pavilion on the University of Wisconsin campus, the governor allowed curiosity and tension to build. All his life he had enjoyed political theater, and this was his opportunity to stage one of the most exciting events of the decade in Wisconsin. Yet the number of people who shared the anticipation was disappointingly small. Although Progressive veterans were curious about what Phil had in mind, they were not enticed by the promise of being provoked into spasms of enthusiasm for any program the governor might offer. "A national third party is inevitable and now is the time to form one," Bob La Follette told reporters shortly before the rally. "Phil and I are back of this jointly as we have been in the past. . . ." But pleading a need to vote against the important Naval Expansion Bill, which he thought represented a threat to American neutrality in a time of international tension, the senator insisted on remaining in Washington.[28]

Other Progressives, who for years had been ready to drop everything to attend conferences that involved decisions on the direction of reform activity, decided to wait and see what developed. When reporters asked Roosevelt if he saw a need for another organization such as the one Phil was preparing to promote, the President replied blandly, "The more liberal forces for liberal policies of the

[27] John E. Miller, "Governor Philip F. La Follette, the Wisconsin Progressives and the New Deal, 1930–1939" (doctoral dissertation, University of Wisconsin, 1973), 310–312; New York *Times*, April 24, 1938; *Capital Times*, April 23, 1938.

[28] New York *Times*, April 25, 26, 1938; Roger T. Johnson, *Robert M. La Follette, Jr., and the Decline of the Progressive Party in Wisconsin* (Madison, 1964; reprinted, Hamden, Connecticut, 1970), 42; Patrick J. Maney, *"Young Bob" La Follette: A Biography of Robert M. La Follette, Jr., 1895–1953* (Columbia, Missouri, 1978), 204–205; entries for March 29, April 18, 1938, in Isabel Bacon La Follette, Political Diary, Philip F. La Follette Papers.

country the better." The only prominent New Dealer who appeared for the rally was Undersecretary of State Adolph A. Berle, and he went at the behest of Fiorello La Guardia, not of FDR. Tom Amlie was the sole Progressive congressman to attend. Though the governor attempted to obtain William T. Evjue's support, the editor published an editorial on the very day of the rally warning that "if repudiation of President Roosevelt is to be a requisite for joining this new venture, The Capital Times is frank in saying it will not go along."[29]

While persons of national influence maintained their distance, the 5,000 people who crowded into the Stock Pavilion found themselves taking part in an affair that met all the expectations of political thrill seekers. Some, in fact, thought it more suitable for Nuremberg than for Madison. National guardsmen directed traffic outside as a drum and bugle corps circled the building. Inside the pavilion, university athletes wearing their red letter sweaters ushered people to their places while a military band played patriotic airs. Flags were everywhere, and behind the podium hung an immense banner bearing a strange device that Phil and his wife had designed for the occasion. In the center of a blue field was a red circle surrounding a blue cross on a white background. The symbol was supposed to represent the National Progressives of America, the new party Phil La Follette intended to launch that evening.[30]

Alvin C. Reis, who had served in the Wisconsin senate before becoming a circuit judge for Dane County, presided over the meeting and delivered a brief speech of introduction. Then Phil La Follette strode to the podium and began an address that was to last an hour and forty minutes. Much of his imagery he had used before, and much of his emphasis on the new party as a popular movement, growing out of the mature deliberations of average men and women, had a familiar ring. Even so, as the governor took pains to point out, he could not pretend to offer a new program complete to the last technicality. He could not satisfy those who expected "someone to shake out of his sleeve a perfected blueprint

[29] Miller, *Governor Philip F. La Follette*, 132–133; *Wisconsin State Journal*, April 24, 28, 1938; *Capital Times*, April 28, 1938.

[30] "Progressives, What Now?" in *Common Sense*, June, 1938, pp. 3–5 (copy enclosed in Alfred M. Bingham to Philip F. La Follette, May 13, 1938, in the Philip F. La Follette Papers); James McMullin, "Progressive—1938 Model," in *The Commentator*, July, 1938, pp. 3–7; Robert Morss Lovett, "April Hopes in Madison," in the *New Republic*, 95 (May 11, 1938), 13–14; La Follette, *Adventure in Politics*, 253–254.

for every detail of every problem for the next twenty years." It was far more important to be sure of the right direction. Then, learning from experience, members of the new party would be in a position to take care of any contingencies that might arise.[31]

Concerned with direction rather than specifics, La Follette at the outset probed for the causes of worldwide discontent during the late 1930's. One fundamental reason for the global malaise stood out over all others: "the failure to produce enough real wealth to support a secure and high standard of living." Recalling once again the lessons he had learned as a student at the University of Wisconsin, he attributed the failure in production to changes that had taken place in the American economy after the closing of the frontier. With the passing of an era of free land, market expansion had come to an end, and demand for the production of farm and factory began to decline. "Capital," observed the governor of Frederick Jackson Turner's native state, "is idle because the machinery that kept it at work became obsolete with the disappearance of the old frontier."

Locked up within financial institutions, capital no longer worked to create abundance for the American people. When old-fashioned capitalism became outdated, the socialists began advocating a new system "that proposes to reward work and achievement on the same basis regardless of individual accomplishment." Yet experience demonstrated "the dangers of giving 'to each according to his needs,' rather than to each according to his contributions." Thus neither the capitalists nor the socialists offered cogent solutions to problems of the Depression. The capitalists failed to see that the world had changed; the socialists recognized that the world had changed, but they failed "to see that *human nature* has not."

While old-fashioned capitalism and socialism both fell short of providing real alternatives for the American people, fascism and communism were even more misleading. Purporting to offer something new, both were in fact founded "on the ancient principle that a chosen few (whether from the top or the bottom of the economic ladder) shall make the decisions and rule by force." Yet the autocratic principle, warned La Follette, violated not only

[31] The summary and the quotations are from the printed version of the address, "A New Movement . . . The National Progressives of America . . . Is Under Way," April 28, 1938, in the Philip F. La Follette Papers.

"every principle of Americanism," but "the best teachings of the human race" as well.

Where, then, were Americans to turn as the world drifted towards war, chaos, and barbarism? Neither the Republicans and Hoover nor the Democrats and Roosevelt had found an appropriate means of using the enormous energies of the American people and the nation's prodigious natural resources to create abundance for all. The reason for the nation's failure to overcome the Depression was, according to Phil, not far to seek: "We have spent so much time squabbling over sharing our wealth that we have lost sight of the essential fact that we can not share wealth unless we have first produced enough real wealth to share." A policy of restricting agricultural and industrial production was based on the mistaken theory that overproduction had brought hard times. In point of fact, Phil argued, "*less* from agriculture, *less* from industry and business, and *less* from labor can only *equal less* for all, *instead* of *more* for all."

The governor quoted Lincoln's famous dictum of 1858: "This nation cannot exist half slave and half free." Now, eighty years after Lincoln spoke, Phil detected a parallel condition. Americans had tried to maintain a high standard of living through deficit financing, but in mortgaging the future, they had lost sight of the truth that "a free nation cannot exist with half of its productive resources at work and the other half idle." American liberty was grounded not in the capacity to borrow against the future, but in the capacity to produce abundance. "The real division in America today is not between Republicans and Democrats," argued Phil. "It is not between workers and farmers. It is not between capital and labor. It is between the earners on the one side and the collectors on the other."

Neither of the two major parties had confronted the fundamental truth that no nation could long exist as a force for good if it denied to a large percentage of its citizens an opportunity to carry on useful work. The Republican party was intellectually bankrupt, and the Democratic party was so torn with dissension that instead of supporting the New Deal, it had "sabotaged, undermined and hamstrung the administration." Precisely because of divisions within the Democratic party, La Follette asserted, the President followed a course that was, of necessity, "confused and confusing." Had FDR used his considerable skills to develop a program that was "clear and fundamental," the Democratic party could never have achieved the consensus needed to carry it out. Roosevelt, driven to obfuscation in order to secure even a part of what he wanted, had been unable to cope with real problems.

Step by step, Phil La Follette led his audience through a process of reasoning that left the formation of a new national party as the only option for reasonable citizens. "There is *no other* course," he insisted. "The time has come when an entirely new movement must go forth to fight for what we believe." Such a movement had already begun under the National Progressives of America, Phil confided; and he promised that the NPA would continue the fight until the American people recaptured their lost heritage. Then, in a burst of enthusiasm, he added what was to become one of his most controversial pronouncements: "Make no mistake, this is NOT a *third* party. As certain as the sun rises, we are launching THE party of our time." Its members were to be bound by no halfway covenant of dissatisfaction; in fact, the NPA would not accept for membership people who had only their bitterness to contribute. The new party required complete conviction, "for the movement that unites America must be itself united."

Believing that he could best explain his new party through the symbol he and Isen had created, Phil turned to the huge blue flag behind him. The cross in the circle, he suggested, represented the ballot and the traditional Progressive principle that "the will of the people shall be the law of the land." Because the ballot imposed no distinctions among races and classes, the cross in the circle also symbolized the equality of all human beings before God. Yet a third meaning derived from using the cross as a mathematical symbol. It was a sign for multiplication, and Phil believed that his policies would multiply wealth. As for the circle, an ancient symbol of unity, it represented concerted action to attain national objectives for all Americans.

In closing, Phil emphasized six basic principles that were to guide the NPA. First, he insisted that money and credit should be under public and not private control. Second, he argued for a restoration of the "absolute right" of every American to earn a living. Third, to improve administrative efficiency and at the same time prevent the abuse of power, he urged a reorganization of the federal government on the pattern that Wisconsin had established. Fourth, he proposed economic security based upon "a definite decent annual income for all." Fifth, he promised that whatever it might cost, he would use the power of government to restore opportunities for individual initiative to every American. (Yet he would "flatly oppose every form of coddling or spoon-feeding the American people.") Finally, with a view towards avoiding the troubles brewing in Europe, he pleaded for hemispheric solidarity. In his view, it was axiomatic that "our hemisphere was divinely destined to evolve peace, security and plenty."

The governor probably should have concluded his address sooner than he did. His six principles seemed repetitious and redundant, a rehash of traditional Progressive positions blended with his own ideas about how to restore prosperity by expanding production. When he finally reached his peroration, he attempted to evoke a spiritual fervor that, despite all the pageantry, was simply out of place in the Stock Pavilion that night. Phil reminded his audience that the Creator had endowed each of them with gifts so that life might become better for all. In doing so, he was attempting to drive home the lesson that citizens with faith in the Progressive vision must necessarily act upon it, for faith without works was dead. But he was ill at ease in using clerical terminology. Concluding his address with a quotation from "that great Crusader, James [the apostle]," he enjoined his listeners to be "doers of the Word, and not hearers only." A great many of the people who attended the NPA rally never fully understood what he meant. Others simply thought him profane. Only a few departed the Stock Pavilion with zeal for the cause to which Phil La Follette had just asked their unswerving commitment. In sum, the event proved one of the strangest occasions in the long history of Wisconsin Progressivism.

* * *

The Stock Pavilion rally received extensive coverage in the nation's press, and the reaction was almost instantaneous. The most enthusiastic response came from those who thought that turning from distribution to production could provide a key to the restoration of prosperity. Curtis Nettels, a historian at the University of Wisconsin, congratulated the governor for his wisdom in basing the party on a "program of production as against scarcity." Joseph R. Farrington, Phil's college roommate, thought his old friend had "struck the Roosevelt administration where it is weakest and demonstrated what is eternally true: that you cannot enjoy a more abundant life by restricting production." Among journalists and publishers, Walter Lippmann, Dorothy Thompson, Frank R. Kent, John Cowles, and William Randolph Hearst all commended at least portions of the speech. Lippmann regarded La Follette as the first Progressive presidential candidate since Woodrow Wilson to suggest using government power "not to supplant, but to liberate, private initiative" through a program of expanded production. Cowles, an associate publisher of the Des Moines *Register and Tribune*, wrote to let Phil know that he anticipated a continuation of poor business conditions if Roosevelt could think of no alternative to redistributing income. He was greatly encouraged to learn that the governor had emphasized "the vital point—the production of more national income."[32]

Yet the overall national response to Phil's message was primarily negative. Even Phil's own supporters thought that promoting the new party would not be easy. His old friend, Francis Brown of the New York *Times*, summarized what struck him as the most important criticisms of the venture. While people did not want a blueprint, suggested Brown, they wanted more details about the NPA program than Phil had provided. Some of the critics had difficulty in distinguishing between the NPA position and that of FDR. Furthermore, they feared "that a third party movement will split the liberal-progressives, placing a Republican or his equivalent in the White House." They worried about the governor's "constant references to the deity" at a time when anti-Semitism and racial prejudices were threatening standards of human decency in Europe. And they found the party symbol disturbing. To some, La Follette appeared to have taken "a page from the Fascist book." The NPA cross-in-circle seemed uncomfortably suggestive of the Nazi *Hakenkreuz*, and critics scorned Phil's use of a "circumcised swastika" as the emblem of his party.[33]

Arthur McNulty, a New York jurist, agreed that many Progres-

[32] See the following letters to Philip F. La Follette in the Philip F. La Follette Papers: Curtis Nettels, April 30, 1938; Joseph R. Farrington, August 9, 1938; and John Cowles, May 2, 1938. For the comments of Lippmann and Thompson, see the New York *Herald Tribune*, April 30, May 2, 1938.

[33] Francis Brown to Philip F. La Follette, May 3, 1938, and Arthur H. Harlow, Jr., to La Follette, April 29, 1938, both in the Philip F. La Follette Papers; Miller, *Governor Philip F. La Follette*, 136. Lloyd K. Garrison supported La Follette, but he was so troubled by the trappings of fascism that he was still fretting over them long after others had forgotten about the NPA. See Garrison to Hans Kohn, July 22, 1940, in the Villard Papers, Houghton Library.

sives were reluctant to desert Roosevelt "because they feel he is the best we can get." The "really liberal Progressives," thought McNulty, were disappointed in "the general tone of the speech." They found nothing in the NPA program "that is even as advanced as Roosevelt," and they argued that Phil's plan of action "should be more forceful and more to the left." Others resented the governor's harsh statement against coddling and spoon-feeding the American people. Whether he meant either to abolish relief or to lower wages, his choice of words did not sit well with organized labor.[34]

The reactions of most critics on both the right and the left were also harsh. In May, 1938, the Central Committee of the Communist Party, USA, issued a thirty-page pamphlet in which it contended that the governor had spoken not with "the voice of the people and of progress," but with "the voice of the rapacious capitalist-agrarian." Instead of supporting a democratic front of Progressives who were standing firm against fascism, ran the CP argument, La Follette had chosen "to make a move of disunity on a program of hostility and opposition to everything the people desire." Communists repudiated the governor because he was abandoning the people "to their worst enemies, to their chief immediate enemy," at a time when it was important to unite "all progressive movements and forces, regardless of political label or affiliation, into one common democratic front." Most of the few remaining Socialists agreed. Though always uncomfortable in associating themselves with the Communists, they also believed that the NPA was moving towards fascism.[35]

"In the camp of reaction and fascism," according to the Communist pamphlet, "the governor's program and his new party have evoked a chorus of jubilation and triumph." The Communist allegation was not entirely wrong, but it overlooked the defensive Nazi response to La Follette's insistence that fascism violated the basic principles of a free society. His denunciation of fascism in

[34] See the following letters to Philip F. La Follette in the Philip F. La Follette Papers: Arthur P. McNulty, May 6, 1938; Arthur H. Harlow, Jr., May 24, 1938; and Harlan Fenske, May 13, 1938.

[35] Communist Party, U.S.A., Central Committee, *The LaFollette Third Party: Will It Unite or Split the Progressive Forces?* (New York, 1938), copy enclosed in Harry A. Jung to Philip F. La Follette, June 8, 1938, in the Philip F. La Follette Papers; Socialist Party of the United States, *Phil La Follette's New Party* (Chicago, [1938]), copy in National Progressives of America pamphlets, SHSW.

the Stock Pavilion address elicited a remarkable reaction from Colin Ross, a German citizen who was a frequent visitor to the United States and a committed National Socialist. Ross replied through an open letter to La Follette published in Berlin in the Nazi periodical *Wille und Macht*. Recognizing that "an American politician who dared to identify himself with Fascist principles would commit political suicide," Ross nonetheless agreed with other commentators that Phil's address "was a purely Fascist or—let us say—a National Socialist speech." Hitler himself had, in fact, already enunciated its basic ideas, and Ross chided the governor for failing to acknowledge the source.

La Follette's Nazi critic confessed that he at one time doubted the possibility of Americans' accepting the principles of national socialism, but the Stock Pavilion rally had strengthened his growing conviction that the United States "will have to decide some day for a type of Fascism or Bolshevism suitable to her own requirements." The very fact that La Follette had formed a new party was but one indication that democracy was "incapable of remedying the economic and social ills of our time." Roosevelt, thought Ross, was bound to fail because he lacked the courage to break with the old order. The mass of Americans wanted the essence of socialism; that is, they were demanding economic security and opportunities for all. But Americans also wanted nationalism, a desire growing out of their consciousness of themselves as a distinct people. The only philosophy appropriate for the new order that the times required was one that combined both socialism and nationalism.

Concluding his open letter, Ross pointed to two alternatives confronting La Follette once he had established the NPA. The governor could, on the one hand, join forces with farmer-labor organizations and with leaders such as Fiorello La Guardia or John L. Lewis. Yet such a heterogeneous combination was likely to become a form of popular front, and the recent failure of popular fronts in France and Spain did not augur well. The other alternative was to seize the day for national socialism in America. If La Follette caught that vision, Ross believed, the National Progressives "may succeed in saving your people from 'chaos and barbarism' and enable them to enjoy the same amount of industrial peace and general content as is enjoyed by my own country thanks to the work achieved by Herr Hitler."[36]

[36] Ross not only provided La Follette with an English translation of his open letter,

Phil La Follette had no more interest in heading a party to promote national socialism in the United States than he had in joining the Communist party. But, in attempting to create a party of moderates with a program for increasing real wealth, he had raised new issues and encountered new problems for which he had no solutions. NPA symbolism provided no real formula for uniting farmers who thought labor unions were getting out of hand, city folk who could not understand how they might benefit from high prices for farm products, and middle-class people in both town and country who grumbled about the boondoggling and something-for-nothing impulses of Americans on relief. In seeking to broaden his support, Phil couched his arguments for expanding production in language that aroused anxieties among the very people on whom he was most dependent. And in proclaiming that the National Progressives of America were launching "THE party of our time," he stirred fear and contempt among radical journalists and others opposed to any political organization that seemed to take a monolithic party as its model. In the setting of the 1930's, the world's experience with single-party states could hardly be encouraging.[37]

Heywood Broun, writing for the *New Republic*, was among the most critical of the many journalists who attacked La Follette and the NPA. Cutting through the vagueness of the Stock Pavilion address, he detected neither a program nor a rationale that merited the support of Progressives. A founder of the American Newspaper Guild and an enthusiastic participant in popular front activities, Broun excoriated La Follette for his failure to place the cause of organized labor at the heart of his program. And he regarded the overtones of mysticism and militarism in the NPA rally as all too suggestive of fascism. "This is no thunder on the left," he asserted,

---

but he also made arrangements to visit the governor in Madison. Colin Ross, "The Cross in the Circle and the Swastika: An Open Letter to the Honorable Philip F. La Follette," translated from *Wille und Macht*, July 1, 1938, and Ross to Philip F. La Follette, December 10, 18, 1938, all in the Philip F. La Follette Papers.

[37] *The Progressive*, June 4, 1938; Paul Y. Anderson, "La Follette's Bid for Power," in *The Nation*, 146 (May 7, 1938), 524–525; McMullin, "Progressive—1938 Model," *The Commentator*, July, 1938, pp. 6–7; and the following, which are all in the Philip F. La Follette Papers: Harlan Fenske to La Follette, May 13, 1938; Everett Case to Robert Maynard Hutchins, May 3, 1938, enclosed in Hutchins to La Follette, May 6, 1938; Thomas C. Brown to La Follette, May 10, 1938; George T. Delacorte, Jr., to William Benton, May 11, 1938, enclosed in Benton to La Follette, May 11, 1938; Alex Gumberg to Freda Kirchwey, June 17, 1938, enclosed in Gumberg to La Follette, June 29, 1938; and Edward F. Dakin to La Follette, June 14, 1938.

"but mere heat lightning well to the right of Roosevelt and the New Deal."[38]

Broun was never the sort of person to enlist in an organization such as the NPA, but *Common Sense* editors Alfred Bingham and Selden Rodman had once been active members of the American Commonwealth Federation and ardent supporters of a third party. They might well have provided Phil La Follette with the sort of journalistic support he needed if he was to make headway with his new party. Yet Bingham and Rodman were as offended by the way Phil established the NPA as were Broun and other critics. Acknowledging that Phil was "a natural democrat so far as social relations are concerned," they agreed with his insistence on increasing the nation's real wealth. They also commended his "avoidance of sharp class emphasis," though they thought that he could not continue to ignore the demands of organized labor. Avoiding a personal attack, they concentrated instead on three counts in their indictment. The governor, they thought, had revealed surprising political ineptitude, had followed undemocratic procedure, and had engaged in inexcusable demagoguery.[39]

Elaborating on each of the three counts, Bingham and Rodman made clear their reluctance to have anything to do with the NPA. Anyone with the governor's training and experience, suggested the *Common Sense* editorial, should have known better than to announce his party "full-blown, name, platform, insignia and all, without taking any of the leaders of the progressive and labor movement into his confidence." The Stock Pavilion rally suggested "not merely political ineptness but a lack of respect for essential democratic procedures." Even if counting noses was a crude way to reach political decisions, argued Bingham and Rodman, it was not a time for "government by decree." The result of acting alone, according to the editorial, was not even good demagoguery, for it showed that the governor underestimated the intelligence of the electorate if he did not actually hold it in contempt. "Somebody ought to

[38] Heywood Broun, "Phil La Follette Sounds Off," in the *New Republic*, 95 (May 11, 1938), 16; Bernstein, *Turbulent Years*, 128–137; Frank A. Warren III, *Liberals and Communism: The "Red Decade" Revisited* (Bloomington, Indiana, 1966), 119–121.

[39] Thomas R. Amlie to Alfred Bingham, May 8, 1938, in the Amlie Papers; "Progressives," *Common Sense*, June, 1938, pp. 3–4; and the following, all in the Philip F. La Follette Papers: Alfred M. Bingham to La Follette, July 28, 1937; La Follette to Bingham, August 7, 1937; and Willard L. Johnson to La Follette, April 13, 1938.

have reminded Phil," remarked the editors, "that a university is more than a place from which to get football 'letter men' as ushers." Returning to the position that Bingham and Rodman had taken during the election of 1936, the editorial concluded by arguing that any new political realignment in 1940 was likely to occur within the Democratic party, and that Progressives in the various states should work to win control of state Democratic organizations.[40]

Phil La Follette and devoted followers who resisted attacks on the NPA were already attempting to establish state parties affiliated with the National Progressives. Yet it was discouraging work. Funds were inadequate, and the response to their appeals for support was disappointing. After the publicity attending the initial Madison rally of the NPA, voters heard less and less about the new party. In states such as Iowa, California, Minnesota, and New York, where Progressive or third-party organizations already existed, the NPA seemed an intrusive or disruptive force rather than an instrument for achieving Progressive solidarity. As the hopeful days of spring lengthened into the twilight of summer, the bloom came quickly off the NPA rose.[41]

* * *

While Phil La Follette struggled to keep NPA hopes alive during the summer of 1938, he gradually became aware of difficulties

[40] "Progressives," *Common Sense*, June, 1938, pp. 4–5; Alfred M. Bingham to Philip F. La Follette, July 28, 1937, in the Philip F. La Follette Papers; Miller, *New American Radicalism*, 146–148.

[41] In the Philip F. La Follette Papers, see: "National Progressive Association Organization Plan"; Ralph M. Immell, address before the Institute of Public Opinion, University of Virginia, July 15, 1938; and John Ernest Roe to Philip F. La Follette, May 31, 1938. For an excellent brief discussion of the NPA in the states, see Miller, *Governor Philip F. La Follette*, 144–149. The Philip F. La Follette Papers contain a great many letters relating to the problems involved in organizing state party affiliates of the NPA. The following deal with the states indicated; all are to Philip F. La Follette except where indicated. *California*: Frank W. Hooper, January 15, 1937; Paul H. Douglas, July 16, 21, October 6, 1937; Raymond Haight to Paul H. Douglas, July 19, 1937; La Follette to Raymond Haight, July 19, 1937; La Follette to John R. Richards, December 2, 1937; John R. Richards, May 18, 1937, June 27, 1938; Elmer A. Benson, February 14, 1938; J. Vernon Burke, March 3, 1938; Herman L. Ekern, March 31, 1938; Al Sessions, April 23, 25, May 4, 5, 1938; Irene Maw Erdman, May 3, 1938; Jerry Voorhis, May 6, 27, 1938; La Follette to Jerry Voorhis, May 18, 1938; Norval C. Fast, May 1, 1938; Harry C. Steinmetz, May 14, June 24, 1938; Walter R. Carter, May 29, 1938. *Idaho*: Ray McKaig, July 20, 1938; M. L. Alsup, August 16, 1938. *Iowa*: John F. Wirds, July 5, 1938; Gordon Sinykin to John F. Wirds, August 25, 1938; W. Howard Chase, September 20, 1938; Ralph Immell to Owen T. Owen, September 26, 1938. *Texas*: Ped Watkins, May 24, June 16, August 17, 1938; La Follette to Ped Watkins, May 29, 1938.

emerging for the Progressives in Wisconsin. Though he had not planned to seek a fourth term as governor, he began to sense that failure to enter the race might lead to his political demise. If the Wisconsin Progressives could not produce a victory in the fall, the chances of building a national organization would virtually disappear. And without Phil at the head of the state ticket, the party seemed unlikely to win. Stalwart Republicans had suffered defeat in four consecutive elections, and they were beginning to discuss with conservative Democrats the possibility of forming a coalition to rid themselves of the Progressive nuisance. Recognizing the threat posed by a Republican-Democratic alliance, party leaders urged Phil to run for an unprecedented fourth term as governor. Even William T. Evjue, much as he disliked the National Progressive effort, favored Phil's entering the gubernatorial race so as to maintain party unity in Wisconsin.[42]

Back in March, a month before the Stock Pavilion rally, veteran Progressive Charles E. Kading had written from Watertown to summarize the arguments for various courses of action that Phil might follow. The considerations justifying another gubernatorial campaign included the belief that any other Progressive candidate might lose, the conviction that the best way to promote the NPA cause was to maintain strength in Wisconsin, and the fear that "without being in the saddle in our own state" Progressives might lose influence in other parts of the country. Bernard J. Gehrmann, congressman from Wisconsin's Tenth District, expressed the prevailing opinion among party leaders when he wrote Phil that his main concern was "to keep our Progressive Organization intact in the State." Party unity, he thought, depended on Phil's heading the state ticket in the coming election.[43]

La Follette responded to the wishes of the Progressive leadership in late July, when he announced his intention to seek a fourth term. At the same time, a test of his ability to maintain party unity began taking shape when two Progressives, Herman Ekern and Thomas R. Amlie, became candidates for a seat in the United States Senate. Ekern, a friend of Old Bob La Follette and for years a staunch supporter of the Progressive party in Wisconsin, had entered the

[42] *Capital Times*, May 8, 1938; Miller, *Governor Philip F. La Follette*, 151; Feinman, *Twilight of Progressivism*, 155.

[43] Charles E. Kading to Philip F. La Follette, March 17, 1938, and Bernard J. Gehrman to La Follette, April 14, 1938, both in the Philip F. La Follette Papers.

campaign at the urging of Evjue. Amlie, with the backing of the Wisconsin Farmer-Labor Progressive Federation, had decided it was time to carry his radical ideas into the Senate.[44]

The Ekern-Amlie contest in the 1938 primary thus became a test of strength between traditional Progressives and younger Progressives identified with a farmer-labor approach. As the representative from Wisconsin's First District, Amlie had worked closely with Alfred Bingham to develop an industrial expansion bill, which he introduced in June, 1937. Cosponsored by Jerry Voorhis of California, Maury Maverick of Texas, and Robert G. Allen of Pennsylvania, Amlie's bill in many ways reflected the same concern for increasing real wealth that shaped the thinking of Phil La Follette.[45]

A more direct inspiration for Amlie's bill, however, was an approach advocated by agricultural economist Mordecai Ezekiel. In 1936, Ezekiel had published a controversial book, *$2500 a Year: From Scarcity to Abundance*, in which he argued that the key to prosperity required a reversal of the Agricultural Adjustment Act's policy of creating artificial scarcities. Instead of subsidizing limitations on production, he recommended using benefit payments to increase production in manufacturing as well as agriculture. Adopting that principle in his industrial expansion bill, Amlie proposed creation of a central agency in which representatives of labor, management, and consumers would co-operate in the planning of production, wages, and prices. To critics, the bill seemed to provide little more than a refurbished National Recovery Act, and little came of it. Still, Amlie found merit in the idea of planning for industrial expansion, and for that reason he seemed more willing to co-operate with Phil La Follette and the NPA.[46]

Unfortunately, the Ekern-Amlie contest in the 1938 primary election produced an extraordinary bitterness indicative of the depth of feeling that divided the Progressives. Ekern charged that Amlie's proposals for industrial expansion resembled nothing so much as

[44] Miller, *Governor Philip F. La Follette*, 152; *Capital Times*, July 3, 8, 11, 22, 24, 1938.

[45] Weiss, "Thomas Amlie and the New Deal," *Mid-America*, 59:32–33; Miller, *New American Radicalism*, 140–141.

[46] Mordecai Ezekiel, *$2500 a Year: From Scarcity to Abundance* (New York, 1936); Thomas R. Amlie, "The Answer to Fascism," in *Common Sense*, August, 1937, pp. 8–10; L. M. Graves, "The Folly of Industrial Planning," in *Harper's Magazine*, 176 (February, 1938), 270–278; Herbert Harris, "This Bill Bears Watching," in *Survey Graphic*, 27 (April, 1938), 227–232, 246–248; Arthur M. Schlesinger, Jr., *The Politics of Upheaval* (Boston, 1960), 215–218.

a Russian five-year plan, and Evjue conjured with visions of a totalitarian state that Amlie's program could produce. For his part, Amlie argued that a dynamic Progressivism required more than rhetorical tributes to the wisdom of Old Bob La Follette. When Amlie defined a conservative as "a man who worships a dead radical," Ekern responded with a stirring reaffirmation of his commitment to old-fashioned Progressivism. The elder La Follette's philosophy, he insisted, "was sound in all respects and is vastly preferable to the panaceas my opponent has been advocating."[47]

Ekern defeated Amlie, but his margin of victory was only 9,091 votes out of 150,679 ballots in the Progressive column. While Amlie pledged his support for the Progressive ticket in the general election, he was obviously disappointed in his failure to inspire enthusiasm for his ideas. Still insisting that the only way to achieve economic recovery was through carefully planned industrial expansion, he attributed his loss in part to Catholic resentment of his decision to support Spanish Loyalists, and in part to the opposition of old-guard AFL leaders in Milwaukee. Even more disturbing was the way factional feuding among Progressives split the party. Ekern's tactics—linking industrial expansion with totalitarian responses to the Depression—aroused an indignation from which Amlie never recovered. Both Ekern and Evjue, he believed, should have known better than to imply that he wished to adopt Soviet solutions or that he identified himself with any alien philosophy.[48]

Deeply troubled by the squabbling among Progressives, and sensitive to the need for Progressive unity, Phil La Follette avoided taking sides in the primary election contest for the Senate nomination. The governor had ample reason to be concerned. Wisconsin's conservative Democrats, after years of political frustration, were at last ready to make common cause with Republicans. Every politician in the state recognized that if the Wisconsin Republican and Democratic parties succeeded in forming a coalition, Phil's chances in the general election would become slim indeed.

The bitterness of the Ekern-Amlie struggle threatened Progressive cohesion, but even more troubling were indications in the primary election returns that conservative Republicans and Democrats

[47] *Capital Times*, September 3, 4, 7, 9, 11–13, 17, 18, 21, 1938.

[48] *Wisconsin Blue Book, 1940*, p. 541; Weiss, "Thomas Amlie and the New Deal," *Mid-America*, 59:34–35; Amlie to Herman Ekern, September 21, 1938, in the Herman Ekern Papers; Amlie to Alfred M. Bingham, September 21, 1938, in the Amlie Papers.

were succeeding in their coalition efforts. Former Democratic State Treasurer Robert K. Henry ran for governor in both Republican and Democratic primaries, and his total vote exceeded that of La Follette. Coalition candidates Walter S. Goodland and John M. Smith, campaigning for lieutenant-governor and state treasurer respectively, ran well ahead of the opposition in both Republican and Democratic primaries. In the race for attorney general, John E. Martin won an easy victory over his Republican rivals and made a good showing in the Democratic column. The only surprise for the coalition was the impressive victory of Julius P. Heil, a German-born industrialist from Milwaukee, who won 55 per cent of the vote for governor in the Republican primary. Because Henry had received but 32 per cent of the Republican vote, he withdrew from the race and endorsed Heil's effort to break the La Follette stranglehold on Wisconsin. In the general election campaign, the coalition backed Walter Goodland for lieutenant-governor, Fred Zimmerman for secretary of state, John M. Smith for state treasurer, and John E. Martin for attorney general. In the campaign for the United States Senate, all anti-La Follette factions united behind Alexander Wiley, who had defeated his closest rival in the Republican primary by 14,000 votes.[49]

While the Republican-Democratic coalition sniffed the exhilarating aroma of victory in the general elections, Phil La Follette was experiencing great difficulties. Nothing seemed to go well for him in 1938. Citizens of Wisconsin responded negatively, if at all, to his call for a new national party. Organized labor, still divided in its sympathies and uncertain of its direction, found little in the governor's program to merit support. Farmers who resented labor militancy, especially when it affected their own operations, were quick to criticize the Wisconsin Labor Relations Act. Unimpressed by the governor's efforts to unite farmers and workers under the aegis of the NPA, rural people instead urged cutting back on programs to encourage the organization of labor.[50]

Overall, in fact, after 1936 the governor had lost heavily in per-

[49] *Wisconsin Blue Book, 1940*, pp. 536–541; *Capital Times*, September 21, 1938; *Wisconsin State Journal*, October 2, 1938.

[50] Gavett, *Development of the Labor Movement in Milwaukee*, 168–169; Haferbecker, *Wisconsin Labor Laws*, 165–166; Backstrom, "Progressive Party of Wisconsin," 427–430; Gaylord C. Loehning to Gordon Sinykin, October 28, 1938, in the Philip F. La Follette Papers.

sonal influence as well as in support for his ideas. He never fully overcame the charges levied against him following the dismissal of Glenn Frank, and he shared in criticism of the way state business had been conducted during the 1937 legislative session. The most damaging personal misfortune occurred in March of the following year, less than two months before the Stock Pavilion rally. While driving from Madison to Milwaukee, Tom Duncan, the governor's trusted adviser, killed a man in a hit-and-run accident. Investigators determined that Duncan had been drinking, and that he did not even know that he had struck anyone. Judge Gullick N. Risjord, who heard the case, found him guilty of first degree manslaughter but imposed a light sentence of only one to two years in the Milwaukee House of Correction. Charges of preferential treatment and political favoritism, similar to the kinds of accusations the La Follettes themselves had often leveled at their opponents, returned to haunt the governor as he stumped the state in 1938. Another and perhaps more important consequence of the episode was that Phil lost the services of a brilliant political tactician.[51]

Stump the state La Follette did, even though he sensed that the mood of voters had changed and that his efforts were probably futile. The Progressive convention met on October 4 and proceeded with grim determination to approve an old-fashioned Progressive platform that made mention of neither the NPA nor industrial expansion. After the governor had opened the campaign with a speech at Baraboo, Glenn D. Roberts, his former law partner, wrote to offer suggestions. "My fault with your position," he observed, "is first, that you do not give me anything tangible which I may fight as an evil and second, that you do not specifically give me a living ideal for which I might give my life if necessary." The prescription Roberts offered as a cure for the apparent apathy of voters in 1938 derived from his experiences in earlier campaigns when La Follette could attack an unresponsive and reactionary legislature or a reactionary state administration. In the campaign underway, however,

[51] *Capital Times*, March 10, 1938; *Monroe County Democrat* (Sparta), March 17, 1938; Milwaukee *Journal*, June 4, 1938; Milwaukee *Leader*, July 1, 1938. Several letters in the papers of Philip F. La Follette expressed dismay over the accident. (Unless indicated, they are to La Follette.) See especially John Gamper, March 10, 1938; W. H. Babcock, March 11, 1938; Joseph A. Padway to Thomas M. Duncan, March 12, 1938; Arthur Johnson, March 14, 1938; A. K. Bentley, March 15, 1938; Ella Vance et al., March, 1938; John Gamper to Charles M. Dow, April 1, 1938; George J. Reid, June 4, 1938; and Henry A. Gunderson, November 29, 1938.

the governor found himself in the unaccustomed position of having to defend the Progressive record, and defense is seldom as stirring or as inspiring as attack.[52]

"The thing that I have been most worried about is the silence," wrote Roy Empey, chairman of the Brown County Progressive Campaign Committee, to Gordon Sinykin on the eve of the election. "It doesn't seem as though you can get any political arguments started in the shops, pool [halls], stores or any meeting places. Everybody seems to be so quiet." The calm proved to be an ominous indication that the Progressives' worst fears were justified. On November 8, citizens went to the polls and voted overwhelmingly to return the Republicans to power. The Progressives lost every state office, the seat in the United States Senate for which Amlie and Ekern had fought, and five of the seven seats they had occupied in the House of Representatives. They fared no better in the Wisconsin legislature, where their representation declined from sixteen to eleven seats in the Senate, and from forty-eight to thirty-two in the Assembly.[53]

In the key race for governor, La Follette lost to Heil by more than 190,000 votes out of 981,560 votes cast. The Republican candidate's winning percentage was 55.4 per cent of the total, while La Follette received but 36 per cent. The remainder went to Harry Bolens, who had run only to keep the Democratic party on the ballot at the next election. La Follette fared worst in the eastern counties that had a heavy concentration of voters with German ancestry. In German Lutheran townships, he won only 37.4 per cent of his 1936 vote, and in German Catholic townships he fared little better in retaining 37.5 per cent. He improved his position in predominantly German towns and cities, but, facing an opposition united behind Heil, he still fell far short of the tally necessary for victory. He won 83.5 per cent of his 1936 vote in Manitowoc, 72.5 per cent in Sheboygan, 68.7 per cent in Oshkosh, 67.4 per cent in Wausau, and only 48.8 per cent in Appleton.[54]

[52] "Comments by Glenn D. Roberts on Phil's Opening Speech at Baraboo," September 26, 1938, in the Philip F. La Follette Papers; Miller, *Governor Philip F. La Follette*, 156.

[53] Roy Empey to Gordon Sinykin, November 7, 1938, in the Philip F. La Follette Papers. Also to be found in these papers are several election postmortems. See especially the following sent to La Follette: Sverre Braathen, November 9, 1938; Ernest Gruening, November 9, 1938; G. C. Sellery, November 10, 1938; Harold Winterhalter, November 13, 1938; Walter D. Corrigan, Sr., November 19, 1938; and Lloyd K. Garrison, December 10, 1938.

[54] Figures relating to the 1936 and 1938 elections are derived from the *Wisconsin Blue*

Even the Progressives' most faithful supporters, the voters of Norwegian ancestry, could not compensate for La Follette's loss of nearly every German voting unit. Stoughton, which had given him 1,411 votes to 737 for Alexander Wiley in 1936, helped elect Heil by casting 828 ballots for him as opposed to 726 for La Follette. While the governor managed to win 54.3 per cent of the vote in thirty-five Norwegian townships of rural Wisconsin, he lost Milwaukee County to Heil by the lopsided margin of 87,916 to 118,617. In sum, the success of Republicans and conservative Democrats in forming an effective coalition, the disputes within the Progressive party and anxieties over the meaning of La Follette's NPA, the residue of ill-will resulting from the dismissal of Glenn Frank, and the shock of Tom Duncan's tragic accident all served to assure Julius Heil of victory. After a decade of intense activity, through which Phil La Follette had become the dominant influence in the politics of Wisconsin, the brilliant and imaginative young governor left public office forever.

* * *

While critics of La Follette and the National Progressives were agonizing over similarities between the NPA and the Nazis, the voting behavior of Wisconsin's ethnic groups in 1938 raised questions about the strength of German identity in Wisconsin. If the state's ethnic Germans remained as sympathetic to the Fatherland as the generation of their parents had been in 1914, it would seem, La Follette should have won far more support than he was able to muster. Had the Wisconsin Germans suppressed their ethnic loyalties after the persecutions of World War I? Did they believe that La Follette's appeal might rekindle anti-German sentiment in the state? And as events moved the world towards an even more terrible conflict, was there anything that either the La Follettes or the state's Germans could do to prevent it?

A God-fearing people, the Wisconsin Germans were much influenced by the theological underpinnings of the churches to which most of them belonged. The German Lutherans thought of salvation as the ultimate goal of their temporal existence on earth. They believed that they could assure their salvation not through good

Book, 1970, pp. 683. The identification and analysis of German and Norwegian voting units relies on the work of David L. Brye, published in his *Wisconsin Voting Patterns*, 57–63, 101–114, 119–123, 400–425.

works, but through the faith that came to them as the gift of God. While individual Lutherans voted and in other ways took part in political activities, the predominantly German synods of Wisconsin and Missouri, as Lutheran church bodies, remained staunchly committed to the separation of church and state. Yet leaders of the German synods often took political positions when organized parties and ideologies posed a threat to their faith. Throughout the Depression thirties, as Roosevelt demonstrated his willingness to experiment with radical solutions for economic problems, Lutheran leaders sought to identify the theoretical basis for policy. Many of them became deeply troubled by the evidences of a Marxian influence in the social thought of the thirties, and they worried about hostility to religious faith far more than they worried about Hitler's persecution of Jews. Indeed, a significant number of German Lutherans were capable of regarding Hitler as God's avenging angel visiting judgment on a people who had rejected the Messiah.[55]

The Lutherans of the Missouri and Wisconsin synods were not virulently anti-Semitic, but they were nevertheless reluctant to condemn the persecution of Jews in Germany. "The Lutheran church, historically considered, has never been a persecuting church and hence not a Jew-baiting church," noted an editorial in the Wisconsin Synod's *Northwestern Lutheran* shortly after Hitler became chancellor. Yet a few weeks later the same writer observed that "we need not hope that a tribe which had rejected repeatedly, consistently, and it would appear finally, the Messiah . . . can ever escape the punishment of a longsuffering Lord and Savior." Exposed to such pronouncements, some German Lutherans tended to regard Jews and Communists as allies of the Antichrist. Walter A. Maier, editor of the Missouri Synod's youth magazine and radio voice of the nationally broadcast Lutheran Hour, argued that it was "Jewish agitators" who had led in the "sovietizing of Russia" and in the defilement of German society after the Great War. By 1939 he was warning that the same "sinister forces" were seeking "to embroil the United States in the forthcoming European war."[56]

[55] Dean Wayne Kohlhoff, "Missouri Synod Lutherans and the Image of Germany, 1914–1945" (doctoral dissertation, University of Chicago, 1973), 26, 193–194, 217, 235–237, 246–247, 258–259; *Northwestern Lutheran*, June 20, 1937, p. 195; Bounduel *Times*, April 8, 1937.

[56] *Northwestern Lutheran*, April 23, 1933, p. 131, and July 16, 1933, p. 229; John G. Mager, "Nazis, Jews, and the War: What the *Lutheran Witness* Said, 1934–1945," in the *American Lutheran*, 47 (November, 1964), 10–13; Kohlhoff, "Missouri Synod Lutherans

The Catholic church in Wisconsin was more sympathetic to the plight of people suffering from Nazi harassment than were leaders of the German Lutheran churches. Yet in considering possible courses of action, Catholic leaders also demonstrated a parochial view of world problems. Early in 1939, Archbishop Samuel A. Stritch penned a circular letter to all pastors of the Milwaukee archdiocese. "Today we are shocked and made indignant by inhuman persecution of those who were once the chosen people of God," he wrote, "the people of the prophets and the patriarchs, the torchbearers of God through long centuries, whose blood flowed through the Sacred Veins of the Master." Stritch pleaded that Catholics do more than oppose the Nazi persecutions. He urged Catholics to pray that Jews might come to see Christ as the Messiah and so enter His Kingdom. He also urged that Americans provide assistance to German Catholics seeking refuge in other lands, but he warned that "with wide unemployment in our midst, we cannot think of offering hospitality to a large number of these exiles." During the summer of 1939, as the Wehrmacht prepared to invade Poland, and as "disturbers of the peace of the world and the propagandists of ungodly systems and philosophies [became] extraordinarily active," the archbishop of Milwaukee asked his pastors "with more than wonted fervor to storm Heaven with prayers."[57]

The ambivalence, hesitancy, or—some would say—ineffectiveness of Wisconsin churches in contributing to efforts directed towards the prevention of another world war were indicative of a widely held belief that war was inevitable and that the best course for the United States was to steer clear of involvement in it. Only a few Wisconsin observers of international affairs were prepared to argue that isolationism represented an ineffective response to the challenge of fascism. Speaking at a workers' rally against war and fascism in Milwaukee in 1935, Meta Berger, the widow of Victor Berger, pointed out that "we are not interested in the imperialism of Europe. We are interested in humanity." Yet she viewed the drift of

and the Image of Germany," 196–197, 210–211, 228–229, 232–233; E. Clifford Nelson, "The New Shape of Lutheranism," in E. Clifford Nelson, ed., *The Lutherans in North America* (Philadelphia, 1975), 472–473.

[57] Archbishop Samuel A. Stritch to all pastors in the Archdiocese of Milwaukee, January 12, 1939; Stritch to all pastors and laity in the archdiocese, January 31, 1939; and (in file 206) Stritch to all archdiocesan priests, July 5, 1939, all in the archdiocesan archives, St. Francis Seminary.

events with realistic comprehension of human behavior. If the European nations became involved in war, she observed, "America has no escape."[58]

Better than most other opponents of America's taking part in another global conflict, Meta Berger knew whereof she spoke. Nevertheless, her words had little effect. Prevailing opinion in Wisconsin on the eve of Hitler's invasion of Poland was that the United States should cut its economic ties with European nations and work to improve the welfare and the security of the American people in their own hemisphere. Observing early in 1937 that the children of England and France were receiving instruction in the use of gas masks, an editorial writer for the Rhinelander *New North* noted with relief that "we still have almost unlimited room in which to grow and no near neighbors who want to take our land away from us." Praising the contributions of Senator Gerald P. Nye's committee to investigate the munitions industry, the *Waupaca County Post* cited the committee's findings in order to emphasize the value of avoiding war. The money expended in waging World War I, noted the *Post*, would have bought every family in Russia, Italy, France, Belgium, England, Australia, and the United States a $2,500 home, on five acres of land, with $1,000 worth of furniture thrown in. And there would have been enough remaining to pay perpetual salaries to 125,000 teachers and 125,000 nurses, as well as to endow 10,000 libraries and 10,000 hospitals. To a people still suffering economic privation after nearly a decade of depression, the Nye committee's findings were a persuasive revelation of the absurd wastefulness of war.[59]

Even before Phil and Isen La Follette began their tour of Europe in 1938, the people of Wisconsin were thoroughly indoctrinated in the message that Phil was to reiterate upon his return. They believed

[58] Kohlhoff, "Missouri Synod Lutherans and the Image of Germany," 263, 267–268; Thomas R. Nevin, "The Protestant Ministry of Wisconsin and the Crisis of Intervention, 1939–1941" (master's thesis, University of Wisconsin, 1968), 30–39; Milwaukee *Leader*, November 11, 1935. The 1935 rally was not the first demonstration against fascism in which Meta Berger played a role. See the *Wisconsin Jewish Chronicle*, March 31, 1933, copy in the Nathan Sand Papers, Wisconsin Jewish Archives.

[59] Rhinelander *New North*, February 11, 1937; *Waupaca County Post* (Waupaca), December 31, 1936. For other expressions of isolationist sentiment in Wisconsin, see: *Waupaca County Post* (Waupaca), October 3, 1935, August 26, 1937, September 7, 1939; *Pierce County Herald* (Ellsworth), January 23, 1936, and October 5, 1939; and the minute book for July 23, 1935–November 9, 1937, pp. 57–58, in the Federated Trades Council Papers, Green Bay Area Research Center.

profoundly that men and women could indeed have work *and* be free. Achieving that dual objective simply required investment of the nation's capital and resources in the constructive enterprises of peace rather than in the destructive activities of war.

It was to assist in achieving full employment in a society at peace that Phil La Follette joined other antiwar Progressives in supporting efforts of the America First Committee. Although Phil never formally joined the organization, created to assist in keeping America out of war, he certainly sympathized with its principal objective. In the rhetoric of the Wisconsin Progressives and in the lessons the La Follettes derived from their political battles over the years, Phil could find ample justification for the basic contention of America First: that the vast investment required to defeat fascism abroad could better be used to promote peaceful enterprise at home. To that contention Phil added the further assurance that peaceful enterprise would turn out to be the surest and most effective means of defeating fascism in the long run.[60]

The problem confronting the La Follettes, the antiwar Progressives, the America First Committee, and other opponents of war was that they could not verify the hypothesis that governed their actions: that withholding support from anti-fascists would in the long run prove the most effective way to defeat the Axis powers. Committed to the hope of avoiding another great war, a hope that nearly all Americans shared, the isolationists seemed absurdly unrealistic as hostilities began. After Hitler launched his blitzkrieg against Poland on September 1, 1939, and after the defeat of France in June, 1940, interventionists could make a much more convincing case for the argument that only with American assistance could the brave but outmanned and inadequately armed British people preserve Western civilization from fascist destruction. As the Wehrmacht conquered country after country, the interventionists and the supporters of aid to Great Britain began winning the moral argument for the American mind.[61]

[60] "Should the Arms Embargo Be Lifted?" in *Town Meeting*, 5 (October 16, 1939), 11, 14–17. For Phil La Follette's association with the America First Committee, see the following in the Philip F. La Follette Papers: R. Douglas Stuart, Jr., to La Follette, July 30, August 5, 1940; La Follette to Clarence A. Dykstra, August 2, 1940; and La Follette to Chester Bowles, August 16, 24, 1940.

[61] Wayne S. Cole has examined isolationist sentiment in four books: *America First: The Battle Against Intervention, 1940–1941* (Madison, 1953); *Senator Gerald P. Nye and American Foreign Relations* (Minneapolis, 1962; reprinted, Westport, Connecticut, 1980);

For several months after Phil La Follette left office, he spoke with conviction in asserting that Americans could have work and be free. Later, in a radio address he delivered over the Mutual Broadcasting network a month after World War II began, he seemed less confident. Reminding his listeners of the "pitiless campaign of abuse" that had raged around his father twenty-two years earlier, Phil recalled that the senator's name had been made "a word of hatred"; in a frenzy of patriotism the senator's critics had burned him in effigy. Yet Old Bob always knew that in voting against war he had voted for "the best interests of America." As Phil would have it, Old Bob's sons were now also working in the nation's best interest. Following his father's example, he warned that "we must not fool ourselves into thinking that we can help fight dictators in Europe and still stay out of war." Furthermore, like his father before him, he expressed deep concern about what war might mean for the American nation. "Make no mistake," he cautioned. "The moment we embark on the road to war, we inevitably take on the trappings of dictatorship."

Phil La Follette's prophetic pronouncements were not the quackish exaggerations of a political mountebank. The United States did become involved in the war as a belligerent, and military necessity did become a justification for taking on some of the marks of dictatorship. The principal reason for the La Follette brothers' opposition to American involvement in another war, however, was their conviction that it would produce an economic calamity the like of which America had never known. "With the enormous debt the world now carries and with the awful increase in the destructiveness of war today," Phil asserted, "you can write it down as a foregone conclusion, that if this is a prolonged war, it will end in the complete collapse of the economic and political systems of every nation which participates in it."[62]

Charles A. Lindbergh and the Battle Against American Intervention in World War II (New York, 1974); and *Roosevelt and the Isolationists, 1932–45* (Lincoln, Nebraska, 1983). Other valuable studies in the vast literature on the subject include: Warren I. Cohen, *The American Revisionists: The Lessons of Intervention in World War I* (Chicago, 1967); Robert A. Divine, *The Illusion of Neutrality* (Chicago, 1962); Manfred Jonas, *Isolationism in America, 1935–1941* (Ithaca, 1966); Warren F. Kimball, *The Most Unsordid Act: Lend-Lease, 1938–1941* (Baltimore, 1969); and John E. Wiltz, *In Search of Peace: The Senate Munitions Inquiry, 1934–1936* (Baton Rouge, 1963).

[62] In the Philip F. La Follette Papers, see: La Follette, "Radio Speech over Mutual Broadcasting Stations" (typewritten), October 3, 1939; Chester Bowles to La Follette, October 4, 1939; and Robert M. La Follette, Jr., "Pending Neutrality Legislation,"

This gloomy forecast did not take into account important differences between the two world wars. Had the second conflict ended as did the first, Phil's dire predictions might have come to pass. Again, however, he was drawing upon his father's wisdom; his thoughts were far removed from principles that were to become the basis for economic policy in the postwar period. Old Bob knew, Phil remarked, "that nations could not destroy millions of productive human beings and billions and billions of dollars of wealth without paying the inevitable price in hard times, poverty and depression." Like many of their contemporaries, the La Follette brothers could not understand in 1939 what the real economic consequences of war would be. With perceptions limited by their own nurture and experience, they were unable to foresee that preparation for war and rebuilding after the war were to provide a stimulus to the American economy. They could not have predicted that, during the war itself and then during the postwar years, the nation's economic performance would exceed the hopes of the most sanguine of Americans.[63]

Before Phil himself went off to war, he witnessed an economic surge in Wisconsin that made his own vision of prosperity seem pallid by comparison. By 1942, the state's defense program had increased the number of jobs for Wisconsin workers to 278,000, almost twice the number available during 1932 at the depth of the Depression, and a gain of 50,000 over the number available in 1940. From 1940 to 1941, average annual payrolls in Wisconsin increased 41 per cent, and in 1941 Wisconsin workers earned more than in any previous year in the state's history. Wisconsin farmers achieved equivalent gains as wartime needs increased demand for dairy products and vegetables, and as Wisconsin became a key state in the "Food for Defense" program. In 1941, Wisconsin produced more than half the cheese, a third of the evaporated milk, and a fourth of the dry milk produced in the United States. A third of the nation's total pea pack—or two cans of peas for every man, woman, and child in America—came from Wisconsin. During the eleven months before Pearl Harbor, Wisconsin poultrymen sold 1.8 billion eggs, enough to load the refrigerators cars of a freight train

---

clipping of radio address, October 4, 1939, from the *Congressional Record*, 76 Cong., 2 sess., 85, part 2, pp. 143–145.

[63] Philip F. La Follette, "Radio Speech over Mutual Broadcasting Stations" (typewritten), October 3, 1939, in the Philip F. La Follette Papers.

ninety-four miles long. "Wisconsin's mighty defense industry, so indispensable to victory, so necessary to peace, moves loyally on," rejoiced R. S. Kingsley, chairman of the Wisconsin Council of Defense, as the nation soberly confronted the task that lay ahead after December 7, 1941.[64]

Citizens of the state, certainly no better informed than the La Follettes, had also not foreseen the economic benefits that war might bring. Nor could they have guessed at the economic consequences of continued international involvement during the generations after the war had come to an end. Although the privation, joblessness, and suffering of the Depression thirties never returned, memories of the hard times lingered. Citizens of Wisconsin were often to become anxious over the way tensions of the years after 1945 might affect the good life they enjoyed in the state they cherished. Like the residents of other states, they rejected the suggestion that war, or the preparation for war, had become economically desirable. In their own way, they sometimes transformed Phil La Follette's confident assertion of 1939 into a question: Could they continue to have work *and* remain free?

For those who best understood Wisconsin and the remarkable diversity and resilience of its people during the difficult times between the two great wars of the twentieth century, the response was always a resounding affirmative.

[64] When war came, Phil accepted a captain's commission in the military police. He was eventually to serve nearly three years as an aide to General Douglas MacArthur. After Harry S Truman succeeded Roosevelt and the Second World War ended, La Follette (then a former colonel) supported MacArthur for President. He had discovered traits in the general, he later recalled, that "kept reminding me of characteristics of my father." See Philip F. La Follette, "MacArthur Has B-R-A-I-N-S," a review of John Gunther's *The Riddle of MacArthur*, in *The Freeman*, 1 (May 7, 1951), 506–507; La Follette, *Adventure in Politics*, 266–270, 274–275, 280; and Miller, *Governor Philip F. La Follette*, 173–176. See also R. S. Kingsley, "Wisconsin in the Defense Program," in the *Wisconsin Blue Book, 1942*, pp. 151–157.

EPILOGUE

The Land Remembers

ALDO LEOPOLD learned to hunt and fish as a boy growing up in Burlington, Iowa, during the last decade of one century and the first decade of another. An apt pupil, he early experienced a sense of wonder at the ways of nature that became the compelling interest of his life. A generation later, across the Mississippi River and to the north, Ben Logan spent his early years on a hilltop farm in Crawford County, Wisconsin, where glaciers had never moved in to level off the irregular terrain. Both men were to leave home, Leopold to study forestry at Yale and become a professor at the University of Wisconsin, and Logan to become a television producer and writer of screenplays. More than thirty years separated them in age, and their career trajectories never crossed, but they held in common a profound respect for the land from whence they came.[1]

Leopold emphasized two important ideas in writing of the "land ethic" that he hoped to make comprehensible to his students and compatriots. He argued, first, "that the individual is a member of a community of interdependent parts," and second, that "the land ethic simply enlarges the boundaries of the community to include soils, waters, plants, and animals, or collectively: the land." To Leopold, then, the land was not merely soil. When he thought of land, he thought of energy flowing through a circuit of soils, plants, and animals. In his view, food chains are simply channels for conducting energy upward; through death and decay energy returns to the soil. The circuit never closes, but is sustained "like a slowly augmented revolving fund of life."[2]

[1] John O. Stark, "Wisconsin Writers," *Wisconsin Blue Book, 1977*, pp. 95–185, provides useful information on nine writers who have lived in Wisconsin and whose works convey an impression of what it has meant to live there. See especially the sections on Aldo Leopold, 135–141, and Ben Logan, 179–182. A full biography, *Aldo Leopold: His Life and Work* (Madison, 1988), by Curt Meine, is gracefully written and provides commendable detail.

[2] Aldo Leopold, *A Sand County Almanac: And Sketches Here and There* (New York, 1949), 203–204, 216; Meine, *Aldo Leopold*, 501–504.

Leopold's sensitive essays won admirers among scholars in the developing study of ecology. When Ben Logan sat down to write his memoirs of the 1930's, he drew upon ideas that Leopold and other ecologists had enunciated. *The Land Remembers*, published in 1975, is a collection of reminiscences about rural southwestern Wisconsin during the years between the two world wars. Appropriately, the author uses a young teacher in a one-room schoolhouse he once attended to announce the theme of his book. "Voice full of emotion," he recalls, she read to him the words of an Indian addressing his people. With a sweeping gesture of his hands the Indian spoke: "We are a People, one tiny fragment. . . . What are we without the corn, the rabbit, the sun, the rain, and the deer? Know this, my People: The *all* does not belong to us. We belong to the *all*."[3]

The thought could lead in opposite directions. One might choose, as did the fascists of the 1930's, to see the most effective social order as one in which individual members sacrificed their own particular interests and served what authorities determined to be in the interest of the whole. Or one might choose, as did the followers of Aldo Leopold, to see the good society as one built on an understanding of the natural order. Such understanding leads not to the domination of one element over all the others, but to respect for the way every element functions in relationship to the others.

Leopold entitled his best-known work *A Sand County Almanac*, and he organized its contents according to the months of the year. Logan's memoir follows the four seasons from spring through winter. Both writers pointed to changes taking place in the environment over time, and yet the structure of their works also suggests the importance of biotic cycles. Like Leopold's allegory of the woodsman's tools, cited in the preface to this volume, the repetitive rhythms of nature may offer a way of coming to terms with the meaning of a segment of time.

Few periods in the history of the state, the nation, or the world have encompassed changes more profound than those of the years from 1914 to 1940. Yet the Wisconsin of 1940 would not have been completely unfamiliar to someone transported from the Wisconsin of 1914. The title of Logan's memoir conveys the idea that for all the changes that came with war, prosperity, and depression, winter will turn to spring, the sun will appear a little higher and a

[3] Ben Logan, *The Land Remembers* (New York, 1975), 4.

little longer each day until midsummer, and the seeds sown in fields and gardens will yield their harvest in the fall. At the close of the 1930's, despite traumatic experiences of war and depression, Wisconsin residents found assurances of a natural order. National needs had encouraged centralizing tendencies in politics and economics, and discoveries in science and technology had created the possibility of disrupting if not destroying the physical environment. Still, even at the conclusion of an agitated and disquieting quarter-century, the land remembered.

APPENDIX A

THE GOVERNORS OF WISCONSIN, 1914–1940

Name	*Birthplace*	*Party*	*Term in Office*	*Birth/ Death*
FRANCIS E. MCGOVERN	Wisconsin	Rep.	Jan. 2, 1911–Jan. 4, 1915	1866–1946
EMANUEL L. PHILIPP	Wisconsin	Rep.	Jan. 4, 1915–Jan. 3, 1921	1861–1925
JOHN J. BLAINE	Wisconsin	Rep.	Jan. 3, 1921–Jan. 3, 1927	1875–1934
FRED R. ZIMMERMAN	Wisconsin	Rep.	Jan. 3, 1927–Jan. 7, 1929	1880–1954
WALTER J. KOHLER, SR.	Wisconsin	Rep.	Jan. 7, 1929–Jan. 5, 1931	1875–1940
PHILIP F. LA FOLLETTE	Wisconsin	Rep.	Jan. 5, 1931–Jan. 2, 1933	1897–1965
ALBERT J. SCHMEDEMAN	Wisconsin	Dem.	Jan. 2, 1933–Jan. 7, 1935	1864–1946
PHILIP F. LA FOLLETTE	Wisconsin	Prog.	Jan. 7, 1935–Jan. 2, 1939	1897–1965
JULIUS P. HEIL	Germany	Rep.	Jan. 2, 1939–Jan. 4, 1943	1876–1949

APPENDIX B

UNDERSTANDING THE LA FOLLETTE ELECTIONS: METHODOLOGY

EMPLOYING statistical methods in historical research enables historians to convert cumbersome columns of data into a few manageable values that describe relationships among variables such as income, religion, ethnicity, and voting behavior. In reality, all the attributes of individuals and societies constitute interwoven matrices of complexly related variables, but as figures in census reports and the like, they are extracted and placed in tables of unrelated independent variables. With contingency tables, multiple regression, and other statistical methods, historians can partially recombine variable relationships that the enumerators separated. Having done that, they may be able to test the accuracy of their theories about past relationships among variables. In this study, PRE (Proportional Reduction of Error) procedures were employed to determine how votes for members of the La Follette family were influenced by ethnicity, religious affiliation, economic prosperity, and place of residence.

Prediction and prediction error are the bases of PRE statistics. In PRE, prediction is simply an estimate or guess of what value any single influence will have on a given variable. Prediction error is the degree or amount that the prediction varies from the actual value. The objective of PRE statistics is to introduce new variables which, in conjunction with the original variable, will reduce the amount of prediction error.

A fundamental measure of prediction error employed in this study is standard deviation. The first step in determining standard deviation is to figure a variable's mean by adding together the values of all the variable's cases ($X_1 + X_2 + X_3 \ldots X_n = \Sigma X$), and then dividing by the number of cases (N) in the variable. Thus the formula: $\frac{\Sigma X}{N} = \bar{X}$. Secondly, the mean of the variable is subtracted from each case to determine how much that case deviates from the mean. This deviation is the amount of error for each case ($X - \bar{X} = \text{error}$). Third, each deviation is squared: $(X - \bar{X})^2$. The squares are then added together, producing the sum of squares: $(X_1 - \bar{X})^2 + (X_2 - \bar{X})^2 + (X_3 - \bar{X})^2 \ldots (X_n - \bar{X})^2 = \Sigma(X - \bar{X})^2$. The sum of squares is then divided by the number of cases in the variable: $\frac{\Sigma(X - \bar{X})^2}{N}$. When the square root of this result is taken, we have the standard deviation (S) of the variable: $S = \sqrt{\frac{\Sigma(X - \bar{X})^2}{N}}$.

The standard deviation tells us how much on average the cases deviate from the mean. In PRE the objective is to reduce the deviation in the dependent variable by taking one or more independent variables into consideration.

To test the hypothesis that there was a strong relationship between the dependent variable (*e.g.*, per cent vote for Robert M. La Follette in 1916) and the independent variable (*e.g.*, per cent Norwegian + Swedish), two steps must be taken. First, using the election returns from all 71 counties, the standard deviation of the La Follette vote alone must be established. The S for the 1916 La Follette vote is 14.11. Second, a modified S must be calculated to take per cent Norwegian-Swedish into account. To accomplish this objective, the Norwegian-Swedish variable may be divided into four categories ranging from high to low in per cent Norwegian-Swedish, and each county may be placed in one of the four categories. The mean is taken for the La Follette vote in the counties placed in each of the four categories. Then four separate standard deviations are established, one for each category. These four S's may be averaged to produce a modified S, which for the 1916 La Follette vote, as influenced by the per cent Norwegian-Swedish, is 7.17. By taking an independent variable into account, then, we have reduced prediction error by 6.94 (14.11 − 7.17). In this form the statistic tells us little but that the error has been reduced. How does this result relate to similar examples? Results may be standardized by reducing all examples to a scale extending from zero to one. The scale represents the proportion of the error that has been reduced and is calculated by dividing the result by the standard deviation of the dependent variable. In this instance, $\frac{14.11 - 7.17}{14.11} = .49$. By taking the per cent Norwegian + Swedish into account, we have reduced by 49 per cent our original error in the 1916 vote for La Follette.

Should we wish to include a second independent variable in the interpretation of data, a simple form of cluster analysis is useful. The new independent variable, *e.g.* Per Farm Production, is divided into four categories as was the Norwegian-Swedish variable. Together the two independent variables form a contingency table with sixteen cells, each cell containing a cluster of counties (Figure 1). On this table, counties in the first cell rank high in per cent Norwegian-Swedish and high in Per Farm Production. Cell 16 contains the counties that rank low in both. The remaining cells represent gradation from one extreme to the other. Each county fits into one of the cells. Adams County, for example, was in the Hi–Med category with its Norwegian-Swedish population and in the Lo category in Per Farm Production. Adams County is therefore a part of the cluster in cell 14. In 1916, Adams County voted 67 per cent for La Follette.

The procedure for eliciting the amount by which per cent Norwegian-Swedish and Per Farm Production reduced the prediction error in the La Follette vote is the same as that described previously. Now, however, we have sixteen categories with sixteen separate standard deviations rather than four. In the case of Adams County in 1916, the amount of error is reduced by 31 per cent.

Regression analysis is similar in theory to the foregoing operations, but it

% Norwegian-Swedish (Hi → Lo); Per Farm Production (Hi → Lo)

	Hi	Hi–med	Lo–med	Lo
Hi	1	2	3	4
	5	6	7	8
	9	10	11	12
Lo	13	14	15	16

FIGURE 1

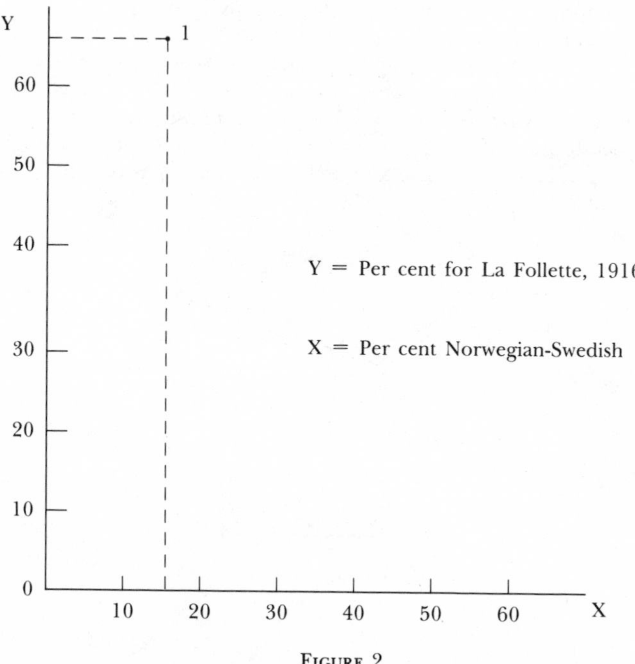

FIGURE 2

uses the regression line rather than the modified standard deviation to determine the amount of reduction of error. As with the procedure using modified *S*'s, regression can be most clearly portrayed graphically. In regression analysis, a two dimensional graph replaces the sixteen-celled contingency table (Figure 2). The data for X and Y are plotted on the graph. For Adams County in 1916, Y = .66, and X = .16. Thus Adams County is located at point 1. When all the counties have been so marked, the result is a scatter plot which depicts the relationship between X and Y (Figure 3). The regression line dissects the points on the graph, forming the mid-line on a plain of points, just as the standard deviation is the mid-point on a line of points. The distance, on average, that the points lie from the line is the estimate of error. In effect, it is the standard deviation from the regression line. The lower the average deviation from the line—that is, the closer the points cluster about the line—the stronger the relationship between the variables. When all points lie on the line, a perfect relationship exists. Conversely, a wide scattering of points indicates a weak relationship (Figure 4).

The most commonly used PRE statistic that employs the regression line is Pearson's *r*, which reveals how much of the original error in Y (*S* of the La Follette vote) is reduced by taking X (per cent Norwegian-Swedish) into account. When $r = .0$ there is no relationship. When $r = 1.0$ there is a perfect relationship.

Multiple regression is a procedure that reveals the amount of error in Y reduced by two or more independent variables ($X_1, X_2, X_3, \ldots X_n$). Multiple regression is important in measuring relationships when more than one independent variable influences Y, as is usually the case in voting behavior. Furthermore, this procedure helps reduce methodological difficulties encountered in studies employing county level data. The *b* coefficient is especially illustrative of relations between variables examined in multiple regression. The *b* is simply the slope of the regression line; it is the amount of change in Y for every unit change in X. To use a homely example, if Y is distance traveled,

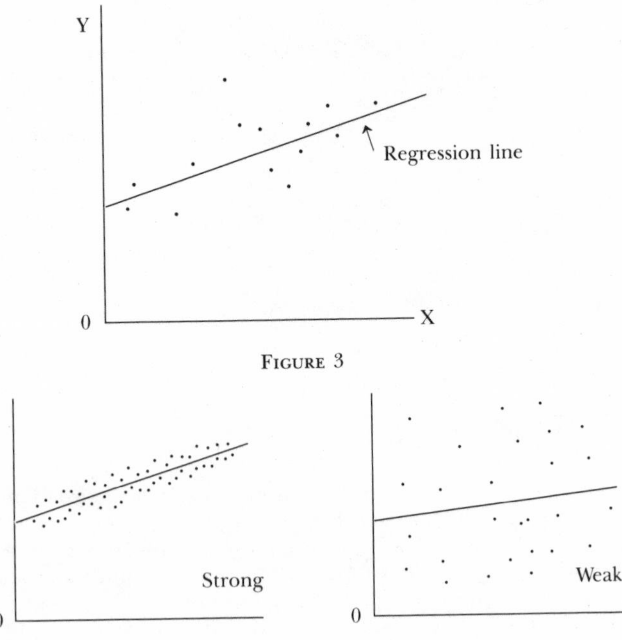

FIGURE 3

FIGURE 4

X is time traveled, and we are traveling at 50 miles an hour, a one-unit (one hour) change in X incurs a 50-mile change in Y. The more change a unit change in X incurs on Y, the stronger the relationship.

Although *b*'s provide a good indication of the impact of X upon Y, *b* is not standardized. It therefore varies in magnitude from example to example. To circumvent that problem, this analysis employed a form of multiple regression known as stepwise regression. Stepwise regression is useful in such studies because it is standardized and consistent. In stepwise regression the first step is to find Pearson's *r* for each of the independent variables in relation to Y. This determines at the bivariate level which X is most closely related to Y. That X is then used as X_1 in subsequent steps. In the second step, each remaining X is regressed on Y and X_1, and the X that most strongly correlated to Y and X_1 becomes X_2. This procedure continues until all X's are ranked in the order by which they came into the equation. Stepwise regression produces a multiple coefficient (*R*) for each variable. The multiple *R* may be interpreted in the same manner as a Pierson coefficient (*r*); it is the square root of the proportionate reduction of error. A large increase in R^2 suggests that a second or third variable may have considerable influence on the dependent variable.

In this study, stepwise regression proved useful in conjunction with the simple cluster analysis just discussed. First a stepwise regression of the major nationality groups in Wisconsin revealed what groups were most influential in each election. Then a second stepwise regression included the influential groups along with a measure of agricultural productivity (Per Farm Production), a measure of manufacturing (Per Capita Value Added by Manufacture), and a demographic variable (Per cent Rural, or the percentage of persons living in places of less than 2,500). In several elections, particularly from 1934 through 1940, Per cent Norwegian and Per cent Swedish appeared as the most influential ethnic variables, and either Per Farm Production or Value Added by Manufacture stepped second. Thus by using Per cent Norwegian-Swedish and either Per Farm Production or Value Added by Manufacture as the two variables in a cluster analysis contingency table, it was possible to depict the results of the stepwise regression. Furthermore, the PRE statistic taken from the standard deviations on the contingency tables, provided a check against the Pearson's *r* used in stepwise regression as well as the partial coefficient (*b*). Several procedures, in other words, served as a means of checking and balancing others.

* * *

The first table exhibited in this appendix provides a summary of stepwise regressions for all of the La Follette primary elections. The charts on subsequent pages include some of the contingency tables used to supplement, explain, or reinforce findings of the stepwise multiple regression. Comments on the multiple regression summary table, presented seriatim from the primary election of 1916 to that of 1940, may aid in the interpretation of data. Similar comments on each of the contingency tables accompany the table.

Explication of the Stepwise Multiple Regression Summary Tables

1916

The stepwise regression supports other findings suggesting that % Norwegian was the most important variable influencing the vote for Robert M. La Follette

TABLE B-1
STEPWISE MULTIPLE REGRESSION SUMMARY TABLE:
THE LA FOLLETTE VOTES, 1916–1940

Primary Elections

Independent variables	*Multiple R*	*Multiple R^2*	*Change in R*
1916 (Senatorial election)			
% Norwegian 1910	.53891	.29043	
Per Farm Production 1910	.61593	.37937	.08894
Value Added Manufacture 1910*	.62692	.39303	.01366
% Rural 1910	.62846	.39497	.00194
1922 (Senatorial election)			
Per Farm Production 1920	.38692	.14971	
% Italian 1920	.39863	.15890	.00919
Value Added Manufacture 1920	.40114	.16092	.00202
% Rural 1920	.40122	.16098	.00006
1925 (Senatorial election)			
% German 1930	.27202	.07400	
Value Added Manufacture 1920	.41048	.16850	.09450
Per Farm Production 1920	.46462	.21587	.04747
% Rural 1920	.46486	.21610	.00023
1928 (Senatorial election)			
Per Farm Production 1930	.45378	.25092	
% Rural 1930	.55923	.31274	.10682
% Norwegian 1930	.61669	.38031	.06757
Value Added Manufacture 1930	.61984	.38420	.00389
1930 (Gubernatorial election)			
% Rural 1930	.63141	.39868	
% Norwegian 1930	.67970	.46199	.06331
Value Added Manufacture 1930	.68741	.47253	.01054
Per Farm Production 1930	.68751	.47267	.00041
1932 (Gubernatorial election)			
% Norwegian 1930	.63498	.40320	
% Rural 1930	.76266	.58166	.17846
Value Added Manufacture 1930	.77961	.60779	.02613
Per Farm Production 1930	.78997	.62406	.01627
1934 (Senatorial election)			
% Norwegian 1930	.52629	.27698	
Value Added Manufacture 1930	.60252	.36303	.09605
Per Farm Production 1930	.60984	.37190	.00887
% Rural 1930	.61132	.37371	.00181
1934 (Gubernatorial election)			
% Norwegian 1930	.52874	.27956	
Value Added Manufacture 1930	.59875	.35805	.07849
Per Farm Production 1930	.60861	.37040	.01235
% Rural	.61100	.37332	.00292
1936 (Gubernatorial election)			
% Norwegian 1940	.53391	.28506	
Per Farm Production 1940	.59257	.35114	.06608
Value Added Manufacture 1940	.60147	.36177	.01063
% Rural 1940	.60263	.36317	.00140

continued

TABLE B-1
Continued

Independent variables	*Multiple R*	*Multiple R^2*	*Change in R*
1938 (Gubernatorial election)			
% Norwegian 1940	.59100	.34928	
Per Farm Production 1940	.71402	.50982	.16054
% Rural 1940	.71708	.51420	.00438
Value Added Manufacture 1940	.72047	.51907	.00487
1940 (Senatorial election)			
% Norwegian 1940	.51681	.26709	
Per Farm Production 1940	.59453	.35346	.08637
% Rural 1940	.60450	.36541	.01195
Value Added Manufacture 1940	.61269	.37538	.00997

*The variable, Value Added Manufacture, is actually the per capita value added.

in his campaign for a third term in the United States Senate. The regression also indicates that the second most important variable, Per Farm Production, was far less important, although perhaps still significant. The economic and demographic variables (Per Capita Value Added by Manufacture, and % Rural) were insignificant in affecting the election.

1922

The regression summary table again reflects other findings. Chapter 11 emphasizes a marked shift among German voters, many of whom opposed La Follette in 1916 but voted for him in 1922. Because Old Bob's support was so great among all groups in all sections of the state in 1922, however, no single ethnic variable appears to have had exceptional importance in determining the outcome of the election. Of all nationality groups, the Italian seems to have had more influence than any other, and it therefore appears in the table. Yet % Italian does not have a significant relationship to the La Follette vote, and neither do the other variables included here. After all, seven out of every ten voters in the Republican primary cast ballots for La Follette. When the support is so overwhelming, the impact of individual variables disappears.

1925

The regression analysis for 1925 reflects the continued insignificance of ethnicity—and for that matter of all other variables considered separately—in influencing the La Follette vote. Per cent German is the most important, but it has a very low correlation with the support for Young Bob. The other variables after Per Capita Value Added by Manufacture contribute little to the equation.

1928

Again, as in 1922, Per Farm Production heads the list of variables influencing the La Follette vote. Furthermore, it is growing in strength of correlation, increasing from .22 in 1925 to .25 in 1928. The rural variable has also become important, adding significantly to the equation from its second position in the stepwise regression. The summary table reflects the trend depicted on the maps, which show a movement of La Follette support away from urban and lakeshore areas to the rural western counties. Also noteworthy is the Norwegian variable, which appears to be regaining its influence.

1930

As in findings other than those in the stepwise regression, % Rural seems to be the most influential variable affecting the vote for Phil La Follette in 1930. In fact, having first appeared as of some significance in 1928, % Rural increased in importance two years later. After 1932 it declined in significance, and during the remainder of the decade % Rural had little effect on the La Follette vote. The emergence of % Rural to importance from 1928 to 1930 coincides with the general trend away from the ambivalence of the mid-twenties. In this table, the remaining variables appear insignificant in 1930, but it is worth noting that % Norwegian continued to increase in importance.

1932

The variable, % Norwegian, is the most important of those affecting the vote for Phil La Follette in a losing campaign for re-election as governor. In fact, the Norwegian variable had more influence in 1932 than did any variable in any other La Follette election in this study. In view of the continued significance of the rural variable through 1932, it is important to note that % Rural and % Norwegian are distinct variables, even though most Norwegians resided in rural areas. The % Rural variable includes much of the northeastern part of the state, which was but lightly Norwegian. A heavy La Follette vote in the Northeast contributed to the importance of % Rural in 1930. In 1932, as the primary election maps suggest, La Follette support began moving westward into the Norwegian/Rural counties, thus increasing the significance of % Norwegian and decreasing that of % Rural.

1934

The votes for Phil in the gubernatorial election and for Young Bob in the senatorial election were nearly identical. They reveal continuation of Norwegian support, although it was slightly less significant than in 1932. The demographic variable, % Rural, disappears completely as an explanation for voting behavior. The relationship between Per Capita Value Added by Manufacture and the La Follette vote is negative, as demonstrated in other findings, and as clearly shown in the contingency table for 1934.

1936–1940

Results of the regressions for these years suggest the establishment of a firm pattern for the later years of the Depression decade. The % Norwegian remains the most significant variable influencing the La Follette vote, with Per Farm Production a strong second. Per Capita Value Added by Manufacture and %

Rural exerted such slight influence on the La Follette vote during these years that they may be disregarded. The relationship between farm productivity and the La Follette vote is a negative one; that is, the more productive farmers were less likely to vote for a La Follette than were the less productive farmers. This finding is borne out in the contingency tables that follow.

Contingency Tables with Commentary

1916 PRIMARY VOTE FOR OLD BOB LA FOLLETTE

Production per farm ↓ / % Norwegian-Swedish →	HI			LO
HI	% La Follette (3 counties) 60.52	% La Follette (3 counties) 45.38	% La Follette (5 counties) 43.96	% La Follette (7 counties) 36.20
	% La Follette (6 counties) 22.40	% La Follette (2 counties) 43.87	% La Follette (2 counties) 36.57	% La Follette (8 counties) 41.87
	% La Follette (4 counties) 60.57	% La Follette (6 counties) 50.04	% La Follette (6 counties) 52.98	% La Follette (2 counties) 43.04
LO	% La Follette (5 counties) 65.83	% La Follette (7 counties) 52.38	% La Follette (5 counties) 53.21	% La Follette *

Standard deviation of the 1916 vote = 14.122
Modified standard deviation = 9.75
Proportionate reduction of error = .31

The table reinforces other findings concerning the importance of the Norwegian vote and farm productivity in the election. The reduction of error of .31 is one of the highest in the study.

1922 Primary Vote for Old Bob La Follette

% Norwegian-Swedish (columns HI → LO); Production per farm (rows HI → LO)

Production per farm	HI			LO
HI	% La Follette (1 county) 71.19	% La Follette (6 counties) 67.29	% La Follette (4 counties) 58.59	% La Follette (6 counties) 72.39
	% La Follette (5 counties) 73.23	% La Follette (4 counties) 67.72	% La Follette (2 counties) 66.29	% La Follette (7 counties) 71.47
	% La Follette (4 counties) 72.92	% La Follette (3 counties) 70.88	% La Follette (7 counties) 74.85	% La Follette (4 counties) 51.54
LO	% La Follette (7 counties) 71.49	% La Follette (7 counties) 72.21	% La Follette (4 counties) 70.13	% La Follette *

Standard deviation of the 1922 vote = 7.66
Modified standard deviation = 6.66
Proportionate reduction of error = .15

Neither farm production nor % Norwegian-Swedish indicate much variation here. All sixteen cells are highly pro-La Follette. Thus the two independent variables are of little importance as determinants of the vote. This does not mean that fewer Swedes, Norwegians and low-producing farmers voted for La Follette. His support was, in fact, so overwhelming that these groups do not appear to have exerted any special influence.

1925 PRIMARY VOTE FOR YOUNG BOB LA FOLLETTE

Production per farm ↓ / % Norwegian-Swedish →	HI			LO
HI	% La Follette (1 county) 61.95	% La Follette (6 counties) 46.67	% La Follette (4 counties) 39.02	% La Follette (6 counties) 62.73
	% La Follette (5 counties) 52.82	% La Follette (4 counties) 47.77	% La Follette (2 counties) 54.76	% La Follette (7 counties) 60.17
	% La Follette (4 counties) 57.64	% La Follette (3 counties) 61.96	% La Follette (7 counties) 60.71	% La Follette (4 counties) 57.78
LO	% La Follette (7 counties) 52.78	% La Follette (7 counties) 58.78	% La Follette (4 counties) 45.85	% La Follette *

Standard deviation of the 1925 vote = 12.57
Modified standard deviation = 11.33
Proportionate reduction of error = .10

The vote for Young Bob shows no real pattern in this table. For the second election in a row, neither ethnic nor economic variables seem to have affected the vote. The demographic variable, % Rural, was also of little importance. The reduction of error of only .10 reflects the political ambivalence of the mid-twenties.

1928 PRIMARY VOTE FOR YOUNG BOB LA FOLLETTE

Production per farm ↓ / % Norwegian-Swedish →	HI			LO
HI	% La Follette (2 counties) 64.66	% La Follette (4 counties) 55.55	% La Follette (5 counties) 55.93	% La Follette (6 counties) 60.84
	% La Follette *	% La Follette (4 counties) 66.06	% La Follette (2 counties) 50.94	% La Follette (9 counties) 60.95
	% La Follette (9 counties) 67.29	% La Follette (2 counties) 61.95	% La Follette (9 counties) 65.04	% La Follette *
LO	% La Follette (8 counties) 70.04	% La Follette (7 counties) 65.60	% La Follette (2 counties) 69.59	% La Follette (2 counties) 57.82

Standard deviation of the 1928 vote = 7.41
Modified standard deviation = 5.48
Proportionate reduction of error = .26

The reduction of error of .26 reflects the return to some significance of the variables influencing the La Follette vote. The table, however, does not depict the increase well unless one examines the bottom row from left to right, which shows a fairly steady drop of 13 percentage points for La Follette. Low-producing Norwegian-Swedish farmers were also more inclined to vote for La Follette than were the more prosperous farmers.

1930 Primary Vote for Phil La Follette

% Rural ↓ / % Norwegian-Swedish →	HI			LO
HI	% La Follette (9 counties) 66.65	% La Follette (5 counties) 67.52	% La Follette (4 counties) 65.25	% La Follette (3 counties) 63.17
	% La Follette (6 counties) 67.01	% La Follette (4 counties) 62.77	% La Follette (4 counties) 63.70	% La Follette (2 counties) 57.10
	% La Follette *	% La Follette (4 counties) 59.50	% La Follette (8 counties) 58.60	% La Follette (4 counties) 60.57
LO	% La Follette (3 counties) 58.28	% La Follette (4 counties) 58.85	% La Follette (4 counties) 53.52	% La Follette (7 counties) 50.54

Standard deviation of the 1930 vote = 8.60
Modified standard deviation = 6.67
Proportionate reduction of error = .22

This table demonstrates the relative importance of rural residence as compared to % Norwegian-Swedish. In fact, % Norwegian-Swedish is less significant in 1930 than in 1928. This is demonstrated in the drop in the reduction of error figure from .26 in 1928 to .22 in 1930. At the same time, the more rural the county, the more likely it was to vote for La Follette.

1932 PRIMARY VOTE FOR PHIL LA FOLLETTE

% Rural ↓ / % Norwegian-Swedish →	HI			LO
HI	% La Follette (9 counties) 57.56 % FDR 60.70	% La Follette (5 counties) 46.82 % FDR 62.23	% La Follette (4 counties) 47.83 % FDR 67.58	% La Follette (3 counties) 32.19 % FDR 76.54
	% La Follette (6 counties) 55.54 % FDR 62.40	% La Follette (4 counties) 45.14 % FDR 60.69	% La Follette (4 counties) 49.85 % FDR 64.29	% La Follette (2 counties) 35.18 % FDR 70.77
	% La Follette *	% La Follette (4 counties) 42.92 % FDR 59.37	% La Follette (8 counties) 37.77 % FDR 69.50	% La Follette (4 counties) 33.05 % FDR 65.03
LO	% La Follette (3 counties) 45.56 % FDR 52.24	% La Follette (4 counties) 42.30 % FDR 64.48	% La Follette (8 counties) 27.59 % FDR 68.24	% La Follette (4 counties) 27.70 % FDR 66.57

Standard deviation of the 1932 vote = 12.76
Modified standard deviation = 8.11
Proportionate reduction of error = .36

It is clear that % Norwegian-Swedish has regained its significance as the most important variable. The Norwegian-Swedish side of the table shows a change of 25% from high to low, while the rural side changes only 12%. The changes are consistent, however, suggesting that both factors are important. The additional data for Roosevelt's vote in the general election indicates that Swedes and Norwegians tended to be restrained in their enthusiasm for him. The reduction of error figure of .36 further indicates the resurgence of Norwegian-Swedish support for La Follette.

1934 PRIMARY VOTE FOR YOUNG BOB LA FOLLETTE

Per capita value added by manufacture ↓ / % Norwegian-Swedish →	HI			LO
HI	% La Follette * 	% La Follette (3 counties) 29.66 % PFL 26.53	% La Follette (4 counties) 21.26 % PFL 18.79	% La Follette (8 counties) 29.40 % PFL 26.28
	% La Follette (6 counties) 34.62 % PFL 32.35	% La Follette (3 counties) 37.80 % PFL 34.91	% La Follette (4 counties) 24.03 % PFL 21.75	% La Follette (4 counties) 18.59 % PFL 16.9
	% La Follette (3 counties) 44.22 % PFL 42.54	% La Follette (8 counties) 36.17 % PFL 32.47	% La Follette (5 counties) 40.92 % PFL 37.31	% La Follette (3 counties) 37.66 % PFL 32.69
LO	% La Follette (8 counties) 50.38 % PFL 45.68	% La Follette (4 counties) 46.63 % PFL 41.35	% La Follette (4 counties) 41.82 % PFL 37.08	% La Follette (4 counties) 25.15 % PFL 22.92

Standard deviation of the 1932 Senate vote = 15.56
Modified standard deviation = 12.90
Proportionate reduction of error = .17

The votes for the two La Follette brothers were so similar in 1934 that they might be considered as one. Phil's percentage of the vote appears in each cell, but it was not considered in other computations. The relationship between manufacturing and the La Follette vote is negative, as demonstrated in other data, and as clearly shown in this table. The 1934 table also shows a stronger relationship between the La Follette vote and % Norwegian-Swedish than does the 1932 table.

1936 PRIMARY VOTE FOR PHIL LA FOLLETTE

Production per farm ↓ / % Norwegian-Swedish →	HI			LO
HI	% La Follette (1 county) 61.07	% La Follette (2 counties) 32.66	% La Follette (7 counties) 23.30	% La Follette (7 counties) 26.62
	% La Follette (4 counties) 49.41	% La Follette (6 counties) 38.41	% La Follette (2 counties) 45.07	% La Follette (7 counties) 26.62
	% La Follette (6 counties) 61.76	% La Follette (3 counties) 32.49	% La Follette (8 counties) 36.60	% La Follette (1 county) 24.71
LO	% La Follette (7 counties) 44.17	% La Follette (6 counties) 45.50	% La Follette (3 counties) 41.03	% La Follette (1 county) 40.87

Standard deviation of the 1936 vote = 19.19
Modified standard deviation = 15.41
Proportionate reduction of error = .20

The 1936 primary election established a pattern that was to hold firm through 1940. The remaining contingency tables may therefore be allowed to speak for themselves. The % Norwegian-Swedish and Per Farm Production variables remain important, while Per Capita Value Added by Manufacture and % Rural variables have lost their explanatory significance.

1938 Primary Vote for Phil La Follette

% Norwegian-Swedish (HI → LO); Production per farm (HI → LO)

Production per farm \ % Norwegian-Swedish	HI			LO
HI	% La Follette (1 county) 47.79	% La Follette (2 counties) 27.42	% La Follette (7 counties) 21.39	% La Follette (7 counties) 14.56
	% La Follette (4 counties) 39.91	% La Follette (6 counties) 26.07	% La Follette (2 counties) 28.53	% La Follette (7 counties) 19.93
	% La Follette (6 counties) 49.66	% La Follette (3 counties) 28.44	% La Follette (8 counties) 28.43	% La Follette (1 county) 38.78
LO	% La Follette (7 counties) 47.95	% La Follette (6 counties) 38.56	% La Follette (3 counties) 35.37	% La Follette (1 county) 7.00

Standard deviation of the 1938 vote = 17.03
Modified standard deviation = 12.10
Proportionate reduction of error = .29

1940 Primary Vote for Young Bob La Follette

Production per farm ↓ / % Norwegian-Swedish →	HI			LO
HI	% La Follette (1 county) 54.31	% La Follette (2 counties) 13.60	% La Follette (7 counties) 14.73	% La Follette (7 counties) 13.32
	% La Follette (4 counties) 29.88	% La Follette (6 counties) 22.83	% La Follette (2 counties) 10.87	% La Follette (7 counties) 14.13
	% La Follette (6 counties) 40.39	% La Follette (3 counties) 30.62	% La Follette (8 counties) 21.65	% La Follette (1 county) 34.33
LO	% La Follette (7 counties) 34.58	% La Follette (6 counties) 32.37	% La Follette (3 counties) 26.48	% La Follette (1 county) 3.23

Standard deviation of the 1940 vote = 16.77
Modified standard deviation = 13.24
Proportionate reduction of error = .21

ESSAY ON SOURCES

THE HISTORICAL PROFESSION is a dynamic one. Concerned with processes of change through time, historians are themselves influenced by changes that modify their perspectives. The discovery of new evidence may require revision of received wisdom, new methods of inquiry may alter modes of analysis, and the daily concerns of a changing world may stimulate interest in new areas of investigation. The dynamic nature of historical inquiry contributes to the excitement that professional historians derive from the work they do; at the same time, historical inquiry provides a constant warning against the assumption that investigation of various truths about the past leads inexorably to the discovery of an ultimate truth. While the labors of historians suggest the limitless possibilities of human endeavor, historical investigation leads finally to a refutation of finality. Bibliographical and historiographical essays may be helpful and instructive, but they can be neither definitive nor exhaustive because few historians can claim to have written the final word on any subject. Nevertheless, readers of this study of Wisconsin from 1914 to 1940 are entitled to direction towards the sources on which it rests, sources that may provide a starting point for further investigation.

Bibliographic Aids and Guides to Research

Because most of the materials cited in the footnotes of this volume are to be found in the collections of the State Historical Society of Wisconsin, the researcher may wish first to consult Clifford L. Lord and Carl Ubbelohde, *Clio's Servant: The State Historical Society of Wisconsin, 1846–1954* (Madison, 1967), a work that serves as a guide to the Society's traditions, goals, and operations. Located on the fourth floor of the building the Society occupies are two important areas for research: the Archives Reading Room, which provides facilities for users of both the manuscript collections and the archives of state and local governments, and the Visual and Sound Archives, containing the Society's iconographic collections. In the reading room the researcher will wish to consult the card catalog, which is organized by subject as well as by collection. Detailed inventories are extraordinarily valuable in locating materials within important collections. Archivists in the iconographic collections are helpful in directing researchers to appropriate materials, and a systematic catalog of photographs and other images facilitates research in the area.

Published guides to manuscript and archival holdings, available in libraries elsewhere as well as in the Society, include Alice E. Smith, ed., *Guide to the*

Manuscripts of the Wisconsin Historical Society (Madison, 1944); Josephine L. Harper and Sharon C. Smith, eds., *Guide to the Manuscripts of the State Historical Society of Wisconsin: Supplement Number One* (Madison, 1957); and Josephine L. Harper, ed., *Guide to the Manuscripts of the State Historical Society of Wisconsin: Supplement Number Two* (Madison, 1966). The most important published aids to research in archival materials and printed government documents are David J. Delgado, ed. and comp., *Guide to the Wisconsin State Archives* (Madison, 1966) and Marcia R. Nettesheim, ed., "Guide to Wisconsin State Agencies and Their Call Numbers" (2nd ed., Madison, 1984). The series entitled *Wisconsin Public Documents* contains the published reports of governors and state executive officers as well as reports of some state boards and agencies. For this volume of *The History of Wisconsin*, the most useful of state government documents was the biennial *Wisconsin Blue Book*, which by 1914 had come to include special articles as well as information for the guidance of legislators. Recent editions of the *Blue Book* contain cumulative lists of special articles appearing in 1919 and after. Other aids to finding materials in this source include *A Guide to the Wisconsin Blue Book, 1853–1962*, Legislative Reference Library, *Research Bulletin*, no. 141 (1963), and Northern Micrographics, *Wisconsin Blue Books and Indexes, 1953–1973* (La Crosse, 1975). For assistance in using materials located in Milwaukee, one should consult John A. Fleckner and Stanley Mallach, eds., *Guide to Historical Resources in Milwaukee Area Archives* (Milwaukee, 1976).

The number of citations to newspapers in the footnotes of this book attests to their value as sources of information on various facets of Wisconsin history. The standard reference is Donald E. Oehlerts, comp., *Guide to Wisconsin Newspapers, 1833–1957* (Madison, 1958), but the researcher would do well to consult the card catalog to the massive collection of newspapers available on microfilm in the State Historical Society.

Doctoral dissertations and master's theses also provide information of inestimable importance. For a bibliography of theses and dissertations related to Wisconsin subjects, see Robert C. Nesbit and William Fletcher Thompson, eds., *A Guide to Theses on Wisconsin Subjects*, comp. Roger E. Wyman (Madison, 1964), and Nesbit and Thompson, eds., *A Guide to Theses on Wisconsin Subjects: A Supplement*, comp. Jeanne Hunnicutt Chiswick (Madison, 1966). A more limited guide to theses is Byron Anderson, comp., *A Bibliography of Master's Theses and Doctoral Dissertations on Milwaukee Topics, 1911–1977* (Madison, 1981). For information on more recent dissertations, the researcher must cull titles either from "Recent Dissertations," regularly published in the *Journal of American History*, or from *Dissertation Abstracts International. A: The Humanities and Social Sciences* (Ann Arbor).

Keeping abreast of published scholarship is as demanding as keeping up with dissertations and theses. Book reviews in scholarly journals are important, but just as useful are guides to scholarly articles and other publications. Thrice yearly, the American Historical Association issues *Recently Published Articles*, a classified bibliography of current essays and scholarly articles. Each number of the *Journal of American History* contains a classified list of recent articles as an accompaniment to its list of recent dissertations. The "Documents and Bibliographies" section of the *American Historical Review* is especially helpful to scholars in search of bibliographical assistance. *Labor History* and *Agricultural History* regularly publish bibliographies of current scholarship in areas of interest to subscribers. The *Wisconsin Magazine of History*, which, since its inception in 1917, has published numerous articles used in this volume, has both annual and decennial indexes available for its first seventy volumes.

During the past decade the publication of topical bibliographies and bibliographical aids has become a thriving industry. An important general guide to available materials is Henry Putney Beers, *Bibliographies in American History, 1942–1978: A Guide to Materials for Research* (2 vols., Woodbridge, Connecticut, 1982).

Recently published bibliographies relating to politics and war include John D. Buenker and Nicholas C. Burckel, eds., *Progressive Reform: A Guide to Information Sources* (Detroit, 1980); Patrick K. Coleman and Charles R. Lamb, comps., *The Nonpartisan League, 1915–22: An Annotated Bibliography* (St. Paul, 1985); Robert U. Goehlert and John R. Sayre, *The United States Congress: A Bibliography* (New York, 1982); D. Stephen Rockwood et al., *American Third Parties Since the Civil War: An Annotated Bibliography* (New York, 1985); and David R. Woodward and Robert Franklin Maddox, *America and World War I: A Selected Annotated Bibliography of English-Language Sources* (New York, 1985).

Guides to research in business, labor, and economic history include William K. Hutchinson, ed., *American Economic History: A Guide to Information Sources* (Detroit, 1980); ABC-Clio Information Services, *Corporate America: A Historical Bibliography* (Santa Barbara, California, 1984); ABC-Clio Information Services, *The Great Depression: A Historical Bibliography* (Santa Barbara, California, 1984); ABC-Clio Information Services, *Labor in America: A Historical Bibliography* (Santa Barbara, California, 1985); and Maurice F. Neufeld, Daniel J. Leab, and Dorothy Swanson, *American Working Class History: A Representative Bibliography* (New York, 1983). For assistance in investigating technology and agriculture, the researcher should consult Stephen H. Cutcliffe, Judith A. Mistichelli, and Christine M. Roysdon, *Technology and Values in American Civilization: A Guide to Information Sources* (Detroit, 1980), and Margaret W. Rossiter, comp., *A List of References for the History of Agricultural Science in America* (Davis, California, 1980).

Bibliographies for ethnic and religious groups, race relations, welfare, and education provide information on a variety of studies in American social history. The researcher should consult the following for references on special subjects: Mark Beach, comp., *A Subject Bibliography of the History of American Higher Education* (Westport, Connecticut, 1984); Steven M. Benjamin, *The Wisconsin-Germans: A Working Bibliography* (Morgantown, West Virginia, 1979); Francesco Cordasco and David N. Alloway, *American Ethnic Groups, the European Heritage: A Bibliography of Doctoral Dissertations Completed at American Universities* (Metuchen, New Jersey, 1981); James P. Danky, ed., *Native American Periodicals and Newspapers, 1828–1982: Bibliography, Publishing Record, and Holdings*, comp. Maureen E. Hady (Westport, Connecticut, 1984); Lenwood G. Davis and Janet L. Sims-Wood, comps., *The Ku Klux Klan: A Bibliography* (Westport, Connecticut, 1984); John Tracy Ellis and Robert Trisco, *A Guide to American Catholic History* (2nd ed., Santa Barbara, California, 1982); Archibald Hanna, comp., *A Mirror for the Nation: An Annotated Bibliography of American Social Fiction, 1901–1950* (New York, 1985); Graham C. Kinloch, *Race and Ethnic Relations: An Annotated Bibliography* (New York, 1984); Francis Paul Prucha, *A Bibliographical Guide to the History of Indian-White Relations in the United States* (Chicago, 1977) and *A Bibliography of Works Published, 1975–1980* (Lincoln, Nebraska, 1982); Walter I. Trattner and W. Andrew Achenbaum, eds., *Social*

Welfare in America: An Annotated Bibliography (Westport, Connecticut, 1983); and Swedish-American Historical Society, *Guide to Swedish-American Archival and Manuscript Sources in the United States* (Chicago, 1983).

The interest in women's history has resulted in the publication of several important bibliographies and guides to research during the past decade. The most important aid to scholars is Andrea Hinding, Ames Sheldon Bower, and Clarke A. Chambers, eds., *Women's History Sources: A Guide to Archives and Manuscript Collections in the United States* (2 vols., New York, 1979). Other bibliographic aids include James P. Danky et al., *Women's History Resources at the State Historical Society of Wisconsin* (4th ed., Madison, 1982); James P. Danky, ed., *Women's Periodicals and Newspapers from the 18th Century to 1981: A Union List of the Holdings of Madison, Wisconsin, Libraries*, comp. Maureen E. Hady et al. (Boston, 1982); Barbara Haber, ed., *Women in America: A Guide to Books, 1963–1975* (Boston, 1978); Cynthia E. Harrison, ed., *Women in American History: A Bibliography* (Santa Barbara, California, 1979); Barbara J. Nelson, *American Women and Politics: A Selected Bibliography and Resource Guide* (New York, 1984); Virginia R. Terris, ed., *Woman in America: A Guide to Information Sources* (Detroit, 1980); Elizabeth and Donald F. Tingley, eds., *Women and Feminism in American History: A Guide to Information Sources* (Detroit, 1981); and Gerda Lerner, *Women Are History: A Bibliography in the History of American Women* (Madison, 1986).

Primary Sources and Contemporary Materials

Most of the manuscript and archival collections used in the preparation of this volume are housed in the State Historical Society of Wisconsin. Of major importance for the war period from 1914 to 1920 are the papers of Governor Emanuel L. Philipp in the manuscripts collection, along with the records of the Wisconsin Defense League, the Wisconsin State Council of Defense, and the Wisconsin Loyalty Legion in the Wisconsin State Archives. Because Richard T. Ely exerted a strong influence on the Loyalty Legion, his papers provide important information on the activities of Wisconsin patriots. Ely's colleague, Edward Alsworth Ross, took a lively interest in international affairs, and his papers offer unusual insights into the ferment in Russia as well as into American attitudes towards the revolution of 1917. The papers of Robert M. La Follette, Sr., for this period are housed in the manuscripts division of the Library of Congress along with the papers of other members of his family except his younger son, Philip.

The papers of Philip F. La Follette and the papers of John J. Blaine constitute the most important collections for gaining an insight into the politics and life of Wisconsin during the New Era. Other collections of importance for an understanding of Progressive politics include the papers of Herman L. Ekern, William T. Evjue, Harold Groves, Ada James, and Edwin E. Witte. All are in the custody of the State Historical Society. Outside Wisconsin, the papers of Oswald Garrison Villard at the Houghton Library, Harvard University, and the papers of Amos R. E. Pinchot and Mercer Johnston at the Library of Congress provide a wealth of information on activities of Progressives during the 1920's. The Howard Y. Williams Papers at the Minnesota Historical Society, St. Paul, are another rich source of information on the independent Progressives.

The papers of Philip F. La Follette constitute the key collection for understanding the decade of the Great Depression in Wisconsin. Other important manuscript sources in the Society include the Thomas R. Amlie Papers, the Wisconsin Cooperative Milk Pool Records, and the Wisconsin State Federation of Labor Papers. The activities of the struggling Democratic party of the state are best covered in the papers of Charles E. Broughton and William B. Rubin.

Other collections that proved useful in the writing of this volume, all in the possession of the State Historical Society, include the papers of the American Federation of Labor, Albert O. Barton, Joseph D. Beck, Albert D. Bolens, Emanuel F. Brunette, John R. Commons, John S. Donald, Matthew S. Dudgeon, Roy Empey, John J. Esch, David Clark Everest, E. H. Farrington, James A. Frear, Arnold Gilberts, Alexander Gumberg, Halbert L. Hoard, Paul O. Husting, the Island Woolen Company, Frank W. Kuehl, Irvine L. Lenroot, Orland S. Loomis, E. L. Luther, Charles R. McCarthy, George A. Nelson, Charles D. Rosa, Albert G. Schmedeman, Samuel Sigman, Algie M. Simons, James A. Stone, James Thompson, Julia Grace Wales, the Wisconsin Council of Agriculture, the Wisconsin League of Women Voters, and the Wisconsin Jewish Archives. Sources from World War I in the Wisconsin State Archives are located in the several series of the State Council of Defense and the War History Commission.

Major collections in the Library of Congress, though not used extensively for this volume, include the papers of Newton Baker, Ray Stannard Baker, William E. Borah, Gutzon Borglum, George Norris, William Allen White, and Woodrow Wilson.

Housed in the University of Wisconsin-Madison Archives are valuable materials relating to activities of the College of Agriculture during the 1920's, to the innovative Experimental College of Alexander Meiklejohn, and to the feud between Philip F. La Follette and Glenn Frank. See the General Subject Files, Administration, College of Agriculture; Student Records, Experimental College, College of Letters and Science; and Secretary of the Regents Papers. Two presidential libraries—the Herbert Hoover Library at West Branch, Iowa, and the Franklin D. Roosevelt Library at Hyde Park, New York—contain materials relating to Wisconsin during the years from 1914 to 1940. Relationships between the two La Follette brothers and the two presidents reveal much about the enormous differences between the New Era and the decade of the Great Depression.

Important published papers include Louis D. Brandeis, *Letters of Louis D. Brandeis. Volume V (1921–1941): Elder Statesman*, eds. Melvin I. Urofsky and David W. Levy (5 vols., Albany, 1971–1978); William Starr Myers, ed., *The State Papers and Other Public Writings of Herbert Hoover* (Garden City, New York, 1934); William Starr Myers and Walter H. Newton, *The Hoover Administration: A Documented Narrative* (New York, 1936); Ray Lyman Wilbur and Arthur Mastick Hyde, *The Hoover Policies* (New York, 1937); Samuel I. Rosenman, comp., *The Public Papers and Addresses of Franklin D. Roosevelt* (13 vols., New York, 1938–1950); Elliott Roosevelt, ed., *F.D.R.: His Personal Letters* (4 vols., New York, 1947–1950); Ray Stannard Baker and William E. Dodd, eds., *The Public Papers of Woodrow Wilson* (6 vols., New York, 1925–1927); and Arthur S. Link et al., eds., *The Papers of Woodrow Wilson* (Princeton, 1966–), a collection of monumental proportions, of which fifty-nine volumes have appeared.

Specific citations for material in government documents and in trade or professional journals are provided in the footnotes. The newspapers cited in the notes require further comment. The most important for the years 1914–1940 are those published in Madison (the state capital) and Milwaukee (the state's largest city). These include the Milwaukee *Journal*, the Milwaukee *Sentinel*, the Milwaukee *Leader*, the Madison *Wisconsin State Journal*, and the Madison *Capital Times*.

The newspapers of smaller towns and cities, while not nearly so complete in their coverage of major events, often carried stories of local importance. It is to them that one must turn for insights into the variety of opinion and interest that characterized Wisconsin during the years from 1914 to 1940. Among the newspapers consulted for this volume were the following: the Antigo *Daily Journal*, the Appleton *Post-Crescent*, the Ashland *Daily Press*, the Beloit *Daily News*, the Bloomington *Record*, the Bonduel *Times*, the Burlington *Standard-Democrat*, the Chilton *Times*, the Eau Claire *Leader*, the Green Bay *Press-Gazette*, the Iron River *Pioneer*, the Janesville *Gazette*, the Kewaunee *Enterprise*, the La Crosse *Tribune and Leader Press*, the Marshfield *News-Herald*, the Merrill *Daily Herald*, the Oshkosh *Daily Northwestern*, the *Pierce County Herald* (published in Ellsworth), the Racine *Journal-News*, the Racine *New Day*, the Racine *Times-Call*, the Rhinelander *New North*, the Shawano *Leader Advocate*, the Sheboygan *New Deal*, the Sheboygan *Press*, the Sheboygan *Times*, the Soldiers Grove *Kickapoo Scout*, the Stevens Point *Journal*, the Superior *Telegram*, the *Taylor County Star-News* (published in Medford), the Two Rivers *Reporter*, the Viroqua *Leader*, the Watertown *Daily Times*, the *Waupaca County Post* (published in Waupaca), and the Wausau *Daily Record-Herald*.

Nearly all the out-of-state newspapers cited in the footnotes are metropolitan papers that contain material of general interest on Wisconsin. They include the Baltimore *Sun*, the Chicago *Tribune*, the Minneapolis *Star*, the New York *American*, the New York *Herald Tribune*, the New York *Sun*, the New York *Times*, the New York *World*, the St. Louis *Post-Dispatch*, the St. Paul *Pioneer Press*, the Washington *Herald*, and the Washington *Post*.

Contemporary articles and editorials appearing in journals of the time are cited in footnotes, but several periodicals merit special mention. Most frequently consulted in the preparation of this volume were *La Follette's Weekly Magazine*, extending from 1909 to 1929, and its successor, *The Progressive*, edited by William T. Evjue from 1929 to 1940. Controlled by the La Follette family, the two weeklies serve as a major source of information on opinions, goals, and activities of the Wisconsin Progressives during the years from 1914 to 1940. A national periodical of considerable importance is *The Nation*. Its editor, Oswald Garrison Villard, was a close friend and admirer of the elder La Follette, and he took an avuncular interest in the careers of La Follette's two sons. *Common Sense*, a non-Marxist but radical periodical begun in the 1930's by Selden Rodman and Alfred Bingham, carried on a long political flirtation with Philip F. La Follette during the Depression Decade. In the long run, Bingham and Rodman's ideas about the proper course for Progressives to take proved to be of little influence, but their journal provides an important perspective on independent liberal activity during the years when Philip La Follette served as governor.

National magazines and periodicals that often carried articles and expressed opinions on political and economic issues are the *Congressional Digest*, *Harper's Magazine*, *The Independent*, *Literary Digest*, the *New Republic*, the *Review of Re-*

views, and *The Survey*. A journal published by the National Association of Manufacturers, *Nation's Business*, reflected the views of its sponsor. A surprisingly valuable source of information on business trends in both Wisconsin and the nation is *Business and Financial Comment*. Issued by the First Wisconsin National Bank of Milwaukee from 1920 to 1929, it was succeeded by *Bankshares Review*, published from 1930 through 1933. The Milwaukee Association of Commerce spread its message through *Civics and Commerce*. Various labor points of view found expression in the *American Federationist*, *Labor*, and *Labor Age*. Journals that had great influence among Wisconsin farmers include *Hoard's Dairyman*, *Equity News*, the *Wisconsin Agriculturist*, and the *Wisconsin Farmer*. The *Wisconsin Educational News Bulletin* and the *Wisconsin Journal of Education* exerted a similar influence among teachers.

General Works and Topical Surveys

The best one-volume histories of Wisconsin are Robert C. Nesbit, *Wisconsin: A History* (Madison, 1973; 2nd ed., 1989) and Richard N. Current, *Wisconsin: A Bicentennial History* (New York, 1977), which supersede William F. Raney, *Wisconsin: A Story of Progress* (New York, 1940). The volume in the New Deal's state guide series compiled by Workers of the Writers' Program of the Works Projects Administration in the State of Wisconsin, *Wisconsin: A Guide to the Badger State* (New York, 1941), offers a useful description of Wisconsin on the eve of World War II. Bayrd Still, *Milwaukee: The History of a City* (Madison, 1948; reprinted, 1965) remains the standard history of Wisconsin's metropolis. *Racine: Growth and Change in a Wisconsin County* (Racine, 1977), edited by Nicholas C. Burckel, contains essays by ten scholars and provides an excellent survey of the county's development. Carrie I. Cropley, *Kenosha: From Pioneer Village to Modern City, 1835–1935* (Kenosha, 1958), contains useful information, as does Howard R. Klueter and James J. Lorence, *Woodlot and Ballot Box: Marathon County in the Twentieth Century* (Wausau, 1977).

Studies that aid in gaining an understanding of Wisconsin's racial, ethnic, and religious groups include Nancy Oestreich Lurie, "Wisconsin: A Natural Laboratory for North American Indian Studies," in the *Wisconsin Magazine of History* (hereinafter *WMH*), 53 (Autumn, 1969), 3–20, reprinted in revised form as a booklet entitled *Wisconsin Indians* (Madison, 1980; reprinted, 1987); Joyce Erdman, *Handbook on Wisconsin Indians* (Madison, 1966); Emmett J. Scott, *Negro Migration During the War* (New York, 1920; reprinted, 1969); Joe William Trotter, Jr., *Black Milwaukee: The Making of an Industrial Proletariat, 1915–45* (Urbana, 1985); John Higham, *Strangers in the Land: Patterns of American Nativism, 1860–1925* (New Brunswick, New Jersey, 1955) and *Send These To Me: Immigrants in Urban America* (revised ed., Baltimore, 1984); Rowland T. Berthoff, *An Unsettled People: Social Order and Disorder in American History* (New York, 1971); Allan H. Spear, "Marcus Lee Hansen and the Historiography of Immigration," in *WMH*, 44 (Summer, 1961), 258–268; Karel D. Bicha, "The Czechs in Wisconsin History," in *WMH*, 53 (Spring, 1970), 194–203; John I. Kolehmainen and George W. Hill, *Haven in the Woods: The Story of the Finns in Wisconsin* (Madison, 1951; reprinted, 1965); John A. Hawgood, *The Tragedy of German-America: The Germans in the United States of America During the Nineteenth Century—and After* (New York, 1940); Gerd Korman, *Industrialization, Immigrants, and Americanizers: The View from Milwaukee, 1866–1921* (Madison,

1967); Theodore Saloutos, "The Greeks of Milwaukee," in *WMH*, 53 (Spring, 1970), 175–193; Theodore C. Blegen, *Norwegian Migration to America, 1825–1860* (Northfield, Minnesota, 1931) and *Norwegian Migration to America: The American Transition* (Northfield, Minnesota, 1940); Carlton C. Qualey, *Norwegian Settlement in the United States* (Northfield, Minnesota, 1938); Victor R. Greene, *For God and Country: The Rise of Polish and Lithuanian Ethnic Consciousness in America, 1860–1910* (Madison, 1975); Donald Pienkos, "Dimensions of Ethnicity: A Preliminary Report on the Milwaukee Polish American Population," in *Polish American Studies*, 30 (Spring, 1973), 5–19, and "Politics, Religion, and Change in Polish Milwaukee, 1900–1930," in *WMH*, 61 (Spring, 1978), 179–209; and Harald Runblom and Hans Norman, eds., *From Sweden to America: A History of the Migration* (Minneapolis, 1976).

Immigration patterns in Wisconsin were important in the formation of religious patterns. The essays in Randall M. Miller and Thomas D. Marzik, eds., *Immigrants and Religion in Urban America* (Philadelphia, 1977) explore that relationship in metropolitan areas. Three books on the Roman Catholic church in America offer insights into the viewpoints and associations of Catholics in Wisconsin. Joan Bland's *Hibernian Crusade: The Story of the Catholic Total Abstinence Union of America* (Washington, 1951) deals with Irish Catholic sensitivity to criticism and efforts to overcome it; Colman J. Barry's *The Catholic Church and German Americans* (Milwaukee, 1953) analyzes rivalries between German and Irish Catholics; and Philip Gleason's *The Conservative Reformers: German-American Catholics and the Social Order* (Notre Dame, 1968) elaborates on the role of the Central-Verein, an association of German Catholic societies in the United States. Myron A. Marty, *Lutherans and Roman Catholicism: The Changing Conflict, 1917–1963* (Notre Dame, 1968) considers the shifting pattern of relationship and antagonism between the two denominations.

The size of the German and Scandinavian immigration into Wisconsin, and the importance of the Lutheran tradition in the background of the immigrants, assured a powerful Lutheran influence in the state. The best one-volume study of the various Lutheran synods is E. Clifford Nelson, ed., *The Lutherans in North America* (Philadelphia, 1975). Excellent treatments of individual synods include: Dean Wayne Kohlhoff, "Missouri Synod Lutherans and the Image of Germany, 1914–1945" (doctoral dissertation, University of Chicago, 1973), microfilm copy in SHSW; Alan Graebner, *Uncertain Saints: The Laity in the Lutheran Church-Missouri Synod, 1900–1970* (Westport, Connecticut, 1975); George M. Stephenson, *The Religious Aspects of Swedish Immigration: A Study of Immigrant Churches* (Minneapolis, 1932); and E. Clifford Nelson and Eugene L. Fevold, *The Lutheran Church Among Norwegian-Americans: A History of the Evangelical Lutheran Church* (2 vols., Minneapolis, 1960).

That there was a connection between ethnicity and voting behavior in Wisconsin during the first half of the twentieth century is amply demonstrated in David L. Brye, *Wisconsin Voting Patterns in the Twentieth Century, 1900–1950* (New York, 1979), the single most important political analysis employed in the preparation of this volume. Concentrating on ethnic influences, Brye provides convincing evidence to support his thesis that ethnicity serves to explain the way Wisconsin voted during the years between the wars. Two other quantitative studies merit consideration. One, by Michael P. Rogin, *The Intellectuals and McCarthy: The Radical Specter* (Cambridge, 1967), argues that the Progressive party of the 1930's provides a link between the Wisconsin Progressives before

World War I and the Wisconsin Democrats after World War II. A second analysis, by Robert R. Dykstra and David R. Reynolds, "In Search of Wisconsin Progressivism, 1904–1952: A Test of the Rogin Scenario," in Joel H. Silbey, Allan G. Bogue, and William H. Flanigan, eds., *The History of American Electoral Behavior* (Princeton, 1978), 299–326, finds serious flaws in Rogin's use of county voting data. Their more sophisticated analysis argues not against continuity but against simplistic, unproved assertions that an unambiguous line of development took prewar Progressivism through the New Deal to the postwar Democratic party of Wisconsin.

The data base employed in this volume was that assembled for *The History of Wisconsin* series. A less extensive collection of county voting data appears in James R. Donoghue, *How Wisconsin Voted, 1848–1972* (Madison, 1974), a volume that tabulates returns on only the presidential, gubernatorial, and senatorial elections during the period 1914–1940. The best readily available sources on voting are the election returns contained in the *Wisconsin Blue Book*.

The political history of the United States from 1914 to 1940 receives attention in three volumes of *The New American Nation* series: Arthur S. Link, *Woodrow Wilson and the Progressive Era, 1910–1917* (New York, 1954); John D. Hicks, *Republican Ascendancy, 1921–1933* (New York, 1960); and William E. Leuchtenburg, *Franklin D. Roosevelt and the New Deal, 1932–1940* (New York, 1963). For the Middle West, one should consult Russel B. Nye, *Midwestern Progressive Politics: A Historical Study of Its Origin and Development, 1870–1958* (2nd ed., East Lansing, 1959). Leon D. Epstein's *Politics in Wisconsin* (Madison, 1958) is valuable, but it concentrates on the years since World War II. Two studies of the Socialist party are useful for gaining an understanding of Wisconsin politics. One is David A. Shannon, *The Socialist Party of America: A History* (New York, 1955); the other is Frederick I. Olson, "The Milwaukee Socialists, 1897–1941" (doctoral dissertation, Harvard University, 1952). Richard C. Haney, *A Concise History of the Modern Republican Party of Wisconsin, 1925–1975* (Madison, 1976) is a brief but useful outline of the Republican party's development over a span of fifty years. Edward N. Doan, *The La Follettes and the Wisconsin Idea* (New York, 1947) focuses on Senator Robert M. La Follette and his two sons, but it may also be read as a study of the Progressive faction of the Republican party. There is no general treatment of Wisconsin Democrats during the years 1914 to 1940. David Burner, *The Politics of Provincialism: The Democratic Party in Transition, 1918–1932* (New York, 1968) contains little information on Wisconsin, and Richard C. Haney's excellent study, "A History of the Democratic Party of Wisconsin Since World War II" (doctoral dissertation, University of Wisconsin, 1970), does not pick up the party's activities until after 1945. Fortunately, three volumes by Arthur M. Schlesinger, Jr., *The Age of Roosevelt*, help to fill a scholarly hiatus. They are subtitled *The Crisis of the Old Order, 1919–1933* (Boston, 1957), *The Coming of the New Deal* (Boston, 1958), and *The Politics of Upheaval* (Boston, 1960).

A good starting point for the evaluation of social and economic developments in Wisconsin during the New Era and the Great Depression is Lewis E. Atherton, *Main Street on the Middle Border* (Bloomington, 1954), which deals with the north-central region of the United States. For the decade of the twenties, the essays in John Braeman, Robert H. Bremner, and David Brody, eds., *Change and Continuity in Twentieth-Century America: The 1920's* (Columbus, Ohio, 1968) offer valuable suggestions on conventional themes. James Warren

Prothro, *The Dollar Decade: Business Ideas in the 1920's* (Baton Rouge, 1954) deals irreverently with businessmen of the New Era. Paula S. Fass, *The Damned and the Beautiful: American Youth in the 1920's* (New York, 1977) focuses on the youth culture of the decade. An extraordinarily valuable study of secondary education is Edward A. Krug, *The Shaping of the American High School* (2 vols., Madison, 1964–1972). Merle Curti and Vernon Carstensen, *The University of Wisconsin: A History, 1848–1925* (2 vols., Madison, 1949) may be taken as a model for other histories in the genre. Useful information on advances in science and technology may be found in John Jewkes, David Sawers, and Richard Stillerman, *The Sources of Invention* (New York, 1969) and in Melvin Kranzberg and Carroll W. Pursell, Jr., eds., *Technology in Western Civilization* (2 vols., New York, 1967). General studies of prohibition include Charles Merz, *The Dry Decade* (Garden City, New York, 1931) and Andrew Sinclair, *Prohibition: The Era of Excess* (Boston, 1962).

Two volumes in the *History of American Life* series, edited by Arthur M. Schlesinger and Dixon Ryan Fox, cover the years from 1914 to 1941. They are Preston W. Slosson, *The Great Crusade and After, 1914–1928* (New York, 1930) and Dixon Wecter, *The Age of the Great Depression, 1929–1941* (New York, 1948). Two comparable volumes in *The Economic History of the United States* series, edited by Henry David et al., are George H. Soule, *Prosperity Decade: From War to Depression, 1917–1929* (New York, 1947) and Broadus Mitchell, *Depression Decade: From New Era Through New Deal, 1929–1941* (New York, 1947). For a valuable symposium to which leading scholars of the time contributed, see the President's Research Committee on Social Trends, *Recent Social Trends in the United States* (2 vols., New York, 1933).

The best one-volume history of the Depression of the thirties is Robert S. McElvaine, *The Great Depression: America, 1929–1941* (New York, 1984). For relationships between Progressives and New Dealers—or differences between them—see Otis L. Graham, Jr., *An Encore for Reform: The Old Progressives and the New Deal* (New York, 1967). For two outstanding analyses of ideas for overcoming the Depression one should consult Ellis W. Hawley, *The New Deal and the Problem of Monopoly: A Study in Economic Ambivalence* (Princeton, 1966) and Theodore Rosenof, *Dogma, Depression, and the New Deal: The Debate of Political Leaders over Economic Recovery* (Port Washington, New York, 1975).

Many works evoke a sense of the Great Depression's devastating impact. Among the best of them are Glen H. Elder, Jr., *Children of the Great Depression: Social Change in Life Experience* (Chicago, 1974); Richard Lowitt and Maurine Beasley, eds., *One-Third of a Nation: Lorena Hickok Reports on the Great Depression* (Urbana, 1981); Alice Lynd and Staughton Lynd, eds., *Rank and File: Personal Histories by Working-Class Organizers* (Boston, 1973); Robert S. McElvaine, ed., *Down & Out in the Great Depression: Letters from the "Forgotten Man"* (Chapel Hill, 1983); and Studs Terkel, *Hard Times: An Oral History of the Great Depression* (New York, 1971).

As one might expect, the decades of prosperity and depression have produced a wide variety of studies dealing with industry, business, labor, and agriculture. The Conference on Unemployment, Committee on Recent Economic Changes, *Recent Economic Changes in the United States* (2 vols., New York, 1929) includes essays on various features of the American economy written by specialists at the close of the New Era. An important general history of Wisconsin industry is Edgar Z. Palmer, *The Prewar Industrial Pattern of Wis-*

consin, UW Bureau of Business Research and Service, *Wisconsin Commerce Studies*, vol. 1, no. 1 (1947). Francis F. Bowman, Jr., *Industrial Wisconsin*, Department of Commerce (1939) is less thorough.

The best point to begin an examination of labor history is with the work by John R. Commons et al., *History of Labour in the United States* (4 vols., New York, 1918–1935). Two books by Robert H. Zieger, *Republicans and Labor, 1919–1929* (Lexington, Kentucky, 1969) and *American Workers, American Unions, 1920–1985* (Baltimore, 1986), provide a recent perspective for dealing with the complex history of labor in Wisconsin. The most useful studies of American labor during the years between the two world wars are those of Irving Bernstein: *The Lean Years: A History of the American Worker, 1920–1933* (Boston, 1960; reprinted, Jersey City, 1983) and *Turbulent Years: A History of the American Worker, 1933–1941* (Boston, 1971). Bernstein's earlier work, *The New Deal Collective Bargaining Policy* (Berkeley, 1950; reprinted, Jersey City, 1975), clarifies a complicated subject.

Studies of American agriculture abound. Among the useful general works are Henry C. Taylor and Anne Dewees Taylor, *The Story of Agricultural Economics in the United States, 1840–1932* (Ames, 1952) and Willard W. Cochrane, *The Development of American Agriculture: A Historical Analysis* (Minneapolis, 1979). The U.S. Department of Agriculture, *Yearbook of Agriculture, 1940: Farmers in a Changing World* (1940) provides a wide-ranging collection of essays on twenty years of agricultural activity. Theodore Saloutos and John D. Hicks, *Agricultural Discontent in the Middle West, 1900–1939* (Madison, 1951) presents much information essential to the preparation of this volume, and Foster F. Elliott's *Types of Farming in the United States* published as a volume in the *Fifteenth Census of the United States, 1930: Agriculture* (1933) is an important guide to farm activities during the period under consideration.

A major work that elaborates on a century of agricultural development in the state is Eric E. Lampard, *The Rise of the Dairy Industry in Wisconsin: A Study in Agricultural Change, 1820–1920* (Madison, 1963). Other extended treatments of particular topics are Orville M. Kile, *The Farm Bureau Through Three Decades* (Baltimore, 1948); John T. Schlebecker and Andrew W. Hopkins, *A History of Dairy Journalism in the United States, 1810–1950* (Madison, 1957); Harold Barger and Hans H. Landsberg, *American Agriculture, 1899–1939: A Study of Output, Employment and Productivity* (New York, 1942); T. Swann Harding, *Two Blades of Grass: A History of Scientific Development in the U.S. Department of Agriculture* (Norman, 1947); Reynold M. Wik, *Steam Power on the American Farm* (Philadelphia, 1953); and Merrill Denison, *Harvest Triumphant: The Story of Massey-Harris* (Toronto, 1949). An excellent collection that emphasizes technological influences is Wayne D. Rasmussen, ed., *Readings in the History of American Agriculture* (Urbana, 1960).

The Great War and the Return of Peace

The remainder of this essay concentrates on studies of Wisconsin subjects and on special subjects of importance to Wisconsin. As indicated in the preface, the year 1914 marks the beginning of the Great War but has no special significance for Wisconsin except insofar as the state became involved in the war effort. American belligerency had repercussions throughout the postwar years;

because of that, any discussion of sources related to World War I must include materials on developments that took place after 1919.

Two excellent master's theses deal with the peace movement in Wisconsin and with the fervent effort to avoid the horrors of war after 1914. They are Jack Frooman, "The Wisconsin Peace Movement, 1915–1919" (University of Wisconsin, 1949) and Ronald P. Formisano, "Demand for a War Referendum, 1914–1917" (University of Wisconsin, 1962). Another study, John P. Finnegan, "The Preparedness Movement in Wisconsin, 1914–1917" (master's thesis, University of Wisconsin, 1961), concentrates on the state's efforts to prepare for the eventuality of American involvement in the conflict. Using some of the materials he uncovered, Finnegan wrote an insightful article, "Preparedness in Wisconsin: The National Guard and the Mexican Border Incident," in *WMH*, 47 (Spring, 1964), 199–213. Samuel Hopkins Adams, "Invaded America: Wisconsin Joins the War," in *Everybody's Magazine*, January, 1918, pp. 28–33, 82, 84, provides a contemporary account of the state's involvement in the war effort. The best means of placing events in a national context is through Arthur Link's magisterial biography of Woodrow Wilson. See, in particular, the volumes *Wilson: The Struggle for Neutrality, 1914–1915* (Princeton, 1960), *Wilson: Confusions and Crises, 1915–1916* (Princeton, 1964), and *Wilson: Campaigns for Progressivism and Peace, 1916–1917* (Princeton, 1965).

Studies of the peace movement and of efforts to avoid American participation in the war include: Merle E. Curti, *The American Peace Crusade, 1815–1860* (Durham, 1929); Charles Chatfield, *For Peace and Justice: Pacifism in America, 1914–1941* (Knoxville, 1971); C. Roland Marchand, *The American Peace Movement and Social Reform, 1898–1918* (Princeton, 1973); and Ernest R. May, *The World War and American Isolation, 1914–1917* (Cambridge, 1959). Domestic responses to American belligerency receive scholarly treatment in David M. Kennedy, *Over Here: The First World War and American Society* (New York, 1980) and in Seward W. Livermore, *Politics Is Adjourned: Woodrow Wilson and the War Congress, 1916–1918* (Middletown, Connecticut, 1966). The most useful study dealing with wartime Wisconsin is Robert S. Maxwell's biography, *Emanuel L. Philipp: Wisconsin Stalwart* (Madison, 1959). The military history of the war may be followed in Basil Henry Liddell Hart, *A History of the World War, 1914–1918* (Boston, 1934) and in Edward M. Coffman, *The War to End All Wars: The American Military Experience in World War I* (New York, 1968).

The heavy concentration of Germans in the state requires special attention. The most helpful studies on Americans of German ancestry are Carl F. Wittke, *German-Americans and the World War* (Columbus, Ohio, 1936), Clifton J. Child, *The German-Americans in Politics, 1914–1917* (Madison, 1939), and Frederick C. Luebke, *Bonds of Loyalty: German-Americans and World War I* (De Kalb, Illinois, 1974). For evidence of national concern over German-American loyalty, see U.S. Senate, Subcommittee of the Committee on the Judiciary, *National German-American Alliance: Hearings Before the Subcommittee . . . on S. 3529 . . . February 23–April 13, 1918*, 65 Cong., 2 sess. (1918). George S. Viereck dealt with German propaganda in *Spreading Germs of Hate* (New York, 1930), but a more recent study of the subject is David W. Hirst, "German Propaganda in the United States, 1914–1917" (doctoral dissertation, Northwestern University, 1962).

An excellent account of how profoundly the mobilization for war affected people in Wisconsin is Lorin Lee Cary, "The Wisconsin Loyalty Legion, 1917–

1918," in *WMH*, 53 (Autumn, 1969), 33–50. Universities and their faculties became involved, as several important studies have shown. See, especially, Carol S. Gruber, *Mars and Minerva: World War I and the Uses of the Higher Learning in America* (Baton Rouge, 1975); George T. Blakey, *Historians on the Homefront: American Propagandists for the Great War* (Lexington, Kentucky, 1970); James R. Mock and Cedric Larson, *Words That Won the War: The Story of the Committee on Public Information, 1917–1919* (Princeton, 1939); and Benjamin G. Rader, *The Academic Mind and Reform: The Influence of Richard T. Ely in American Life* (Lexington, Kentucky, 1966).

The persecution of people suspected of disloyalty and the wartime threat to civil liberties are treated in Horace C. Peterson and Gilbert C. Fite, *Opponents of War, 1917–1918* (Madison, 1957); Joan M. Jensen, *The Price of Vigilance* (Chicago, 1969); Donald O. Johnson, *The Challenge to American Freedoms: World War I and the Rise of the American Civil Liberties Union* (Lexington, Kentucky, 1963); William Preston, Jr., *Aliens and Dissenters: Federal Suppression of Radicals, 1903–1933* (Cambridge, 1963): and Harry N. Scheiber, *The Wilson Administration and Civil Liberites, 1917–1921* (Ithaca, 1960).

A wartime publication, the University of Wisconsin's *War Book of the University of Wisconsin: Papers on the Causes and Issues of the War by Members of the Faculty* (Madison, 1918), sought to justify American involvement and to inspire enthusiasm for its prosecution. At the close of the conflict, two commemorative books praised the state's contributions to the Allied victory: Fred. L. Holmes, *Wisconsin's War Record* (Madison, 1919) and Rutherford B. Pixley, *Wisconsin in the World War*... (Milwaukee, 1919). With the Armistice, the *Wisconsin Magazine of History* published a series of reminiscences and reflections on the war, and as new materials come to light it continues the practice. The following have all appeared in the *WMH*: Kenneth Conant, "An Artist in Battle," 2 (December, 1918), 194–198; Glenn Garlock, "A Description of Shell Fire," 2 (December, 1918), 190–191; Morris Davis, "Madison Artilleryman Gets Mustard Gas," 2 (March, 1919), 309–312; Sara E. Buck, "A Woman 'Y' Worker's Experiences," 3 (December, 1919), 241–244; William G. Haan, "The Division as a Fighting Machine," 4 (September, 1920), 3–26; Karen Falk, "Public Opinion in Wisconsin During World War I," 25 (June, 1942), 389–407; John M. Work, "The First World War," 41 (Autumn, 1957), 32–44; Ira Berlin, ed., "A Wisconsinite in World War I: Reminiscences of Edmund P. Arpin, Jr.," 51 (Autumn, 1967), 3–25, (Winter, 1967–1968), 124–138, and (Spring, 1968), 218–237; and John O. Holzhueter, "Pvt. Treptow's Pledge," 67 (Autumn, 1983), 2–16.

The historical literature on the close of the Great War and the abortive effort to establish a lasting peace is too vast to permit summary in these pages. Yet keeping in mind the attitude of Wisconsin's two senators—Bob La Follette opposed the Versailles settlement and Irvine Lenroot sought a compromise—it is possible to comment on studies that clarify the two positions. For such purposes, the most informative works are biographies: Belle Case La Follette and Fola La Follette, *Robert M. La Follette* (2 vols., New York, 1953) and Herbert F. Margulies, *Senator Lenroot of Wisconsin: A Political Biography, 1900–1929* (Columbia, Missouri, 1977). Two other biographies assist in making sense of the Senate debate on the treaties: John A. Garraty, *Henry Cabot Lodge: A Biography* (New York, 1953) and Arthur Walworth, *Woodrow Wilson* (2 vols. in one, 3rd ed., New York, 1978). Walworth has also written a volume on international developments under the title *America's Moment, 1918: American Diplomacy at the End of World War I* (New York, 1977).

Other studies which treat matters related to the difficult process of peacemaking include: Ruhl J. Bartlett, *The League to Enforce Peace* (Chapel Hill, 1944); Paul Birdsall, *Versailles Twenty Years After* (New York, 1941); Denna Frank Fleming, *The United States and the League of Nations, 1918–1920* (New York, 1932); and Thomas A. Bailey's two volumes, *Woodrow Wilson and the Lost Peace* (New York, 1944), and *Woodrow Wilson and the Great Betrayal* (New York, 1945). While these studies differ in their assessments of Wilson's role in the treaty debate, all of them represent shadings of opinion that later underwent radical revision during the years of the Cold War. One of the founders of a new school of historiography that became prominent during the 1960's, William Appleman Williams, first published *American-Russian Relations, 1781–1947* (New York, 1952). Then, in subsequent studies, Williams helped to modify not only the focus of debate over the treaties of 1919 but also the focus of debate over the American position in world affairs during the twentieth century.

In some respects, Williams' analysis was similar to that of Robert M. La Follette during the war period. It ran counter to prevailing opinion, but it nonetheless won adherents. An important study by N. Gordon Levin, Jr., *Woodrow Wilson and World Politics: America's Response to War and Revolution* (New York, 1968), relies in part on the new approach in arguing that Wilson sought to win a settlement that might avoid the extremes of atavistic imperialism on the one hand and Bolshevism on the other.

In the preparation of this volume, the study that proved most helpful in working out the meaning of the peace settlement for the people of Wisconsin was Ralph Stone, *The Irreconcilables: The Fight Against the League of Nations* (Lexington, Kentucky, 1970). For one thing, Stone delved deeply into the sources and derived his hypotheses from them. For another thing, he carefully examined each of the major participants in the debate over the League of Nations, and that meant that he provided the clearest, most unambiguous analysis of the thinking behind the positions taken by Senators Lenroot and La Follette.

The struggle over ratification of the treaty and the bitter conflict over the League of Nations did little to relieve the fear of radicalism that produced the Red Scare of 1919–1920. In two important volumes, Theodore Draper tells the story of the formation of the American Communist party and its association with programs and policies of the USSR: *The Roots of American Communism* (New York, 1957) and *American Communism and Soviet Russia: The Formative Period* (New York, 1960). The popular response to the perceived threat of radicalism is the subject of Robert K. Murray, *Red Scare: A Study of National Hysteria, 1919–1920* (Minneapolis, 1955). Stanley Coben concentrates on the person most responsible for the hysteria in *A. Mitchell Palmer: Politician* (New York, 1963), and he deals with the social hysteria in "A Study in Nativism: The American Red Scare of 1919–20," in the *Political Science Quarterly*, 79 (March, 1964), 52–75. Harold M. Hyman concerns himself with the threat to civil liberties in *To Try Men's Souls* (Berkeley, 1959), and Paul L. Murphy provides a more extensive constitutional history in a volume of the *New American Nation* series, *The Constitution in Crisis Times, 1918–1969* (New York, 1971). Manifestations of the Red Scare in Wisconsin receive attention in Edward J. Muzik, "Victor L. Berger: Congress and the Red Scare," in *WMH*, 47 (Summer,

1964), 309–318; Charles A. Nelson, "Progressivism and Loyalty in Wisconsin Politics, 1912–1918" (master's thesis, University of Wisconsin, 1961); and Dana Lee Gisselman, "Anti-radicalism in Wisconsin, 1917–1919" (master's thesis, University of Wisconsin, 1969).

Some of the same influences that produced the Red Scare help to account for resurgence of the Ku Klux Klan in the postwar years. The best general treatment of the new Klan movement is Kenneth T. Jackson, *The Ku Klux Klan in the City, 1915–1930* (New York, 1967), which replaces older works such as John M. Mecklin, *The Ku Klux Klan: A Study of the American Mind* (New York, 1924). The most important study of the Klan in Wisconsin and other midwestern states is Norman F. Weaver, "The Knights of the Ku Klux Klan in Wisconsin, Indiana, Ohio, and Michigan" (doctoral dissertation, University of Wisconsin, 1954). Robert A. Goldberg published "The Ku Klux Klan in Madison, 1922–1927" in *WMH*, 58 (Autumn, 1974), 31–44, then turned his attention to Colorado in *Hooded Empire: The Ku Klux Klan in Colorado* (Urbana, 1981).

Experiences of the war years brought support for two measures that reformers had long advocated: woman suffrage, and the prohibition of alcoholic beverages. With the ratification of the Eighteenth and Nineteenth amendments, it seemed, the United States could proceed to create a just and happy society. The story behind the "noble experiment" with prohibition is well told in Norman H. Clark, *Deliver Us From Evil: An Interpretation of American Prohibition* (New York, 1976) and in Andrew Sinclair, *Prohibition: The Era of Excess* (Boston, 1962), previously mentioned. An older work by Peter H. Odegard, *Pressure Politics: The Story of the Anti-Saloon League* (New York, 1928), contains much basic information that remains useful, as does Charles Merz, *The Dry Decade* (Garden City, New York, 1931). The Anti-Saloon League's *Year Book*, published annually, provides abundant materials for assessing the progress of temperance reformers in their war against alcohol. Ernest H. Cherrington, who headed the Anti-Saloon League's educational campaign, wrote a valuable summary of the movement: *The Evolution of Prohibition in the United States of America: A Chronological History of the Liquor Problem and the Temperance Reform in the United States from the Earliest Settlements to the Consummation of National Prohibition* (Westerville, Ohio, 1920; reprinted, Montclair, New Jersey, 1969).

For the prewar antecedents of the Eighteenth Amendment, one should consult: Jack S. Blocker, Jr., *Retreat from Reform: The Prohibition Movement in the United States, 1890–1913* (Westport, Connecticut, 1976); Ruth B. A. Bordin, *Woman and Temperance: The Quest for Power and Liberty, 1873–1900* (Philadelphia, 1981); Joseph R. Gusfield, *Symbolic Crusade: Status Politics and the American Temperance Movement* (Urbana, 1963); and James H. Timberlake, *Prohibition and the Progressive Movement, 1900–1920* (Cambridge, 1963).

An important reassessment which takes seriously the problem of alcohol addiction, and which finds prohibition more effective than scoffers believed, is J. C. Burnham, "New Perspectives on the Prohibition 'Experiment' of the 1920's," in the *Journal of Social History*, 2 (Fall, 1968), 51–68. Mark Edward Lender and James Kirby Martin probe drinking habits and the extent of alcohol consumption in *Drinking in America: A History* (New York, 1982). David E. Kyvig considers the reasons for the reaction against the Eighteenth Amendment and the formation of organizations to secure repeal in *Repealing National Prohibition* (Chicago, 1979).

For studies of the temperance movement and prohibition in Wisconsin, see Peter R. Weisensel, "The Wisconsin Temperance Crusade to 1919" (master's thesis, University of Wisconsin, 1965); Jeffrey Lucker, "The Politics of Prohibition in Wisconsin, 1917–1933" (master's thesis, University of Wisconsin, 1968); and Paul W. Glad, "When John Barleycorn Went into Hiding in Wisconsin," in *WMH*, 68 (Winter, 1984–1985), 119–136. An important work on the brewing industry of Wisconsin is Thomas C. Cochran, *The Pabst Brewing Company: The History of an American Business* (New York, 1948).

During the recent past, women's history has assumed an increasingly important place in university classrooms and in American historiography. A useful guide to work that has been accomplished is Estelle B. Freedman's historiographical essay, "The New Woman: Changing Views of Women in the 1920s," in the *Journal of American History*, 61 (September, 1974), 372–393. The broadest survey of the often conflicting roles women have played in American history is Carl N. Degler, *At Odds: Women and the Family in America from the Revolution to the Present* (New York, 1980). William H. Chafe concentrates on a crucial half-century in *The American Woman: Her Changing Social, Economic, and Political Roles, 1920–1970* (New York, 1972), and J. Stanley Lemons offers a perceptive analysis of women during the post-suffrage decade in *The Woman Citizen: Social Feminism in the 1920's* (Urbana, 1973).

Participants in the campaign for woman suffrage were conscious of the importance of what they were doing, and they were conscientious in keeping records of their activities. Elizabeth Cady Stanton, Susan B. Anthony, Matilda Joslyn Gage, and Ida Husted Harper edited six hefty volumes on the *History of Woman Suffrage*, published at various locations between 1881 and 1922, which together have proved to be a mine of information for historians. Adding to that record, Carrie Chapman Catt and Nettie Rogers Shuler wrote *Woman Suffrage and Politics: The Inner Story of the Suffrage Movement* (New York, 1923), and Inez Haynes Irwin wrote *The Story of the Woman's Party* (New York, 1921; reprinted, 1971). At the end of the 1920's, Marguerite M. Wells reflected on "Some Effects of Woman Suffrage," in the American Academy of Political and Social Science *Annals*, 143 (May, 1929), 207–216. And at the outset of the Great Depression, Sophonisba P. Breckinridge contributed *Women in the Twentieth Century: A Study of their Political, Social and Economic Activities* (New York, 1933).

Then, during the Depression and World War II, scholars appeared to lose interest in examining the activities of women in American life. One of the few serious books to appear during the thirties and forties was Ernest R. Groves, *The American Woman: The Feminine Side of a Masculine Civilization* (2nd ed., New York, 1944). Fortunately, the interest in women's studies revived, and works on women's history began to crowd the bookshelves of libraries. Among the first important books published during the revival of interest were William L. O'Neill, *Everyone Was Brave: The Rise and Fall of Feminism in America* (Chicago, 1969) and Aileen S. Kraditor, *The Ideas of the Woman Suffrage Movement, 1890–1920* (New York, 1965). Both stirred lively debate, and a new vitality began to characterize the study of women's history.

Historians have accomplished much in the fields of women's history and the history of the family, but much remains to be done. Four articles that have appeared in the *Wisconsin Magazine of History* emphasize the political activities of women: Charles E. Neu, "Olympia Brown and the Woman's Suffrage Movement," 43 (Summer, 1960), 277–287; Marilyn Grant, "The 1912 Suffrage Referendum: An Exercise in Political Action," 64 (Winter, 1980–1981), 107–118; Lawrence L. Graves, "Two Noteworthy Wisconsin Women: Mrs. Ben Hooper and Ada James," 41 (Spring, 1958), 174–180; and James Howell Smith, "Mrs. Ben Hooper of Oshkosh: Peace Worker and Politician," 46 (Winter, 1962–1963), 124–135. The years between the wars, it appears, were not years in which Wisconsin women played a vigorous role in affairs of the state. If that is the case, it is important to investigate the activities women did feel compelled to undertake, and what is more important, why they felt compelled to undertake them.

THE NEW ERA OF THE 1920'S

Any investigation of the New Era of the 1920's must begin with the conclusion of World War I. Dixon Wecter, *When Johnny Comes Marching Home* (Boston, 1944; reprinted, Westport, Connecticut, 1970) deals with social aspects of reconversion, while Paul A. Samuelson and Everett E. Hagan, compilers for the U.S. National Resources Planning Board of *After the War, 1918–1920: Military and Economic Demobilization of the United States, Its Effect upon Employment and Income* (1943), concentrate on economic problems of the postwar period. Burl Noggle, *Into the Twenties: The United States from Armistice to Normalcy* (Urbana, 1974) is an excellent general treatment of the transition from war to peace.

In addition to the political studies already mentioned, there are several biographies that provide insights into major political activities of the period. Robert K. Murray's revisionist interpretation, *The Harding Era: Warren G. Harding and His Administration* (Minneapolis, 1969), portrays a president who was far from being a buffoon whose peccadilloes undergraduates find amusing. Donald R. McCoy's *Calvin Coolidge: The Quiet President* (New York, 1967) is a thorough, workmanlike treatment by a scholar whose knowledge of New Era politics is unsurpassed. Burl Noggle examines the far-reaching implications of the major political scandal of the twenties in *Teapot Dome: Oil and Politics in the 1920's* (Baton Rouge, 1962). Senator Robert M. La Follette's role in initiating the investigation receives appropriate emphasis.

Since the opening of the Herbert Hoover Presidential Library in 1966, scholars have been working to familiarize themselves with one of the twentieth century's least known but most important chief executives. The first volume of George H. Nash's definitive biography, *The Life of Herbert Hoover: The Engineer, 1874–1914* (New York, 1983), closes with the outbreak of war in 1914. Two important shorter biographies and several more specialized studies have, however, already appeared. The biographies are Joan Hoff Wilson, *Herbert Hoover: Forgotten Progressive* (Boston, 1975) and David Burner, *Herbert Hoover: A Public Life* (New York, 1979). Facets of Hoover's career receive attention in Gary Dean Best, *The Politics of American Individualism: Herbert Hoover in Transition, 1918–1921* (Westport, Connecticut, 1975); Craig Lloyd, *Aggressive Introvert: A Study of Herbert Hoover and Public Relations Management, 1912–1932* (Columbus, Ohio, 1972); Donald J. Lisio, *Hoover, Blacks, & Lily-Whites: A Study of Southern Strategies* (Chapel Hill, 1985); and Jordan A. Schwarz, *The Interregnum of Despair: Hoover, Congress, and the Depression* (Urbana, 1970). Useful anthologies are Martin Fausold, ed., *The Hoover Presidency: A Reappraisal* (Albany, 1974); Lawrence E. Gelfand, ed., *Herbert Hoover: The Great War and Its Aftermath, 1914–23* (Iowa City, 1979); and Ellis W. Hawley, ed., *Herbert Hoover as Secretary of Commerce: Studies in New Era Thought and Practice* (Iowa City, 1981).

A mining engineer who had achieved impressive triumphs in business and commercial activities, Hoover became a major influence as secretary of commerce during the Harding and Coolidge administrations. His own short essay, *American Individualism* (Garden City, New York, 1922), became a tract of the times, and in *The Revolt of the Engineers: Social Responsibility and the American Engineering Profession* (Cleveland, 1971), Edwin T. Layton dealt with many of the ideas Hoover represented. The thinking of businessmen in the New Era is the subject of Morrell Heald's article, "Business Thought in the Twenties: Social Responsibility," in *American Quarterly*, 13 (Summer, 1961), 126–139. Heald enlarges on the theme of welfare capitalism in *The Social Responsibilities of Business: Company and Community, 1900–1960* (Cleveland, 1970). An essay that explores the relationship between Wisconsin progressivism and values of the marketplace is Stuart Morris, "The Wisconsin Idea and Business Progressivism," in the *Journal of American Studies*, 4 (July, 1970), 39–60. A broader treatment of the point of view promulgated by businessmen is Alan R. Raucher, *Public Relations and Business, 1900–1929* (Baltimore, 1968).

The image of the New Era conveyed in Frederick Lewis Allen's *Only Yesterday: An Informal History of the Nineteen-Twenties* (New York, 1931) is one that retains its clarity in the popular mind. (That image is not entirely false. When Isabel Bacon was a student at the University of Wisconsin, she delighted in thinking of herself as a "flapper," and she wrote home about her hopes of "vamping" another student named Phil La Follette.) Robert S. and Helen M. Lynd's investigation of Muncie, Indiana, to which they gave the title *Middletown: A Study in Contemporary American Culture* (New York, 1929), provided Allen with some of the material he used in his evocative account. Later works, such as Frederick J. Hoffman's *The Twenties: American Writing in the Postwar Decade* (New York, 1955), might be read as a gloss on *Only Yesterday*. Nevertheless, William E. Leuchtenburg, *The Perils of Prosperity, 1914–32* (Chicago, 1958) provides a more balanced popular treatment.

The young artists, writers, and intellectuals who lived for a time as expatriates in Europe were, in fact, few in number. Yet they captured the imagination of young Americans at home, and thus Ernest Hemingway, F. Scott Fitzgerald, and others came to represent the flights of fancy among rebellious youth in Oshkosh and Sheboygan, as well as New York and Chicago. An extraordinarily insightful examination of the expatriates is Warren I. Susman, "Pilgrimage to Paris: The Backgrounds of American Expatriation, 1920–1934" (doctoral dissertation, University of Wisconsin, 1958). Glenway Wescott, who lived in France during the twenties and whose *Good-Bye, Wisconsin* (New York, 1928) expressed ambivalent feelings about his home state, has been the subject of three useful literary and biographical analyses: Sy M. Kahn, "Glenway Wescott: A Critical and Biographical Study" (doctoral dissertation, University of Wisconsin, 1957); William H. Rueckert, *Glenway Wescott* (New York, 1965); and Ira Johnson, *Glenway Wescott: The Paradox of Voice* (Port Washington, New York, 1971).

Two biographies of Wisconsin academics provide invaluable insights into the period 1914–1940. Julius Weinberg's *Edward Alsworth Ross and the Sociology of*

Progressivism (Madison, 1972) traces the long career of a leader in the discipline of sociology. Theron F. Schlabach's painstaking study, *Edwin E. Witte: Cautious Reformer* (Madison, 1969), presents the life and thought of one of Wisconsin's most influential public servants. Regrettably, there is no adequate biography of John R. Commons, with whom Witte studied when he was a graduate student at the University of Wisconsin. Commons' autobiography, *Myself* (New York, 1934; reprinted, Madison, 1963), reveals more of the author's general ideas than of his specific contributions to the development of institutions. There is also no full-length biography of John J. Blaine, who served three terms (1921–1927) as governor of Wisconsin before sitting for a single term as United States senator. The richness of his papers suggests that his career provides more insight into the New Era than scholars have assumed. James H. Daffer treats Blaine's early life in "Progressive Profile: John James Blaine from 1873 to 1918" (master's thesis, University of Wisconsin, 1951), and Patrick G. O'Brien provides a useful profile in "Senator John J. Blaine: An Independent Progressive During 'Normalcy,' " in *WMH*, 60 (Autumn, 1976), 25–41.

By the time peace returned to Wisconsin, the state's lumber industry was declining in relative importance, and concerned citizens increasingly turned attention to problems of land use and conservation. Raleigh Barlowe's article, "Forest Policy in Wisconsin," in *WMH*, 26 (March, 1943), 261–279, focuses on the formation of a forestry program. John M. Gaus published "Conservation in Wisconsin" in the *Wisconsin Blue Book, 1933*, pp. 69–83, and F. G. Wilson's "Forestry in Wisconsin" appeared in the *Wisconsin Blue Book, 1942*, pp. 177–185. By far the most useful work on the subject, however, is Vernon R. Carstensen, *Farms or Forests: Evolution of a State Land Policy for Northern Wisconsin, 1850–1932* (Madison, 1958). Arlan Helgeson, *Farms in the Cutover: Agricultural Settlement in Northern Wisconsin* (Madison, 1962) focuses on the attempt to expand farming into northern Wisconsin after the timber had been cut, and Lucile Kane published an article, "Settling the Wisconsin Cutovers," in *WMH*, 40 (Winter, 1956–1957), 91–98.

The best analyses of Wisconsin agriculture and the exciting research at the University appear in Edward H. Beardsley, *Harry L. Russell and Agricultural Science in Wisconsin* (Madison, 1969). The years after the war were difficult ones for farmers in Wisconsin, as they were elsewhere. An early study of their problems is Benjamin H. Hibbard, *Effects of the Great War upon Agriculture in the United States and Great Britain* (New York, 1919). Looking back from a perspective of nearly forty years, James H. Shideler provided a more scholarly treatment in *Farm Crisis, 1919–1923* (Berkeley, 1957; reprinted, Westport, Connecticut, 1976). Responding to the perceived need for a scientific approach to agriculture, researchers at the University of Wisconsin were leaders in scientific investigations. The story of their accomplishments is well told in Paul de Kruif, *Hunger Fighters* (New York, 1928); Franklin C. Bing and Harry J. Prebluda, "E. V. McCollum: Pathfinder in Nutrition Investigations and World Agriculture," in *Agricultural History*, 54 (January, 1980), 157–166; and A. Richard Crabb, *The Hybrid Corn-Makers: Prophets of Plenty* (New Brunswick, New Jersey, 1947).

In the meantime, under the leadership of Dean Harry L. Russell, the College of Agriculture at the University of Wisconsin sought to extend its services to farmers of the state. The direction of the college's efforts is indicated in the many communications and publications distributed from Madison. See, especially, Harry L. Russell, "The Stability of Wisconsin's Agriculture," in Wisconsin Bankers' Association, *Proceedings*, 1921, pp. 131–136; Harry L. Russell and F. B. Morrison, *New Pages in Farming*, UW Agricultural Experiment Station, *Annual Report*, 1920–1921, in *Bulletin*, no. 339 (1922); Benjamin H. Hibbard and Guy A. Peterson, *How Wisconsin Farmers Become Farm Owners*, UW Agricultural Experiment Station, *Bulletin*, no. 402 (1928); and Chris L. Christiansen, *Wisconsin—Then and Now*, UW Agricultural Extension Service, *Circular*, no. 180 (1936). Ernest L. Luther traces the history of an important activity in "Farmers' Institutes in Wisconsin, 1885–1933," in *WMH*, 30 (September, 1946), 59–68.

The mechanization of farming had important consequences for the manufacturers of agricultural machinery as well as for farmers themselves. Reynold M. Wik provides excellent discussions of the subject in *Steam Power on the American Farm* (Philadelphia, 1953), mentioned above, and *Henry Ford and Grass-Roots America* (Ann Arbor, 1972). Persons interested in agricultural technology should also consult Robert E. Ankli, "Horses vs. Tractors in the Corn Belt," in *Agricultural History*, 54 (January, 1980), 134–148, and the relevant portions of Walter F. Peterson, *An Industrial Heritage: Allis-Chalmers Corporation* (Milwaukee, 1978).

Frederick Lewis Allen emphasized the development of the internal combustion engine and the automobile's popularity as important phenomena of the postwar decade, and historians have written extensively on both. John B. Rae provides commendable detail in *American Automobile Manufacturers: The First Forty Years* (Philadelphia, 1959). His shorter work, *The American Automobile: A Brief History* (Chicago, 1965), is a more general treatment, as is David L. Cohn, *Combustion on Wheels* (Cambridge, 1944). Bernard A. Weisberger's *The Dream Maker: William C. Durant, Founder of General Motors* (Boston, 1979) is a superb biography. James J. Flink has contributed two important books on the influence of the automobile on American society: *America Adopts the Automobile, 1895–1910* (Cambridge, 1970) and *The Car Culture* (Cambridge, 1975). Flink's "Three Stages of Automobile Consciousness," in *American Quarterly*, 24 (October, 1972), 451–473, is a thought-provoking essay. Michael L. Berger, *The Devil Wagon in God's Country: The Automobile and Social Change in Rural America, 1893–1929* (Hamden, Connecticut, 1979) and Warren J. Belasco, *Americans on the Road: From Autocamp to Motel, 1910–1945* (Cambridge, 1979) deal with social responses to the automobile.

Two general treatments of highway promotion and policy after development of the internal combustion engine are Frederic L. Paxson, "The Highway Movement, 1916–1935," in the *American Historical Review*, 51 (January, 1946), 236–253, and Charles L. Dearing, *American Highway Policy* (Brookings Institution, Institute of Economics, *Publication*, no. 88, Washington, 1941). More important for researchers concerned with construction of the Wisconsin highway network is a joint publication of the Wisconsin State Highway Commission and the United States Public Roads Administration, *A History of Wisconsin Highway Development, 1835–1945* (1947).

Special topics in business history and geography receive scholarly attention in four useful studies: John W. Alexander, "Geography of Manufacturing in the Rock River Valley" (doctoral dissertation, University of Wisconsin, 1949); John E. Brush, "The Trade Centers of Southwestern Wisconsin: An Analysis of Function and Location" (doctoral dissertation, University of Wisconsin,

1952); Steven B. Karges, "David Clark Everest and Marathon Paper Mills Company: A Study of a Wisconsin Entrepreneur, 1909–1931" (doctoral dissertation, University of Wisconsin, 1968); and James M. Rock, "The Wisconsin Aluminum Cookware Industry Prior to World War II" (doctoral dissertation, Northwestern University, 1966). Rock has published *The Wisconsin Aluminum Cookware Industry Prior to World War II* (Chicago, 1967) and an article, "A Growth Industry: The Wisconsin Aluminum Cookware Industry, 1893–1920," in *WMH*, 55 (Winter, 1971–1972), 87–99. The value of such studies in business history should induce scholars to examine other Wisconsin firms. Forrest McDonald, *Let There Be Light: The Electric Utility Industry in Wisconsin, 1881–1955* (Madison, 1957) surveys an industry that affected nearly all forms of manufacturing in the state, but it tends to become an apology for the utilities.

Radio broadcasting had it origins in the postwar period, and the influence of radio in Wisconsin, as in the nation, was enormous. Gleason L. Archer's *History of Radio to 1926* (New York, 1938; reprinted, Salem, New Hampshire, 1971) is useful, but scholars will find Erik Barnouw's *A History of Broadcasting in the United States* (3 vols., New York, 1966–1970) a more thorough study. Another early work on radio, S. E. Frost, Jr., *Education's Own Stations: The History of Broadcast Licenses Issued to Educational Institutions* (Chicago, 1937; reprinted, Salem, New Hampshire, 1971), is encyclopedic in its coverage, but it provides only basic information. Hadley Cantril and Gordon W. Allport, *The Psychology of Radio* (New York, 1935; reprinted, Salem, New Hampshire, 1971) is an effort to assess radio's influence on listeners. Henry Ohl, Jr., "The Robotization of Art," in *Wisconsin Labor*, 1929, pp. 11 and 13, is a critical assessment by a prominent labor leader. Philip T. Rosen, *The Modern Stentors: Radio Broadcasters and the Federal Government, 1920–1934* (Westport, Connecticut, 1980) contains useful information. An interesting article on an early independent broadcaster is James I. Clark, "Early Broadcasting in Wisconsin: Clyde S. Van Gorden and Station WTAQ," in *WMH*, 41 (Winter, 1957–1958), 90–98.

The development of radio broadcasting brought rural Wisconsin under influences of the metropolis, but tensions between urban and rural ways of life remained powerful during the years between the two world wars. Don S. Kirschner, *City and Country: Rural Responses to Urbanization in the 1920s* (Westport, Connecticut, 1970) deals largely with Iowa and Illinois, but many of its general observations apply to Wisconsin as well. The proceedings of a 1929 symposium, Conference on Problems of the Small City and Town, *The Small City and Town: A Conference on Community Relations*, edited by Roland S. Vaile (Minneapolis, 1930), contain useful materials.

One of the best ways to assess the relationship between town and country is through fiction, as Irma H. Herron recognized in writing *The Small Town in American Literature* (Durham, 1939; reprinted, Brooklyn, 1970). Among Wisconsin writers, the one most identified with rural communities was Zona Gale, whose books about "Friendship Village" won a following in small towns of the state. The best study of Gale is August Derleth, *Still Small Voice: The Biography of Zona Gale* (New York, 1940), but the interested reader should also consult Harold P. Simonson, *Zona Gale* (New York, 1962) and Henry James Forman, "Zona Gale: A Touch of Greatness," in *WMH*, 46 (Autumn, 1962), 32–37. Robert R. Dykstra explores the importance of town and country rivalries in his article "Town-Country Conflict: A Hidden Dimension in American Social History," in *Agricultural History*, 38 (October, 1964), 195–204.

Labor unrest in postwar America drew attention to another sort of rivalry as the strikes of 1919 gave way to management efforts to reassert control over workers. David Brody, *Labor in Crisis: The Steel Strike of 1919* (Philadelphia, 1965; reprinted, Westport, Connecticut, 1982, and Champaign, 1987) provides a good introduction to labor's problems in the twenties, and Mark Perlman, *Labor Union Theories in America: Background and Development* (Evanston, 1958; reprinted, Westport, Connecticut, 1976) establishes a framework for consideration of those problems. Selig Perlman and Philip Taft's *Labor Movements* (New York, 1935), the last volume in John R. Commons et al., *History of Labor in the United States, 1896–1932* (4 vols., New York, 1918–1935), is an important survey written during the Great Depression. Edwin E. Witte, *The Government in Labor Disputes* (New York, 1932; reprinted, Salem, New Hampshire, 1969) reflects many of the ideas of Witte's mentor, John R. Commons.

The decade of the twenties produced a steady flow of labor studies. Among the most useful in formulating the ideas advanced in this book are John R. Commons, *Industrial Goodwill* (New York, 1919; reprinted, Salem, New Hampshire, 1969); John R. Commons, ed., *Trade Unionism and Labor Problems* (Boston, 1921; reprinted, New York, 1967); Sidney Howard, *The Labor Spy* (New York, 1924); Sumner Slichter, "The Current Labor Policies of American Industries," in *Quarterly Journal of Economics*, 43 (May, 1929), 393–435; George William Taylor, *Significant Post-War Changes in the Full-Fashioned Hosiery Industry* (Philadelphia, 1929) and *The Full-Fashioned Hosiery Worker: His Changing Economic Status* (Philadelphia, 1931).

For many years after arrival of the Great Depression, a popular historical generalization held that the New Era had been a period of reaction when reform activities all but disappeared. In a famous essay, "What Happened to the Progressive Movement of the 1920's?" in the *American Historical Review*, 64 (July, 1959), 833–851, Arthur S. Link corrected several misapprehensions in arguing that, contrary to popular belief, Progressive reformers retained enthusiasm for many of their favorite causes during the decade. Clarke A. Chambers supported that thesis in *Seedtime of Reform: American Social Service and Social Action, 1918–1933* (Minneapolis, 1963; reprinted, Westport, Connecticut, 1980), a work that demonstrates the Progressive commitment to social welfare. Moving beyond social welfare, Eugene M. Tobin's more recent study, *Organize or Perish: America's Independent Progressives, 1913–1933* (Westport, Connecticut, 1986), contains a wealth of information on the ways that independent reformers confronted a broad range of issues during the postwar decade. The studies of Tobin and others, while exploring new areas of investigation, recognize the enduring value of the best of earlier scholarship. Theodore Saloutos and John D. Hicks, *Agricultural Discontent in the Middle West, 1900–1939*, a study already mentioned in this essay, is an example of such scholarship. Saloutos' article, "The Wisconsin Society of Equity," in *Agricultural History*, 14 (April, 1940), 78–95, in fact remains a very important brief work on the subject.

Several works on the Nonpartisan League suggest the historiographical trend towards greater sophistication through the examination of an increased variety of sources. Early studies of the Nonpartisan League include Herbert E. Gaston, *The Nonpartisan League* (New York, 1920; reprinted, Westport, Connecticut, 1975) and Charles E. Russell, *The Story of the Nonpartisan League: A Chapter in American Evolution* (New York, 1920; reprinted, Salem, New Hampshire, 1975). Drawing on those accounts, but probing beyond them, Robert L. Morlan produced a far more satisfactory analysis in *Political Prairie Fire: The Nonpartisan League, 1915–1922* (Minneapolis, 1955; reprinted, Westport, Connecticut, 1975, and St. Paul, 1985). Then, using previously unexamined materials, Lowell K. Dyson brought rural radicalism into sharper focus in *Red Harvest: The Communist Party and American Farmers* (Lincoln, Nebraska, 1982). In sum, the historiography related to reform activities during the 1920's has been less concerned with revising older interpretations than with enlarging the subject and clarifying perspectives.

Biographical studies often serve as a means of producing new interpretations of historical phenomena. Among the important works that have led to greater understanding of Progressivism in the 1920's are Gilbert C. Fite, *George N. Peek and the Fight for Farm Parity* (Norman, 1954); Richard Lowitt, *George W. Norris: The Persistence of a Progressive, 1913–1933* (Urbana, 1971); LeRoy Ashby, *The Spearless Leader: Senator Borah and the Progressive Movement of the 1920's* (Urbana, 1972); and Michael Wreszin, *Oswald Garrison Villard: Pacifist at War* (Bloomington, Indiana, 1965).

Because taxation became a focal point of attacks on the way Progressives dealt with state problems, the Progressive tax program is a matter of importance in the political as well as the economic history of Wisconsin. Three contemporary articles providing basic information include Thomas E. Lyons, "The Wisconsin Tax System, in the *Wisconsin Blue Book, 1923*, pp. 79–102; W. J. Conway, "Taxation in Wisconsin," in the *Wisconsin Blue Book, 1927*, pp. 115–138; and Harold M. Groves, "The Wisconsin State Income Tax," in the *Wisconsin Blue Book, 1933*, pp. 51–67. A later sophisticated analysis of the effects of Progressive taxation in the state appears in W. Elliott Brownlee, *Progressivism and Economic Growth: The Wisconsin Income Tax, 1911–1929* (Port Washington, New York, 1974). Arguing that the Wisconsin reform movement represented the short-sighted interests of farmers as opposed to manufacturers, and that the Progressive tax program hindered economic growth, Brownlee supported his thesis in two articles published after the appearance of his book. The articles are "Income Taxation and the Political Economy of Wisconsin, 1890–1930," in *WMH*, 59 (Summer 1976), 299–324, and "Income Taxation and Capital Formation in Wisconsin, 1911–1929," in *Explorations in Economic History*, new series 8 (Fall, 1970), 77–102.

The political ferment of the postwar years and Robert M. La Follette's presidential campaign of 1924 have received attention from many historians uneasy with sweeping generalizations about the conservative, business-oriented politics of the New Era. Kenneth Campbell MacKay, *The Progressive Movement of 1924* (New York, 1947; reprinted, 1966) remains the standard work on the subject, but more recent scholarship has enriched understanding and provoked lively discussion. The interested reader will wish to consult, in addition to works already cited, James H. Shideler, "The La Follette Progressive Party Campaign of 1924," in *WMH*, 33 (June, 1950), 444–457; James H. Shideler, "The Disintegration of the Progressive Party Movement of 1924," in *The Historian*, 13 (Spring, 1951), 189–201; Paul W. Glad, "Progressives and the Business Culture of the 1920s," in the *Journal of American History*, 53 (June, 1966), 75–89; and Alan R. Havig, "A Disputed Legacy: Roosevelt Progressives and the La Follette

Campaign of 1924," in *Mid-America*, 53 (January, 1971), 44–64. For the activities of Socialists and militant groups to the left of the Progressives, one should consult James Weinstein's "Radicalism in the Midst of Normalcy," in the *Journal of American History*, 52 (March, 1966), 773–790, as well as his more extended treatment, *The Decline of Socialism in America, 1912–1925* (New York, 1967; 2nd ed., New Brunswick, New Jersey, 1984). The Wisconsin Socialists receive particular attention in Scott D. Johnston, "Wisconsin Socialists and the Conference for Progressive Political Action," in *WMH*, 37 (Winter, 1953–1954), 96–100.

No name figures more prominently in the history of Wisconsin Progressivism than does that of the La Follette family, yet scholarship on the La Follettes is less voluminous than one might expect. Not until 1970, with the opening of the La Follette Family Papers at the Library of Congress and the removal of restrictions on the Philip F. La Follette Papers in the State Historical Society of Wisconsin, were researchers free to use all the materials necessary for a scholarly treatment of the La Follette family's influence. Before 1970, only the La Follettes themselves had access to important family documents. Fortunately, Belle Case and Fola La Follette used their materials with care in writing *Robert M. La Follette* (cited earlier), and their biography still remains the best study of La Follette *père*.

Because manuscripts from the first phases of La Follette's career are housed in the State Historical Society of Wisconsin, most of the works that appeared before the opening of the La Follette Family Papers in Washington focus on the years before 1906. Edward N. Doan, *The La Follettes and the Wisconsin Idea* (previously noted) is the only work to deal with both father and sons, but in part because of restrictions on sources, the study lacks depth. Fred Greenbaum, *Robert Marion La Follette* (Boston, 1975) and David P. Thelen, *Robert M. La Follette and the Insurgent Spirit* (Boston, 1976; reprinted, Madison, 1986) are short, thoughtful works published after the Library of Congress papers became accessible; but a full-scale scholarly biography of Old Bob remains to be written.

For persons interested in the history of Wisconsin between the wars, studies related to the two sons of Robert M. La Follette are more helpful than are studies related to the father. Yet the problem of sources has been just as difficult. In writing *Robert M. La Follette, Jr., and the Decline of the Progressive Party in Wisconsin* (Madison, 1964; reprinted, Hamden, Connecticut, 1970), Roger T. Johnson relied heavily on interviews with surviving Progressives as well as on newspapers, periodical literature, and other materials from the interwar period. Although Theodore Rosenof's article, " 'Young Bob' La Follette on American Capitalism," in *WMH*, 55 (Winter, 1971–1972), 130–139, appeared after the opening of the La Follette Family Papers, the author rested his case principally on materials in the *Congressional Record* and in *The Progressive*. Finally, eight years after removal of restrictions on the family papers in the Library of Congress, Patrick J. Maney published his excellent *"Young Bob" La Follette: A Biography of Robert M. La Follette, Jr., 1895–1953* (Columbia, Missouri, 1978), the first authoritative treatment of the La Follettes' elder son.

During the last years of his life, Philip F. La Follette spent many hours in the State Historical Society in an effort to complete his memoirs. Unfinished at the time of his death in 1965, they were ably edited by Donald Young and published under the title *Adventure in Politics: The Memoirs of Philip F. La Follette*

(New York, 1970). While the volume contained valuable insights into the working of Phil's mind, it obviously lacked a historian's perspective. The first scholarly work to make full use of Philip La Follette's papers, as well as papers in the Library of Congress and in the Roosevelt Library at Hyde Park, was John E. Miller's *Governor Philip F. La Follette, the Wisconsin Progressives, and the New Deal* (Columbia, Missouri, 1982). Originally written as a dissertation at the University of Wisconsin in 1973, it is a careful and perceptive study, and it provides a firm basis for further examination of Wisconsin Progressivism during the Depression Decade.

The inaccessibility of manuscript sources doubtless delayed full historiographical recognition of the La Follettes' influence in twentieth-century American politics. Yet it did not prevent the completion of several theses and dissertations that provide a wealth of information on the La Follettes and their followers. Even with the availability of new sources, that information remains useful for scholars. The theses and dissertations that deal with the La Follettes' activities during the years from World War I to the New Deal include L. David Carley, "The Wisconsin Governor's Legislative Role: A Case Study of the Administrations of Philip Fox La Follette and Walter J. Kohler, Jr." (doctoral dissertation, University of Wisconsin, 1959); Sherman E. Harrington, "Senator Robert M. La Follette, Jr.: His Senate Record and Program of Realistic Reform for America" (master's thesis, University of Wisconsin, 1936); Padraic Kennedy, "La Follette's Foreign Policy Reconsidered" (master's thesis, University of Wisconsin, 1960); Alan E. Kent, "Portrait in Isolationism: The La Follettes and Foreign Policy" (doctoral dissertation, University of Wisconsin, 1957); Karl E. Meyer, "The Politics of Loyalty: From La Follette to McCarthy in Wisconsin, 1918–1952" (doctoral dissertation, Princeton University, 1956); and Theodore Rosenof, "The Ideology of Senator Robert M. La Follette, Jr." (master's thesis, University of Wisconsin, 1966).

The Great Depression

Whatever the flaws in this volume of *The History of Wisconsin*, it would have been a very different study, and probably less valuable, had the Philip F. La Follette Papers not been open to researchers. The collection is fundamental to an understanding of the effects of the Great Depression, the ways in which people of Wisconsin responded to hard times, the relationships between Wisconsin Progressivism and the New Deal, and the troubled international affairs of the years before World War II.

General works and topical surveys previously cited provide the basic information necessary for placing Wisconsin's response to the Depression in a broad national context. In addition to works already noted, two studies directed towards a general readership are helpful in understanding the causes of the devastating stock market collapse of 1929. They are John Kenneth Galbraith, *The Great Crash, 1929* (Boston, 1955; 3rd ed., 1972; reprinted, New York, 1980) and Robert Sobel, *The Great Bull Market: Wall Street in the 1920s* (New York, 1968). An exceptionally helpful economic analysis of the Depression, Lester V. Chandler's *America's Greatest Depression, 1929–1941* (New York, 1970), is both concise and lucid.

Insights into the economic thought of the time and reactions to the Depression may be derived from Adolf A. Berle, Jr., and Gardiner C. Means, *The*

Modern Corporation and Private Property (New York, 1933; reprinted, Buffalo, 1982) and from Charles A. Beard, ed., *America Faces the Future* (Boston, 1932). Examples of various ways the people of Wisconsin responded to the coming of hard times may be found in Milwaukee County, Citizens' Committee on Unemployment (and the Public Employment Office of Milwaukee), *Annual Report*, 1932; Kimball Young, John L. Gillin, and Calvert L. Dedrick, *The Madison Community*, University of Wisconsin, *Studies in the Social Sciences and History*, no. 21 (1934); Paul C. Glick, "The Effects of the Depression on Wisconsin's Birth Rates" (doctoral dissertation, University of Wisconsin, 1938); and William D. Knight, *Subsidization of Industry in Forty Selected Cities in Wisconsin, 1930–1946*, UW Bureau of Business Research and Service, *Wisconsin Commerce Studies*, vol. 1, no. 2 (1947).

A good introduction to the way Wisconsin farmers responded to conditions in agriculture during the 1930's is Walter H. Ebling's short essay, "Changes in Wisconsin Agriculture Since the Last Census," in the *Wisconsin Blue Book, 1933*, pp. 133–139. Herbert Jacobs' "The Wisconsin Milk Strikes," in *WMH*, 35 (Autumn, 1951), 30–35, deals with the violence that spread throughout rural areas of the state. A more scholarly treatment of the farmers' protest movement early in the Depression is A. William Hoglund, "Wisconsin Dairy Farmers on Strike," in *Agricultural History*, 35 (January, 1961), 24–34. Hoglund provides important information on the Wisconsin Cooperative Milk Pool, while John L. Shover's *Cornbelt Rebellion: The Farmers' Holiday Association* (Urbana, 1965) concentrates more on the larger Farmers' Holiday Association. Lowell K. Dyson's *Red Harvest*, already cited, includes both groups in exploring the dimensions of rural radicalism of the 1930's.

Understanding the activities of organized labor and policies formulated to deal with working-class concerns requires an appreciation of the ideas of institutional economists, especially John R. Commons. An excellent introduction is Joseph Dorfman et al., *Institutional Economics: Veblen, Commons, and Mitchell Reconsidered* (Berkeley, 1963). Robert Ozanne's sympathetic essay, "The Labor History and Labor Theory of John R. Commons: An Evaluation in the Light of Recent Trend and Criticism," appears in Gerald G. Somers, ed., *Labor, Management, and Social Policy: Essays in the John R. Commons Tradition* (Madison, 1963). The most useful contemporary analyses are Selig Perlman, *A Theory of the Labor Movement* (New York, 1928; reprinted, New York, 1966, and Philadelphia, 1979), and John R. Commons and John B. Andrews, *Principles of Labor Legislation* (4th ed., New York, 1936; reprinted, 1967). Gordon M. Haferbecker, *Wisconsin Labor Laws* (Madison, 1958) provides a valuable summary of important labor legislation in the state, and Thomas W. Gavett concentrates on Wisconsin's metropolis in his *Development of the Labor Movement in Milwaukee* (Madison, 1965).

Passage of Wisconsin's unemployment compensation law in January, 1932, represented the state's most important early reponse to the problems of unemployment during the thirties. Elizabeth Brandeis, who took an active part in securing the legislation, wrote an article on its provisions, "Wisconsin Tackles Job Security," in *The Survey*, 67 (December 15, 1931), 295–296, and her husband, Paul A. Raushenbush, published another positive assessment, "The Wisconsin Idea: Unemployment Reserves," in the American Academy of Political and Social Sciences, *Annals*, 170 (November, 1933), 65–75. Years later, they collaborated in writing *Our "U.C." Story, 1930–1967* (Madison, 1979).

Daniel Nelson wrote a brief article on the law, "The Origins of Unemployment Insurance in Wisconsin," in the *WMH*, 51 (Winter, 1967–1968), 109–121, and then went on to publish a superb extended analysis, *Unemployment Insurance: The American Experience, 1915–1935* (Madison, 1969).

The election of Franklin D. Roosevelt in 1932 and the coming of the New Deal greatly modified the relationships between the states and the national government. An important study of that shift is Jane Perry (Clark) Carey's *The Rise of a New Federalism: Federal-State Cooperation in the United States* (New York, 1938; reprinted, 1966). Another perceptive examination of the subject is Morton Grodzins, *The American System: A New View of Government in the United States*, ed. Daniel J. Elazar (Chicago, 1966). Thomas R. Dye placed earlier scholarship in broad context in his *Politics in States and Communities* (Englewood Cliffs, New Jersey, 1969; 6th ed., 1988). In the writing of this volume of *The History of Wisconsin*, the most valuable and suggestive works were James T. Patterson, *The New Deal and the States: Federalism in Transition* (Princeton, 1969; reprinted, Westport, Connecticut, 1981) and Barry D. Karl, *The Uneasy State: The United States from 1915 to 1945* (Chicago, 1983).

The most thorough biography of Roosevelt, not yet completed, is that of Frank Freidel, *Franklin D. Roosevelt*. The four volumes so far published are subtitled *The Apprenticeship* (Boston, 1952), *The Ordeal* (Boston, 1954), *The Triumph* (Boston, 1956), and *Launching the New Deal* (Boston, 1973). The best single-volume studies of FDR during the Great Depression are James MacGregor Burns, *Roosevelt: The Lion and the Fox* (New York, 1956), and Rexford G. Tugwell, *The Democratic Roosevelt: A Biography of Franklin D. Roosevelt* (Garden City, New York, 1957). The most comprehensive single-volume study of the New Deal is William E. Leuchtenburg, *Franklin D. Roosevelt and the New Deal, 1932–1940* (New York, 1963), and the most provocative is Paul K. Conkin, *The New Deal* (New York, 1967; 2nd ed., Arlington Heights, Illinois, 1975). An important account of Roosevelt's political activities in the 1920's and early 1930's is Alfred B. Rollins, *Roosevelt and Howe* (New York, 1962). For the relationship between persons active in the Progressive movement and the New Deal, see Otis L. Graham, Jr., *An Encore for Reform: The Old Progressives and the New Deal*, previously mentioned.

New Dealers who worked closely with Roosevelt could not help being influenced by his magnetic personality. Frances Perkins' *The Roosevelt I Knew* (New York, 1946) is an admiring account of her role as secretary of labor under FDR's leadership which contains much valuable information. In addition to writing *The Democratic Roosevelt*, Rexford Tugwell published *The Brains Trust* (New York, 1968) and *In Search of Roosevelt* (Cambridge, 1972). Equally thoughtful, but propounding a different point of view, are Raymond Moley's two books: *After Seven Years* (New York, 1939; reprinted, Jersey City, 1972) and *The First New Deal* (New York, 1966). A fascinating and candid account of the inner workings of the New Deal is Harold L. Ickes, *The Secret Diary of Harold L. Ickes* (3 vols., New York, 1953–1954; reprinted, Jersey City, 1974). Katie Louchheim, ed., *The Making of the New Deal: The Insiders Speak* (Cambridge, 1983) is a collection of reminiscences. Especially useful for this volume were those of Thomas H. Eliot and Wilbur J. Cohen on the advent of Social Security.

Among the many useful biographical studies of New Dealers and Americans prominent during the 1930's are Linda J. Lear, *The Aggressive Progressive: The*

Political Career of Harold L. Ickes, 1874–1933 (New York, 1981); Bernard Sternsher, *Rexford Tugwell and the New Deal* (New Brunswick, New Jersey, 1964); Searle F. Charles, *Minister of Relief: Harry Hopkins and the Depression* (Syracuse, 1963; reprinted, Westport, Connecticut, 1974); J. Joseph Huthmacher, *Senator Robert F. Wagner and the Rise of Urban Liberalism* (New York, 1968); Richard B. Henderson, *Maury Maverick: A Political Biography* (Austin, 1970); Francis L. Broderick, *Right Reverend New Dealer, John A. Ryan* (New York, 1963); T. Harry Williams, *Huey Long* (New York, 1969); and Edward Blackorby's biography of William E. Lemke, *Prairie Rebel: The Public Life of William Lemke* (Lincoln, Nebraska, 1963).

Excellent studies of New Deal programs, the persons who administered them, and the regulations they promulgated provide important insights into the way the Roosevelt administration pursued its objectives of relief, recovery, and reform. In discussing the National Recovery Administration, economic planning, and the antitrust program of the later New Deal, Ellis W. Hawley made an impressive contribution with *The New Deal and the Problem of Monopoly: A Study in Economic Ambivalence*, previously cited. Thomas K. McCraw, *TVA and the Power Fight, 1933–1939* (Philadelphia, 1971) provides important perspectives on struggles over purposes and programs of the Tennessee Valley Authority. Wisconsin's "little TVA" is the subject of Samuel Mermin's *Jurisprudence and Statecraft: The Wisconsin Development Authority and Its Implications* (Madison, 1963.) Thomas K. McCraw's chapter on James M. Landis in his masterful, Pulitzer-prize-winning study, *Prophets of Regulation: Charles Francis Adams, Louis D. Brandeis, James M. Landis, Alfred E. Kahn* (Cambridge, 1984), places the Securities and Exchange Commission in the broad regulatory tradition, a tradition that the author sees as having succeeded only when it took economic realities into account. Another work that deals with regulation, but from a different perspective, is Frances Fox Piven and Richard A. Cloward, *Regulating the Poor: The Functions of Public Welfare* (New York, 1971).

Because of Wisconsin's importance as an agricultural state, four books merit consideration. They are Van L. Perkins, *Crisis in Agriculture: The Agricultural Adjustment Administration and the New Deal, 1933* (Berkeley, 1969); Gilbert C. Fite, *George N. Peek and the Fight for Farm Parity*, previously cited; Richard S. Kirkendall, *Social Scientists and Farm Politics in the Age of Roosevelt* (Columbia, Missouri, 1966); and Paul K. Conkin, *Tomorrow a New World: The New Deal Community Program* (Ithaca, 1958).

In part because of Wisconsin's unemployment compensation program, the state's Progressives became deeply involved in both the drafting and the administration of the Social Security Act passed by Congress in 1935. The most comprehensive treatment of the subject is Daniel Nelson's *Unemployment Insurance: The American Experience, 1915–1935*, already cited. Theron F. Schlabach, *Edwin E. Witte: Cautious Reformer*, also cited above, is an excellent biography of the man celebrated in Wisconsin as "the father of Social Security." Witte's own account of the battle for social security legislation appeared as *The Development of the Social Security Act: A Memorandum on the History of the Committee on Economic Security and Drafting and Legislative History of the Social Security Act* (Madison, 1962); and Robert J. Lampman edited *Social Security Perspectives: Essays* [by Edwin E. Witte] (Madison, 1962).

Other contemporary analyses, along with the recollections of participants in the debate over the law, provide a sense of the diversity of thought on the program. Interested readers will especially wish to consult Paul H. Douglas, *Social Security in the United States: An Analysis and Appraisal of the Federal Social Security Act* (New York, 1936; reprinted, Salem, New Hampshire, 1971, and Westport, Connecticut, 1972) and Abraham Epstein, *Insecurity, a Challenge to America: A Study of Social Insurance in the United States and Abroad* (New York, 1936; 3rd ed., 1968). Charles McKinley and Robert W. Frase later provided useful information in *Launching Social Security: A Capture-and-Record Account, 1935–1937* (Madison, 1970). Arthur J. Altmeyer, who served on the Social Security Board and as commissioner of Social Security, linked the program with Wisconsin in "The Wisconsin Idea and Social Security," in the *WMH*, 42 (Autumn, 1958), 19–25, but his most important contribution to an understanding of the law is his book, *The Formative Years of Social Security* (Madison, 1966).

Because Wisconsin includes a relatively large number of Indians—at least 15,000 people—New Deal Indian policy is a subject of considerable importance in the history of the state during the Great Depression. The key document establishing a basis for modification of American Indian policy is the celebrated report of Lewis Meriam et al., *The Problem of Indian Administration* (Baltimore, 1928), written for the Brookings Institution's Institute for Government Research. To place the report and the Indian Reorganiztion Act of 1934 in context, one should first consult Francis Paul Prucha's monumental study, *The Great Father: The United States Government and the American Indians* (2 vols., Lincoln, Nebraska, 1984), and Theodore W. Taylor's important work, *The Bureau of Indian Affairs* (Boulder, 1984).

An early essay on the effort to revise the policy of assimilation is Randolph C. Downes's article, "A Crusade for Indian Reform, 1922–1934," in the *Mississippi Valley Historical Review*, 32 (December, 1945), 331–354. More recently, Michael T. Smith published "The Wheeler-Howard Act of 1934: The Indian New Deal," in *Journal of the West*, 10 (July, 1971), 521–534. Significant books on the campaign to modify policies embodied in the Dawes Act include William H. Kelly, ed., *Indian Affairs and the Indian Reorganization Act: The Twenty Year Record* (Tucson, 1954) and Graham D. Taylor, *The New Deal and American Indian Tribalism: The Administration of the Indian Reorganization Act, 1934–45* (Lincoln, Nebraska, 1980). Focusing on John Collier's role in bringing about a change in government policy are Kenneth R. Philp, *John Collier's Crusade for Indian Reform, 1920–1954* (Tucson, 1977) and Lawrence C. Kelly, *The Assault on Assimilation: John Collier and the Origins of Indian Policy Reform* (Albuquerque, 1983).

That Wisconsin is a state well suited for the study of American Indians is the thesis of Nancy Oestreich Lurie's article, "Wisconsin: A Natural Laboratory for North American Indian Studies," in the *WMH*, 53 (Autumn, 1969), 3–20, reprinted in revised form as a booklet entitled *Wisconsin Indians* (Madison, 1980; reprinted, 1987). Nevertheless, the scholarship on Wisconsin Indians in the 1930's is disappointing in volume. The only tribal studies dealing with the decade are Lurie's own work, "The Winnebago Indians: A Study in Cultural Change" (doctoral dissertation, Northwestern University, 1952), microfilm copy in SHSW; Edmund J. Danziger, Jr., *The Chippewas of Lake Superior* (Norman, 1978); and Patricia K. Ourada, *The Menominee Indians: A History* (Norman, 1979). Students of the Depression Decade would benefit from more investigations such as the one Donald L. Parman conducted for "The Indian and the Civilian Conservation Corps," in the *Pacific Historical Review*, 40 (February, 1971), 39–56, and for his more extensive work, "The Indian Civilian Conservation Corps" (doctoral dissertation, University of Oklahoma, 1967), microfilm copy in SHSW.

The CCC was a New Deal agency that exerted an important influence in Wisconsin during the Depression Decade. John A. Salmond, *The Civilian Conservation Corps, 1933–1942: A New Deal Case Study* (Durham, 1967) provides an excellent survey of the agency, and George P. Rawick views it as an expression of the New Dealers' concern for young people in "The New Deal and Youth: The Civilian Conservation Corps, the National Youth Administration, and the American Youth Congress" (doctoral dissertation, University of Wisconsin, 1957). Less scholarly works are Leslie Alexander Lacy, *The Soil Soldiers: The Civilian Conservation Corps in the Great Depression* (Radnor, Pennsylvania, 1976) and Perry H. Merrill, *Roosevelt's Forest Army: A History of the Civilian Conservation Corps, 1933–1942* (Montpelier, Vermont, 1981).

Environmental concerns provide a theme for Roderick Nash's valuable study, *Wilderness and the American Mind* (New Haven, 1967; 3rd ed., 1982), and for A. L. Reisch Owen's more limited work, *Conservation Under F.D.R.* (New York, 1983). University of Wisconsin Professor Aldo Leopold established a reputation as one of the giants in the conservation movement of the thirties. Two of his books, *Game Management* (New York, 1933) and *A Sand County Almanac: And Sketches Here and There* (New York, 1949), became classics in the field of ecology. Susan L. Flader, *Thinking Like a Mountain: Aldo Leopold and the Evolution of an Ecological Attitude Toward Deer, Wolves, and Forests* (Columbia, Missouri, 1974) is a detailed account of Leopold's ideas, and Anthony Wolff, ed., *The Sand Country of Aldo Leopold: A Photographic Interpretation by Charles Steinhacker; Essay by Susan Flader; Selections from Writings of Aldo Leopold* (San Francisco, 1973) adds further dimension to the appreciation of Leopold's point of view. Curt Meine's *Aldo Leopold: His Life and Work* (Madison, 1988) is a splendid book, and as close to being "definitive" as any study is likely to be.

The establishment of New Deal programs neither overcame the Depression nor silenced the critics of American society, and despite Roosevelt's enormous popularity, the Depression Decade was one of great political ferment. Donald R. McCoy's early study, *Angry Voices: Left-of-Center Politics in the New Deal Era* (Lawrence, Kansas, 1958; reprinted, New York, 1971), established a foundation for later investigation of radical protests during the 1930's. More recently, Ronald A. Mulder has examined the reactions of Progressive senators to the New Deal in *The Insurgent Progressives in the United States Senate and the New Deal, 1933–1939* (New York, 1979). The activities of dissident reformers outside the Congress are the subject of Donald L. Miller's study, *The New American Radicalism: Alfred M. Bingham and Non-Marxian Insurgency in the New Deal Era* (Port Washington, New York, 1979). Ronald L. Feinman, *Twilight of Progressivism: The Western Republican Senators and the New Deal* (Baltimore, 1981) contains a perceptive discussion of the brothers La Follette and the activities of Wisconsin Progressives.

In the investigation of Wisconsin Progressives during the 1930's, Donald McCoy again led the way with the publication of his article, "The Formation of the Wisconsin Progressive Party in 1934," in *The Historian*, 14 (Autumn, 1951), 70–90. Lester F. Schmidt expanded the time frame of his research for "The Farmer-Labor Progressive Federation: The Study of a 'United Front'

Movement Among Wisconsin Liberals, 1934–1941" (doctoral dissertation, University of Wisconsin, 1955), and Charles H. Backstrom concentrated on the state's Progressive party organization in "The Progressive Party of Wisconsin, 1934–1946" (doctoral dissertation, University of Wisconsin, 1957). The congressman from Wisconsin's First District, Thomas R. Amlie, served as national chairman of the National Farmer Labor Political Federation. He is the subject of two excellent articles: Theodore Rosenof, "The Political Education of an American Radical: Thomas R. Amlie in the 1930's," in the *WMH*, 58 (Autumn, 1974), 19–30; and Stuart L. Weiss, "Thomas Amlie and the New Deal," in *Mid-America*, 59 (January, 1977), 19–38. Hugh T. Lovin examines the appeal of independent political action among workers and labor leaders in "The Persistence of Third Party Dreams in the American Labor Movement, 1930–1938," in *Mid-America*, 58 (October, 1976), 141–157.

The labor struggles of the late thirties greatly exacerbated the problems that the Wisconsin Progressives confronted in dealing with demands for a new, independent political party. For a discussion of interpretive difficulties in the labor history of the decade, see David Brody, "Labor and the Great Depression: The Interpretative Prospects," in *Labor History*, 13 (Spring, 1972), 231–244. The best studies of labor problems and policies during the New Deal era are Irving Bernstein's volumes, previously cited: *The New Deal Collective Bargaining Policy* and *Turbulent Years: A History of the American Worker, 1933–1941*. A valuable collection of essays edited by Milton Derber and Edwin Young, *Labor and the New Deal* (Madison, 1957; reprinted, Jersey City, 1972), contains several important essays, including Robben W. Fleming's "The Significance of the Wagner Act," 121–155. Jerold S. Auerbach's superb study, *Labor and Liberty: The La Follette Committee and the New Deal* (Indianapolis, 1966), indicates clearly why New Dealers believed new labor legislation to be a necessity, and why Young Bob La Follette became a great favorite among workers. Two studies dealing with labor in Wisconsin are Walter H. Uphoff's *Kohler on Strike: Thirty Years of Conflict* (Boston, 1966) and Robert H. Zieger's *Madison's Battery Workers, 1934–1952: A History of Federal Labor Union 19587* (Ithaca, 1977).

In an atmosphere of labor conflict at home and anxiety over international rivalries abroad, the dispute between Governor Philip F. La Follette and University of Wisconsin President Glenn Frank attracted great national attention. Aware of the governor's political ambitions, many Progressives believed it was more than a tempest in a teapot and that it raised questions about the future of democracy in America. Discussing the episode in *Some Ferments at Wisconsin, 1901–1947: Memories and Reflections* (Madison, 1960), George Clarke Sellery makes clear that he was no admirer of Frank. In *The President Wore Spats: A Biography of Glenn Frank* (Madison, 1965), Lawrence H. Larsen argues that while Frank had undeniable abilities as a journalist, he lacked the scholarly credentials to be an effective university president. Steven D. Zink's carefully researched article, "Glenn Frank of the University of Wisconsin: A Reinterpretation," in the *WMH*, 62 (Winter, 1978–1979), 91–127, attempts to rescue Frank's reputation.

The fact is that both sides lost credibility as a result of the squabble. Frank lost his job, and Phil La Follette aroused concern among defenders of academic freedom and among persons who detected similarities between the governor's tactics and those of the fascists. In part because of doubts raised by the feud with Frank, La Follette's attempt to gain national political influence came a cropper. The governor's perception of national needs receives careful attention in John E. Miller, "Governor Philip F. La Follette's Shifting Priorities from Redistribution to Expansion," in *Mid-America*, 58 (April–July, 1976), 119–126, and Donald McCoy analyzes his attempt to form a new party in "The National Progressives of America, 1938," in the *Mississippi Valley Historical Review*, 44 (June, 1957), 75–93. Sidney Hyman touches on the participation of one of La Follette's supporters in *The Lives of William Benton* (Chicago, 1969).

The best works on the effort to avoid involvement in a second world war, an effort the La Follettes and many of their followers supported, are those of Wayne S. Cole: *America First: The Battle Against Intervention, 1940–1941* (Madison, 1953); *Senator Gerald P. Nye and American Foreign Relations* (Minneapolis, 1962; reprinted, Westport, Connecticut, 1980); and *Roosevelt and the Isolationists, 1932–45* (Lincoln, Nebraska, 1983). John E. Wiltz has provided a useful survey of the historiography of isolationist activities in his short study, *From Isolation to War, 1931–1941* (New York, 1968). For a careful examination of the forces that brought defeat to the antiwar effort, one should consult William L. Langer and S. Everett Gleason, *The Challenge to Isolation, 1937–1940* (2 vols., New York, 1952; reprinted as *The Challenge to Isolation: The World Crisis of 1937–1940 and American Foreign Policy*, 2 vols., New York, 1964, and Gloucester, Massachusetts, 1970). In Walter Johnson's *The Battle Against Isolation* (Chicago, 1944; reprinted, Jersey City, 1973), William Allen White's biographer makes clear that his sympathies lay with the interventionists. A more balanced treatment is Mark Lincoln Chadwin's later study, *The Hawks of World War II* (Chapel Hill, 1968; reprinted as *The Warhawks: American Interventionists Before Pearl Harbor*, New York, 1970). An interesting approach to the isolationist-interventionist debate in Wisconsin is Thomas R. Nevin, "The Protestant Ministry of Wisconsin and the Crisis of Intervention, 1939–1941" (master's thesis, University of Wisconsin, 1968).

With the onset of World War II, the people of Wisconsin joined other Americans in a massive stock-taking effort. They took great pains to determine where events of the interwar years had taken them, how they had comported themselves in a time of uncertainty, and what the future held for them. When the war ended, the process of historical interpretation began in earnest, and the process continues to this day. For a full-dress history of Wisconsin in wartime and the postwar period, the reader is referred to the successor volume in this series, William F. Thompson's *The History of Wisconsin. Volume VI: Continuity and Change, 1940–1965* (Madison, 1988).

INDEX

A. J. Monday: 235
Academic freedom: and Glenn Frank ouster, 504–506
Adamic, Louis: 446
Adams, Samuel Hopkins: 33
Addams, Jane: 5, 6, 288
Advance-Rumely Corporation: 150
Agricultural Adjustment Act (AAA): 408, 417, 418, 553
Agricultural Credits Act (1923): 275
Agricultural Experiment Station: 165–167, 175
Agricultural economics: 179–180
Agricultural implements: 143–151
Agriculture: 165–194 *passim*; postwar problems, 133–136; as business, 142–143; farm implements industry, 143–151, 154–155; proposed government price controls, 151–153; co-operatives, 152, 153; highways and, 155–164; rise of scientific approach to, 165; at University of Wisconsin, 165–170; and banking, 170–171; increased production, 171–172; scientific research in, 172–174; resettlement in Cutover, 202–207; effects of Depression on, 357–362. *See also* Farmers
Ajax (automobile): 140
Alexander, A. S.: 171
Alexander, Louis M.: 236
Alfonsi, Paul: 517–518
Alford, W. H.: 314
All-Crop harvester: 150
Allen, Robert G.: 553
Allen, William Harvey: 176
Allen-A Hosiery Company: labor strife at, 245–246
Allis-Chalmers Manufacturing Company: rebuilt by Otto Falk, 148–149; and farm implement industry, 149–151; paternalism towards labor, 238–239; AFL-CIO dispute, 531–532
Allis Mutual Aid Society, 238
Altmeyer, Arthur J.: 346, 391; compiles unemployment data, 380; role in Social Security legislation, 452, 453, 455, 457, 459, 463–464
Aluminum cookware: 210
Amalgamated Clothing Workers: 244
America First Committee: 527, 562
American Association for Labor Legislation: 391
American Commonwealth Political Federation: 476n, 478, 536, 537, 550
American Constitutional League: 72
American Country Life Association: 164
American Expeditionary Force: 25
American Farm Bureau Federation: 134, 178, 274
American Federation of Full Fashioned Hosiery Workers: 245, 430
American Federation of Labor (AFL): 247, 290; attempts to organize Kohler Company: 429–430; elitism of, 529; and CIO, 530; in Wisconsin, 530–533; competition with CIO, 533–534
American Labor party: 268
American Legion: 72, 375
American Lutheran Conference: 343, 344
American Medical Association: 115, 453
American Newspaper Guild: 549
"American Plan": 235, 236, 239, 240, 450–451
American Protective League: 31, 36
American Society of Equity: 394
Americanization: as postwar phenomenon, 72–79; in education, 256–258
Amlie, Thomas R.: 437, 439, 441, 477, 478, 528, 537, 541; elected to Congress, 445; role in farmer-labor alliance, 475,

476n; opposes Communists, 479; 1938 senatorial primary, 552, 553–554
Anderson, Henry W.: 102
Anderson, Knute: 142
Anderson, Sherwood: 230
Andrews, John B.: 391, 392
Angell, Norman: 283
Animal breeding: 172
Anti-Saloon League: role in Prohibition, 88–89, 90, 92, 93, 94–95, 96, 300; during wartime, 58
Anti-Semitism: of Ku Klux Klan, 121; during Depression, 368; in 1932 gubernatorial primary, 401n; in Germany, 406; among German Lutherans, 559
Apostle Islands: 215
Appleton Chamber of Commerce: 236
Armistice: celebration, 55; effect on labor movement, 232
Arndt, William: 155
Ashe, William: 519
Ashland: fervency of World War I patriotism, 32
Association Against the Prohibition Amendment: 103
Association of Agricultural Colleges: 171
Association of American Agricultural Colleges and Experiment Stations: 169–170
Association of Catholic Women's Clubs: 112
Association of University Women: 110
Augustana Synod: 91, 344
Austrians: and World War I, 1
Automobile industry: early history, 136–142; in Wisconsin, 136, 137–138, 139–140, 141, 142; during Depression, 356, 372

Babbitt (novel): 196
Babcock, C. A.: 236
Babcock, Stephen M.: 166, 173, 181–182, 185
Bacteriology: 173
Bad River Reservation (Ashland County): 489
Baker, Newton D.: 102
Baker, Ray Stannard: 25–26, 33
Bakken, Henry H.: 180
Ball, Bert: 170
Ballard, C. B.: 268
Banachowicz, John: 531, 532
Banking industry: and automobile industry, 141; and New Era prosperity, 141–142; and agriculture, 170–171
Bankruptcy: 362
Banting, Frederick Grant: 185n
Barber, Mildred: 118n
Barkley, Alben: 524
Bartlett, John H., Jr.: 389
Barton, Albert O.: 218
Bassett, A. K.: 155
"Battle of Durham Hill" (Waukesha County): 417
Bear Brand Hosiery Company: 372
Beard, Charles A.: 387
Beaver Dam (Dodge County): labor convention at, 530
Beck, Joseph: 320, 321
Becker, John A.: 513
Beer: availability during prohibition, 100–102
Belmont, Alva: 110
Belmont, O. H. P.: 110
Beloit College: 193
Bennett, Edward: 189
Bennett, J. Henry: 123
Bennett Law: 77
Benson, Elmer: 507
Bentley, Arthur: 278
Benton, William: 538
Berger, Meta: 110, 289n; and pacifist movement, 8; opposes isolationism, 560–561
Berger, Victor: opposition to World War I, 11; 1918 senatorial campaign, 47, 48, 49–50; *Leader* suppressed, 49; denied seat in Congress, 53; during Red Scare, 68; opposes Ku Klux Klan, 124; supports La Follette in 1922, 280, 293; on Robert La Follette, Jr., 309
Berle, Adolph A.: 541
Bicyclists: 156
Biemiller, Andrew: 475, 478, 514–515, 517, 518
Bingham, Alfred: 437, 473, 476n, 477, 479, 481, 537, 553; critical of National Progressives of America, 550–551
Birge, Edward A.: 499–500
Black, Hugo: 510
Blacks. *See* Negroes
"Black Thursday": 350, 351
Blaine, John J.: 135; in 1918 elections, 51, 52, 53; and prohibition, 97–98, 103; elected to U.S. Senate, 103; supports equal rights, 112, 113; opposes abolition of National Guard, 117; opposes Ku Klux Klan, 123; and postwar unemployment, 132; vetoes gasoline tax bill, 162; vetoes state park bill, 214n; vetoes private detective agency bill, 242; and crim-

inal contempt case, 244; and educational reforms, 260; wins 1922 senatorial election, 278, 279; position among Progressives, 299, 307; gubernatorial candidacy supported by Old Bob La Follette, 300, 303; and prohibition, 300–301; and taxation, 302–303; and highways, 304, 306; 1924 gubernatorial campaign, 305–307; 1926 senatorial campaign, 313–315; supports Progressive unity campaign, 318; delegate to 1928 Republican convention, 319; endorses Al Smith, 321; aids Phil La Follette's gubernatorial campaign, 323; 1932 senatorial campaign, 401; New Deal appointment, 409; appoints Zona Gale to UW Board of Regents, 500
Bliss, C. H.: 519
Bloodgood, Wheeler P.: 26, 28
Blue Mound Road (Milwaukee County): first concrete road in state, 159–160
Blumenthal, Lottie: 368
Boardman, Charles: 18
Boerner, Martin: 512
Boileau, Gerald: 445
Bolens, Albert D.: 229
Bolens, Harry: 557
Bolshevism: 54, 67, 69, 71, 73, 75
"Booster spirit": 196–199, 225, 228; and onset of Depression, 352–354, 365
Borah, William E.: 231, 318, 436, 460, 477
Bouck, William: 286
Bowles, Chester: 538
Boys Working Reserve: 38
Brager, Henry: 195
Brandeis, Elizabeth: 378, 381, 384, 391, 392, 402; role in Social Security legislation, 450, 451
Brandeis, Louis D.: 287, 378; espouses social programs, 449–450, 451, 454, 464
Branson, Eugene C.: 177, 179
Brewing industry: opposes Anti-Saloon League, 89; opposes prohibition amendment, 96; during prohibition, 100; opposition to woman suffrage, 106, 108
Brisbane, Arthur: 351
Brittingham, Thomas E., Jr.: 185
Brody, Lawrence J.: 305
Brookings Institution: 488, 490
Brooks, Hellen M.: 118n
Broughton, Charles E.: 401
Broun, Heywood: 549
Browder, Earl: 460
Brown, Francis: 546
Brown, Olympia: 107, 108
Brown, Timothy: 185
Bruce, George: 197
Bryan, Charles: 291–292
Bryan, William Jennings: 43n, 291
Budenz, Louis: 245–246
Budget: legislation concerning state's, 512–513
Bull Traction Machine Company: 145
Bureau of Indian Affairs: 486, 487, 488, 490, 491
Bureau of Markets: 154
Burke, Michael E.: 28
Burmeister, William: 31
Burtis, Ira E.: 390, 394
"Bush, The" (Madison): 101–102, 124
Business: postwar, 129–142 *passim*; postwar depression, 129–133; installment buying, 140–142; and tourism, 160; postwar rhetoric of prosperity, 252–252, 273
Business and Financial Comment (Milwaukee): 133, 141
Butter: 185–186

Cabot, Richard C.: 242n
Callahan, John M.: 443, 444, 445, 503
Camp Douglas (Juneau County): National Guard trains at, 18, 23–24
Camp MacArthur (Texas): 24
Camping: 216–217
Cannon, F. A.: 155
Cannon, Raymond J.: 470
Capper-Volstead Act: 275
Carhart, John W.: 136
Carnegie Endowment for International Peace: 385
Cary, Charles P.: 224, 257–258
Cary, William J.: 53
Case, Harry Woodburn: 506
Case, J. I., Company. *See* J. I. Case Company
Catholics: schools, 75; and Americanization, 75–77; opposition to prohibition, 89–91, 93, 95; Irish support prohibition, 90; opposition to woman suffrage, 106; opposed by Ku Klux Klan, 123–124; sponsor labor conference, 238; voting patterns, 342; voting patterns in 1938, 557; oppose Nazi anti-Semitism, 560
Catt, Carrie Chapman: 108, 109
Causey, James: 405, 509
Central Co-operative Association: 411
Central-Verein: 90

Central Wisconsin Conservation District: 496
Chafee, Zechariah: 35
Chain Belt Manufacturing Company: 74
Chain stores: 199, 227–230
Chambers of commerce: 196
Chapple, John C.: 38n, 401, 402, 403, 444, 445, 501
Chevrolet, Louis: 139
Chevrolet Motor Car Company: 139, 147
Childs, Marquis: 483–485
Chippewa tribe: 487, 489
Christ, Peter: 244
Christensen, Parley P.: 272, 273
Christoffel, Harold: 531–532
Chrysler, Walter P: 139
Church League of Industrial Democracy: 279
Cities: effects on rural demography, 219–225 *passim*
City Club (Washington): 279
City Club of Milwaukee: 191, 198
Civil War veterans: 195
Civil Works Administration: 467, 492
Civilian Conservation Corps (CCC): 408, 491, 492–499
Clark, Bennett Champ: 461
Clarke-McNary Bill: 208
Clausen, Frederick H.: 390, 394
Clausen, Leon R.: 148
Cleveland, Grover: 19
Clifford, Eugene A.: 403
Cohen, Wilbur J.: 453n
Cole, Leon J.: 168, 172
Coleman, William: 239
Collective bargaining: 246, 425, 426–427, 433
College of Agriculture (UW): 151, 165–187 *passim*; theoretical vs. practical research, 167–168; General Extension Division, 169; opposition to, 176–181; audited, 176–177; agricultural economics, 179–180; ethical problems of scientific research, 181–183; research foundation established, 183–187; and radio, 193–194; and settlement of Cutover, 204–205
Collier, John: 488, 489
Comings, George F.: 255, 256; elected lieutenant-governor, 300, 301; opposes Blaine on prohibition enforcement, 300; 1924 gubernatorial campaign, 303–304, 307
Committee for Industrial Organization: 530
Committee of Forty-Eight: and search for viable third party, 268–269, 270–271, 272–273, 279, 386
Committee on Economic Security (COES): 452, 457, 458, 459, 463
Committee on Public Information: 25, 38, 43
Commons, John R.: 29, 40, 232, 237, 362; role in unemployment compensation, 378, 390, 391, 392; evolves labor theory, 420–423
Communist Labor party: 268
Communist party: 268, 280, 478–479; repudiates National Progressives of America, 547
Communists: in Farmer-Labor party, 284–286; feared by Progressives, 285–286; and unemployment demonstrations, 368–369; public perception of, 369, 370; opposed by Phil La Follette, 542
Concrete: as paving material, 159–160
Conference for Progressive Political Action (CPPA): 279–282, 286–288, 289
Congress of Industrial Organizations (CIO): formation of, 530; in Wisconsin, 531–533; competition with AFL, 533–534
Connery, William P., Jr.: 451
Conservation: 200–202, 207–210, 492–496
Constitution (state): prohibits borrowing for internal improvements, 156–157, 201, 468, 514
Construction industry: during Depression, 356, 357
Consumerism: 249–250, 252–254
Consumers' League: 112
"Continental Sunday": 90
Continuous Mediation Without Armistice: 4–6
Coolidge, Calvin: 231, 286, 292, 293, 318; vetoes farm legislation, 152
Cooper, Henry Allen: 53, 286
Cooper, John: 303
Cooper, William John: 265
Co-operation: in business, 195–199
Co-operatives: 152, 153, 175, 177–178, 409
Corn: 173
Corporations Auxiliary detective agency: 242, 243
Costello, Emil: 531, 532–533
Costigan, Edward P.: 408, 442
Cottrell, Frederick Gardner: 183
Council of Defense: 129

Council of Grain Exchanges: 170
Council of Jewish Women: 110
Cowles, John: 546
Credit: during New Era, 140–141
Croly, Herbert: 288
Cronon, Edward: 38
Crowder, Enoch: 24
Crowley, Ada Fuller: 119–120
Crowley, Leo T.: 352
Crownhart, Charles H.: 42, 322
Crownhart, J. G.: 190
Cubberley, Elwood P.: 177
Cudahy, John: 27
Cutover: 127, 198, 364n; agricultural resettlement, 202–204, 205–207; stump removal, 204–205; reforestation, 207–210; and recreation, 211–220 *passim*; Indian farming in, 487
Cutting, Bronson: 406, 408

Dahl, John L.: 302, 303
Dairy farming: effects of Depression on, 358, 409–412; dairy strike, 409–410, 413–419; farmers' organizations, 412–413
Dammann, Theodore: 439, 445, 481, 513, 516
Daughters of the American Revolution: 112
David Adler Clothing Company: 244
Davidson, James: 20
Davidson, Jo: 283
Davidson, Walter: 27
Davies, Joseph E.: 1918 senatorial campaign, 47, 48–49
Davis, John W.: 287, 291, 292, 293; 1924 vote compared with 1932 vote, 403–404
Dawes Severalty Act: 486
Dawes, Charles G.: 231
DeLong, J. E.: 519
Delwiche, Edmond J.: 172
Democratic party: in decline after 1894, 19–20; and Poles, 76; postwar conservatism, 297; Depression improves prospects, 398–400; 1932 victory, 403–404; distrust of Progressives, 404; and Roosevelt's endorsement of Robert La Follette, Jr., 443; liberal wing allies with Progressive party, 443–444; criticized by Phil La Follette, 543; makes peace with conservative Republicans, 552, 554–555
Dempsey, C. E.: 420n
Denney, John M.: 509
Dennis, Eugene: 478
Department of Farmers' Institutes: 166
De Pere (Brown County): first sawmill at: 199
Depression (1920–1921): 129–132, 274–275
Depression, Great: and farmers, 163, 357–362; Wisconsin reaction to Crash, 350–355; business' reaction to, 351–355; bankruptcies, 362, unemployment and relief, 363–365, 367–386, 390–395; effect on dairy industry, 410–411; effects on labor movement, 425–426; Phil La Follette on causes of, 542–543
Detective agencies: and labor movement, 233–234; and labor strife, 242–243
Deutsche, Fred J.: 304
Dewey, John: 93, 258
Dill, Clarence C.: 451
Dithmar, Edward F.: 53, 312
Do Our Bit Club: 8
Doheny, Edward L.: 282
Donaghey, John T.: 305, 380
Doudna, Edgar G.: 260
Douglas, Paul: 435, 450
Doyle, W. H.: 141
Draft: World War I, 24
Drought: 358
Du Bois, W. E. B.: 288, 436
Dudgeon, Matthew S.: 69, 176
Duffy, F. Ryan: 401, 403, 443
Duncan, Thomas M.: 246, 379, 446; Phil La Follette's most trusted aide, 476; hit-and-run accident, 556, 558
du Pont, Irenee: 139
du Pont, Pierre S.: 139
Durant, William C.: 138; and tractor industry, 146
Duranty, Walter: 409
Dykema, Peter W.: 6
Dykstra, Clarence: 506
Dynamite: 204

Economy: postwar, 129–136; agricultural, 133–136; effects of expansion, 141–142; postwar boom, 248–250. *See also* Depression, Great
Eddy, Sherwood, 435–436
Education: Americanization of, 73–75; postwar religious tensions, 78–79; postwar reforms and expansion, 251, 256–263; business influence, 257; classroom reforms, 258–259; regional disparities, 259–260; opposition to reforms, 259–261; vocational, 257, 262–265
Eighteenth Amendment (prohibition): 87, 247n; opposed by Germans, 94–95; rat-

ified, 96–97; enforcement, 98, 101–102; skepticism towards, 99; effects of, 99–102; repeal of, 103, 104; and tourist industry, 218; politics of enforcement, 300–301
Ekern, Herman: 285, 314, 320, 439; 1938 senatorial campaign, 552–554
Elections: analysis of 1916–1940 La Follette family votes, 298, 327–345, 571–588; Wisconsin system described, 325–326
Electrification: 382–383, 386
Eliot, Thomas H.: 451, 454, 459, 460
Ellis, L. S.: 180
Ellsworth (Pierce County): efforts to reduce unemployment, 374
Ely, Richard T.: 129; hyperpatriotic spokesman, 40, 42–43, 54; and League to Enforce Peace, 59; and agricultural economics, 179
Emergency Board: 512
Emergency Highway Act (1931): 380
Emergency Peace Conference (1915): 5
Emergency Relief Act (1932): 395–396
Emergency Relief Appropriation Act: 467, 468
Emergency Relief Bill (1933): 407n
Employers Mutual Liability Insurance Company of Wisconsin: 211
Employment: postwar, 131–133; during New Era, 248–249, 250, 252. *See also* Unemployment
English language: 74–75
Epstein, Abraham: 450
Esch, John J.: 49, 276
Esch-Cummins Act: 276, 281, 312
Esperanto: 264n
Espionage Act (1917): 35, 37
Eugenics: 24n
Everest, David Clark: 211, 236, 237, 519
Everett, James A.: 175
Evjue, William T.: 47n, 52, 64, 303, 363, 401n, 523; and prohibition, 95n; criticizes Wisconsin Alumni Research Foundation, 186; endorses Franklin Roosevelt, 403; chairs Progressive convention, 440; supports Roosevelt over Phil La Follette, 538, 541; favors fourth term for Phil La Follette, 552; supports Ekern candidacy, 553; opposes Amlie's industrial expansion bill, 554
Ewing, Mark C.: 236
Explosives: in stump removal, 204–205
Ezekiel, Mordecai: 553
Faast, Ben: 204
Falk, Otto H.: 314; and Allis-Chalmers, 148–149
Falk Corporation: 148
Fall, Albert B.: 282
Family: changes in attitudes towards, 253–254; affected by postwar amusements, 254–256
Farm bloc: and postwar politics and legislation, 274–275, 277, 278
Farm Holiday Association. *See* National Farmers' Holiday Association
Farm prices: impact of Depression on, 357–358, 362
Farmall tractors: 147
Farmer-Labor and Progressive League: 441, 476n, 478; delegates attend labor conference, 476
Farmer-Labor party (FLP): 272, 279, 280; Communists in, 284–286; attacked by organized labor, 285
Farmer-Labor Political Federation: 473, 475. *See also* Wisconsin Farmer-Labor Political Federation
Farmer-Labor Progressive Federation (FLPF): 476, 478; relationship with Phil La Follette, 517–518, 520. *See also* Wisconsin Farmer-Labor Progressive Federation
Farmers: and postwar depression, 133–136; and farm implements, 143–145, 147, 150, 151; and McNary-Haugen Bill, 152, 153; and trucks, 154–155; support highway improvements, 156, 157, 158, 161–163; allied with Progressives, 175–176; opinions of urbanites towards, 231–232; midwestern farm bloc, 274–275, 277, 278; endorse Blaine for governor, 300; bankruptcies, 362; and unemployment compensation, 393–394; dairy strike, 409–410, 413–419; resentment towards organized labor, 555; contributions to World War II, 564–565
Farmers' Equity Union: delegates attend labor conference, 476
Farmers' institutes: 166
Farmers Union: 181, 412, 413, 417, 441
Farrington, E. H.: 133
Farrington, Joseph R.: 545–546
Fascism: opposed by Phil La Follette: 542; and National Progressives of America, 546, 547
Fechner, Robert: 493, 498
Federal Aid Road Act (1916): 157, 158
Federal Board of Farm Organizations: 178

Federal deficit: 130
Federal Emergency Relief Act: 464
Federal Emergency Relief Administration (FERA): 464–465, 466, 467
Federal Highway Act (1921): 160
Federal Land Bank system: 275
Federal Reserve Board: 131, 351
Federal System of Bakeries: 240
Federal Trade Commission: 312
Federated Trades Council. *See* Milwaukee Federated Trades Council
Fiction: as mirror of New Era, 79–84, 196, 230–231, 483
Filene, Edward A.: 500
Filene, Lincoln: 451
First Wisconsin National Bank of Milwaukee: 133, 229, 254, 349–350
Fish, Carl Russell: 40, 198, 500
Fisher, Irving: 93
Flamm, William: 260, 363n
Flexner, Abraham: 505
Flu. *See* Influenza epidemic (1918)
Fons, Leonard: 379
Fontaine, A. B.: 315
Food: during World War I, 29
Food Administration: 29, 171, 178
Ford, Henry: 6, 140, 231, 261; and tractor industry, 145–146
Ford Motor Company: 138
Fordson tractors: 145–146, 147
Forest Crop Law (1927): 208
Forest Products Laboratory: 201, 496
Forestry: 200–202, 207–210
Forrest, William L.: 363
"Four Minute Men": 27, 38
Fourteen Points: 61–62, 65, 76
Frank, Glenn: 499, 556, 558; supports public radio, 194; appointed UW president, 500–502; confrontation with Phil La Follette, 502–503; dismissal, 504–506; cost to La Follette, 523
Frankfurter, Felix: 387, 454, 481
Franksville (Racine County): cannery strike in, 536
Frazier, Lynn: 270, 277, 279, 318, 442
Frear, James A.: 53
Fred, E. B.: 173
Freeman, R. E.: 519
Frey, John P.: 273
"Friendship Village" (stories): 230–231
Fritz, Oscar M.: 116
Froker, Rudolph K.: 180
Fuel: during World War I: 29–30
Full Fashioned Hosiery Workers: 245, 430
Fuller, Oliver C.: 130
Furuseth, Albert: 402
Future Farmers of America: 226
Future Trading Act: 275

Gaillardet, L. P.: 305
Gale, Zona: 230, 268, 436; opposes National Guard, 117; "Friendship Village" stories, 230–231; on motion pictures, 255–256; and Glenn Frank, 500
Galpin, Charles J.: 179
Ganfield, William: 277
Garfield, James R.: 288
Garner, H. L.: 352
Garrison, Lloyd K.: 378, 433, 505, 546n
Gasoline tax: 162–163, 304, 305
Gaus, John M.: 378, 522
Gehrman, Bernard J.: 393, 552
Geline, Max: 534
General Federation of Women's Clubs: 117
General Motors Company: 138, 139; and tractor industry, 146–147
General Synod: 343–344
Genetics: 172
German-American Alliance: 12–14, 89
German language: opposition to during World War I: 32, 38
Germania-Herold (Milwaukee): 16
Germans: and World War I, 1, 3, 10, 12–15; loyalty questioned, 15; anti-German hysteria, 16, 32, 41, 44, 54; accused of causing influenza epidemic, 57–58; postwar attitudes towards, 67; Americanization among Lutherans, 77–78; and prohibition movement, 89, 90–92, 94–95, 96; switch from Democratic party to Progressive party, 277–278; postwar voting patterns, 342–343; voting patterns in 1938, 557; ethnic and religious identities, 558–560
Germany: Phil La Follette visits, 526
Gettelman, Bernhard: 243, 445
Gilberts, Arnold: 413, 415, 418, 419
Gimbel Brothers: 192
Glover, A. J.: 185
Goff, Emmett S.: 166
Gold standard: 408
Gompers, Samuel: 260, 529
Good-Bye Wisconsin (novel): 84
Goodland, Walter S.: 33–34, 555
Goodnight, Scott H.: 218
Goodwill tours: 195–196
Gordon, Edgar B.: 193
Gottlieb, Laurence R.: 309
Government: efforts to provide employ-

ment and relief, 376–380, 384–397 *passim*; centralization during Depression, 448–449; role in Social Security, 450–464; role in emergency relief, 464–469; Phil La Follette's ideas on role of, 519, 521–522; reform legislation, 521–522
Government Reorganization Act: 521–522
Graass, Frank H.: 517
Grady, Daniel: 503
Grandine, Joseph G.: 209
Grau, Phil: 197
Graunke, Walter: 475, 528
Great Lakes Naval Training Station: 57, 189
Green, William: 425
Greene, Howard: 445
Griffith, Edward Merriam: and state forestry program, 200–201, 202, 208
Grobschmidt, John: 379, 517
Gross, Edward J.: 303
Groves, Harold: role in unemployment and relief, 378, 379, 381, 384, 390, 392, 475, 478
Groves Bill: 392–393, 394
Gruening, Ernest: 308–309, 402
Gruenwald, Hannah O.: 206
Gunderson, Henry A.: 481, 516

Haas, Francis J.: 534
Hackett, Francis: 14
Hadley, F. B.: 168
Haight, George I.: 184
Hall, Harry B.: 366
Halpin, James J.: 174
Hammersley, Charles: 325
Handley, John J.: 363, 390, 426–427, 441, 532
Hanks, Lucien: 185
Hanks, Stanley C.: 352
Hansen, Alvin H.: 40, 453
Hansen, Charles E.: 302
Hanson, Frank H.: 306
Hanson, J. P.: 307
Hanson, Malcolm: 189–190
Hard, William: 267
Harding, Warren G.: 132, 275, 277, 286
Hart, Charles W.: 144
Hart, Edwin B.: 173, 174
Hart-Parr tractors: 144–145
Hartford (Washington County): automobile industry in, 138; impact of Depression on, 372–374
Harvesters: 150–151
Harvey, E. L.: 73
Hatch, Kirk L.: 163, 169
Haugen, Gilbert N.: 152
Haydon, A. E.: 296
Hayes, Max: 268
Hearst, William Randolph: 546
Hebenstreits Furniture Company: 373
Hefty, T. R: 352
Heil, Julius P.: 298; 1938 gubernatorial campaign, 555; defeats Phil La Follette, 557–558
Henderson, Norman B.: 124–125
Henry, Robert K.: 162, 555
Henry, William A.: 166
Hibbard, Benjamin H.: 153, 180, 206
Hickock, Lorena: 465
Highways. *See* Roads and highways
Hill, Charles L.: 420
Hillman, Sidney: 481
Hillquit, Morris: 5, 280
Hirst, Arthur R.: 304–307
Hitler, Adolf: 405, 483, 485, 497, 523, 526, 527, 537, 548, 559, 561, 562
Hitt, Arthur: 419
Hoan, Daniel: 280, 367, 370, 470; and U.S. entry into World War I, 12
Hoboes: 261
Hochstein, Irma: 113–114
Hoffman, Conrad: 173
Hohlfeld, A. R.: 37n
Holman, Charles: 178
Holmes, Fred L.: 222
Holmes, Harvey: 411
Holmes, W. E.: 78
Holt, Hamilton: 5
Holt, William A.: 389
Holway, Orlando: 23
Home Protection party: 105
Hooper, Jessie Jack: and suffrage movement, 116; and peace movement, 117–118; 1922 senatorial candidate, 277
Hoover, Herbert Clark: 323, 326, 351: U.S. food administrator, 29; and prohibition, 101, 102; and postwar unemployment, 132; supports co-operative business ventures, 196–197; and postwar prosperity, 252; as spokeman for business and class differences, 274; 1928 presidential campaign, 318–319, 321; fails to restore prosperity, 367; loses support, 390; defeated by Roosevelt, 403; reluctance to undertake economic reforms, 448
Hopkins, Harry: 454, 465, 469, 471, 481
Hopkins, J. A. H.: 268
Horlick's malted milk tablets: 57
Horner, Henry: 507

Hosiery industry: labor strife, 245–246
Hoskins, William: 183
Hough, Emerson: 199
House, Edward M.: 14
Houston, David F.: 158
Huber Bill: 390, 391, 392
Hughes, Charles Evans: 20, 21, 509
Hull, Merlin: 27, 51, 52, 53, 445
Humphrey, George C.: 173
Hurley, Charles: 507
Husting, Paul O.: 15, 27, 37, 45–46, 60
Hutton, R. P.: 96
Hydroelectric power. *See* Public utilities

Ickes, Harold: 288, 469
Illinois Division of Highways: 160
Immell, Ralph: 416, 471, 492, 538
Immigration: and disease, 58; and "Americanization," 72–79; restriction of, 74; opposed by Ku Klux Klan, 124; Negroes from South, 125–126
Income tax: first in state, 301–302; reformed, 310–311; federal, 449
Indian Defense Association: 488
"Indian New Deal": 488
Indian Pageant Corporation: 215
Indian Reorganization Act: 488, 489, 490
Indians: status during New Era, 486–491
Industrial espionage: 233, 241–243
Industrial expansion bill: 553
Industrial Workers of the World (IWW): 27, 72; public perception of, 368–369
Industry: postwar expansion, 129–151; impact of Depression on, 356–357; hurt by 1937 recession, 525; contributions to World War II, 564–565
Influenza epidemic (1918): 53, 57–58
Injunctions: as anti-labor device, 233–234, 243–247
Installment buying: 140
Interchurch World Movement: 242n
Internal combustion engine: and automobiles, 136; and farm machinery, 144–145, 147
Internal improvements: and state constitution, 156–157, 201, 468, 514
International Association of Machinists: 279
International Congress of Women (1915): 5
International Harvester Company: 147, 148, 150
International Stamping Company: 373
International Unemployment Day: 368
Irish: and prohibition movement, 90, 91
Irish, Lucina G.: 363
Iron Horse (tractor): 146–147
Isolationism: 527, 560–561
It Can't Happen Here (novel): 483

J. A. Craig Company: 146
J. I. Case Threshing Machine Company: 138, 144, 145, 147–148, 150
James, Ada: 108, 268, 303
James, David G.: 107–108
Janesville (Rock County): automobile industry in, 139
Jeffery, Thomas B.: 137, 139
Jenkins, Ab: 149
Jennings, Frank B.: 252
Jews: as viewed by Lutherans, 559; as viewed by Catholics, 560. *See also* Anti-Semitism
John Deere and Company: 148, 149, 150
Johnson, Axel: 79
Johnson, Hugh S.: 152, 153, 430
Johnson, Magnus: 283
Johnston, William H.: 279, 286
Jones, Lewis Ralph: 168
Jones, Richard Lloyd: 47
Jordan, David Starr: 5, 6–8
Judd, Charles H.: 263
Junior Loyalty Legion: 39
Jury trial: and labor strife, 243, 244, 246, 247

Kading, Charles E.: 552
"Kane-Pennington Hot Air Engine": 137
Kannenberg, Roland E.: 514
Kansas Agricultural College: 169
KDKA (radio station): 191
Keating, Edward: 280, 512
Kellogg, Frank B.: 277, 279
Kellogg, Louise Phelps: 8
Kelly, Fred C.: 474
Kelly, W. A.: 236
Kelly, William: 498
Kendall, Edward C.: 185n
Kennedy, R. A.: 311n
Kenosha: automobile industry in, 137; labor dispute, 245–246; effects of Depression in, 349
Kenosha County: in Liberty Loan drives, 44
Kent, Frank R.: 546
Kettenhofen, J. F.: 207
Keynes, John Maynard: 283
King, Franklin H.: 166
Kingsley, Ralph S.: 366, 565
Kirchwey, Frieda: 446

Kirkpatrick, C. W.: 498–499
Kissel, Louis: 138
Kissel Industries: 373
Kissel Motor Car Company: 372
Kisselkar: 138
Kleczka, Leonard: 503
Kohler, Walter J.: 209, 298; 1928 gubernatorial campaign, 320, 321; popularity as governor, 321; defeated in 1930 gubernatorial campaign, 321–325; failure to cope with unemployment, 377; 1932 gubernatorial campaign, 400, 401, 403; plumbing-ware business, 427–430; response to workers' demands, 431
Kohler (Sheboygan County): strike at, 427, 431–435; model community, 428
Kohler Company: strike, 427, 431–435
Kohler Improvement Company: 428
Kohler Workers' Association: 430, 433–434
Kraft Cheese Company: 373
Krumrey, Henry: 268
Kruszka, Michael: 76
Kruszka, Wenceslaus: 76
Kryszak, Mary: 118n
Ku Klux Klan: 2, 85–86, 88, 100, 306; in Wisconsin, 120–125; enmity towards Catholic church, 123–124; fraternal activities, 125
Kuhn, Arthur: 431
Kull, George F.: 38n, 39, 314, 377
Kuryer Polski (Milwaukee): 76

Labor: in post-World War I period, 69–70; and radicalism, 70; opposes equal rights law, 113; hostility towards Negroes, 126; on farm prices, 151; opinions of farmers, 231–232; postwar opposition to, 232, 235–237; postwar optimism, 232–233; legislation concerning, 233–235, 242–244, 246–247; and private detective agencies, 233–234, 242–243; union membership figures, 234; open-shop movement, 235–237, 239–240; relations with employers, 237–239; self-promotion, 240–241; litigation concerning, 244–246; labor code revised, 246–247; abundance during New Era, 248–249; shorter workweek, 249–250, 252; fears concerning educational reforms, 260; supports vocational education, 264–265; attacks on Farmer-Labor party, 285; AFL supports La Follette presidential campaign, 290; deserts Progressives, 291, 292; endorses Blaine for governor, 300; origin and nature of in America, 420–424; welfare capitalism, 424–425; and National Industrial Recovery Act, 425–426; rights uncertain under New Deal legislation, 426–427; Kohler strike, 427–435; Wisconsin Labor Relations Act, 510–512; Phil La Follette's attitudes towards, 528; and Progressive party, 528, 529; AFL-CIO struggle and attendant problems, 529–534; and recession of 1937–1938, 535; rural hostility towards, 536; unsympathetic to Phil La Follette, 555
Labor colleges: 264–265
Labor Forward Movement: 232
Labor party: 270, 271, 272–273
La Budde, Otto: 47
La Crosse: impact of Depression on, 364
La Follette, Belle Case: and peace movement, 8, 9; and suffrage referendum campaign, 108; declines to run for office, 308
La Follette, Isabel (Isen): 405, 541, 544
La Follette, Philip F. (Phil): signs revised labor code, 246; campaigns in Minnesota, 283; mirrors father's principles, 297; early career, 315–316; endorses Al Smith, 321; 1930 gubernatorial campaign, 321–325; elections analyzed, 327–345 *passim*, 571–588; becomes governor, 346, 377; forms National Progressives of America, 347, 538–545; supports five-day workweek, 372; works to reduce unemployment, 377–386; "kitchen cabinet," 378; invokes Frederick Jackson Turner, 379, 542; advocates public power, 382–383; anti-Depression program, 386–387, 388–389; sponsors unemployment compensation, 394–395; defends Progressive principles on radio, 396–397; 1932 gubernatorial campaign, 400–402; seeks influence outside Wisconsin, 404–405; possible cabinet appointment, 405, 406; visits Europe, 405–406, 409; confers with Franklin Roosevelt, 407–408; and League for Independent Political Action, 436, 437; and Progressive party, 438–441; 1934 gubernatorial campaign, 442–443, 445–446; power of "La Follette name," 445–446; espouses social welfare legislation, 464–472; confers with Roosevelt, 466, 468, 469, 477; manages federal appropriation, 468–472; relationship with Roosevelt, 473,

526; wary of forming third party, 474; avoids endorsing radical groups, 476–477; 1936 gubernatorial campaign, 479–482; and Marquis Childs's *Sweden: The Middle Way*, 483–485; advocate of consensus, 485–486, 519–520; urges integrated CCC camps, 498; and Glenn Frank ouster, 501–506, 523; anti-Depression measures, 506–507; supports Supreme Court reorganization proposal, 508–510; labor legislation, 510–512; budget-balancing legislation, 512–513; public power legislation, 513–517; relationship with Farmer-Labor Progressive Federation, 517–519; calls special session of legislature, 518, 520–521; reorganizes state government, 520–521; derided by disgruntled legislators, 522–523; confers with Roosevelt, 524; ambitions for post-Roosevelt years, 524–526; ponders formation of third party, 525–526, 527–528, 535–536; 1938 European tour, 526; opposes national socialism, 526–527; difficulties with third party formation, 537–538; breaks with Roosevelt and forms National Progressives of America, 538–545; speech and rally at Stock Pavilion, 542–545; reaction to new party, 545–551; 1938 gubernatorial campaign, 551–552, 554–557; loses election to Heil, 557–558; isolationism of, 561–563; prophecies about World War II, 563–564; serves in war, 565n

La Follette, Robert M., Jr. (Young Bob): 243, 272; opposes Communists, 285; works with CPPA, 289; mirrors father's principles, 297; seeks father's Senate seat, 308–310, 311–312; confers with Blaine, 313; early career, 315–316; party affiliation controversy, 317; plan for Progressive unity, 318; 1928 senatorial campaign, 318–319; attends 1928 Republican convention, 319; elections analyzed, 327–345 *passim*, 571–588; on radical groups, 369; anti-Depression legislation, 387–388; defends Progressive principles on radio, 397; endorses Franklin Roosevelt, 403; lack of personal ambition, 405; confers with Roosevelt, 406–407; and New Deal programs, 408–409; and League for Independent Political Action, 436; and founding of Progressive party, 438–439, 441–442; 1934 senatorial campaign, 442–443, 445–446; seeks to amend Social Security bill, 460–461; confers with Roosevelt, 466, 477, 524; relationship with Roosevelt, 473; and Marquis Childs's *Sweden: The Middle Way*, 483–485; suggests Dykstra as UW president, 506; supports Supreme Court reorganization proposal, 508; possible successor to Roosevelt, 524; chairs Senate Civil Liberties Committee, 528–529; and organized labor, 528–529; and formation of National Progressives of America, 540

La Follette, Robert M., Sr. (Old Bob): efforts opposing World War I, 2, 9–10, 21, 22, 24; and National Guard, 17; leader of Progressives, 19–20; election of 1916, 20–21; opposes arming merchant ships, 21; opposes declaration of war, 22; opposes conscription, 24; opposed by Wisconsin Loyalty Legion, 37; denounced by University of Wisconsin faculty, 42; accused of disloyalty, 42–43; opinion of armistice, 55–56; opposes peace treaty, 60–61, 65; opposes military intervention in Russia, 69; leader of Progressives during New Era, 128, 251; opposes privilege, 266; 1920 Republican platform, 271–272; sensitivity to postwar changes, 274; and farmers, 274–275; and railroad brotherhoods, 275–276; 1922 senatorial campaign, 276–279; excoriates Frank B. Kellogg, 277; and Conference for Progressive Political Action, 279–282, 286; 1924 presidential campaign, 283, 284, 286–295; European tour, 283–284; courted by Farmer-Labor party, 284–286; deserted by labor, 292; supported by Socialists, 293; analysis of 1924 presidential voting, 293–295; funeral, 296; supports Blaine's gubernatorial campaign, 300, 303; son Philip aids presidential campaign, 316; elections analyzed, 327–345 *passim*, 571–588; 1924 vote compared with 1932 vote, 403–404; aids Menominee tribe, 490

La Follette for President Committee: 286

La Guardia, Fiorello: 442, 477–478, 481, 541, 548

Lamfrom, Leon B.: 235

Landon, Alfred E.: 477, 480

Lane, Franklin K.: 78

Language: postwar political issue, 74–75, 76, 77, 78–79

Larson, J. F.: 180
Larson, Lawrence: 516
Laubenheimer, Jacob: 367
League for Independent Political Action: 436–437, 438
League for Industrial Democracy: 280
League for Industrial Rights: 235
League of American Wheelmen: 156
League of Nations: 58, 60, 84, 88, 483; Wisconsin opposition to, 63–65
League of Nations Disarmament Conference: 117
League of Women Voters: 109, 110, 114, 115–116, 118
League to Enforce Peace: 58–60, 62, 500; supports peace treaty, 65
Legislative Reference Library: 178
Lehman, Herbert H.: 507
Lehner, Philip: 305
Leisure: postwar debate over, 249, 250, 253–255
Leith, Benjamin D.: 172–173
Leman, Monte M.: 102
Lenin, V. I.: 280
Lenroot, Irvine L.: 313, 315; supports war effort, 27; 1918 senatorial campaign, 46, 48–49; supports Treaty of Versailles, 60, 61–62, 66; during prohibition, 103
Leopold, Aldo: 495–497
Lescohier, Don D.: 40, 377, 379–380
Lever Food and Fuel Control Act: 94
Levitan, Solomon: 363, 481, 516
Lewis, Charles B.: 121
Lewis, David J.: 451
Lewis, John L.: 530, 548
Lewis, Sinclair: 196, 224, 230, 231, 483
Liberty League: 508
Liberty Loans: 43–45
Lighty, William H.: 193, 509
Lilienthal, David E.: 409
Lincoln, Abraham: 543
Lindbergh, Charles A., Jr.: 231, 261
Lindbergh, Charles A., Sr.: 270
Lippmann, Walter: 102, 504–505, 546
"Little New Deal": 522
"Little Wagner Act": 511
Lodge, Henry Cabot: 62
Long, Huey: 460, 466, 469
Longworth, Alice Roosevelt: 66
Loomis, Orland S.: 378–379, 481, 513
Lovett, Robert Morss: 436, 475
Lowell, A. Lawrence: 65
Loyalty Legion. *See* Wisconsin Loyalty Legion
Loyalty pledges: 36–37
Lueck, Albert: 479, 481
Lueck, Martin: 307
Luick Ice Cream Company: 372
Lumber industry: 199–200, 202, 210; during Depression, 356; among Indians, 487, 490; decline spurs conservation efforts, 492
Lundeen, Ernest: 460
Lusitania (ship): 16, 17, 43
Luther, Ernest L.: 143, 187, 362
Lutheran Free Church: 344
Lutheran Synodical Conference: 343, 344
Lutherans: opposition to League of Nations, 63; and Americanization, 75, 77–79; attitudes towards prohibition, 89–93, 95; opposition to woman suffrage, 106; voting patterns, 343–344; voting patterns in 1938, 557; and national socialism in Germany, 558–559

MacArthur, Douglas: 565n
MacDonald, Angus: 208
MacDonald, Duncan: 286
MacDonald, Ramsay: 284
Machinery industry: during Depression, 356
Madison: during prohibition, 101–102; engine plant, 145; reaction to stock market crash, 352; unemployment in, 363–364, 368; dairy striker killed near, 419; National Progressives of America rally in, 541–545
Madison Ministerial Union: 124
Maguire, J. W.: 431, 432
Mahoney, William: 284
Maier, Walter A.: 559
Mail-order merchandising: 227–228
Manchester, Harry S.: 352
Manly, Basil: 275, 279, 285
Manufacturing and industry: effects of state tax system on, 309–310
Marathon County: industry in, 210–211
Marathon Paper Mills Company: 211
Marcantonio, Vito: 475n
Marquette University: 193
Marshall, Roujet D.: 201
Marshfield: efforts to provide relief, 374
Martin, John E.: 555
Martin, Patrick H.: 28
Marx, Karl: 422
Masons (fraternal organization): 123
Masters, Edgar Lee: 230
Matheson, Alexander E.: 112
Matheson Bill: 300
Mauthe, Carlton: 379

Mauthe, William: 393
Maverick, Maury: 509, 553
McAdoo, William Gibbs: 43, 45, 281, 282, 286
McCarthy, Charles: 177, 178, 179, 263; 1918 senatorial campaign, 47; on Bolshevism, 69
McCollum, E. V.: 173, 174
McCoy, R. B.: 300
McDonald, Duncan: 268
McElroy, Robert McNutt: 41
McGovern, Francis: 393; elected governor in 1910, 20; withdraws from senatorial campaign, 46
McHenry, A. C.: 278
McHenry, Wendell: 228
McNall, P. E.: 180
McNary, Charles: 152
McNary-Haugen Bill: 152–153
McNulty, Arthur: 546–547
Mead, George H,: 177, 319, 321
Mellon, Andrew: 319
Mencken, H. L.: 319
Menominee County: created, 491
Menominee tribe: 487, 489; status during New Era, 490–491
Meriam, Lewis: 488
Merritt, Harry C.: 149–150
Messmer, Archbishop Sebastian G.: 75; opposes prohibition, 95
Metalworking industry: during Depression, 356
Methodist Federation of Social Service: 279
Mexican Revolution: 9–10, 18
Meyer, Ernest: 502
Meyer, Lou: 149
Michigan: auto industry in, 137, 142
Mickelsen, Gunnar: 432
Milk: postwar legislation, 275. *See also* Dairy farming
Milk Pool. *See* Wisconsin Cooperative Milk Pool
Miller, Anton M.: 390
Miller, R. J.: 514
Milton College: 193
Milwaukee: Socialist opposition to World War I, 11–12; preparedness efforts, 16; armistice celebration in, 55; Poles, 76; during prohibition, 96, 99, 102; Ku Klux Klan in, 120, 121; Negroes migrate to, 126; unemployment in, 363, 367–368, 374
Milwaukee Association of Commerce (MAC): 74, 197, 203–204, 215, 236–237; opposes government regulation, 366–367
Milwaukee Association of Industrial Advertisers: 349
Milwaukee City Club. *See* City Club of Milwaukee
Milwaukee County: in Liberty Loan drives, 44
Milwaukee Employers Council: 235
Milwaukee Employment Bureau: 133
Milwaukee Family Welfare Association: 363
Milwaukee Federated Trades Council: 126, 239–240, 348, 530, 531–532
Milwaukee Peace League: 8
Milwaukee School of Engineering: 193
Milwaukee Travelers' Aid Society: 363
Milwaukee Welfare Association: 370
Minkley, Carl: 497
Minnesota Federation of Labor: 270
Missouri Synod: 78, 95
Mitchell, Jonathan: 497
Mitchell & Lewis Wagon Company: 138
Mitchell Motor Car Company: 138, 139
Moehlenpah, Henry A.: 203; loses 1918 election, 53; on postwar farm problems, 134; on auto industry, 140
Moline Plow Company: 152
Montgomery Ward: 227
Moore, J. G.: 39
Moore, Ransom A.: 172
Moran, Arthur J.: 417
Morgan, William: 278
Morgenthau, Henry, Jr.: 65, 459
Moriarity, Joseph: 27
Morrill Act (1862): 165
Morris, George P.: 60
Morrison, F. B.: 134, 180
Morrison, Henry C.: 259
Mortenson, W. P.: 180
Mortgages: on farms, 362
Motion pictures: 187; viewed as threat to family values, 255–256
Mulberger, Charles: 97
Mulberger Act: 97
Munro, Dana C.: 42–43
Murray, Merrill: 391
Muscle Shoals power plant: 312
Mussolini, Benito: 284, 523, 527, 537
Muste, A. J.: 436

Nash, Charles W.: 139, 355, 356, 365
Nash Light Six (automobile): 140
Nash Motors Company: 139, 349, 355, 364

National American Woman Suffrage Association: 109–110
National Association of Employment Managers: 233
National Association of Manufacturers (NAM): 113, 389, 425–426, 429
National Broadcasting Company: 192, 396
National Catholic Welfare Council: 279
National Choral Peace Jubilee Committee: 6
National Commission on Law Observance and Enforcement: 101–102
National Conference on Economic Security: 456–457, 458
National Council of Defense: 28
National Defense Act (1916): 18
National Education Association: 257
National Farmers' Holiday Association: 413, 414, 415, 418, 441; delegates attend labor conference, 476
National Federation of Cooperative Livestock Shippers: 180
National Guard: 17–19; in World War I, 23–24; proposed abolition of, 117; mobilized during strikes, 416, 417, 432
National Industrial Conference Board: 309
National Industrial Recovery Act: 408, 414, 425, 427
National Labor Board: 430, 433
National Labor Relations Board: 433–434, 536
National League of Women Voters. *See* League of Women Voters
National Lutheran Council: 343
National Progressives of America (NPA): 347; formation of party, 541–545; basic principles, 544–545; party symbol, 544, 546; reaction to formation of party, 545–551; Nazi response to, 548; Phil La Follette defeated (1938), 557–558
National Radio Forum: 397
National Recovery Administration: 408, 428, 429, 430
National Security League: 16, 37, 73
National Socialism: 406; opposed by Phil La Follette, 526–527; and National Progressives of America, 547, 548; anti-Semitism, 559, 560; rise to power, 483; youth camps, 497
National Trade Union Unity League: 368
National Travel and Outdoor Life Exposition: 215–216
National Woman's Party: 110, 112, 113
National Women's Trade Union Lague: 114
Naval Appropriations Act (1915): 17
Naval Expansion Bill: 540
Nazis. *See* National Socialism
Negroes: migrate to northern cities, 86, 88, 124, 125–126; in the CCC, 498
Nekoosa-Edwards Paper Company: 236
Nelson, Adolphus P.: 205
Nelson, John Mandt: 53, 289, 303
Nelson, Philip E.: 510
Nettels, Curtis: 545
Neville, Ella H.: 8
New Deal: 346–347, 351; Young Bob La Follette's opinions on programs, 408–409; programs and legislation, 448–449, 450, 464–465, 466, 467, 473
New Era: 111, 118, 127–128
Nicholas II of Russia: 68–69
Niebuhr, Reinhold: 436
Night Outlasts the Whippoorwill (novel): 79–82
Nineteenth Amendment (woman suffrage): 87–88, 109, 110, 111
9XM (radio station): 189–190
Nixon, Robert A.: 379, 390
Nonpartisan League (NPL): 51, 269–270, 273, 279, 280, 281, 292
Norman, Ed: 495
Norris, George W.: 289n, 317, 318, 321, 387, 399, 436, 442, 507, 525; wins 1928 primary, 319
Norris-Sinclair bill: 281
North, Sterling: novel about postwar America, 79–82
North Dakota: NPL origins, 269
Northern Forest Park: 214, 214n
Northern Paper Mills: 236
Northern States Power Company: 192
Northern Wisconsin Resort Association: 214
Northwestern College (Watertown): 148
Northwestern Radio Company: 192
Norwegian Lutheran Church in America: 343–344
Norwegians: voting patterns, 328, 342–343, 344; support Schmedeman in 1934 gubernatorial campaign, 444; voting patterns in 1938, 557
Nunn, H. L.: 389, 519
Nutrition: 173
Nye, Gerald P.: 318, 442, 561

Office of Road Inquiry: 137
Ohl, Henry, Jr.: 254–255, 532

Oil: postwar scandals, 282, 283n
Oklahoma Southern Tenants Union: 509
Oldfield, Barney: 149
Oleomargarine: 185–186, 358n, 396
Oliver Farm Equipment Company: 145
Olson, Floyd B.: 444
Oman, Carl: 414–415
Oneida County: efforts to reduce unemployment, 374
"Open" primaries: 325–326
Open-shop movement: 235–237, 239
Oregon (state): pioneers gasoline tax, 162
Osborn, C. M.: 246
Osborne, A. L.: 393
Oshkosh: efforts to reduce unemployment, 374
Oshkosh, Reginald: 490–491
Otto, Max: 378

Pabst, Fred: 103
Packers and Stockyards Act: 274–275
Padway, Joseph A.: 242, 433, 434
Paine, Robert F.: 66
Palmer, A. Mitchell: and Red Scare, 70–71
Paper industry: 211
Parker, Alton B.: 43n
Parker, George S.: 355, 356
Parr, Charles H.: 144
Patents: and university research, 182–183
Patriotic Press Association: 37
Patriotism: manifestations and excesses during World War I, 30–54 *passim*; manifestations after World War I, 72–73; and postwar education, 256–258
Pattison, E. S.: 305
Paunack, A. O.: 352
Peace movement: in World War I era, 1, 4–9; failure of, 22–23; women support, 117–118. *See also* Isolationism
Peavey, Hubert H.: 27
Peck, George W.: 399
Peek, George N: 152
Pennington, Edward Joel: 137
People's Legislative Service: 275, 276, 279, 280
Pepper, John: 284–285
Perkins, Frances: role in Social Security legislation, 451, 452, 453, 457, 463
Perlman, Selig: 429, 529; analysis of American worker, 423–425; on role of government, 435
Pershing, John J.: 231
Peterson, W. H.: 173
Pfister and Vogel Leather Company: 74
Philipp, Emanuel: supports arms embargo, 14; supports arms buildup, 17; elected governor, 20; re-elected in 1916, 20–21; arms National Guard, 23–24; opposes conscription, 24; defense efforts, 29; moderation during war crisis, 31–33, 45; fails to gain senatorial appointment power, 46; attacked by Roy Wilcox, 50, 300; 1918 gubernatorial campaign, 50–52; wins primary, 52; wins election, 53; visited by prohibitionists, 58; and Cutover, 205, 207
Phonographs: 254–255
Pidcoe, L. L.: 352
Pierce, Dante M.: 134
Pierce Engine Company: 138
Pierce-Racine automobiles: 138
Pinchot, Amos: 268, 271, 272, 273
Pinkerton detective agency: 242, 243
Plant breeding: 172–173
Platt, Chester: 303
Plumb, Glenn E.: 276
Plumb Plan: 276, 281
Poles: resist assimilation, 75–76; in post-World War I society, 76–77
Police: women as, 116–117
Polish Housewives League: 112
Political Equality League: 108
Polonia: 76
Popular Front: 478, 479
Populists: 88
Post, Louis F.: 288
Pound, Roscoe: 500
Powell, William V.: 65
Power. *See* Public utilities
Prentice Park (Ashland): 217
"Preparedness": 4, 16–17
Primary elections. *See* "Open" primaries
Progressive party: origins, 435–441; 1934 campaign, 441–445; alliance with liberal Democrats, 443–444; significance of 1934 victories, 445–447; delegates attend labor conference, 476; aids Roosevelt in 1936 campaign, 477–478; avoids affiliation with Communists, 478
Progressive Republicans: 399, 400
Progressives: oppose U.S. entry into World War I, 1, 9; pre-World War I optimism, 3; and woman's movement, 110; support Wisconsin Society of Equity, 175; postwar reforms, 251, 266–267; postwar reorganization, 267–274; and Committee of Forty-Eight, 268–269; and agrarian radicals, 269–271; and 1920 Republican convention, 271–273; 1924 platform,

284; 1924 presidential campaign, 283, 284, 286–290; divisions among, 297, 299–300; endorse Blaine for governor, 300; 1928 gubernatorial campaign, 320; growing disenchantment with Republican party, 326; importance to La Follette family, 326–327; analysis of 1916–1940 La Follette elections, 327–345; support New Deal programs, 346–347; support five-day workweek, 372; efforts against unemployment, 381–382, 384; 1932 gubernatorial campaign, 400–402; support Franklin Roosevelt, 403–404; distrust of Democratic party, 404; form third party, 438–441; ties with Roosevelt, 470–472, 473; and Glenn Frank, 501–503, 506; and organized labor, 528, 529; factionalism among, 553, 554; losses in 1938 elections, 557. *See also* National Progressives of America

Prohibition movement: World War I affords opporunity for reform, 84–85, 88–93; exploits influenza epidemic, 58; opposition to, 89–91, 94–96. *See also* Eighteenth Amendment

Property tax: 301–302

Public service commission: 383

Public utilities: Phil La Follette supports, 382–383; legislation concerning, 513–517

Public works: Phil La Follette's program defeated, 465–472

Public Works Administration: 408

Puelicher, John H.: 237

Putnam, Mabel: 112

Quaker Oats Company: 184, 186

Quick, William J.: 307n

Quinn, Robert: 507

Racine: automobile industry in, 136, 137, 138; effects of Depression in, 374

Racine County: in Liberty Loan drives, 44

Radicalism: hysteria over in post-World War I era, 67–68; and labor, 70; opposed in Wisconsin, 71–73. *See also* Communists

Radio: as advertising medium, 149; postwar developments, 187–194; strengthens family ties, 254–255; utilized by Phil and Robert La Follette, Jr., 396

Railroad brotherhoods: 275–276, 279, 280, 281

Railroad Commission of Wisconsin: 154

Railroads: competition with highways, 157, 158; as postwar political issue, 276; grade-crossing improvements, 380

Railway Labor Board: 276

Rainbow Lake (Waupaca County): 525

Rambler (automobile): 137

Rauschenbusch, Walter: 378n

Raushenbush, Paul A.: 378, 381, 384, 391, 392, 450, 451, 461

Rawleigh, William T.: 283, 286, 290,306

Reading Formula: 430

Recession: of 1937–1938, 525, 535

Reconstruction Finance Corporation: 409, 468

Record, George: 268, 271

Recreation: movies, 187, 255–256; in Cutover, 211–220; in rural communities, 225–226; radio, 254–255

"Red Arrow" Division. *See* 32nd Division

Red Cross: 36, 37, 39, 42; and 1918 influenza epidemic, 57

"Red Flag" bill: 73

Red Scare: 67–68, 70, 203, 232; in Wisconsin, 71–72

Reed, James A.: 231

Reedsburg (Sauk County): effects of Depression in, 348

Reform: political effects of postwar boom, 250–251, 267

Reid, A. H.: 244

Reis, Alvin C.: 541

Reno, Milo: 413, 415, 418, 419

Republican National Committee: 277

Republican party: in Wisconsin, 1865–1916, 19–20; Stalwarts vs. Progressives, 19–21; 1918 general election, 53; and Treaty of Versailles, 60; regulars oppose La Follette presidential bid, 291–292; claims Young Bob La Follette as member, 317; dominant party in postwar Wisconsin, 326, 398; break with Progressives, 439; criticized by Phil La Follette, 543; coalition with Democrats, 552, 554–555; gains in 1938 elections, 557. *See also* Stalwart Republicans

Republican Voluntary Committee: becomes force in Republican party, 309, 315, 320, 323

Research Corporation of New York: 183

Research foundations: 182–184

Retailing: installment buying, 140–142; chain stores, 227–230

Revell, Aldric: 518

Reynolds, John W.: 27–28

Rhinelander (Oneida County): ban on

dancing and jazz, 262; efforts to provide relief, 374
Rice Lake (Barron County): efforts to reduce unemployment, 374
Rich Vogel Shoe Company: 373
Richberg, Donald: 481
Richland Center: labor incident in, 536
Risjord, Gullick N.: 556
Roads and highways: postwar developments and funding, 155–164; as political issue, 304–307
Roberts, Glenn D.: 378, 556
Roberts, J. E.: 38–39
Roberts, Owen: 509
Robertson, T. Brailsford: 183
Rock County: setting for novel, 81
Rockefeller, John D.: 95
Rodman, Selden: 437, 475, 537; critical of National Progressives of America, 550–551
Roe, Gilbert: 268, 272, 285
Rogers, Alf: 322
Roosevelt, Franklin Delano: 295, 326; and Wisconsin Progressives, 346–347, 351, 470–472, 473; 1932 presidential campaign, 398–401, 403; analysis of 1932 vote, 403–404; and Wisconsin political factions, 404; and La Follette brothers, 404–405, 406–408; cabinet appointments, 405, 406; scapegoat of activist farmers, 418; and management-employee relations, 430; acts to prevent strike violence, 433; supports Young Bob La Follette, 443; reluctance to centralize welfare programs, 448; speaks at economic security conference, 456, 458; endorses tax-offset law, 457; and Social Security legislation, 461, 462, 463; confers with La Follette brothers, 466, 477, 524; and relief programs, 466–467; approves federal appropriation for Wisconsin, 469; 1936 election campaign, 477, 480, 481–482; and Indian affairs, 488; and conservation, 493, 498; cuts back on federal appropriations, 507; threatens to pack Supreme Court, 507–510; political methodology compared to Phil La Follette's, 526; popularity diminishes during 1937–1938 recession, 535; cool towards National Progressives of America, 540–541; criticized by Phil La Follette, 543–544; criticized by Nazi writer, 548
Roosevelt, Theodore: 268, 288; supports "preparedness" and war, 16–17, 26; favors League of Nations, 58
Rosa, Charles: 52
Rosenberry, Marvin B.: 237
Ross, Colin: 548
Ross, Edward Alsworth: 60, 93, 155; opinions on World War I, 3, 23, 24n, 40
Roth, Filibert: 202
"Round-robin" letter: castigates Old Bob La Follette, 42
Rowlands, E. Myrwyn: 379
Rubin, William B.: 245n, 247n, 272, 401, 401n, 414
Rural Electrification Administration: 513
Russell, Harry L.: 177, 203–204, 205, 206; and postwar farm crisis, 134; encourages university research, 166–171, 174–175, 176; relations with farm organizations, 178, 179–180; and establishment of WARF, 183, 185, 186
Russia: 69, 407, 409
Rutz, Henry: 536
Rykov, Aleksei: 283

St. Adalbert's parish (Milwaukee): 76
St. John's Military Academy: 39
St. Louis Proclamation: 11
St. Norbert College: 193
Saloons: women in, 55; closed during flu epidemic, 67
Samson Sieve-Grip Tractor Company: 146
Sanders, J. G.: 168
Sauthoff, Harry: 445
Scandinavians: attitudes towards prohibition, 91; voting patterns, 328, 342, 343, 344, 557
Schafer, John: 303
Schlesinger, Arthur, Jr.: 463–464
Schmedeman, Albert G.: 368, 393, 401n, 473; defeated in 1928 gubernatorial election, 321; elected governor, 403; and dairy strike, 415–416; faith in New Deal programs, 417; and Kohler strike, 432; praised by Roosevelt, 443; 1934 gubernatorial campaign, 444, 445; reluctance to institute economic reforms, 465
Schmitz, A. J.: 268
Schneider, George: 445
Schoenfeld, C. J.: 306
Scrip: 469
Sears, Roebuck and Company: 227, 373
Seelman, J. J.: 103
Selective Service Act (1918): 37, 94
Sellery, George C.: 40, 501

Senate Civil Liberties Committee: 528–529
Sensenbrenner, Frank J.: 236, 238, 389
Settlement: in Cutover, 202–204, 205–207
Severson, Herman J.: 98, 300, 302, 303, 511, 518
Severson Act: 98, 103
Shannon, F. J.: 39
"Share Our Wealth" program: 460
Sheppard-Towner Act: 115
Shipstead, Henrik: 277, 279, 318, 442, 444
Shons, W. H.: 306
"Short Course" (UW): 166
Shuler, Nettie Rogers: 108
Sigman, David: 517, 518, 528
Sigman, Samuel: 441, 475, 528
Simons, Algie M.: 11, 27, 53n
Simons, May Wood: 78
Sinclair, Upton: 466
Single Taxers: 280
Singler, Walter M.: 412–414, 417
Sinykin, Gordon: 473, 505
Sixteenth Amendment. *See* Income tax
Slacker, The (film): 27
Slagg, Stanley: 379
Slichter, Charles S.: 40, 184
Slichter, Sumner H.: 239
Smith, Al: 320n, 321, 326, 443
Smith, John M.: 171, 555
Smith, Peter J.: 390
Smith-Hughes Act (1917): 262
Smith-Lever Act (1914): 169
Snell, Chester D.: 501
Social Democratic party: 68
Social feminism: 105–107, 112
Social Security: 346; rival plans, 450, 451, 458, 459–460; legislative struggle for, 450, 452–464; passage, 460–461; provisions, 461–463; credited to Arthur Altmeyer, 463–464
Social Security Board: 461, 463
Socialism: opposed by Catholics, 75
Socialist party: opposes U.S. entry into World War I, 1, 11–12; pre-World War I optimism, 3; theory of war and imperialism, 10–11; and woman suffrage, 107; and Ku Klux Klan, 124; breaks ties with organized labor, 232; postwar decline of, 267–268; represented at Conference for Progressive Political Action, 279, 280; comes to support Old Bob La Follette, 280–281; endorses La Follette's presidential bid, 287, 292–293; opposes Young Bob La Follette's candidacy, 309; lack of support for, 311; public perception of, 368–369; delegates attend labor conference, 476; opposes CCC, 497; repudiates National Progressives of America, 547
Soil Conservation Service: 494
Sommers, William: 475
South: commercial ties with, 195–196
Southern Publicity Association: 120
Spanish flu. *See* Influenza epidemic
Stacey, Peter: 155
Stalwart Republicans: 19, 399, 400, 402, 404; postwar realignments, 296–297; shift tactics after La Follette senatorial victory, 313–315; 1928 gubernatorial campaign, 320; growing disagreements with Progessives, 326; align with conservative Democats, 552, 554–555
Stamp, Josiah: 405
State Aid Road Law (1911): 157
State Board of Forestry: 200
State Board of Vocational Education: 262
State Conference of Social Workers: 110
State Council of Defense: 28–33, 44, 45, 129
State ex rel. Owen v. Donald: 201, 207
State government: efforts to provide employment and relief, 376–380, 384–397 *passim*; reorganization, 521–522
State Highway Commission: 215, 304, 306–307; created, 157; and State Trunk Highway System, 158–159, 160–161; and gasoline tax, 162
State Highway Fund: 162
State Historical Society of Wisconsin: 215
State Regional Planning Committee: 467
State Trunk Highway System: 158–159, 161
Steam engines: 144
Steel industry: 133
Steele, Harold: 245
Steenbock, Harry: 173, 174; and research on vitamin D, 182–184, 185, 186
Steffens, Lincoln: 283, 297, 298
Stern, Leo: 15
Stock market crash: 346, 350–355
Stock Pavilion (UW): National Progressives of America rally at, 542–545
Stone, James A.: 100, 348–349
Storrow, James J.: 139
Story, H. W.: 366
Stout Institute: 193
Strange, John: 299n
Straub, Edna: 219

Stresemann, Gustav: 283
Strikes: 426; in paper industry, 236; in Milwaukee clothing plant, 244–245; in Kenosha, 245–246; increase during Depression, 346; by dairy farmers, 409–410, 413–419; at Kohler Company, 427–435; during conflict between AFL and CIO, 533–534; in Franksville, 536
Stritch, Archbishop Samuel A.: 560
Studebaker, J. W.: 495
Student Army Training Corps: 42
Studer, Norman: 436n
Stump removal: 204–205
Submarines: 1, 10, 16, 21, 57
Suffrage. *See* Woman suffrage
Superior (Douglas County): during prohibition, 101
Superior State Teachers College: 193
Supreme Court: Roosevelt's efforts to reorganize, 499, 507–510
Sussex (steamer): 10, 21
Sweden: economic success, 484–485; similarities to Wisconsin, 485
Sweden: The Middle Way (book): 483–485
Sweet, Arthur: 303
Swenson, Magnus: 29
Swope, Gerard: 388–389

Taft, Philip: 435
Taft, William Howard: favors League of Nations, 58, 59, 65
Talmadge, Eugene: 469
Taxes: property, 161–162, 383; gasoline, 162–163, 304, 305; on Cutover lands, 206; under Forest Crop Law, 208–209; politics of, 301–303, 309–310; highway, 304, effects on manufacturing and industry, 309–310; 1925 reform, 310–311; on chain stores, 383; on oleomargarine, 396
Taylor, Henry C.: 153, 79
Taylor County: efforts to reduce unemployment, 374
Tchitcherin, Boris: 283
Teapot Dome: 282
Teigan, Henry G.: 284
Temperance movement: during World War I, 2; opposed by German-Americans, 12–13. *See also* Prohibition movement
Tennessee Valley Authority: 408, 409, 513
Terry, Earle M.: 189, 190
32nd Division ("Red Arrow"): 24–25
Thomas, Norman: 436, 497, 529
Thomas B. Jeffery Company: 139
Thomas Kane and Company: 137
Thompson, Carl D.: 382
Thompson, Dorothy: 546
Thompson, Helen F.: 118n
Thompson, James: 1918 senatorial campaign, 46–47, 48; declines to run for governor, 51
Thorpe, Merle: 349
Tittemore, James N.: 180; 1918 gubernatorial candidacy, 51–52
Titus, William A.: 207–208
Torkelson, Martin W.: 159
Tourist industry: 211–220; and support for improved highways, 160
Townley, Arthur C.: 269, 292
Townsend, Francis E.: 458, 459, 466
Townsend Plan: 459–460
Tractor industry: 143–150, 154
Trade associations: 195–196, 388, 389
Trade Union Label Department: 240
Trades and Labor Council (Kenosha): 246
Treaty of Versailles (1919): 58, 60–62; Wisconsin support for, 64–65; fails, 66–67
Truck Equipment Company: 373
Trucks: 154–155, 163
Tugwell, Rexford: 451, 457, 469
Turner, Frederick Jackson: 203, 379, 421, 422; invoked by Phil La Follette, 379, 542
Turner, Glenn P.: 132
Twenty-first Amendment (repeal): 104

U-boats. *See* Submarines
Unemployment: post-World War I, 70; during Depression, 356, 363–365, 367–386, 390–395; demonstrations against, 367–368; community efforts against, 369–376; government efforts against, 376–386, 390–395; legislation concerning, 380–381; solutions proposed by legislative committee, 390–394; unemployment insurance enacted, 394–395
Unemployment insurance: 233, 346, 388, 389–392, 394–395, 448, 450–458, 462, 519. *See also* Social Security
Union of Kohler Workers No. 18545: 430–431, 433–434, 435
USSR. *See* Russia
Unions. *See* Labor
United Auto Workers: 531
United Danish Evangelical Lutheran Church: 344
United Mine Workers: 529–530
U.S. Bureau of Labor Statistics: 130

United States Chamber of Commerce: 389
U.S. Department of Agriculture: 178
United States Employment Service: 29, 70
United States Food Administration: 202
U.S. Senate: and Versailles Treaty ratification process, 60–63
United States Steel Corporation: 133
United States Supreme Court: Roosevelt threatens to reorganize, 499, 507–510
United Taxpayers Cooperative Association of Wisconsin: 516
Universal Military Training League: 37
University of Wisconsin: peace movement at, 4–5, 6–7; loyalty organizations, 40–41; accusations of disloyalty, 41; contribution to war effort, 41–42; Americanization program, 74; during prohibition, 102; research foundations, 182–184; radio station at, 189–190; presidency of Glenn Frank, 499–506. *See also* College of Agriculture; Stock Pavilion
University of Wisconsin College of Agriculture. *See* College of Agriculture
Urbanization: 220–223

Values: postwar changes, 253–256
Van Devanter, Willis: 510
Van Gorden, Clyde S.: 191–192
Van Hise, Charles R.: 6, 15, 42, 167, 499; work for peace movement, 59
Vansittart, Robert: 405
Van Vleck, Edward B.: 40
Veblen, Thorstein: 288
Victory Loan: 131
Viereck, George Sylvester: 89
Villages: effects of urbanization on, 223–226, 231; recreation in, 225–226; merchandising in, 227–230
Villard, Oswald Garrison: 64, 65, 288, 436, 505, 506, 537
Vincent, Jack: 495
Violence: as part of wartime hysteria, 31–32, 45; during Kenosha strike, 246; over dairy prices, 346; during unemployment demonstrations, 368; during dairy strikes, 416–417, 419; during Kohler strike, 432
Viroqua (Vernon County): during prohibition, 98–99, 101; Ku Klux Klan in, 123
Vitamins: 173–174, 182–184, 185
Vocational education: 257, 262–265
Voigt, Edward: 99
Volstead, Andrew J.: 97
Volstead Act (1919): 87, 97, 103, 218
Voluntarism: and effects of Great Depression, 374–376, 377
Voorhis, Jerry: 553
Voting patterns: analyzed, 298, 325–345, 571–588

WAAK (radio station): 192
Wages: effects of postwar boom, 248–252 *passim*; and attitudes of American working class, 420, 422
Wagner, Robert: 377, 433, 451
Wagner Act (1935): 427n, 510, 528
Wagner-Lewis Bill: 451, 454–456
Wales, Julia Grace: 118; role in peace movement, 4–6, 7, 8, 17
Walker, Frank: 469
Wallace, Henry A.: 418
Wallace, Henry C.: 152, 153
Walsh, Frank P.: 442
Walsh, Thomas J.: 282, 283, 406
War and Peace Society: 6
War Finance Corporation: 275
WARF. *See* Wisconsin Alumni Research Foundation
Waukesha County: dairy strike violence in, 417
Waukesha High School: 39
Wausau Group: 211
Webb, Edwin Y.: 35
Webb-Kenyon Act: 93
Weber, Frank J.: 132, 239, 240, 242, 264; predicts Great Depression, 348; opposes Communists, 369n
Weeks Act (1911): 208
Wehr, Henry: 55
Weiss, Harry: 391
Welfare: 448, 449, 454. *See also* Social Security; Unemployment
Welfare capitalism: 238–239, 424–425
Wescott, Glenway: 83–84, 256
West Allis Works: 238
West Bend Aluminum Company: 373
Western Paper Manufacturers Association: 236
Weyenberg Shoe Manufacturing Company: 373
WGAY (radio station): 192
WHA (radio station): 190, 192–193, 194
Wheat: 172
Wheeler, Burton K.: 287–288, 442
Wheeler, J. Russell: 170
Whelan, Charles E.: 123
White, William Allen: 65–66
Wickersham, George: 101
Wieseman, William: 121

Wilcox, Roy P.: 300, 309, 311; 1918 gubernatorial candidate, 50, 52
Wiles, Russell: 183
Wiley, Alexander: 479, 481, 555, 558
Wilkie, Harold M.: 503, 504
Willard, Frances: 105
Williams, Burt: 135
Williams, Howard Y.: 436, 437, 473–474
Williamson, Charles A.: 40
Wilson, Woodrow: 297, 399; and peace movement, 5, 6, 8; mistrusted by La Follette, 9–10; neutrality supported by German-Americans, 14; supports arms buildup, 17, 21; election of 1916, 21; asks for declaration of war, 22; favors conscription, 24; endorses Davies in 1918 senatorial campaign, 48–49; announces armistice, 55; postwar course criticized by La Follette, 56; concludes peace treaty, 58; followers support peace treaty, 61; Versailles Treaty rejected, 66–67; supports League of Nations, 84; beer proclamation, 94; supports woman suffrage, 109; returns railroads to private ownership, 276
Winnebago County Agricultural School: 169
Winnebago tribe: 489
Winnipeg (Manitoba): tractor trials, 145
Wipperman, R. O.: 514
Wisconsin Agricultural Authority: 521
Wisconsin Alumni Association: 184
Wisconsin Alumni Research Foundation (WARF): 185–186, 496
Wisconsin Bankers' Association: 170–171, 176, 203, 207, 229; and postwar auto industry, 140, 141–142
Wisconsin Brewers' Association: 89, 96
Wisconsin Chamber of Commerce: 486
Wisconsin Citizens' Committee on Employment: 377
Wisconsin Colonization Company: 204
Wisconsin Committee for Unemployment Reserves Legislation: 391
Wisconsin Conservation Commission: 496
Wisconsin Cooperative Milk Pool: 441; organized, 411; role in dairy strike, 412–414, 415–416, 417, 418, 419; delegates attend labor conference, 476
Wisconsin Council of Defense: 565
Wisconsin Dairymen's Association: 165
Wisconsin Defense League: 26–29, 33, 35, 36
Wisconsin Department of Agriculture and Markets: 412
Wisconsin Department of Markets: 194
Wisconsin Development Authority: 383, 514–517
Wisconsin Equal Rights Law (1921): 112–114
Wisconsin Farm Bureau: 178, 180
Wisconsin Farm Bureau Federation: 394
Wisconsin Farmer-Labor Political Federation: 536–537
Wisconsin Farmer-Labor Progressive Federation: 510, 528, 536–537, 553
Wisconsin Farmers' Holiday Association: 413, 419
Wisconsin Federation of Women's Clubs: 110, 114
Wisconsin Finance Authority: 468–471, 514
Wisconsin Free Library Commission: 69
Wisconsin Good Roads Association: 155
"Wisconsin Idea": 181, 386, 506
Wisconsin Idea, The (book): 47
Wisconsin Industrial Commission: 29, 391, 395; and postwar unemployment, 132
Wisconsin Labor Relations Act: 511–512, 519, 534, 555
Wisconsin Labor Relations Board: 533–534
Wisconsin Land o' Lakes Association: 214, 215
Wisconsin League for Good Roads: 156
Wisconsin League of Municipalities: 470
Wisconsin League of Women Voters: 115–117, 119. *See also* League of Women Voters
Wisconsin Legislative Interim Committee on Unemployment: 364
Wisconsin Loyalty Legion: 11, 33–40, 42, 44, 59, 72, 486
Wisconsin Manufacturers' Association: 72, 236, 309, 310, 389–390, 391, 515
Wisconsin Municipal and Highway Contractors' Association: 304
Wisconsin National Guard. *See* National Guard
Wisconsin Peace Society: 4, 6
Wisconsin Plan: 531
Wisconsin Pure Milk Products Cooperative Association: 394
Wisconsin Rural Electrification Coordination: 513
Wisconsin Society of Equity: 51, 175–178, 179, 180–181, 203
Wisconsin State Federation of Labor: 233, 239, 240, 264, 378, 381, 391, 392, 426,

427n, 434, 476; and AFL-CIO struggle, 530–531, 532, 533
Wisconsin State Industrial Union Conference: 533
Wisconsin Supreme Court: 201
Wisconsin Synod: 63, 78, 92, 95
Wisconsin Unemployment Compensation Act (1932): 395
Wisconsin Valley Electric Company: 211
Wisconsin Wheel Works: 138
Wisconsin Woman Suffrage Association: 107
Wisconsin Women's Progressive Association: 110
Withrow, Gardner: 445
Witte, Edwin E.: 346; and state tax system, 310; role in unemployment compensation, 378, 385, 394; role in Social Security legislation, 453–457, 458, 459, 460, 461, 463, 464
Witte, Edwin: 534
WLBL (radio station): 194
Woll, Matthew: 375
Woman suffrage: 85, 104–106; during World War I, 2; in Wisconsin, 106–109; statewide referendum on, 108–109
Woman's Peace party: 8
Women: and peace movement, 5–6, 8; in saloons, 55; and prohibition, 104, 105; suffrage movement, 104–109; during World War I, 109; societal perceptions of, 111; inequities in workplace, 114, 118–119; expansion into new societal roles, 115–117; opposition to National Guard, 117–118; as legislators, 118
Women's Christian Temperance Union: 105, 110
Women's movement: fragmentation after suffrage amendment, 111; equal rights movement, 112–114; Wisconsin equal rights law, 112–114
Women's Progressive Association: 112
Women's Trade Union League: 110
Work, Hubert: 488
Work, John: 280
Workers Alliance: delegates attend labor conference, 476
Working People's Nonpartisan League: 270
Workmen's compensation: 233, 388, 519
Works Progress Administration: 471, 492, 513
World Court: 312
World War I: 1–54 *passim*; diversity of opinion on, 3, 25–27; Wisconsin opinions on, 3–4; U.S. entry into, 22–23; "Red Arrow" Division in, 24–25; casualties, 25; stateside defense efforts, 26–41; hyperpatriotism during, 31–37, 40–41, 42–43, 45, 48–49, 50–51; Liberty Loans, 43–45; reaction to armistice, 55–56; peace treaty, 58–67; unites Poles, 76; and woman suffrage movement, 109; economic stimulus, 129
World War II: inevitability of, 560; isolationists oppose, 561–563; return of prosperity during, 564
Wrabetz, Vojta: 534
WRAL (radio station): 192
Wright, Ivan M.: 411
WTAQ (radio station): 191
Wylie, Fred M.: 210

Yellow-dog contracts: 244, 246
Young Communist League: 368
Young Men's Christian Association: 37
Young Women's Christian Association: 112
Youth: during World War I, 39

Zimmerman, Fred: 303, 555; supports co-operative business ventures, 198; and Allen-A labor dispute, 246; 1926 gubernatorial campaign, 314–315
Zimmerman, H. E.: 155
Zinmey, Arthur: 510
Zoning: in northern Wisconsin, 209
Zucker, T. F.: 185n

Index prepared with the assistance of
Barry Christopher Noonan

ABOUT THE AUTHOR

Paul W. Glad is Regents' Professor of History at the University of Oklahoma in Norman. Born in Salt Lake City, Utah, he grew up in Geneva, Illinois. He obtained his baccalaureate degree from Purdue University and his Ph.D. degree from Indiana University. From 1966 to 1978 he taught courses on twentieth-century American History in the University of Wisconsin in Madison.

ABOUT THE BOOK

The text was composed in Baskerville by Impressions, Inc., of Madison on an Autologic, Inc., APS-μ5 CRT typesetter. The book was printed by offset lithography on a long-lived paper called Glatfelter Supple Offset. It was bound in Joanna Western Arrestox.